Police
Administration

Police Administration

Fourth Edition

O. W. Wilson
Late Dean Emeritus, School of Criminology
University of California, Berkeley, and
Superintendent of Police (Retired), Chicago, Illinois

Roy Clinton McLaren
Chief of Police
Arlington, Virginia
and former Director, Field Operations Division,
International Association of Chiefs of Police
Gaithersburg, Maryland

McGraw-Hill Book Company
New York   St. Louis   San Francisco   Auckland   Bogotá   Düsseldorf
Johannesburg   London   Madrid   Mexico   Montreal   New Delhi   Panama
Paris   São Paulo   Singapore   Sydney   Tokyo   Toronto

Police Administration

Copyright © 1977, 1972, 1963 by McGraw-Hill, Inc. All rights reserved. Copyright 1950 by McGraw-Hill, Inc. All rights reserved. Printed in the United States of America. No part of this publication may be reproduced, stored in a retrieval system, or transmitted, in any form or by any means, electronic, mechanical, photocopying, recording, or otherwise, without the prior written permission of the publisher.

0DODO898765

This book was set in Times Roman by Black Dot, Inc. The editors were Lyle Linder and Barry Benjamin; the copy editor was Pamela Haskins; the cover was designed by Rafael Hernandez; the production supervisor was Angela Kardovich. The drawings were done by J & R Services, Inc.
R. R. Donnelley & Sons Company was printer and binder.

Library of Congress Cataloging in Publication Data

Wilson, Orlando Winfield, date
  Police administration.

  Includes bibliographical references and index.
  1. Police administration. I. McLaren, Roy Clinton,
joint author. II. Title.
HV7935.W48   1977   363.2   76-56177
ISBN 0-07-070726-X

To Orlando Winfield Wilson
1900–1972
and to August Vollmer
1876–1955

Contents

PREFACE   ix

PART ONE   **Police Responsibilities and Relationships**

  1   The Crime Problem and the Police Role in Society   3
  2   The Relationship of Police to Government and Politics   15
  3   Police Leadership in the Community   30
  4   Regional, State, and Federal Law Enforcement Planning   39
  5   Consolidation, Regionalization, Sharing of Services, and
      Relationships with Other Agencies   51

PART TWO   **Administration**

  6   Management Theory and Organizational Behavior   63
  7   Organization for Police Service   69
  8   Direction   117
  9   Interpersonal and Behavioral Aspects of Management   149
 10   Planning and Research   157
 11   Management Information   182
 12   Inspectional Services   198

viii CONTENTS

13 Public and Community Relations 221
14 Personnel Management 244

PART THREE Operations

15 Team Policing 315
16 Patrol 319
17 Allocation and Distribution of Operational Manpower 357
18 Criminal Investigation 363
19 Organized-Crime and Vice Control 384
20 Crime Prevention, Suppression, and Resistance 410
21 Special Operational Problems 428
22 Traffic 435

PART FOUR Auxiliary and Technical Services

23 Information Services and Control 461
24 The Crime Laboratory 503
25 Other Auxiliary Services 510
26 Buildings and Equipment 525

PART FIVE Appendix

A Outline of Items of Use in the Development of a Comprehensive
Law Enforcement Plan 551
B Daily Activity Report Program Budget Coding Program
Budget Summary Sheets 565
C Consolidated Daily Report—Monthly General Activity Report 571
D Statement of Departmental Goals, Arlington County Police
Department, Arlington, Virginia 576
E Purpose and Nature of Inspection 582
F Guide to Performance Evaluation 585
G Baltimore Police Department, 755-Hour Program, Police
Recruit Training Curriculum Outline 609
H Field Training Guide 613
I Shift Rotation Schedule and Sign-Up Sheet 630
J Excerpts for Distribution of Police Patrol Force 633
K Allocation and Distribution of Police Patrol Manpower 656

BIBLIOGRAPHY 673

INDEX 681

Preface

On October 18, 1972, several months after the publication of the third edition of this book, Orlando Winfield Wilson died at his home in Poway, California, at the age of seventy-two. To the police of the world, the loss of O. W. Wilson has been immense. Internationally, he was widely known as the greatest authority in the history of police administration. In the United States, only August Vollmer, Bruce Smith, and J. Edgar Hoover approached him in stature as an influence for good in American law enforcement.

During the course of his brilliant career, O. W. Wilson achieved the highest success in several different but related fields in police administration. To many of us, he was Dean Wilson — the founder of the School of Criminology at the University of California. To a great many others, he was Superintendent Wilson, who brought about a near miracle as the head of the Chicago Police Department. To others he had been Colonel Wilson, who as much as anyone else was responsible for shaping the enormously successful pattern for civil policing in West Germany following World War II.

To his professional contemporaries and personal friends he was "O. W." Finally, to a fortunate few who had the opportunity to work directly for him and with him, he was known simply as the Chief.

The Chief commenced his career in 1921 as a police officer in Berkeley, California, where he served under August Vollmer, the father of professional

PREFACE

American law enforcement. More than any other person in the police field, August Vollmer influenced the thinking of O. W. Wilson, and to the credit of both men, that influence persisted strongly throughout his career.

While he worked as a police officer, O. W. Wilson was also a student at the University of California and, following his graduation with a bachelor's degree, he was appointed chief of police in Fullerton, California, in 1925.

His next position was as chief of police of Wichita, Kansas, beginning in 1928. During the period from 1928 to 1939, he introduced many new methods and policies, including techniques for the allocation and distribution of patrol manpower, a comprehensive planning program, a new records and communications system, advances in recruitment, selection and training, and many other innovations.

In 1939 Chief Wilson returned to the University of California as a professor of police administration in the Political Science Department, and in 1950 he was named dean of the newly created School of Criminology. For several years the University of California remained one of the few schools in the country to offer a baccalaureate degree with major work in the police field. The School of Criminology also offered other specialties within the criminal justice system, and thus anticipated the current emphasis on the criminal justice curriculum now in vogue in the United States by about twenty years.

Prior to World War II, and intermittently afterward, the Chief directed a number of police management and reorganization studies as a consultant for Public Administration Service, and in the course of this work he was able to apply and refine the results of both his practical and academic backgrounds.

During the war he served as a Lieutenant Colonel and Colonel in the Army, and served as Chief U.S. Public Safety Officer, Region III, Italy, and later held the same position in the U.S. zone after the defeat of Germany. To a great extent he was responsible for the rapid development of responsible civilian policing in West Germany, a factor which undoubtedly played a part in the rebirth of the country.

After his return to the university, he continued with his writing in the police field. He had already completed *Police Records* in 1942, then wrote *Police Planning* in 1952, with a new edition in 1958. He wrote *Parker on Police* in 1957, and *Police Administration* in 1950, with new editions in 1963 and 1972.

In 1960, he was asked to head a special panel to select a new commissioner for the Chicago Police Department, in the wake of a police burglary scandal. After interviewing a number of applicants, the panel requested him to resign so they could consider him for the position. He was immediately appointed as superintendent. In the next few years he transformed a department with a national reputation for corruption and mediocrity into one of the finest major city police departments in the world.

When he began his administration in Chicago, a great many skeptics doubted whether a man with his professional background and visionary ideals would last long in the environment which surrounded the department at that time. To

PREFACE   xi

those of us who knew him, however, there was no question that he would succeed.

He immediately selected several key assistants from outside the department and began a complete reorganization of personnel, introducing totally new administrative and operational concepts. Although he had a great capacity for making deliberate, well-planned decisions appear to be sudden and decisive, a large measure of his success was due to his ability to make important decisions with great conviction.

He had trememdous energy and walked through the hallways with great, bounding strides that conveyed a sense of movement and progress. His mind was like a steel trap, and he had an uncanny ability to detect weaknesses in a plan or a proposal. More than anything else, he combined an exhaustive knowledge of his profession with an overwhelming belief that what he was doing was right.

The Chief was not without his detractors, but they were few. Some of his concepts were initially labeled controversial, but not many remained that way. Although a great number of his innovations at one time seemed even radical, they are widely accepted today. (In the few areas where his ideas did not meet wide acceptance, however, he learned the art of compromise — such as on the question of fire-police integration.) He was said by some to be a traditionalist — perhaps because he continued to support the concepts of Vollmer as well as his own ideas, all of them remarkably ahead of their time in the first place — but those who really compare these principles with the current state of affairs in policing will realize that such a statement borders on blasphemy.

The law enforcement profession has not yet achieved O. W. Wilson's vision of excellence for the police service, but we are nevertheless far better off today because of his presence. His loss to us is enormous, but let us be reassured in the knowledge that his influence will remain, and that his ideals will live on.[1]

Although the "Essential O. W." of prior editions is intact in this work, a conscientious effort has been made to change those things which the Chief would have modified himself. Above all, he was an innovator and was forever in support of constructive change in the police field.

During the work on the third edition, there was an opportunity to see, firsthand, the great range and depth of his knowledge. His ability to grasp a new idea was unexcelled; although he had retired from active police administration at the time of our collaboration for the third edition, his knowledge of the issues at that time left no doubt as to the direction his ideas on current problems would have taken if he were still living.

O. W. Wilson would have wanted to continue with most of the wording of the

---

[1] Adapted from an article by R. C. McLaren, "A Memorial to the Chief," *The Police Chief*, January 1973, p. 12.

preface contained in the third edition, partly because of its dedication to August Vollmer. It is therefore appropriate to incorporate the language of that preface here.

Roy Clinton McLaren

This book has been written primarily for the police administrator and executive. However, the authors believe that establishing the police executive as the primary audience also makes the book more useful to the critical student of police management, regardless of rank or station. The principles underlying its recommendations are unchanging, and the goal is still the professionalization of police service. It is clearly apparent that this goal cannot be achieved without superior leadership, and it is for this reason that administrative and leadership functions continue to be stressed in the revisions of the work.

For the administrator the book is offered as a guide to superior practice. The authors have had the personal opportunity to test the value of the concepts and procedures recommended in this text in many progressive police agencies.

The original encouragement and guidance given by the late August Vollmer of the Berkeley Police Department can never be forgotten. Both of us served in the department, and along with many others in his city, his country, and his profession, we are grateful to have personally received the benefit of his wisdom and inspiration.

O. W. Wilson
Roy Clinton McLaren

Police
Administration

Part One

Police Responsibilities and Relationships

Chapter 1

The Crime Problem and the Police Role in Society

The progress of mankind over the past few millennia must be regarded as grounds for optimism in many respects. The quality of life has improved significantly in terms of increased life expectancy, broadened distribution of wealth, improved social welfare, vastly increased productivity, and technological advancement. People live longer, and the hazards and problems of primitive life—such as disease, tribal combat, exposure to extremes of climate, scarcity of food, and the need to expend enormous amounts of energy just to contend with these difficulties from day to day—have largely disappeared from Western cultures.

Although we must acknowledge these undeniable signs of the gradual improvement in the quality of life, there are countervailing and rapidly increasing manifestations of potential disaster for our recently acquired civilization.

The threat of nuclear holocaust is of course foremost among the potential horrors which we—as civilized beings—have created for ourselves. In its total form, war is capable of destroying civilization within a few hours, and all mankind within weeks. Ranked only behind war (if that is a comfort) are five other major threats to modern society, which are in many ways interrelated and

3

at the same time potentially dangerous as the precursors to war. These modern specters are crime, environmental pollution, exhaustion of natural resources, overpopulation, and social intolerance.

THE CRIME PROBLEM

Next to war, crime is a greater immediate threat to lives and property than the other issues. The failure of society to diminish criminality imposes great hardships on our people, not only in terms of loss of life and property, but also in terms of fear and suspicion, which detract from our peace of mind and comfort. The cost of crime is staggering. If this money could be directed into education, medical and social research, efficient production, conservation of resources, and protection of the environment, the welfare of our society would be immeasurably increased.

Economic losses directly attributable to criminal activities are heavy, but nevertheless they are only a part of the total cost of crime. To them must be added the cost of administering criminal justice. Police, prosecutors, criminal courts, probation and parole agencies, and correctional institutions all create heavy drains on the public economy; further, their costs seem to increase out of proportion to the cost of maintaining other government functions. In addition, unproductive lives wasted in criminal activities and in penal institutions represent a tremendous loss.

Causal factors in criminality and social disorders are so numerous and occur in such an infinite variety of combinations that their isolation, analysis, and evaluation become extremely difficult. Genetic inheritance, behavior, imprinting during infancy and early childhood, family relationships, social interaction, and community and institutional influences have varied effects on the personality and behavior of individuals. The prevention of criminality, therefore, cannot be the exclusive task of one community agency. The administration of criminal justice, including treatment such as institutionalization, parole, and probation, may be made more effective, efficient, and speedy by good legislation, sound court decisions, and progressive management—but the prevention of behavior which requires such treatment is much more basic and must be accomplished through improvement of the quality of family life and through amelioration of economic and social conditions in the community.

(improvement)

Crime in Perspective

People have a tendency to seek simple solutions to complex problems, and a recent posture of society has been to think in terms of solution to "street crimes"—to assume that if we could somehow stop the offenders who are now committing robberies, burglaries, thefts, and rapes, our crime problem would be solved. The truth is, however, that long-term improvement can be achieved best through the upgrading of inadequate education, the elimination of poverty and unemployment, and the betterment of poor family relationships, rather than through the action of any single component of the justice system. The

THE CRIME PROBLEM AND THE POLICE ROLE IN SOCIETY

various agencies making up the system should realize their responsibility for properly identifying these causes of crime and social disorder.

Many people mistakenly believe that street crime can be treated as an isolated phenomenon. Actually, dishonesty in business, price-fixing, embezzlement, tax evasion, and fraud are widespread in our society. The losses attributable to white-collar crime of this sort are far greater than the combined losses from burglary, robbery, and street theft. The effect of white-collar crime—and of the hypocrisy generated by it—upon the people who commit street crime also deserves speculation. The solution to the crime problem must involve a reappraisal of the very definition of criminality and an attack on all kinds of crime—not just the crime committed by the poor and the violent.[1]

The Etiology of Crime Although a considerable amount of crime is generated by people who have a clear perspective of right and wrong, some crime is committed by people who are pathologically disposed to criminality and violence, and still more of it by people who have been subjected to delinquency-producing influences.

Theories as to the etiology of crime are by no means universally agreed upon by scholars in the field, and therefore no one presentation of theories could be looked upon as authoritative. Nevertheless, the police practitioner and the criminal justice student should be aware of some basic thoughts relating to the origins of criminal behavior. The following paragraphs are thus intended not to be authoritative but rather to encourage further study and discussion.

Genetic Factors The pathology may in rare cases stem from genetic problems, such as an apparent tendency for some men who are born with an extra Y chromosome to be predisposed toward crimes of aggression. Other inherited traits may have a slight bearing on criminality, such as personality type, intelligence, and even physical appearance.

Imprinting The little-understood phenomenon of imprinting causes a significantly larger number of problems of crime and social deviance than the genetic factors. The process of imprinting is actually a natural stage in the development of higher forms of animal life, in which the infant is exposed to influences (many of them parental) that tend to mold the behavior of the young animal. An example of proper imprinting is the development of normal attitudes toward establishing and sustaining friendships—through a combination of physical contact, affection, sensory stimulation, and playacting between parent and infants or between infants. In controlled experiments with animals, researchers have discovered that depriving the infant of parental touching and fondling can result in the failure to imprint positive or adaptive behavioral patterns and at the same time can often result in potentially maladaptive behavior such as suspicion, aggression, and anxiety, along with downright manifestations of terror, frigidity, depression, and other neurotic or psychotic symptoms.

[1] Ramsey Clark, *Crime in America*, Simon and Schuster, New York, 1970, p. 38.

POLICE RESPONSIBILITIES AND RELATIONSHIPS

While more responsive to correction than genetically acquired behavior, the imprinting process can be extremely difficult to reverse. Deviant behavior due to imprinting, such as that of the psychopathic thief, the habitual child molester, and the compulsive arsonist, is not readily corrected by any known therapy in current psychiatric practice.

Long-Term Social and Environmental Influences A considerable cause of criminality—perhaps the most significant in terms of sheer numbers—is the result of factors which can be described best as long-term social or environmental influences. Youth-gang relationships, the effect of marital discord, long-term poverty, racial discrimination, and continuing neglect or abuse by parents in later childhood and adolescence—all these are examples of the long-term social and environmental influences which generate crime and delinquency.

Fortunately, this kind of criminal and delinquent behavior responds much more easily to corrective means than the deviance due to genetic inheritance or imprinting. Education, group and individual counseling, vocational training, probation and parole supervision, the deterrence factor resulting from effective police action, prompt trial, and appropriate sentencing are examples of treatment methods which produce results, either individually applied or in some combination.

Short-Term Influences This category of factors includes the immediate influence of associates who urge participation in crime, the influence of alcohol and drugs, lack of money, critical incidents (such as those which start riots), and so on. Short-term influences are often interspersed with other factors mentioned above, and, in the opinion of most criminologists, for most offenders there may be combinations of long-term and short-term factors.

THE ROLE OF THE POLICE

Whenever crime is discussed, the role of the police is conspicuously identified. Thoughtful students of police administration, as well as most observers of the crime phenomenon who view the problem systematically, realize that the police have been assigned a disproportionate amount of responsibility for both the present level of crime and the efforts to cope with it in the future. Nevertheless, the police role is obviously significant in considering short-range solutions to the crime problem. For the greatest impact on crime *right now*, the following changes are required:

- Crime-prevention programs at the neighborhood level, with full community support
- Improved, vigorous, and conspicuous tactical surveillance by greater numbers of police in the locations where crime is most prevalent
- More public prosecutors and public defenders and increased activity by them
- Increased capacity of the court system, including an increase in the number of judges, and administrative improvements such as extension of

THE CRIME PROBLEM AND THE POLICE ROLE IN SOCIETY

working hours and the elimination of senseless postponements, routine plea bargaining, and inadequate or inconsistent sentencing

• An increase in the number and capacity of correctional facilities of various kinds so that there would be a realistic alternative to probation and suspended sentences in dealing with offenders having little potential for responding to lenient treatment

• Massive educational programs and enforcement pressure against the use of heroin and those who are engaged in its traffic

It seems unlikely that criminality will be so diminished in the next few years that agencies presently engaged in the administration of criminal justice may be disbanded. As long as there are criminals, the police must attempt to protect society from their depredations. If the preventive efforts fail, the police must arrest the offenders for the immediate purpose of keeping them in custody as a protection to society and, it is hoped, to give the criminal justice system an opportunity to carry out rehabilitation.

The Philosophy of Police Service

The primary purposes of a police department are the protection of life and property against crime, the preservation of peace and order, the safe movement of traffic, and the provision of emergency services. In carrying out secondary goals, the police render a host of miscellaneous noncriminal services and are charged with the enforcement of a wide variety of state and local laws, ordinances, and regulations. Some of the laws are designed to safeguard the morals of the community, and through their enforcement the police department becomes the principal agent of society in attempting to eliminate the opportunity for immoral conduct. On the other hand, the traditional American response to any offensive behavior has been the enactment of a law against it, with the result that statute books and city ordinances are filled with prohibitions against conduct that many persons have come to regard as innocuous.

The American faith in government by laws, the reluctance of most states and cities to evaluate and modify these laws, and the failure to recognize the difficulties of their enforcement make the tasks of the police departments and criminal justice agencies more arduous. A constant dilemma facing the police is the problem of what to do about the enforcement of laws which have become unpopular, perhaps with a majority of the people. It would seem that the police have a responsibility to inform the public of the consequences of the violations of these laws and then to ask the public to help the police attach priorities to their enforcement, such as through the selective allocation of manpower to deal with particular kinds of crime. Most police officers, furthermore, are acutely aware of what the public will tolerate in the way of enforcement pressure, and they will exercise considerable discretion in the enforcement of unpopular law, even in the face of management policy to the contrary. Police leadership should therefore ask the public—by direct contacts, through the news media, and through communication with legislators—to change a law when there is a

POLICE RESPONSIBILITIES AND RELATIONSHIPS

general lack of support for it, not only by the public, but also by the police themselves.

Noncriminal Police Work Load   A great percentage of police work is noncriminal, if random patrol activity is considered to be in that category. The police deal constantly with traffic congestion, vehicle accidents, lost property, missing persons, family conflicts, citizens who are locked out of their houses, barking dogs, frightened persons, suspicious noises, and a host of other problems which the public has come to expect the police to solve.

Social Service Role   A broadened concept of social responsibility on the part of the police has resulted in a more positive philosophy of service. Police work now includes many aspects of social service for which the police are particularly well suited; some cases have more than ordinary social welfare significance, notably those involving the mentally defective, the very young, the very old, and family relationships which result in conflict or crises. Police service today extends beyond mere routine investigation and disposition of complaints; it also has as its objective the welfare of the individual and of society. If society is to be protected against crime in an effective way, the police must actively seek out and destroy delinquency-inducing influences in the community and must assist in providing suitable treatment for the maladjusted.

Police Code of Ethics   The need for a statement of police responsibilities and conduct has been recognized and is summed up in the code of ethics adopted by the International Association of Chiefs of Police in 1957:

As a law enforcement officer, my fundamental duty is to serve mankind; to safeguard lives and property; to protect the innocent against deception, the weak against oppression or intimidation, and the peaceful against violence or disorder; and to respect the Constitutional rights of all men to liberty, equality and justice.

I will keep my private life unsullied as an example to all; maintain courageous calm in the face of danger, scorn, or ridicule; develop self-restraint; and be constantly mindful of the welfare of others. Honest in thought and deed in both my personal and official life, I will be exemplary in obeying the laws of the land and the regulations of my department. Whatever I see or hear of a confidential nature or that is confided to me in my official capacity will be kept ever secret unless revelation is necessary in the performance of my duty.

I will never act officiously or permit personal feelings, prejudices, animosities, or friendships to influence my decisions. With no compromise for crime and with relentless prosecution of criminals, I will enforce the law courteously and appropriately without fear or favor, malice or ill will, never employing unnecessary force or violence and never accepting gratuities.

I recognize the badge of my office as a symbol of public faith, and I accept it as a public trust to be held so long as I am true to the ethics of police service. I will constantly strive to achieve these objectives and ideals, dedicating myself before God to my chosen profession . . . law enforcement.

THE CRIME PROBLEM AND THE POLICE ROLE IN SOCIETY

Adherence to such a code is the first step toward true professionalization of police service.[2] Many departments now refer to the code of ethics in the language of the oath of office; others require their members to sign this or a similar code and keep it where frequent reference to it may be made.

Police Problems of Today

Police tasks of today differ widely from those of a hundred years ago, although the fundamental purpose remains the same. The adaptation of modern technology to criminal use brings new problems and added threats to the peace, comfort, security, and welfare of citizens. The vastly increased use of the automobile by delinquent youth as well as by adult offenders has affected the crime rate. Cargo planes filled with hundreds of pounds—sometimes tons—of contraband are able to sift through border defenses almost at will. Traffic accidents and congestion demand a large part of police attention, and transient populations resulting from rapid and easy transportation have added to the growing list of problems.

Problems of cultural assimilation continue, but they have become internal and intramural rather than international; in the United States, for example, ethnic and cultural discrimination has shifted from problems of the Irish, Jewish, and Italian immigrant to the difficulty being experienced by native American minorities. Family unity is less frequently the ideal than formerly, and responsibility for child training is often delegated to schools, organizations, and other parent surrogates, sometimes even to television sets. New attitudes toward the young, particularly toward teenagers, have resulted in their greater freedom to participate in adult activities without at the same time having to assume responsibility for their actions. These new attitudes are reflected in the changing morality of a large part of today's youth, particularly with reference to the use of marijuana and other dangerous drugs and narcotics and in regard to freer sexual expression. Alliances between criminals and ostensibly law-abiding citizens and complacency toward organized crime involving corruption, bribery, extortion, and murder all contribute their share to the increase in crime.

An additional problem facing the police today is based on the difficulty in overcoming public opposition to police authority even while the public demands protection from criminal elements. Although the crime crisis of the past few years has resulted in an upsurge of support for the police by the so-called silent majority, a large percentage of the public still feels the police are worse than they actually are. A growing radical minority, taking advantage of this feeling, has openly sought to discredit all police. A still smaller but highly militant minority is bent on assassination of police officers and attacks on other visible symbols of authority.

Contrary to the thinking of some die-hard police officers and others who believe that harsh and often brutal police methods used in the past would be

---

[2]Don L. Kooken, *Ethics in Police Service*, Charles C Thomas, Publisher, Springfield, Ill., 1957.

effective with today's problems, the difficulties we now have were in some measure caused by these same backward methods, carried out by unprofessional people. As the succeeding paragraphs indicate, two side effects of the unprofessionalism of the past have been the enactment of restrictive legislation and the development of adverse public opinion.

Police leadership has failed until recently to insist on higher qualifications for recruitment and higher ethical standards for all personnel. In years past, the police have also occasionally ignored procedural law in their zeal to enforce the criminal law, resulting in legislation and court decisions which so restrain the police in their interrogation of suspects and in their search for, and seizure of, evidence that they often lose cases on mere technicalities. While the goal of ending police abuse of authority is certainly worthy, the effect of this method of attaining it has been questionable.

Some judges have openly stated that adverse rulings are intended to be a means of keeping the police in order. The ultimate effect of these decisions is to punish the public rather than the police. Furthermore, it cannot be demonstrated that these decisions have a deterrent effect on those police officers who are prone to abuse their authority. Such deterrence must come from a concerted effort of the police agencies themselves, police associations, municipal officials, bar associations, and legislative and judicial bodies to define the limits of reasonable search and seizure and to devise constructive methods of selecting, controlling, and disciplining all police personnel.

Changes in Police Methods

Police methods have changed greatly during the past 100 years. The police today use almost every conceivable means of transportation and communication. The horse patrol and "nightstick on the pavement" have given way to automobiles containing computer terminals and teleprinters, helicopters with television, and jet flying belts. Modern communication centers tape-record telephone messages and complaints as well as radio dispatches, both outgoing and incoming, and record the time periodically so that should the substance of any message be questioned, the true facts may be established. Police dispatchers now have access to computer-based visual-display terminals giving identification data, records of wanted persons and property, the call numbers of the nearest available patrol cars, and other information of great tactical value. Patrol officers can now dictate police reports into automatic recording machines from any telephone, and these reports can be transcribed onto reproduction masters, from which any desired number of copies of the report may be made.

These systems are gradually replacing the typing of reports by the officers themselves as well as eliminating the frequently illegible copies of reports that resulted from the use of carbon paper. Television-based filing and retrieval systems now permit nearly instantaneous capture, storage, and random-access retrieval of documents with resolution high enough to permit classification of fingerprints transmitted by the system.

THE CRIME PROBLEM AND THE POLICE ROLE IN SOCIETY

Automated data-processing systems lead to greater speed and accuracy in crime analysis and statistical studies so useful in the direction and control of department resources, particularly in the wise deployment of manpower, the most important and expensive of all police resources. Large, progressive departments now use data-processing equipment for payroll preparation and daily attendance reports, thus eliminating the laborious typing of the names of all officers on duty on each watch. The daily attendance reports can be reproduced by business machines with great rapidity; the unit or watch commander then needs only to make corrections or indicate whether an officer is off duty and for what reason.

Principles and techniques developed in the physical sciences have long been employed in the identification of criminals through the study of evidence found at crime scenes and through the employment of techniques of interrogation in conjunction with the polygraph and other instrumentation. Research continues in laboratory methods which have their application not only in the identification of offenders but also in many of the lifesaving services the police are called upon to render. Modern apparatus such as the spectrograph, gas chromatograph, and diffraction x-ray are in common use; toxicological and chemical studies are routine, and the training and talents of the pathologist and other scientists are available for assistance in the reconstruction of crime scenes. The modern police laboratory is a far cry from the old "ballistics room" of the past. There is a trend toward the establishment of procedures which will ensure a more prompt and thorough search of crime scenes for physical evidence, with provision of facilities for its identification, recording, and transportation to crime laboratories in an unaltered, uncontaminated condition; these procedures require the assignment of evidence technicians on patrol around the clock.

It is impossible for the average patrol officer to be skilled in all the diverse requirements of police service, and consequently the specialist has appeared. The laboratory examiner or criminalist, the evidence technician, the polygraph operator, the personal-identification expert, the radio technician, the fiscal officer, the legal officer, the data-processing systems analyst, the police planner, the training officer, and the personnel analyst are all specialists who have been brought into police departments since the turn of the century.

The continuous adaptation of science and technology to police use and the introduction of improved administrative practices are essential to modern police management. Potential applications require constant scrutiny and wise policy decisions by the police administrator, as well as support from local government for ideas which hold promise.

POLICE AND THE TOTAL SYSTEM OF JUSTICE

In the past decade several national commissions have focused on the crime problem or have paid significant attention to the police role in the control of crime and violence.

POLICE RESPONSIBILITIES AND RELATIONSHIPS

The President's Commission on Law Enforcement and Administration of Justice was established in 1965 as a result of the crime issue. Treatment of the police and discussion of police responsibility occupied a significant portion of the efforts of the Commission and the resulting report. The thrust of much of the thinking reflected in the report is that if police forces are improved and the quality of law enforcement is increased, our crime rate will accordingly decrease.

The immediate benefit of the Commission's report was not so much the direct adoption of recommendations by police agencies as it was the focusing of national attention on the problem. The most practical result of the report was the stimulation of legislation to create the Office of Law Enforcement Assistance and its successor organization, the Law Enforcement Assistance Administration (LEAA), in the U.S. Department of Justice. The creation of LEAA, established through the Omnibus Crime Control and Safe Streets Act of 1968, has had a more far-reaching impact on law enforcement and the administration of justice than any other single event in modern law enforcement history since the establishment of the national system of fingerprinting. Specifically, the most important activity generated by the Crime Control Act has been the financing of comprehensive state law enforcement planning and the massive grants and action programs resulting therefrom.

In 1967 President Lyndon B. Johnson appointed the National Advisory Commission on Civil Disorders, which emphasized the great need for improvement of police–community relations and for increased police training in dealing with minority groups. A year later the President established the National Commission on the Causes and Prevention of Violence. That group also directed attention to the need for police improvement.

At the urging of the U.S. Department of Justice, the federal government sponsored the National Advisory Commission on Criminal Justice Standards and Goals, which in 1973 produced a voluminous series of reports containing findings, goals, and standards in the criminal justice field. The volume on police was approved by a task-force committee headed by Edward M. Davis, Chief of Police of Los Angeles, with staff work and draft writing by a team of police officers under the direction of Vernon Hoy, a deputy chief in the Los Angeles Police Department. The police standards set forth by the Commission are, on the whole, quite good.

At the same time the National Advisory Commission was compiling its recommendations, the American Bar Association (with the cooperation of the elected officers of the International Association of Chiefs of Police) produced a series of standards for police entitled *The Urban Police Function*. The ABA standards are more concerned with police operational policies and the police role in criminal procedure than those of the National Advisory Commission, but many of the standards are common to both reports and should be adopted by police departments.

The most recent national commission to focus on the police is the National Commission on Productivity, which in its initial efforts has concentrated on the means by which police effectiveness can be improved. The Commission

THE CRIME PROBLEM AND THE POLICE ROLE IN SOCIETY

defines productivity improvement in a broad way, and so the *quality* of police work, as well as the *quantity,* is a matter of concern to the group. The National Commission on Productivity is sponsored by the federal government, with Commission representation by leaders in government, industry, commerce, and organized labor.

During the past 50 years the country has experienced several other important investigations and reform movements, most notably the Wickersham Commission in 1929 and the American Bar Foundation's Survey of the Administration of Justice in 1956, but these efforts lacked the pressure of crime as an urgent national issue and did not have the immense impetus resulting from massive federal spending.

A central theme occurs repeatedly in the original work by the President's Commission on Law Enforcement and Administration of Justice and throughout most of the planning efforts carried on by the federal government and other organizations: the realization that the various functions of the law enforcement and criminal justice process can no longer be considered isolated activities, unrelated to one another. Perhaps there is no better proof of the need for a systems approach to criminal justice than this: In the entire United States the realization of the idea of the various criminal justice agencies operating under a single government at the local level is practically unknown.

Related to the need to consider the system of justice as an entity is the urgency for a recognized discipline or field of study which encompasses the law enforcement and criminal justice system as a whole. Until recently, no college or university in the United States offered a degree in the administration of criminal justice—that is, a generalized degree covering expertise in police, courts, and corrections.

In 1968 the International Association of Chiefs of Police recommended the following goals for law enforcement (i.e., as defined by the Crime Control Act to mean police, courts, and corrections) in a planning report to the Commonwealth of Massachusetts:

- The ultimate goal of law enforcement in society should be to reach a level of citizen compliance with the law through voluntary means with minimal enforcement.
- The various components in the system of justice should consider themselves as a part of an integrated whole rather than as autonomous subdivisions. Plans submitted by these components should therefore consider the impact and relationships of the entire system.
- All plans should take into account the desirability and feasibility of consolidation, regionalization, and sharing of resources, in terms of both geographic integration and integration of each component of the system into a whole.
- Crime, disorder, and hazards to public safety have multiple causes, and they require multiple solutions. Planning should therefore consider a variety of approaches and solutions.[3]

---

[3]*Guidelines for the Establishment of a State Law Enforcement Planning Agency for the Commonwealth of Massachusetts, Part I*, International Association of Chiefs of Police, Washington, D.C., 1968, p. 16.

POLICE RESPONSIBILITIES AND RELATIONSHIPS

In the initial news release publicizing the creation of the Police Foundation,[4] the president of the parent Ford Foundation reiterated the widespread belief in police as the focal point in the reduction of crime:

> Obviously a fundamental attack upon crime will require a long-term national effort not only to reform and reinforce the whole system of law and justice but also, and perhaps more fundamentally, to remove the conditions that breed crime, poverty, illiteracy, ill health, and slum housing. But one major present point of leverage for change is the police, as the President's Crime Commission pointed out in ample detail and careful analysis.

It is also entirely possible that the conditions which are contributing to our rapidly accelerating crime rate will continue to get worse—such as the alarming increase in narcotics and drug abuse, urban overcrowding, the gap between affluence and poverty, unemployment and economic recession, racial discrimination, the decay in family life, the increase in crime inspired by revolutionary activists, and the hypocrisy generated by corruption at high levels in government. The result may be that our present crime crisis will be insignificant when judged by tomorrow's criteria, and in that event society may have to depend on truly innovative solutions.

[4]The Ford Foundation established the Police Foundation as a funding agency to stimulate innovation and improvement in the police field.

Chapter 2

The Relationship of Police
to Government and Politics

In contrast to the prevailing pattern found in the rest of the world, the criminal justice "system" in the United States and Canada is a peculiar combination of national, state, and local agencies. In the United States, the task of description is compounded by the existence of some 55 state and territorial jurisdictions and as many separate criminal-law and procedural codes. Federal agencies operate under limited police powers, carefully regulated by constitutional restrictions but with wider jurisdiction in the area of courts and corrections. At the state level, although the various components of the criminal justice system all exist as state functions, they are controlled by different branches of government; state police and highway patrols are overwhelmingly organized as part of the executive branch of the state government, whereas the court system is within the judicial branch. Suspects who are arrested by the state police (the executive branch) become defendants in the court system (the judicial branch). However, as an offender moves through the court system to the state correctional system, he or she again returns to an agency which is under the control of the executive branch of government.

At the local level the criminal justice process is complicated by the almost complete concern of municipal government with only the police function. Municipal administrators—city managers, mayors, council members, and so

POLICE RESPONSIBILITIES AND RELATIONSHIPS

on—are obligated to concern themselves only with the part of the process relating to police. The next phase of the process—the courts' function—is controlled by various combinations of the judicial and executive arms of government, but very often at a different level, such as through a county prosecutor or state-administered lower court. An offender completing a passage through the system may again return to a local-government agency— the county sheriff—for incarceration in the county jail.

Since most policing in the United States and Canada is carried out by municipal police forces, much of the discussion about the relationship of the police agency to the government and politics will be oriented to conditions which exist at the municipal level.

TOP-LEVEL CONTROL

During the development of policy, the question often arises as to the relative degree of control and responsibility exercised by officials at various levels of the governmental hierarchy. Unfortunately, many city charters or city ordinances are ambiguous on the question of control, and in some cases the management of a police department is simultaneously vested in a city council and/or police commission, a mayor, a city manager or administrator, a director of public safety, and a chief of police.

In few cities has the solution for the problem originated with the legislative body, such as the city council. In fact, because its members often have had little or no experience in municipal government, this body must share a great part of the responsibility for some of the present confusion about determination of policy and assignment of responsibility.

Some organizations devoted to municipal management, such as the National League of Cities and U.S. Conference of Mayors and the International City Management Association, have attempted to promulgate policy guidelines for any given issue. However, there has been relatively little effort to establish the bounds for policy determination by each successive level of the municipal hierarchy.

Some of the problem can be traced to inadequacies in the city charter or the governing ordinance itself. An ordinance which is overspecific about details relating to police management, and at the same time ambiguous as to who actually exercises control, is frequently found to be at fault in many communities. Consultants of the International Association of Chiefs of Police have often encountered police ordinances which set out in detail the organizational structure of the department, including the numbers of personnel to be assigned to each rank and such matters as salaries and working conditions, as well as rules and regulations for the conduct of departmental business.

A detailed ordinance is unnecessary and undesirable. The best kind of ordinance is brief and general, as illustrated in Figure 2–1, showing the model ordinance developed by the IACP staff.

THE RELATIONSHIP OF POLICE TO GOVERNMENT AND POLITICS

(Section) Police Department

There is hereby created a Police Department for the City of _____ which shall consist of a Chief of Police and as many employees as the City Council may designate from time to time.

(Subsection) Appointment and Removal of the Chief of Police. The Chief of Police shall be appointed by the (Mayor) (City Manager) with the approval of a majority of the City Council, from a list of eligible candidates supplied by the Civil Service Commission (or central personnel agency). The Chief of Police shall serve at the pleasure of the (Mayor) (City Manager) and may be removed by the (Mayor) (City Manager) at any time thereafter with the consent of a majority of the City Council.

(Subsection) Supervision and Control of the Chief of Police. The (Mayor) (City Manager) shall be the immediate supervisor of the Chief of Police, and all policies, directives and orders from the City Government to the Chief of Police shall be made by or transmitted through the (Mayor) (City Manager) as the executive head of the City Government. The Chief of Police shall report directly to the (Mayor) (City Manager) and not to the City Council, to individual members thereof, or to (any other committee or commission).

(Subsection) Powers and Duties of the Chief of Police. The Chief of Police shall direct the administration and operations of the Police Department, and in addition to policies transmitted to him by the (Mayor) (City Manager), shall establish such other policies, directives, rules and regulations for the administration and operations of the department as he sees fit. The Chief of Police shall serve as appointing authority for appointment to any position within the department other than his own, and shall have the power to suspend or dismiss any employee, consistent with the provisions of the (State law or City Charter).

Budgeting

(Other ordinances should relate to municipal budgeting and fiscal management. Any such ordinance should provide for annual budgets to be submitted by each department, and that approval of expenditures should not require a second action by the full City Council, as long as the department's expenditures do not exceed monthly or quarterly allocations.)

Personnel Management

(Other ordinances should relate to municipal personnel management, disciplinary action, and employee benefits in general. However, specific salaries for each position should not be set out in ordinance form. Salaries should be mentioned only in the annual budget or by resolution.)

Figure 2–1 Model police ordinance. *(Prepared by the International Association of Chiefs of Police.)*

When the department is encumbered by a detailed ordinance which infringes on the authority of the chief of police to carry out day-to-day operations, the chief should take the initiative to have a simpler form adopted, such as the model ordinance mentioned above. This kind of ordinance is also usually acceptable to city managers and mayors, since it gives them more control than would be the case if the police ordinance were highly detailed. The manager or mayor may thus be receptive to bringing the ordinance problem to the attention of the city council. In some cases, a poor police-charter provision can be changed only by an election, which may require the support of a

POLICE RESPONSIBILITIES AND RELATIONSHIPS

citizens' group or charter commission before the change can be realized. The chief should not hesitate to recommend the change because of fear that people will misconstrue his attitude as being motivated by a desire to be independent and not under the control of the legislative body. If this feeling is strong, he should enlist the aid of influential citizens and persons in the government who can present the case without identifying the chief as the initiator.

A proper ordinance or charter should set out the chain of command for control of the department and for reporting purposes. Even when the ordinance or charter fails to specify the proper chain of command, the chief should attempt to secure agreement by the manager or mayor and the council through a written memorandum or a directive which serves the same purpose.

Much of the concern over who controls the police department—and to what extent—centers on the degree of emphasis on vice control or on some of the forms of policing which are subject to discretion. The fact is that most laws of any consequence which must be enforced in any locality are state laws rather than city ordinances, and so the question of enforcement really is academic; a department which does not want to enforce state laws in the face of public sentiment to do otherwise will run the risk of scandal and official censure. The only local laws of any importance for police relate to parking control and traffic flow, licensing (such as the regulation of taxi-cab drivers and operators of businesses such as massage parlors), and other matters of similar significance. Of these ordinances, by far the most significant are those which deal with the question of morality.

The City Manager and the Mayor

There are two predominant forms of municipal government which ought to be discussed here, i.e., the city-manager system and the strong-mayor system. The relationship of the chief of police to the executive head in each of these forms is slightly different.

The principal difference between these two forms is the method of selection of the executive head. Most mayors are selected by popular election and as a result often feel that they must reflect public opinion to a greater extent than a manager. The disadvantage of the strong-mayor–council form (i.e., with the mayor independently elected and having responsibility for the executive branch) is that there is no assurance in most situations that the mayor will have even a minimum level of qualifications. The advantage of the system is that the strong mayor has complete executive control during his incumbency. When the mayor is competent, the system is probably superior to a city-manager form of government in which the manager is of equal competence.

The advantage of the city-manager system, on the other hand, is that the average level of competence of managers is probably superior to that of the incumbent in the strong-mayor system because of selection standards which can be imposed upon an appointed office but not on an elected office in government. The disadvantage of the city-manager concept is that the manager is often forced to keep himself in check to satisfy a majority of council

THE RELATIONSHIP OF POLICE TO GOVERNMENT AND POLITICS

members and often administers by offering his council members a choice between alternatives. The manager must also frequently relay the policies of the majority of the council to city department heads as if these policies were his own ideas. The system works beautifully until the philosophy of the council is at variance with his own concepts, and in that case he must decide when an issue or series of issues justifies his resignation.

Most city managers view the administration of the police department with more concern and apprehension than they feel toward other city departments. Part of the reason is that the majority of managers achieve their positions through a combination of academic training and a period of apprenticeship in an assistant administrative position. They are thus shielded to some extent from the rough-and-tumble politics which many mayors have experienced in their careers. Moreover, most city managers have backgrounds in general public administration, fiscal management, or engineering, but seldom in law enforcement. As a result, they tend to be more aloof from the affairs of the police department than many mayors, who often are elected because of prominence within a community or because of past experience in city councils or ward politics. Most of these areas are likely to place them in closer contact with police or with policy decisions affecting police.

Many city managers therefore believe in giving police-department heads a wide latitude for action except in regard to policies which affect all city departments, such as those concerning promotional procedures, personnel management, budgeting, and other administrative matters. On the other hand, most city managers refrain from attempting to make policy in such traditional police matters as scheduling, assignments, beat layouts, departmental rules and regulations, operational policy, internal record keeping, and communications procedures.

Developing Good Relationships   Some of the problems which develop in the relationship between the police administrator and the mayor or city manager can be attributed to faulty personal communication. This topic is explored in greater detail in Chapter 9, but several guidelines are set out here.

The police chief should report regularly to his supervisor through a combination of verbal and written communications. When a conversation results in policy change, it should be reduced to writing. Written verifications of verbal commitments are, unfortunately, a necessary evil in any well-run organization. However, the tone and content of memos from the chief should not give his supervisor the impression that the latter's memory is faulty or that the chief is "building a case" against the mayor or manager.

A disadvantage of promotion from within to the rank of chief of police is that it is sometimes difficult for the new police administrator to establish the right kind of friendly rapport, which is in contrast to the reserved pattern of communications—or perhaps none at all—between the mayor or manager and the chief prior to his appointment. This situation can be helped when the new chief makes the first few contacts with the manager or the mayor in the presence of other, more experienced department heads, such as at an informal staff luncheon.

A practical means for overcoming some of the potential conflict between the chief and the manager is an advance agreement between the two to present the chief's differing point of view to the city council as a means of appeal. The city manager should be expected, of course, to present his opposing views. This kind of arrangement should be discussed well before the development of problems themselves, preferably during the hiring interview at the time the chief of police is selected.

Police administrators should use a positive approach in their communications with their supervisors; they should emphasize successful activities rather than negative ones. However, when a deficiency or problem must be discussed, the chief should offer a solution (or perhaps several alternatives) along with the problem.

Bad news should not be delayed until it gets out of hand. For example, when the police administrator fails to notify the manager or mayor of a festering grievance (perhaps stemming from a questionable policy established by the manager) until a committee from the police association is en route to the city council, the manager is placed in a vulnerable position which may not be deserved.

Some difficulties between the manager and the chief may arise because the problems or needs of the department are not communicated by the manager beyond his own level to the city council or the legislative body. When this happens, and then when there is a subsequent feeling on the part of the city council that the facts should have been transmitted to the council by the chief, it is tempting for the police administrator to think about short-circuiting the usual line of communication through the manager. This can be a special problem during the budgeting process. The budget which is prepared by the chief of police must be reviewed by the city manager, who then makes his own recommendations in the light of the demands and needs of other city departments and the state of revenues. The city manager may or may not convey to the council the police chief's recommendations as to the amount of money to be spent for various programs in the budget. In some cases, the struggle for control over the budgeting of programs is at the heart of the control over the entire fiscal apparatus of the municipality.

In the city-manager form of government, it is important for the police administrator to remember that the manager does not expect the chief always to confide totally in him. The chief should understand that what is said to the manager may have to be reported to the city council. It is unfair to disclose a confidence to the city manager and then expect him to refrain from discussing it with the city council.

Deciding what should be reported to the city administrator on an exception basis is not an easy task; the degree of reporting is related to the size of the city. Generally, a police administrative matter or internal problem should be discussed immediately with the manager if it is likely to be newsworthy to the community. Operational situations, such as a single crime or a series of crimes or accidents, should have a high threshold. In most communities, headline-news items, as well as operational situations which have captured the attention of a substantial number of citizens, ought to be communicated above the departmental level.

Differences in Opinion   People often succumb to the temptation to think of a simple difference in opinion as a breakdown of communication. At times, disagreement in philosophy or concept has to be acknowledged. No mutually agreeable solution may be possible except to explore each other's point of view in detail to see what motivates each view. When the issue involves major policy (and not a superficiality, in which case the city administrator should not have been concerned anyway), the mayor or city manager has the right to prevail. The police executive (as in the case of the city manager who is in conflict with a city council) must decide whether an unfavorable decision on the issue justifies his resignation or whether he should accede to the higher authority.

When the operation of the department is proceeding smoothly without disturbing problems, it is easy for the city administration to lapse into the widespread but oversimplified belief that the chief is to "run the department" as long as he performs in a satisfactory way and that the only alternative is to fire the chief if he does not do a good job. As indicated earlier, there are times when a position or an action by a department head must be specifically overruled by his supervisor. The manager should be expected to resolve serious differences between his own thinking and that of the department head in favor of his own best judgment. When he does this, of course, he relieves the department head of the consequences of the immediate effect of the action. At the same time, the manager must realize that he cannot usually be as technically competent as some of his subordinates or have the depth of experience of all his department heads. He should therefore allow the department heads to have correspondingly greater authority and responsibility over their respective subordinates than the manager has over the department heads.

This should be especially relevant to the police department for several other reasons. First, the chief is the highest-ranking member in the city government with peace-officer status. Second, the position of chief of police is a traditionally powerful and responsible office. More than any other person in a local government, the chief is typically *expected* by the public to control crime and vice. In many states and cities the chief is given statutory authority as the principal law enforcement officer, and the term "chief of police" itself has a certain implication of the finality of his authority. Third, in any organization with a well-developed hierarchy, the highest-ranking member with experience in all the ranks usually finds he has greater disciplinary authority and responsibility than his counterparts who have not had this experience. This is particularly true in a semimilitary organization whose members operate under conditions requiring firm control of personnel.

The Director of Public Safety

Some public safety departments are relatively old and, in fact, predate the expansion of the city-manager movement. The position of director of public safety in Pittsburgh, Pennsylvania, is a charter office which was established in 1901. The concept cannot be universally categorized, therefore, as part of a trend to overcome the inadequacies of an incumbent chief of police by appointing someone to supervise him. Unfortunately, many public safety directorships created today are expressly designed to do just this. At times, in the presence of a totally inadequate chief of police and an unsatisfactory civil service system which prevents the chief's removal, the device has some justification. In most cases, however, the technique must be deplored as a subterfuge for failure to take more acceptable corrective action, such as the use of disciplinary or personnel remedies which already exist, or the failure to exercise reasonable courage and conviction in dealing with the chief.

For the few local governments in the country which are fortunate enough to have several of the criminal justice functions organized as a part of one government, the new position of director of criminal justice seems to have more promise than the concept of public safety director. The police have much more in common with the prosecutor and many more relationships with the court than with members of the fire department and some of the other functions which have been traditionally placed within the department of public safety. Also, the director of criminal justice is much more easily able to relate to some of the agencies and activities which are not really a part of the criminal justice system itself but are closely allied with it, such as social service agencies, both public and private, and community organizations which are interested in delinquency prevention and control.

The public safety concept has some validity at the state level of government; many state organizational structures are poorly designed, with the result that the governor is burdened with a multiplicity of departments which he must supervise in the absence of a consolidation or grouping of functions. In this case there is ample justification for establishing a department of public safety which combines state police, the state fire marshal, beverage control, weights and measures, civil defense, motor-vehicle inspection, and related functions.

The Police Commission and Other Forms of Control

The police-commission structure is found in some parts of the United States, and it has several variations in structure and responsibility. One of the versions of the police-commission concept is the small group of part-time officials (usually an odd number) appointed by the city council or mayor. The police commission is often given responsibility for the promulgation of rules and regulations and for the administration of personnel rules, with duties similar to those of a civil service commission. In some cases the police commission is an appeal body only for disciplinary and personnel matters, and in other instances it has direct statutory control over the entire operations of the department.

THE RELATIONSHIP OF POLICE TO GOVERNMENT AND POLITICS

There is little justification for the existence of a police commission if it is given any responsibilities other than those of acting as an appeal board or as a civil service or personnel-regulating body.

On occasion, a multiple-member commission has been converted to a single-member "commission." The police commissioner in the New York City Police Department has now become the equivalent of chief of police and is the executive head of the agency, but the position developed historically as the surviving commissionership from a multimember body. In other cases, the term "police commissioner" is simply used in place of the title "chief of police," or there may be a "commissioner" in addition to the chief.

Regardless of the structure of the commission, problems and conflicts stem primarily from poorly worded or deficient statutes or regulations. A typical ambiguity can be seen in the following example:

> The chief of the department shall have the authority, under the supervision of the commissioner, to suspend any member of his department. . . .

and

> The police department should be divided into shifts at the discretion of the chief with the approval of the commissioner.[1]

This sort of conflict is by no means rare, and it appears in ordinances, charters, and rules and regulations with frequency. At times the dilemma caused by the existence of the single police commissioner who is not actually the executive head of the department or the multiple-member police commission can be resolved only through basic reform of the governmental structure.

In the commission form of government, each city commissioner acts as head of a city department. That form of government has gradually disappeared over the past few decades and is rarely found today. If the elected police commissioner administers the department directly, the system is no more and no less effective than the elected sheriff at the county level. In addition, the system suffers from vulnerability to "logrolling" among commissioners and from other disadvantages long recognized by students of public administration.

POLICE AND POLITICS

The literature of police administration gives little attention to the problems of the police administrator who encounters "politics," as the word is commonly used in the derogatory sense. Many police officials, moreover, believe that a forthright discussion of police and politics is somehow on the forbidden list of thoughts which must remain in verbal form only.

The police administrator and key members of the department are sometimes given visible support by well-meaning citizens who thereby actually

---

[1]*Rules and Regulations for the Department of Police, Cairo, Illinois*, pp. 3–4.

hinder the cause of the chief and the department. During budget hearings, for example, certain council members may oppose suggestions for expansion of the budget for what the chief believes to be essential police purposes. Citizens who support the department head's point of view can then endanger the chief's standing with these same council members by being overaggressive, thus shifting the emphasis from the issue itself to one of personal conflict.

There may be attempts by misguided members of the department to influence members of the city council on an individual basis. This practice is to be avoided and, if necessary, should be dealt with by disciplinary action. In one extreme instance of this kind, a supervisor in a police department asked his priest to influence a recalcitrant councilman during the next confessional dialogue between the priest and the councilman. Fortunately, the priest had better sense than the supervisor.

A problem which sometimes arises in municipal police departments and which is of concern to mayors, city managers, and chiefs of police is created by individual council members who wish to influence the department or to obtain favors. Some states, such as California, restrict the authority of individual council members by giving only the collective group the authority to make decisions. In other cases, this kind of control is established by the city charter or is a result of the council's own deliberations. In any event, the chief of police must sometimes decide whether a direct contact by an individual council member should be discouraged. The issue is a delicate one, and the manner in which it is handled often determines whether a chief of police remains in his position.

An example of a proper charter provision governing the activity of council members in this regard is shown in Figure 2–2.

Dealing with Difficult Situations

Ideally, any chief of police or executive head of the department should have enough independence, courage, and integrity to consider himself to be "bigger than the job." In other words, if he is asked by the city manager or mayor to carry out an unethical order or if he is placed in an untenable position, the chief should be prepared to resign if he is unable to effect a change in the direction of events. Unfortunately, of course, the chief of police may not always have this strength. Moreover, because of the prestige inherent in the position of chief of police, there will doubtless be others to take his place who are more willing to accept compromise. In such a situation the chief of police should feel no hesitation about enlisting public support in his behalf.

The chief who considers his action solely *a matter of principle* is usually referring to his pride and stubbornness. Principles and objectives must be weighed on the scale of expediency, provided there is no compromise with crime or corruption. The police chief must keep his main objective in view but yield a secondary objective when to remain stubborn threatens the success of his program. He must not adopt so inflexible an attitude as to create situations

THE RELATIONSHIP OF POLICE TO GOVERNMENT AND POLITICS

Sec. 4.04. Council and council members not to interfere in appointments or removals or direction of personnel.

Neither the council nor any of its members shall direct the appointment of any person to or his removal from any office or employment by the city manager or by any of his subordinates, except as specifically provided in this Charter. Except for the purpose of inquiry, the council and its members shall deal with the administrative services solely through the city manager, and neither the council nor any member thereof shall give orders either publicly or privately to any subordinate of the city manager. Any councilman violating the provisions of this section or voting for a motion, resolution or ordinance in violation of this section shall be guilty of a misdemeanor and upon conviction thereof shall cease to be a councilman. Provided, however, that nothing herein contained shall be construed as prohibiting any councilman from discussing with the city manager any appointment or removal.

Figure 2-2 Charter provision governing interference by city council members, Alexandria, Virginia. *(Source: The City Charter of Alexandria, Virginia.)*

that will forever block the attainment of his purpose. When insistence against powerful community opinion jeopardizes what has already been accomplished, it is folly not to yield, especially when the point at issue is relatively unimportant.

The world cannot be reformed or a police department reorganized in a day; an act directed toward either of these ends that might fail today may be acceptable tomorrow. Police chiefs should develop their programs and their departmental and community support by doing the easiest things first. Nothing succeeds like success, and as the chief succeeds with the less difficult, the more difficult becomes easier to accomplish. Police chiefs must not compromise with criminals; neither should they initiate action for which the community has not been prepared. Undertaking premature action that may cost the chief his job is not an intelligent approach to the task of providing the community with the best possible police service. When the attitude of the public toward change in general is not well known, perhaps the best advice is to suggest that the chief test public reaction to several new or controversial ideas in order to probe the willingness to change.

Avoiding Unnecessary Issues The great number of influences that are brought to bear on the police may place the chief at some time or other in opposition to influential persons in the community, and in consequence some hostility may be created which can result in a temptation to expand an issue or to meet it head on, merely as a show of force. Such temptation should be resisted. The chief should avoid an issue when the main thing to be gained is a moral victory; he has little else to gain and much to lose by such action. If he loses, he may find himself out of office; if he wins, he has gained nothing beyond the development of a hostility to the point where it will never be dissipated.

The Trap of Inflexibility   Police resistance against "politics" is sometimes so strong that even when political figures in the legislative body have engaged in their rightful role of broad police determination, the police are unable to view it favorably. The police must not build up such a "sales resistance" to outside influence as to be unable to consider worthwhile proposals. Constant guarding against pressures and frequent denial of requests tend to establish a behavior pattern that prompts the police to say "no" when they might better say "yes." They must guard themselves against putting on such a thick, defensive armor that they cannot distinguish between influence and wise suggestions and advice. The police should not say "no" until they have studied all the facts.

The Power Structure

Communities differ in the composition of the so-called power structure. The term is meaningless when it refers to the sum total of the business community, the heads of all civic organizations, the press, and the elected and appointed officials of the community. On occasion, however, the prime source of power can be much more specifically identified with a group, such as a single civic organization, citizens who share a special interest such as membership in a club, and so on. For example, the power structure in some rural communities is found in the volunteer fire department.

When the power structure in a community is concentrated in an identifiable organization which the police executive may conscientiously join (such as Rotary, Kiwanis, the Lions, or—even though he may lose face temporarily in some quarters—the volunteer fire department), he should make an effort to participate actively in the organization. A few veteran police chiefs have stated facetiously (but not without some truth) that public opinion in the community is controlled by bartenders and barbers. Regardless of who exercises the power of opinion, the chief of police should make certain that he is aware of their collective views so that constructive influence by the police department can be carried out.

The police administrator may meet or come into contact with city hall habitués who, because of personal idiosyncrasies or because they represent unethical interests, have a particularly troublesome influence over policy makers. In some cases government officials can be misled into thinking that the city hall habitués and/or lobbyists truly do represent the majority of citizens. The department and the community can suffer from the consequences. For example, some of the habitual city hall visitors may have a more-than-average tolerance for gambling and the "open city." Their repeated suggestions can cause the police to reduce enforcement pressure or the number of personnel assigned to vice activity. Similarly, city hall lobbyists can influence council members to reduce expenditures to the point of endangering the safety of the community. The city policy makers, and particularly the police administrator, must be careful to distinguish between what the community as a whole should have and what representatives of special interests would have.

The Power of the Press

While the entire public must be kept informed, some individuals in the community exert such a powerful and widespread influence as to deserve special attention. The police chief is frequently justified in taking them into his confidence and discussing his proposed plans with them in order to ensure their understanding and approval and to gain their assistance in informing and winning the support of others and in meeting opposition to the plan. Especially important is the support of the press. The chief should discuss his plans frankly with members of the press in order to avoid criticisms that sometimes spring from ignorance of the purpose and nature of the operation and to obtain the active help of the newspapers in disseminating information to the public.

Community newspapers often have a strong influence in determining whether the chief is retained or dismissed. There are instances in which a local newspaper has developed hostility for the police chief in particular and the department in general because the police have criticized and rebuked the press for inaccurate reporting of crime news. The police administrator should never allow such situations to escalate to the point of hard feelings, and he should personally make frequent contacts with the publisher or editor to discuss sensitive or political issues relating to the department.

Community Control

The question of community control is a dilemma for many urban police chiefs. Simply defined, the term "community control" means the transfer of decision-making authority over police policy from the local government at large to smaller neighborhood units within the area encompassed by that government.[2]

Alienation and abuse of minorities, lack of influence in setting enforcement priorities, imbalance in vice-law enforcement, and inability to secure a rightful share of police resources are prominent among the problems cited by community-control advocates. These advocates state that many of these problems affecting urban residents can be alleviated if the means of control are directly in the hands of neighborhood representatives rather than indirectly in the hands of representatives who are elected by the citizens at large. While they admit on occasion that such arrangements may not be as efficient as centralized control by established government, the advocates of community control state that their chief concern is legitimacy, not efficiency.[3]

The greatest difficulty with decentralized community control for police is that the regularly constituted legislative body is of course the legitimate, democratically elected mechanism for representative government. Second, there is no assurance that leaders who emerge from neighborhood organizations have that much more legitimacy with all the citizenry in the neighborhood

---

[2]Alan A. Altshuler, *Community Control: The Black Demand for Participation in Large American Cities*, Pegasus Publications, New York, 1970, pp. 64–65.

[3]Ibid., p. 40.

than a city-council member elected from the same political ward, or even a council member or mayor who is elected at large. Third, a community-control mechanism which deals with police policy determination, but not with other government services, is at best an awkward arrangement which is likely to encourage conflicts with the regularly constituted legislative body.

Nevertheless, advocacy of community control has focused some needed attention on these problems and has pointed the way for improvements which may correct some of the abuses which actually do exist.

A police department which attempts to keep the department "open" to the citizenry tends to have fewer problems in coping with demands for greater citizen participation. Departments which have a more traditional approach may frequently be a target for demands of this sort. The closed department can often be identified by the following descriptors:

1 Having a traditional "institutional-style" department which stresses equal and impartial law enforcement. The honest, incorruptible, institutional-style department may even resist attempts by the mayor and members of the city council to influence basic police policies, maintaining that such efforts are "political" and are thus to be resisted.

2 Having a press policy which basically is one of noncooperation.

3 Having an attitude of defensiveness of police officers charged in citizen-complaint investigations in which officers should have been disciplined.

The closed institutional-style department is not without its benefits. Some reasonably effective police organizations have developed under these conditions, achieving high morale and carrying out good work as far as the members of the department are concerned, even though much of the community is dissatisfied.

The police administrator may therefore want to move toward a comprehensive citizen-participation program which will permit the traditional policy-making apparatus in the city to retain control, while giving citizens a genuine opportunity to see what is going on in the department, and to provide input into department policy making without controlling it. A comprehensive program for citizen participation is described in Chapter 12.

Partisan Politics

The influence of partisan politics on the police remains one of the great handicaps to effective police management. Although the enactment of civil service law has curtailed the flagrant turnover of government employees under the old political-spoils system, there is still an unacceptable amount of firing and hiring of police administrators on the basis of their political affiliations.

Professional administrators owe it to their departments to refrain from partisan political campaigning in any form. A police chief who supports a candidate for local office in any overt way perpetrates a gross administrative evil and, of course, runs the risk of being turned out of office if the candidate loses.

The incidence of purely political turnover of the chief's job seems to be receding. Fortunately, some areas of the country have nonpartisan local government. Several states, such as California, operate under "little Hatch Acts" which effectively discourage partisan political campaigning.

Although police administrators are well-advised to stay away from political campaigning, they should not go so far as to avoid speaking out to the public and to politicians about the issues themselves.

However, because of the nature of contemporary politics, the police administrator must often decide whether to take sides in a partisan situation or on an issue which is seemingly favorable to the department's point of view at the moment. Chiefs of police and police labor unions have sometimes aroused the enmity of a majority of the city council because they openly supported the position of a minority of the council with views closer to their own. The problem is usually one which arises not from the right of the chief to express his viewpoint, or even from the issue itself, but from the manner in which the viewpoint is expressed. Administrators should be especially cautious about avoiding the appearance of favoritism for one side or another to the degree that they are apparently suggesting the defeat of opposing council members in the next election.

Chapter 3

Police Leadership in the Community

Every police chief is responsible for leadership in two broad areas. He must provide leadership within the department, and as the head of the force he must represent it in relations with the administrative head of the city and, through the administrative head, with the municipal council and the public. In other words, the chief must provide the leadership on law enforcement issues for the entire community. Exercising community leadership in law enforcement is uncomplicated and straightforward when there are no controversial issues at stake or when there are no threats to vested interests, business profits, or public convenience.

THE PROMOTION OF PROGRAMS

Programs and objectives which experience the least difficulty are those which are both noncontroversial and inexpensive. Few adults would question the police chief's advocacy of educational programs against drug abuse among schoolchildren or the chief's interest in prevention of street crimes through simple redistribution of the patrol force.

The next level of difficulty is the program which has commendable

POLICE LEADERSHIP IN THE COMMUNITY

objectives—such as the reduction of armed robberies by increasing the size of the patrol force or the recruitment of officers with high qualifications—but which encounters resistance from the city government and taxpayers because it is too expensive and results in increased taxes through higher payroll costs.

The third level of difficulty may be the program which affects the interests, profits, or convenience of a special group or of the public at large but which is not necessarily expensive. An example of this is the installation of metered parking, which is self-supporting but nevertheless controversial.

Finally, of course, the highest level of difficulty is the program which not only has controversial objectives but also is considered too expensive by the people who control the budget.

The police administrator has important responsibilities in winning support for departmental programs, even those of the first level. The chief's task is much easier, of course, when the city administration or legislative body approves the program; he then has only to convince the public (and, at times, the members of his department) as to its merits.

The Program Which Has Top Governmental Support

Part of the leadership responsibility is to provide positive educational information, but some effort must also be expended in neutralizing outside influences that are in opposition to the public good. For example, if a recently enacted antipinball-machine ordinance seems threatened by complaints from proprietors of places where these machines are in use, and if it appears that the pressure for repeal is coming from organized-crime interests, the newspapers and other sources of influence should be informed.

Moreover, the police should enlist the support of influential groups at the start. An influential citizen or group committed in favor of a policy or plan will not ordinarily oppose it later.

General community support is based on understanding: the police cannot progress beyond the understanding of their superiors and the public. Everyone should be kept informed regarding the nature and purpose of police policies and plans because those who do not understand will not approve, and those who do not approve are likely to resist and sometimes actively oppose the operation.

Public understanding, in turn, must be based on facts, and the first step is to disseminate those facts which assisted in reaching department-level decisions so that they may be used to help others in reaching an understanding of the police purpose and method.

The facts gathered by the police must also be interpreted by them in order to ensure that correct conclusions are drawn from their consideration. The police likewise have a responsibility to interpret their acts and policies to the public so that all may know the reasons on which they are based, the results obtained, and the probable consequences of failure. The following are examples: (1) the reasons for conspicuous patrol cars, for restricted use of foot patrol, and for search for physical evidence at crime and accident scenes; (2)

the relationship between enforcement and education, on the one hand, and the accident rate, on the other; (3) the relationship between commercialized vice and organized crime; and (4) the reasons for the youth-crime-control program.

Acting without Higher Governmental Support

The police chief is faced with the dilemma of whether to act when he feels that his immediate supervisor is not exercising enough leadership or is opposing programs which the chief feels are in the public interest. The problem is more common in the city-manager system than in the strong-mayor form of government because many city managers operate under the concept of the consensus, viewing their role as merely carrying out the policies of the city council. The chief often thus finds himself to be the first level of responsibility in counteracting what in his opinion are trends which would endanger the quality of police service or public protection.

When the police administrator makes an appeal to a legislative body, his presentation should be unemotional, well organized, brief, and forceful. He should not try to cover all the galling or petty issues which may be disturbing him, but only the important topics which prompted the appeal. Expressing a sense of humor in this kind of situation is a good idea if not overdone, and it can actually provide a face-saving breakthrough or outlet for tension which may prompt an immediate move in his favor.

Appeal to the Public

Even when a program is rejected by the legislative body, the chief can take the message to the public reasonably well by describing the disease but not the treatment. For example, the chief can point out a rise in street crime without relating it to the need for more officers, or he can describe the delays encountered in answering incoming calls without mentioning the need for a new communications complex.

Under the strong-mayor form of government, the mayor and the chief often take a more vigorous stand in the face of budget setbacks and issue strong public statements on the failure of the council to act. Elected sheriffs find it necessary to do the same thing with respect to boards of supervisors at times. This kind of posture is not recommended, however, in systems in which the legislative body can remove the police administrator without cause—unless he is planning to leave anyway.

The Need for Leadership in Enacting New Legislation

The chief of police is often in the best position to suggest new legislation to cope with a particular kind of problem facing the department. While it is generally considered to be the domain of state and local legislatures to formulate new laws, most legislators freely admit that they need the advice of persons who deal with the problems on a day-to-day basis.

Perhaps even more important than the need for changes in criminal statutes is the need for changes in administrative law which would affect the

POLICE LEADERSHIP IN THE COMMUNITY

management and operation of the department. Examples are the need for the police administrator's input in laws affecting a local or state system for selection of police officers, disability and retirement provisions, and police disciplinary procedures.

The administrator who suggests a change in law, either in the state law or in a local ordinance, should first review his recommendations with appropriate members of the police command staff and with members of the city manager's staff who may be affected by the change. For example, the chief's initiative in proposing changes in the retirement system should be discussed with members of the police department, the city personnel agency staff, and the city fiscal-department staff if the changes affect benefits of officers. Similarly, a recommended change in legislation such as a new state standard for entrance medical requirements should be discussed with the examining physician in the city personnel or health department.

New legislation may be introduced by submitting suggestions to members of state legislatures who represent the local region or to legislators who are known to be sympathetic to the kind of new laws being proposed. Legislation may also be introduced by presenting ideas to local and regional police planning commissions or councils for their endorsement so that these commissions or councils can then transmit the requests to the legislature, either through local representatives or to the legislature directly, such as through a legislative committee.

At times, of course, the chief may want to support new legislation, even though he is not the person who actually suggests it. The chief may thus advocate new laws through press releases, contacts with civic organizations, and public appearances. His comments can often influence public opinion which is uncommitted or weakly committed to an idea.

Citizen Surveys and the Determination of Citizen Opinion on Issues

Regardless of whether a survey of citizen opinion is associated with new legislation, obtaining the views of the citizenry on police problems is an essential step in the assumption of leadership within the community. The views of citizens may temper the opinions of a police administrator whose ideas are somewhat out of phase with community thinking, and in the event the chief has misgivings about a particular position but on balance feels that it would be wise to adopt a course of action in a certain direction, a citizens' survey may provide the chief with a source of strength and realization of purpose which may not have been there to begin with. For example, the chief of police may feel, perhaps mistakenly, that most citizens want to have massage parlors in the community, although he believes that the presence of massage parlors would lead to the growth of organized crime, the spread of venereal disease, and an upsurge in prostitution. Obtaining the opinion of citizens may prove to be refreshing when he finds that most people agree with him about massage parlors.

Neighborhood Police–Community Councils

A proved vehicle for exerting leadership in the community is the neighborhood police–community council.[1] By presenting new concepts to each neighborhood council, the police administrator can usually win the support of interested citizens who are members of the council or who attend neighborhood meetings. In terms of the percentage of citizens who are represented in council meetings, the number is typically quite small; their true value, however, is their influence on the many people with whom they come into contact and the effect of their endorsement as described in newspaper articles and television coverage. Further, neighborhood councils can very often offer worthwhile suggestions to the administrator, in terms of either changes in laws or the adoption of new programs being advocated by the chief.

The Role of Regional Organizations in Community Leadership

Many states now have regional police planning organizations which have been established to carry out the aims of the state law enforcement planning agency. The regional organization often has a variety of committees, such as a police chiefs' committee or a council, commission, or committee which is created for the purpose of reviewing, coordinating, and approving law enforcement grants. These regional committees or councils can be an effective vehicle for transmitting the police administrator's ideas to persons outside the department, through the regional committee's endorsement of proposals as a part of the grant process. Also, by ascending to office in the regional organization, the chief can make statements or releases on issues on behalf of the regional committee, including, of course, issues related to his own grant applications.

Some of these points also apply to regional organizations which have nothing to do with the law enforcement planning grant process, such as a police chiefs' organization in a multistate area or an association of state chiefs of police. For example, a chief who is president of a state association of chiefs of police can usually, because of the office, have more impact on state legislators than would otherwise be the case.

Civic Associations and Organizations

Neighborhood civic associations, taxpayers' associations, and service clubs can be of value in helping the police administrator achieve support for new programs and in recognizing problems affecting the community. In some cities various civic associations and clubs have their own coordinating organization which can be known by a variety of titles, such as the "Interclub Service Council" or the "Federation of Civic Associations." The chief should seek regular contact with such a coordinating group, particularly if there is a subcommittee established to cover the police or criminal justice area.

[1] The concept of the police–community council is described in Chap. 13.

The Importance of a Statement of Goals

Taking public positions on difficult issues is a wise procedure and is one of the essential elements in leadership. Coupled with statements of goals for the benefit of departmental personnel, public statements on issues are helpful for the following reasons:

- They force the administrator to go through the necessary planning which has to be done if such statements must stand up to scrutiny.
- Goals which cannot stand the test of public scrutiny are probably not worthwhile; concepts which are poorly planned or conceived may thus be exposed as a result of making them public, and if the police administrator can realize that fear of failure is a natural condition which affects many executives—and in fact, is considered by some management authorities to be one of the characteristics of a successful manager—he can freely admit that his organizational goal was wrong, and a more appropriate goal can be established in its place.
- A public statement of goals helps resolve questions on which the administrator or the department was not taking prompt or effective action.
- The essence of leadership is to be the first person in the community to take a position on a certain issue, as opposed to concurring with popular opinion. If other people take positions first, then the chief follows and is not a leader, in the truest sense of the word, with respect to that particular issue.
- The statement of a goal is often the first real step in the solution to a problem, since the processes of formulating a goal, planning its execution, and actually adopting it are often inseparable.

THE SUBSTANCE OF LEADERSHIP IN THE COMMUNITY

The preceding paragraphs in this chapter have dealt with the methodology for achieving leadership within the community. Attention should now focus on some of the specific elements of a sound police administrative program which are best achieved through community leadership or which should be made known to the public:

- The substantial and immediate gains to be realized from the application of sound police practice cannot be obtained solely through action by the police. Citizen participation in crime prevention is essential, and without a substantial change in the number of people who refrain from committing crimes on moral grounds or from the standpoint of enlightened self-interest, a truly significant reduction in crime will not be possible.
- The police department must be suitably staffed. Conditions of service must be made attractive, and the best persons available must be selected for appointment and promotion. A high level of performance must be assured by recruit and in-service training and by discipline. Incompetent and otherwise unqualified officers must be removed from the service. Police officers must be indoctrinated in a philosophy based on community service, and continuous attention must be given to the relationship between the police and the public.

- Changes brought about in a police department should have a strong and direct relationship to operational effectiveness and efficiency. Both citizens and members of the department should understand that the police operations which offer the greatest promise for increased productivity are those which employ the greatest number of officers in the activities which consume the greatest number of man-hours.
- If it is assumed that police are productively employed, the community must realize that any new program or activity has to receive additional funding so that manpower and other resources are available to carry it out; otherwise, the new activity must necessarily supplant some other existing activity.
- The force must have the most modern equipment. The public should understand that police service is "labor-intensive" and that equipment is a small percentage of overall police cost. The difference between the very best equipment and the poorest sort of equipment is negligible in terms of the percent of the total budget. Modern equipment to conserve manpower must be utilized in police patrol, traffic, and investigative operations.
- The community should recognize that operational manpower should be deployed according to need and in proportion to called-for services. Foot patrol should be restricted to areas where conditions make automobile patrol unsuited. Two-man patrol cars should not be used except where and when conditions would require foot-patrol officers to operate in pairs. Patrol cars should be conspicuously marked for the most part, and the technique of hazard-oriented, aggressive preventive patrol should become the basic police operation.
- The force must be organized in a manner to ensure effective direction, coordination, and control. Organizational units must be carefully articulated so that the force will operate as a whole; relationships between the units must be precisely defined. All police duties must be assigned to someone, and all organizational units must have unavoidable and clearly understood responsibilities. Controls must be established to ensure that each member is held accountable for the use of authority. Procedures for authoritative line and staff inspections and supervision must be established.
- Systems and procedures must be established that will ensure the compilation and analysis of facts that relate to every field of police service so that action may be wisely planned and so that operating personnel can make direct use of information.
- Department procedures must be outlined to guide in the performance of every police operation and in meeting every situation that may arise. Manuals should be published, records operations and reporting regulations outlined, and field procedures and tactical plans prepared.
- The community must be organized to support police programs and assist in the solution of police problems, especially in the fields of traffic, organized crime, and juvenile-crime control.
- Procedures must be developed and manpower organized and directed toward the apprehension and prosecution of criminals and the recovery of stolen property.
- Organized crime must be driven from the community and prevented from reappearing by the stringent suppression of gambling, prostitution, and

POLICE LEADERSHIP IN THE COMMUNITY

narcotics traffic and by the strict supervision and control of the retail-liquor trade.

• Motorists and pedestrians must be controlled with a minimum of inconvenience and penalty in a manner to ensure maximum speed consistent with safety in traffic. Attention must also be given to public education. Public compliance with regulations must be won with minimum punitive enforcement.

• Delinquency-inducing conditions in the community must be eradicated and replaced by wholesome activities; attention must be given to the discovery and treatment of the delinquent child and to those exposed to situations that may cause maladjustments and consequent antisocial behavior. The social welfare aspects of police service should be emphasized. Treatment should be obtained for the physically, mentally, and emotionally ailing.

• The patrol force should be recognized as the backbone of the department and should be held responsible for the attainment of most police objectives. Although special divisions must be created for planning and staff direction, their activities at the level of execution should be restricted to tasks that may be performed substantially better by the specialist than by patrol officers and to those which, when performed by patrol officers, interfere with regular patrol duties.

• The force must be steeped in a sound philosophy of public service, such as that embodied in the following British police principles:

a. To prevent crime and disorder, as an alternative to their repression by military force and by severity of legal punishment.

b. To recognize always that the power of the police to fulfill their functions and duties is dependent on public approval of their existence, actions, and behavior, and on their ability to secure and maintain public respect.

c. To recognize always that to secure and maintain the respect and approval of the public means also the securing of the willing cooperation of the public in the task of securing observance of laws.

d. To recognize always that the extent to which the cooperation of the public can be secured diminishes, proportionately, the necessity of the use of physical force and compulsion for achieving police objectives.

e. To seek and to preserve public favor, not by pandering to public opinion, but by constantly demonstrating absolutely impartial service to law, in complete independence of policy, and without regard to the justice or injustice of the substance of individual laws; by ready offering of individual service and friendship to all members of the public without regard to their wealth or social standing; by ready exercise of courtesy and friendly good humor; and by ready offering of individual sacrifice in protecting and preserving life.

f. To use physical force only when the exercise of persuasion, advice, and warning is found to be insufficient to obtain public cooperation to an extent necessary to secure observance of law or to restore order; and to use only the minimum degree of physical force which is necessary on any particular occasion for achieving a police objective.

g. To maintain at all times a relationship with the public that gives reality to the historic tradition that the police are the public and that the public are the police;

the police being only members of the public who are paid to give full-time attention to duties which are incumbent on every citizen, in the interests of community welfare and existence.

h. To recognize always the need for strict adherence to police-executive functions, and to refrain from even seeming to usurp the powers of the judiciary of avenging individuals or the state, and of authoritatively judging guilt and punishing the guilty.

i. To recognize always that the test of police efficiency is the absence of crime and disorder, and not the visible evidence of police action in dealing with them.[2]

[2]Charles Reith, *A Short History of the British Police*, Oxford University Press, New York, 1948, pp. 64–65.

Chapter 4

Regional, State, and Federal Law Enforcement Planning

The federal Crime Control Acts and other federal and state laws affecting comprehensive law enforcement planning have added an important new responsibility for the police administrator. The police executive plays a key role in determining the nature of projects or programs which can be funded in whole or in part from outside sources. For the next several decades it is likely that the chief who does not aggressively seek outside funding assistance will be subjected to criticism.

Some chiefs of police are fortunate enough to be members of law enforcement planning agencies or commissions at the regional or state level. This situation is healthy because it tends to keep the chief advised of contemporary projects and grant application policies, thus allowing the department to be competitive. The selection of the chief as a member of a planning agency or commission is usually influenced by the size of the city, however, and the small police agency has less chance for such representation. In any event, police chiefs should aggressively seek the involvement of their agencies in regional or statewide law enforcement planning and should make certain that they themselves or other representatives of their departments attend planning and information sessions. In the department which has sufficient size to justify

39

POLICE RESPONSIBILITIES AND RELATIONSHIPS

its own research and development or planning staff, of course, the responsibility for continuous departmental planning to take advantage of federal and state funding plans belongs to the formal staff unit.

Application of the proper technique for "grantmanship" requires a special skill, particularly in view of the various sources of financing. As of the moment, funds are available from a number of federal departments: Housing and Urban Development; Health, Education, and Welfare; Transportation; and Justice. Grants are also available from foundations and state agencies themselves.

Assistance to a police department from federal or state resources can be considerable. In many demonstration-agency or prototypical projects, the department is supplied with massive amounts of expertise and money which would have been impossible to realize otherwise for such purposes. Even if a police department is not able to secure a grant or a satisfactory level of funding, the department can certainly benefit from projects which have been carried out elsewhere. The police administrator should therefore encourage other departments and the planning agencies themselves to disseminate the results of this kind of assistance.

GUIDELINES FOR COMPREHENSIVE PLANNING AT THE STATE LEVEL

Before presenting material on state law enforcement and criminal justice planning, it is appropriate to review some of the important features in the Omnibus Crime Control and Safe Streets Act of 1968 (the initial legislation which established the Law Enforcement Assistance Administration) and the amendments through 1976.

Provisions of the Crime Control Act

The act specifies that the state planning agency shall develop a comprehensive statewide plan for the improvement of law enforcement (i.e., police, courts, and corrections) throughout the state.

The state planning agency is also responsible for defining, developing, and correlating programs for the state and the units of general local government in the state and for establishing priorities for programs to improve law enforcement throughout the state.

The act authorizes grants for comprehensive state plans which cover:

1 Public protection and general crime reduction
2 Recruiting and training of law enforcement personnel
3 Public education relating to crime prevention
4 Construction of buildings and facilities
5 Combating organized crime
6 Prevention and control of riots and civil disorders
7 Recruiting and training of community-service officers
8 The establishment of criminal justice coordinating councils for cities (or groups of cities) with a population of 250,000 or more

REGIONAL, STATE, AND FEDERAL LAW ENFORCEMENT PLANNING

9 The development of community-based delinquency-prevention and correctional programs

10 The establishment of interstate metropolitan regional planning units

The plan itself must generally provide for the machinery to administer a grant program to state and local agencies. It must also allow for substantial distribution of funds to local governments; it must provide for a means for taking local needs into account; and it must emphasize innovations. The act also requires the plan to contain an outline of priorities for improvement and coordination of all aspects of law enforcement, including descriptions of:

- General needs and problems
- Established systems
- Available resources
- Machinery for implementation of the plan
- Relationship of the plan to relevant state and local plans

Finally, and most important of all, the plan must indicate the direction, scope, and general type of improvements in the future.

State and Regional Criminal Justice Planning Agencies

All states in the nation, as well as four territories and the District of Columbia, have comprehensive law enforcement planning agencies.

In the original Omnibus Crime Control and Safe Streets Act, the term "law enforcement" was used in a broad sense to mean police, courts, and corrections. This use of the term has never been successful; "law enforcement" has been used improperly even by members of the Law Enforcement Assistance Administration staff to mean police, and the greatest objection to the term has been that it encourages a feeling on the part of police that the entire Law Enforcement Assistance Administration and its programs are primarily for the benefit of police, i.e., "law enforcement" in the pre-LEAA days.

The term now endorsed by LEAA as well as the state organizations concerned with criminal justice planning is "criminal justice" by itself or "law enforcement and criminal justice." State planning agency administrators, further, want to call their organizations "state criminal justice planning agencies" as a generic term.

State criminal justice planning agencies have established an association of administrators entitled, appropriately enough, the National Conference of State Criminal Justice Planning Administrators. The organization was formed in 1971, and for the first several years operated on a committee basis, with preparation of correspondence and distribution of guidelines and position papers carried out by working committees consisting of several state criminal justice planning agency administrators who volunteered for the purpose.

In 1974, however, the Conference established a small headquarters staff in Washington, D.C. The staff prepares most of the work formerly done by the committees, although there is a two-member committee which approves documents prepared by the staff. The Conference has developed a position paper on minimum standards for state criminal justice planning agencies, covering several policies and procedures common to most agencies. These procedures cover planning, auditing of action grants, monitoring of action projects, evaluation, the basics of a grant management-information system, grant administrative procedures, and time frames for disbursement procedures. The minimum standards specify that an agency shall have a full-time professional director and further specifies that each agency shall have full-time professionals assigned to planning, research, program development, and fiscal operations.[1]

The standards do not establish recommended organizational structures or specific staffing levels but urge that the following factors be considered in determining staff levels: size of state, the number of active project applications, the range of duties, the degree to which state criminal justice planning agencies offer technical assistance to local and state agencies, and the manner in which grants are processed.

The standards also recommend several specific internal or administrative programs for the state criminal justice planning agencies—that each agency provide a formal training and staff-development program for its headquarters, regulatory, and supervisory board council personnel, including a minimum of 25 hours of in-service training a year for all persons designated as professional staff. A second program area recommended is public information—that each agency shall have on its staff or readily available to it a public information officer having access to policy-making individuals in the agency and maintaining liaison with the public and with information specialists in other agencies in the criminal justice system.

According to the standards, each state criminal justice planning agency should establish a technical assistance program to ensure the availability of adequate technical experts for criminal justice within the state.[2] Because of the limitations of staff size and money, many of the smaller state criminal justice planning agencies necessarily require their staff members to carry out two or more dissimilar functions. For the 15 largest state criminal justice planning agencies, however, the similarities in responsibility and function would seem to make it possible to recommend a structure which would be useful in any of the 15 agencies, notwithstanding the fact that there is a tendency for the organization of SCJPAs to fall into one of two broad patterns, the first featuring strong local and regional orientation or control (such as in California) and the second featuring stronger control at the state level.

No state criminal justice planning agency has a true criminal justice operational responsibility—that is, the delivery of a criminal justice line function such as police, court administration, or correctional administration—

---

[1]Memo dated Jan. 30, 1975 from Richard N. Harris, Chairman of the National Conference of State Criminal Justice Planning Administrators.
[2]Ibid.

with the exception of several state criminal justice planning agencies which have been administering the state criminal justice information systems. One agency conducts jail inspections, and several states perform organizational surveys for police departments and other work related to technical assistance.

In the State of New York, the Department of Criminal Justice Services contains several agencies of both staff and operational nature, but the state criminal justice planning agency is actually a division within the Department of Criminal Justice Services.

Foundation in Law About 20 of the 55 state criminal justice planning agencies are established according to state or territorial law. The other 35 exist primarily through executive order. The Law Enforcement Assistance Administration itself has no position on this issue. The argument for establishing the state criminal justice planning agencies through executive order by the governor is that the governor is then able to retain complete control over the state criminal justice planning agency without interference from the legislature.

Since the governor has ultimate control over criminal justice planning in all states anyway, it seems more logical to give the state legislature a role in the organization of the state criminal justice planning agency, rather than to permit complete dominance by the executive branch.

Supervisory Boards The original Omnibus Crime Control and Safe Streets Act and its subsequent admendments have not required state criminal justice planning agency supervisory boards per se. The act states merely that the state planning agency should be "representative" in character. Federal criminal justice planning agency *guidelines*, however, are much more specific and require not only that there must be a "representative board" but also that the board must be supervisory as opposed to administrative in character.

Despite the specific guideline, there is considerable latitude in the degree to which the various state criminal justice planning agency boards actually supervise. Some state laws or executive orders are more specific than others in setting out the responsibility of the supervisory boards; some directives state merely that the boards shall supervise state criminal justice planning policy but are silent as to whether the board is responsible for day-to-day administration of the headquarters staff. In any event, the governor in each state has the ultimate authority over the state criminal justice planning agencies; in some states, furthermore, the governor is chairman of the board.

In every state and territory, the governor appoints the head of the state criminal justice planning agency staff.

Regional and Local Criminal Justice Planning Agencies Regional criminal justice planning agencies are found in 46 of the 55 states and territories. Their development came about because the Crime Control Act mentions regional representation and regional priorities. Further, the guidelines established for internal fiscal administration of the state criminal justice planning agencies mention "local agencies or *combinations thereof*" in describing the allocation of funds to state criminal justice planning agencies, regions, and local agencies. Before enactment of the Crime Control Act of 1968, there were also regional councils of government structures in most states. It thus became relatively easy for existing councils of governments to absorb the new responsibilities for law enforcement and criminal justice planning. (In about half the states a dual set of bureaucracies exists for regional planning purposes—the regional criminal justice planning districts and regional planning districts for general purposes.) Finally, several states have accomplished the same effect as geographic regionalization of planning by placing localities into groupings according to population or demographic data.

Regardless of the form of the regional structure (whether as coterminous with council-of-government boundaries, as separate criminal justice regions, or on the basis of demographic groupings), the principal reason behind regional planning is simply to avoid diffusing money.

There are some difficult problems associated with administration of regional planning agencies. First, in many states there are too many regional planning agencies, and in some cases staffs in regions with vastly smaller populations are the same size as the agency staffs in the larger regions. But the fundamental problem with regional planning agencies is that the purposes they serve are not completely useful. The regional agencies are not allowed to administer operational activities and serve simply as grant-processing agencies. Larger local agencies frequently have criminal justice planning staffs which prepare grant applications that are merely approved at the regional level and sent on to the state criminal justice planning agency. Logrolling is another frequent complaint about the regional agencies, and few representatives of local agencies serving on a regional board will risk denying a grant application of a member agency for any reason because to do so is to invite retaliation. The regional process then becomes largely a rubber-stamp operation which consumes a considerable portion of the overall planning dollar in the country.

Finally, in almost every state there is a struggle between the state machinery and the regional staffs. This struggle stems for the most part from attempts by the regional staffs to secure delegation of power to the regions.

Many of the local and regional planning directors have joined a national organization entitled National Association of Regional Councils, and in addition to that group there is a National Association of Criminal Justice Planning Directors, which is made up exclusively of regional directors, as opposed to state employees.

Relationships between State Agencies and the Law Enforcement Assistance Administration   In a continuation of a trend which began in 1971 and was in evidence again in the 1973 and 1976 amendments to the Crime Control Act, there are now more congressional stipulations and conditions. The state criminal justice planning agencies, on the other hand, have reacted against these conditions as a threat to their autonomy. The state criminal justice planning agencies are also threatened to some extent by pressure from larger cities, who have asked Congress for exemption from state grant procedures so that the cities can deal with LEAA directly.

Several years ago, before the development of the state criminal justice

REGIONAL, STATE, AND FEDERAL LAW ENFORCEMENT PLANNING

planning agencies and the regional structure in each state, it appeared that the regional offices of LEAA would be more influential in determining law enforcement and criminal justice policy. Instead, regional offices of LEAA—and, indeed, LEAA headquarters itself—have been concerned largely with procedural compliance rather than with the development of performance standards and objective criteria for the evaluation of plans and results of action programs.

Throughout the United States, there are frequent disputes between the state criminal justice planning agencies and the regional Law Enforcement Assistance Administration offices, who, in the opinion of the state people, often operate outside their authority but receive little disciplinary guidance, as a rule, from LEAA headquarters. State criminal justice planning agency administrators complain that even after a correction of a regional LEAA condition by LEAA headquarters, the regional office may be allowed to make the same error all over again.

According to a study by the U.S. Advisory Commission on Intergovernmental Relations,[3] the block grant program administered by LEAA needs some very fundamental reorganization, including consolidation of many regional planning agencies.

Perhaps the most fundamental problem associated with the Law Enforcement Assistance Administration and the network of state and regional planning agencies has been the failure to unify the criminal justice system. Representatives of the various components—such as police chiefs, prosecutors, judges, and correctional administrators—are often willing to participate in comprehensive planning, but when money is in short supply, the desire to fund one's own projects often supersedes the desire to cooperate. More importantly, coordination between the various components to carry out a specific crime-reduction program is often impeded by the refusal of judges to participate, on the grounds that their cooperation is prejudicial to their role as neutral referees.

Recommended Organization of State Criminal Justice Planning Agencies

In the first draft of guidelines prepared by LEAA, it was anticipated that a "supervisory" board would have direct charge of the executive head and the staff of the state planning agency. This would have precluded the role of the board as an advisory body only and would have made it necessary for the governor to supervise the executive head of the agency through the board. LEAA later modified this position. The regulation now requires the board to have responsibility for reviewing and maintaining general oversight of the state plan, but it is silent on the matter of supervision of the executive director.

The supervisory or advisory board should be considered a part of the state criminal justice planning agency. It should have a chairperson and members selected by the governor. Tenure of the chairperson and committee members should be indefinite, subject to the discretion of the governor. Board composi-

[3]U.S. Advisory Commission on Intergovernmental Relations, *Safe Streets Reconsidered: The Block Grant Experience, 1968–1975*, Government Printing Office, Washington, 1976.

tion should reflect the total criminal justice system, and because the police component of the system accounts for such a large share of the total cost of the system, police representation should be stressed.

The state criminal justice planning agency should be established by law. The law should delineate the roles of the board and the agency staff, but it should not attempt to describe the organizational structure or detailed responsibilities of the agency.

The board should establish a schedule of meetings and should be available for special consultation at the request of the governor. Members should not receive compensation except for honoraria, travel, and living expenses for meetings. A simple majority vote of those present at a meeting should be sufficient to decide policy and issues which must be resolved.

The state criminal justice planning agency staff should be headed by an executive director, who should be directly responsible to the governor. The director should be appointed and removed by the governor and should have a thorough understanding of the theory, legal foundation, organization, and administration of all elements of the criminal justice system, including police, prosecution and defense, courts, corrections, and release procedures. The director should also have sufficient background and experience to be able to deal with federal, state, and local agencies and with various associations and professional organizations. The director should be responsible for appointing the agency staff and for directing its work and should also serve as the staff's representative at meetings of the board.

Two general trends have emerged in the organizational structure of state criminal justice planning agencies. The first trend is toward strong state control of planning. State criminal justice planning agency staffs in the strong version are larger and more complex. The second approach is to establish the state planning agency as a smaller coordinating staff, with most of the power for approval of grants delegated to regional and local levels. Obviously, the basic nature of the criminal justice planning agency must be considered in deciding upon the proper structure.

Other questions having a bearing on the structure must be considered: Should the structure be divided first into categories such as "police," "courts," and "corrections," or should the top level of the structure be organized first in terms of methodology and then by subject matter? In the interest of unified

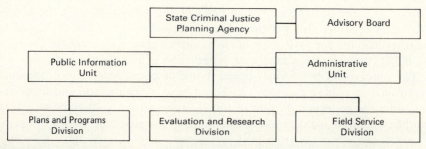

Chart 1 Recommended structure. (State Criminal Justice Planning Agency.)

handling of administrative and management matters, the latter alternative, depicted in Chart 1, is recommended.

A state criminal justice planning agency can logically consist of the following major organizational units.

Plans and Programs Division   This division should be responsible for the accounting of funds, the development of comprehensive planning, the establishment of priorities, and the evaluation of local plans for general acceptability; it should also be responsible for seeing that the plans are in conformance with the comprehensive plan approved by the advisory board.

The staff work at the state level for the development of the comprehensive state plan should be carried out by the plans and programs division after consultation with local and regional planning groups and with periodic advisory review by the board. The comprehensive state law enforcement plan should first advocate several general principles to guide overall system planning. The plan should then logically deal with more detailed statements of policy, and finally it should suggest specific policies and goals in the various disciplines which make up the criminal justice system.

The division should establish priorities, as required by LEAA guidelines and the Crime Control Act. The agency should have the authority to procure contracts for any necessary work in planned development and agency operation, consistent with LEAA regulations. The plans should consider all aspects and levels of the law enforcement and criminal justice system, including noncriminal police services. The plans and programs division should seek the application of all appropriate planning agency staff expertise to assist in the planning process.

Evaluation and Research Division   A division of work should be evaluating projects, compiling statistics, compiling and disseminating research information, conducting experimental research and development, and preparing studies in the general field of criminology, law enforcement, and crime prevention.

The first broad responsibility of the division should be the evaluation of grant-funded projects—a process which depends largely on compilation of law enforcement and criminal justice statistics.

The next function of the evaluation and research division should be the compilation of general statistics, statewide, within the criminal justice system. Guides for this activity should be as follows:

- The statistics should have wide application and should cover the entire criminal justice system.
- The statistical system should be automated.
- Information should be accessible to local agencies.
- The system should include noncriminal and administrative statistical information (i.e., for budgeting and manpower deployment).
- National definitions and classifications should be used when possible.
- "Exception" reporting should be used when possible.

- The system should include interfaces with the criminal-justice information system of the state and other record sources.
- There should be legislation to require mandatory reporting by local agencies for criminal, traffic, and administrative information.
- Statements concerning the volume of crime should take into account, and if necessary be modified by, studies relating to unreported crimes, self-reported crimes, and so on.

The third general responsibility should be experimental research and development:

- The division should be the administrator for a statewide central storage file for technical and research material, and it should disseminate information about the material.
- The division should test and evaluate products and otherwise carry out applied research.
- Depending on the size of the state, there should also be a nondirective research program.
- Research files of the division should be accessible to local agencies, and periodic reports covering product evaluation and research should be made available to these agencies.

Finally, the division should undertake research studies in criminology. An interdisciplinary staff should conduct studies and research in various aspects of crime causation, prevention of criminality, police administration and operations, criminal procedure, corrections, and so on.

Field Service Division   As indicated in Chart 1, this division can logically be responsible for certification of training programs and individual competence, development of training, recruiting, and selecting standards; the conduct of training courses and seminars; field consultation; and assistance in local plan development by direct visits to the field.

Note that the divisions in Chart 1 have been given responsibility without regard to clientele—that is, the field service division will conduct work in certification of training not only for police but also for corrections, probation, and parole agencies. In terms of the number of agencies and the probable need for field services, however, the bulk of this effort will be directed at police departments.

The planning agency should also have appropriate support units, such as a public information unit to issue releases to the news media and to assist in preparation of bulletins, speeches, and other material going outside the agency; in addition, it should have an administrative unit for housekeeping functions, such as internal budgeting, purchasing, personnel management, and maintenance.

In states not having separate police-officer standards and training agencies, this division should develop a statewide program of standards and training for law enforcement and criminal justice officers. This should be carried out by several separate but coordinated programs, through the development of training curricula, selection standards, and a certification program, thereby establishing certain levels of training, education, and experience. The certification plan should consider the desirability of lateral entry among law enforcement agencies in the state. It should also stress the desirability of a broad general education for law enforcement personnel and should consider the feasibility of several levels of professional competence such as community-service officer, police officer, and police agent. The division should also administer the work of the Police Standards Council, as recommended by IACP, and other provisions contained in the Council program.

Part of the work of a field service division should be devoted to providing technical assistance and consulting. Consulting for local agencies can include the following:

- Analysis of currently available crime statistics
- Study of existing reports and literature
- Interview of agency heads, community leaders, and other appropriate representatives of the law enforcement and criminal justice system
- On-site assistance for law enforcement administration and operations through direct observation, reading of reports, and interviews with operating personnel
- Dissemination of questionnaires soliciting this information to supplement field visits
- Preparation of reports containing facts, analyses, and recommendations

Auditing Some states distinguish between (1) the disbursement and accounting of funds for ongoing grants and (2) the audit of vouchers from local agencies or post-grant audits to ensure compliance with state or federal regulations. As indicated in Chart 2, Virginia's Division of Justice and Crime Prevention has a separate auditing unit which reports independently to the director. The separate unit facilitates internal auditing of the planning agency's own funds as well.

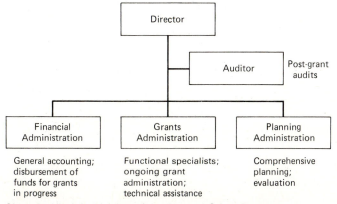

Chart 2 Virginia Division of Justice and Crime Prevention.

Advisory Board The advisory relationship of the board is depicted in Chart 1 as well. The board, in compliance with LEAA guidelines, should have the review authority for the overall plan.

Composition of the advisory board in a state criminal justice planning agency should be influenced primarily by the need for technical expertise and a balanced representation from each element of the criminal justice system. There is a growing trend toward appointing more generalist managers and executives on advisory boards. This trend is based partially on the theory that providing for both functional representation and regional representation would make the boards so unwieldy in size that only through appointment of city managers or mayors could there be representation of the various functions. This may be true if the board is supervisory rather than advisory; however, since the main purpose of the board should be the review of the overall plan for technical soundness, there should be adequate representation from the parts of the criminal justice system which are the largest and most complex.

Regional Planning within the State

Some states have decentralized the primary responsibility for law enforcement planning by delegating the process to regional organizations.

The regional concept in planning should not be confused with the movement toward regionalization of services, as discussed in the next chapter; the two phrases may not have anything in common other than the root word "region." If regional planning has little relationship to consolidation or regionalization of services, the concept can add another level of administrative hierarchy without contributing to unified state planning. In a system based on giving a high degree of authority to regions (for deciding on the composition of the state plan as well as for making judgments as to the suitability of grant applications), there is a great need for coordination between regional staffs.

At some time in the future, federal funding of law enforcement and criminal justice planning may cease. It would seem to be incumbent on local agencies to continue to develop the local administrative machinery for planning so that even in the absence of federal funds the benefits of the planning and coordination of various agencies in the system can continue. In some areas, regional planning would be the only way this could be done effectively.

Guidelines for the Comprehensive Plan

This text will cover guidelines in the area of police administration and operations, but it will not deal with specific guidelines for prosecution, defense, court, correctional, and release-procedure planning.

A list of specific items which will facilitate the development of the police portion of the comprehensive plan, as well as some general comments related to other functions of the criminal justice system, is found in the Appendix.

Chapter 5

Consolidation, Regionalization, Sharing of Services, and Relationships with Other Agencies

The existence of thousands of understaffed, ill-trained, and poorly equipped small police forces is a continuing major deficiency in police service in the United States. Some of the reasons for the collective deficiency of many smaller agencies can be identified. Foremost among them are problems relating to personnel quality, training, and standards:

- Small agencies often limit recruiting to their immediate vicinity. The pool of prospective applicants may therefore contain few qualified personnel because of the small size of the potential field.
- Many small local governments have limited budgets for recruiting and selection and often have inadequate procedures for the selection of personnel.
- Salaries in small agencies are traditionally lower, with the result that many potential candidates gravitate toward larger cities.
- Training budgets, personnel benefits, and other inducements are similarly lower and noncompetitive.

Second, because of the low frequency of need, small agencies are seldom able to offer specialized police services, such as in criminalistics, technical communications, identification, crime analysis, and specialized investigations.

Third, small agencies have even smaller amounts of money to spend on development and research than agencies of moderate to large size—and the latter are certainly not outstanding models in research expenditures. As a consequence, small agencies often find themselves lagging behind the larger departments in the technical field and are forced to copy what is being done by them.

Fourth, a small department often has a wasteful ratio of supervisors to patrol officers. In the ideal situation, a sergeant should supervise from five to eight officers. In the smaller agency, however, the supervisory ratio may be one sergeant to one patrol officer, or in some cases, of course, there may be only one patrol officer on duty.

Fifth, it is easier for the criminal element to identify the location of officers in a small agency. The offender may know, for example, that the department has only one or two police cars to cover the entire city or village. When he sees both vehicles out of service or can otherwise account for both, he can be reasonably certain that the community is left unprotected in terms of immediate response.

Related to the last item is the inability of the small department to mobilize a large number of officers to cope with emergency situations or tactical problems requiring the presence of many officers. The large agency may very infrequently need to mobilize 100 or more personnel to cover such a situation, but when the need arises, the mobilization can be carried out. In the small community, mobilization of this sort is impossible without formal mutual-aid agreements with neighboring agencies.

Finally, many small agencies are caught up in petty disagreements, conflicts, and jealousies which hamper coordination. There is often a serious limitation on interdepartmental communications. Radio monitoring and teletype networks are far from universal, and there are frequent examples of the existence of two agencies, side by side, with no contact whatever—either among officers at the operational level or through official means of communications.

Some of the other conditions which prompt the need for consolidation are not related to size. There is often considerable duplication of effort because of the division of a natural region into artificial political areas. For example, the Detroit Police Department and the Wayne County Sheriff's Office maintain separate identification and fingerprint files in buildings located across the street from one another. For years, arrested persons processed through the Detroit Police Department were photographed and fingerprinted prior to delivery to the Sheriff's Office. Upon booking at the jail, the process was repeated, and nearly identical file systems were established. This situation is still quite common in other parts of the country, although in recent years the FBI and state bureaus of identification have attempted to reduce the number of fingerprints resulting from a single arrest.

CONSOLIDATION AND REGIONALIZATION

All these problems have led to a recent intensive interest in consolidation and regionalization of services. Consolidation was identified as a key issue in the *Task Force Report: The Police*.[1] In general, consolidation is most practical in the areas which are also relatively noncontroversial in terms of the exercise of local control. Few governmental officials or police administrators will question the desirability of pooling resources for the establishment of a consolidated or regional crime laboratory or training facility. On the other hand, there is much more apprehension about pooling patrol service and criminal investigation, which form the backbone of local policing.

But perhaps the greatest obstacle to consolidation is the unwillingness of small-city executives—both in the local government and in the police department itself—to relinquish authority. The administration of field services (patrol, investigative, and traffic functions and other related activities) on a regional basis in the United States can probably never be truly effective unless there is a consolidation of governments as well. In the United States there is a traditional fear of strong central government—an interesting situation in view of the strength of the federal government and the country's power in the world, and one which does not exist to the same degree in most other nations.

In England, for example, the fear of centralized police strength has not been a deterrent to consolidation. Through a well-planned program carried out in the past few years, the smaller police forces have been merged into the larger, more effective agencies. In 1976 the smallest force in England had more than 600 personnel, and in the course of the next few years additional consolidation will take place.

Regionalization of Information

Regionalization of information service is perhaps the most widespread form of consolidation. Great strides are being made in the statewide information systems which are now proliferating throughout the United States and many other countries. Several states now have real-time capability (that is, the files are updated at the same time the agency receives the information so that an inquiry at any given moment reflects the actual status of the file) to handle information on wanted persons, stolen vehicles and property, driver information, vehicle registration, data from offense reports, and the status of individuals within the criminal justice system.

Several information systems also carry the promise of providing regional management information—principally for the reporting of crime and accident data, but also to report administrative information, such as data for salary determination, budgeting, purchasing, operating expenses, and other facts of concern to administrators, which heretofore have been derived through questionnaires and subsequent manual tabulation.

---

[1]The President's Commission on Law Enforcement and Administration of Justice, Government Printing Office, Washington, 1967, p. 68.

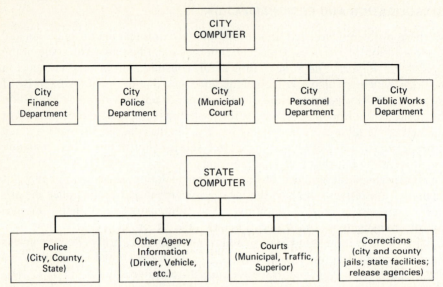

Chart 3 Criminal justice versus local-government orientation for computer-based information systems.

The most recent trend in the orientation of police-information systems has been the tendency for police to participate in two systems simultaneously—first as a part of the regional or statewide criminal justice system and second as a part of a general local-government system. Chart 3 shows these two systems.

Some observers have criticized the waste which is evident if police participate in two systems, i.e., having a dedicated (agency-controlled) computer for participation in the regional or state-level criminal justice system, while having simultaneous access to a computer controlled by local government to fulfill management-information needs.

In the next few years the question may become academic, since future generations of computers may be of such size and sophistication as to handle a great many systems regardless of orientation.

Sharing Personnel Services

Another promising area for regionalization of service relates to personnel recruitment and selection. Although training expenses and facilities have been shared for many years, only recently has there been any effort to pool the recruitment and selection of manpower. An increasing number of agencies have agreed to have joint advertising campaigns, a common examination procedure, and common eligibility lists. Agencies operate a common eligibility system by asking candidates to list the departments in which they would be willing to accept employment. The agencies then agree to alternate choices or "draws." An example of cooperative personnel-recruitment effort is the Northern Virginia Police Minority Recruitment Office, operated jointly by personnel on loan from the police departments of Alexandria, Arlington, and

Fairfax County, Virginia. The staff engages in field recruiting by visiting college campuses, conducts recruiting campaigns through radio and newspaper advertising, and gives entrance tests to candidates. Recruiters give each candidate information about each agency, and the candidate then selects one or more agencies as his or her preference.

State Services for Local Agencies

There is increasing use of state services in the police area by local governments. Many states have for years supplied local law enforcement agencies with specialized help in such areas as narcotics enforcement, personnel selection, training, vice investigation, criminalistics, and identification services.

The State of California has supplied local governments with most of these services, and in the past few years it has added free police-management consulting to this list. Several other states now offer management consulting to local police agencies. The first to do so was the State of New York, followed by California, New Jersey, and Florida. Efforts of this kind should be encouraged, provided that the state is willing to engage in criticism of local government and does not weaken its work by emphasizing improvement of noncontroversial technical and support services to the detriment of recommendations in the more important and controversial aspects of police management.

Contract Services

Many cities contract with nearby agencies for part or all of their police services. The practice is quite common in California; the Los Angeles County Sheriff's Department provides total policing service for many cities in the county, which pay for a specific number of patrol cars to be assigned to the city. The Sheriff's Department also supplies investigative service and all technical and administrative support which may be necessary.

Determination of the cost for contract service requires careful thought and good accounting methods. For example, the contract ought to specify the cost of whatever services the city *would have received* (if any) without having entered into a contract. This amount, of course, should be deducted from the contract price. Another consideration which must be kept in mind in contract service between a city and its county is that city taxpayers usually pay the same county taxes as the residents of unincorporated areas within the county. Yet in most cases the city resident receives far fewer direct benefits from the county police agency; the city resident does not receive patrol or investigative service by sheriff's deputies and, in some cases, even pays for the care of city prisoners in the county jail.

THE PROSECUTION AND JUDICIAL FUNCTIONS

Effective law enforcement requires that the police maintain a good working relationship with both the prosecutor and the courts. These relationships are discussed in the following paragraphs.

The Prosecutor

With the exception of the judges who try criminal cases, prosecuting attorneys have a greater influence on the criminal justice process than any other element of the system. If the prosecutor's office has adequate staffing through the use of full-time lawyers who earn adequate salaries, the prosecutors can thereby gain enough experience to become real assets in the preparation of cases and in presentation before the court. Too often, though, the prosecutor's staff consists of young lawyers who take these jobs because they are among the few positions which are available to lawyers without experience. Equally unrewarding is the situation in which the prosecutor's staff consists of a number of part-time prosecutors who are allowed to retain their own private practices.

In either case, the result is likely to be the situation in which the "pretrial conference" between the police investigator and the prosecutor is a hurried conversation in whispered tones carried on in the corridors of the courthouse. Under these circumstances the police are justifiably quite bitter if inadequate prosecution results in a high percentage of dismissals or acquittals.

If the lack of staff and inadequate preparation by inexperienced or part-time prosecutors are identified as the major complaints by police, then the next most common area of grievance is the tendency for the prosecutor in some cases to influence police operational policy. At times, the influence can be subtle and indirect, for example, the failure to prosecute certain kinds of cases. In other situations, the prosecutor—perhaps for political advantage—may simply tell police that he wants to carry out specific police objectives.

In some jurisdictions county prosecutors take an active part in the investigation of crimes committed in their bailiwicks in order to ensure suitable law enforcement. The number of investigators employed by the prosecutor, the types of crimes investigated, and the extent of the investigation conducted by his office are influenced by his evaluation of the quality of investigation by local police agencies. The prosecutor's appraisal of the political value of such investigations and of the improved record of convictions that results, as well as his personal interest in crime prosecutions, is also a factor that influences his participation in this work.

The need for the investigation of crimes by the prosecutor's office exists in communities where police investigations are ineffectual because of detective incompetence. Inadequate training, inferior recruitment procedures, unsuitable methods of selecting from the force those best qualified as detectives, lack of leadership with resultant ineffective direction and control, and indifference on the part of detectives are all weaknesses which lead to greater use of investigators assigned to a prosecutor's office.

At times there is justification for having one or two investigators assigned to a large prosecutor's office to act as investigative coordinators and to handle certain kinds of cases (such as nonsupport) which may not originate with the police department. In this situation, the investigators should be on the payroll of the prosecutor rather than assigned temporarily from the police department.

Active investigation of crimes by the prosecutor's office may often strain

CONSOLIDATION, REGIONALIZATION, SHARING OF SERVICES 57

the relationship between the police and the prosecutor's staff investigators, and consequently the resulting investigations are often unsatisfactory. The desirability, if not the actual necessity, of a close and friendly relationship between the two offices is reason enough for the police to make a determined effort to provide a quality of service and a degree of cooperation that will be satisfactory to the prosecutor. The most important step in this direction is for the police to be sure that the investigation of each case is correct and complete in every detail and that the prosecutor is provided with a summary of all information which he needs to prepare his case and to present it to the court.

The police should attempt to gain the support of the prosecutor and the public defender in presenting arguments for administrative changes affecting the relationship of these functions with the courts. For example, an argument to replace a system of mandatory appearance by arresting officers is most likely to fail if the prosecutor's staff disagrees with the idea because of lack of communication.

The Courts

A poor relationship exists between police and the courts in many jurisdictions of the United States, and there is repeated and widespread police criticism of judicial action—or the lack of it—throughout the country. Indeed, the police chief who admits privately that he is satisfied with the court in his jurisdiction is rarely found.

Theoretically, the police are not supposed to be unduly concerned with the status of a person who is arrested, once the subject leaves police custody. Practically, the police *should be expected* to express concern over situations which unnecessarily reduce police capability to cope with crime.

Police criticism of the court function usually falls into three categories: first, deficiencies in the administration of the court system; second, leniency and inconsistency in sentencing; and third, overzealous or improper rulings affecting admissibility of evidence.

The first problem often relates to unnecessary delays in hearing criminal cases, adding even more work load to crowded calendars. Often the backlog of cases awaiting trial results in delays of six months to one year or more for many kinds of offenses, such as murder, armed robbery, or felonious assault. This means, of course, that a defendant is either on bail during this time or in custody in a city or county jail—neither of which is desirable for an extended period. At times the court may attempt to reduce backlogs by wholesale dismissal or reduction of charges, rather than by increasing the staff and capacity of the system or by lengthening working hours. Obviously, this approach does not serve justice and causes morale problems among police.

The police should become staunch advocates of a two-stage appearance system for misdemeanor arrests so that police officers need go to court only when a defendant pleads not guilty. A system which requires a mandatory court appearance by an officer for each traffic citation or misdemeanor arrest is backward, out of date, and a waste of police manpower.

The problems of leniency, inconsistency, and improper rulings are more difficult to solve, of course, because they relate to judicial discretion, which the court values so dearly. The short-range solution, if there is one, must certainly include increased communication between judges, the prosecutors and public defenders, and the police administrator. An effective device (beyond simple meetings and office contacts) consists of inviting judges to address groups of police officers in round-table or seminar-type discussions which encourage a two-way flow of information. These sessions often have a secondary value in providing constructive information from the court to the police in the improvement of investigations.

In larger agencies there is a trend toward creating police legal advisors as full-time members of the department. The legal advisor is in an ideal position to participate in dialogues with the court and its related agencies.

On occasion a difficult problem involving the courts can be overcome through press publicity on deficiencies and improper actions. This kind of solution should not ordinarily be initiated by the police because of the resentment it creates.

The Local Criminal Justice System Plan

Most localities are many years away from having a criminal justice "system" in which the various components—such as police, prosecutor, and courts—work for a common supervisor. Indeed, the local "criminal justice department" may never become a widespread practice as long as there is a continuation of the traditional separation of executive, legislative, and judicial functions at the local level. In the face of this pessimism, the best hope for the immediate future is to achieve some measure of cooperation by establishing local criminal justice coordinating councils and by preparing a system description or plan which identifies existing relationships between the various components. The description or plan can also make recommendations for improvement of the activity of any one component, or it can suggest areas in which two or more agencies can achieve better coordination.

Although a local criminal justice system description or plan can be prepared by some group other than the council and although the council can operate independently of the group which prepared the description, it is certainly far more effective to have the description or plan endorsed or prepared by the coordinating council.

In Arlington, Virginia, the criminal justice coordinating council is chaired by the county manager, with the prosecuting attorney serving as vice chairman. The police chief, the head of the state probation and parole office, the director of human resources, the sheriff, the court administrator, judges, and several citizen representatives are also members of the council. The group meets regularly for discussion of system problems, for review of agency grant requests, and in general for coordination of the system. In this last capacity the council has completed a description of the system, which in itself is a worthwhile achievement.

Part Two

Administration

This part of the book is concerned with management-related responsibilities and emphasizes those functions which ought to be of more immediate concern to the administrator than operational activities best carried out by line personnel. Our objective is to provide guidelines for effective management and to encourage evaluation and improvement of administrative procedures.

It is tempting to add a disclaimer at this point to suggest that the reader should always remember that proper administrative procedures and management techniques are not ends in themselves, but simply the means for achieving improved police protection and service at the operational level. The truth is, however, that the police service is in no immediate danger of overmanagement. On the contrary, there is an increasing need for police administrators to recognize that a sound organizational structure and good management procedures are essential to the effectiveness of a police agency.

In the past few years it has been fashionable for many people to view technological advancement as the panacea for all law enforcement problems. A significant number, on the other hand, have felt that most police problems can be solved simply by increasing the size of the force or by giving officers on the street more pay or better equipment. Any of these approaches is unsatisfactory by itself. Most progressive administrators have realized that policing has been and will remain a personal service. Law enforcement is almost totally concerned with the problems of people, not of machines or equipment. Effectiveness of a police agency depends more upon the development of a highly motivated force and upon good supervision and management carried out by enlightened leadership than on the number of police officers and their pay and equipment.

Police departments are directed for the most part by administrators who have emerged from line operations. This may explain the preoccupation of many chiefs of police with operational activity and a corresponding lack of attention to such vitally important functions as planning, budgeting, internal inspection and control, fiscal management, and (perhaps most important) personnel management and career development. Over the past 50 years, in fact, some of the progress that has been made in these areas has taken place despite police leadership rather than because of it, and it has been necessary in some cases for governments to appoint nonpolice executives to important positions in an attempt to introduce management skills.

Terminology In the public service, the terms "administration" and "management" are practically synonymous. They will be used interchangeably in this text.

Administration has been classically defined by Luther Gulick in his famous acronym POSDCORB, which stands for the initial letters in *P*lanning, *O*rganizing, *S*taffing (or personnel management), *D*irecting, *CO*ordinating, *R*eporting, and *B*udgeting.[1] In a text on police administration, naturally these functions of administration and management are fundamental. Each of them will be presented in the text, although not in the order of their appearance in the acronym.

There are various ways to categorize the terminology used in police service. The method used by the Field Operations Division of the International Association of Chiefs of Police is to think of the police function as consisting of either (1) operations or (2) administration. The term "operations" embraces the traditional line (or primary) functions for which the agency was established—patrol service, criminal investigation, traffic control, vice enforcement, and various other activities having a direct effect on crime prevention and law enforcement. Administration, on the other hand, embraces everything else—support, staff or auxiliary services, technical services, personnel management, internal investigations and inspections, and all the other responsibilities mentioned by Gulick.

The concept of "line" and "staff" is similar to IACP usage but different in some respects; one characteristic of the "line" is that it usually describes the entire chain of command in a line unit, such as a field operations bureau. As a result of military influence, the commander of the bureau would be known as a line officer even though his duties are totally administrative. Furthermore, the

[1]*Papers on the Science of Administration*, Institute of Public Administration, New York, 1937.

ADMINISTRATION 61

term "staff" differs from "administration" in that the former does not suitably describe top-level executive responsibilities, including those of the chief executive. Staff duties encompass only those duties performed by staff officers who, in contrast to line officers, exercise no direct authority (authority in their own right) over operating or line personnel. Line officers, however, may perform staff duties, and when they do so, they act in the capacity of staff officers. The tasks of the personnel officer, the training officer, the report-review officer, and the dispatcher when he is not the officer in direct command are examples of staff duties.

Administration includes the management of support services or auxiliary functions. All services which assist operational personnel in the immediate performance of their duties are designated as auxiliary, secondary, or support services.

The term "direction" is often used synonymously with words such as "leadership" or "control." Many writers in the administration and management field, however, prefer to give "direction" some overall qualities which may include some similar terms. As used in this text, "direction" will include leadership, command, supervision, control, and other related meanings. "Leadership," on the other hand, will be used in a more restricted sense; it will relate to the characteristic of setting examples—of doing things first so that others may follow.

Administrative Responsibilities of the Chief The principal task of the chief is to see that the resources of the department are so managed that its objectives—preservation of the peace, protection of life and property, and enforcement of the law—are achieved economically and effectively. Success depends on the performance of administrative duties; some should remain within the office of the chief or closely tied to it; while others may be freely assigned to operating and service units, depending on the size of the agency. Some duties must be carried out personally by the chief in the small agency. In a larger department the chief may delegate authority to administer these duties. The police administrator carries out his task through the organization of the department, by exercise of direction and supervision, by policy determination and planning, by control and inspection, and by development of personnel. The chapters in Part Two of this text are concerned with these responsibilities.

Chapter 6

Management Theory and Organizational Behavior

Although people have engaged in managing other people since the time of earliest recorded history—and no doubt much earlier in prehistoric life—the development of modern management theory was slow in coming. The works of Henri Fayol and Frederick Taylor, for example, were pioneer efforts in the field, but they appeared no earlier than the second decade of the twentieth century.[1]

The reasons for the slow growth are varied. Part of the problem, no doubt, is that modern management theory is based on social enlightenment and democratic idealism, both of which were in short supply before the eighteenth century. Businesses themselves were uncomplicated and did not require complex solutions to simple problems. Further, the existing sciences in the seventeenth and eighteenth centuries were relatively unconcerned with matters outside their specialties; there were no sociologists or psychologists available to express opinions on management subjects. Finally, there has always been—until recent years—an inexhaustible supply of cheap labor.

As if to make up for lost time, those who are interested in the history of

[1]H. Koontz and C. O'Donnell, *Management: A Systems and Contingency Analysis of Managerial Functions*, McGraw-Hill Book Company, New York, 1976, p. 25.

63

ADMINISTRATION

management have been speculating on the origin and development of management theory and organizational behavior. Some of that theory has been presented in the following pages.

The Evolution of Management Behavior

It has been said that human beings by nature are social, territorial, and familial, but above all organizational. This pattern of interrelated characteristics may stem, perhaps, from our apparent background as a clan animal, a creature who has depended on group action for survival. In every known human culture people have organized themselves into families, clans, tribes, teams, and committees. In almost every case, these groups have been organized into hierarchies, with a small unit of leaders (often just one leader) determining what the rest of the group may do or think.

The exact nature of ancestral groups is of course speculative—but a clue to the organization of primitive societies of thousands of years ago may be the organization of the few remaining primitive cultures on earth today. These primitive groups have some characteristics in common. The size of the basic tribal hunting or agrarian group seldom exceeds a certain number of individuals, reporting to a leader or chief. Once the size of the group exceeds this number, the tribe or clan tends to develop subordinate leaders who follow a key tribal figure or chief. A second common characteristic is that the subordinate leaders, together with the chief, often form a tribal council. In some societies the council is a group of elders, and in others it is made up of the most wealthy or learned. Also, for some unknown reasons, many societies appoint a medicine man, wise man, or grand vizier who acts as a resource to the group.

In addition to the study of present-day primitive societies, accounts of Indian life in America from the sixteenth to the eighteenth centuries offer some interesting insights into the nature of tribal organizations. It is apparent that in the tribes which were known to European settlers—in the days when Indians were relatively unaffected by European ways—there was a great range in the characteristics of tribal leaders. For example, some Indian chiefs were described as wise and judicious, and others were described as reckless and brutal. The same kind of observations can be made with regard to the primitive societies which still exist today.

As societies grew larger, organizational relationships in the tribe or clan became more complex. Agriculture developed, allowing the creation of the first permanent settlements that were independent of the need to hunt or herd. It provided the opportunity for the evolution of villages, artisans, tradespeople, and soldiers. These specializations created, in turn, the need for different kinds of leaders and in different numbers.

The predominant management style throughout recorded history has been consistent with the assumptions of Theory X, as described by Douglas McGregor. Theory X assumes that the average human being has an inherent dislike of work, and to achieve adequate productivity must be closely controlled or threatened. Theory X adherents are often linked with a set of related personality traits as well, a pattern also described as a Type A personality. Theory X-Type A managers are often assertive, hard-driving and may be less concerned with the product than with the rewards attained in pursuit of it. They may be disliked, but nevertheless may be successful because those whom they lead are fearful of the consequences of not following their leadership.

The Theory Y leader,[2] on the other hand, stresses participatory management. Theory Y assumes that human beings will exercise self-direction and self-control to further objectives to which they are committed, and under proper conditions will not only accept but seek responsibility. Theory Y may also attract those with benign and easy-going dispositions, or Type B personalities. Theory Y-Type B managers may offer leadership in its truest sense; that is, they do a thing first so that others can follow as opposed to ordering them to do.

Of course, many contemporary managers may combine several of these styles and behaviors. However, the trend seems to be toward the leadership style of Theory Y, which lends itself in particular to the process which has come to be known as management by objectives—a process which emphasizes results rather than the means, the establishment of mutual goals and "contracts" between management and employees, monitoring of progress, evaluation of results, feedback, adjustment of goals, and repetition of the cycle. Without the enlightened management style advocated by those who believe in Theory Y, the process of management by objectives would not be very effective.

The Theory of Self-Management

In a given group of human beings, a certain percentage seem to be driven by some inner force rather than by a supervisor or leader. These people seem to do their best even under adverse circumstances. Many managers and leaders are thought to be the sort of people who have a great deal of self-direction. They are the kind of people for whom the desk slogan "The Buck Stops Here" was coined. They want to have responsibility, even though it may at times go unrewarded.

Most other individuals tend to react more strongly to conditions surrounding their place in society or their work. The great majority of individuals are thus affected by such things as low pay, poor working conditions, and poor supervision. Their productivity can be affected by these factors. When times are right and conditions are good, they are highly productive. When things are bad, however, they are demoralized and unproductive.

One of the current mysteries of the psychology of management concerns whether self-management and self-actualization can be cultivated or whether they are innate personality characteristics. Abraham Maslow, in his pioneering works on the psychology of management behavior,[3] described the attitude of

---

[2]Douglas McGregor, *The Human Side of Enterprise*, McGraw-Hill Book Company, New York, 1960, p. 33.

[3]A. H. Maslow, *Eupsychian Management*, Richard D. Irwin, Inc., Homewood, Ill., 1965.

The Hierarchy of Needs and the Theory of Motivation

some of his students who felt that because they wrote about or accepted the premise of self-actualization, someday a "bell would ring and they would somehow have been transformed into self-actualizing individuals."

The Hierarchy of Needs and the Theory of Motivation

To some extent, managers and workers share the same characteristics in relationship to motivation and, in Maslow's terms, the hierarchy of human need.[4] In this theory, individuals develop a healthy personality to the extent that they realize what psychological health really is and to the extent that they understand their full potential. According to Maslow, human needs are arranged in the following hierarchy in order from lowest to highest:

1 Physiological (such as the need for food and shelter)
2 Safety (the need for security and the absence of threat)
3 Affiliation (the need for close, affective relationships)
4 Achievement and esteem (the need for self-respect)
5 Self-actualization (the need to develop one's skills and responsibilities to the maximum)

Maslow also proposed that these elements in the hierarchy are not equally influential on the individual at any given time; rather, as the needs on a lower level are satisfied, the next succeeding level, or salient, becomes the next objective until the final level—that of self-actualization—is reached. Further, as the needs on a given level become more satisfied, the needs on the next highest level grow stronger.

In this concept, employees who are only partially satisfied at one of the lower levels of the hierarchy of needs are not dissatisfied at not achieving a higher level. In other words, you don't miss what you never knew you didn't have.

THE EFFECT OF MANAGEMENT BEHAVIOR ON ORGANIZATIONS

Up to this point the discussion has centered on organizational behavior in groups in general. What we are concerned with in a text on police administration, of course, is the effect of management on the behavior of a group of individuals organized to do work—a unique kind of work, law enforcement.

Students of industrial psychology have long known that the productivity of workers can be influenced enormously by the kind of management in the organization. This is particularly true in the sort of organization in which much physical activity and repetitive action are factors in production. Both the Theory Y management style and the Theory X management style are effective in this kind of environment. In fact, in one study mentioned by Peter Drucker,

---

[4]A. H. Maslow, *Motivation and Personality*, Harper & Row, Publishers, Incorporated, New York, 1954.

the coercive type of manager had a slight edge over the manager with a democratic style when the work product was based on physical activity and repetitive performance on a production line.

Police work, however, is much different from production-line activity. First, it is essentially work which is carried out in the absence of supervision. Second, the police organization is dependent largely on outside circumstances (the proclivities of criminals or the circumstances of the weather) as determinants of work load. One of the basic police activities, aggressive preventive patrol, is only slightly more effective when carried out by an inspired self-actualized patrol officer than by the mere movement of a patrol car from point to point by an uninspired, unmotivated officer who is moving about his or her beat for an entirely different reason; in many cases the potential offender is unable to distinguish between the behavior of the aggressive, highly motivated officer and the wanderings of the unmotivated one. At first glance, the potential offender or the citizen who views their activity at a distance is often unable to tell the difference.

Psychological Health and Management Effectiveness Maslow has also speculated that good managers tend to be in good psychological health and, in fact, to be superior in almost every other way—in terms of physical health, intelligence, creativity, and so on. Conversely, he finds that the inferior manager often suffers from a lack of these same characteristics. What, then, will happen if inferior managers are provided with training and therapy to overcome their psychological problems and with good food and medical treatment to surmount their physical shortcomings? According to Maslow, an inferior manager may improve considerably as a result of such measures, and the organization may be considerably better off because of the improvement; however, the one-time inferior manager will never be quite as good as the superior manager who started off with all the advantages.

Motivation and Reinforcement A fundamental premise in motivational theory is the *principle of reinforcement*—the idea that management rewards employees for the kind of behavior it wants to perpetuate (positive reinforcement) and punishes acts or behavior which should be eliminated (negative reinforcement).

Negative reinforcement, despite its undesirable connotations, has always been (and perhaps always will be) a necessary part of motivation. Even in the most successful applications of Theory Y management, employees must be aware that negative performance, if left unchecked, may lead to destruction of the organization or its programs long before the application of positive influences can counteract the negative behavior.

Negative behavior can have characteristics which range from the personal derelictions of individuals (being absent from work, insulting citizens, or assaulting one's supervisor) to an action taken by a group of employees (such as demanding a salary which—either through a strike or through the disadvantageous competitive position created by exceptionally high wages—causes a collapse of a program or the business organization itself).

Positive reinforcement, on the other hand, is said to be the motivational basis for most successful organizations—at least in private industry. Positive reinforcement rewards the employee for good performance, and then a series of mutually advantageous reinforcements take place—first, a higher salary for better work, which in turn produces a better product and a more competitive position, and so on.

As the level of expectations increases, financial incentives alone may not be enough to sustain positive performance for many employees, particularly for those who aspire to be managers. It then becomes reasonable to reward these employees through greater personal recognition and improvement of status.

Because of the nature of the work, police departments should attempt to hire people with a heightened sense of their own personal worth and their own ethics—in other words, those who can be described as moving toward self-management or self-actualization. Further, the search for potential police managers should focus on those who have superior characteristics in most aspects of their total behavior—in their work production, in their physical and psychological health, and so on. Finally, failing in our attempts to recruit all our managers from this group of people with superior characteristics, we should attempt to do the best we can—through training and supportive management—to assist those people whose management behavior and personal characteristics are less than superior.

Chapter 7

Organization for Police Service

The act of organizing is indispensable to proper management, and without some form of organizational structure, most police operations could not be carried out. If the organizational structure is poor and if organizational concepts are poorly understood or applied, the efficiency of the department will be severely affected.

There is a distinction between the *simple organizational structure* of an agency and the application of *principles of administrative organization.* While the two are obviously related (a good structure usually depends on conscious application of the principles), they are not one and the same. An agency can often operate adequately—quite well, in some cases—with a deficient structure, but an agency with a seemingly good structure can very seldom operate with efficiency if a basic principle of administrative organization, such as the need to adhere to channels of communication, is consistently ignored. Further, the process of organizing ought to include thoughtful consideration of many of the other principles of administration. For example, if establishing an organizational structure requires that attention be given to the assignment of responsibilities, then by extension there should be concern about whether these responsibilities are necessary or what changes should be made in existing procedures.

69

ORGANIZATIONAL TERMINOLOGY

An understanding of the organization and its component parts requires a definition of terms. Police titles and ranks and some other terms are also defined in the following paragraphs.

Police Titles and Ranks

The police administrator should realize that there is considerable regional variation in titles and ranks. The rank or grade of authority is commonly shown by military-style designations, but no uniform terminology has been adopted by the American police service, with the result that confusion sometimes occurs when police visitors bearing the same rank as local officers have quite different duties and authority. Communication between departments in the discussion of salaries and levels of responsibilities is also confused; consider the plight of the chief in a large Eastern city who is interested in justifying his budget request for higher pay for his inspectors (a higher rank than captain). If he writes to a department in California, he may be told that its inspectors receive slightly more pay than sergeants but less than lieutenants, who naturally earn less than captains.

Above the rank of captain there is such wide variation in the use of police titles that it is impossible to fix upon a uniform terminology. Some departments use military titles, such as "major," to designate heads of functional divisions in cities having district stations or as the title for the assistant to the chief; others have supervising captains; and still others designate as "assistant" or "deputy chiefs" those officers who are assistants to chiefs. The head of the department may be called "chief of police," "superintendent," or "commissioner."

The following ranks are in reasonably wide usage throughout the United States (except for the rank of major, which is found primarily in the Middle West and South) and will be used in this text in the interest of standardization and uniformity:

Chief of police
Deputy chief of police
Assistant chief of police } used only in larger departments
Police major
Police captain
Police lieutenant
Police sergeant
Police officer

Titles are sometimes unnecessarily confused with rank. A title often designates an assignment rather than rank. A captain who heads a detective operation may, for example, sign correspondence by affixing his name and his rank (captain), or his title (commander, criminal investigation division). Other

ORGANIZATION FOR POLICE SERVICE

assignments are commonly given titles, which in some systems also carry rank as well. Examples are detectives or investigators, dispatchers, desk sergeants, and jailers. Creation of specialist ranks should be avoided, as indicated in Chapter 14.

Organizational Titles and Other Terminology

Lack of uniformity in naming functional, territorial, and time units in police departments also results in confusion.

Functional Units   The following terms are suitably descriptive, represent common practice, and consequently are used throughout this book.

Bureau   The largest organic unit within a large department. Each bureau consists of a number of divisions.

Division   A primary subdivision of a bureau or of the office of the chief. A division has a departmentwide function either for general police service or for specialized activity. In moderate-sized to large departments having no district stations, each division is usually commanded by a captain; in departments having district stations, a division is usually commanded by a major, a director, or a supervising captain. In smaller departments the division head is often a lieutenant.

Section   A functional unit within a division. The duties of some divisions call for additional specialization, and in consequence personnel must be further classified according to their duties. Such extensive subdivision is found only in large departments. In a large detective division the personnel may be divided among a number of sections to investigate certain classes of crimes. For example, there may be a homicide section, a robbery section, an auto-theft section, and so on. The traffic division may have sections devoted to accident investigation, intersection control, and meter enforcement. The records and communications division may have the following sections: communications, identification, records, and statistics.

While the rank of the officer in charge of a section is logically that of lieutenant, this individual is not invariably so designated because rank depends largely upon the size and responsibility of the position.

Unit   When further specialization is needed, the section can be divided into units. The term "unit" can also be used to describe an organizational subdivision which is too small in size to be afforded any other status, and it especially applies to a small subdivision which carries out housekeeping duties. The term "unit" can also be used as a synonym for any organizational subdivision.

Territorial Units   Territorial divisions of the department are described as follows.

Post   A fixed point or location to which an officer is assigned for duty, such as (1) an intersection or crosswalk for traffic duty; (2) a spot or location for general guard duty, observation, and surveillance or for the apprehension of a person wanted for, or about to commit, a crime; or (3) a designated desk or office.

Route   A length of street or streets, designated for patrol purposes. A route is most frequently used for the assignment of traffic officers, although it is sometimes used for the assignment of foot-patrol officers. A route is also sometimes called a "line beat."

Beat   An area (in contrast to a length of street) assigned for patrol purposes, whether foot or motorized. It is also sometimes used for the assignment of motorized traffic officers instead of a route.

Sector   An area containing two or more beats, routes, or posts. The squad of officers assigned to a sector is headed by a sergeant.

District   A geographic subdivision of the city for patrol purposes, usually with its own station. A district is usually commanded by a captain who is charged with the basic responsibility for administering, directing, and controlling the patrol force in his district.

Area   A section or territorial division of a large city, each comprised of designated districts. In some departments, area commanders are appointed to exercise close command and supervision of district commanders. In other departments this echelon of command is eliminated by having areas supervised and controlled by deputies of the patrol-division head, operating directly under his control and out of his office.

Team-Policing Terminology   No clear pattern of terminology has yet emerged for departments organized for team policing, and the following terms seem to be used as equivalents.

District, Sector, Team Area   The geographic area in which a single team operates. Generally the team is commanded by a lieutenant, with five or six sergeants, a number of detectives, and nine to as many as forty patrol officers.

Division, Area   Groupings of several teams, usually under a captain or major.

Beat, Response Zone, Zone   The area within a district which is the responsibility of a single officer, when there are several officers working at the same time in the district. Also, the area for which an officer is responsible for the conduct of follow-up investigations within the district.

Time Units   Police personnel are apportioned throughout the day in the following manner.

Watch or Shift   A time division of the day for purposes of assignment. Shifts may be consecutive eight-hour periods, or they may overlap to meet unusual or peak loads.

Platoon   Personnel assigned to one shift or watch. The platoon, ordinarily commanded by a lieutenant, may serve the entire city or a district thereof. It may be composed of several squads assigned to sectors of the city or the district. Divisions that have personnel on duty for more than one shift divide them into platoons on the basis of the hours of the day they are on duty,

ORGANIZATION FOR POLICE SERVICE

without regard to the number on duty or the rank of the supervising officer. This procedure facilitates making assignments.

Other Terminology   The following additional definitions are provided to avoid misunderstanding in the use of these terms throughout this book.

Member   A person on the police-department payroll, whether an officer or a civilian employee.

Civilian Employee   A member who has not taken the oath of office and is not authorized to make arrests.

Sworn Officer   A member of the police department who has taken an oath of office and who possesses the police power of arrest.

Superior Officer   An officer who has supervisory responsibilities, either temporarily or permanently, over officers of lower rank.

Commanding Officer   An officer who is in command of the department or of a bureau, a division, a section, an area, a district, a squad, or any other subdivision of the department.

Ranking Officer   The officer having the highest grade or rank within a given group or at a particular location. Officers of the same grade should rank according to the date of their appointment to that grade, unless otherwise ordered by the chief of police. For a special detail and for a specific period, an officer may be designated by the commanding officer to take command without regard to rank. The beat officer is generally the ranking patrol officer when others are dispatched into the beat.

PRINCIPLES OF ORGANIZATION

An examination of the structure of public, commercial, military, and industrial organizations may reveal the application of some principles which can be considered fundamental. They should be kept in mind by the chief when organizing his force in the manner described in the following chapters. These principles are listed below:

1   Tasks, similar or related in purpose, process, method, or clientele, should be grouped together in one or more units under the control of one person. In order to facilitate their assignment, these tasks may be divided according to (*a*) the time, (*b*) the place of their performance, and (*c*) the level of authority needed in their accomplishment.

2   Specialized units should be created only when overall departmental capability is thus significantly increased; they should not be created at the expense of reduced control and decreased general interest.

3   Lines of demarcation between the responsibilities of units should be clearly drawn by a precise definition of the duties of each, which should be made known to all members so that responsibility may be placed exactly. Such definition avoids duplication in execution and neglect resulting from the nonassignment of a duty.

4   Channels should be established through which information flows up

74   ADMINISTRATION

and down and through which authority is delegated. These lines of control permit the delegation of authority, the placing of responsibility, the supervision of work, and the coordination of effort. Lines of control should be clearly defined and well understood by all members so that all may know to whom they are responsible and who, in turn, is responsible to them. Exceptions to routine communication of information through channels should be provided for emergency and unusual situations.

    5   Structure and terminology should facilitate the understanding of the purposes and responsibilities of the organization by all its members.

    6   Each individual, unit, and situation should be under the immediate control of one, and only one, person, thus achieving the principle of unity of command and avoiding the friction that results from duplication of direction and supervision.

    7   The span of control of a supervisor should be large enough to provide economical supervision, but no more units or persons should be placed under the direct control of one person than he or she is able to manage.

    8   Each task should be made the unmistakable duty of someone; responsibility for planning, execution, and control should be definitely placed on designated persons.

    9   Supervision should be provided for every member of the organization and for every function or activity. (If the supervision is not immediately available at the actual level of execution, it should be obtainable through referral to a predesignated authority.)

    10   Each assignment or duty should carry with it commensurate authority to fulfill the responsibility.

    11   Persons to whom authority is delegated should be held accountable for the use made of it and for the failure to use it.

Grouping of Similar Tasks

This concept is the *sine qua non* of the process of organizing. As indicated earlier, tasks may be grouped if they are similar or related in function, process, method, or clientele or if there is a need to group them by time of day, place of execution, or level of authority. Each of these elements can be termed a *basis of organizational grouping.*

Organizational terminology itself should ideally reflect the nature of the work being performed. The name given to a subdivision should enable someone outside the department to make a reasonable assessment of its responsibilities.

Grouping of tasks should be logical and consistent. For example, the responsibilities of an administrative division should not include an operational activity. Neither should there be overlap in the assignment of responsibilities for which accountability is attached. Many of the problems relating to overlapping or conflicting responsibilities in an organization can be attributed to the use of two or more different bases on the same level.

Efforts of the department are most easily coordinated and most effectively directed when the force is organized to facilitate the assignment and performance of tasks on the basis of type of duties and time and place of performance.

ORGANIZATION FOR POLICE SERVICE

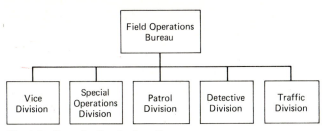

Chart 4 Organization by function.

Function The force should be organized primarily according to the nature of the tasks to be performed; i.e., it should be divided into groups so that similar and related duties may be assigned to each. For example, most members will be assigned to patrol duties, but some may be assigned to traffic control, others to crime investigation, and so on, as shown in Chart 4. These divisions encompass all the field services to the public that must be provided by the police department. This chart thus does not include the organic units designed to perform auxiliary and administrative tasks. (The factors that should be considered in ascertaining the need for the desirability of these functional divisions will be discussed later.)

Time The units are divided into shifts or watches according to the time of day, as shown by Chart 5. This is the most elementary form of police organizational structure when it is applied to a small department. Any large functional unit can also be organized according to time if the demand exists.

Place A territorial distribution of a platoon, accomplished by assigning patrol officers to beats, is necessary to facilitate the direction and control of the officers and to ensure suitable patrol service at every point within the jurisdiction. The territorial distribution of a platoon is shown by the dashed lines in Chart 6. Patrol officers on street duty are usually under the supervision of a patrol sergeant. When the number of patrol officers is great, it may be desirable to group them into squads assigned to specific sectors of the jurisdiction, with a sergeant in charge of each sector.

A large city is divided into geographic districts, and the patrol force is apportioned among them; the organization of the force then reflects the

Chart 5 Organization by time.

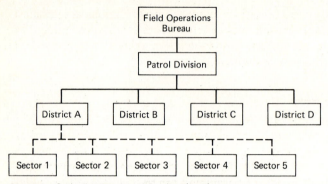

Chart 6 Organization by place (territory).

organization of the territory, as shown in Chart 6. In some departments, personnel engaged in one or more of the specialized tasks (crime investigation, traffic, vice control, and juvenile-crime control) are apportioned among the several districts, with their control vested in the district commanders; in others, the head of each functional unit retains direct control over all personnel performing tasks in his field, even though they may be physically decentralized by being housed in district stations.

Level of Authority A police department is always divided according to the level of authority; i.e., there will be some patrol officers, some sergeants, some lieutenants, and so on, as illustrated in Chart 7. Vertical combinations of superior officers, with each rank at a different level of authority from any other, form channels through which operations may be directed and controlled. These chains of command, or lines of direct control, facilitate the delegation of authority and the placing of responsibility; supervision is thus ensured, and coordination effected. Problems relating to organization for command and control are dealt with in subsequent pages.

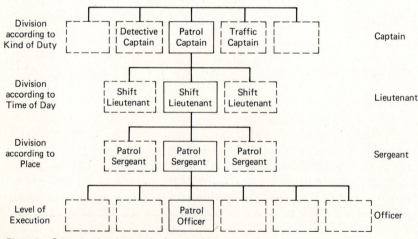

Chart 7 Organization by level of authority.

ORGANIZATION FOR POLICE SERVICE

Chart 7 also illustrates that tasks in most police organizations are grouped by function, time, and place, as well as by level of authority, in combination. In general, however, the same basis for organizational grouping should be used on any given level within a bureau or division.

Specialization Based on Need

Specialization is the natural result of the division of work by function. The degree of specialization, in turn, is determined by the size and sophistication of the department, by the number of special units created, and by the extent to which each has exclusive responsibility for the performance of tasks within the special field. A special unit need not be created for the performance of each group of operational tasks, and even if it is, most of the duties in the special field may be performed by the patrol division. For example, in spite of the creation of a traffic division, most street-traffic duties should be performed by the motorized-beat-patrol officer. Similarly, while a detective division may be established, much of the work of investigating crimes may be performed by beat officers.

Decisions relating to specialization are extremely important in police administration and will greatly affect the operation of the department. Specialization has a direct bearing on relationships of members in their performance of police duties; it also complicates direction, coordination, and control. Many of the significant variations in police organization and operating methods in this country are traceable to diverse decisions in respect to the degree of specialization. For example, the centralization of police operations is somewhat in proportion to the extent of specialization because specialists have a strong impulse to retain complete control of all operations in their field and to oppose the delegation of authority for the performance of these operations to a unit having general police responsibilities. They feel that no one else is as competent to perform these special tasks.

Specialization Grows with the Growth of the Department The development of specialization in the police department of a rapidly growing city today is similar to the gradual historical development of specialization that occurred in the modernization of police organization. The chief investigates crime in the small department, but as the amount of work increases, one or more officers may spend part or full time at this task. The increased number of police and the greater amount of work to be done in larger departments result in still further specialization in those fields of police activity where the importance and nature of the task seem to require special attention, ability, and training.

Chart 8 illustrates the similarity of functions carried out by police departments and points out the diversity of activity, even in the smallest of forces, which lends itself to the trend toward specialization as the department grows. Note that the chief of police in the small city may actually carry out the duties which would be assigned to a specialized division in a larger agency.

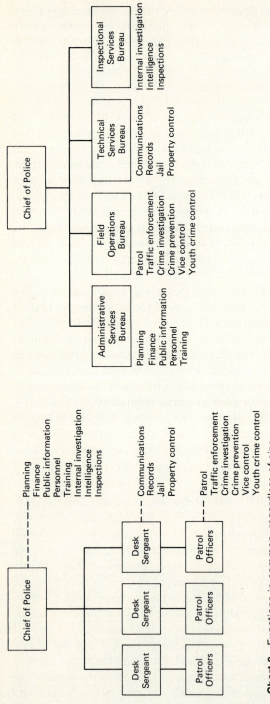

Chart 8 Functions in common, regardless of size.

ORGANIZATION FOR POLICE SERVICE

Determining the Need for Specialization An examination of police practices indicates that specialization has not always been soundly based; wide variations in the proportion of the force devoted to patrol and to the special branches of the service are found among cities of every population group, in every geographic division of the country, and in departments in both the upper and lower brackets of personnel strength. Equally pronounced variations are found in the proportional strength of such special branches of the services as detective, vice, traffic, juvenile-crime control, and communications and records. It does not seem likely that varied conditions within individual communities justify such wide variations in practice; neither does it seem likely that such widely varying practices can be equally effective—some must be better than others.

Sound decisions on the need for, and the nature and degree of, specialization are vital to the creation of an effective organization. Careful consideration should be given to all aspects of the question, and the advantages should be weighed against the disadvantages before a decision is made.

Lines of Authority and Chain of Command

Communications should ordinarily go upward and downward through established channels in the hierarchy. Diverting orders, directives, or reports around a level of command usually has disastrous effects on efficiency of the organization if the level which is bypassed is ordinarily capable and responsible. The bypassed supervisor has no official knowledge of the nature of a directive going downward. Since this supervisor is unaware of a directive, he or she can hardly be held responsible for enforcing it. A secondary loss, of course, is that the organization does not receive the benefit of the supervisor's services. However, the greatest disadvantage is the loss of control and power over subordinates.

Diversion of reporting around a supervisor in the upward direction is far less of a problem, since the bypassed supervisor, if competent, can usually stop the practice through pressure on subordinates. The bypassed supervisor usually has more difficulty in coping with a situation in which a higher level encourages the supervisor's subordinates to bypass the chain of command. The police administrator should be alert for indications of problems in either direction.

Command outside the Pyramid of Authority Officers from different units are sometimes engaged together in an operation, and if the project is to be under effective command, one superior must exercise control for that particular operation. Police operations, like combat in war, sometimes require instant decision and action. For a ranking officer under these circumstances to have to appeal to higher authority before seeking control of members of units not under his or her command would be inconsistent with the purpose of organization; the procedure is so cumbersome and time-consuming as to jeopardize the objective.

While superiority of rank does not ordinarily authorize officers to assume command over subordinate members of the force outside their unit, there are two circumstances in which this action is warranted. The first includes (1) situations involving unsuitable or improper action on the part of an officer of lesser rank and (2) emergency situations, such as at the scene of a crime, explosion, or other catastrophe, where the superior may demand, and should receive, assistance in performing essential tasks from any lesser officer regardless of the unit to which he or she is regularly assigned. These situations demand immediate action in order not to jeopardize the police purpose and the reputation of the department. The second circumstance is routine dispatching and giving of orders by officers in a staff capacity, i.e., without authority in their own right, but actually in the name of someone else, even though that person is not designated in the giving of the order.

Authority through Departmental Directives The exercise of command over personnel outside the pyramid of authority under the circumstances described above must not violate the principle of unity of command. In theory the principle is not violated because the superior officer is, in a sense, speaking for the commanding officer of the subordinate, ordering him to do what his commander would require of him were he present in person. In practice it is not violated if the command is exercised in conformity with departmental directives which automatically grant an officer confronted with a situation requiring immediate action the authority to cut across the usual lines of control. These out-of-the-ordinary relationships should be formalized in regulations to avoid misunderstanding and confusion. For example, regulations should define the situations in which superior officers may exercise direct command outside their usual pyramid, namely, all those in which the police purpose or reputation is jeopardized.

Duty of Subordinate to Obey The superior officer must appraise the emergency that confronts him and decide on his justification for assuming command over subordinates outside his unit. The subordinate has no alternative; he must obey the order, but he or his commander may later protest the misuse of authority. The superior must not interfere with the performance of routine duties by subordinates not in his unit except under the conditions mentioned above. A superior officer is frequently tempted to assume command over a lesser officer outside his unit who is performing a routine task in which the superior has an interest. This he should not do, although he may discuss the matter with the lesser officer; if this does not correct the situation, he may seek correction at a higher level.

Unity of Command

In police service it is important (1) that only one person be in complete command of each situation and (2) that only one person be in direct command or supervision of each officer. Confusion is created when more than one

ORGANIZATION FOR POLICE SERVICE

superior undertakes independent command of an operation performed by several subordinates or when a subordinate receives orders from more than one superior. In such circumstances the orders given are not likely to be harmonious, and conflicting orders confuse subordinates and make the coordination of their efforts more difficult. Generally, it is unwise for a police executive or commander to appear at the scenes of incidents on a routine basis unless he plans to take personal command. If he is present and does not act, he runs the risk of abdicating his authority and serves no purpose with his presence except to tempt his subordinates to refer the matter to him. If he does act, the regular field supervisor on the scene becomes a spectator.

Difficulty in the interpretation of the principle of unity of command often occurs at the sergeant–police officer level. In some cases, especially in small departments, an officer is supervised by the regular sergeant of the squad for three shifts a week but receives supervision from a relief sergeant for the remaining time. The student may argue that the practice is a violation of the principle, but the key to proper understanding of the concept is the word "direct." In these situations, a relief supervisor should obviously exercise control for events taking place during his or her own tour of duty. However, departmental directives should establish the policy to decide which supervisor is responsible for the subordinate in such matters as authorization of annual leave, performance evaluation, and the conduct of disciplinary investigations not requiring immediate action.

Span of Control

The ability of one person to direct, coordinate, and control immediate subordinates—the span of control—has physical limits because an individual can be in only one place at one time and cannot work 24 hours a day. There are also definite mental limitations to successful command as the number of immediate subordinates grows larger. In addition, as the number is increased, particularly if the subordinates are separated from the superior by time or space, the tasks of command increase.

The proper span of control is determined by such factors as native ability; the complexity of the tasks to be performed by subordinates; separation of the superior from immediate subordinates by time or place; the time demanded by the public for speeches, ceremonies, and personal appointments; and the time taken in official extradepartmental conferences. Consequently, no effort is made to establish an arbitrary number as the optimum which can be universally applied.

Many executives attempt to exercise a span of control beyond their capacity, with a resultant loss of effective direction, coordination, and control. Two factors may cause administrators to make such an error: (1) an overestimation of their own ability and (2) an inability or unwillingness to delegate authority because of a desire or real need to exercise a close control over operations. The desire may originate in the executive's sense of his or her own indispensability and in a conviction that subordinates are incapable of making

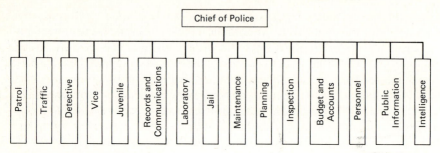

Chart 9 Broad span of control.

wise decisions; the need may arise from the incompetence of poorly selected or inadequately trained subordinates.

A broad span of control, as illustrated by Chart 9, requires the chief to make numerous decisions and to participate in operating details. Because of the large number of officers reporting directly to the chief, the task of coordination is increased. The chief's time is likely to be so occupied that there is little time left to perform the primary administrative tasks of planning, inspection, and other management duties. There is grave danger that the burden of details will be overwhelming, thus preventing the chief from exercising a positive, creative, and imaginative leadership.

The span of control may be reduced by the use of additional levels of supervisory officials, thus lengthening the chain of command. The line of control necessarily divides at each level of authority in the chain, since at each level the power of command is delegated to subordinates. A rise in the number of immediate subordinates increases the difficulty of command, whereas the utilization of an intermediate level of authority, as illustrated by Chart 10, relieves the head of much of the burden of command and gives him more free time to inspect the department and plan improvements. The extra level of

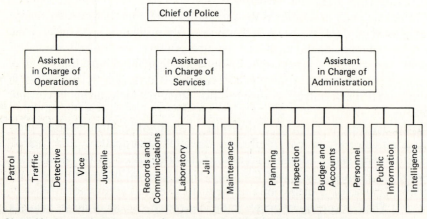

Chart 10 Narrowing the span of control by lengthening the chain of command.

ORGANIZATION FOR POLICE SERVICE   83

authority, however, lessens the leader's personal participation in police operations, impedes somewhat the easy and rapid flow of information up and down the channels of control, limits his ability to control operations, and may diminish the effectiveness of his personality and add to departmental red tape. Lengthening the chain of command is not, therefore, an unmixed good. Each added level of authority removes the chief by one more intermediary from actual operations and consequently from the opportunity personally to direct, coordinate, and control the efforts of the force.

Optimum Span of Control   In the organization of the force, therefore, the chief must decide on the relationships that are to prevail in the distribution of subordinates; i.e., the chief must decide on the relative width of the span of control and the length of the chain of command. A similar decision must be made within each pyramid of command at every level of authority. Are the pyramids to be short and broad or tall and narrow? There is no standard optimum ratio between the span of control and the length of the chain of command applicable at each level of authority and in every situation. The height and width of each pyramid will be determined by conditions that prevail in particular situations, such as time available for administrative tasks, the competence and reliability of subordinates, and the ability of the head to delegate authority. Ideally, the people who are in positions of leadership should have a combination of personality, education, training, and experience which would permit the choice of a broader span of control.

Delegation of Authority

The necessity for the grouping or division of personnel according to the level of authority arises from the human limitations of the leader. If all duties were performed by half a dozen officers working on the same shift and in the same room, one person could easily direct, coordinate, and control them. As the number is increased and as they are separated by time and place, the chief has greater and greater need for assistance in commanding his force. The superior officer of each functional, time, and place group aids the chief in his command duties by directing, coordinating, and controlling the members assigned to his unit. Each superior officer must be held responsible for the performance of tasks assigned to him and consequently must be given the necessary control over personnel and matériel in his unit to enable him to discharge this responsibility. This necessity justifies the following rule of command: *A person cannot be held responsible for the accomplishment of an order unless he or she has been delegated the authority necessary for its accomplishment.* When this rule is observed, the giving of an order (placing of responsibility) is a delegation of essential authority.

Authority of Unit Heads   The superior officer of each organization unit has command of every person within the organization pyramid beneath him. The chief is at the apex of the pyramid and has command over all members of the force; he is responsible for the attainment of all police objectives without regard to function, time, or place, even though the department is divided according to major objectives into patrol, traffic control, and so on. The head of the patrol division, in turn, has command over all patrol personnel and is responsible for all patrol functions, even though the patrol force is divided into districts and into platoons according to time. The commander of a district likewise is responsible for all patrol functions in his jurisdiction regardless of the time of day. A platoon commander is responsible for patrol operations in his district during the hours of his shift or watch.

Varieties of Delegated Authority The division of the tasks of command among the officers of the various units is known as *delegation of authority*. The authority that the chief delegates to a superior officer is not the total authority of the chief; rather, it is limited to the command of members within the pyramid of that officer's authority. That officer, in turn, delegates the authority given to him to the heads of smaller subordinate units. This process is continued to the lowest level—that of execution. The delegation of authority may be divided into policy formulation, direction, supervision, and execution.

Policy Formulation Policy is the broad, general plan or principle underlying methods of procedure or the conduct of the department's affairs. It affects all levels of personnel in the department and influences all aspects of the department's performance. For example, policy decisions must be made about methods of patrol as well as the treatment of the youthful offender; the policy statement will say *what* is to be done but not *how* it is to be done.

Policy may be handed to the chief in the form of legislation or an administrative order from the head of the city or of a board. Other policy may be formulated by the chief himself. His expression of authority may be principally in the form of broad statements of action to be followed by the department.

Direction To carry out the policies of the chief, decisions must be made about procedures: what is to be done, who is to do it, and when, where, and how it is to be done. To implement the policy, a large number of people located in various organizational units, according to the nature, time, and place of their duty, must be given specific directions so that the efforts of all members may be coordinated and the force may work as an integrated team toward the accomplishment of its purpose. The essence of direction is assignment; it consists of directing someone to do something.

Supervision Supervision of officers engaged in carrying out their assigned tasks is essential; assistance and guidance must be provided to ensure successful performance. It is the duty of supervisors to see that the job is done properly in accordance with the directions given.

Execution Authority is also expressed at the level of execution. Authority is more than a right or a privilege to perform a task; it is accompanied by a responsibility to do so—a requirement that it be done.

ORGANIZATION FOR POLICE SERVICE

The processes of policy formulation, direction, supervision, and execution are not each limited to a specific level of authority. Policy decisions of less importance, for example, may be made at every level of authority, including the lowest, that of execution. Direction will likewise be effected at every level by actual or implied commands. Supervision and execution must be provided at each level; each officer, regardless of the amount of authority he or she has, is responsible for, and must be supervised in, the execution of some task.

Common Sense in Using the Principles

These principles of administrative organization are intended to facilitate the operation of the force, not to hamper it. Performance seemingly hindered by their application is not proof of their invalidity; it may simply be evidence of their misuse in actual practice.

For example, a too rigid adherence to lines of control might inhibit the chief, or other commanding officer, from entering a district station or other police facility at a late hour of the night in the absence of all officers in the chain of command between himself and the watch commander. It is important that all commanding officers be free to circulate and observe operations anywhere within their pyramid of authority in the absence of their subordinate commanders and supervisors. In fact, they have an obligation to do so. The supervisor in command, however, has a responsibility to report to his immediate superior that the higher commander has been present on a tour such as this.

The improper use of command channels results in unnecessary delay and red tape. The test as to whether subordinates should use command channels lies in whether their superiors must be kept informed of the particular transaction under consideration. Routine reports and requests which do not require the attention of, or decision by, those in higher authority should not be sent through command channels. To do so results only in clogging those channels, delaying important decisions, and involving superior commanders in useless paperwork. Subordinates of one bureau should make liaison or communicate directly with subordinates of another bureau when decisions by superiors are not required. This is called *lateral communication*.

Actions in furtherance of a staff responsibility usually do not require the use of command channels. For example, the traffic division, which has staff responsibility in traffic matters, may give advice and guidance to other elements of the department without going through command channels. If such supervision reveals a situation requiring corrective action which advice and guidance cannot bring about, then the traffic division would normally recommend such action to higher authority, which would direct corrective action through command channels.

When a superior gives an order or discusses a matter with a subordinate without the knowledge or presence of an intermediate commander, it is the responsibility of the subordinate to inform the intermediate commander of any decision reached or of any order given to the subordinate by the superior.

Adherence to officially established lines of authority may seem to cause needless delay, and the process of control may appear to be unduly cumbersome and involved. Desire to get on with the job sometimes leads to cutting across lines of control in violation of the principle of unity of command. The same desire tempts the executive to undertake an unreasonable span of control in order to provide a more direct access to those engaged in the performance of a task. Friction and loss of control then result. When the principles are disregarded, the force operates without organization, and its effectiveness becomes dependent on the judgment and good will of its members.

The organizational structure by itself, because it is a static, mechanical device lacking intelligent discretion, will not help the force to deal effectively with live and constantly changing situations. In order for it to do so, the organization must be considered a dynamic group, readily adaptable to any situation that confronts it. Its adaptability is influenced by the relationships that are established between the component units. Proper relationships, defined by departmental policies and procedures, will prevent friction, delay, and other obstacles to free and easy operation and at the same time will facilitate conformity to the principles of administrative organization, with a resultant increase in the effectiveness of the force.

Essential flexibility is obtained by creating procedures that make it unnecessary to adhere to formal channels for supervision and control in every case. Adaptability to meet emergency needs is provided by defining situations that automatically cause a shift in command. Deviations from rigid lines of control are thus possible without violation of the administrative principles.

THE PROCESS OF REORGANIZATION AND THE APPLICATION OF ORGANIZATIONAL PRINCIPLES

In the application of organizational principles, the administrator is dealing, in an overwhelming majority of cases, with an existing department and its problems rather than with a newly created agency. A fundamental step in the organizational process, therefore, is the study of the existing structure.

Guidelines for the Analysis of the Existing Organizational Structure

There are several techniques which can be used to analyze a police organizational structure. The first and most obvious method is the examination of existing charts. Unfortunately, as many consultants have discovered, most police departments do not have accurate charts or tables of organization. In many medium-sized and small agencies, a chart does not even exist.

Examination of a chart should give some preliminary attention to questions which can save time and energy later:

- Is there more than one version of this same chart? If so, why?
- Who made the chart? In some cases, inaccurate charts are sometimes

ORGANIZATION FOR POLICE SERVICE

offered in annual reports, budget documents, and other reports presented to government officials or the public. The inaccuracies are sometimes calculated, but they often result from chart making by someone (such as a budget clerk) who has no appreciation of proper chart making or no in-depth knowledge of the actual structural relationships.

- Is the chart outdated?
- Is the chart only a plan for intended organization?

The next step is the "testing" of the chart, if it exists, or—if it does not—the gathering of information so that the actual relationships can be depicted. The technique is the same for both.

The testing and information-gathering process can be used by the new administrator (whether promoted from within or selected from outside the department) or by a staff officer acting on behalf of the chief. The process should involve review of written directives and manuals, but it depends primarily on verbal questioning of employees at each level as follows:

- To whom do you report?
- Do you report directly to anyone else?
- Who reports to you?
- Do they report to anyone else? If so, under what circumstances?
- What are your personal duties or responsibilities?
- What are the overall responsibilities of your unit (i.e., the people reporting to you)?
- What are the exact actual titles of (1) the unit headed by your direct supervisor, (2) the unit you supervise, and (3) the units reporting to you?
- What are the ranks and titles of the supervisors of each of the units mentioned above?

Understanding the actual structure has great value, since it points the way toward solutions while it permits description of the deficiencies; the mere identification of a structural problem often leads to cure.

It is difficult to separate the organizational process into discrete parts, since the study and analysis of the existing structure and the development of ideas for the new structure often blend into one another. For example, the discussion of the present structure often concerns the following key analytical questions:

- Why is the function or responsibility carried out by the unit?
- Could it be carried out better by some other organizational arrangement?

Also, the analysis of the structure considers the same basic organizational principles which have already been presented earlier in this chapter and which—in applied form—are used to establish the new structure.

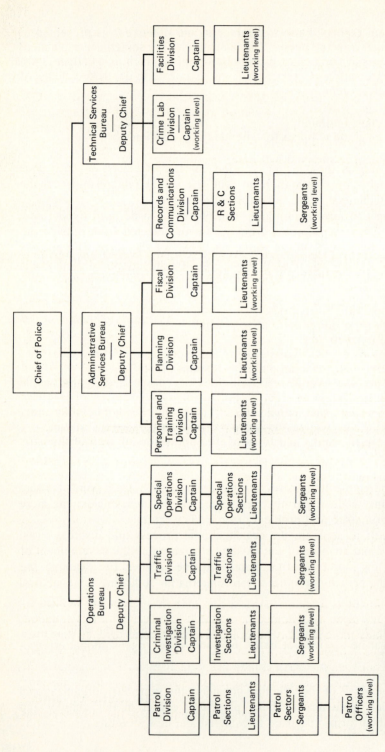

Chart 11 Department A. Extreme structure based on equal rank at all levels. (Note the large number of captains and lieutenants and the use of supervisors at the working level.)

ORGANIZATION FOR POLICE SERVICE

Consideration of Organizational Principles in Reorganizing the Structure

There are a great many considerations to be kept in mind in the development of organizational structures. There are variations which are due simply to the size of the agency and the resulting level of complexity of the task which must be organized. Certainly, the basic function or clientele of an agency is of paramount importance in developing the structure; the organizational structure for the U.S. Drug Enforcement Administration must necessarily differ from the structure of a small county sheriff's office located in a rural region.

It may seem as if the application of organizational principles would result in identical structures for agencies of the same size that have similar police problems. As the reader will note in the succeeding pages, organizational structures may differ for many valid reasons.

Reasons for Variation The need to accommodate specialized functions and to provide unique services to the public is a fundamental reason for variation in structure.

Individual differences in the capability of employees and the general quality of personnel must also be taken into account. These differences cause variations in structure. Since the purpose of organization is to make the best use of all available talent and energy, the personality, interest, native ability, skill, and experience of each member are important factors to be considered in making assignments.

The special qualifications of top members of the department have a greater influence on organizational structure than those of the rank and file. There are more positions at the lower levels of authority, and individual differences usually may be taken into account in making assignments. At the higher levels, however, there are increasingly fewer positions and, therefore, less opportunity to make assignments in which the particular skills of the individual may be used to best advantage. Consequently, changes in the organization of the force may at times be necessary because of the special qualifications or limitations of the available officers, but in making such changes, care must be taken not to violate sound principles of organization.

Differences in procedures sometimes necessitate further variations from a model organization. For example, the need for close supervision of the dispatcher by an officer who is qualified to make important decisions on the spur of the moment is lessened when the dispatcher's duties are defined by regulation and his tasks are outlined in prepared broadcasts. In this situation, the dispatcher may more logically be assigned to the records division than to an operating division. Differences in tasks assigned to the operating units also result in variations in the basic functional organization. For example, the assignment to the patrol division of basic responsibility for the preliminary investigation of crimes and accidents and for the enforcement of moving-traffic violations will influence the organization and size of the three divisions involved in these activities.

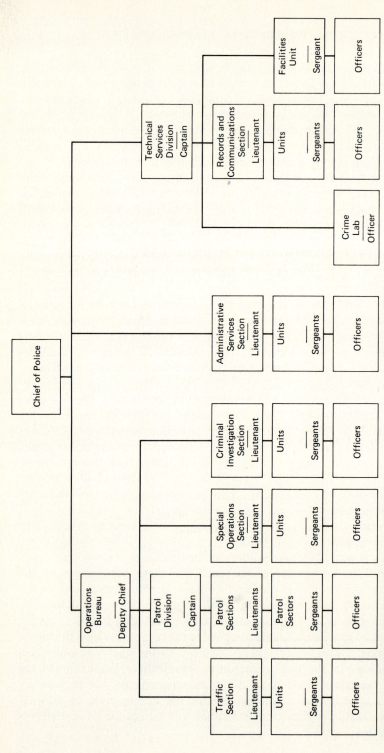

Chart 12 Department B. Extreme structure based on minimum rank required for supervision. (Note the absence of uniformity of rank in positions reporting directly to the chief.)

ORGANIZATION FOR POLICE SERVICE

State laws are highly significant in the determination of organizational differences. At the state level itself, the law may strictly limit the powers of the force. In some states, the state may impose organizational restrictions or mandates which affect local police. Finally, charters and ordinances often have a profound effect on the structure of departments at the local level.

Consideration of Rank in the Organizational Process Some functions in a police department are obviously of greater importance than others, and this difference may be reflected in the number of personnel and the supervisors assigned to the function. The nature of the organizational structure in a police department does not permit a perfectly uniform relationship of rank to subdivision staff size for the simple reason that there are greater numbers of people to be supervised in the operating divisions, particularly patrol, and a greater depth of supervision is necessary. If the titles of subdivisions and the ranks of supervisors were determined by the size of the subdivisions and the minimum number of supervisors necessary for adequate span of control, the organization would have the distorted structure shown in Chart 11 for an imaginary force, Department A.

On the other hand, the organization for imaginary Department B is based on equating ranks at every level, regardless of the complexity of the job. This structure, shown in Chart 12, is equally bizarre and results in a staggering oversurplus of rank.

It is obvious, then, that a balanced structure must respect several contradictory tendencies, with several of them desirable in moderation but destructive if carried to an extreme:

1 Economy of supervisory manpower (i.e., the tendency toward broad span of control)
2 Effectiveness of supervision (the tendency toward narrow span of control)
3 Equal rank for subordinates supervised directly by the same supervisor
4 Basing the structure on the minimum number of supervisory levels necessary for the control of each successive rank
5 Rewarding difficult and complex positions by giving them higher rank even though the supervisory responsibilities are minimal
6 Utilizing lower ranks for higher-level responsibilities

Broad Span of Control versus the Single Executive Assistant When the number of immediate subordinates (division heads) is high and the administrative duties of the chief become heavy, as in a large department, a reorganization of the top level may be necessary in order to provide assistance to the chief and to give him time for more important tasks. The reorganization may take one of several forms: (1) The chief may narrow his span of control by the creation of intermediaries between himself and his present immediate subordinates; (2) he may consolidate functions (which may involve demotion of some subordinates if they are currently all of equal rank); or (3) he may retain his present span of control and obtain assistance in the form of an aide who is not in the line of command. Any one of these solutions can be used successfully under the right circumstances.

At times, however, the chief may be tempted to reorganize by creating a single assistant or executive officer who is in the line of command. This structure is not recommended for several reasons. First, the administrator's span of control is reduced to one, which is both uneconomical and unrealistic. Second, if the single subordinate is strong, there is a tendency for this person to absorb most of the chief's problems—including the same problem of excessive span of control which existed before. Third, an extra command step is created between the operational forces and their commander. As a result, communication to all elements in the organization may be diffused or even blocked.

The Influence of Specialization

Some of the principal considerations relating to specialization in the organizational process were mentioned earlier. Since specialization plays such an important part in the determination of structure, the subject will receive additional emphasis here.

Development of Specialization The metropolitan police force created in London, England, by Sir Robert Peel in 1828 provided a day and night patrol, the jurisdiction being divided into beats and each officer devoting his attention exclusively to patrolling his district.[1] Detectives were not created until 1843. When police services were first established in this country, all tasks were performed by men on patrol. Crime investigation and rudimentary forms of traffic and vice control were performed by the watch, which was created primarily for the purpose of preserving the peace and protecting life and property by repressive patrol.

From this simple organization emerged the modern department with its high degree of specialization. The need for a separate unit for crime investigation gradually became apparent, and detective divisions were created for this purpose in the larger departments. For example, the Boston Police Department, created in 1854, consisted of about 250 officers, of whom 6 were attached to the chief's office and 5 were detectives.[2] The proportion of the force devoted exclusively to crime investigation was relatively small at the beginning, but the number of officers assigned to this task had been greatly increased by the turn of the century. Demands were already being made for other specialized activities, but the trend toward specialization did not become pronounced until later with the coming of the automobile, when the problem of traffic control became increasingly acute. Specialization in traffic control has been followed by specialization in delinquency prevention; both were preceded and accompanied by specialization in vice control.

---

[1]W. L. M. Lee, *History of the English Police,* Methuen & Co., Ltd., London, 1901.
[2]Edward H. Savage, *Boston Watch & Police,* J. E. Farwell and Company, Boston, 1865, p. 94.

ORGANIZATION FOR POLICE SERVICE

Specialization in Small Departments In the small department, patrol officers must be jacks-of-all-police-trades. They must patrol their beats for conditions that may jeopardize the comfort, safety, and welfare of the people, and they must take action to correct those conditions. They should exert influence on young people to aid their development into worthwhile citizens. They must repress the criminal activity of those so inclined; and when crimes are committed, they must personally conduct investigations to make arrests, recover stolen property, and aid in the preparation of the cases for presentation in court. They must inform citizens of regulations, warn them of violations, and arrest those who persist in transgressions; they must also regulate vehicular and pedestrian traffic in order to prevent accidents and congestion. They must provide innumerable services to the public, giving information, assistance, and comfort to those in distress. This is the service provided by police officers in a small town today—service similar to, but much more extensive than, that given by their predecessors, the night watch, 100 years ago.

Advantages of Specialization In any organization, civilian or military, business or government, there are definite advantages to be gained by specialization, i.e., the assignment of particular tasks to special units or individuals in the organization. The major advantages are listed below.

Placement of Responsibility Definite fixing of responsibility is the first rule of effective operation. Through specialization, responsibility for performance of a task can be placed on a specific individual or unit.

Development of Experts Personnel qualified by training or special ability may be selected for particular tasks; constant repetition of a task develops a high degree of skill and ability, which are further increased in a narrowed field of interest and attention.

Improvement of Training Persons assigned to a specialized field may be given more intensive training than would be feasible for the entire force, and the narrowed field of interest also promotes study and research by individual members.

Promotion of Esprit de Corps A small group which is made responsible for the performance of a specific task tends to form a cohesive unit with high morale and pride in its accomplishments. When members of the special unit are selected on the basis of special ability and become highly skilled through training, repetition, and attention to a restricted field, they invariably develop enthusiasm and a strong esprit.

Stimulation of Special Police Interest Because of their definite responsibility, specialized personnel develop a proprietary interest in department operations that relate to their field. Their consequent concern causes them to participate actively in departmental operations and press for authority, personnel, and matériel to meet their needs. The demand by special units for adequate facilities is desirable as long as it does not result in a disproportionate allocation of the resources of the department.

Arousal of Public Interest Similarly, specialized units arouse and organize public interest and support of police activities. Within limits, such public support is desirable; it aids in securing necessary funds for improvements or increased police strength.

Disadvantages of Specialization The evils of specialization in some cases may outweigh the advantages. When specialization is carried to excess, it seriously injures departmental operations. The following disadvantages may result from specialization.

Limitation of Usefulness Every police matter referred to an officer deserves the officer's immediate attention and usually receives it when he or she is unquestionably responsible for its performance. As a department becomes more specialized, however, many police matters can no longer be directly and promptly disposed of by the officer immediately concerned, but must be referred to designated individuals and units in the organization for decision and action. Responsibility is thus divided between the patrol officer and the specialist. Specialists may hesitate to take action outside their own field because their skill and ability in other activities are usually not so great. Further, specialization frequently affords both the specialist and the nonspecialist a convenient excuse for not undertaking a task that may involve some inconvenience, time, and energy.

Restriction of General Police Interest Participation in a special activity by all members of the department creates among them an interest that is lost when the operation is performed exclusively by specialists. For example, when patrol officers have no responsibility in vice, traffic, and juvenile-crime control, they are not likely to have much interest in these primary police tasks.

Complication of Tasks of Command As specialization is increased, interrelationships multiply alarmingly; these interrelationships are areas of potential conflict and friction that greatly increase the problem of integration. Specialization requires that each special unit be assigned certain responsibilities and that concomitant authority be delegated. This, in turn, necessarily limits the authority delegated to all other units and thereby complicates the tasks of coordination, supervision, and control. Unity of command is also jeopardized by bringing into conflict individuals not under a common leadership in operations, such as at serious crimes and severe explosions, fires, and other catastrophes that require the services of specialists and members from other divisions of the force.

Creation of Other Administrative Problems The swivel-chair executives and private offices that frequently accompany specialization present other problems. The influence of specialists tends to grow out of proportion to their responsibility. They exert every effort to establish their position more firmly and to enhance its importance. Unless their demands for more personnel, equipment, office space, and records facilities are checked, the result may be a department of generals with no troops left to do the fighting. Specialization promotes further specialization. The special unit frequently urges the necessity of an independent records system and of a specialized patrol superimposed on

ORGANIZATION FOR POLICE SERVICE

the regular patrol. Specialists may also develop their own pressure groups in the community, and these groups may embarrass rather than aid the administration.

Hampering of Development of Well-rounded Police Program The conditions just described promote lopsided programs with unjustified emphasis on special fields of police work. This results when the personality and influence of the specialist, rather than the need for service, are the determining factors.

Diminishing of Territorial Coverage Specialization invariably results in a less-intensive general patrol, if overall strength remains the same. Manpower devoted to the specialty must be subtracted from the personnel strength of the generalists in patrol, who must cover the same territory with fewer officers.

Determining Factors The evils as well as the benefits of specialization must be considered in reaching a decision concerning the extent to which any branch of police service should be specialized. The question is largely one of degree; a fixed stand for or against specialization under all circumstances would be highly arbitrary. Some of the factors to be considered are discussed in the succeeding paragraphs.

Quality of Personnel The higher the quality of police personnel, as determined by selection and training, the less the need for specialization; the greater range of ability of competent officers makes it possible for them to perform successfully a greater variety of tasks. On the other hand, the range of tasks which may be assigned to officers of lesser ability and inferior training is substantially smaller.

Need for Special Skill and Ability Certain police tasks require special skills and abilities that only specialization can provide. For example, the operation of a camera, lie detector, and devices for chemically testing the degree of intoxication, as well as the performance of laboratory tasks, requires highly developed skills. Also, specialization within the detective division is justified for certain types of crime investigation that require special skill and ability.

Importance of the Job The importance of a task is ascertained (1) by the need, as indicated by study of such reliable factors as crime and accident rates, juvenile-crime indexes, vice conditions, or the percent of crimes cleared by arrest and property recovered; and (2) by the demand for a particular service. The demand for service does not necessarily reflect actual need; it may be artificially stimulated by pressure groups, by public opinion, or by police officials or higher authority. Special units are frequently established in response to either or both of the above factors.

Amount of Work to Be Done A task may not be especially important or require special skill and ability, but if the amount of work, concentrated in time and place, is sufficient to occupy the full time of one person, specialization may be justified. An example is the officer who devotes full time to the enforcement of time-limit parking regulations.

Need for Readily Available Services Specialization may be justified to make certain services readily available, even though there may not be sufficient work to occupy the full time of one person. For example, in a small department the identification officer or the laboratory technician frequently provides 24-hour service in photographing crime scenes and searching them for physical evidence. As the amount of work increases, this arrangement becomes unsatisfactory because the officer sacrifices an undue portion of his or her off-duty time. Also, investigation is sometimes impaired because others hesitate to infringe on the officer's off-duty time. Under these circumstances there is need for a skilled evidence technician on each shift, even though his or her full time may not be devoted to these duties. The remainder of this officer's time may be spent in patrolling troubled areas where more than the usual amount of concentration of police attention is desirable.

Intermittent Emergency Needs The creation of a special unit may be justified when the unit is used as an emergency reserve to meet irregular, intermittent needs. For example, enforcement of moving-traffic regulations may be the responsibility of the patrol division, thus making it unnecessary to create an enforcement squad in the traffic division. Unusual needs for traffic control created by parades, athletic events, and other public functions, however, require the intermittent attention of a number of traffic officers. Intermittent need created by unusual criminal activity also requires special details of officers. Without a unit for this purpose, officers either must be withdrawn from their regular beats, which is unwise, or must work overtime, which is also undesirable. These irregular needs may justify the creation of a task force in a large city or, in a smaller one, of a traffic squad which will be available, when not on special assignments, to supplement the selective enforcement of moving-traffic regulations by the patrol division.

Need for Maintaining Skill There may be an insufficient amount of work for all members to maintain skill through performance, thus justifying specialization so that suitable skill need be maintained only by a few officers. Photographic work is an example. All officers may be competent to learn photography of crime and accident scenes and of physical evidence under varying conditions, but there is insufficient photographic work to keep each officer in practice. Consequently, there is need for one or more specialists in these and related tasks.

Need for Planning and Control The amount of planning that is necessary in any field of activity may justify specializaton, and the desirability of placing responsibility for supervision of the execution of the plans as well as for control of the specialists involved may provide further justification. For example, in a department in which street-traffic duties are performed by members of the patrol division, a superior officer (such as a platoon lieutenant) may be responsible for planning police traffic control in addition to his other duties; he may also supervise, in a staff capacity, the execution of his plans. With the growth of the community, his patrol and traffic duties will finally increase to the point where he cannot perform all of them satisfactorily. It may be necessary to assign traffic duties to an officer who will devote full time to traffic control. This assignment usually marks the origin of a traffic division.

ORGANIZATION FOR POLICE SERVICE

\ *Dissimilarity of Tasks to Other Duties* Some duties are sufficiently dissimilar to all others to justify specialization, even though special skills are not required. For example, the tasks of an officer assigned to a fixed traffic post and the duties of service units, such as records, communications, and identification, are all dissimilar to the usual police tasks. Dissimilarities are also found in certain types of investigations, such as those involving stolen automobiles, worthless checks, and commercialized vice, whereas preliminary investigations of crimes and arrests for traffic violations are not markedly dissimilar to other duties performed by patrol officers.

\ *Attitude of Personnel toward the Tasks* An uncooperative attitude on the part of police officers toward a particular task frequently results in its neglect and may cause it to be assigned to a special group who are interested in the program and enthusiastic about its promotion. There have been instances in which patrol personnel have been unsympathetic, or actively opposed, to such programs as control of juvenile crime, vice, or even traffic. Once the wisdom of the program has been successfully demonstrated, opposition to it may disappear, and the need for specialization will then be diminished.

\ *Interference with Usual Duties* When the performance of a task interferes with the usual duties of an officer, there may be justification for relieving the officer of this task and assigning it to a special individual or unit. For example, a patrol officer may conduct criminal investigations up to the point where the amount of time spent at such work interferes with the performance of his regular patrol duties. If the investigation takes him from the vicinity of his beat to some distant location or if it requires him to spend considerable time at headquarters or in buildings where his services are not available for regular patrol, he should receive assistance for these tasks. Interference with usual duties must also be considered when placing responsibility on a superior officer in the patrol division for staff planning and control in a specialized field. The same holds true in making assignments to desk officers, dispatchers, information clerks, and others assigned to posts for the performance of infrequent, but important, duties.

\ *Size of the Force and Area of Jurisdiction* Little specialization is justified in a small department; but as its size increases, the need for specialization grows. The area covered by the police force also affects the degree of specialization. A state police force of 500 troopers must necessarily be less specialized than a municipal force of equal size. A state trooper is often responsible for all crime investigation, vice control, and traffic regulation in his district, whereas in many cities one group of officers regulates traffic, another controls vice, and a third makes crime investigations, thus relieving the patrol officer of some responsibility in these specialized fields.

RECOMMENDED ORGANIZATIONAL STRUCTURES

This portion of the book is devoted to recommendations on the overall structure of police agencies of various sizes. An attempt will be made here to depict proper relationships at the highest levels of the hierarchy, but the details of the recommended structure below the division level will be presented in appropriate chapters elsewhere in the text.

Top-Level Organization

In the medium-sized and large departments, a logical method of organization is the assignment of broad functional responsibilities to three or four assistants, with one assistant in charge of operations, one responsible for administrative functions, one assigned to technical services (sometimes called "support services" or often just "services"), and (in larger agencies) one assistant in charge of inspectional services. When units with similar or related duties are assigned to an assistant, some of the advantages of specialization are achieved, and the problem of coordination is also minimized. Nevertheless, a clear and precise definition of the duties of each assistant is essential to effective operation.

As previously pointed out, however, deviation from a plan of rigid classification of functional units may be justified by unusual qualifications (personality, native ability, experience, and so on) of an individual assistant.

The Executive Aide   The duties of this officer are to shield the head from unwanted detail by screening all matters intended for his attention, making decisions (when the aide knows how the chief would make them), and disposing of inquiries and requests personally or by referring them to other officers. The executive aide exercises no command in his own or her own right and consequently does not have direct control of any functional unit except in the chief's name; the aide is purely a staff officer, with rank below that of assistant chief. An executive aide may also sometimes be used advantageously in large departments having assistant chiefs in charge of functional units, as shown in Chart 10. Substantial advantages are gained from this arrangement when the executive aide clearly understands his or her true relationship to the chief and to the rest of the department. Regardless of the structure, an executive aide must have an extremely close relationship to the chief and know how he would decide most matters; the executive aide's loyalty to the chief must be unquestioned. Unless these conditions can be met, this form of organization is not advised.

Organization of Administrative Functions

The need for separate units to perform administrative tasks is influenced by the size of the department and the desirability for direct access to the chief. Since these are the tasks of management which would otherwise be the specific responsibility of the administrator, the organic units created for their performance are logically placed in or adjacent to the chief's office. While these tasks must be performed, a separate unit is not absolutely essential for each; often two or more may be grouped together for performance by a single unit.

Need for a Separate Personnel Division   In only the small department will

ORGANIZATION FOR POLICE SERVICE

the police chief have the time necessary to perform the important personnel duties, and even then some outside technical assistance may be needed. In larger forces a police personnel officer should be appointed to assist the chief in the performance of these tasks. In departments of fewer than 100 members, the police personnel officer may also perform other duties; in larger forces, however, this officer should work on a full-time basis, and in the largest he or she will require assistants.

Departmental training should be the responsibility of the personnel officer, except in the largest departments, where a separate division will be required. The time the personnel officer will spend in actual instruction is dependent on the time that must be devoted to administrative tasks, the number of qualified instructors in the department and in the community, and the personnel officer's own experience and training as an instructor in the police field.

Need for a Public Information Unit   The chief of a small department must personally direct public information activities, while in larger departments he will delegate these responsibilities to one or more subordinates. He may, for example, assign these tasks to his personnel director or to his training officer.

Continuity of policy, purpose, and program, essential to satisfactory progress, is dependent on the permanency of assignment of public information responsibilities. The importance of the job, the amount of work to be done, its dissimilarity to all other police duties, the special skill and training required, and the need for placing responsibility for the performance of these tasks make specialization imperative. Since public information duties are administrative tasks, the unit should report directly to the chief or to the chief's assistant in charge of administration and should not be a part of an operating or a technical service bureau. In departments of approximately 250 personnel, the amount of work in public relations justifies the establishment of this task as a specialized assignment.

Need for a Budget or Finance Office   Large departments need a professionally trained finance officer to assist in the preparation of the budget, to formulate justifications for budget items, to supervise requisitions and disbursements, to prepare payrolls, and to carry out other work which requires the keeping of financial records. In the largest departments this officer should be attached to the office of the chief or the assistant in charge of administration. In smaller departments having a planning unit, the function may be assigned to it, since planning is so closely related to the formulation of the budget and to the determination of fiscal needs. In the smallest departments, a records officer may be given these responsibilities.

The purchasing function has a close relationship to the storage of supplies, inventory control, and other warehousing activities. In medium-sized and large departments, the property-management function can thus be made a part of a fiscal division. In the largest departments, a separate property-management division may be necessary.

Need for a Police Legal Advisor   Many police departments in the United States employ a full-time legal advisor. The position was strongly recommended by the President's Commission on Law Enforcement and Administration of Justice, and the establishment of legal advisors has been assisted by grants from the Law Enforcement Assistance Administration. Legal advisors usually have responsibility for reviewing departmental policies and written directives for their legal sufficiency, consulting with officers on specific cases, attending staff meetings, and advising uniformed forces in the field in times of civil disturbance and at protest demonstrations. They also conduct in-service legal-training programs, update preservice curricula, and maintain liaison with the city attorney, the county prosecutor, and the courts. Legal advisors normally do not prosecute criminal cases, defend civil actions, or act in an adversary role in departmental disciplinary trials; however, their advice often prevents later reversal of cases and civil suits against the department and its officers.

Most legal advisors report directly to the chief, although they are available for consultation to officers of all ranks. The confidential relationship which ought to exist between the advisor and the chief may be eroded by placing the legal advisor in a planning or administrative division. Departments of 200 personnel or more can justify a legal advisor, and larger departments can support additional personnel assigned to the legal advisor's staff.

Need for a Planning Unit   Small departments may not need a staff planning unit. Planning must be done, however, regardless of the size of the department, and provision must be made for it.

In small departments in which there are no specialized divisions for traffic, vice, or youth control, thought must be given to the need for operational planning in these fields. Experience has shown that the patrol division may become so engrossed in the more fundamental police tasks involved in the repression of criminal activities that it neglects to develop plans in special areas and to follow up on their execution. To ensure proper attention, the chief may assign an officer, in a staff capacity, to plan and inspect in each of the special fields. Usually this assignment may be given to an officer in command of a post that requires attendance but not full-time attention. For example, a platoon lieutenant in command of the early-morning shift will be available for emergencies and for making decisions on the disposition of suspects but may devote his free time to staff planning and inspection of a traffic program. Other superior officers may be given similar responsibilities in special areas of activity, even though they may have no direct control of the personnel engaged in the execution of the tasks.

In departments that do not have a planning unit, the responsibility for staff planning may be given to ad hoc committees appointed to deal with specific problems or to an officer in addition to his or her other duties; the choice of the officer is influenced by the nature of the planning that must be done and the relative competence and interest of the several staff and line officers. These considerations are of more importance than the rank of the officer chosen. For

ORGANIZATION FOR POLICE SERVICE

example, the personnel officer may be designated in some instances, whereas in others, it may be that the head of patrol, records, or some other division is best suited to meet the requirements of the task.

The planning unit may be under the control of an assistant chief in charge of administration, as shown in Chart 10, or it may be a part of the chief's office or closely connected to it, as shown in Chart 14 (page 111).

Organization of Technical Services

The need for separate divisions for the performance of each of the technical or auxiliary services is influenced by the size of the department and the desirability of combining some closely related tasks for assignment to one division.

Need for a Records and Communications Division   The size of the police department is the most important factor influencing the organization of the records division. In small departments, usually those with fewer than 20 officers, the records duties are all performed by the desk officers. In a very small department, where these tasks can be accomplished by one desk officer working on only one shift, a formal records division need not be organized. However, when the amount of work requires the assignment of records tasks to desk officers on two or more tours of duty, the work must be planned and directed; procedures must then be outlined, and responsibilities assigned. In a department of this size, a head of the division is usually needed to deal with these administrative problems.

In a small department the officer supervising desk operations will work on the day tour and provide functional supervision of the records work on the other shifts. The desk officer in departments of this size also books prisoners and serves as jailer, complaint officer, and dispatcher.

As the department increases in size, routine desk duties and records tasks increase to such an extent that the desk officer is not able to handle them alone. This officer may first obtain a part-time assistant, perhaps a police officer who does the fingerprint work, or an officer who devotes an hour or two each day to the report-review operation.

In still larger departments one or more persons, assisted by the desk officer, may devote a full tour of duty exclusively to records tasks. The supervision of records functions then passes from the daytime desk officer to the full-time officer who directs all records and communications activities in his or her capacity as the head of the services division. Usually the first full-time person to be appointed to records work will be an identification officer who may devote an hour or more a day to identification records and the remainder to complaint and arrest records. A department of 20 officers or more usually warrants this scheme of organization.

The propriety of including communications tasks under the control of the records division is sometimes questioned because the intimate relationship of these activities is not always clearly understood. Most police records originate with reports transmitted by some form of communications facility, and information to be added to the records is received from time to time in a like manner.

Scarcely a police action is taken that does not involve some form of communication. Nearly all requests for police service are made by telephone, police officers on street duty frequently report to headquarters by telephone, and radio communication is maintained between headquarters and officers in the field. The facts contained in these messages and the resultant action should be immediately recorded. Accurate and honest initial recording of requests for service is, in fact, the key step in successful records management and a principal control point for all operational activities. The need to coordinate communications with records is so compelling that some departments have adopted the term "information division" in lieu of the term "records and communications division."

Need for a Data-processing Division Another reason for the use of the name "information division" is the need for a term which embraces electronic processing of information as well as maintenance of conventional documents and records. Most large police departments now have computers or, at least, personnel who are responsible for computer input into a system operated by some other department of the government.

During the development of a data-processing unit, the function can be assigned logically to the planning or research and development division; much of the developmental work will require very close attention by personnel assigned to the planning unit. Once the function is well established, it can be transferred to the technical services bureau—either as a part of a records-information division or by itself. Additional material on the application of data processing to the records and communications function will be found in Chapter 23.

Need for a Separate Jail Division In small departments, desk officers may perform some or all jail duties. There are, however, advantages to establishing a separate jail division in large departments. Removal of the jail from the control of the units that make arrests lessens the danger of prisoner mistreatment, and the concomitant "covering up" is greatly reduced. Such separation also permits the selection of personnel best qualified to be custodians.

Need for a Police Laboratory While in many departments the laboratory has developed under the stimulating guidance and enthusiasm of an identification officer, sooner or later it should be removed from his control, since in his true capacity he is concerned primarily with the identification of persons from records (see Chapter 23).

The laboratory provides a service to all operational units, and there is, therefore, some advantage in not attaching it to any one of the line divisions. If the laboratory function has several full-time employees, it should be given the status of a separate service unit reporting to an assistant in charge of auxiliary or technical services, especially in large departments. This arrangement tends

ORGANIZATION FOR POLICE SERVICE

to group technical functions and provides a measure of protection from the influence of the operating divisions.

Need for a Separate Maintenance Division In small departments the operating personnel take a more active part in the supervision of maintenance and repair services than in larger ones. For example, the communications officer may service and repair police radio equipment in addition to his regular communications duty; a traffic officer may supervise the maintenance of signs, signals, and markings; or a patrol officer may oversee auto maintenance and repair. In small or medium-sized departments, maintenance functions and central service or support activities can all be carried out by a services division.

In larger departments advantages are gained by combining all maintenance and repair service under one employee, the head of the maintenance division. Police personnel are then relieved of these duties, and the qualifications of a maintenance specialist usually result in an improvement of service. The coordination thus effected also makes it possible to use maintenance personnel to better advantage by transferring them from one duty to another to meet special needs.

In the largest departments, it will be necessary to divide the maintenance functions still further by establishing separate units for radio maintenance, automotive maintenance, and building maintenance. Each of the heads of these units will report directly to a division head in the auxiliary or technical services bureau.

Need for Centralized Support Services Auxiliary services are provided in a number of fields, and in departments of suitable size these services may be brought together under one head, for efficiency of administration, to form a central service division. This division might include an evidence and recovered-property section, a reproduction and graphic arts section, a mail-delivery section, an automotive-pound section, and an animal-shelter section. In a department requiring this degree of specialization, prisoner custody may be included.

Organization of Inspectional Services

Best results are obtained from continuous inspection of the operation of the force and of the condition of personnel and matériel, but the chief does not have time for this type of inspection except in the small department. Provision must therefore be made for an aide to carry on this task. Because of the open manner in which inspections are made, the person who performs this duty for the chief must have sufficient rank to command the respect of all members and should report directly to the chief or an assistant chief. Since the aide's primary duty is staff inspection, the title of "inspector" is appropriate.

Ascertaining needs is a purpose of inspection and a first step in planning, and since research and analysis are common to both inspection and planning, there are some advantages to combining both operations in one unit or under the control of one person, i.e., the inspector. This provision is shown in Chart 14.

Such combination affords some further advantages. It permits smaller departments to obtain greater specialization in planning and inspection by employing one highly qualified person to perform both functions. Further, when combined, each process stimulates the other—the person or unit that develops a plan or procedure is more interested in checking on its operation than one that played no part in its development; likewise, the person or unit responsible for meeting a need is most apt to be diligent in searching for the need and best qualified to detect and appraise it. Finally, combining the planning and inspectional personnel brings them both closer to operating personnel, thereby creating a better relationship than would otherwise prevail.

In the largest departments a bureau of inspectional services may be formed, in which would be included a division of field inspections responsible for general inspection of personnel and matériel, an internal investigations division concerned with the integrity of the force, an intelligence division to keep the chief informed on criminal and noncriminal activities of certain individuals and security problems of the community, and a division concerned with organized crime and staff supervision of department vice-repression activities (see Chapters 12 and 19).

In small departments the vice division may perform the duties of the intelligence division in keeping the chief informed, and internal investigation responsibilities may be carried out by operational supervisors or by the chief.

Organization of Operational Functions

The expansion of team policing in the past few years has required a completely new outlook on the organizational relationships of those functions which have been traditionally considered to be operational in character—patrol, criminal investigations, traffic control, crime and delinquency prevention, vice control, and so on. Although the organization of administrative and technical service functions (as described in the preceding pages) is affected somewhat by team policing, the impact upon the operational functions is immense. For this reason, all the organizational relationships described in the balance of this chapter will relate to *conventional*, i.e., *non-team*, policing. (Organizational material for team policing will be found in Chapter 15.)

Factors to be considered in establishing the responsibility of the patrol force and the relationships between it and specialized operational units are discussed in detail in the chapters devoted to these activities. The size of the department is also an important influence on the need for any specialization. Detective and traffic divisions are needed in fairly small departments, but vice- and youth-control units of more than one person usually are not created in departments of fewer than 50 personnel. Large departments should have separate organizational units for each of the primary police tasks, i.e., patrol, traffic, detective, vice, youth, and tactical operations.

ORGANIZATION FOR POLICE SERVICE

In the creation of functional units for the performance of the primary police tasks, the following concepts should be kept in mind: (1) The patrol force is the backbone of the department; it carries out the primary operational activity for which the department is created, and it is responsible for the basic police services. (2) Specialized units are justified only when performance is definitely improved thereby. (3) The principal purpose of the specialized unit is to assist the patrol force in the field of special interest and to undertake tasks that it is able to perform substantially better than the unspecialized patrol force. (4) Specialized operational units should not relieve the patrol force of the special activity.

Although a specialized technical or administrative unit at headquarters may well exercise executive responsibility for the execution of its tasks, the specialized operational unit often does not. Neither is it completely relieved of tasks that do not relate specifically to its purpose. This is so because of the nature of police work; violations of every kind usually must receive immediate attention when observed by an officer in the field, regardless of the unit to which he or she is attached. Improved service results when most members of the department have some responsibility in the accomplishment of primary police tasks.

Organization of the Patrol Division   The patrol division is on 24-hour duty, divided into platoons for each shift. In larger departments, the division is often under the supervision and control of a patrol captain. Each platoon is under the command of a lieutenant who is responsible to the captain for the conduct of his officers and for all crimes committed in his jurisdiction during his tour of duty. The duties of the second (daytime) platoon lieutenant may be performed by the patrol captain in departments of such size that his regular duties as a captain do not interfere. Each lieutenant has direct control over one or more patrol sergeants and a staff supervision over the dispatcher and members of other divisions in the absence of their supervising officers.

In small departments such a large command group may not be required. In the smallest departments the duties of the patrol captain may be performed by the chief of police, and the tasks of the platoon lieutenants by desk sergeants in direct command of patrol officers on street duty. As the size of the department increases, the inadequacy of the supervision of patrol officers by a desk sergeant necessitates the appointment of a patrol sergeant. The patrol sergeant then assumes the duties of the platoon lieutenant and exercises a staff supervision over the dispatcher when that officer is properly assigned to the records and communications division. Before the department attains a size that justifies more than one patrol sergeant on duty on the largest shift, it will be found desirable to appoint a platoon lieutenant with a patrol sergeant to aid in the street supervision of patrol officers.

Need for a Traffic Division   The creation of a traffic division stimulates effective police traffic control by placing responsibility for its accomplishment on one or more officers who devote full time to this task. A traffic division ensures attention to traffic problems in proportion to their importance by providing a broad, well-rounded, continuous, and effective program. It increases the application of police effort to traffic control by enlisting the services of the nontraffic police. It provides some advantages of specialization, viz., the selection of qualified officers, the promotion of skill and ability, and the development and application of special techniques and procedures.

A traffic division may be necessary before the need to supervise street personnel engaged in traffic control justifies its creation. The patrol division may perform street-traffic duties under the indirect control of a supervisor who is responsible for traffic planning and for coordination of traffic activities. These staff duties may require the establishment of a small, specialized unit in larger departments, even though the performance of traffic tasks remains the duty of the patrol division or (as it is often called in such cases) the uniformed division.

Usually, however, when the appointment of a full-time supervisor is justified to plan and inspect police traffic activities, there are a number of officers devoting full time to the performance of traffic duties, such as accident investigation in serious cases, selective enforcement, and intersection control. These officers then usually become the street personnel of the traffic division. To this group are added other personnel required to perform necessary analytical and educational tasks, such as the operation of public-address equipment, the supervision of the junior traffic patrol, and in some departments the maintenance of signs, signals, and markings. (Relationships between the patrol and traffic divisions are discussed in Chapter 22.)

Need for a Detective Division In a small department the chief may perform all the duties of the detective division; in a somewhat larger one, with one or two officers devoting full time to crime investigations, the chief may direct their activities, thus making the creation of a detective division unnecessary. When the direction and control of officers who devote full time to crime investigation become burdensome, the chief is justified in creating a detective or criminal investigation division with one of the detectives designated as the head to direct and coordinate the crime-investigative activities of both detectives and patrol officers.

Need for a Vice Division The attitude of the public toward vice control and vice conditions in the community should be taken into account in considering the creation of a vice division and in determining its size. Usually, a department of 50 members should have one person devoting full time to vice control.

In large cities, specialization within the vice division is sometimes desirable. One or more officers may be assigned to gambling, another squad to liquor control, another to narcotics, and a further group to the control of prostitution.

The vice division need not provide 24-hour service. It usually operates

ORGANIZATION FOR POLICE SERVICE

most effectively on a flexible, single tour of duty with the hours arranged by the head of the division to meet immediate needs; on some days of the week, the division may operate during certain hours, and on other days a different schedule may be used. Also, individual members of the division may work different hours according to the immediate need.

Need for a Youth Division The police must participate in delinquency prevention, whether a special division is created for this purpose or not. The need for a special unit in all but the smallest departments is clearly indicated by the amount and importance of work to be done; also, the skills and techniques required in some delinquency-prevention tasks are markedly dissimilar to those needed in other police undertakings. Success in delinquency prevention can keep people out of jail, whereas other operating personnel often believe they have a fundamental responsibility to put people into jail. This difference sometimes results in clashes, especially between youth and detective divisions.

The difficult task of coordinating delinquency-prevention activities with other police activities is the responsibility of the chief; the youth division should be a separate unit within a field operations bureau and on a par with the patrol, detective, traffic, and vice divisions, if it is to operate most effectively. To place this unit at any other level will often result in its program being hampered by objectives not in accord with its purposes. For example, the presence of a youth section in a criminal investigation division often results in conflict. Detectives frequently recognize no treatment except jail, insist on prosecution in every case, and quarrel with the juvenile court for not sending all offenders to the reformatory. If the thinking of detectives cannot be altered from this inflexible attitude, the delinquency-prevention objective invariably is subordinated.

Need for a Tactical or Special-Operations Division In medium-sized and large departments, there is often a need to establish a specialized tactical force for selective patrol operations, saturation patrol, stakeouts, massive application of manpower, and so on.

When the need exists, the tactical force can be established as the primary function of a special-operations division within a field operations bureau. The division can also be used for crowd and riot control, air and sea patrol, rescue operations, and other specialized activities.

Need for Conventional District Stations The use of conventional district stations (as opposed to "team offices" under team policing) has many disadvantages, among them the resulting complications in planning, directing, coordinating, and controlling decentralized police operations. In many instances the district stations are in fact little police departments which operate almost autonomously. Even when the feeling of autonomy is not so apparent, the complex relationships which result are in sharp contrast to the relatively simple ones that exist when the department is operated entirely from one station. The

ADMINISTRATION

physical separation is a disintegrating force that weakens control over members assigned to the separate station. On the other hand, efforts to tighten the control jeopardize the authority of the district command.

While the chief may be able to shield his force from improper vertical pressures applied through him, a police district is a point at which lateral pressures are applied by community groups and individuals which the district command may not successfully resist. Such pressures threaten the chief's control of his force and the successful execution of his program.

Distance also complicates the transmission of information, instructions, and records, as well as the custody and transfer of prisoners, property, and evidence. District stations are costly because the site and the building with its communications, office, jail, and equipment represent a large capital investment; also, the operation of the station necessitates additional personnel, utility, and other operating expenses. Fortunately, the need for district stations has been reduced as improvements in automobiles, communications equipment, and recording methods continue.

In jurisdictions of large area, district stations may be needed to provide greater public convenience and improve the quality of police operations. Other reasons for the use of district stations may be the limited motorization of the force, the off-center location of headquarters, or topographical obstacles to easy travel, such as bodies of water, cliffs, ravines, mountainous areas, undeveloped sections, or railroad tracks without grade crossings, which have the effect of extending the area of jurisdiction. Sometimes communities within the municipality want their own district station. Because of civic pride a formerly autonomous suburban community presently annexed to a larger jurisdiction may demand the continued use of its police station; this may persist for many years, even though there is no other justification for the station's existence.

District stations are considered a public convenience that saves the local residents travel time in order to get information, register complaints, post bail, pay fines, and obtain recovered property. Analysis of the public convenience so provided, however, indicates that it is not great. Information is obtained and complaints are registered almost invariably by telephone; on the other hand, calls for service or assistance which should be directed to the central communications room are sometimes held up for a considerable time because they must be relayed from the district to the dispatcher in another area. Few cities with district stations decentralize the acceptance of fines. Recovered property is likewise usually stored and controlled at headquarters, and the speedy transfer of prisoners from district-station lockups to the main station requires most jail personnel to be located at headquarters.

Many citizens mistakenly believe that the physical presence of a district station has a great influence in reducing crime. Anyone who has examined an accurate crime "spot map" in a large city knows better. The map may show a decrease in street crime within several hundred feet of a station, but beyond these limits there is very little influence on crime. The station itself cannot respond to calls for service, nor can it render aid in an emergency. Prompt police service depends on the presence of motorized-patrol officers on their beats.

Nevertheless, some police operations are unquestionably simplified, and the quality of service correspondingly improved, by the creation of a district station. The district station saves police time in bringing in found property and physical evidence, witnesses and suspects for interrogation, and prisoners for booking and incarceration. Also, patrol officers may be more readily posted at shift changes because they have a shorter distance to travel to their beats. These advantages are not compelling, however, because a more complete motorization of patrol diminishes these needs except where the distances are great; when foot-patrol officers are used in the area, they may be transported by a motorized officer or be permitted to report directly to their beats, going to headquarters only at the end of their tour of duty.

Measuring Need for District Stations District stations should not be created until studies of the time saved in operations indicate that the decentralization is economically sound. Police departments in large communities undoubtedly need district stations. An examination of the need for presently existing district stations in many cities, however, indicates that they should be abandoned or reduced in number by consolidation; the small number of citizens who call there in person for police service and the slight saving of time in police operations do not justify the expense.

Model Organizational Structures

The International Association of Chiefs of Police has developed several model structures for departments of various sizes. These structures have been provided to IACP's management consultants as useful guides, rather than as mandates.

The model structure for a small municipal department is shown in Chart 13. In agencies of this size, organization by time of day is sufficient. If more than one officer is on duty during shifts 1 and 3, a senior officer or sergeant should act as shift supervisor. The chief may want to supervise personnel directly on the day shift. This structure can accommodate as many as six or seven patrol officers per shift, with a sergeant in charge. However, if the number of patrol officers exceeds this level, so that more than one supervisor is necessary on each shift, it is likely that a simple organization by time will be inadequate.

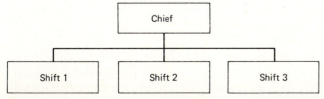

Chart 13 Model structure, small department (up to about 25 personnel).

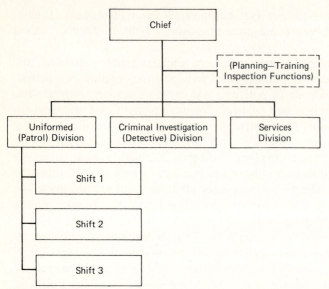

Chart 14 Model structure, small to medium-sized department (as few as 20 to about 100 personnel).

Departments larger than 20 to 25 personnel should be organized functionally, as shown in Chart 14. The uniformed or patrol division should be the largest by far, and it requires a second- or third-level supervisor in charge. A typical chart for a department of 100 personnel might indicate a captain in command of the uniformed division with lieutenants in charge of each shift, a lieutenant in charge of the detective division, and another lieutenant heading the services division. Further subdivision by function would be unnecessary.

Chart 14 also illustrates the beginning of the planning, personnel, training, and inspections functions, and it shows these functions as staff activities closely associated with the chief's office. The duties can be apportioned in various ways if they are assigned to more than one staff officer.

In the next stage of development (shown in Chart 15), the growth of administrative functions may require the establishment of a full-fledged organizational subdivision to group fiscal, personnel, training, property-management, and possibly public information or community relations activities.

Technical services functions can also emerge at this stage as a grouping of records, identification, communications, laboratory, technical maintenance, and other technical activities.

In the uniformed division the usual organization of personnel by shift is depicted, along with the development of specialized traffic and tactical forces. It is at this stage of growth that the term "uniformed division" is most appropriate, since it seems somewhat inappropriate to place a traffic unit within a patrol division.

ORGANIZATION FOR POLICE SERVICE

At the top level, the planning and inspections functions remain as staff activities having a close relationship to the chief, but they are not yet of divisional stature.

Chart 16 illustrates the recommended pattern of growth toward the creation of bureaus containing several divisions each. The criminal investigation division is grouped with patrol and traffic personnel to form a field operations bureau. Tactical and juvenile officers become a part of the field operations bureau through the creation of the special-operations division and the youth or juvenile division.

The administrative services division depicted in Chart 15 is seen as a fully developed bureau in Chart 16, with separate divisions for personnel, training, fiscal management, and community relations. The latter function is often placed in an administrative grouping because press relations and public information activities are traditionally administrative in nature. Some aspects of the community relations function, however, are undoubtedly operational in nature, such as crime-resistance education.

Chart 16 also shows the planning function as a research and development division (which is the preferred title in commercial and industrial organizations, as well as in an increasing number of public agencies). In a medium-sized

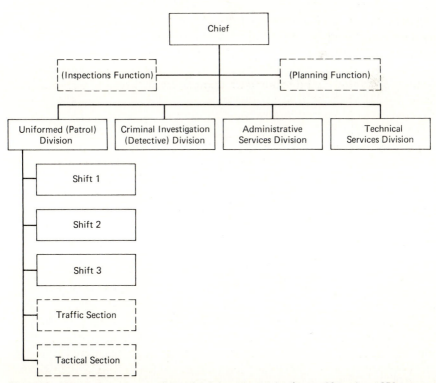

Chart 15 Model structure, medium-sized department (as few as 80 to about 250 personnel).

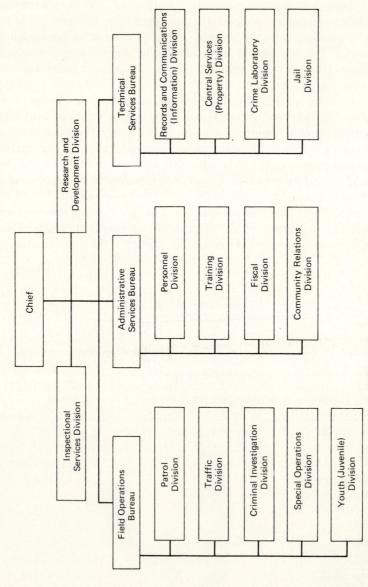

Chart 16 Model structure, medium-sized to large department (as few as 200 to about 1,200 personnel).

ORGANIZATION FOR POLICE SERVICE

department, the research and development division can handle some of the responsibilities, such as the administrative filing system, carried by the chief's office staff in the very large agency. More importantly, a research and development division in a department of this size does not have excessive layers of supervision; the head of the division is personally involved in the work and can thus take maximum advantage of the close relationship to the chief's office. In a very large agency, on the other hand, the need for several layers of supervision in a large research and development division tends to minimize this advantage; communication between the chief and staff personnel actually engaged in planning work might as well go through another level of supervision—the head of the administrative services bureau. (See Chart 17.)

In the medium-sized to large agency, the inspections function appears as an inspectional services division, encompassing field inspections, intelligence, vice control, and internal investigations. In an agency of this size, the inspectional services function should (with rare exceptions, as described in Chapter 12) be directly associated with the chief. It should be the last of the major administrative responsibilities to remain organizationally linked to the chief's office. The size of the inspectional services staff in a very large agency will require bureau status, as indicated in Chart 17.

Chart 17 shows the fully developed organizational structure at the division level. Except for executive aides and office personnel, there are no division-level activities having a direct relationship with the chief's office. Administrative responsibilities are carried out through deputy chiefs.

The student of police administration is sometimes tempted to confuse the appearance of relationships on the chart with the actual physical relationships of the office space within the building; the depiction of major bureaus in separate boxes on the chart tends to make the student think of these activities as somehow removed from the sensorium of the chief—as if these major functions were located in separate buildings. Actually, the major bureau heads should all be considered assistants to the chief, and there should be a close physical relationship between their offices and those of the chief, as well as close personal communications between them. An understanding of the proper relationships can help the student avoid difficulties caused by the assumption that only those activities which are linked to the chief's office with a lateral line can be considered "close" to him.

The placement of several functions is sure to result in controversy whenever police administrators discuss organizational structure. For example, the vice-control function is operational in character for the most part, and in many police agencies today it is located totally within the operations bureau or the criminal investigation division. As depicted in Chart 17, however, the vice-control division emphasizes those aspects of the vice-control function which are inspectional in character, although the division would no doubt engage in major investigations. Other questionable or controversial placements involve the location of property-management and maintenance functions. If the activity of a property unit stresses internal control and management rather than

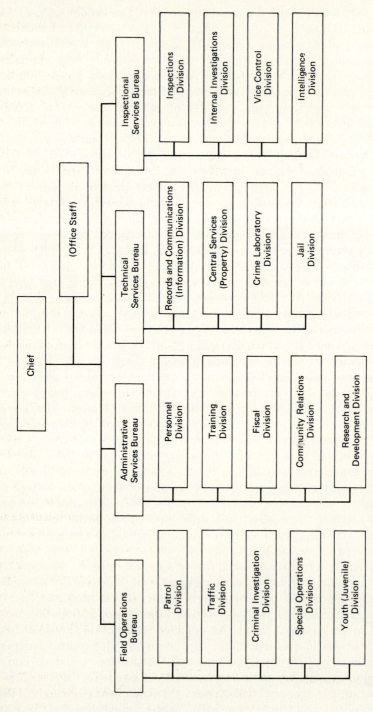

Chart 17 Model structure, large department (1,000 personnel and up).

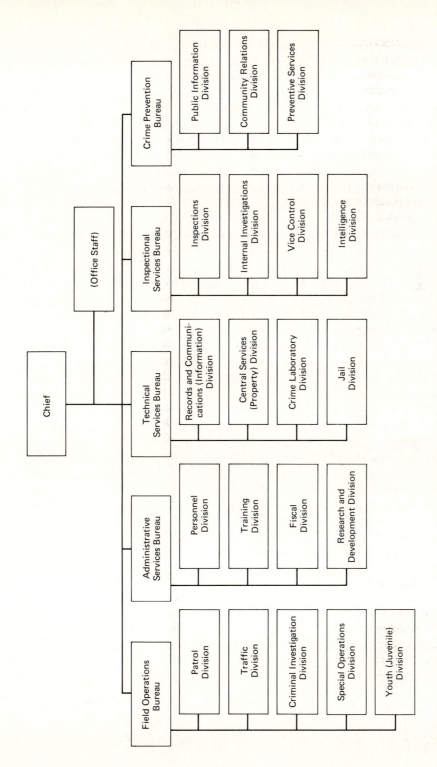

Chart 18 Alternate model structure, large department (illustrating a crime-prevention bureau as a major organizational subdivision).

the operational aspects of the function, it is better placed in the administrative services bureau than in the technical services bureau. For example, if the department has greater problems in the control of purchasing and inventories for administrative supplies than it does in the control of evidence, the function could be placed logically in administrative services.

Chart 18 illustrates a recommended alternate structure in a large agency. It stems from the growing trend to recognize the obligation of the police in the field of long-range crime prevention. This structure also permits the grouping of several quasi-operational activities such as public information and community relations, which otherwise must be placed in divisions or bureaus which are clearly administrative in other respects.

Structures for County Police and Sheriff Organizations   The organizational requirements of county police agencies are the same as those of municipal police departments. Sheriff's offices, on the other hand, must consider the responsibility for civil process. The prevailing organizational pattern in the United States is the grouping of the sheriff's-office functions into two basic divisions—civil and criminal—or, as a variant, three divisions—civil, criminal, and jail. This grouping, however, tends to place too much responsibility on the head of the criminal division. The civil activity in most sheriff's offices can be added simply as another division to the structure depicted in Chart 17 or as a responsibility of the operations bureau with the basic structure patterned after Chart 16 or 17.

The State Police or Highway-Patrol Organizational Structure   Organizational principles guiding the development of the police structure at the municipal or county level can obviously be applied at the state level. There are a great many other requirements and considerations, however, which affect the state structure in actual practice; there are so many, in fact, that model structures for state police and highway-patrol organizations in this text would be inadvisable. First, states vary greatly in the number of functions which are assigned to the state police agency. Second, there are significant differences in the nature of the overall state structure. Almost half of all such state agencies are a part of a larger agency, such as a department of safety, of motor vehicles, or of highways.

Chapter 8

Direction

Although the percentage of police administrators with formal training in management has steadily increased over the past few decades, the police service is still far behind private industry in this respect. Progressive city managers and mayors have tended to appoint chiefs with education or training in administrative and management subjects, but for the most part chiefs continue to be selected on the basis of other characteristics, including their ability to control and discipline their subordinates. Indeed, because many administrators today have had no training in administration or management, their strength tends to depend on these aspects of direction. Although skill in direction may seem to be an inherent quality which derives from personality or basic character, the effectiveness of direction by any administrator almost always can be improved measurably.

LEADERSHIP WITHIN THE DEPARTMENT

For the police administrator, the most important aspect of direction is leadership.

In Chapter 3 some of the needs for police leadership in the community were described. When leadership is discussed in the context of the community, there is seldom any uncertainty about what the term means. Certainly, it does not connote command or supervision or control—instead, it clearly means leadership in its truest sense, that is, doing things first so that others in the community may be inspired to support and adopt the programs of the department.

When the term "leadership" is discussed in the context of the department, however, it begins to assume a stronger meaning; often the word is used as a synonym for direction itself or for command or control. The use of the term in this stronger sense will be avoided in this discussion.

The police service rarely experiences the kind of activity which lends itself to true field leadership by the head of the agency or by top-ranking command officers. While the military general can achieve leadership by physically mingling with the troops in the field in the midst of an assault or by exhorting his personnel prior to a great battle, the police leader must realize that the work carried out by people under his command is for the most part routine and that even in those situations where field leadership is possible, most of it can and should be assumed by second- or third-line supervisors rather than by administrators. At times, however, there are justifications for the appearance of the chief of police or head of the agency to assert field leadership—such as at a major riot or disaster or in situations requiring mobilization of the entire department. The chief should make the most of these times and should be certain that he does not appear at the scene of a major disorder or crisis as a mere observer. If he is there, he should assume the leadership; otherwise, he should stay away. The chief can lose more than he can gain by making an appearance in the field and then allowing his subordinates, who may be used to dealing with crises in the field, to make major decisions which the chief ought to make himself.

The Command Presence   There is no substitute for the administrator's physical presence in all departmental facilities at various times of day and in all locations within the city. Officers tend to resent a chief who stays in his office and who does not communicate with personnel in any way at their work stations or in the field.

Actually, what the police administrator learns from visits to various locations within a department and the community is substantial in itself; thus there are two basic reasons for exerting command presence—the generation of a feeling of esprit de corps on the part of personnel and the benefit of the knowledge gained by the chief from visits into the field.

The Proper Orientation of Leadership

Because the situation requiring field leadership seldom exists, the police manager must think in terms of leadership in *ideas and concepts*, in energy and enthusiasm, and in high principles and integrity.

The quality of leadership is reflected in the appearance, spirit, bearing,

DIRECTION

demeanor, words, actions, and work of subordinates. The members of a force under superior leadership tend to enjoy doing their work, to have a feeling of elation on its accomplishment, to be proud of their department, to praise their superiors, to carry out instructions and requests cheerfully and willingly, and to work tirelessly for long hours under uncomfortable conditions without question or complaint. In contrast, subordinates under inferior leadership tend to be frequently dissatisfied with their jobs, to dislike their duties, to resent instructions and requests from their superiors, and to avoid accepting new responsibilities. They sidestep routine tasks at every opportunity or perform them with a feeling of resentment amounting almost to hatred, often protesting assignments and instructions or accepting them sullenly. Good leadership is a catalytic agent that transforms indifferent, dissatisfied, disloyal, and inefficient officers into loyal, agreeable, hardworking, interested, and efficient employees who derive great satisfaction from the accomplishment of their jobs. Under good leadership the harmonious and effective effort of all members is directed in maximum degree toward the accomplishment of the police purpose.

Leadership is not the exercise of authority through the issuance of commands and threat of punishment for noncompliance. Some police chiefs erroneously assume that the strength and frequency with which commands are barked and the exclusive use by the executive of the power of decision are evidences of strong leadership. The good executive makes fewer, rather than more, decisions; the strong leader directs and coordinates more by inspiration and enthusiasm than by the authority of command or by threat of disciplinary action. Success is often dependent on the leader's ability to persuade subordinates to get the job done with maximum harmony and effectiveness.

In exercising their power of command, leaders should distinguish between the tone and style of written and verbal orders and similarly, between orders given under combat conditions and those not given under the necessity of immediate and decisive action. Written orders should be concise and unambiguous; verbal orders given in the field, where time is essential, and in all radio broadcasts must also be unequivocal and precise. Orders under other conditions, however, are preferably presented as requests or wishes rather than as peremptory orders, with opportunity invariably given for clarification to ensure that they are understood.

In investigating the need for disciplinary measures, leaders should initiate action promptly. Before disposing of a case, however, they should invariably insist on having all the facts with special reference to the cause of the incident in order to discover whether it resulted from faulty instruction, poorly conceived procedure, or inadequate or otherwise unsuited supervision. Leaders will discuss a problem with their subordinates privately, and in reaching a decision or suitable disposition, they will consider the welfare of the individual as well as the good of the service.

The chief should establish friendly relationships (in keeping with the proper bearing required of the leader) with all members of the force and should circulate through the department and attend roll calls in order to have personal contacts with officers at work. The chief should never be too busy to speak to an officer whom he meets either on the street or at police headquarters. These contacts, however, should not be of such duration and frequency as to weaken supervisory control by first-line supervisors.

Qualities of the Successful Leader   The qualities of the leader that induce subordinates to render their best service vary widely, since they reflect the leader's total personality. Personalities vary, and the successful leader does not act out of character by aping the characteristics of another in the belief that such behavior will automatically result in superior leadership. However, successful leaders *do* have some attributes in common: They are usually above average in intelligence, emotionally stable, and psychologically strong. While they may not all demonstrate enthusiastic, forceful, or outgoing personalities, many of them have considerable enthusiasm for their own ideas and great forcefulness or drive in setting and achieving goals.

PROMOTION OF CONFIDENCE, LOYALTY, AND INTEREST

In addition to these qualities, or as the result of them, successful leaders have the ability to win the confidence, inspire the loyalty, and maintain the enthusiastic interest of subordinates. These three abilities are so vital to leadership as to deserve particular study.

The leader must win the confidence of his subordinates concerning his ability, principles, and programs. Qualities of the leader that tend to induce such confidence include:

- A strong belief in his own competence to deal successfully with any situation that may develop and an ability to display this self-confidence in a natural and acceptable manner
- Knowledge and skill relating to his own job and to the work of subordinates
- An insistence on having all the facts before taking action
- Soundness of judgment
- A willingness and ability to accept responsibility and especially to accept liability for failures without passing the blame on to subordinates
- An ability to maintain poise (mentally, physically, and emotionally) under criticism and attack
- The initiative to investigate unsatisfactory conditions and the courage to take corrective action
- The absence of prejudices, especially in reference to race, politics, religion, and labor
- Unquestioned personal integrity and an insistence that the department be free of graft, including petty handouts
- An uncompromising attitude toward crime and corruption, coupled with a recognition of the necessity for correct timing in dealing with outside forces over which he exercises no direct control
- Energy and a willingness and ability to work hard

DIRECTION

121

- Physical and emotional strength to withstand the strain of demands on his time, energy, and patience
- The ability to make subordinates feel that he has the courage to represent the agency and its personnel in issues that threaten it or its members

The last point, which is perhaps the most significant element of leadership, is worth elaboration. Many things can threaten the department or its members, such as the potential loss of pay or benefits, handicaps imposed by the court system on police investigations, shortages of manpower and equipment as a result of legislative indifference, or attacks against the police by dissident elements of society. In issues of this sort, the chief must convey the impression to his subordinates that he is willing to resign rather than compromise his ethics and principles.

The chief's personal actions and attitude are an important factor in sustaining employee confidence. He must not allow the strain of criticism and administrative difficulties to be reflected in his demeanor, voice, facial expression, language, or conduct. Subordinates are quick to sense subtle changes and to overemphasize their significance; they are prone to lose some confidence in a leader who, in their opinion, gives evidence of not being able to stand the pace. For this reason the leader must give attention to his state of health and nerves. He must also avoid being placed in an unfavorable light which may cause him to lose prestige in the eyes of his subordinates. He should be discreet, temperate, conscientious, honest, and energetic if he asks the same of his subordinates. It is not unreasonable to expect the chief to exhibit a higher overall capacity for these characteristics than anyone else in the department. He should likewise be observant for evidence of weakness in his supervisory staff that may result, under stress, in injudicious acts.

The chief must inspire loyalty to himself and to his department. Loyalty is a feeling or an attitude resulting from an emotional rather than an intellectual process and consequently is induced in one person by the feeling or attitude of another. Loyalty creates loyalty, and the leader will win loyalty somewhat in proportion to the loyalty he manifests to his subordinates. Loyalty is similar to friendship in that both thrive on reinforcement. The personal relationships between the leader and his subordinates influence the feeling between them. Actions that unnecessarily jeopardize a feeling of loyalty between them are to be avoided; actions that stimulate this feeling of loyalty are to be encouraged.

At times the chief may find that a position he takes on an issue or a new procedure he advocates is unpopular to the point that loyalties to him and the department are put to a severe test. The chief must always remember that if he acts within the framework of good conscience and according to principles for fair play, most of these situations will be resolved. The administrator should therefore exercise patience and restraint when a stand on an issue or a new procedure threatens to disrupt loyalties. Some chiefs react personally to surface manifestations of disloyalty and thereby escalate the problem to the point where a change in loyalty cannot be obtained.

It is an important task of leadership to create and maintain the enthusiastic interest of members of the force in their jobs and the satisfaction which comes from a sense of accomplishment. The interest that an employee demonstrates in his or her work is often in proportion to the interest shown by the supervisor in that same work. In fact, no other management or supervisory technique has so positive an effect on motivation as the manifestation of interest on the part of a supervisor in the work being carried out by a subordinate. If the supervisor finds the work interesting, it is natural for a subordinate to begin to feel the same way about it.

Interest on the part of personnel is stimulated by the interest and concern expressed by the chief in their personal welfare, accomplishments, and problems. Their interest is greatly stimulated by the willingness and ability of the leader to take them into his confidence so that they may see and understand problems and their solutions. He must make them partners in the police venture so that their routine tasks will be more interesting. A partnership is not a one-man show. The chief must seek and utilize subordinates' suggestions in order that each member may feel that he or she has a vested interest in the department and its operation. The leader must permit subordinates to participate in decisions and in the development of plans and to share in department problems, criticisms, and commendations. He must delegate authority freely, permitting subordinates an opportunity to exercise their initiative, judgment, and authority.

Conferences Conferences are effective devices for sustaining and promoting confidence, loyalty, and interest on the part of all members of the force. Active participation at meetings enables subordinate members to air their grievances and make criticisms or suggestions regarding policies, procedures, techniques, equipment, space, working conditions, training, and other matters relating to the organization and its operation. Conferences provide an effective means for building morale, they promote the flow of information relating to department activities, and they bring subordinates into a more active participation in the administration of police affairs. The interest of subordinates in their work and in the affairs of the department is thereby increased.

Commendation The desire for recognition is a key factor which motivates many employees, and the chief must take advantage of this to increase the effectiveness of the department. Commendation and praise are often more effective as tools of leadership than criticism and disciplinary measures.

Commendation may be given in a number of ways. Leaders should use every opportunity to call the attention of others to outstanding accomplishment. This may be done by personal praise in conferences or in the presence of others or by commendatory notes on the daily bulletin that all members may read and thus know that their efforts are recognized and appreciated. Department publications and the public press are also effective devices for calling attention to outstanding individual and unit accomplishments.

Supervising and command officers should watch for and report commend-

DIRECTION   123

able acts to the chief, and the chief himself should be alert to discover officers who deserve praise. Care should be taken to avoid giving one officer undue praise to the exclusion of others having equal claim to credit. Successful supervisors give full credit to the officers of their unit and do not seek commendation for themselves.

The effectiveness of the commendation is sometimes reduced by ritualization, formality, and excessive use. If commendations become perfunctory and commonplace, their value is lost. Praise is most valuable when it is meaningful, not necessarily when it is formal.

In departments of fewer than 200 members, the chief can make mental notes of individual accomplishments and mention them casually when meeting the officer here and there. When this extends to work not publicized, it is an even greater morale builder because the feeling grows within the department that the chief knows what takes place and gives credit where credit is due.

Democracy in Leadership   Although this phrase might seem to contain contradictory terms, the successful leader usually wins the support of his force for his policies, plans, and procedures before placing them into effect. The arbitrary imposition of procedures on protesting personnel is a mark of poor leadership, and it often results in failure. Even the most excellent plan will not be carried out satisfactorily by unsympathetic police officers.

The chief should therefore not inflict policies and procedures on the members of the department when they are not prepared to approve and accept them. He should first win their approval. When his proposals are sound, the approval is usually gained without difficulty; resistance to the plan may be evidence of its unsuitability and may indicate the need for a reassessment or modification of it.

Attitude toward Subordinates   The development of morale and the maintenance of a suitable esprit de corps are important leadership responsibilities of the chief and other supervisory officers. Pride in the organization and in its component members, self-confidence and confidence in other officers and supervisors, and camaraderie among the officers are essential elements the establishment of which deserves close study and attention by supervisors.

The supervisor must be fair and friendly toward his subordinates, but he must not permit undue familiarity. While he should demonstrate that he is squarely behind his officers in the proper performance of their duties, he should not allow them to believe that he will support them in derelictions of duty or violations of department rules. He must have a clear concept of the difference between loyalty to his superiors and to the department and loyalty to his subordinates, and he should not be permitted to interpret the protection of subordinates in misconduct as a desirable loyalty.

The leader must not be arbitrary or capricious; he should instead maintain a reasonable and open-minded attitude which reflects a willingness to discuss the pros and cons of any question. He should maintain an open-door policy toward all members of the force, urging them to discuss with him any matter of interest to them and welcoming them when they call. Should this practice occupy too much time, the busy executive should set aside one morning or afternoon each week for this exclusive purpose.

COMMAND AND SUPERVISORY CONTROL

Whereas *leadership* provides direction primarily by inspiration, *command* is the process of transforming direction into effect through executive action.

Line of Direct Control, Command, and Coordination

The line of direct control (chain of command) is the channel through which the power of command passes. Command affects those in the vertical line extending from the top to the level of execution; coordination affects two or more persons who must work in unison and who are usually on an equal level of authority and sometimes under a different immediate command. In any given pyramid of authority, coordination among several officers or organizational units will be the responsibility of the first supervisor in common for the officers concerned. The base of the pyramid broadens as coordination must be achieved between geographical, chronological, and functional groups; as this occurs, the level of authority capable of achieving coordination will be higher.

Direction by Command It is neither feasible nor possible for the chief personally to give every command to every officer who is engaged in an operation. Chiefs cannot be in two places at one time; they cannot work 24 hours a day; and, finally, they do not have the time (or, in some cases, the ability) to make all the decisions needed in the course of an operation and to work out the details involved in the formulation of each order. Instead, the chief gives the signal to go. The order to put the plan in operation is given to each unit head who, in turn, prepares more detailed instructions for his or her own subordinates, as necessary. The subordinates have questions, and consequently decisions must be made. These subordinates, in turn, will formulate orders for their subordinates—more questions will be asked, and more decisions must be made. When a question is asked that cannot be answered or when the officer in charge is unwilling to accept the responsibility for making a decision on an important matter, he refers the problem to his immediate superior, who in most cases will make the decision, although in some instances it may be referred up the various levels of authority to the chief. The directions to the officers who do the job thus come down the line of control. This flow of direction from one head to his subordinates is shown in Chart 7.

Coordination of the Force Efforts of the force must be coordinated if the plan is to operate satisfactorily. Coordination requires teamwork, the harmonious combination of the efforts of two or more persons toward a common end. The need for coordination arises from the fact that police duties are less

DIRECTION

amenable to sharp lines of demarcation than police personnel are. The organization of the force is a structure built of units of manpower, the least common denominator being one person; consequently, each officer must be assigned to only one unit. Police duties, however, do not fall into such a rigid pattern of kind, or place, or time. A police operation may extend over the 24 hours of the day and over the entire area of the city. Since police incidents frequently involve several types of violations, it may not be possible to classify the operation as purely traffic, vice, crime investigation, or patrol. Under such circumstances, the members of more than one division, of more than one platoon, and of more than one district or beat may be assigned to tasks involved in the operation. Since the relationship between patrol and each of the specialized divisions is influenced by the effectiveness of patrol service, the following paragraphs discuss the coordination of the efforts of the various patrol units to ensure superior performance.

Coordination of Geographical Patrol Units The coordination of the work of officers dispatched to a house being burglarized requires that they be sent at the same time and that they be deployed so as to cut off escape. Coordination of the efforts of officers on several beats on the same tour of duty, as in this example, presents no serious problem in the conventional (i.e., non-team-policing) structure. Lines of direct control are clearly established (see circle A, Chart 19), and the relationships, being simple, are easily understood. The principle of unity of command is not jeopardized, and the efforts of patrol officers within a platoon are easily integrated and directed toward a common objective. The coordinating authority is vested in the officer in command, who is aided in its application by the dispatcher, who in turn performs this service by virtue of the power of command delegated to him.

Two questions are involved in the coordination of geographical units: (1) Should a service extending beyond the limits of one beat be completed by the officer on whose beat the need originates, or should such tasks be assigned to the officer on the second beat? A decision must be made in each case on the basis of such variables as distance and the relative present work loads of the two officers and their relative competence. The intricacy of the task is also an important determining factor; more time might be spent in giving the second officer instructions and the background of explanation necessary to its success-ful accomplishment than would be required by an officer already informed on all details of the case. (2) In a city divided into police districts, should officers from one district be dispatched into another to aid in disposing of incidents that occur near the dividing boundary? The urgency of the case is an important factor here; a nonemergency incident can more easily be deferred and thus handled by the regular beat officer in the interest of continuity and responsibili-ty. The advisability of doing so in emergency situations is apparent, and the practice is the natural one when dispatching is centrally initiated and con-trolled.

Coordination of Platoons The continuance or completion by a relieving platoon of a service previously initiated presents another coordination prob-lem, illustrated by circle B, Chart 19. Two units are involved, each with its own

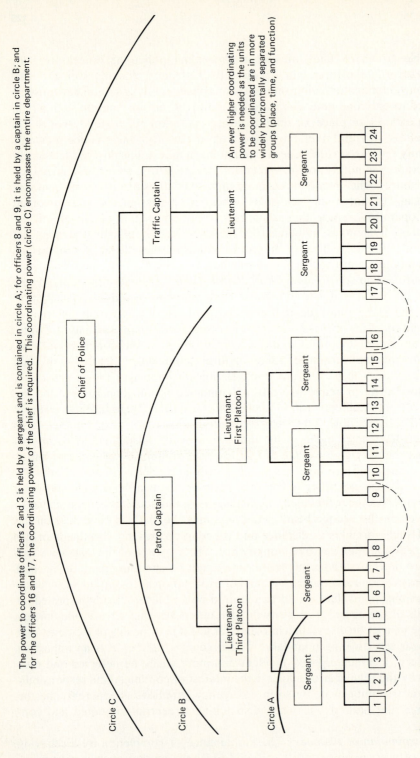

Chart 19 Levels of coordination.

DIRECTION

commanding officer, which necessitates including their common superior in the relationship if the full coordinating power of authority is to be utilized. Since this superior will usually not be present in person, the full force of his authority is absent, and some difficulty may be experienced in coordinating the effort of the two platoons. The difficulty has three sources: (1) The definiteness of the objective is blurred. Facts lose vitality in being reported; regardless of how accurately and in what detail information is passed from one platoon to another, the relieving platoon commander and his subordinates will not have as vivid and complete an understanding of the task as those who initiate it. (2) Platoon commanders are of equal rank and authority; thus the relieving commanding officer may use his authority to change the plan of operation, sometimes with resultant delay and interference in the continuity of the operation. (3) The sense of responsibility is somewhat dulled; a feeling may exist that, since the task was initiated by another platoon, it should have been completed by its personnel.

Continuity of service between platoons is essential to effective operation. Machinery must be provided for accurately transmitting facts, for placing responsibility for the satisfactory continuance of uncompleted tasks, for inspectional report review to ensure proper operation, and for the delegation, by department regulations, of authority to one platoon lieutenant to direct the lieutenant of a succeeding platoon to complete an unfinished task. For example, the lieutenant being relieved should pass on to the lieutenant relieving him any information concerning special assignments or duties, any case to be worked on, or any other information that might assist in department operations. The relieving lieutenant, when notified of a plan of action initiated but not completed by the preceding platoon, should be held responsible for lack of success resulting from his failure to carry it out as planned.

Coordination of Functional Units   Difficulty in coordinating the efforts of separate functional units is increased because of the diversity of their purposes and tasks and because of the higher position in the chain of command usually occupied by their heads. For example, the efforts of officers 16 and 17 in Chart 19, since they are in separate functional units, may not be coordinated at any level below that of their commanding officers' superior. In all but the largest departments the coordinating officer would be the chief, and the coordination takes place within circle C.

The problem of the coordination of functional units could be eliminated by the imposition of artificial limits to prevent one unit from engaging in any way in an activity assigned to another; in poorly organized and weakly administered departments, the problem is sometimes solved in this way. However, more effective police service usually results when the efforts of several functional units are directed toward an important objective. Most larger departments are organized functionally and utilize as many functional units as may be necessary or desirable. Effective operations may require a high degree of functionalization, which increases the problem of coordination. The type of relationship between the functional units that promotes coordination is described later (see page 133).

128   ADMINISTRATION

Coordination in Team Policing   Coordination of the force in team policing is critical. A disadvantage of district team policing is that in a major police incident the actions which were formerly carried out by a single platoon of officers are now conducted by separate teams reporting to different supervisors. For the overwhelming percentage of police incidents, one or two officers can safely carry out the assignment, and it is toward this high percentage of cases that team policing is oriented. In the remaining cases, where a larger number of officers is required, the traditional method of organizing a patrol force is inherently more effective than the district team concept *unless* an effort is made to plan for coordination in such situations. The plan can consist of the designation of a higher-ranking supervisor to act as coordinator in situations requiring deployment of personnel from more than one team. In simple cases, the beat officer in charge of the area where the incident occurs can be designated as officer in charge. In more complex situations, the supervisor in charge of the district of occurrence (for example, the sergeant on duty within the team) can be designated as in command if it is necessary to deploy personnel from several districts.

Line and Staff Command

Command is essential to successful direction. For the purpose of this discussion, commands may be considered to be of two kinds: line and staff. Both types of command involve the active use of authority delegated by the chief.

Line command is the exercise of the authority delegated by the chief to his immediate subordinates and by them to their subordinates down the line of direct control to the lowest level. Line command is simple in operation and involves no difficult relationships when the channels of control are clearly established and understood; it consists of the superior officer's directing the efforts of his immediate subordinates by written or verbal orders and instructions.

However, the direction of a police force, because of the nature of its work, presents some problems which do not exist in most business organizations. (1) Field personnel usually operate without the actual and continuous presence of a superior officer. (2) Calls for service are most frequently received at headquarters, and consequently orders for the performance of such services must come from headquarters. (3) Several orders must be given to each subordinate on each tour of duty; in the aggregate, many commands must be given as compared with the number necessary in directing the more routine tasks of business. If they personally issued all orders, commanding officers would have little or no time for other equally and sometimes more important tasks. Commanding officers, therefore, must have assistance in communicating their orders.

Staff command is the giving of orders by an agent who has no authority in his own right but who performs the routine tasks of command as a service for his principal. The agent may be a secretary, an aide, or an assistant who says, in effect, "The chief says that you shall do so and so." When staff command is used frequently, reference to the principal is omitted, especially in routine

DIRECTION 129

operations where the relationships are clearly understood, as in the case of the dispatcher's giving directions to beat officers. Even in an emergency situation in which no plans for the contingency have been established, the dispatcher acts on behalf of a commanding officer.

Other staff officers in the department may carry out staff command, such as planning or training officers or inspectors who must give instructions during the course of their work to personnel not under their direct control.

Departmentwide Command

A coordinating power transcending that of the heads of divisions or districts is needed in situations that require the services of most of the on-duty members of several or all divisions. This supreme coordinating power belongs to the chief or to someone authorized to act for him. The need for having only one person in command of each situation makes it essential to divide the 24-hour-a-day, seven-day-a-week command responsibilities of the chief into several time segments so that one person who has the effective power will be in a position to control any police situation requiring the use of large numbers of personnel or involving a serious incident calling for more than routine supervision. This person's office will be the command post during the hours when the chief's office is closed.

While the problem of departmentwide command is concerned with identical principles regardless of the size of the community, it is more easily and simply solved in departments without district stations than in those with district stations. For this reason, this section is limited to a discussion of the former. The problem of departmentwide command in larger departments is discussed in the next few pages.

The chief's coordinating power can be made available throughout the 24 hours by investing this authority in operating personnel who are constantly on duty and therefore immediately available to assume command of emergency situations. The patrol division is the only operating division that invariably provides 24-hour service, and it is easier to integrate the work of other divisions having fewer members with that of the patrol force, which has the largest membership. In addition, it is usually the first to learn of emergency calls and to reach the scene of action; and since its duties encompass the entire police field, it has broader powers and greater responsibility than any other division. The highest-ranking patrol commander on duty should therefore be invested with extraordinary powers of command in emergency situations; this authority is then an extension of this officer's power of administrative supervision.

In district team policing, the solution to the problem of providing citywide command coverage during night and weekend hours is more complicated. Depending on the size of the force, night command officers either should be designated for the assignment on a more or less permanent basis (in the larger departments) or, in small agencies, should be on an "on-call" basis. In any event, the night commander under team policing will usually have no direct line of control over the people he will be supervising during a large-scale incident or emergency.

Any delegation by department regulations of the chief's power of command over the entire force should contain restrictions on its unnecessary use in order to minimize interference with routine operations. The line of control under every possible circumstance must also be established.

Some departments appoint one or two assistant chiefs to be in charge during the hours when the chief is not on active duty, a practice that is unsound for several reasons. While rank has a favorable effect in contacts with other departments and some citizens, who may insist on talking to a top-ranking officer, prestige of commanders may be bolstered by other means, and these reasons appear to be inadequate justification for the assignment of an assistant chief to night duty. In addition, the undesirable night hours are a poor reward for an officer who has proved valuable enough to be promoted to the next-to-the-top position in the department.

More importantly, an assistant chief on duty at night, by reason of his rank and free time, almost invariably exercises direct control over the platoon lieutenants, even though department regulations may undertake to restrict his action to the infrequent situations that require his coordinating power. This violation of the principle of unity of command impairs the control by division commanders of their subordinate personnel and creates confusion and dissension. Since there are no duties relating to either operations or services that an assistant chief may perform during the absence of division heads without violating the principle of unity of command, assistant chiefs should work during the daytime, not at night.

Command during Full Mobilization   When a force is mobilized in the field during an emergency such as a disaster or riot, regular command relationships are inappropriate. In the aftermath of the riots in 1967 and those following the assassination of Dr. Martin Luther King, Jr., critiques of police field operations revealed two almost universal deficiencies—the failure to adopt an emergency-oriented command hierarchy and the absence of practice or training in command under the emergency structure.

Routine command systems have too long a chain of command for emergency conditions. Many departments, forced to operate for extended periods during full mobilization, have found that the simultaneous presence of patrol officers, sergeants, platoon commanders, watch commanders, division heads, and bureau chiefs, as well as the chief himself, frequently resulted in extremely unwieldy situations in the field and that a temporary reorganization of the command structure had to be devised on the spot.

The police administrator should therefore be very much aware of the need for alternative command structures and should provide for orientation and training in the use of the command structure designed for situations requiring full deployment of departmental personnel.

Division and District Command

Police service is provided 24 hours a day, and the chief is responsible for all police acts and for crime conditions without regard for hour. Division and district heads also are responsible for the operation of their units at all hours of

DIRECTION   131

the day and night. Neither the chief nor the division heads are physically able to remain on duty 24 hours each day of the year. Provision must be made, therefore, for the performance of the command duties of these key figures during their absence.

Within each division or district, during hours when the division head is ordinarily not on duty, commanding or supervisory officers are usually in charge of members then on duty. The patrol division (and, usually, the records and communications division) provides 24-hour service and consequently should have a commanding officer for each shift; in departments of appropriate size, one of three lieutenants is in charge of each platoon, and he is authorized to take all necessary action to ensure the performance of the duties of his force. Department regulations should require the patrol lieutenant to notify his captain of any unusual event or grave crime.

The need for continuous service by other divisions varies. Detectives, traffic, and youth-division officers usually are not on duty throughout the 24 hours; and the vice division, except in the largest departments, is a single squad that works irregular hours, varying its schedule from day to day according to need. Service by supervisory and command officers of the specialized divisions is almost always less continuous than that by officers at the level of execution. When the number of persons on duty does not justify the assignment of a supervising officer, no competent authority from the specialized unit is available to make decisions and initiate action, and continuous supervision becomes more difficult. For example, the youth division may have one or more officers on duty during the evening hours when their supervising officers are off duty; the traffic division may have two or more officers assigned to downtown traffic control with no traffic sergeant on duty in the area; and records and communications officers may be on duty at night in the absence of their supervising officers.

Administrative Supervision   The cost of assigning a supervisory officer from each division to meet a less-than-full load is ordinarily not justified. Instead, the supervisory staff of the patrol force, available 24 hours a day, may be used in one of two ways to provide supervision in the absence of superior officers of other divisions. In the first instance, special personnel may be attached to the patrol division under the direct control of its supervisory officers but devote full attention to their special tasks. However, when this plan is used, patrol supervisors may interfere with the techniques used or assign other time-consuming duties that impair the performance of the special tasks. Also, they may divert personnel from the special duty to meet an emergency or other unusual need and fail to reassign them to the original task when the need has ended. This arrangement, therefore, does not work well when the superior officers of the patrol division are not in complete sympathy with the special task or when the need for specialization is great—as when the task is highly technical, the amount of work is considerable, or the duties are important.

The alternative procedure eliminates these disadvantages by leaving the specialists under the direct control of their own division and delegating their supervision to the patrol division. This is delegated or administrative supervision of the employee without regard to the quality or method of performance of his or her task; it is a general supervision relating to the time of reporting on and off duty, attention to work, and compliance with department regulations.

District Command in Team Policing Traditional district-command concepts do not apply in the case of team policing. In district team policing, each district commander is responsible for most police services within the district, and thus conventional functions such as patrol on the one hand and investigations on the other are no longer carried out by separate divisions. Further, as indicated on page 128, *division* command under team policing is simply an extension of the concept of the district team, i.e., that in each division there are several district teams having general responsibility for almost all police service.

Problems of Command with Traditional District Stations District stations create difficult problems of command. Relationships must be established that will fix responsibility on the district command for conditions within the district and for dealing with incidents that require police action. The district command, therefore, must be given commensurate authority. District authority is strongly influenced by district relationships with members of the special divisions (whether these divisions are decentralized or not) and by procedures for the receipt and recording of complaints and the radio dispatching of officers as well as the control of call boxes and records kept at the district stations.

There are two approaches to the organization of a decentralized traditional force (i.e., one without district team policing). The most common system is based on the assignment of a district commander to be in charge of all three shifts in his district. This method facilitates placement of responsibility for enforcement and makes coordination of station housekeeping easier, but it has the disadvantage of fostering an independent attitude on the part of district commanders and their personnel and—at times—creating powerful "kingdoms" which have strong local political support. The second approach is based on assigning citywide responsibility to a shift commander, and *then* decentralizing command. In Dallas, Texas, a captain in headquarters is placed in charge of each shift and is given citywide responsibility for supervising the five lieutenants on duty in the five district stations. The system causes some problems in the coordination of housekeeping activities in the station—such as cleaning, maintenance, storage, and so on—but makes interdistrict cooperation on a given shift far easier, discourages the tendency to build domains, and facilitates communicating information to and from headquarters. (The exact opposite of this situation is found in the district team concept as developed by the police departments in Los Angeles, California, and Charlotte, North Carolina. In Los Angeles, division stations are under the command of a single supervisor who has 24-hour responsibility for the area encompassed by the division. Further, individual teams operating out of the station have 24-hour responsibility for their respective team areas.)

Coordination when Patrol Division Is Decentralized Consideration will be given first to cities in which only the patrol division is decentralized

DIRECTION   **133**

among district stations, with the members of the other functional divisions continuing to work from headquarters. Since each station is controlled by a district commander, with lieutenants in charge of some of the shifts, the commander of the patrol division for the entire city should have a title which clearly distinguishes his rank from that of a district commander. In some cities this title is that of "major" or "assistant chief"; in cities in which the head of the department is called "superintendent" or "commissioner," the head of the patrol division may be given the title "chief of patrol."

Since each district commander is responsible for the 24-hour performance of all patrol duties and for all conditions in the district, the command power of the head of the patrol force is divided territorially by districts. Any operation that requires the coordination of two or more districts has the attention of the head of the patrol force during his tour of duty, and likewise patrol operations may be coordinated with the action of other divisions by a higher power when the chief of the department is on duty.

In departments that do not have district stations, the coordination of all on-duty members during the absence of division heads is usually carried out by the highest-ranking patrol supervisor on duty. The creation of district stations complicates the relatively simple coordination by the subordinate of the head of patrol because, instead of one platoon lieutenant having jurisdictionwide command, decentralization requires a lieutenant in each station with authority limited to his district. In the absence of the head of patrol, therefore, a new problem is presented in the coordination of patrol operations that involve more than one district and of emergency operations that require performance by members of all divisions. The principle of unity of command requires that only one person be in charge of an operation.

Under the conventional system for decentralizing command, the problem can be satisfactorily solved only by delegating the command power of the head of the patrol division to officers assigned to his office at headquarters during the night shifts.

Unless these officers are well grounded in their relationships with personnel of districts and other divisions, they will violate the principle of unity of command and create the previously described confusion that results when assistant chiefs are assigned to night shifts. This danger is lessened by the fact that they have a rank lower than that of assistant chief. They may have the rank of captain in large departments having district stations and the rank of lieutenant in smaller departments with only two or three stations. Department regulations should establish the staff character of their service and their superiority to district lieutenants in emergency situations.

In the largest departments, however, a coordinating power is needed above the level of captain or patrol lieutenant. In these departments, the coordinating power may be assigned to the chief's office, with high-ranking personnel on duty throughout the 24 hours. These officers then serve as the department command post and are available to provide coordination and decision-making authority at headquarters. In addition, they may have the duty and authority to go to the scenes of incidents which in their judgment require their presence, in

134 ADMINISTRATION

order to ensure that adequate police service is being rendered, to determine the need for additional manpower or equipment and to summon such assistance when needed, to coordinate the participation of the several divisions of the department through the highest-ranking officers of each of the divisions at the scene, and to take command of police personnel at the scene in the absence of officers of higher rank when they deem it desirable to do so. They are expected to observe and inspect operations of the department and to take steps to correct inadequacies in both the performance and supervision of personnel.

Some quite large cities operate without district stations. Because of their size, these departments may also maintain a 24-hour command post in the office of the chief or a deputy chief.

Coordination when Other Divisions Are Decentralized In conventional police organizational structures, the personnel of special units should not be decentralized unless the advantages to be derived from this clearly outweigh the disadvantages that are inherent in the resulting complicated relationships and lines of control. When decentralization does take place, one of two relationships is then justified. First, the specialized force in the district may be supplied with its own supervisory and command staff, and then it would operate independently of the patrol district command. The extent of physical independence will vary. Actually, independence from the patrol district command may be established without complete physical separation, although close proximity and joint use of some office facilities create opportunities for friction and may tempt some officers to violate the principle of unity of command.

Under the second arrangement, the force of specialists in the district is detached from the specialized division, except for functional supervision (such as review of reports) by headquarters specialists. Specialists in the district are thus placed under the direct control of the district commander.

The choice between the two feasible arrangements is based on the degree of responsibility it is desired to place on district commanders. When district command is to be held responsible for the enforcement of parking regulations, for example, it should be given direct control over the officers assigned to this task. If, on the other hand, the specialized division is to retain this responsibility, it must provide supervisory and command staff over officers assigned to these duties. The desirability of retaining complete control in the special divisions is influenced by the specialization-determining factors discussed in Chapter 7.

The plan used by some departments is to give district commanders administrative supervision over members of specialized divisions on duty in their districts in the same manner that such supervision is made the responsibility of platoon lieutenants in departments having no district stations. This plan does not work as satisfactorily as the two methods described above because separation by distance and the larger number of commanders involved weaken the control of the special divisions over members assigned to districts and complicate the maintenance of satisfactory working relationships with district commanders. This less-desirable plan should be restricted to fields where the technical requirements of the tasks are beyond the capacity of district platoon

DIRECTION 135

commanders and where the small number of specialists makes it impractical to assign a supervisor from the specialized division.

In summary, officers performing specialized duties should be under the direct control either of the specialized division or of the district command. Sometimes these two arrangements should be used in combination, one division retaining complete control of all its members, while another assigns personnel to a district commander for the performance of one or all of the tasks of the division during one or more shifts. This flexibility permits an arrangement based on need instead of arbitrary rule created merely to ensure uniformity.

ORDER OF RANK

The order of rank should be established in department regulations with the stipulation that this sequence in rank will prevail in all ordinary circumstances and that, in the event of the incapacity of the chief or any of his subordinates, the mantle of authority will descend the ranks in the indicated manner. Officers of every rank may thus know (1) what their command responsibility is and (2) who their superior is from whom they may seek decisions.

Regulations should also provide for deviations from this sequence in order to meet unusual situations. Two activities require such deviation: (1) the performance of all administrative duties over a period of time, as when the chief is out of town or incapacitated, and (2) field operations by members of several divisions involving the search for, or apprehension of, a criminal; the handling of crowds at accidents, fires, explosions, parades, public meetings, athletic events, and other assemblages; and the protection of life and property during a riot, flood, earthquake, storm, or other catastrophe.

The skills needed in these two types of situations vary considerably, and the order of rank, therefore, may not be the same for each. Consequently, regulations establishing the line of direct authority must be drafted on the basis of the personalities, skills, experience, and abilities of individuals and the nature of the tasks to be performed.

Administration of the Department   The best-qualified assistant or deputy chief, usually the one in charge of operations, should be selected to act during the protracted absence of the chief. When there are no assistant chiefs, such as in smaller departments, an acting chief must be chosen from the bureau or division commanders. In agencies having divisions as the highest organizational units, the head of the uniformed or patrol division (who usually has had the broadest experience and should outrank the others) is the logical one to serve as acting chief of police. In some departments, however, differences in personality and ability may justify the chief's deviating from the usual procedure by appointing one of the other assistants or captains to serve in his absence.

Order of Rank in Emergency Situations   In field operations involving an emergency situation or unusual condition, an officer from a division other than patrol who is superior in rank to the officer in command of the situation may come upon the scene. Such officers are not in the normal hierarchy of command, but their rank establishes their authority and imposes upon them a responsibility to take command when, in their judgment, the condition warrants this action. Their decisions should be based on the seriousness of the situation, the suitability of the action being taken by subordinates, and their own experience in dealing with such a situation. For example, if a patrol lieutenant were coping with a condition in a satisfactory way, the captain of another division with limited experience in such matters would not presume to interfere; action would be required of the captain, however, if the situation were clearly out of hand, thus jeopardizing the police purpose and the reputation of the department. The heads of such divisions as vice, youth, and records may have had only limited experience in other types of activities. The detective captain in the case of a serious crime, and the traffic captain in the event of an emergency jeopardizing the free flow of traffic, however, would have a real interest in the respective problems and might, if they thought that the patrol lieutenant needed their assistance, offer suggestions or take command. The principles involved here are the same as those discussed earlier on page 79, under "Command outside the Pyramid of Authority."

THE FORMAL DIRECTIVE SYSTEM

The police administrator who depends solely on direction through personal and informal communication with subordinates to get things done runs the risk of inconsistency, lack of coordination, and subordinates' failure to follow instructions—which are certain to stem from the absence of a formal directive system. On the other hand, clear identification of policy through directives is often recognized as the hallmark of the leader who is able to establish goals and pursue them tenaciously.

The formal directive system comprises both verbal and written systems. The formal verbal system consists of staff conferences and briefings, which should take place within the various levels of the organization. This system will be discussed in succeeding paragraphs. First, however, there is a need to describe the written directives system since it is fundamental to goal setting and the establishment of policy.

The Written Directives System

Written directives are the agents of the director. They assist in setting goals, and they define policy, establish procedures, and set forth the rules and regulations of the organization. They are intended to guide the efforts and objectives of the department so that all activity is characterized by a singleness of purpose. Directives can be categorized in several ways. Specificity is the basis for classifying directives into the categories of *goals*, *policy*, *procedure*, and *rules*. Grouping by format results in *manuals*, *memorandums*, *bulletins*, and *written orders*. Classifying directives by seriousness and permanence of subject matter results in *general orders*, *special orders*, *instructional material*, and *memorandums*.

DIRECTION

Classification by Specificity Depending on the degree of restrictiveness, directives can be grouped as follows.

Goals Goals and policies have much in common in an organization, and it is sometimes hard to distinguish between the two. In most cases, however, the term "goal" has a meaning which includes achieving an unmet objective. Also, according to some authorities, a goal ought to have some measurable characteristic. A policy, on the other hand, is often a broad statement as to the method to be used in achieving goals.

Chapter 3 emphasized the importance of setting law enforcement goals for the community. Equally important is the need to establish internal goals for the department, and for the same reasons expressed earlier.

As indicated in Chapter 3, statements of goals established for the benefit of the community should be in writing, and the same principle applies in goal setting for the department. A clear statement of goals can therefore be a logical part of the written directives system.

An example of a written statement of goals can be found in Appendix D.

Policy Although "policy" can be defined to mean a guideline for carrying out even the most detailed action, the term usually refers to the broad statement of principle. Unless a policy is further defined and restricted, it allows a degree of flexibility within the limits set out by the policy maker. The following is an example of a policy statement:

> Driving in a hazardous manner causes traffic accidents, and accidents are reduced by vigorous enforcement of traffic laws, particularly when enforcement is concentrated at the times and locations where accidents have occurred in the past and upon the kind of offenses which have caused accidents.

This policy does not establish fixed rules for enforcement, nor does it describe the procedure for writing out a traffic citation. However, it does provide the framework within which more detailed procedures can be drafted.

Policy should be reduced to writing and should become a part of duty manuals, general orders, and instructional material. Placing departmental policy in written form is by no means easy; the tedium of the process is sometimes relieved only by the arguments which it causes among staff officers. When the work is finished, however, the results more than make up for the difficulty. A common form of policy statement is the general order, which often combines an opening statement of principle, followed by procedural guidelines. Additional discussion of general orders can be found in the next few pages.

The question of who should set operational policies for the department is often crucial for the police administrator. An aggressive mayor, manager, or city council may want to establish policy for the department, but ordinarily the policy they establish—and they have an inalienable right to establish it—is not troublesome if it is broadly stated or unless the policy is contrary to the chief's ethics or to good management practice. Generally speaking, operational policies (such as the traffic-enforcement policy mentioned above) should be the responsibility of the chief of police, although many others may assist in their preparation.

The method of developing policy is important. The actual work may be performed by a staff officer or planning group, such as the research and development division, but the process should include all ranking supervisors who might be affected by the policy. This "review and comment" process provides an opportunity for commanders to contribute to the final product, and it permits review and discussion which build support for the policy.

Procedure More specific than a goal or a policy but less restrictive than a rule or regulation, a procedure describes a method of operation while still allowing some flexibility within limits. Instructional material and manuals are composed largely of procedural directives.

Rule Still more specific and restrictive is the rule or regulation which is intended to cover situations in which no deviations or exceptions are permitted. For this reason, the rules and regulations of a department should be limited to situations which can result in disciplinary action if a rule is violated. If there is justification for a rule, it is because there is an unchanging feature in the matter which prohibits anyone from taking leeway. For example, the "no smoking" regulation in certain areas of hospitals may exist because of the flammable or explosive nature of materials that are present. No individual, whether hospital administrator, doctor, patient, or visitor, may be allowed an exception to the rule. In this instance, the positive inflexibility of the rule has great merit. The same lack of flexibility, however, removes the opportunity for individual discretion, initiative, and judgment. When continuously prohibited, these qualities in human beings will eventually atrophy. Employees are often offended by unnecessary rules and may regard them as an indication that management considers employees unfit to exercise discretion in the affairs of the organization. Subordinates begin to look upon themselves as simply "bodies" rather than as partners in the enterprise. Instead of accepting responsibility and contributing worthwhile ideas, such employees simply perform as directed without particular regard to the success or failure of the organizational objectives.[1]

Classification by Format Written directions are found in a variety of formats, roughly classifiable into two categories: (1) the collection of directives known variously as the duty manual, general order manual, manual of rules, and so on, and (2) individual directives, which may range from formal general orders intended to become a part of a manual to informal instructions placed in a daily bulletin.

The Manual Statements of goals, permanent policies, procedures, and rules should be placed in manual form both as a convenience to members of the department and to ensure control over dissemination and revision. The format of the manual should facilitate revisions. For this reason the manual should not be printed on odd-sized paper or on both sides of the page, nor should it be permanently bound. The best format, even in large departments, utilizes

---

[1]Part of the material in the paragraphs describing the directive system has been taken from *A Survey of the Police Department, Baltimore, Maryland,* International Association of Chiefs of Police, Washington, D.C., December 1965, p. 121.

DIRECTION   139

conventional multilith printing on one side of 8½- by 11-inch paper, held together with heavy-duty three-post binders.

In large departments, manuals can be produced in several versions—particularly when there is a considerable volume of well-developed procedures of greater interest to certain major bureaus than to the department as a whole. A recommended classification is shown below:

- General duty manual (containing goals, general policy, procedures, rules, and regulations requiring the attention of all members of the department, as well as a section for general orders which have not yet been codified into the manual)
- Field operations manual (containing standard operating procedures and instructional material of interest to operating personnel)
- Administrative services manual
- Technical services manual
- Inspectional services manual

Individual Directives   There is a need for individually produced directives in addition to the manual. The individual directive provides a means for immediate updating or revision of orders which eventually will be placed in manual form, and is the principal means for conveying information of temporary or special interest or for material intended only to explain previous directives or to inquire. The following excerpt from an IACP survey report illustrates a recommended system of individual directives:

General Orders.   These should define policy and direct procedures for the indefinite future and for the department as a whole or for subordinate elements within the department. They should be codified and indexed for inclusion in a police manual. Revisions to the manual should be reproduced and disseminated to each member, who should be required to sign his name on a receipt sheet. A concise announcement of the nature and intent of the order should also be placed in the Daily Bulletin for three consecutive days so that any officer's regular days off are overlapped.

Examples of the type of directive found in the general order are as follows:

- Permanent policies and rules; for example, investigation procedures, reporting procedures, procedure and policy relating to arrest and to persons in custody.
- Permanent personnel policies affecting training, promotion, transfer, ratings, discipline, grievance, working conditions, and retirement—but not including individual changes in status.

Special Orders.   Their intent is to define policy and direct procedure for special situations or events. Included should be orders covering temporary or self-cancelling circumstances. A synopsis of the special order should be prepared and directed to the records division (if the order has wide applicability) for inclusion in the Daily Bulletin as in the case of general orders, and copies should be sent to the addressees. One copy should be routed to the administrative file. The second should be retained in the office of origin, filed by subject. Any division or district

140 ADMINISTRATION

shift commander should be given the authority to issue special orders for the personnel of his respective unit. The file copy should be reviewed by all others in the chain of command, including the chief, before being placed in the administrative file. Examples of the uses of special orders are shown below:

- Specific instructions for the accomplishment of a specific purpose. Once accomplished, there will be no need for continuing instructions. Examples might be the redesignation and assignment of police vehicles, or establishment of working schedules—assignment of days off, meal times and so forth, for specific officers.
- Temporary procedures designed to cover a specific occurrence or event which is of a self-cancelling nature. An example might be instructions for the use and deployment of manpower to a particular public gathering, such as a parade route, including the assignment of individual duties. (Note: The general policy for this type of duty should be contained in a general order.)

Instructional Material. This category should include instructional and training material which ordinarily would be found in manual form in many police departments. The tone and form of instructional material is less rigid and more flexible than in general and special orders. Instructional material can include training guides and training bulletins. This material should form most of the bulk of manuals. Ordinarily, violations of instructional matter, per se, should not be considered as grounds for disciplinary action.

Memoranda. These should be considered primarily as a device to inform or inquire, and secondarily to direct. Memoranda are also more personal in nature and thus oriented to one person or a restricted number of persons. When directed to the entire department or a substantial number of employees, memoranda can be distributed in exactly the same manner as special orders; otherwise the original copy of a memorandum should be directed to the person receiving it. A second copy can also be directed to the recipient, and on this copy a reply can be noted. The third copy should be retained by the sender. The second copy can be directed to the administrative file immediately, or after disposition of the item providing the subject matter is important enough to warrant this. Uses of the memorandum may be classified as follows:

- To disseminate information or instructions which do not warrant a formal order, such as notice of an outside training program available to police personnel, or an announcement of a promotional examination and procedures for applying.
- To direct the actions of subordinates in specific situations or circumstances at a level of command or supervision not authorized to issue general or special orders. Such directions should not deviate from or conflict with established policy or procedure.
- To explain or emphasize portions of previously issued orders.
- To inform members of the actions or policies of other agencies.
- To inquire.
- To record matters relating to the quantity and quality of subordinates or of work projects assigned to a member.

Personnel Orders. (Although personnel orders are technically in the category of special orders, they deserve separate mention here.) These are prepared when appropriate over the signature of the chief and on personnel action forms for the following reasons: appointment, transfer, promotion, demotion, change-in-pay status, formal reprimand, suspension, dismissal, resignation, retirement, and restoration to duty following prolonged absence.[2]

Verbal Direction

Much of the process of directing is verbal—in the form of simple instructions to subordinates, the initial formulation of policy before it is placed into written form (sometimes, regrettably, in lieu of its ever being put into writing), or detailed and informal instructions at the level of execution.

Staff Conferences The conference permits the executive to carry out verbal direction and also to engage in a degree of personal leadership because of the interplay of personalities. Most importantly, however, the proper staff conference enables dialogue and interaction—the building of one idea upon another—and permits freedom of expression, which in itself tends to have a beneficial effect on employee morale.

Formal staff conferences should be conducted in a businesslike manner in order to utilize the time of all members to best advantage. Conferences should be planned with an agenda prepared and made known in advance to all conferees; they should convene and adjourn promptly, and a conclusion, clearly understood by all, should be reached on each item of business, or if agreement cannot be reached, the matter should be either tabled or postponed for further discussion when more facts are available. The leader must stimulate the active participation of the members by asking questions and by encouraging the presentation and discussion of divergent views. He or she must keep the discussion under control, however, and not permit it to wander afield from the problem under consideration; on the other hand, the leader must permit members to bring up for discussion at the opportune time matters in which they have an interest or grievance. Suitable action should be taken to implement conclusions reached, and a brief résumé of the conference should be prepared and distributed among the members.

The chief should conduct conferences so that the officers may come to know him personally and to have an opportunity to discuss with him matters of common interest. The membership and frequency of conferences will be influenced strongly by the size of the department and its organization. The chief should confer informally each day with his immediate subordinates, setting aside a time each morning for this purpose, although attendance should not be compulsory when pressing matters interfere. Attendance should be compulsory, however, at more formal weekly meetings that the chief should hold with his immediate subordinates and the next lower echelon. For example, in a large department with several assistant chiefs, the chief should meet informally each day with his assistants and each week more formally with the assistant chiefs and the division heads; in a smaller department, he should confer informally each day with division heads and more formally each week

---

[2]*A Survey of the Police Department, Dallas, Texas,* International Association of Chiefs of Police, Washington, D.C., September 1967, p. 104.

with division heads and their lieutenants (or, in still smaller departments, with sergeants also present at the weekly meeting).

Division heads should hold conferences with their supervisory personnel in much the same manner. In smaller departments the chief should hold quarterly or semiannual meetings of all off-duty members. In larger departments, this general conference may need to be held in more than one section, and limited time may restrict the number of general conferences that can be scheduled, although at least one section meeting should be held each week. A general conference should be conducted regularly in district stations for district personnel in departments so organized.

Departments having district or 24-hour team policing find that team meetings or conferences are essential to communication among team members and to the development of esprit de corps within the team. Most agencies that have adopted team policing have found it necessary to provide for overtime or compensatory time for officers who are required to attend team meetings.

Vertical Staff Meetings A superior way for assuring that the policy developed by the chief or the command staff is actually conveyed to the people on the operating level is to conduct what are popularly known as "vertical staff meetings." In the vertical staff meetings conducted by the Los Angeles Police Department, the chief of police convenes a representative of each rank all the way to the level of the patrol officer in the field—in other words, he talks to a patrol officer in a given division or team and to the patrol officer's sergeant, lieutenant, captain, and so on up through the higher ranks. The loss of information which is so often the result when traditional directives are issued is thereby minimized; in describing a vertical staff meeting the chief of the Los Angeles Police Department recites the following experience:

I used to meet with deputy chiefs and inspectors. When asked, "How are things going?" their response would be, "Oh great, Chief." They'd smile, I'd say, "Is there any problem?" "No, no, Chief." "You're doing a great job." I finally figured out that, hell, they don't know what's happening. And that's true. So I conceived of the idea of the vertical staff meeting. I'll meet with five captains, their area chief, and assistant chief, and with a commander who's sort of a functional coordinator. In this way, all five levels are at the meeting. I'll look at those five captains, and I'll say, "You got any problems?" They'll say, "You got any time?" And then they start unloading on me. Then I'll turn to a guy on my right who is paid $50,000 a year and say, "I thought we took care of that a year ago." "We did," he will say. Then he turns to the guy next to him and says, "Didn't you take care of that?" "No, we never heard about it," is the typical answer. We have a vertical staff meeting from the bottom—policemen, sergeants, and lieutenants—so that every level in the hierarchy is represented. I personally meet with selected members at these levels so I can find out exactly what's happening. I know I'll never get it in written progress reports. Why? Because my brass doesn't know unless they do the same thing that I do. Unless every one of them does the same thing, they'll never know. We do have controls, you know, in terms of crime data and so forth. But only the human beings on the front line can really tell you what's happening.[3]

[3]Edward M. Davis, "Team Policing," *The Police Yearbook*, International Association of Chiefs of Police, 1975, p. 185.

DIRECTION 143

Informal Verbal Orders   In some departments there is a tendency to give orders in direct, military fashion—often to the point of harshness. Few people can work at their best under a steady barrage of direct orders; enlightened administrators, who do not have to resort to authoritarian control to know their own strength, use suggestion and polite phraseology in achieving compliance with their instructions.

The supervisor should not place responsibility for an order on some higher authority, but should give orders as though they emanated from the supervisor's own mind; otherwise, the higher authority's support is weakened. The practice of giving orders in the name of a superior is poor form and a sign of weakness, and it raises doubt in the minds of subordinates as to the confidence of the supervisor in the wisdom of the order.

GENERAL SUPERVISION

A consistent, nagging, and troublesome problem confronting police administrators—particularly in the largest departments in the country—is the difficulty in transmitting policy to personnel at the operational level because of the mechanics of communication and the breakdown of policy and procedures as a result of deficient supervision. The problem is widespread and has multiple causes. Poor supervision stems partially from inadequate leadership at the top (resulting in faulty identification of objectives, poor morale, and lack of motivation), deficient directive systems, poor selection of patrol officers (who may become supervisors in a few years despite their lack of qualifications), inadequate promotional procedures, and lack of supervisory training.

The Administrator's Role in Improvement of Supervision

The cure for the supervisory dilemma, like the cause, is multiple. The cure depends on maintaining a strong written directives system; providing continuous policy briefings by means of formal staff meetings and verbal contacts; defining supervisory responsibilities at each level; avoiding excessive changes in procedures; ensuring a suitable span of control; making certain that supervisors are trained in supervisory skills and the etiquette of supervision; improving the educational level of personnel (both those already on the force and those who will enter); improving control procedures, including staff inspection; giving supervisors enough authority to carry out their responsibilities; and, above all, having the courage to hold supervisors responsible for the actions of their subordinates.

The police administrator cannot hope to have his policies carried out unless the objectives and methods of their attainment are clearly understood from the top of the organization down to the level of execution. When the officer on the street does not understand what is being done and why it is being done as it is, he is not likely to be in sympathy with the operation and consequently will have little incentive to perform his tasks effectively. The success of the most excellent plan is then jeopardized. The superior officer who does not understand the purpose and nature of a plan usually does not support it; this attitude, quickly reflected in the officer's subordinates, almost invariably causes the plan to fail. The administrative staff has a grave obligation to see that its policies and procedures are understood and harmoniously followed throughout the entire department.

Sergeants must direct and control their officers. They should not confuse their role with that of a shop steward who joins hostile subordinates in resisting management. Sergeants are an integral part of the management of the department and as such are concerned with the achievement of the police purpose. They must win the support of their officers by interpretation of policies and procedures.

Sergeants stand between the administrative and command groups who develop plans and order them into operation and the officers who are engaged in carrying out the procedure. In this position they have important responsibilities to both groups. To subordinates, they must interpret the purpose of the plan, explain its desirability, and instruct and assist in its execution; for superiors, they must be alert to discover evidence of the success or failure of the plan, to detect weaknesses, and to recommend changes to meet actual needs which may fluctuate as a result either of the effectiveness of the program or of changed or unanticipated conditions.

Continuous, well-planned, and wisely directed supervision is essential in the effective administration of any unit within the police department. Without it, the best and most carefully planned program will miscarry. Day-by-day checks must be made to keep the program adjusted to changing needs. Unless careful supervision is maintained, misinterpretations and misunderstanding will creep in, and if they are permitted to continue without correction, the purpose of the plan may not be attained.

The execution of a well-rounded program is dependent upon the well-balanced daily program of the individual officers in charge of carrying on the work. Police officers are prone to be individualists, each having his or her own ideas regarding the relative importance of various tasks in any program.

The supervising officer must also scrutinize the day-by-day activity of each subordinate to ensure that police energy is directed into the most useful channels. It would be naive to assume that the old stereotype of the lazy police officer was entirely without foundation. The police service has always attracted its share of lazy individuals who should be encouraged either to perform or resign.

By constant observation and study of their officers, supervisors should be able to detect the officers' strengths and weaknesses. On detecting a weakness or dereliction, supervisors should take immediate action to overcome it. This does not necessarily involve punitive measures. A friendly discussion with the officer may accomplish more.

The principal supervisory task—the *sine qua non* of the job—is advising subordinates of ways in which their performance can be improved. A supervisor should discuss the performance of subordinates with them, if only to let them know they are doing superior work. If their work can be improved, on the other hand, a supervisor who does not discuss the need for improvement is simply not doing what he or she is paid to do. Additional comment on

DIRECTION   145

supervisory techniques which can be used to assess performance will be found in Chapter 16 in the section on patrol supervision.

Supervision of Civilian Employees

Civilian employees may be under the direction of a sworn member of the department or under another civilian. In either case, the work of civilians must be inspected, they must be trained in the techniques of their assignments, they must be instructed in the rules and regulations of the department, and their value to the department must be periodically evaluated. The supervisors of civilian employees can be assisted by the personnel officer, who should provide them with brief training bulletins, devise evaluation-report forms, and assist in an investigation of, and in conferences with, an employee who is charged with inefficiency or whose dismissal is being sought for any other reason.

Supervisors should provide their subordinates with concise and clear instructions, should devise work loads which are fair and as nearly equal as possible, should confer frequently with individual employees concerning their performance and progress, and should offer constructive criticism as well as encouragement and praise when they are deserved.

Relationship of Supervision to Discipline

The word "discipline" must be used carefully to avoid confusing its several meanings. When used in its positive sense, discipline can be defined as a characteristic which embodies willingness to conform and a feeling of self-restraint, coupled with dedication and perseverance. Used in a negative way, discipline is synonymous with correctional or disciplinary action.

The term "discipline" by itself is used in this book only in the positive sense; the phrase "disciplinary action" will connote the negative meaning. The positive type, properly provided, results in a police force which voluntarily conforms to departmental policy, procedures, and rules.

Even in departments which have good discipline, there are times when disciplinary action must be exercised. In recommending disciplinary action, supervisors must make important judgments about the motive and intent of the offender. They must attempt to determine whether the violation resulted from deliberate defiance of department rules and regulations or inadvertently from ignorance or carelessness. When the offense stems from the latter source, the recommended action should be aimed at retaining the officer and assisting him to improve his value to the service. When the violation is a willfully defiant act or has an immoral or dishonest motive, disciplinary action should consist of stronger corrective measures or separation. In many cases, separation is the only effective way of dealing with the incompetent or lazy officer, and it is the only acceptable method of dealing with confirmed patterns of brutality or dishonesty by individual officers.

Consequences of Lax Disciplinary Action   Lax disciplinary action often has evil consequences that impair the effectiveness of the force. Members of the force lack esprit de corps; they suffer from damaged morale and have a lackadaisical attitude toward their work, their superiors, their department, and the public. The entire force and each unit in it suffer from a lack of direction or objective. Incompletely trained members are inattentive to duty and guilty of violating department regulations. They disregard the rights of the general public, and as a group they have the characteristics of a mob rather than of an organized force. When the head of a force avoids applying corrective action except when compelled to do so by an indignant public, he loses the confidence of the people, and his force loses the prestige so necessary for maintaining good public relations. When police officers are brutal or dishonest, accept gratuities, or are guilty of discrimination against some persons because of race, creed, color, or social or economic status, the evidence of poor leadership is undeniable and calls for drastic correction from the top down. Discipline is the responsibility of supervising officers and cannot be expected to develop from the level of patrol officer up through the ranks.

Forms of Disciplinary Action Disciplinary action by supervisory officers may be punitive or nonpunitive. Punitive action may involve the imposition of overtime duty without compensation, suspension without pay, loss of some part of weekly and annual leaves, and, finally, separation from service. Punitive action is seldom constructive, but when necessary, it frequently has a salutary effect on all members of the force and sometimes, but not always, on the person against whom it is directed.

Nonpunitive action includes all efforts short of punishment made by a superior to correct a weakness in a subordinate. It is essentially a training method, is usually applied first, and is more constructive and desirable than punitive action. When suitable use is made of nonpunitive forms of discipline, it is rarely necessary to apply punitive measures.

The Sergeant: Key to Good Discipline Sergeants play a more important role as department disciplinarians than any other rank. Wisely selected superior officers need corrective action less frequently than patrol officers and others at the level of execution. Sergeants supervise the greatest number of subordinates, including officers who are inexperienced and who have not been completely trained on the job and those who have lost promotional opportunities because of weaknesses that need correction. Successful control of subordinates by the sergeants is reflected in an improved quality of work and in improved public relations; when the sergeants maintain a close and firm supervision, the likelihood of citizen complaints is lessened considerably. In addition to these immediate advantages, subordinates under wise supervision are thus schooled to become more effective superior officers, an important long-range advantage.

Disciplinary Responsibility of the Immediate Superior The immediate superior has three important responsibilities: (1) to discover the weakness, deficiency, failure, or overt act of a subordinate that indicates the need for corrective action; (2) to analyze all the factors involved in order to decide the most suitable action; and (3) to initiate and, in most instances, to carry out the disciplinary action. In discharging these responsibilities, the superior must act promptly, decisively, and wisely, being guided by the best interest of the community. Superiors should resist a temptation to postpone action in the hope that it may not be needed. When a subordinate repeats a mistake after the superior has ignored the first one, the most recent mistake is the fault of the supervisor. Procedural weaknesses on the part of officers may be discovered by inspection as described in Chapter 12. Such weaknesses and an account of the action taken by each superior officer should be recorded in the officer's personnel file and used in the manner previously described in evaluating his or her accomplishments as a superior officer. Supervising officers who discover no weaknesses in subordinates and take no corrective action are not performing their duties as supervisors. Each higher-ranking officer, in turn, is responsible for seeing that his or her immediate subordinates seek evidences of weaknesses and for taking suitable action when they fail.

Analysis of the Situation In order to apply correctional action wisely, the supervisor must analyze intelligently all factors involved in the situation. Has the situation developed from a weakness or failure beyond the control of the subordinate—for example, a defective departmental procedure, absence of a procedure to serve as a guide, deficient training, or failure on the part of the supervisor? If one or more of these conditions apply, the subordinate cannot be held completely responsible.

When the cause is not an outside fault but is found within the subordinate, the superior is responsible for ascertaining its nature and how it may be corrected. The fault may grow out of a failure on the part of the subordinate to keep informed in a manner prescribed by regulation, such as by reading the daily bulletin or other files; it may result from an improper attitude toward the public or from a lack of self-control; it may be in the form of inattention to duty as a result of laziness or lack of interest in the job; or it may have been engendered by bad examples set by older officers. Whatever the cause, the supervisor should evaluate its source and seriousness before taking action.

Application of Corrective Action After analyzing the problem, the supervisor must immediately take such action to correct the cause of the undesirable situation as lies within his power. The immediate supervisor should have the authority, and be required, to take and report prompt remedial action in all cases that in his opinion should be disposed of by nonpunitive action. When in doubt on this point, his decision should be confirmed by his own superior. The objective of the immediate supervisor in taking corrective action should not be to punish or humiliate the subordinate by reprimand or ridicule but to remedy the weakness by constructive action, almost invariably in the form of a frank, private discussion of the problem with the subordinate.

In some cases, complaints against officers may grow out of financial or domestic difficulties or stem from situations that relate to their social welfare rather than specifically to their performance of duties. The complaints may be investigated by a staff officer or the internal investigations division. They should, however, almost invariably be discussed by the investigating officer with the officer's superior because his or her understanding and knowledge of the problem may be vital in helping to find a solution.

Authority to Suspend or Jail   Actions by subordinates may be so serious as to necessitate immediate suspension. Authority for such action should rest with a supervisor in direct command of the subordinate. The condition of the subordinate may disable him for continued police duty, as when he has the odor of alcohol on his breath; his immediate superior should, under all ordinary circumstances, arrange for the commanding officer to examine the offending subordinate and approve the proposed action. The suspension is usually limited to several days and is subject to continuance or other action by the chief or the chief's assistant. Over weekends and holidays it may be desirable for the division commander to rule on the continuance or discontinuance of the suspension.

The subordinate's actions may constitute an offense that raises a question about the advisability of formally booking him and lodging him in jail. Such action should not be undertaken without prior clearance with the chief or an assistant; the offending officer may be held in a police office until a decision is reached.

Documentation of Action   In order to support separation from service of both civilian and sworn members, notes should be made of all discussions, oral reprimands, and private talks between supervisors and subordinates. When these talks are ineffective, they should be followed by a written reprimand, a copy of which is to be kept by the supervisor, in which the supervisor outlines precisely the reasons for the reprimand and what is expected of the subordinate. Further unsatisfactory performance should be sufficient cause for more severe disciplinary action, which should be recorded in departmental personnel files as well as in the city's central personnel agency.

Chapter 9

Interpersonal and Behavioral Aspects of Management

Many casual students of administration (as distinguished from the highly sophisticated student) are prone to think of the structure of an organization—and thus the people within it—as something that can be varied as easily as pencil lines can be drawn on a paper chart. They fail to recognize that the strength of the organization is dependent on the attributes of the people within it. These human strengths, in turn, are in part dependent on the ability to satisfy the human needs of the members of the organization and the need for effective communications among them.

Human Relations

Thoughtful administrators have recognized for some time that an organization made up of human beings must be considered not as a collection of robots but as a dynamic group of individuals with as many different combinations of capability, energy, motivation, attitude, and interest as there are people in the organization. There is increasing realization that the administrator must take into account (1) the differences in capacity and behavior of individuals and (2) the viewpoints of personnel, both individually and in groups—partly because it

149

is the practical and economical thing to do in the long run and partly because it is more humane and reasonable.

Consideration of Individual Differences It seems clear enough that the behavior of human beings can be attributed to a variety of influences—inborn traits which are common to the species, predisposition and capacity inherited from immediate forebears, imprinting of behavior patterns at a very early age, parental influence and childhood family training, the influence of siblings and friends, formal education, the church, and the collective influence of an individual's entire interaction with the balance of society.

It seems equally clear that some of these factors in the continuum of human development are less easily changed than others. Some, indeed, are being recognized by members of the scientific world as basic to human nature—for example, the tendency to relate to territory, the tendency to develop a social hierarchy, and the apparent predilection toward violence as a means of solving problems. Yet some of the other elements—especially those acquired recently—can be influenced quite heavily by retraining or motivational persuasion. A police employee can be taught new techniques which are easily acquired (and just as easily forgotten), but the aggregate of the employee's characteristics which are relatively immune to change—his or her basic, inherited human tendencies; individual inheritance of capacities; and relatively fixed and imprinted personality patterns—must become a primary concern of the police executive.

Consideration of individual differences and attitudes can have a significant influence in almost any area of administration, such as organizing, planning, directing, or staffing. To illustrate the value of considering personal differences, let us describe a theoretical situation involving organizational relationships in a medium-sized to large municipal police agency. In this department, supervisors of the rank of captain have approximately equal qualifications in terms of job knowledge, skill in work planning, and ability to motivate the performance of subordinates—but with one exception: Captain A, in contrast to his peers, is far less able to handle a large number of subordinates because of personality difficulties in relating to others. He does have, on the other hand, a much greater capacity for imaginative planning, a very high degree of job knowledge, and great dedication and energy.

Under these circumstances the administrator would be justified in considering a departure from a rigid, consistent organizational structure when it comes to placement of Captain A; he could justifiably assign to the captain an executive officer as second in command beneath him with responsibility for handling the relationships with his subordinates. The administrator also has several other reasonable alternatives when he is confronted with this kind of situation. He could reduce the span of control for Captain A; he could make certain that the subordinates assigned to Captain A have benign personalities so that his supervisory problems would be minimized; or he could assign him to (or create for him) a specialized position which could make the most of Captain A's talents.

INTERPERSONAL AND BEHAVIORAL ASPECTS OF MANAGEMENT

The administrator should adjust his treatment of subordinates to a degree which will result in the maximum efficiency of his organization, but not to the extent which would harm morale or lead to claims of favoritism or partiality. One successful technique that can be used as a guideline is to treat subordinates as individuals to the extent necessary in personal relationships and private conversations, but in written directives or public action to avoid any appearance of individual treatment.

Consideration of Group Attitudes and Feelings The concept of participatory management or democratic leadership is probably more widespread in the public service than in private business—especially a business which has developed as the personal creation of one all-powerful individual. Participatory management is found in greater frequency in organizations—both public and private—with higher staff educational levels, such as school systems, universities, and the management of large corporations. There is a difference, of course, between participatory management and simple consideration of the feelings of the group, but the difference is actually one of degree rather than of kind.

Self-made business people and police executives who have risen through the ranks because of their ability to assert themselves might well ask what advantages can accrue either from having members of the organization express their opinions or from having them participate in decision making. The advantages appear to be as follows:

1   Most human beings feel the need for recognition and belonging, and in some cases these needs are more important to an individual than higher pay or other benefits. Consideration of the group's feelings and attitudes can result in higher morale and increased productivity. As indicated in Chapter 6, rewarding employees through the acceptance of their ideas and the recognition of their contributions can be part of the reinforcement process which is at the heart of employee motivation.

2   The group may have correctly identified problems, solutions, and goals and can thus make a substantive contribution to improvement of the department.

3   Even if the advantages listed above do not produce greater efficiency, the process of making conditions more pleasant for employees can be justified simply as the humane thing to do.

A succinct expression of the aspirations of employees was presented more than 20 years ago by Professor Fritz J. Roethlisberger, of Harvard University:

They have feelings. They like to feel important and to have their work recognized as important. Although they are interested in the size of their pay envelopes, this is not a matter of their first concern. Sometimes they are more interested in having their pay reflect accurately the relative social importance to them of the different jobs they do. Sometimes even still more important to them than maintenance of socially accepted wage differentials is the way their superiors treat them.

They like to work in an atmosphere of approval. They like to be praised rather than blamed. They do not like to have to admit their mistakes—at least publicly. They like to know what is expected of them and where they stand in relation to their boss's expectations. They like to have some warning of the changes that may affect them.

They like to feel independent in their relations to their supervisors. They like to be able to express their feelings to them without being misunderstood. They like to be listened to and have their feelings and points of view taken into account. They like to be consulted about and participate in the actions that will personally affect them. In short, employees, like most people, want to be treated as belonging to and being an integral part of some group.[1]

In the period following the disclosure of the famous Hawthorne experiments[2] and in the years following World War II, the zeal to embrace human relations as a panacea for management problems steadily increased, causing some management authorities to caution against overexuberance. Among their comments are the following:

1 Although many leaders effectively use democratic techniques, democracy and leadership tend to be contradictory in principle.
2 Most great advances in any field are achieved by individuals or individually dominated organizations, and not by groups whose members have equal status.
3 The avoidance of friction and competition can lead to complacency.
4 It is as difficult to train someone to put human relations into practice as it is to train someone to be kind and gentle.

Although training in human relations can enhance qualities which may already be present in the executive, it cannot hope to develop attitudes which do not exist at least in embryonic form. Attitudes toward employees—like those which concern race relationships—are difficult to simulate.

The Human Aspect in Police Decision Making Professor Roethlisberger's listing of human aspirations did not mention a unique need of most police employees—one, in fact, which probably stems from the basic police concern with justice and morality; that is the desire to have their supervisors act ethically. (The same attitude is not always found, however, with respect to the ethics of fellow officers, for whom the group bond at times becomes para-

[1]Fritz J. Roethlisberger, "The Human Equation in Employee Productivity," speech before the Personnel Group of the National Retail Dry Goods Association, 1950, as published in H. Koontz and C. O'Donnell, *Management: A Book of Readings*, McGraw-Hill Book Company, New York, 1964, p. 336.
[2]During the 1920s, researchers at the Western Electric Company plant in Hawthorne, New Jersey, engaged in experiments to test reactions of a small group of production workers to changes in the physical environment, such as the level of lighting. To their surprise, productivity increased despite all changes in physical environment, causing the researchers to conclude that the higher productivity was generated by the feelings of identity and increased status on the part of the workers.

INTERPERSONAL AND BEHAVIORAL ASPECTS OF MANAGEMENT

mount.) Some of the other aspirations mentioned earlier are also worth considering when the merits of a decision are being evaluated:

- Is the decision ethical and fair? Are there hidden or unexplained motives behind it?
- Is it wise (not only the idea itself but also the method to be utilized)?
- Have all consequences of the action been examined? Would the expense outweigh the effect? Is the change to be brought about too insignificant in terms of results?
- Are chances of success good? Will action resulting from the decision receive high-level support and public acceptance?
- Has it been explained properly to both those who must carry it out and those who are affected by it?
- Is the timing appropriate? Does the decision or change come on the heels of a previous unsettling change? Does the decision follow a mistake by someone, making it appear to be a reaction rather than an independent step initiated by the leadership in the department?

Bristow and Gabard[3] have commented on the value of explanation in advance and the consideration of timing in the announcement of decisions. Advance explanation is necessary for securing the support and understanding of officers in the department and the citizenry as well. Many morale problems stem from inadequate explanation, particularly when directives are issued in terse, military style. (On occasion, officers with poor morale may react to thoughtless direction by carrying out instructions to the letter, hoping to cause embarrassment to the administration.) Of course, no amount of advance explanation is capable of rectifying an unethical or unwise decision.

Timing is sometimes critically important to the success of a decision, especially when a change is sought in public conduct. For example, initiating a clampdown during the week before Christmas on overtime parking violations (brought to light as a result of the seasonal demand for parking) could have a disastrous effect on community support. As another example, the chief should not exhort personnel to adhere to a policy on time and attendance just after the force has overextended itself in coping with an emergency situation requiring an unusual amount of overtime.

Personal Communications

Much has been written in the past few years about the apparent failure of people to communicate with one another. There certainly are, of course, numerous instances in which a breakdown in communications is responsible for inefficiency or failure in a police operation. Police departments work on a shift basis, which means that at certain times communications have to be relayed from one watch to another. The work is also very often decentralized,

[3] Allen P. Bristow and E. Caroline Gabard, *Decision Making in Police Administration,* Charles C Thomas, Publisher, Springfield, Ill., 1961, p. 80.

which adds to the problem. Finally, personal communications in a well-developed hierarchy often suffer because of the transformation of information as it goes through a lengthy chain of command. In some cases, information communicated from the highest level of management to the operating level can become so distorted that the end result has the basic effect of carrying out just the opposite of top management's original intentions. Finally, communication to and from a supervisor or a subordinate is not always the same as communication among personally affected parties. A subordinate will often fail to reveal his or her true feelings in conversations with an immediate supervisor, who may believe that quiet compliance is the same as agreement. The supervisor may then make rash decisions based on what is essentially false information.

Although there are perhaps limits on the accuracy and depth of information which can be obtained by a supervisor through personal conversation with a subordinate, there is absolutely no other reasonable substitute for it. All supervisors—and, most particularly, the chief of police—should from time to time talk personally to employees who are in every subordinate rank. Vertical communication is one of the sure ways the administrator has for determining whether departmental policy is being understood by operational-level employees (see page 142).

A discussion of the communications problem would not be complete without mentioning what is partly responsible for many difficulties in conveying information—the failure to listen properly. This subject was ignored in schooling until recently, when educational authorities recognized the need to develop the art of listening in the primary and secondary grades. Even among mature adults, special courses can enhance the ability to listen.

Improvement in comprehension of written material is also necessary. Perhaps the best way to increase reading comprehension is through certain rapid-reading methods which train the reader to eliminate "subvocalization." The vastly improved reading efficiency then permits the reader to pay more attention to the relationship of one thought or concept to others, and it allows for greater retention and comprehension. Speed reading, furthermore, helps solve the increasing problem of the avalanche of books, monographs, research reports, periodicals, and letters which overwhelms most police administrators today.

Many of the problems attributed to poor personal communications are misrepresented; they are the result not so much of difficulties in communication as of simple disagreements between people. Too much energy can be expended in attempting to resolve the difficulties by looking for a solution to the communications problem and not giving enough attention to the real differences which may account for the apparent communications problem.

Communication need not be extensive to be effective. Some people in working situations have excellent relationships with one another but scarcely communicate at all because they may be in perfect agreement in their methods and objectives. Under these circumstances articulation of the information is really not necessary.

INTERPERSONAL AND BEHAVIORAL ASPECTS OF MANAGEMENT

Rumors Rumors are a frequent source of problems in police service. Police work lends itself to the development of rumor perhaps more than any other calling, partly because of the shift work, decentralization, and the lengthy chain of command which impedes the flow of communication, and partly because the nature of police work may have an effect on the personalities of those engaged in it. Speculation is a necessary part of the investigative process, as is the willingness to be suspicious. Police often deal with sordid persons and situations and must learn much of their information as rumor or gossip. The effect of all these influences can mean that a police department can become a true "rumor mill."

The best means of prevention, of course, is widespread dissemination of factual circumstances before rumors can be started. The harmful effect of rumor can be at least partially overcome by adopting a well-developed written directives system, by reducing the vulnerability to rumor through positive training, and by producing information bulletins which simply and pointedly counteract rumors while they are being spread. Several major city police departments, including those in Chicago and Baltimore, have devoted part of the space in the departmental newsletter to countering rumors.

An item which appeared several years ago in a counter-rumor column in the *Baltimore Police Department Newsletter* reads thus:

CURRENT RUMORS

Certain rumors have been circulating and should be cleared up as soon as possible. They are as follows—with answers:

"A general 'shake up' of Captains in the offing, many are to be transferred—one Captain will be promoted to exempt position to fill the old, discontinued position of Night Commander."

Answer: No basis in fact for any of these rumors. There are no transfers contemplated and the position of Night Commander will not be reactivated.

"Another Bureau will be instituted in the Department."

Answer: There is no basis in fact for this rumor. The Department is functioning quite well within the framework of its present organizational structure.[4]

Training in Personal Communications Discussion of personal communications is an essential part of the recruit-training and in-service curriculum, and such a subject might well include some instruction in semantics—not only to improve personal communications but also to enhance the quality of written reports.

The formal study of communications skills will ordinarily lead to the presentation of various factors which make up the process. One management authority cites reception, sensation, perception, evaluation, decision, and action as the key steps.[5] The instructor should point out the need for understanding the different terms.

---

[4]*Baltimore Police Department Newsletter,* Baltimore, Nov. 20, 1968.

[5]J. Campbell Connelly, *A Manager's Guide to Speaking and Listening,* American Management Association, New York, 1967, p. 11.

Informal Paths of Communication   Very often the informal leader derives strength from the channels of personal communication selected or from the method used to disseminate information. One of the reasons informal leaders sometimes fail when they become official leaders may be the collapse of their informal communications system. When the chief considers informal leadership capability in a subordinate who is slated for promotion, he should explore the possibility that the new supervisor may no longer be effective because of the change in relationships with his or her former associates.

Chapter 10

Planning and Research

The act of planning is an inseparable part of the administrative process. Successful police administrators plan continuously whether they realize it or not, since the function is necessary before any new program, system, or effort can be introduced. Planning is essential to the successful conclusion of any serious undertaking. In fact, planning has a beneficial effect which is similar to the act of goal setting; once planning is accomplished, much of the struggle to implement the plan is already overcome. Planning is necessary for the development of improved practices and procedures as well as for their application in actual operations. Planning is necessary at all supervisory levels since each supervisor and commanding officer must determine how to accomplish tasks and must ascertain needed resources and procedures.

In a progressive department, all beat officers, traffic officers, detectives, youth officers, and vice officers are given some discretion in the performance of their duties and consequently must engage to some extent in planning their work. Each division and many of its subordinate units must also plan their operations. In some, where wide and frequent fluctuations in the need for service require frequent reassignment of officers, with an outline of their duties in each new assignment, the planning operation is so continuous and of such magnitude that planning units are sometimes justified. They may be called "operations analysis sections" to distinguish them from the central planning

157

division of the department. For example, the traffic division must plan the details of parades and other public events, and the task force must plan the day-to-day operations of its tactical and details sections. In a large city, the patrol division must also engage in much operational planning, and, where security is involved, so must the detective division. Patrol-division operations directed at the control of youth activities will involve planning by the youth division, which will also be engaged in planning its own independent operations.

In most of such routine planning of operations, the planning division will not participate, although it is available should an operations section desire its assistance. On the other hand, the planning division may very properly have assisted each of the operations sections to develop a definition of its functions and the details of procedures to be followed in its day-to-day activities.

Resistance to Formal Planning   In spite of the general recognition of the necessity for planning, many police chiefs undertake to manage their departments, or permit them to run themselves, without planning. They rely on operating personnel to deal with situations as they arise. Such failure to plan may invalidate budget requests and jeopardize budgetary control; it may also destroy public confidence, lower morale, and lead to general confusion and deterioration. Without planning, an eventual loss of control over personnel will result, with a concomitant decrease in effectiveness.

Whenever the planning process is formalized, resentment may tend to build up in the minds of people who somehow view the formal planning unit as unnecessary and a waste of time. Part of the responsibility for this feeling is based on the relative newness of the idea of formal planning units. Other planning efforts have suffered because the heads of such formal units have attempted to expand and broaden the natural power that emanates from this office if not conscientiously controlled by both the chief and the staff planners themselves.

Total Resources of Department Essential in Planning   The planning process is intimately tied up with operations, and operating personnel should participate in planning to the fullest extent possible. The planning unit should therefore consider stimulation of the planning process throughout the department to be a first responsibility. It should not attempt to relieve the operating units and personnel of their obligation to participate in planning—to do so would result in impractical proposals or loss of confidence in the success of the plan.

Although the formulation of plans may be made the responsibility of one person or of a large planning division, all units in the department that may be affected by a plan must be actively involved in its preparation. Participation in the development of a plan will stimulate interest in its operation and promote an understanding of its purpose and application. It is essential that those who are affected by plans should consider them practical and acceptable. Those

PLANNING AND RESEARCH

who contribute to the development of plans usually find them workable and sound and give sympathetic support to their implementation. In addition, this participation will lead to further awareness on the part of operating personnel of the need to recognize or seek out areas where planning is needed, thus keeping the planning function alive at a level below that of the central planning unit.

Plans relating to personnel management, for example, should be prepared with major input from the personnel officer or with his or her assistance and guidance. Also, the planning should benefit from the experience of line officers in detecting needs and in establishing objectives and standards for selection, promotion, training, rating, discipline, and welfare if the plan is to be satisfactory. Likewise, the finance officer may develop and operate the mechanics of a budget and of accounting and purchasing procedures; but present and future personnel, equipment, supplies, and building needs as well as their specifications can be identified and interpreted only in the light of the experience of operating personnel. Plans relating to records-division operations should be developed through major input by the records-division staff, or under their guidance, and special operating procedures should be developed by personnel engaged in the work to which they apply. The chief, in turn, needs the experience of the entire department in predicting the probable results of any proposed modification of organization, policy, or procedure.

Planning has a very close and fundamental relationship with such other administrative tasks as inspections and training. The inspection process can serve to reveal the flaws which generate the need for remedial planning. Since the end result of planning is very often the introduction of new techniques, their successful implementation depends on training and indoctrination of members in the new methods.

In short, for plans to be meaningful, the total resources of the department must be utilized in their preparation; plans must reflect the experience of line officers, the findings of the statistician, the conclusions of the crime and methods analysts, the counsel of staff inspectors, and the advice of every organic unit that may make use of them.

THE PLANNING PROCESS

Some consideration should be given to the kinds of plans which may be developed by the department. First, plans may be thought of as short-range or long-range. Long-range planning, expressed simplistically, is nothing more than the establishment of programs or goals. Short-range plans, on the other hand, are a matter of immediate concern to all supervisory personnel and include scheduling, consideration of manpower and resources, immediate budget preparation, and other activities which generally can be carried out within a few weeks or months.

From another perspective, planning can be considered to be oriented to management (administration) or to be operational. Management plans obviously relate to the functions described in this portion of the text, whereas operational plans generally mean tactical plans such as those involved in the development of a blockade plan, disaster plan, or riot-control plan. Planning can also be considered in terms of tactical planning (already mentioned) or strategic planning. Strategic planning usually means the development of long-term or overall operational policies, such as long-range control of vice or organized crime, and other police operations which hinge on the existence of strategy for coping with a situation.

The Philosophy of Planning   The student of police administration should understand that the planning function is a part of the larger process of administration. The activity is found throughout the organization. The idea of a staff planning unit carrying out all planning in the department is no more sensible than suggesting the creation of a "direction" division for carrying out all activity related to direction.

The role of the staff planning unit should be carefully described in writing. Idealistically speaking, the planning unit should view its role as carrying out the chief's responsibility for planning rather than the sergeant's. Emphasis should be on management planning rather than on operational planning; upon the strategic rather than the tactical; upon long-range plans rather than short-range ones; upon research rather than inspection or control; and upon staff coordination rather than direct involvement. In actual practice, of course, matters are not nearly so clear-cut—hence the reason for suggesting carefully defined, written policy statements.

The staff planning process really involves a state of mind rather than an adherence to a rigid set of principles to guide the activity. It can utilize the application of the scientific method—the statement of a problem, development of a hypothesis, testing, and the conclusion. The process can certainly involve the test of efficiency: Is the operation in question being handled in the best way possible? Can it be done in any other way? Can it be done for lower overall cost? With greater efficiency? With greater safety? The process also is concerned with the general application of the "consulting" method, which is to describe past practice, current status of the problem, and good practice in general; to analyze alternatives (including if appropriate, past attempts at solutions); and to make specific recommendations for future action.

The concept of "completed staff work" has an important part in the production of planning and research reports. This has been defined as the study of a situation and the statement of recommended action in such a form as to allow the administrator to make a prompt and effective decision. The concept has been distilled to the following elements:

1   A brief statement of the problem or topic
2   Elaboration of the problem or topic, containing factual information and detailed explanations, if necessary
3   Analysis of alternative courses of action and their consequences,

PLANNING AND RESEARCH **161**

taking into account the comments of other staff members and supervisors affected by the work

4 Final conclusion and recommended action, ready for approval or disapproval

5 Enabling directives or general orders, ready for signature

6 Appendix items, if appropriate, consisting of detailed reports having a bearing on the work but not essential to the conclusion; detailed statements of concurrences or objections of staff; exhibits; and examples or mock-ups

Items 3 and 6 in the above list mention review by members of the staff or supervisors who are affected by the plan. A proposed action given review in this way is said to have been "staffed," and the purpose is the same as indicated in Chapter 8 under the discussion of written directives. The process stimulates the development of ideas by middle management, including alternatives perhaps not envisioned by planning officers. It exposes the plan to the reality of applied use. Inaccuracies are readily identified. It encourages acceptance of the plan when it is adopted. Finally, the process cultivates the feeling of unity of purpose and encourages members of the department to act as a team.

The Initiation of Planning There are several ways of initiating the planning carried out by the planning or research and development division. Much of the work, it is hoped, will be generated by ideas coming from the chief. Part of the effort will be initiated by the planning staff as a purposeful activity. Some of the input should be expected to come from the staff inspections unit. An increasing number of requests for work will be made by other divisions, especially when the planning staff has demonstrated the usefulness of its products to the department.

As indicated in the introduction to this chapter, the inspections function has an important bearing on the planning process. The first step in planning is the determination of needs, and some form of inspection must be employed for this purpose. The need for the plan must be recognized before the plan can be developed; this recognition may occur at any level in the organization. Attention may be called to the need by failures resulting in injury to officers, prisoners, or private citizens or by sudden decreases in effectiveness as measured by percentage of stolen property recovered or of cases cleared by arrest. It may be recognized by the operating divisions in the routine performance of their duties. As a rule, however, the recognition of need for a plan results from the use of inspectional devices that will ensure an examination of all aspects of the department's operations.

Discovery of needs in their own fields is the responsibility of the operating units. The head of the unit cannot shift this responsibility any more than the chief can, but he may charge his subordinates to be on the alert for evidence of such need. Evidence may be found at any level of authority, but when the operating unit fails to discover it, the final responsibility rests with the chief. For this reason, and because operating personnel may be unwilling or unable to recognize or anticipate needs and problems, the administrative head will find it advantageous to conduct a continuing appraisal of police objectives and of the machinery and methods designed for their attainment. In larger departments a specialized staff inspections unit will be needed for this purpose. Personnel assigned to conduct inspections should always be alert for situations requiring new plans.

Once the usefulness of planning has been demonstrated, the planning unit may have some difficulty in coordinating requests for service when they originate directly from operating units. Requests should therefore be channeled through the chain of command so that intermediate and higher levels may be informed and so that they may have the opportunity to coordinate requests.

Steps in Planning   The concepts presented under "The Philosophy of Planning" are all useful in understanding the actual planning process. Planning involves finding facts and analyzing them to determine present and future needs and then developing procedures and resources to meet these needs. The plan is the detailed outline of the procedure to be used. The following steps must be taken in its development: (1) The need for the plan must be recognized. An apparent need must be verified by a more intensive investigation and analysis. (2) The objective must be stated, and the general method of operation (the manner in which the objective is to be attained) must be determined. (3) Data necessary in the development of the plan must be gathered and analyzed. Included will be answers to the questions of "what," "where," "when," "who," and "how." (4) The details of the plan must be developed: personnel and equipment must be provided and organized, procedures developed or applied, schedules drawn, and assignments made. (5) Planning reports must be prepared, utilizing the concepts mentioned in the description of completed staff work. (6) Planners should participate in a staff capacity during implementation, if this is requested by persons carrying out the plan. (7) Plans must be reviewed, and modified if necessary, to accommodate changes in need and technology.

ORGANIZING AND STAFFING THE RESEARCH AND DEVELOPMENT FUNCTION

Police departments which have had experience with formalized planning units have found that the best position of this unit is as close, and with direct access, to the chief of police as possible when inadequate attention has been given to planning functions in the past. During the infancy and development of a planning unit, strong support from the chief of police is needed to ensure departmentwide acceptance and understanding. Not all subordinate management personnel will be immediately sympathetic to the need for such a unit. Furthermore, locating the planning unit in a subordinate bureau or division may tend to isolate it from the decision-making process.

On the other hand, if the planning unit is well established and functions without the need for continuing support from the chief and if the chief is able to delegate the planning effort to a deputy chief who is sympathetic to the planning process and at the same time has good communication with the chief, the planning function can be made a part of an administrative services bureau.

Personnel Assigned to Research and Development The success of the planning or research and development unit, even in a small department, will be dependent on the qualifications of its staff members. They must have a sound knowledge of police administration bolstered by good judgment, initiative, enthusiasm, and persuasiveness. They must have imagination in order to conceive fresh solutions to problems which may have their roots in traditional, stultified practices. Since a part of their task consists of gaining concurrences on plans, they must be personable and work well with other people.

In large departments, some posts in the research and development division may be filled more effectively and economically by civilians than by police officers. For example, methods and forms analysts, programmers, and data-processing personnel all need special background and training. The required skills are not exclusively applicable to law enforcement and are not frequently found in police personnel. Junior members of the planning unit may be drawn from universities and colleges that offer courses in public administration. They must, of course, be guided and directed by someone who has had more practical experience.

In addition to the permanent staff of the planning unit, members from various branches of the department may be assigned on a temporary basis to work on problems in their fields of special competence and interest. This is especially important when large numbers of officers will be affected by the plan, since their acceptance of it is necessary for its successful operation. A representative who understands the point of view of the operating units can anticipate objections to, and recognize the weaknesses of, proposals before they become incorporated into plans.

Organization of Responsibilities in the Large Department

The recommended structure for a research and development division in a large department is depicted in Chart 20. Although no subdivision of the planning unit is normally suggested below the division level in medium-sized departments, some of the responsibilities and functions may merit temporary

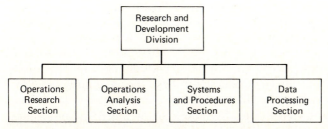

Chart 20 Organization of a research and development division, large department.

subdivisional status during developmental stages. For example, a data-processing section may be formed within the research and development division during a period of heavy staff work. Later, the section may be discontinued if the programming and planning work load declines.

Systems and Procedures The systems and procedures section is concerned with the preparation of departmentwide directives and general orders, special orders, and memorandums. It performs the research necessary for the preparation of drafts for review by the chief and his staff. This section has the responsibility for indexing and cataloging department publications and supplying these indexes to department personnel. It also reviews each order issued at any level in the department in order to eliminate any conflicts or inconsistencies with other directives.

The systems and procedures section is also concerned with the development of procedural manuals and with forms control. The latter is an extremely important function which ensures clarity, uniformity, and brevity in recording and communicating all kinds of information. Specific tasks include cataloging and indexing every form in use in the department and devising flowcharts to show where the forms originate, who sends them, where they go, and what use is made of them. In addition, the office conducts a continuing review of forms to make sure that they conform to department policy and to determine whether combinations of forms would be feasible and economical. All orders for forms from any unit in the department must go through this office so that it may review the number ordered and restrict this number to no more than can be used in one year. The section should maintain a suspense file on requests for changes in order to study these suggestions before a new design is ordered. When the forms-control unit prepares a new form or redesigns an old one, it submits the proposed form to the units that will be using it for comments or concurrence. When the form finally leaves this section, all aspects of its design and content have been completed, and it is ready for reproduction or printing.

The development of procedural manuals is a continuing process closely allied with forms control and with paperwork simplification. A constant check is necessary to prevent duplication of files and inefficient methods of originating or routing records and other material.

Operations Analysis The operations analysis section studies daily reports of serious crimes in order to determine the location, time, special characteristics, similarities to other criminal attacks, and various significant facts that may help to identify either a criminal or the existence of a pattern of criminal activity. Such information is helpful in planning the operations of a division or district. For example, a department which has a canine corps or a tactical unit is enabled to plan assignments and procedures for these special groups when the nature of offenses can be clearly delineated and spot-mapped from day to day. An actual spot map produced by the planning unit of the Baltimore Police Department is illustrated in Figure 10–1.

PLANNING AND RESEARCH

Figure 10–1 Spot map. *(Prepared by the Staff Planning Unit, Baltimore Police Department.)*

In its survey of the Chicago Police Department in 1970, IACP recommended separation of operations analysis tasks into two categories: (1) long-range or strategic operations analysis intended to predict crime trends and probably manpower and resource requirements and (2) short-range or tactical operations analysis, including preparation of crime-analysis bulletins and spot maps for day-to-day use. The short-range activity was placed in the bureau of field operations, and the long-range activity was retained in the research and development division.

There is some dispute as to whether operations analysis is a fit subject for a planning unit, but nevertheless many major-city planning units deal with the subject, which is the systematic examination of the time, geographic distribution, and frequency of crime and traffic problems. The involvement of planning units in this area stems from the use of the scientific method as a problem-solving device and from the fact that planning personnel are often the most familiar with the methods used in sophisticated statistical systems.

Data Processing Today's decision-making process depends heavily on electronic and mechanical handling of data, the storage and retrieval of information, and the generation of reports. The data-processing function should be located within the planning unit during its infancy in the department for the same reason that planning itself should be placed under the control of, or as close as possible to, the office of the chief. Much of the initial work in the data-processing area will require continuous effort by the personnel of the research and development division, with constant review, revision, and updating of techniques. Ultimately, however, some of the routine processes can be transferred to another division in the department, with only the design and development phase of future projects remaining a responsibility of the planning unit.

It should be kept in mind that a computer is really a practical tool to be considered in much the same light as a typewriter or calculator, and as the need for computer use begins to increase in many of the divisions of the department, there will be growing justification for placing its operation in a service bureau rather than in a research and development division.

Operations Research   There should be a section responsible for operations research and for general planning and development activities not described in references to the work of other sections.

The report of the President's Commission on Law Enforcement and Administration of Justice was most emphatic in recommending the establishment of operations research capability in larger police departments:

> It might seem that the most important contribution that science and technology could make to public safety would be to develop equipment for law enforcement with the same degree of ingenuity that it has demonstrated in a great variety of human needs. But advanced "hardware" is only one aspect of the promise that science and technology hold for the police. One of the most promising contributions, yet one most obscure by present standards of adoption, is that which involves operations research.
>
> As an important mechanism for innovation within police agencies, it is urged that police departments of one thousand or more employees establish an operations research group comprising professionally trained scientists, mathematicians and engineers, including at least one person with a broad statistics background, and at least one with electronics competence. There are today about 37 state, county and local forces of one thousand or more personnel.
>
> An operations research group once formed would study the organization of the department, provide technical guidance to the department management, analyze operations, and assess the effects of all experimentation within the department. Such groups, which have proven extremely effective in industry, the Federal Government, and the military, should prove to be a significant force for experimentation and innovation. The group need not be large; depending upon the size of the force, it may include up to about seven professionals. The dollar investment for thus significantly improving the effectiveness of over one thousand men is small compared to that of most other operations of this sort and size.[1]

The work of an operations research section should obviously involve the use of operations research techniques. The term "operations research" has

---

[1]President's Commission on Law Enforcement and Administration of Justice, *Task Force Report: The Police*, Government Printing Office, 1967, p. 61.

been adopted by business management and military management to mean a systematic, method-oriented, basic inquiry into the structure, characteristics, functions, and relationships of an organization. Its techniques provide the administrator with a scientific basis for solving problems in terms of the best interests of the total organization. Some of the techniques which have potential police use are linear programming, game theory, statistical analysis, and simulation. In the application of operations research technique, for example, there must be the collection of relevant and pertinent data. The analysis of the collected data must be so detailed and valid as to provide a model of the real-time situation. Next, there must be a manipulation of the model to estimate what will occur under varying circumstances. Selection of the optimum course of action can then result from the testing. A continuing check must be made on the validity of the model in the light of any new data which are developed.[2]

The kind of planning needed most in a large, modern, and complex police agency is long-range in nature and involves in-depth analysis and research. In order for comprehensive long-range planning to be possible, the goal which the planning is meant to achieve must be formulated. In summary, long-range planning must itself be planned.

The operations research section should furnish the administrator with current and regular reports on significant management problems, including information needed to direct and control programs and projects. To carry out this responsibility, the section should develop a management-information system. Such a system would identify management problems; identify controls which are needed to manage more effectively; aid the planning, monitoring, and progress of programs and projects; provide timely progress reports to identify areas where actions may be required; identify areas where utilization may be improved; improve the quality and content of data on which management decisions are based; and identify the factors which influence the decisions. Various types of basic reports should be developed by the system such as management-analysis reports, master-employee reports, and program- or project-status reports.[3]

This section should conduct studies to determine the most economical types of equipment for efficient performance and the most economical schedules for replacement. Operations research techniques are ideally suited to this kind of problem solving.

THE IMPACT OF DATA-PROCESSING AND COMPUTER TECHNOLOGY ON PLANNING

The great majority of reports produced by police computers are statistical in nature and are intended to present routine administrative or crime-reporting

---

[2]*A Survey of the Police Department, Chicago, Illinois,* International Association of Chiefs of Police, Washington, D.C., June 1970, pp. 141–142.

[3]Ibid., p. 143.

information for immediate use rather than to provide long-range management information for making policy decisions or on-line operational support for field personnel.

Unfortunately, the use of computers in many departments has been prompted by the desire of the city to enter what is now a fashionable field. This situation has certainly not been helped by the aggressive sales policies of computer manufacturers, who will not usually turn down the opportunity to sell or install their hardware even when there is reasonable doubt about the practical value of the equipment.

Data-processing and computer technology can affect the planner in several major areas:

1   The planner *may use the technology directly as a tool in management planning* related to manpower and material resources, including applications of O.R. techniques described earlier.

2   The planner's involvement with data-processing and computer technology *may consist of design input* into operational or real-time computer systems.

3   The planner *may have to control and coordinate requests* from various divisions for adopting procedures utilizing data processing.

4   The planner who acts in a staff capacity may sometimes be asked to *generate material for day-to-day crime or operations analysis.* This is especially true when the staff planner has been involved already as the system designer and has the computer located physically within the planning unit.

The first three of these areas are logical responsibilities of a staff planning unit, but the use of planning personnel to generate routine crime analysis should be avoided unless the computer is operated by the planning unit.

MANAGEMENT PLANS

There is a subtle distinction between the act of planning and the plans themselves. The word "plan," when used as a noun, conveys a sense of formality and finality; it is the end result of planning. To put it another way, "planning" is a more pervasive function, to be found almost anywhere and at any time that management is being carried out; a formal plan, however, may not necessarily result from planning.

Some management plans describe the future course of action involved in the organization and management of personnel and matériel and in the procurement and disbursement of money. Such administrative planning relieves the chief and his command group of burdens that otherwise would require so much of their time that they would be unable to carry out their functions of direction, coordination, and control.

Since management planning is concerned with the tasks that are more particularly the chief's responsibility, it will involve the personnel of his office.

PLANNING AND RESEARCH

In a large department having directors of finance, personnel, and training, planning in these areas may be performed by these directors with or without the assistance of the planning division. Their tasks are discussed here because they do present problems in planning without regard to the persons or units that actually do the planning.

Budget Planning Future needs for personnel, equipment, and capital improvements must be estimated and justified if appropriations are to be obtained. Budgeting involves planning in order to ascertain future requirements; surveys must be conducted to determine the need for replacing worn and outmoded equipment or to meet increased demands in transportation, communications, weapons, laboratory, traffic control, maintenance, accounting, and jail.

Other Fiscal Plans Accounting procedures must be established and expenditure reports provided to assist in making administrative decisions and in holding expenditures within appropriations.

Specifications must be drawn for equipment, and purchasing procedures must be established that ensure a check of deliveries with the prescribed specifications. Plans and specifications must be drafted for new buildings and for the remodeling of old ones.

Personnel Plans Procedures must be established to ensure implementation of the department personnel program, described in detail in Chapter 14. For example, the steps in the recruitment procedure should be completely outlined, from the announcement of examinations to the final appointment of the successful candidates. Procedures and forms must be devised to ensure an accurate record of the accomplishments of individual employees. A rating form should be developed and procedures adopted to ensure a periodic evaluation of all officers.

A career-development plan is an essential part of the police personnel program. The plan should list requirements and opportunities.

Allocation of Manpower A highly important planning task is the allocation of manpower. In the very small department, resource allocation often becomes one of the major tasks of the chief of police himself at budget time, when he must convince the city administration of the need to increase the size of the force. The degree of success in this undertaking is often regarded as the hallmark of the ability of an administrator. In a department of any size, the technique of justifying increased manpower should not be trusted to chance or guesswork, but instead should be supported by factual information related to increases in crime or services or through comparisons with agencies of comparable size. The latter technique is the least desirable expedient and should be carried out only when there is an absence of other information.

As discussed in Chapter 17, the preferred method for determining manpower requirements is to base estimates on actual and projected work-load requirements. This sort of system can be worked out manually in a very small department and through the application of machine processing in the larger agency. The technique is often carried out by the data-processing personnel assigned to the research and development division, sometimes because the personnel in that unit developed the technique in the first place.

Staffing Plan and Table of Organization   Plans must be made to reflect the distribution of personnel among the various units of the department. Forms in table format should be prepared which will enable the administrative head to know at a glance from day to day the number of personnel actively working in each unit so that it will be possible to detect any dangerous depletion of manpower in one unit owing to relief days, illness, and transfer. The plan for allocation and distribution of patrol manpower is depicted graphically in the form of beat maps. The planning unit or research and development division can participate in beat studies and the preparation of beat maps.

Training Plans   Recruit, in-service, and roll-call training should be planned, as well as curricula, schedules, lesson plans, and examinations. In-service training programs must be integrated into the work schedule. Guides and checklists should be prepared for field instructors to ensure complete coverage of all training subjects by explanation and demonstration and to assist them in supervising the patrol work of recruits (see Chapter 14).

Community Relations Plans   In addition to establishing sound and constructive relationships with all other departments involved in the administration of the city government, it is desirable that plans be made to organize community agencies and individual groups and societies for cooperative efforts with the police department. The public information officer or community relations unit officer will play a role in the development of these plans (see Chapter 13).

Comprehensive Law Enforcement and Criminal Justice Plans   Many of the aspects of the comprehensive state law enforcement plan (see Chapter 4) can have a direct effect on local police management, and management-planning efforts resulting in funding must obviously avoid conflict with the state plan. Regions, counties, and cities (particularly larger agencies) also contribute proposals for specific projects which often become a part of the state comprehensive plan, or they may be required to submit a comprehensive, generalized plan for their own region or agency which technically becomes a part of the state plan.

Management Planning through Consulting Police-management surveys conducted by consulting firms can usually be described as general plans for the improvement of the department. In most cases, consultants emphasize management improvement. Consulting reports prepared by the International Association of Chiefs of Police, Public Administration Service, and private consulting firms tend to stress recommendations for improvement and development of management functions such as leadership and direction, planning, and personnel management.

OPERATIONAL PLANS

Although it is the responsibility of each line division to plan operations in its field and to carry them out, these plans must necessarily be developed within a framework previously set up by the planning unit with the approval of the chief. For example, the research and development division, the chief, and the chief's immediate subordinates will have studied the needs of operating divisions such as patrol, traffic, detective, vice, and youth. For each of these divisions a decision must be made concerning the number of officers needed to provide effective service, the distribution of these officers throughout the hours of the day and the days of the week, their territorial distribution throughout the city, and the operating methods best suited to each. Furthermore, each line-division commander has the responsibility of working out with his subordinates the assignments of the allotted officers, of developing plans to meet the day-to-day and the unexpected needs, of selecting personnel best suited to perform specific tasks, of arranging for their supervision, and of discovering areas in which further planning and research may improve the service the division is rendering. The research and development division then again enters the picture to perform basic research and continuing studies to assist in the development of new techniques of prevention and enforcement and to provide commanding officers with factual data, interpretations, and recommendations on the basis of which they may form their decisions.

Plans for the operation of the line divisions are of two kinds: (1) those designed to meet routine, everyday, year-round needs and (2) those designed to deal with intermittent, and usually unexpected, variations in activity.

Regular Operating Procedures Operating divisions must have specific plans to meet current needs. The manpower of each must be distributed throughout the hours of operation and throughout the area of jurisdiction in proportion to need. The most desirable shift hours must be determined, the patrol and traffic forces must be distributed among the shifts, and the jurisdiction must be divided into beats for each shift. Assignments have to be devised that will allow certain officers to meet intermittent needs and yet provide for their productive use during the hours when they are not so occupied. Schedules must be prepared that integrate such factors as relief days, lunch periods, and the hours, nature, and location of regular work. Supervision becomes more difficult when regular assignments are interrupted in order to deal with short-time, periodic needs; nevertheless, plans must be made to ensure that suitable supervision is provided.

Specialized assignments must be worked out by the supervisors in both the detective and youth divisions to provide approximately equal work loads, taking into consideration variations in the importance of cases and the average time required to investigate them. Assignment of officers to a division should be on the basis of need, and within divisions they should be made on the basis of special ability and interest but also in proportion to need. The planning division may also participate in organizing the nature and extent of specialized assignments, but such activity is very close to the basic "reason for being" of investigative commanders. In any case, the unit commander should be free to fill the assignments.

Programs must be developed to meet particular needs in each field of activity. For example, the traffic division needs programs of enforcement, public education, and engineering. Each of these may comprise several individual parts; for example, the public education program will require diverse approaches, depending on whether it is directed at pedestrians, motorists, schoolchildren, churchgoers, elderly people, or people residing in a given district. A large department may have a safety-education unit to plan such programs. The youth division needs operational plans intended to eliminate certain delinquency-inducing factors in the community. Programs designed to make better citizens of delinquent and predelinquent children and minors or to promote better relationships between officers and adolescents will be required. This division will also need plans to obtain assistance from all community agencies in the diagnosis and treatment of certain delinquents.

Meeting Unusual Needs

Regular operating programs of the field divisions are based on the assumption, proved valid by experience, that the nature, frequency, time, and place of occurrences that call for police action may be predicted. It should be realized that such predictions are possible because the hazards which result in these occurrences do not change quickly: street layouts, obstructions to vision, the nature of business enterprises, and the character of the residents in a given area remain fairly stable over a relatively long period of time. When the offenses that occur within the area are plotted on maps by means of pins or other devices, the concentration of accidents and of each class of crime will be found in approximately the same position from one year to the next. The police are thus able to plan with considerable consistency a program of prevention and enforcement in any field of police activity based on an average need. Criminal activity and unusual situations and circumstances have no respect for averages, however, and create irregular, out-of-the-ordinary, short-term demands for police service.

PLANNING AND RESEARCH   173

In the investigative divisions, the unusual need is nearly always met by temporary adjustment of regular assignments, and it will seldom be necessary to augment the strength of these divisions. For example, a sudden surge of burglaries may result in a case load beyond the capacity of the detective, or detectives, assigned to handle this type of crime. Some of these cases may be given to other investigators whose current load may be lighter than usual.

Unusual needs in the traffic and patrol divisions may also be met by such internal adjustments, except on occasions, such as community events, which create demands beyond the capacity of manpower normally adequate for the regular operating programs. The patrol division may encounter unusual criminal activity, such as a series of robberies, burglaries, or other crimes committed by one or more persons, usually during the same hours of the day, on the same days of the week, and in the same section of the city. Plans must be made to meet these situations without loss of time through last-minute readjustments of assignment schedules.

A mobile reserve unit or task force should be available to strike at or otherwise meet such out-of-the-ordinary needs in cities where they occur frequently; this condition is likely to be found in cities of more than 200,000 inhabitants. Such a task force is described in Chapter 21. A task force may receive planning assistance in the form of operations analysis carried out by a unit attached to the field operations bureau. In some cities the planning unit has the responsibility of analyzing the crime situation so that it may detect areas in which patterns of criminal activity demonstrate the need for this kind of operation.

Contingency Plans   Every police department should develop and maintain contingency plans for the handling of such things as floods, blizzards, airplane crashes, explosions, and other disasters, both natural and man-made. One of the most important contingency plans is that which relates to civil disorders and riots. Another essential plan concerns barricaded persons and subjects who are holding hostages. Input from operational personnel is most important in the development of these plans. Procedures must be prepared to meet varying degrees of emergencies while at the same time providing continuing police coverage of areas not affected by the emergency. These should actually be a series of plans to cope with progressively intensified needs, but they should be outlined and presented in such a way that a simple request for a plan by its number will set it into action immediately. For example, plan 1 may call for the utilization of five patrol cars and a sergeant's car from the district of the occurrence, but when the emergency increases or is originally of great proportions, a call for plans 2, 3, and so on would automatically send additional cars from adjacent and other districts, but never unduly reducing the strength of any one district.

In the formulation of such plans, arrangements must be made for the establishment of a command post (usually the first patrol car on the scene) at a location to which other cars can readily report. The command post should keep a log of vehicles reporting and should handle all radio communications with the central complaint room.

Proper handling of a large-scale disaster or civil disorder may require total mobilization of the department for protracted periods. Obviously, plans must be carefully developed, comprehensive, and thoroughly understood. They should be distributed in the form of general orders to ensure departmentwide circulation and comprehension. There may be a need for several variations of the full-scale mobilization plan to cover the differing demands of the several kinds of disasters or disorders which may affect the community, but any such plan should establish the nature of the emergency command structure, the method of initiating and terminating the plan, clarification of authority and responsibility for summoning outside assistance, and provision for coordination and liaison before and during emergencies.

Certain specific locations, such as airports, docks, and munitions plants, are sites of potential disaster. Plans to meet these possible emergencies must be available at all times. They must be specific in terms of outlining the actual roads and arteries which are to be closed to traffic, which hospitals are to be alerted, how the scene is to be isolated, and which other agencies are to be called upon for assistance. The mission must be clearly understood, i.e., to control traffic, isolate the scene, preserve life, and protect property.

Specific emergency plans can operate under a *move-up* system, which is based on the application of general emergency plans to specific situations; i.e., they call for the activation of one or more of the emergency plans. As pointed out earlier, these would automatically include the strength of each plan number below it, but they would not unreasonably deplete any district or area of its police coverage. Strength is drawn from the task force and from ever-widening circles of districts within the city.

Procedures for coping with specific situations at known locations should also be planned. Included in this category are plans for dealing with attacks against buildings equipped with alarm systems and against police or other public buildings by violent dissidents and mobs. Plans must also be made for blockades and jail emergencies and for special community events, large public meetings, athletic contests, parades, political rallies, and protest demonstrations.

Routine Operational Planning

Much of the routine operational planning should be carried out by supervisors and other personnel in the operating divisions, with staff coordination and support by the planning unit. Operational plans should deal with reporting, dispatching, stopping suspicious persons, techniques of arrest, conducting raids, and so on. These are plans that affect all, or nearly all, members of the department at one time or another. They must be clearly and concisely stated so that no confusion exists in their application.

Each of these areas of planning calls for continuous study and research, and frequent modifications of plans may be necessary. This is the function of planning, although it may not be possible to outline in exact detail the actions to be taken in every possible situation. Human conduct is subject to infinite variation and cannot be predicted with accuracy; therefore, some freedom to make quick decisions on the spot is desirable. Planning should be so complete, however, that nothing that can be decided in reflective study is left to the impulsive decision of an individual officer.

Standard Operating Procedures There is no distinct demarcation between a plan and an operating procedure. In a sense, all procedures and directives are plans, since they guide future action. However, so that there is a practical limit to the extension of this concept, operating procedures are not discussed in this chapter, which is devoted primarily to formalized planning. As stated in Chapter 8 and earlier in this chapter, operating procedures and instructional material should be placed in a manual. In larger departments several manuals—such as a field operations manual and a technical services manual— may be necessary, and the staff work for written directives and manuals can be assigned to the research and development division.

Field Operations Analysis The term "operations analysis" is used by many police departments to describe the identification of crime trends and patterns (as well as traffic-accident and enforcement patterns) through statistical treatment of information and through examination of actual investigative reports. The term should be used with care to avoid confusion with "operations research," which has no particular relationship to police field operations; the words "crime analysis" or "traffic analysis" should be used as appropriate, or the term should be prefaced by the word "field" so that there is no confusion.

The technique of field operations analysis is an effective service for patrol officers in helping them concentrate their activity at the proper locations and times and on the appropriate subjects. It has a very practical use for a detective during the interrogation of a suspect in the search for crimes that may be attributable to that suspect. There is a close relationship between crime analysis and the *modus operandi* search. The latter usually results from a request by a detective to the records division (or *modus operandi* unit within that division, if one exists) to search the files in an attempt to link an unknown offender's method of operation with the patterns and habits of persons who are known to the police. Often the crime analyst will discover characteristic patterns connecting seemingly isolated cases. He can then initiate a *modus operandi* search or alert field investigators as to the potential value of the search.

In too many cases the technique of field operations analysis is not carried out at all, even though it is applicable to medium-sized and larger departments.

In others, an examination of crime or traffic reports is not conducted until a problem situation arises. In the more sophisticated departments, however, various formal systems are used to analyze crime or traffic trends and patterns.

In the Chicago Police Department, the crime-analysis function is carried out by detectives assigned to the Criminal Investigation Division's headquarters offices. There are "desks" established for each of the primary crime categories, such as robbery, auto theft, and burglary. Each crime analyst is equipped with spot-map boards for pinning the location of each incident and a desk file into which are placed copies of reports according to a detailed classification system. The basic product of the analyst is a crime-analysis bulletin, which is a brief one- or two-page document containing dates, times, locations, and circumstances reflecting patterns or trends. The bulletin is specific and is addressed only to the beat officers and investigators in the districts or areas where patterns have been established. A sample of a crime-analysis bulletin recommended in an IACP management study is shown in Figure 10-2. The bulletin is patterned after the system utilized in the Chicago Police Department.

In a small department, crime analysis can be carried out by physical examination of crime reports to identify crime patterns and to establish crime trends. A common method is to assign the activity to a report-review officer who also administers the report follow-up system. The officer can categorize crime reports and then produce spot maps, crime-analysis bulletins, and other information that may be of value to patrol officers and investigators.

Other cities carry out crime analysis or field operations analysis at the level of the field operations bureau or in the planning unit itself. The treatment of crime analysis in a planning unit should focus on "strategic analysis" as opposed to the "tactical analysis" carried out by field operations personnel.

Although crime analysis appears to be an effective operational device, the function is time-consuming and costly when performed manually. In large agencies the personnel cost can be considerable, and so departments are advised to consider utilizing computer technology to generate crime- or traffic-analysis patterns.

RESEARCH

Most research carried out within police agencies today is restricted to a few of the larger municipal, county, and state police departments. Other nonprofit research is conducted by universities and institutes—some of it supported by state law enforcement planning agencies or the federal government itself. This research, even so, usually involves the application of the problem-solving method to well-known situations requiring solutions—not experimental or basic research in the pursuit of new techniques. Research is often limited to product testing or evaluation or the troubleshooting process in problem solution.

PLANNING AND RESEARCH 177

13 May 1976

From: Crime Analysis Section

To: Patrol Division; Sectors 1-10 and 2-10; Beats 1-12
1-11 and 2-12

Crime Pattern — Stripped Autos Recovered   #76 - A T - 81

Beat	Type of Auto	Recovery Location	Time	Date	Number
1-12	73 Chevrolet	1251 S. Monroe (rear)	0150	1 May	31511
1-12	73 Chevrolet	1328 S. Jefferson	0649	1 May	30363
1-11	75 Ford	1532 S. Adams	0655	4 May	34329
2-12	73 Pontiac	1356 S. Spring (alley)	1045	6 May	36487
1-11	72 Chevrolet	4300 W. Main	0040	7 May	30536
2-12	76 Ford	1555 S. Spring	1005	7 May	37843
2-12	76 Chevrolet	1904 S. Fillmore (alley)	0900	11 May	38839
2-12	75 Chevrolet	1845 S. Fillmore	1200	12 May	44774

Remarks: Each of above autos was recovered stripped of transmission, motor or a
combination of both. Times of recovery would suggest these autos were
dropped at recovery locations early on the 1st watch or late on the 3rd
watch. Crime Pattern #76-A T-77 listed other autos recovered in the
South Side with stripping of this type. Be on the alert for late model
autos either being pushed or towed in the area west of Fillmore especially
during the hours of darkness.

Commander - Crime Analysis

Notify the Crime Analysis Section if an arrest results from this information or if an arrest
is made by normal patrol or investigation which would affect the continuance of the pattern.

Figure 10–2   Sample crime-analysis bulletin.

Very little experimental research is carried out by smaller units of
government; in fact, the police system in the United States finds itself looking
in every direction for leadership in this field. The reasons for this difficulty are
several: Few legislative bodies can conscientiously allocate funds for research
efforts because the practical benefit may be difficult to point out to the
taxpayers. In the smaller agency, providing meaningful resources to carry out
research is practically impossible. Second, the police have traditionally lacked

the specialists and scientists who can perform the work. Third, experimental research involving "control" situations in the field, or the analysis of differential application, can be dangerous.

Until the creation of state law enforcement planning agencies and the establishment of the Law Enforcement Assistance Administration's National Institute (which is concerned primarily with fostering research), much of the pure research that existed was carried out by universities rather than by police agencies themselves. These efforts have been of recent origin anyway, and before World War II there was little research of any kind in the police field, in or outside the university.

Research in the police field can be categorized in several ways. First, the subject matter can be divided broadly into two areas: research relating to the behavior of human beings and research in technology and equipment. Second, the work is oriented either toward improvement of administration and management or toward operational improvement. Finally, police research can be classified according to its position on a scale embraced by pure research on one extreme and practical research on the other.

These relationships can be depicted in matrix form (see Figure 10–3), which serves a useful purpose in illustrating the dimension of the task:

Abstract versus Applied   As used in this matrix, *abstract* refers to pure, basic, or nondirective research—to experimentation without knowing precisely what the final result or objective may be. It can also mean the invention of a new solution or concept to solve an existing problem. Its opposite, *applied* research, refers to the testing or evaluation of products or methods already in use or to the application of a fully developed idea outside the police field to specific police use. Most police research can thus be described as tending toward the applied rather than the abstract. As in the other scales described below, the placement of an activity along the scale is often indefinite or uncertain.

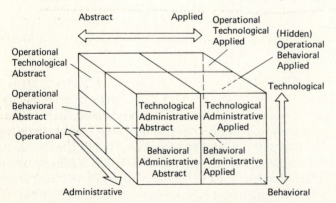

Figure 10–3 Matrix illustrating the dimension of police research.

PLANNING AND RESEARCH

Technological versus Behavioral In Figure 10–3, *technological* refers to the physical sciences, to equipment, or to products. *Behavioral*, on the other hand, relates to research in the social sciences and human relationships. Again, there is no sharply defined line between the two; most technological research involves consideration of the human beings who will use the technology or be affected by its use.

Operational versus Administrative Operational embraces the activities which justify the existence of the police function—line activities such as patrol, investigation, and the prevention of criminality. At the other end of the scale, *administrative* refers to management and to the services which support operations.

As indicated in the following compendium, there are eight possible mission areas. Examples of research topics or programs in each area are also shown:

1 (Technological–Administrative–Abstract) Experimentation with new concepts for automatic vehicle locators (which are essentially supervisory in nature); exploration of administrative uses for newly discovered computer or operations research techniques

2 (Technological–Administrative–Applied) Development of computer formats; application of management-systems engineering; testing office equipment

3 (Behavioral–Administrative–Abstract) Conduct of experiments in innovative management; exploration of ways to enhance employee motivation; theorization on career-development systems

4 (Behavioral–Administrative–Applied) Development of improved promotional examinations; application of improved supervisory methods

5 (Operational–Technological–Abstract) Development of concepts for nonlethal weaponry; examination of newly discovered scientific phenomena for possible application in the criminalistics laboratory

6 (Operational–Technological–Applied) Study of effects of weaponry already developed; testing of operational equipment, such as personal radios and mobile teleprinters; evaluation of locks, hardware, and alarm systems

7 (Operational–Behavioral–Abstract) Identification of causes of criminality; basic research in programs for the reduction of criminality; conduct of victimization studies; biomedical research

8 (Operational–Behavioral–Applied) Evaluation of the effect of various field operations; conduct of studies of innovative operational methods; evaluation of programs intended to improve police relationships with the community

Directions for Technological Research At the present time there are a number of promising applications of technology in the police field, and all of them offer ample opportunity for further research and development.[4] Some of them can be categorized as a part of "command and control" technology. They

---

[4]Some of these applications will be discussed further in later chapters.

include computer-assisted dispatching, automatic car locators, frequency shift keying (a device which will permit nearly instantaneous transmission of digital messages), mobile teleprinters, mobile digital terminals, and other communications improvements. Some technical advances relate more closely to information systems—both management and operational applications—through increased use of computers and data-transmission and storage devices such as high-speed random-access video-tape files, or the optical scanning and automated classification of fingerprints. Still other advances can be categorized as extensions of human senses, such as sensing instruments to locate and identify objects or persons by size or movements and odor-sensing devices which duplicate a dog's ability to classify trace odors left by human beings at the scene or to detect dangerous or contraband substances. Further advances can be expected in nonlethal weaponry or riot-control devices and in many other areas.

Because of the nature of our free-enterprise system, the police have the advantage of commercial pressure behind technological research; there is money to be made from the sale of sophisticated equipment. The police can therefore concentrate research efforts on guiding the work of manufacturers along certain lines and on making sure that manufacturers are aware of user requirements.

Directions for Behavioral and Social Science Research Unfortunately, the commercial pressure behind the technological advancement does not exist to the same degree in the behavioral and social science areas. There is simply not enough money to be made by commercial organizations to warrant research efforts on their part in such areas as the influence of poverty and discrimination, the effect of personality imprinting during early childhood, the value of corrective education and training, the diagnosis of predisposition toward crime or violence, and the development of biomedical solutions to the problem of criminality.

Research in the biomedical field is an important area which has tremendous application to crime prevention and law enforcement. Much of this work undoubtedly will always remain out of the reach of law enforcement agencies, but the work should be encouraged by police and others in the criminal justice system.

Role of the National Institute of Law Enforcement and Criminal Justice LEAA's National Institute of Law Enforcement and Criminal Justice has fostered police research and developmental work in a number of important areas. The institute has sponsored major projects such as the Kansas City Patrol Experiment (see page 322) and has issued a number of reports and monographs, including the "Prescriptive Package" series, ranging from team policing to management of rape investigations.

Recent work by the institute has included a study of patrol response time

PLANNING AND RESEARCH

in Kansas City, a model disciplinary procedure (in conjunction with IACP), a study of the investigative process (with the Rand Institute), research in the application of computer algorithms to mug-shot identifications, field trials of body armor, and many other diverse projects.

The institute plans to continue the present stress on technology and research in behavioral applications in law enforcement. The institute will study the problem of corruption in licensing and regulating agencies, the effect of crime on the aged, the lack of guidelines for investigating white-collar crime, the technique of family-crisis intervention, and the improvement of the personal relationship between police and victims.

The institute has added a heretofore missing dimension in law enforcement research—the guidance, coordination, funding, and evaluation by a federal agency—to the existing expertise in research and development available through larger police departments, private and industrial research organizations, professional associations, and universities.

Chapter 11

Management Information

This chapter is concerned with the group of functions which are known collectively as the *management-information system*. In its broadest terms this system is concerned with the total flow of data which reaches police chiefs to help them plan future policy and direction and to control resources and activities. In business and industry, however, the management-information system relates primarily to the kinds of planning and control with which business executives are most concerned—budgeting, accounting, and administrative reporting. We shall use the term in this restricted sense.

BUDGETING AND FISCAL MANAGEMENT

The task of providing appropriate resources for the administration and operation of the department ranks among the most important responsibilities of the police executive. Achieving a proper budget is, in fact, one of the informally recognized measurements of success used by police chiefs when they rate one another.

The Integrated Approach to Management Information   Budgeting is essentially a planning process, and there must be close ties with the formal planning unit and with division heads during the development of the budget. Part of

182

the fiscal-management process relates to control of expenditures, an area of concern to division heads but of less moment to the planners who participate in long-range forecasting. Feedback from inspection of facilities and procedures is related to planning. Reporting of departmental performance is also an essential ingredient in control. All these management tasks should be considered part of an integrated system even though they may be carried out by different units within the department.

Concepts in Budgeting

As indicated earlier, the ability of the administration to obtain the proper manpower and resources can be a key factor in the success of the department. Less obvious, however, is the importance of proper methodology in budgeting. Few cities are so financially well off that departmental requests for funds are accepted wholly without argument.

As a consequence there is considerable competition among city departments for the available money. The city department which justifies its requests with sound, factual logic is most likely to get results. City managers, mayors, and city councils appreciate being given the kind of information which can be used to make sound decisions. If those who decide the size of the budget are deprived of the opportunity to assess the department's programs, they are much more likely to base decisions on personal relationships, subjective feelings, or their reaction to misguided pressure from special-interest groups.

The budget is nothing more than the work program of the department stated in terms of the money needed to carry it out. When budget requests are based on a combination of existing and proposed work programs, they tend to be more precise; the budget which has been determined by simply inflating last year's figures by a fixed percentage is often dealt with, in kind, by an across-the-board percentage reduction.

Budget requests can be justified and defended best on the grounds that if the funds are not provided, there must be a corresponding reduction in services provided to the public. Some operations which are essential for the conduct of police affairs cannot be reduced even though the budget request is cut; they are at an irreducible minimum. Reductions of budget requests are therefore usually reflected in the line operations—the services to the public—and most frequently in patrol and traffic control. This fact must be made apparent to the appropriating authority: The reduction in the amount appropriated will result in a reduction in service to the public.

Descriptions of programs and the activities which go into each program should be extensive, and the cost of each activity should be determined. Then when city management or the city council advocates a reduction in the amount, they must concurrently announce publicly, in effect, that a service to which the community has been accustomed is being curtailed. City councils do not, as a general rule, like to be associated with reductions in service, and so they will often refrain from making hasty budget cuts if programs are adequately and extensively described.

Figure 11–1 Comparison of budgeting systems.

COMPARISON OF BUDGETING SYSTEMS

VALUE
Good
↕
Poor

Budget Execution and Accountability

Program Formulation

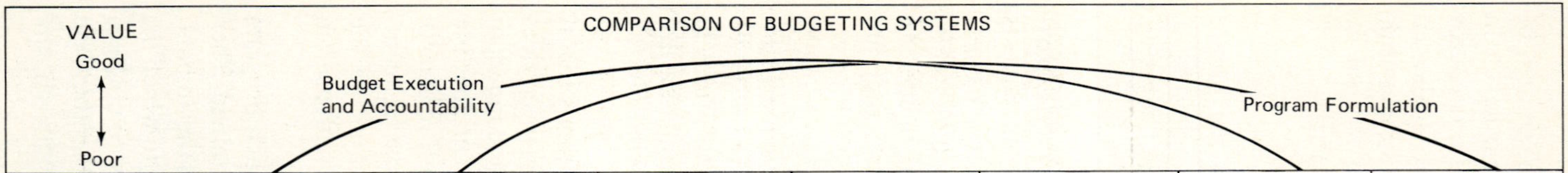

	1	2	3	4	5	6	7
Type:	Object (Line-Item)	Departmental	Object, with Departmental Breakdown	Performance (Program) and Object Combination	Performance	Program	Functional
Purposes and usefulness:	Fair for execution and accountability	Fair for execution and accountability plus some program formulation	Best for execution and accountability, plus good program formulation	Best balance; execution and accountability good, program formulation good	Good program formulation, good accountability	Good program formulation, fair for execution and accountability	Fair for program formulation
Typical descriptive headings found in budget document:	I. Salaries A. Chief B. Captains C. Lieuts., etc. II. Op. Exps. A. Gas & Oil B. Off. Supp. C. Utilities, etc. III. Capital Outlay A. Vehicles B. Cap. Equip., etc.	A. Patrol Division B. Traffic Division C. Central Records & Communications Division D. Etc.	I. Salaries A. Patrol Division B. Traffic Division C. Etc. II. Op. Exp. A. Patrol Division B. Traffic C. Etc. III. Capital Outlay, etc.	I. Salaries A. Patrol Service 1. Store Security 2. Routine Patrol, etc. B. Traffic Regulation 1. Parking Control 2. Accident Invest., etc. II. Op. Exp., etc.	A. Patrol Service 1. Store Security 2. Routine Patrol, etc. B. Traffic Regulation 1. Parking Control 2. Accident Invest. 3. Etc.	A. Patrol Service B. Traffic Regulation C. Investigations D. Etc.	Protection of Persons and Property

MANAGEMENT INFORMATION

Objectives of Budgeting The major objectives of the budgeting process can be summarized as follows:

Formulation

- From the viewpoint of the department head: to obtain the necessary funds for the administration and operation of the department and to assist in planning the work of the department
- From the viewpoint of the city administration and the legislative body: to control the basic programs and expenditures of the department

Execution (after the budget is adopted)

- To make sure the appropriation for the budgeted item is not overdrawn
- To check the attainment of objectives during the fiscal period

A budget system can achieve all or just one or two of these objectives, depending on its methodology. A comparison of several different systems is shown in Figure 11–1.

The most frequently encountered method is *object*—or *line-item*—*budgeting.* In its most typical form the budget is divided into three categories during the formulation phase: salaries, operating expenses, and capital outlay. Under this system the salary section is very often broken down into full-time versus part-time employees or a listing of the number of personnel in each rank or classification. The operating-expense section, in its typical form, consists of lines or categories as shown in Figure 11–2, with object headings such as "office supplies," "travel," "utility services," and "repairs." In other variations (the true line-item budget), each category of expense is shown on a separate line, and the amount for that line is entered in columns along the right-hand side of the budget document. For example, under "office supplies" items for "paper" and "pencils" will be found, and so on. Finally, the capital-outlay portion of a line-item budget usually consists of a listing of each of the capital items to be purchased along with its price.

Object budgeting may be accompanied by supplementary pages containing detailed explanations of new and existing expenditures. Even so, it is basically unsatisfactory because it is not designed to achieve all the objectives previously mentioned. It has only fair value for the formulation of programs. Its best use (and only in its more detailed forms) is to establish accountability during the execution phase of the budget.

A so-called *departmental budget* is a logical outgrowth of object budgeting. It classifies proposed expenses by department or division. Some of the typical headings shown in a departmental budget are depicted in Figure 11–1. Examples are "patrol division," "traffic division," and "records and communications division." A departmental budget in its simplest form (that is, with no additional categories other than appropriations by division) is rarely found. However, a combination of departmental and object budgeting, as shown in column 3 of Figure 11–1, can be a very effective system. When this budget is

Account Code	PURPOSE	Actual 1975-76	Approved Budget Estimate 1976-77	Revised Budget Estimate 1976-77	Actual Estimated 1976-77	Recommended City Mgr. 1977-78	Approved Budget
100	Personnel Services						
101	Departmental Payroll	$ 82,347	$ 89,579	$ 75,889	$ 75,824	$ 90,168	
102	Overtime	1,228	2,000	2,800	2,800	2,500	
	Total	$ 83,575	$ 91,579	$ 78,689	$ 78,624	$ 92,668	
200	Contractual Services						
201	Printing	$ 0	$ 75	$ 75	$ 75	$ 450	
206	Dry Cleaning	588	1,000	600	550	650	
208	Uniforms	2,042	1,800	1,500	1,500	1,800	
224	Consultant	3,500	0	0	0	0	
236	In Service Training	360	400	300	300	325	
	Total	$ 6,490	$ 3,275	$ 2,475	$ 2,425	$ 3,225	
300	Materials and Supplies						
301	Office and Traffic Supplies	$ 151	$ 200	$ 190	$ 225	$ 380	
353	Target Ammunition	194	0	29	29	100	
	Total	$ 345	$ 200	$ 219	$ 254	$ 480	
400	Maintenance						
401	Office and Radar Equipment	$ 28	$ 200	$ 150	$ 105	$ 200	
500	Miscellaneous						
502	Dues and Publications	$ 51	$ 100	$ 75	$ 70	$ 100	
503	Other	64	50	50	45	50	
	Total	$ 115	$ 150	$ 125	$ 115	$ 150	
600	Capital Outlay						
601	Two Police Cruisers(Replacements)	$ 8,485	$ 1,800	$ 1,962	$ 1,962	$ 6,000	
	Total	$ 8,485	$ 1,800	$ 1,962	$ 1,962	$ 6,000	
	Total Police	$ 99,038	$ 97,204	$ 83,620	$ 83,485	$102,723	

Figure 11–2   Typical object-budget format.

cut, those who do the cutting are thus forced to be aware of the specific unit within the department which will have decreases in the salary or operating-expense category.

The *performance budget* (see column 4 of Figure 11–1) is oriented toward proposed programs and services to be performed. It is actually an extension of the object budget but includes performance and program information. The performance budget which contains object categories is a well-balanced, effective system.

The performance budget in its pure form is intended to show unit costs for various activities, with performance goals varying in proportion to expense. As far as we know, there are no major police departments in the United States which operate under the pure performance-budgeting concepts shown in column 5 of Figure 11–1.

A form of performance budget, often known as a *program budget*, shows less detail and uses broader descriptive headings. The terms "performance" and "program," in fact, are often synonymous when used in the context of budgeting. The program budget is intended to identify the programs of the department, such as patrol service and traffic regulation. It is possible that a pure program budget does not exist in police service. Budgets commonly identified as "program" are in reality "departmental" budgets, as shown in column 2 of Figure 11–1. The difference is profound and should be understood; in a true program budget, a program such as criminal investigation includes the cost for conducting criminal investigations by patrol-division officers as well as

MANAGEMENT INFORMATION

those conducted by detectives in the criminal investigation division. The department or divisional budget, on the other hand, projects the cost for the entire operation of the division, regardless of the activities of those who are assigned to the division.

The difference between the two is even more pronounced if an attempt is made to break down programs into subprograms—e.g., from "criminal investigation" to "crimes-against-property investigation" and further to "burglary investigation." The departmental style of budget is utterly unable to cope with this sort of program definition, but the system which can make the basic, true program budget possible can easily be extended to provide for subprograms of all kinds.

Zero-base budgeting is a new form of program budgeting which differs somewhat from the conventional program format. In zero-base budgeting, the city council or manager establishes several potential levels of expenditure, and the operating department is then expected to describe the services it can perform at each level of expenditure for each program or activity. More about this form of budgeting will be presented in later pages.

The broadest theoretical extension of the program concept is the *functional budget,* mentioned in column 7 of Figure 11–1. It is the exact opposite of the line-item budget and has some value in program formulation but none at all for control during execution of the budget.

The Conventional Budget in Operation

More than any other aspect of police management, the budgeting process in the police department must conform to the budgeting and fiscal procedures in use in the general government for the jurisdiction. Most cities and counties and all states have some sort of organized system for development of the budget and its subsequent execution. Some units of government require a significant amount of advance planning, including presentation of preliminary budgets and estimates, and adherence to schedules. Usually, the executive head of the government—such as the mayor or city manager—takes a leadership role in setting out the schedule for budget preparation and in actual development of the budget, with strong support by the government's fiscal officer. The initial effort may well be a policy statement by the mayor or manager, intended to give constraints and guidelines to department heads, followed by a budget-development schedule.

In most cities, the department heads have an important role in budget development. The chief of police, for example, is expected to present a justifiable budget in complete detail, accompanied by arguments substantiating significant increases or changes in services or programs. (Theoretically, this includes recommendations for decreasing services or expenditures.) The chief is expected to put this information into standardized format. Obviously, the budget submitted by the police department must be compatible with the rest of the system. Giving detailed advice about a general governmental fiscal and budgeting system is beyond the scope of this book. The reader is referred to

ADMINISTRATION

such texts as *Management Policies in Local Government Finance*[1] for more information.

After the chief of police receives the budget message and schedule, he should issue his own instructions to bureau and division heads and to the staff planning and fiscal units. These instructions should reiterate the overall scheduling requirements and should explain the need for proper detail and justification in preparing budget items.

Bureau and division commanders should be brought into the budget-planning process in the earliest possible stages. Their ideas and proposals should be carefully considered in the preliminary development of the budget. Division commanders should, of course, have some responsibility for controlling budget expenditures for their units and also for submitting new or modified program and activity proposals. Commanders should submit their estimates to the administration shortly before the development of the formal budget document.

Justifying the Budget Regardless of the format of the budget, it will be no more effective than the arguments within it. While the chief may occasionally be able to persuade the decision makers through the strength and forcefulness of his personality, in the long run, he will require logic, care, and reason as allies in his cause.

The heart of the budget is found in the portion of the document intended for detail or substantiation. Justifications need not be lengthy, but they should clearly indicate the reason for the increased expenditure, as shown in the following example:

207 *Gasoline.* The increase is due to an estimated increase of 250,000 patrol miles because of additions to the number of patrol cars last year, plus a rise in gasoline cost.
250,000 miles $\div$ 12 miles/gal = 20,833 gal $\times$ 58¢ per gal = \$12,084

Similar justifications should accompany each code or item.

Adopting the Program or Performance Budget

Ever since the Hoover Commission first coined the term "performance budgeting," there has been a marked increase in the discussion (if not the use) of the concept at all levels of government. While the system is especially applicable to large cities with well-developed accounting procedures, the principles can be adopted to a city of any size, provided sophisticated machinery exists for processing information.

Needless to say, this form of budgeting cannot be utilized if the city as a whole has not adopted the concept. If it has, however, there are some unique

---

[1] J. Richard Aronson and Eli Schwartz, eds., *Management Policies in Local Government Finance*, International City Management Association, Washington, D.C., 1975.

MANAGEMENT INFORMATION

189

considerations which ought to be presented here because of the unusual demands of police operation; although many municipal work tasks can be thought of as highly discrete (for example, a water-meter reader may do nothing else but read meters and may do it all day long), the basic police task—patrol operation—depends upon the activity of the patrol officer and varies widely from minute to minute. At one minute the officer may be engaged in routine preventive patrol and in the next instant be engaged in criminal investigation; minutes later he may be rendering a noncriminal service such as helping a woman locked out of her home to gain admittance.

The difficulty in adapting the concept to police service is based on the extreme dependence on detailed activity sheets prepared by police officers themselves (backed up by command and control information, to be sure, but nevertheless dependent on individual reports from officers).

Once this difficulty is overcome, performance and effectiveness can be related to cost per unit. For example, the decision maker can decide whether he wants 20 percent clearance of burglaries at X dollars per unit of time or 30 percent clearance at Y dollars.

Adoption of a meaningful performance-budgeting system demands infinite patience and careful planning. Police employees and legislators alike must understand the objectives and advantages of the system, and both will have to adjust their activities to accommodate it.

The performance or program budget does not eliminate the need for detailed, written justifications in support of the budget. In fact, written statements justifying the budget make better sense with the program concept than with the line-item system. The program budget can be criticized by city councils when the programs are stated too broadly, without divisional or activity breakdown or without written justifications when they are appropriate. According to its advocates in other areas of government, the program budget actually improves legislative-executive relationships and promotes better planning, better public relations, improved decision making, and an overall increase in efficiency and economy. Finally, the system makes it possible to adopt a method of reporting which compares actual accomplishments with the budget plan. Monthly reports can be presented in terms of achievements in addition to dollar figures. Also, although program budgeting is sometimes opposed because of installation and operating costs, if the agency already has data-processing facilities this objection can be minimized.

Development of the System   Initially, the new budgeting concept should be operated simultaneously with the old procedure so that the two systems are parallel. In the first year, usual estimates and budget documents should be prepared. The appropriations for many programs will have to be estimated. Estimates with a margin of error of up to 10 percent will probably occur and should be expected. During each succeeding year's budgeting, however, it will be possible to refine estimates even more. At the end of five years, budgeting by major program should be made more accurate, and program costs should be clearly identifiable.

Each appropriation or allotment should be identified by object and by program code. Naturally, some expenditures will apply to more than one program, and an estimate of the cost for each program should be given a separate entry into the data bank. For example, a certain percentage of the salary portion of the budget should be earmarked for crime prevention and suppression, a certain percentage allocated to traffic control, and so on. How much of the actual output will prove to be spent for crime prevention and suppression can be resolved only when the budget is actually placed into operation and daily-activity reporting commences.

During execution, each expenditure (including salary expenditures) should show the same sort of coding—that is, by department, bureau, and division; by object; and finally by program. The Appendix gives an illustration of a code-numbering system recommended in IACP management studies. It should be stressed that the numbers are illustrative only and that a similar system can be developed which should be compatible with the account-numbering system used by any city having the machinery for program budgeting.

A key device in successful program budgeting in a police agency is the use of a detailed daily-activity report (see Appendix B). This is the only means by which personnel time can be identified by program and activity. When this system is adopted, each member of the department should complete the daily-activity report or have it completed for every day worked. After supervisory review, reports should be key-punched and information stored in the data bank. Information extracted from the report will be used in part of the preparation of the consolidated daily report (see Appendix B), which is an essential part of the management-information system, but its main purpose will be the formulation of the budget.

A summary report form designed to show the status of the budget is also illustrated in Appendix B. This two-page form is intended to show the status of the budget both by object and by program. Ultimately, this form should be modified by the addition of program activities shown in the suggested code-numbering guide. When this has been done, another column can be added to the right-hand margin of the form to show unit cost for many of these activities. The budget summary statement should be prepared monthly, semiannually, and annually. Semiannual statements (as well as statements for previous years, once the system is in operation) will, of course, be instrumental in preparing the next budget.

In the second year of operation, the department will not have to estimate program cost by pure guesswork. Personnel working on the budget will have a series of monthly statements from which they can prorate annual cost estimates for the next budget.

Execution of the budget during the second year will also be more accurate than the first year's experience. After about three years of this budget operation, a department can expect refinement and accuracy of program estimates. The budget should then serve as a planning device which translates programs into personnel, space, and equipment requirements and a reasonably accurate projection of the amount of money involved.

MANAGEMENT INFORMATION

Zero-Base Budgeting As indicated earlier, this concept is a new form of program budgeting. In zero-base budgeting, programs and subprograms are identified in much the same way as in regular program budgeting, described above. During the budget-formulation process, however, the city budget-making authority (such as the city council or city management) establishes several levels of expenditure for operating agencies to use as "targets."

For example, department heads may be asked to describe what level of services could be provided, say, for 85 percent of the current budget, for each activity now being contemplated. At the same time, the department may be asked to describe what could be provided for 100 percent of the current budget. A third level of expenditure is usually requested as well, for example, the level of service which could be provided for 115 percent of current funding.

Each combination of activity and funding level is called a "decision package." The decision package contains a brief description of the objectives of the activity, a section on resources required, and a section describing the services which can be performed at the specified level of expenditure.

When the decision packages are completed, the operating departments are expected to assign priorities to the various packages, arranging them in order of importance as determined by the department head. The decision packages and the priority list are then forwarded to the city manager or his staff for coordination with other departmental requests, additional assigning of priorities, and transmission to the authority which actually decides upon the budget.

Zero-base budgeting allows the budget-making authority to pick a level of services which fits the occasion and the resources of the city. For example, some programs in the police department might be viewed as requiring 115 percent funding, while others would be budgeted at the 85 percent level. Similarly, packages from some other city departments could be funded at various other levels.

Figure 11–3 illustrates a version of a decision-package format used in Arlington, Virginia.

Role of the Staff Planning Unit A great part of the budget planning and development work in the first year should be assumed by the research and development division. This unit can assist the fiscal officer with the program analysis, which is basic to this kind of budgeting, and aid in the integration of this process into an already-existing system of budgeting.

Purchasing

Most police departments use a purchasing system which is consistent with the practice followed in the other departments of the municipal government. Some concepts ought to be set out, nevertheless, so that the police administrator can influence the change for the better. A proper purchasing system usually begins with the preparation of a purchase requisition. Format ordinarily calls for a description of the item, its cost, the name of the vendor or vendors, the account number, and some reference to the division doing the purchasing. The form itself can suggest various instructions or regulations controlling the purchasing

DEPARTMENT _____ DIVISION _____ PAGE NUMBER _____ OF _____

ACTIVITY _____

CURRENT ACTIVITY PURPOSE, DESCRIPTION & OBJECTIVES:

PERSONNEL (MAN-YEARS) SERVICE CLASSIFICATION	FY '76 ACTUAL	FY '77 BUDGET	FY '78 RECOMM.	FISCAL SUMMARY	FY '76 ACTUAL	FY '77 BUDGET	FY '78 RECOMM.
				COST:			
				PERSONNEL			
				NON-PERSONNEL			
				TOTAL			
				REVENUE:			
				FEES			
				GRANTS & OTHER			
				TOTAL			
				NET GENERAL			
				FUND SUPPORT:			
				% CHANGE FROM FY '77			
TOTAL:				% OF DEPARTMENTAL			
TEMPORARY FUNDS (DOLLARS):				LOCAL BUDGET:			

PERFORMANCE MEASURES	FY '75	FY '76	FIRST HALF OF FY '77

ALTERNATIVE 1 – DESCRIBE CHANGE, IMPACT AND CONSEQUENCES:

PERSONNEL (MAN-YEARS) SERVICE CLASSIFICATION	FY '78 RECOMM.	FY '78 ALT. 1	FY '78 CHANGE	FISCAL SUMMARY	FY '78 RECOMM.	FY '78 ALT. 1	FY '78 (CHANGE +/−)
				COST			
				PERSONNEL			
				NON-PERSONNEL			
				TOTAL			
				REVENUE			
				FEES			
				GRANTS & OTHER			
				TOTAL			
				NET GENERAL			
				FUND SUPPORT:			
TOTAL:				% CHANGE FROM FY '78 RECOMMENDED......			
TEMPORARY FUNDS (DOLLARS):				% OF FY '78 RECOMM. BUDGET:			

ALTERNATIVE 2 – DESCRIBE CHANGE, IMPACT AND CONSEQUENCES:

PERSONNEL (MAN-YEARS) SERVICE CLASSIFICATION	FY '78 RECOMM.	FY '78 ALT. 2	FY '78 CHANGE	FISCAL SUMMARY	FY '78 RECOMM.	FY '78 ALT. 2	FY '78 (CHANGE +/−)
				COST			
				PERSONNEL			
				NON-PERSONNEL			
				TOTAL			
				REVENUE			
				FEES			
				GRANTS & OTHER			
				TOTAL			
				NET GENERAL			
				FUND SUPPORT:			
TOTAL:				% CHANGE FROM FY '78 RECOMMENDED......			
TEMPORARY FUNDS (DOLLARS):				% OF FY '78 RECOMM. BUDGET:			

Figure 11–3 Example of a decision-package format, zero-base budgeting.

MANAGEMENT INFORMATION 193

process, such as stating that a purchase below a certain amount need not have a formal purchase requisition at all or that an item costing more than a specified amount requires that a bidding procedure be invoked.

An important part of the purchasing procedure for major items is the inclusion of justification for the purchase. The justification should not be elaborate if the purchase is being made pursuant to an item which was requested in the police budget. It makes little sense to justify approval of an expenditure twice—first when the budget is approved and again at the time the purchase is being made. This is especially true in a conventional line-item type of budget system, in cases where each item is justified or explained. Justifications for any purchase should be brief and to the point and should be oriented more to identifying the proper account number than to examining the reason for the purchase.

Additional justification is required when a specified brand name for a unique product is sought. Purchasing agents very rightly resent the request of department heads or other employees who order a particular brand-name item which must be purchased separately, rather than a stock item from the warehouse, only because they saw the name in a certain vendor's catalog. Very often the purchaser within the department will use a brand name as a convenience in ordering an item, failing to realize the complications this may cause.

The purchase order itself is prepared after the requisition form is processed, and it is the document which authorizes the vendor to bill the city or the department. Whereas the requisition form can deal in generalities, the purchase order has to be exact in its description of merchandise. The typical purchase-order form carries instructions to the vendor for invoicing the city and often sets conditions of payment as well as delivery information.

Before the purchase requisition can be converted to purchase-order form, the transaction usually has to be checked against the budget to see that there is sufficient money for the purchase or, if an allotment system exists, to see that the purchase does not exceed the allotment for that period.

Approval of Invoices

An important part of the administrator's financial responsibility is the approval of invoices received from vendors so that the city can be assured the proper product was received and that it was delivered in good working order. In a small department this task might be carried out by the chief himself about once a month. If invoices are processed by a city fiscal department, sets of them can be physically brought to the police chief so that he can approve each expenditure. A rubber stamp can help in this process by providing a space for recording the proper department and the account number.

In larger departments, verifying the accuracy of invoicing must be carried out by personnel assigned to the department fiscal office. Many times these same people participated in the processing of purchase requisitions and

194 ADMINISTRATION

therefore have some knowledge of the transaction, but often they must call an operating division or other unit in the department to make certain that a product has been received in good condition.

Financial Statements

A necessary part of the management-information system is the preparation of timely financial statements so that the status of the budget items is readily apparent. The trend today, with more and more systems based on automated data processing, is to summarize budget accounts which are overexpended or close to being expended. A glance at the report can therefore disclose accounts which are "in trouble" on an exception basis. A budget item which is not in financial trouble would obviously not require checking before the requisition is made.

Usually, there should be a close relationship between the unit in the department which is responsible for purchasing and the property-and-stores system; having items in plentiful supply would obviously affect a decision to purchase.

If the government itself has a well-developed purchasing and warehousing system, some of the requirements for storage of property at the departmental level will be minimized. Departmental stores then need be concerned only with supplies and equipment which are in constant use in a department or which are highly specialized.

In automated management-information systems, the status of a budget account can immediately be queried through a terminal device. As a purchase requisition and a purchase order are processed, the deduction from a budget account can be made on a real-time basis. The system can also produce machine printouts of purchase orders as a by-product.

The ultimate in convenience for the preparation of a program budget is the computerized linkage of the daily-activity reporting system described earlier, with payroll information, so that printouts contain not only the man-hours necessary for carrying out each program and activity but also personnel cost.

ADMINISTRATIVE RECORDS AND FILING

There are perhaps as many systems for filing administrative papers as there are police departments. All departments, regardless of size, eventually require some means for classifying and filing the many papers, documents, memos, and letters which come in and out of the department and yet have very little to do with actual case reporting or other operational records. For example, if there is an administrative services bureau, most general administrative records should be placed within that bureau.

Failure to set up an adequate administrative file usually means that material is misfiled and difficult to locate, and the resulting searches waste time and energy. The failure is not critical, and for this reason administrative filing systems take second priority and often are undeveloped.

IACP usually recommends an administrative file based on classifica-

MANAGEMENT INFORMATION 195

tion by subject matter rather than by the name of the person who is sending the material or to whom it is to be sent. The file should also contain such subdivisions and further breakdowns to permit rapid search and proper cross-indexing.

An important part of the administrative file relates to personnel management. In an agency having a personnel division as part of an administrative services bureau, the location of personnel records is fairly unimportant. In cities separating the two functions, there is much more justification for departing from the concept of centralized records so that personnel records are maintained by employees of the personnel division itself because of their frequent need to refer to these documents.

Another exception which should be permitted is the location of internal investigations files if the function is not a part of an administrative services bureau. Although such files must be considered administrative in nature, they should be maintained by the personnel assigned to the internal investigations function.

Subsidiary Files In large departments there is often a need to establish some uniformity in the format of subsidiary files which are maintained at bureau, division, and sometimes section level. Bureau and division commanders must have some means for filing copies of correspondence they originate on administrative matters and for filing documents that are specifically directed to them. A convenient means for doing this is to require each of these subsidiary files to follow the major or primary classifications in the main administrative file in headquarters. This practice makes it far easier to adjust when a commanding officer is transferred from one unit to another, and it facilitates the task of supervisors and inspectors when the filing system is inspected.

ADMINISTRATIVE REPORTING

An essential part of a management-information system is the process of summarizing both administrative and operational facts so that trends can be identified and comparisons made to review weaknesses and to assist in the development of plans.

Fiscal reporting has already been discussed. The purpose of the following pages is to present some of the other reports which can be used to influence management decisions.

The use of data-processing equipment provides flexibility, speed, and accuracy in the compilation of data for monthly reports, for other summaries, and for the statistical studies so frequently requested by police executives and by outside agencies. Data-processing equipment is essential for the compilation of statistical summaries in departments of more than 150 officers, and while desirable in smaller ones, it is not essential, since all data may be tabulated by clerks either by continuous daily entries on master sheets or by reference to the original records and indexes at the time of compilation. Master sheets are not recommended except for very small departments because they present an unusual opportunity for errors that are hard to locate without starting a new sheet and because their accuracy is difficult to check.

The Daily Report   The consolidated daily report is an essential document in medium-sized to large departments. The police administrator and the commanding officers need current information on major crimes, accidents, and arrests and on officers not available for duty. This information should be tabulated in convenient form as a daily summary with columns to carry statistics for the current day and the current and previous months to date. Copies should be placed on the desks of the chief and the division heads before they report for duty. (The consolidated daily report is shown in Appendix C.)

Although some data might well be compiled on a weekly basis—particularly if they represent an activity which is newly developed or troublesome—most management information can be summarized on a monthly basis.

The Monthly Report   When police departments ultimately achieve true program budgeting, the kind of monthly summaries depicted in Appendix B will be highly significant. Such summaries will contain up-to-date material relating to basic departmental programs as well as to detailed subdivisions as necessary. For example, the amount of work for the "investigation-apprehension" program can be determined as well as the amount of time required to handle specific classifications within this general program. Comparisons can also be made for the various commands in larger departments. Until true program budgeting is in effect, however, monthly reports should be in a form convenient for analysis and comparison so as to reveal crime trends and the effectiveness of police units, procedures, and policies. The monthly report should include statistical summaries of complaints and other cases, arrests, traffic accidents and enforcement, juvenile offenses and police activities related thereto, laboratory accomplishments, identification-records activities, personnel matters, and maintenance costs and other expenditures. Tabulations should be carried in columns for the current month and the current and previous years to date.

Specialized Reporting   Keeping regular monthly statistics may not be necessary for certain administrative matters. For example, showing the progress of personnel recruiting may be necessary only every six months or so or if there is a shift in a trend.

One of the most wasteful practices in police departments today is the generation of near-useless statistical information. If the information is not used for any practical purpose, it should not be placed in the form of statistical summaries. Also, some administrators keep statistics solely for defensive purposes, i.e., "in case someone asks" about a situation or procedure. If this is the only reason the statistics are kept, they should be abandoned.

MANAGEMENT INFORMATION

The Annual Report The annual report usually consists of a summary of the monthly reports, and consequently most of the annual-report tables correspond to those of the monthly report, differing only in column arrangements and headings. Data considered not valuable enough to compile monthly usually are not compiled on an annual basis. One of the purposes of the annual report is to provide comparisons with the year just passed and previous years. The data for five-year comparisons can be presented satisfactorily when the annual report is printed. Limitations of space or the desire for greater simplicity, however, may limit the data to three years. Data for the current year and the year immediately preceding are invariably shown. The third column may be devoted to either the third or the fifth year.

Spot Maps Spot maps are useful to indicate the locations of police hazards and to furnish supervising officers with evidence of weaknesses in police service. The location of crime and accident hazards on maps aids in the direction of enforcement efforts and shows individual officers where their attention is most badly needed. Surveys of traffic hazards, supplemented by spot maps, frequently reveal highway-accident-inducing factors that may be eliminated by regulation or by change in roadway design.

Charts of Accomplishment Graphs showing accomplishments of the department as a whole, of the various divisions, and of individual officers are valuable in stimulating interest in the job, in developing competition, and in directing attention to operations in which the department appears to be weak. A competitive spirit is not limited to competition between individuals; an officer, a unit, or the entire department may attempt to improve a previous record.

Monthly totals and data for the current and previous years to date may be recorded by simple line graphs or bar charts or by thermometers or dials. If placed in a location where they may be reviewed by the public, these charts are useful in public reporting. Those which show the records of individuals, however, should not be on public display, although they may be posted at headquarters, where they may be reviewed by the persons concerned.

A detective-division chart may portray, month by month for each crime classification, the percentage of cases cleared by arrest, the percentage convicted, and the percentage of recovery of stolen property. The percentage for each of the preceding five years may also be shown for purposes of comparison. The accomplishment of the detective assigned to each class of crime is thus provided for the stimulation of the officer and the guidance of his or her supervisors.

Charts that show comparisons between months of the current and previous years and between previous yearly totals may be advantageously used for tabulating a variety of data: index crimes classified according to type; fatal, personal-injury, and property-damage motor-vehicle accidents; citations and notices of violation; arrest or enforcement indexes; and so on.

Chapter 12

Inspectional Services

The administrative functions of inspection and control permeate the entire organization. They are not performed exclusively by any one supervisor but are in process throughout the department. At each level of authority, supervisors must plan and direct the work of others. Thus must they inspect and control the activities of subordinates—from the chief down through each successive level to the officer who performs the task.

The extent to which police administrators should participate in the processes of control cannot be defined exactly because it is influenced by the organization and size of the department. In practice, their participation is influenced by the amount of time they must have available, their concept of the importance of a particular task, their interest in it, their confidence in the ability of their subordinates, and their own ability to delegate authority. Their responsibility for their successful accomplishment, however, must be emphasized.

Misdirected or capricious use of authority may do great harm; therefore, controls must be provided so that all who exercise authority will be held responsible for the consequences of their actions. "Control," states Gulick, "consists in seeing that everything is carried out in accordance with the plan which has been adopted, the organization which has been set up, and the orders

198

INSPECTIONAL SERVICES   199

which have been given . . . control is in a sense the consequence of command in action."[1] Authority cannot be delegated safely without this check.

ORGANIZATION AND STAFFING FOR INSPECTIONAL SERVICES

In most modern police departments, the activity embraced by the term "inspectional services" may include inspection of persons, property, and procedures; the investigation of personnel; and (with less regularity) intelligence or vice control. Although the first two functions are seemingly similar, in actual practice the role of the inspector is very different from that of the internal investigator. Both functions are nevertheless logically grouped under one commander in a major department, even though it may be necessary to have personnel with different aptitudes assigned to the two functions.[2]

The head of the department must keep informed on matters that vitally affect police operations. Some relevant facts are reflected in police records, but the chief must have firsthand information in order to operate successfully. In all but the small departments the chief needs assistance in order to have this information available at all times, and in the largest departments these inspectional duties may be so continuous and of such broad scope that a separate bureau may be required. Students should keep in mind the analogy mentioned in relation to Chart 8 when studying Chart 21—that is, they should understand that the functions implicit in the titles of the various sections must usually be performed to some degree in every department by someone.

Staffing the Inspections Unit

In medium-sized departments, the formal inspections function may be assigned to one or more staff officers who can be given the working title of "inspector." If there are several inspectors, their duties should be divided according to the functions inspected rather than territorially or by time of day. Platoons in both the territorial and functional units are inspected by the heads of their districts and divisions, and the inspector likewise should deal with the work of the district or of the functional unit as a whole. Inspectors are more likely to do so when they have the responsibility for inspecting the operation throughout the 24 hours.

In larger departments it may be necessary to "overrank" the inspection functions to enable inspectors to carry out their responsibilities. Although inspectors are theoretically staff officers acting on behalf of the chief of police, inspectors who have substantially lower rank than the supervisors of the units most often inspected will encounter difficulty in being objective and may suffer from not being able to react to criticism and pressure from people who outrank

[1]Luther Gulick, *Papers on the Science of Administration,* Institute of Public Administration, New York, 1937, p. 78.
[2]Additional information on internal investigation will be found later in this chapter. Intelligence and vice-control activities are covered in Chap. 19.

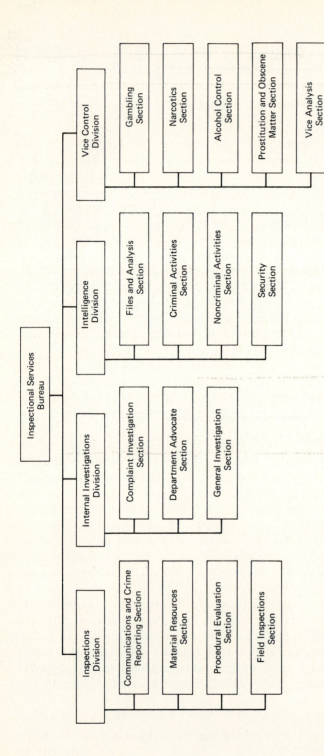

Chart 21 Organization of an inspectional services bureau in a large department.

200

INSPECTIONAL SERVICES

them. Persons assigned to the inspectional services bureau, and in particular to the inspections division, should have adequate rank to carry out their purpose. For example, if the common rank for platoon commander of the patrol division is lieutenant and if it is obvious that inspectors will be required to be in contact with platoon lieutenants in each district, the officer assigned to inspectional duties should be a captain or higher.

Staffing Other Inspectional Services Units

The considerations for rank mentioned above should not have a great bearing on the staffing of the internal investigations, intelligence, and vice-control functions unless the department has substantial problems involving unethical activity and dishonesty among high-ranking officers. Most personnel investigations involve officers of lower rank. There is, however, an urgent requirement for strength of character, loyalty, and absolute integrity in those selected for these investigative assignments.

Division of responsibilities among internal investigators can be made on the basis of whether the activity performed is overt or covert in nature, and in very large departments it is possible to assign officers to specialized units, such as the investigation of brutality cases and bad-debt cases.

INSPECTION AS AN IMPLEMENT OF CONTROL

Accountability of Command

Although they may free themselves of the actual performance of the tasks involved, superior officers cannot rid themselves of an iota of responsibility for the accomplishment of these tasks. They may delegate to a subordinate the authority to perform a task, and they may tell the subordinate that he or she is responsible for successful conclusion of the assignment, but they remain accountable for its final accomplishment.

Rule of Control Authority is delegated by some form of command; responsibility is effectively placed by some form of control. Delegated authority should be accompanied by accountability, but the responsibility lies dormant until the consequences of the use of authority are ascertained. Until then there is no basis on which to hold the user accountable. The effective placing of responsibility or the act of holding accountable involves an evaluation of the manner in which the authority was exercised, hence the rule of control: *The person who gives an order must ascertain that it has been properly executed.*

It is relatively easy to delegate authority by giving a command, but to determine the manner in which the order was carried out so that the subordinate may be held responsible is often difficult. The process of inspection is the one key to this determination.

Control, therefore, is implemented by inspection, i.e., a critical review or examination involving careful scrutiny and analysis. In some cases inspection may be accomplished by simple observation; in other instances, it may involve inquiry or the analysis of records and statistics.

Need for Inspection   Since law enforcement is almost entirely a personal service, every condition in a police organization and its environment is traceable in a large measure to the acts of police officers and to the success or failure of their operations. If every member of the force were a paragon of virtue, industry, and judgment as well as omniscient in matters of department procedures and regulations, there would be no need for control of personnel; orders would be carried out exactly as planned, and inspections would be pointless.

This not being the case, police officers are subject (though to a lesser degree) to the usual frailties of mankind; consequently, periodic inspections are necessary. Failures and errors may thus be corrected before they assume serious proportions, and weaknesses may be ferreted out and often overcome by modifying procedures or instructions. Even more important than this is the wholesome effect that inspection has on officers who know that their work will be scrutinized critically. They become more painstaking in their efforts and are less likely to be guilty of neglect, errors, and poor judgment. Similarly, inspections raise morale because members of the force can then expect to receive credit for good work.

Purpose of Inspection   The purpose of inspection is fourfold: (1) To learn whether the task is being performed as outlined. Are regulations and procedures being complied with? Has the operation developed as planned? (2) To learn whether the anticipated results are being realized. Does the operation accomplish what was expected of it? (3) To discover whether the resources of the department are being utilized to the best advantage. (4) To reveal the existence of need, thus accomplishing the first step in planning.

Although inspection may uncover an unsatisfactory condition that is evidence of need, the condition by itself may not reveal the exact nature of the need. For example, noncompliance with regulations and procedures, unsatisfactory results and conditions, and failure to use department resources to best advantage may indicate a need for additional or modified organization, regulations, procedures, equipment, manpower, training, direction, or leadership; but further study and analysis by the planning division and the operating units concerned will usually be necessary to determine in which of these areas the primary weakness lies.

Scope of Inspection

Everything relating to the police department must be subject to control, and consequently inspection must be made of everything involved in the police organization and its manifold operations. Conditions, situations, and actions that contribute to the success or failure of police operations are exposed by the inspection of persons, things, procedures, and results. Obviously, the inspection process cannot be sharply divided among these four classifications because of the interrelationships involved. The following examples of inspection make this fact apparent.

INSPECTIONAL SERVICES

Persons Determination of the health and physical appearance of the force calls for an examination of individuals. Compliance with regulations on grooming, diet, and fitness may be ascertained by a casual visual (and sometimes olfactory) inspection, whereas matters of health may require a thorough medical and laboratory examination. Morale and personality, both important factors in successful police operations, may be appraised only in part by observing the individual officer; a more accurate appraisal may require examination of the things the person uses and of his or her thoughts, attitudes, actions and reactions, and accomplishments.

Things The physical inspection of things indicates whether repair and replacement are needed; it may also reveal the extent of compliance with regulations. This inspection cannot be allowed to become casual or superficial. Every item and aspect of the police building, offices, cell spaces, and corridors; all police vehicles and the police garage; the laboratory and its equipment; department and privately owned weapons; uniforms and uniform equipment; records, files, and other office equipment; officers' notebooks; radio and communications equipment; supplies of every kind; physical evidence; prisoners' property—all must be regularly inspected to determine whether they are in good condition and suitably cared for as required by the particular regulations governing their maintenance and use.

Procedures and Actions Conformity with procedures designed for use during the tour of duty, such as the inspection of hazards, the questioning of suspicious persons, the handling of violators, the investigation of crimes or accidents, the interrogation of suspects and witnesses, and the search and transportation of prisoners, may be determined more accurately by observation of acts than by analysis of the results or study of reports covering the particular incident. Obviously, not every action can be observed; the observation of some, such as the stopping of suspicious characters and the arrest of violators, will be difficult and infrequent. It is nevertheless important that inspections be made often to determine whether department procedures are being followed.

Results An examination of results indicates the success of the operation; it also indicates whether each task was performed in the manner outlined and whether the resources of the department were used to best advantage. In addition, it may reveal needs not previously discovered. The inspection of results includes the analysis of statistics, the examination of reports of incidents, and the determination of public reactions. In research and analysis, inspection goes hand in hand with planning.

Line and Staff Inspection

Inspection is of two kinds: (1) an authoritative or line inspection, conducted by those in direct control of the persons and things being inspected, to see that tasks are satisfactorily performed; and (2) a staff inspection conducted by those who lack this direct control but who have the responsibility to determine whether the job has been satisfactorily completed by those who do the work and how well the authoritative inspection has been carried out. In the latter case, results and findings of the inspection must ordinarily be reported to someone in direct command for action, whereas in the former, the one making the inspection should apply the rule of control; it is this person's duty to take direct action to see that the job is properly performed.

Line Inspection Line inspection, made by superior officers charged with responsibility for the completion of an operation, is the more or less continuous inspection of the process of doing the task, which is essential if the superior officer is to ensure satisfactory accomplishment by holding his or her subordinates to account. Control, inherent in command, follows the channels of authority, and consequently none of the problems that might arise is distinct from those of command.

As long as the chief gives an order directly to the person who is to execute it, as in a small department, inspection is fairly simple, since it is a part of the task of supervision. As the chain of command is lengthened, however, the inspectional process becomes more complicated because those responsible for seeing that the task is accomplished are further removed from the one who actually performs it.

For example, in a small department, the chief might order a patrol officer to enforce a certain regulation and would ascertain by personal inspection that the order was being carried out. In a large department such an order, emanating from the chief, would not be given directly to the patrol officer but would descend through several levels of authority—an assistant chief, captain, lieutenant, and sergeant—and each level is accountable to a superior. This delegation down the chain of command involves no complications; but knowledge of the results, necessary if those at each level of authority are to be held accountable, ascends to the chief with difficulty.

Application of the Rule of Control The chief's main interest is to know that his order has been executed, which is his application of the rule of control. He is not interested primarily in ascertaining the suitability of the orders issued on the basis of his command. The urgent nature of most police operations makes it impossible for the chief to preview each order issued by his subordinates, and limited time makes it impossible for him to review each order. Neither does he care to know that the orders were issued, and consequently he would not expect subordinates to report the fact of issuance; that is not the essence of the responsibility. His primary concern is that his order has been carried out—not the form and methods used in its execution.

Inspection of Direction and Supervision How, then, is each officer in the chain of command to ascertain that the order which he has issued has been complied with so that the rule of control may be applied at each level? The sergeant's day-by-day supervision enables him to obtain this information by

INSPECTIONAL SERVICES   205

frequent and regular inspection. The lieutenant, also responsible for the accomplishment of the task, delegates the necessary authority to his sergeant, but he can hold the sergeant responsible only by ascertaining that the task has been performed. He could personally supervise its performance, but his limited time makes this impractical; that is why lieutenants have sergeants. They must therefore discover by some other means whether a task has been accomplished. They will watch for reports that may indicate lack of attention, and they will make sample inspections to learn whether a regulation is being enforced. This inspection is essential if sergeants are to be held responsible for the authority granted to them. Captains have recourse to the same inspectional procedures to determine whether lieutenants are holding their sergeants responsible. Inspection is essential at each level of authority to ascertain that the job has been done. At each successively higher level, the amount of inspection by sampling is decreased, and thus the justification for staff assistance is increased. More importantly, the chief will need to know whether his line commanders are carrying out their responsibilities for line inspection at every level.

Staff Inspection   Staff inspection itself is divided into two categories. The first relates to, or may be part of, *functional supervision* and is most commonly encountered when the line commander lacks the necessary technical skill (sometimes accompanied by a lack of interest) to inspect technical work carried out by subordinates. For example, the crime laboratory may inspect the work and equipment of evidence technicians assigned to a field operations bureau. Lack of time may also result in staff inspection used in this sense; for example, a vehicle-maintenance unit may routinely carry out inspection ordinarily handled by patrol sergeants. Similarly, a records officer may be assigned to review case reports on behalf of the line supervisor.

Staff inspection in this first category also includes the informal interest and supervision which exist when one operating division develops a procedure which is then carried out by another or when one division's work is the outgrowth of another's—such as the dependence of follow-up criminal investigations upon the quality of patrol-division preliminary investigations. In this case, staff inspection must be carefully controlled and coordinated so that effective and friendly working relationships are maintained. Affirmative action taken as a result of informal inspection of this sort must be carried out by a common supervisor.

The second category of staff inspection relates to the *general requirement to conduct inspections on behalf of the chief* by a formal staff inspection unit (or a staff officer assigned to inspections) to ensure control over the total operation of the department and its personnel and to make certain that line supervisors are effectively discharging their responsibilities. The balance of this section will be devoted to the function of formal staff units intended to fulfill this requirement.

Inspections by the Staff Unit

The functional assignment of duties, as shown in Chart 21 under "Inspections Division," encompasses all phases of inspectional needs discussed earlier, i.e., conditions, situations, and actions as they are affected by persons, things, procedures, and results. The inspections undertaken by the inspections division should not duplicate those performed by the intelligence unit, the internal investigations unit, and the vice-control division. They will, however, often enhance the effectiveness of the work of these divisions. For example, the inspector who discovers discrepancies in some area of crime reporting may at the same time be uncovering evidence of a breach of integrity in some member of the force. This is not the primary aim of the inspector, however, who is interested chiefly in discovering and pinpointing specific areas where irregularities or weaknesses occur and in keeping supervisory officers informed about them so that corrective action may be taken.

The inspections listed in the first three sections under "Inspections Division" in Chart 21 are conducted continuously but largely on an unscheduled spot-check basis. Field and headquarters inspection teams, on the other hand, make scheduled, simultaneous inspection of these aspects of the department's operations. They may spend several days inspecting a district station, for example, and will examine in minute detail every phase of building maintenance, care of equipment, and records of every kind, as well as check on methods of handling calls for service, and so on.

Because of the nature of their duties, inspectors should have flexible working hours; each day they should select the hours that will prove most productive. They should submit in advance weekly schedules showing the hours to be worked, but deviations from these should be expected when conditions require it. They should report matters that deserve present or future attention as they are discovered.

A Straightforward Process   Inspection conducted by the line supervisor is usually informal, without a sharp distinction between the casual observation involved in supervision and the somewhat more orderly observation which is characteristic of inspection. When inspection is formalized, however, it should be conducted in an open, straightforward way—whether carried out by line supervisors or staff inspectors. Inspection carried out by stealth (such as searching lockers in the absence of the tenants) is certain to have undesirable effects on morale, and the conditions which the inspector tries to observe will be driven underground. Also, the staff inspector should not operate in such a manner as to lull personnel into thinking he is not actually inspecting. *The staff inspector should never allow employees to believe he is doing anything else but inspecting.*

The Inspector's Relationships   One of the inspector's important duties is to report to the chief, for corrective action, unsatisfactory conditions that can be disposed of in no other way.

INSPECTIONAL SERVICES 207

The inspector's relationship with the chief, best established by regularly scheduled conferences, is influenced by the extent to which the chief wishes to participate in corrective action. The inspector should not, in his desire to shield the chief, fail to reveal information of great importance and also information of less importance that he has reason to believe the chief might want. In order to establish a suitable relationship, the inspector must learn to recognize the type of information wanted by the chief and should err on the side of providing too much rather than too little.

The inspector must establish a relationship with operating personnel that will enable him to deal frankly and directly with them, using persuasion, suggestion, and personal request rather than commands to correct irregularities without the assistance of high authority. To establish this relationship, it is necessary that inspectional duties be performed by a police officer whose maturity, experience, morality, integrity, judgment, character, and personality command the respect and admiration of all members of the force. A desirable relationship is further promoted by an attitude of friendliness reflected in the officer's demeanor, voice, and facial expression and evidenced by a willingness to be helpful and by an interest in the welfare and personal problems of the members of the department.

The inspector must be circumspect in relations with both commanding officers and subordinates in order to avoid friction. The inspector's findings and any resultant suggestions or requests to subordinates should be reported punctiliously to the commanding officer with further recommendations. Care must be used in making suggestions and requests, especially to subordinates, to avoid creating the impression that they are commands. A good relationship between operations personnel and those engaged in staff inspections is vital to the success of this kind of supervision. The relationship is a delicate one, and desirable results are achieved only when it is worked out to the satisfaction of all concerned.

Since the officer who makes a staff inspection lacks direct control over the subject of the inspection, what is this officer to do when an unsatisfactory condition is discovered? In order to effect correction, someone must call the matter to the attention of the officer at fault. A too literal interpretation of the principle of unity of command may lead to the conclusion that the officer engaged in staff inspections should be restricted to reporting the matter through official channels to the superior officer who has command of both the operating and the inspecting officers. In all but the large departments, this procedure would necessitate reporting nearly all matters to the chief and, consequently, would defeat one of the important purposes of staff inspections. The evils of unnecessarily delaying corrective action and the desirability of lessening the routine duties of commanding officers justify cutting across the lines of direct authority when this may be done without jeopardizing harmonious working relationships. For example, the report-review officer cuts across the lines of authority by reporting matters directly to the immediate superior of the officer involved. The lines can be successfully cut across only by friendly discussion—not by command. The level at which this can be done without friction is influenced by the personalities involved, their willingness to give and take, and the esprit of the organization.

Operating personnel should be instructed in the true character of staff inspection and should recognize it as a service rather than as a device for catching them in a dereliction of duty. When all members of the force understand the purpose and character of staff inspection, it can be used to the fullest extent to relieve commanding officers of heavy burdens and to promote a constructive and harmonious relationship between personnel of various units.

Appraisal of Intangibles The inspector should spend most of the time inspecting operations and conditions concerning which there is no other way to receive reliable information. It is in the inspection of these latter, less tangible things that the inspector will render the greatest service to the chief.

Personal observation will enable the inspector to ascertain the fidelity with which department procedures are being followed, to appraise the officers' morale and their attention to duty, to evaluate public reactions to the police and their programs, and to determine the conditions on the streets, in headquarters, and in station houses at all hours of the day or night. Rather than being restricted to what can be seen, the inspector will discuss duties and the manner of their performance with subordinate and superior officers alike and in this way will discover the competence of officers, the adequacy of training, and the suitability of department procedures, as well as the personnel and equipment needs of the department.

Concentration on Important Matters The inspection process can suffer needlessly when inspections are directed toward meaningless or perfunctory activities. Even when the inspection is carried out with the best of intentions, it can be subject to misinterpretation and downright exaggeration if caution is not exercised regarding the importance of the subject matter. Several years ago, for example, a newly established inspectional program in the Metropolitan Police Department in Washington, D.C. (which is subject to a measure of control by the United States Congress), was severely criticized by an influential member of the Senate, who rebuked the new unit for making an incidental reference to a station clock face which was so dirty that it was difficult to tell the time. The senator criticized the inspectional effort on the grounds that police had more important business than to look for dirty clocks. The lesson to be learned here is that an inspector should consider things in the context of what is immediately important and what can wait.

Timeliness of Inspection When possible, inspection should be concurrent, or at least close in time, with an event. Inspection carried out long after an incident or act takes place is analogous to shutting the barn door after the horse has gotten out. Corrective action is also more meaningful when memories are fresh.

INSPECTIONAL SERVICES

The Concept of Control Points A "control point" is a logical or natural point in any process which lends itself to review. Quite often a control point occurs when an action is documented (such as the recording of complaint information on a case-control form by the dispatcher) or when responsibility shifts from one person to another. For example, the review of reports by a sergeant and the matching of reports with information received initially by the complaint officer or dispatcher are natural control points. Concentration of formal inspection at control points already established is therefore an effective device.

Control Points Should Be Widespread Inspection of a total operation is seldom possible, making it necessary to concentrate on a few control points. However, these points should be distributed widely so that effort is not focused solely on one phase of operation to the neglect of another. These points can and should be varied from time to time to avoid unnecessary predictability of the process.

Control Points Should Emphasize the Important As indicated earlier, paying attention to unimportant details can be risky in terms of public and legislative support, and it is usually detrimental to department morale. Using a relatively unimportant procedure as a control point should be avoided. In many cases during IACP surveys, consultants have found that departmental inspectors have rigorously checked such things as the freshness of the ammunition in patrol officers' service revolvers but have ignored personnel disciplinary infractions and lapses in supervision which were taking place directly in front of them.

The Cost of Inspections It must be mentioned that the cost of carrying out any inspectional service (or, for that matter, any administrative or staff activity) must be weighed against the benefit. For example, if it costs $25 to describe a deficiency and the deficiency itself accounts for only a $20 waste of taxpayers' money, it makes little sense to go to such an expense to describe or correct it unless the deficiency is likely to be repeated.

For example, regular inspections to ascertain that employees are making economical use of a product—such as the proper grade of paper—are unjustifiable if the inspection process costs more than the difference in the cost of paper.

Frequency of Inspection The interval between inspections can be very important to the process. Such key activities as reviewing crime-report classification and spot-checking follow-up investigation reports should take place on a weekly basis. Other activities, such as the inspection of facilities, can take place quarterly or semiannually. Of course, the degree of the problem has a strong bearing on the frequency of inspection; if an activity or process is being done well, the need for inspection is less critical.

Staff Inspection of Line-Inspection Reports The inspector should promote the inspectional process throughout the organization, and his or her activities should stimulate, rather than retard, inspections by other members of the force.

Daily inspections of some aspects of the condition of personnel and matériel should be made by line officers. For example, at the beginning of each tour of duty, sergeants should inspect the jail and the department-owned vehicles.

Weekly or monthly formal inspections by line officers should also be carried out and should be documented by means of checklists which form a record of inspectional activity. These records can then be made available to staff inspectors as well as line commanders.

Police inspectors should rely heavily on reports submitted by operating personnel on these periodic inspections in order to lessen their own work load and to ensure a more complete inspection. Suitably designed reports, when correctly and accurately prepared, promptly submitted, and used according to wisely conceived procedures, reveal much essential information and diminish the need for additional inspectors. Also, through the use of suitable reports that can be occasionally spot-checked, the inspector has more free time for making the personal inspections that will ensure that conditions are satisfactory or reveal that some need correction.

A major advantage of the review of operational-inspection reports is that they stimulate the interest and attention of operating personnel by forcing them (1) to make periodic inspections that might otherwise be neglected and (2) to state that conditions are either satisfactory or unsatisfactory. For example, if a patrol officer is required to submit a periodic report on the vice conditions on his beat, he will make a greater effort to learn whether such conditions exist. One of his principal tasks is to know the conditions on his beat, and failure to know is as much a dereliction of duty as failure to take action in the face of such knowledge. When he states that vice exists on his beat, he is then bound by department regulations to take some action against it or to report it to the vice division. If he periodically reports that vice is present on his beat at a certain location and that he has reported the condition to the vice division, then the inspector must ascertain why the vice division has permitted the condition to persist.

One purpose of the inspector's performing the personal inspection is to be assured of the accuracy of the reports of the operating personnel. Inaccuracies will arise from carelessness and indifference in inspection or in preparation of the report or from a deliberate misrepresentation of facts. Additional instructions for the person making the inspection and preparing the report and for his or her supervising officer should eradicate the former; removal from the force may be necessary in the case of deliberate misrepresentation. Either of these actions, of course, would be initiated by order of the chief.

Follow-up　A key element for the success of a formal inspection system is the certainty of action taken to remedy a deficiency. If the inspection process

INSPECTIONAL SERVICES

continually reveals inadequacies which remain uncorrected, the system will soon become perfunctory.

Many times, operating personnel will bring attention to a matter which they feel inspectors should report to higher authority. Although reporting back to operating personnel is not within the scope of duties of inspectors, the administrator should make certain that the results of corrective action are made known to the inspectors—not only so that they can, if necessary, inform operating personnel of action to be taken but also to satisfy the inspectors themselves. In a large department, several months may go by before an inspection schedule brings the team into the same areas for repeat inspections. The quality of work of inspectors is improved when they realize that constructive action is taken with respect to their views.

Inspection Procedures Inspection procedures for the guidance of the inspections-unit personnel should be outlined in the same manner as procedures for all other police operations. When adequate inspection procedures have been established, the chief may be more confident that the entire organization is operating as planned.

A listing of the purpose and nature of inspections is presented in Appendix E. This material can become the basis for a general order establishing an inspections program.

Inspection Standards Every inspectional observation must be accompanied by a judgment as to whether a predetermined standard is being met. The standard in some cases might be simply compliance with the law or a police regulation rather than a performance standard. It follows, therefore, that inspection of procedures and operations will not be fully effective unless such standards exist—either formally or informally. The inspectional services staff can render a most useful service by assisting other units in the development of performance and operational standards.

INTERNAL INVESTIGATION

Over the past decade there has been considerable sentiment expressed by persons outside law enforcement to establish civilian review boards to investigate or adjudicate allegations against police. Undoubtedly a part of the reason for this has been the tendency of police to avoid making fair and vigorous investigations of wrongdoing within their ranks. What has been described as the "blue veil of protection" has all too often been drawn over police transgressions. There are numerous reasons for this, among them the feeling among police that they are vilified by a growing segment of the public and therefore must band together for self-protection. Some misguided administrators may believe that conducting a vigorous internal investigation is tantamount to admitting failure. The opposite, of course, is closer to the truth.

It is clearly apparent that if the police do not take a vigorous stand on the matter of internal investigation, outside groups—such as review boards consisting of laymen or other persons outside the police service—will step into the void.

When a complaint is registered against a police officer by a supervisor, a slightly different attitude is likely to prevail. Departments often pursue cases of this sort with more enthusiasm than they exhibit when handling a complaint initiated by a citizen, since the element of insubordination is often present, or at least there is the probability that a supervisor in the department has a vested interest in seeing that disciplinary action is taken.

Police work is unlike any other vocation in a number of ways, all of which contribute to the problem of misconduct and the frequency of complaints:

- Police service is one of the few occupations in which a substantial part of the clientele does not appreciate the service, and police are sometimes asked by others to ignore violations of the law for one reason or another.
- Most police are conspicuous in attire and in their vehicles, making their actions—both good and bad—more noticeable.
- Enforcement of the law often creates resentment, which sometimes becomes vindictive and personal.
- Police officers are exposed to temptations not often found in other forms of work.
- Officers in the field usually work without direct supervision, a fact that creates additional opportunity for misconduct.
- The public tends to be more critical of police, who are expected to exhibit a higher level of conduct and behavior than others. When they do not exhibit this higher degree of good conduct, complaints are justifiable.
- The nature of the work occasionally attracts persons who have antisocial or brutal tendencies.
- Emotion-charged situations are frequently encountered during police contacts such as arrests and interviews at crime scenes. The emotion can obscure the reason and judgment of both police officers and citizens.

Personnel complaints, both justified and unjustified, will be made from time to time. Police administrators should realize that the practice of smothering a complaint, depending upon a complainant to supply all the initiative, or failing to take formal investigative action, will ultimately lead to the type of situation which the administration may have sought to avoid in the first place—loss of public confidence and police morale.

Organization of the Formal Internal Investigations Function

Disciplinary control ordinarily commences at lower levels of supervision. In most departments, sergeants generally handle minor transgressions on an informal basis. More serious transgressions are traditionally handled by higher-ranking officers in the hierarchy.

INSPECTIONAL SERVICES   213

In the absence of a formalized internal investigations unit, this sort of investigation should usually be carried out by line personnel in the chain of command in which the offender is located. Investigations of this sort should not be assigned to detective personnel or other operating personnel.

In large departments, an internal investigations division should be established to exercise staff supervision over all internal investigations and to conduct the actual investigations in selected cases. The internal investigations unit should have the responsibility for recording, registering, supervising, and controlling the investigation of complaints against officers and for ferreting out evidence of corruption within the force. The operation of this unit protects the reputation of the department by establishing, through complete and objective investigation, that any allegation of misconduct made against a police officer, regardless of the source, is either sustained by evidence or not so sustained; that, although the alleged act did occur, the officer was exonerated; or that the act did not occur and the case was unfounded.

In departments of fewer than 1,000 officers, the internal investigations function can be carried out without the need for further subdivision of the unit. In larger agencies, however, it is necessary to group the activities of the unit in some logical way, such as shown in Chart 21. Other variations are possible, as indicated below. In its survey of the Metropolitan Police Department in Washington, D.C., IACP recommended the following division of duties in the internal investigations unit:

- Complaint investigations section. The responsibilities of this section include staff supervision of the investigations carried out by line commanders and the investigation of most serious complaints made against departmental personnel.
- Administrative section. The purpose of this section is to receive, file, and process all complaints against departmental employees and to serve as liaison with the trial board and complaint-review board.
- General investigations section. This section should be given the responsibility of conducting confidential investigations affecting departmental personnel, with work to be initiated at the direction of the chief of police. Since personnel are required to work covertly at times, security should be observed in the operations of such a unit and in reporting the results of its activities.

The Internal Investigations Process

Creation of an internal investigations unit does not relieve command personnel of the need to maintain discipline. On the contrary, it strengthens it by providing assistance to commanders, on request, in the investigation of alleged misconduct of their subordinates. In addition, this investigative unit supervises, for the chief, all disciplinary investigations by commanders.

The existence of this investigative unit should be given publicity in order to lessen the tendency of the public to condemn all police officers because of failure to punish one wrongdoer. Its function and its role must be completely explained to the members of the department; they must understand that the internal investigations unit is as eager to establish innocence as guilt.

In the course of investigating persons engaged in vice and organized crime, the intelligence and central vice units may discover indications of possible involvement of members of the force that justify thorough examination. Such discoveries should be reported immediately by the head of the unit to the chief so that he may assign an investigation either to his internal division or to an investigator selected for this specific assignment.

Ferreting Out Violations The department may learn or suspect that unidentified officers are accepting gratuities for special favors, ignoring violations by favored persons, soliciting or accepting bribes, giving forbidden information to lawyers and bond brokers, stealing or extorting money from prisoners, "rolling" drunks, working in league with vice operators, and so on. The internal investigations unit must use various undercover techniques to ferret out violations of this nature and to produce evidence that will bear out allegations against the officers. When such evidence is found, the chief or the commanding officers of the accused should proceed as with any other complaint against a member of the force, and where the seriousness of the offense warrants it, an arrest should be made and charges preferred.

Registration A register should be kept at a constantly manned post in the division. All commanders and supervisors should be required to report by telephone within an hour any alleged or suspected violations of law, ordinance, or department rules by members or employees and to obtain a register number. The register should contain spaces for the registration number, name, rank, badge number, and duty assignment of the alleged violator; the date and hour of the first entry and of receipt of the first written report; the date the case was considered by the department disciplinary board; and the date of the final action by the chief. There should be no index to the book, and access to it should be limited to the chief and to his highest-ranking commanders in the internal investigations unit.

Supervisors and commanders must exercise some discretion in registering rule violations that are observed by them and disposed of by oral reprimand, in contrast to violations that are reported to them by citizens. It should be within the rights of unit commanders to give written reprimands and to excuse an officer from one tour of duty without pay or to require the officer to work gratis on one or two off-duty days without having to preprocess such decisions through the department's disciplinary machinery. Such actions, however, in contrast to oral reprimands, should be reported to the internal investigations division for review to ensure their justification and for processing so that they will be recorded in the personnel file. In the event that an action is found to be

INSPECTIONAL SERVICES   215

unjustified, it should be rescinded by the chief, and the officer should be compensated for any loss that may have been sustained.

In many agencies, there is no appeal available to an officer for oral or written reprimand which remains at a lower level in the department (i.e., not in the officer's departmental or city personnel-office file). But when the disciplinary action consists of formal written reprimand which can have an effect on promotion or failure to receive a pay increase or when loss of pay is involved, appeal is usually provided as a remedy.

Investigations Each district or division should conduct investigations initiated by it or assigned to it by the internal investigations unit. When the charges are very serious or relate to a criminal act, the assistance of the internal investigations unit may be requested. This unit may retain control of the investigation in cases of alleged misconduct that come to its attention other than by report from the officer's supervisor or commander.

The investigation usually will encompass several stages, and the watch commander who initiated it should be required to submit a report to the internal investigations division and to submit a copy through normal channels before going off duty. A report should be obtained from the accused officer, and finally a report of the findings of the investigation and a recommendation for action must be made.

The first recommendation for action should come from the lowest command level so that in the case of an officer's having been found guilty of the charge, he or she will not feel that a summary sentence has been given. The recommendation should pass up the channels to the chief, each level reviewing all previous recommendations. The various suggestions may then be assessed and reevaluated by the internal investigations unit before the case is finally presented to the chief.

When a charge against an officer is not sustained by the investigation, he or she should be notified in writing of the final disposition, and the case should be closed. No records should be placed in the personnel file to show that the officer has been the object of an investigation. When charges are sustained, the disciplinary action taken should become part of the officer's personnel record, but the record of the investigation will remain with the internal investigations unit.

Disciplinary Action

When severe disciplinary action has been recommended, the chief should appoint a department disciplinary board composed of members of the force, none having a rank below that of the officer charged, to review the facts of the case, to make further investigation when necessary, and to submit a recommendation for action. While department regulations may establish the relative ranks of board members, it is best that they be selected by the chief on the basis of their competence and fairness. Before disciplinary action is imposed, an officer should be accorded the right to a hearing before the department disciplinary board, if he or she so desires.

The use of a disciplinary board in this manner relieves the chief of some of the onus of disciplinary action, and it diminishes the likelihood of capriciousness and hastiness. On the other hand, since it makes only a recommendation to the chief, the board does not deprive him of his power of control over his personnel. For example, the Los Angeles Police Department designates a commissioned officer to serve as department advocate. This officer is charged with the pretrial investigation of disciplinary cases and their presentation to a department trial board known as the "board of rights." This board then makes the recommendation to the chief of police, who has total and final disciplinary power.

The chief should have unrestricted disciplinary power subject only to the general direction and approval of the administrative head of the city. The chief should guard this power zealously and use it so temperately and wisely that its continued use will not be jeopardized.

Appeal from Disciplinary Action of the Chief   A central personnel agency, operating independently of the administrative head of the city, or an independent appeal board may be authorized to hold a hearing to ascertain the true facts on appeal by a subordinate who has been suspended, demoted, or dismissed. The appeal board should not be authorized to increase the disciplinary action taken by the chief; its authority should be restricted to sustaining or reducing the action taken by the chief. The final level of appeal described by law should rest with the highest executive in the government, such as the mayor or the city manager. Such a process provides a suitable safeguard against capricious disciplinary action by the chief.

Departmental Disciplinary Board   Ideally, the departmental disciplinary board should consist of five members of the department, with four appointed by the chief and one by the accused officer. The board should have no investigative power and should handle only those cases referred by the internal investigations division or the chief of police. Its jurisdiction should be cases not handled by means of summary punishment, cases directed to the board by the chief, and cases in which the accused requests a hearing, regardless of seriousness.

A board hearing is an administrative proceeding in which evidence and arguments are heard and, on the basis of them, a decision is made. Administrative hearings do not usually require legal formality or adherence to courtroom procedure. Various courts have declared some basic principles governing hearings, however:

1   The nature of the charge must be made known to the accused.
2   The accused must be given reasonable notice of the time and place of the hearing.

INSPECTIONAL SERVICES   **217**

3 The accused must be given the opportunity to call witnesses, to cross-examine opposing witnesses, and to testify in his or her own behalf.
4 The accused is entitled to have the hearing before those who are to decide the issue.

Of course, if procedures of this kind are specified in civil service laws, the accused officer is entitled to have the laws strictly followed.

Although an administrative hearing is quasi-judicial in character and thus need not be strictly formal, it should be conducted in a dignified manner, free of distraction and interruption. The rules for the hearing should be reviewed carefully so that the accused is fully aware of the items listed above and the rules themselves. The procedure should include provision for opening statements for both the accused and the department advocate, provision for cross-examination, questioning by board members, and other ground rules.

Because criminal trials require *proof beyond reasonable doubt*, police officers may confuse violations of regulations with violations of law. They are not the same, of course, nor does the same procedure necessarily apply. A police officer who receives an adverse decision based on evidence which does not result in proof beyond reasonable doubt may therefore erroneously believe that his or her rights have been abridged. Also, in an administrative hearing, the outcome will not result in a prison sentence, heavy fine, or loss of life. At the most, the officer's job is at stake.

The board should have a presiding officer, who should be knowledgeable concerning the procedure and familiar with parliamentary rules. Both the presiding officer and the department advocate (who should not be a member of the board) should be able to confer with the city attorney or police legal advisor.

The board should end its deliberation by making its decision, accompanied by a statement summarizing the essentials of the hearing and findings. Each charge (if there are several) should receive a separate finding.

If the decision sustains a charge, one of the following dispositions can be recommended:

- Oral reprimand
- Written reprimand
- Loss of time or of annual leave in lieu of suspension
- Suspension up to 30 days (but no longer)
- Removal from service

Summary Disciplinary Action   The disciplinary system should provide for a simple way to dispose of minor infractions which require some sort of formal action but which are not serious enough for a trial-board appearance. For example, a repeat violation of uniform regulations might require a supervisor to recommend summary action, which should be approved by a second-line supervisor. Summary action should not exceed more than two or three days' loss of leave or pay. The accused officer should have the right to appeal any action to the disciplinary board. Review of summary action should be a responsibility of the internal investigations unit.

Emergency Action   First-line supervisors should have the authority to suspend subordinates until the next business day for certain violations, such as drinking on duty, which preclude the officer's remaining on the job until disciplinary action is taken. Sergeants should also be authorized to send officers home (without pay, if necessary) to secure missing equipment such as a handgun or a flashlight. In larger departments, this authority can rest with platoon or shift commanders.

RELATIONSHIPS OF INSPECTIONAL SERVICES TO VICE CONTROL AND INTELLIGENCE

The relationship of organized crime to vice is well known, and since the purpose of an intelligence unit in a police department is to gather information on vice activity as well as on organized crime, the two functions have much in common. There is also at times a strong relationship between police internal investigations and vice control. Although vice and intelligence divisions deal with operational rather than administrative information for the most part and thus technically do not belong in an inspectional services grouping (see Chapter 19), the similarity of work and the nature of the clientele make it desirable to group vice control, intelligence, internal investigations, and field inspections into one major bureau.

Breaches of integrity are frequently related to vice and organized crime and may be discovered when they are investigated. Appraising the integrity of the force involves an investigation of complaints made against members by other officers as well as by individuals outside the department. Such investigations will not unnecessarily duplicate those conducted as an essential part of the function of command when they are restricted in intent to discovering the existence of graft and moral turpitude in the department and to establishing the evidence necessary for successful trial-board action or criminal prosecution.

Police Corruption

In this chapter there have been several references to some of the causes of police corruption, including the characteristics of law enforcement which contribute to officer misconduct.

Although corruption is by no means unheard of in the rest of the criminal justice system and although there are many other occupations which are susceptible to it throughout the world, police corruption is for several reasons more dangerous to our society than other forms. First, the police have a unique position with respect to the use of force and the capacity to deprive people of

INSPECTIONAL SERVICES

their freedom. Second, those people outside the police service who benefit from police corruption are in a position to do greater damage to the welfare of the citizenry than, say, the recipients of the corrupt relationships between headwaiters and their preferred customers.

Corruption in law enforcement can take many forms. It can be isolated and individualized, or it can be conspiratorial and widespread in the organization. The corruptive alliances can exist between the highest officials of the department and the leaders of organized crime or between records clerks and private detectives. The degree of corruption can range from the personal involvement of police officers in crimes to the willingness of a beat officer to look the other way when the restaurant owner who gives the officer free coffee has committed a minor traffic infraction.

The corruption of an individual officer is occasionally a possibility, even in the best of departments, but the worst kind of corruption involves many officers, all of whom know that it is going on.

Institutionalized Corruption Certainly, corruption involving large numbers of officers is less common now than it was a few decades ago. Nevertheless, the problem of institutionalized corruption is still with us, and it is still insidious. Furthermore, bureaucracies are slow to change, and if there are employees on several different levels of supervision who are involved, the disease is not easily cured or prevented.

Patrick V. Murphy, president of the Police Foundation and reform commissioner of the New York City Police Department during a period in which police corruption received intensive investigation, has expressed concern about the failure to recognize the seriousness of the problem:

> For too long corruption has been the skeleton in the police closet. Failure to discuss corruption openly has permitted it to flourish. A dearth of research on the subject handicaps police administrators, elected officials, journalists, and citizens anxious to address the problem of corruption.
>
> The reduction and control of police corruption can be complex. Many well-meaning police administrators have been unable to master the uses of power, unable to obtain public support, and unable to control a large bureaucracy in ways sufficient to achieve substantial control of corruption. Holding top and middle management strictly accountable through the use of powerful sanctions is essential if the police administrator is to deal successfully with corruption and avoid the high risk of personal blame for its existence. Yet, the environment engendered by the civil service mentality can protect the echelons immediately beneath the chief while the chief is held accountable for corruption. Therefore, despite civil service restraints, the chief must find ways to make his subordinates in management actively participate, and hold them strictly accountable, for a positive approach to the control of corruption.[3]

---

[3]Foreword to Herman Goldstein, Police Corruption: A Perspective on Its Nature and Control, Washington, D.C., Police Foundation, 1975, p. i.

The Outlook for the Future The elimination of corruption will require courageous actions in several directions by a number of people, with emphasis on the leadership of the chief of police. First, obviously, the chief must make plain to the members of the department and to the public at large that police corruption will not be tolerated—that in no way will the administration of the department give a wink and a nod to any form of corruption. Second, proper police selection standards (particularly those relating to character and education) must be established and followed. Third, the department must be organized so that inspections and internal investigations can be carried out effectively. Fourth, command officers and supervisors must be held accountable for the corrupt acts of police officers. Murphy states that police chiefs often hesitate to make their subordinates accountable for police corruption and that the importance of accountability in controlling corruption is either not understood or ignored in most United States police departments where the problem is encountered.[4]

Finally, citizen resistance to corruption must be developed through public education and information, so that tolerance of corruption by the community is no longer acceptable. It is particularly important for police chiefs fighting corruption to have the support of city officials, prosecutors, and the news media. These are important elements in mustering total community support against corruption.

[4]Patrick V. Murphy, "A Decade of Urban Police Problems," speech delivered at the Sixteenth Annual Wherrett Lecture on Local Government, Institute for Urban Policy and Administration, University of Pittsburgh, 1974, p. 4.

Chapter 13

Public and Community Relations

The decade of the 1960s was marked by widespread riots, civil disorder, violent protests, increasing street crime, an explosion in the use of narcotics, assassination of public officials and national figures, and other manifestations of a troubled society. Although the unrest centered in densely populated urban areas and on college campuses, few areas of the nation escaped its effects. The police were suddenly forced to consider the subject of "public relations" or "community relations" in a new way. As a result of the agonizing experience of these years, some fundamental concepts must now be recognized.

POLICIES AFFECTING PUBLIC AND COMMUNITY RELATIONS

The emphasis in this field has shifted from a concentration on building the public image toward achievement of a comprehensive set of objectives and policies:

- Public support is essential to effective police administration.
- The motivation for increasing public support should be not so much to receive praise and support per se as to secure the benefit of the support in terms of increased finances and backing to do a better job.

- The only long-term way to improve the image of the police is to provide effective, enthusiastic, fair, and just service in as professional a manner as possible. Communicating the news of progress in this direction, however, should be deliberate and immediate.
- The police must realize that improvement in police services and the police image can be neither achieved overnight nor enhanced by adoption of superficial community relations programs. If the public senses that community relations programs are insincere, the efforts will probably fail.
- Improvement of police services can be facilitated through dialogue with the community.
- The community relations effort should emphasize crime resistance and public education programs.[1]
- Fair and just treatment of all citizens should be a fundamental policy of the department.

Public Support Essential in Police Administration

Public cooperation is essential to the successful accomplishment of the police purpose. The support of the public is necessary for the enforcement of major laws as well as of minor regulations, and with this support arrests are made and convictions obtained that otherwise would not be possible. A public that observes laws and complies with regulations relieves the police of a large share of their burden. Difficult programs can be carried out with strong public and community support, and preferred techniques can be used successfully in friendly communities. Progressive programs and increased efficiency result in a greater public appreciation of police efforts. Public commendation and praise build police morale, which leads to increased efforts and an improved service. Without public support, budgetary requirements for needed buildings, equipment, and personnel are difficult to obtain. Police salaries, leave, retirement benefits, and other conditions of service are also favorably influenced by a friendly and cooperative public.

A hostile public, on the other hand, will make conditions disagreeable. Citizens may censure police without good cause or may criticize plans or programs to the point of their termination. When the activities of the police are misunderstood and construed as wrong, their morale is damaged, the maintenance of esprit de corps is made difficult, and they develop a negative attitude that causes them to be fearful of undertaking any constructive work. Also, faced with a critical, antagonistic public, the police unfortunately tend to develop a hostile attitude which only worsens public relations.

Relationship between the Police and the Public   Public support and cooperation are influenced by the relationship between the public and their police, that is, by the actions and conduct of each toward the other. The nature of any relationship is determined by the attitudes of the parties involved because the actions of each are determined by his or her own attitudes and influence the

[1]The operational aspects of crime prevention and public education are discussed in Chap. 20.

attitudes and conduct of the other. Each must have a correct attitude, therefore, if a desirable relationship is to be created and maintained. The public's attitude toward the police is molded and built by them and, in turn, reflects the police attitude.

While the police themselves are the most important factor in creating public attitudes, there are other influences in constant play. The press, motion pictures, and television exert a powerful influence in molding public opinion, and they may, through misrepresentation, create a climate of feeling which is unfriendly and unfair. Strong personalities within a community, if not converted to the police point of view, may likewise do much to destroy public confidence in the police, to build resentment, and to prevent the creation of a desirable rapport between the police and the public. The police, however, may influence even these factors by proper attitudes.

The Police Attitude   The police must scrutinize their own viewpoint to be certain that it is a proper one. Their attitude will be influenced by their concept of the police function—of their duty to the public. All members of the force must recognize that the people, through their representatives, hire and pay the police and that, as in any other employment, there must exist a proper employer-employee relationship.

The police must understand that the essence of a correct police attitude is a willingness to serve, but at the same time they should distinguish between service and servility and between courtesy and softness. They must be firm but must avoid even a hint of rudeness. They should develop a position that is friendly and unbiased—pleasant and personal in all nonrestrictive situations and firm and impersonal in situations calling for regulation and control. They should understand that the primary police purpose is to prevent violations, not to arrest people. And they should recognize the line of demarcation between police and court functions.

The Public Attitude   A public that cooperates with the police, supports them in their efforts, and observes laws and regulations may be said to have a desirable attitude. The police administrator is confronted with the task of creating and maintaining this attitude. Its development is impeded by a traditional fear of the police, by errors of judgment on the part of individual police officers, by unpopular police action in the enforcement of laws and ordinances that offend individuals, by the consequences of granting or refusing to grant special favors to important persons, by press attacks and political pressures, by an uninterested public, by an unsavory police reputation, and sometimes by the need to overcome such a reputation.

The problem is similar to that encountered daily in business and industry. Employees desiring a promotion work harder and make it evident that they are doing a superior job; they bend their efforts toward establishing a suitable relationship with their employer. Merchants wishing to increase their sales try to build good will; they sell better merchandise, increase the demand for it through advertising, and satisfy their customers. The principles involved in creating the desired relationships between the police and the public are simple and readily applied, although the hoped-for results are not always easily and quickly achieved.

Building Good Will and Avoiding Resentment   Good will is as essential to success in police operations as it is in commercial enterprises. Business firms expend large sums of money in developing good will, and they train their employees carefully in procedures designed to promote good feeling and to eliminate those situations which provoke resentment. They have found that employee courtesy pays big dividends. Police departments should undertake similar programs.

Public good will is developed by positive action; it is not wished into being by hopeful thinking. Methods and procedures that will bring about agreeable relations with the public must be carefully developed and planned. A department guilty of bad practices toward its citizens in the past may meet apparently impenetrable resistance when wholesome changes are proposed, but the greater the resistance, the more important to break it down. There are many activities that have special value in building good will, and small courtesies and special services will go far toward improving the standing of the police in the eyes of the community. The British police have long recognized the importance of such services; in the words of Charles Reith:

> The police have kindly words and helpful advice for anyone in doubt or trouble who comes to them . . . they fulfill an immensely beneficial social function in finding relief for the destitute, in tracing missing relatives, and in smoothing out family quarrels, misunderstandings, and estrangements of every kind.
>
> It may be argued warmly, in some quarters, that the rendering of such service is not part of the duties and functions of the police. The answer is that the friendliness, confidence, respect, trust, and affection they receive from the people are almost the sole basis of the power and efficiency of the police of Britain. Whatever tends to strengthen this relationship, strengthens and maintains the vitality of true democracy in Britain. Whatever tends to loosen the bonds of the public's relationship with the police . . . must lessen, also, the power which the police derive from the public's appreciation of them. Any material decrease of this power will quickly lead to their increased dependence on the use of physical force: to the need, by central authority, of endowing them with despotic powers to enable them to fulfill their tasks; to police dependence, not on being liked by the people, but on being feared by them; and to the opening of a short road for the transference of their organization into the only alternative form of police which is available.[2]

INFORMING THE PUBLIC

Failures in police administration are frequently traceable to a lack of public support arising from citizen misunderstanding of police purposes and methods. Resentment and distrust change to friendliness and respect on closer public

[2]Charles Reith, *A Short History of the British Police,* Oxford University Press, New York, 1948, pp. 112–113.

PUBLIC AND COMMUNITY RELATIONS 225

acquaintance with the police; antagonism gives way to cooperation when each understands the other's point of view. Successful police administration invariably rests on a sound foundation of public support.

The police themselves are often the victims of two common misconceptions that hinder their activity in keeping the public informed: (1) that such activity is unethical and (2) that the public will misconstrue it as an effort to build personal prestige rather than to improve police service. These misconceptions are based on the failure of the police to understand that their success is dependent on public cooperation and that keeping the public informed is therefore an integral part of their job.

While informing the public is related to the public relations function of the individual officer vis-à-vis the people, it is on a different level; it is the relationship of management to stockholder, in a sense. The government cannot move ahead of the people, just as a business cannot move independently of those who have a financial responsibility for, and interest in, the enterprise. It is essential that the head of the department take the people of the community into his confidence and that he tell them the problems of his department, what is being done to solve them, and, most importantly, why a specific solution is being used.

The Public Information Officer   In larger departments, the chief's responsibility for dissemination of information to the public should be delegated to a public information officer or to a staff unit organized to gain public support for the department.

The public information function may be divided into five broad categories: (1) evaluating public opinion and attitudes with respect to the policies, methods, and personnel of the department; (2) advising the chief with regard to the public relations aspects of new or revised department programs, policies, procedures, and activities; (3) planning and carrying out programs aimed at keeping the public informed on police activities; (4) furnishing a staff supervision of all police activities that may influence public support; and (5) assisting in crime resistance and public safety education.

The public relations mission can be successful only when the officer charged with its accomplishment understands the necessity for developing and maintaining public support and knows the factors that influence support both favorably and unfavorably. The chief must also be alert to the reactions of the public and must use his public information officer to maintain a constant liaison between himself and the public. He must not wait until the attitudes of the community have become fixed and rigid before he takes action to remedy an unfavorable response, nor must he fail to take action on suggestions which come to him from the citizens.

Personnel assigned to public information duties must be aware that the policies, programs, activities, and operating methods of the several divisions strongly affect public relations. They must be scrutinized, evaluated from their public relations aspect, and perhaps modified (see Chapter 20).

The public information officer should therefore participate in general staff meetings and planning conferences and should be encouraged to visit division heads periodically for informal conversations regarding departmental activities. This officer must also be in complete agreement with the concepts expressed earlier in this chapter and, of course, must have an ability to write well.

The principal responsibility of the public information officer is the dissemination of information outside the department. Most of his or her efforts will be concentrated on general dissemination of information to the public, rather than on contacts with specific agencies or individuals. Informed citizens are nearly always cooperative. They understand the need for control, the purpose of regulations, and the reasons for police policies and procedures; in consequence, they comply readily with regulations and assist also in the solution of police problems. The more effective the educational program, the less enforcement is necessary to maintain suitable compliance.

While public information regarding the purpose and justification of police practices and procedures is intended primarily to promote public support, it is also aimed at educating the public to cooperate in the most effective manner with the police. Citizens are taught traffic safety to make them safer drivers and more cautious pedestrians; they are also taught how to reduce opportunities for the commission of crimes by professional or occasional criminals who may attack their families, homes, or property, and they learn how to assist the police in the apprehension of criminals.

The public information officer has a responsibility to department members as well as to the public and to the chief. He can assist in interpreting changes and innovations in the department, and he can dispel the unfortunate effect of rumor and gossip by the use of the department bulletin or newsletter for the dissemination of factual material. He can encourage the circulation of department publications, promote welfare and recreational programs, and provide speakers for appearance at group meetings of officers. He has the facilities for adding importance to such things as creditable mentions, safety or heroism awards, and promotions. He can substitute, for the cold announcement of retirement or death, a dignified, warm expression of good wishes or condolence; when he does so, he strengthens the bonds not only between the chief and the force but also between the members of the force. The public relations officer has a two-way role: He must stimulate favorable public reaction to the police, but he must remember that such attitudes are reciprocal and must do everything possible to promote a friendly attitude among the police.

The Police and the Press

Because of its influence on public opinion, the press with a genuine interest in the public good can assist in improving the quality of police service by pointing out the need for improved personnel practices, for better equipment, and for adequate manpower. Amicable relations with the press also afford many other advantages to the police. Newspaper facilities can then be used for reporting department activities to the public and for disseminating information relating to department programs and procedures. A favorable press can enlist the aid of the public in crime and traffic-control problems; it can help in instructing the public regarding the nature and purpose of new regulations and in educating citizens in procedures designed to minimize opportunities for criminal acts and accidents.

Most newspapers are willing to devote all the space requested to police subjects because these matters are of human interest and sometimes provide material for some form of newspaper campaign. The editorial staff, of course, may have its own ideas about what constitutes news and what material is suitable for publication; generally, however, a frank discussion of police problems and proposed solutions will produce the necessary editorial assistance. In those frequent instances where the editorial staff remains unsympathetic, a talk with the publisher may bring about the desired results. When the newspaper is unfriendly to the administration, the chief should explore these remedies before taking irreconcilable action. In the face of prolonged antagonism, however, the administration may need the aid of local groups and influential persons in the community to counteract the press.

The police should remember that the public media are not usually controlled or owned by a majority of the citizens they serve. Furthermore, the power of the press can be overrated if its policies are out of step with the vastly underestimated power of face-to-face communication, particularly by the decision makers of the community. One authority in the field of political communication has noted that there can be a discrepancy between "newspaper strength" and real strength, not at the grass roots but *at the decisive middle level of communication and decision*[3]—those positions which are removed a sufficient vertical distance from rank-and-file members of the social, economic, and political communications and command hierarchies of the community to permit the incumbents to influence large numbers of people, but which are not so far removed as to be out of touch with grass-roots sentiment.

The police are occasionally the victims of unfair, and sometimes malicious, press attacks, and the public good then suffers. The police are in a vulnerable position in regard to the press; since they deal with human beings, it is easy for the news media to criticize almost every police act and be assured of sympathetic support at least from those citizens who have been subjected to some police control.

The police administrator has the responsibility and duty to establish relationships with the press that will protect the honest and ethical officers of the force and will lessen the likelihood of unfair criticisms. This will require adopting a policy of complete fairness and frankness with the newspapers and their representatives. Police administrators should not attempt to conceal departmental weaknesses or the derelictions of individual police officers; they should receive from the press, in return, a fair presentation of the facts and a

---

[3]Karl W. Deutsch, *The Nerves of Government: Models of Political Communication and Control*, paperback ed., The Free Press (Macmillan), New York, 1966, p. 154.

critical analysis of the causes. The press should not condemn the department or the police generally for the acts of individual officers; rather, it should point out the weaknesses in the system which permitted unqualified personnel to become members of the department and should develop a public demand for improved procedures of recruitment and training that would lessen the possibility of such errors in the future.

The police should welcome honest criticism based on facts when that criticism is constructively designed to improve police service. On the other hand, the press should not criticize without having all the facts, and its criticism should not be an attack on personalities but a constructive attempt to improve procedures and policies.

The Press Conference In many departments, and particularly in the larger ones, police chiefs will find it advantageous to arrange periodically to meet with the press representatives in their city. It is usually better to have this meeting following a morning conference at which decisions regarding police, disciplinary problems, and personnel changes may have been made. These decisions can then be announced in an authoritative way that precludes the circulation of rumors and speculation, and all representatives of the press have an equal opportunity to present questions on matters of current concern.

When holding such a conference, the chief should establish from the outset that it will be conducted in a dignified, formal manner with no feet-on-the-desk, smoke-filled-room atmosphere of popular tradition. The chief should use the time judiciously and should expect the reporters to do the same. The press representatives should be seated comfortably, either around the chief's desk or at a conference table. After presenting the announcements briefly and concisely, the chief should open the floor to questions.

Except for occasional "in-studio" appearances, most television coverage is not as formal as the conference with newspaper reporters. Television reporters often prefer outside interviews in the daylight (to avoid paying lighting specialists), with the informal question-and-answer approach most often used. Television coverage is more personal and accurate; although content may be edited in the cutting room, distortion is much less likely.

Regardless of the format of the news conference, the chief should answer all queries frankly and openly when he has the information, and he should take note of problems which are brought to his attention by the reporters. A policy of not answering hypothetical questions will save time and avoid injudicious conjectures and statements. A reply amounting to "no comment" (although that specific phraseology should not be used, since it antagonizes many journalists) should be given to questions regarding his reaction to statements or actions of other public officials or figures. Such a response, politely stated, will prevent the chief from becoming involved in issues that lie outside his jurisdiction. He should be physically and emotionally relaxed and should not allow himself to become angered or flustered by any unexpected or unwelcome questions. He must keep his sense of humor and composure. Reporters

PUBLIC AND COMMUNITY RELATIONS

appreciate the opportunity to meet in this way with the chief and ordinarily will respond to his friendly manner and attitude in kind.

Police Press Policy

Newspapers and other public media usually carry three types of stories relating to the police department. First, they are interested in crime news—either in terms of specific incidents or in relation to trends. Second, personnel or administrative changes, internal politics, intragovernmental controversies, and the relationship of the police department to other agencies have always been newsworthy items in most cities. Third, the press may be interested in public service features which are intended to improve relations with the community or which may have preventive or educational value.

A comprehensive police press policy must cover all three of these areas.

Crime News It is sound policy to make information on crimes and other incidents generally available to the public media. Press representatives must rely on police sources for their views. Any attempts to restrict these sources invariably fail, sometimes disastrously for the chief. A policy should be established that will ensure accessibility by press representatives to the daily bulletin and some other police records so that the press will obtain promptly all spot news which is routine in character; at the same time the police must protect against the divulgence of information that might interfere with the successful conclusion of an investigation or with the apprehension of a criminal. Obviously the press should not have access to records relating to national-security and vice investigations or information relating to current investigations, the publication of which might jeopardize their successful conclusion. Procedures should be developed and instructions given to operating personnel that will enable reporters to gather their news facts rapidly, accurately, completely, and promptly following the receipt of the information by the police. All policies and procedures designed to aid the press should be explained to all members of the force so that they may assist in carrying out the police purpose.

Press contacts with individual officers, however, should be as few as possible in order to lessen the interference with work, to simplify control and coordination, and to avoid embarrassment when officers are asked for information that they are not certain should be released. When the police establish procedures that facilitate the collection of news, press representatives unconsciously reduce their number of contacts with members of the force.

Competitor papers are jealous of their news rights and resent any evidence of news being withheld from release until after their deadline. The only course for the chief under any circumstances, whether dealing with a friendly or an unfriendly press, is to arrange for the release to be made as cases are reported. The chief should also watch closely for any evidence of newspaper favoritism on the part of members of the force.

Individual reporters sometimes prepare feature articles and discuss them with the police, who should honor this confidence by not revealing the plan to competitive reporters. On the other hand, a reporter may discover that the chief has been withholding information from the press in regard to a future action in order that its release may be in more complete detail or be well timed in reference to other phases of the operation. When questioned about such a plan, should the chief decide to give any relevant information to the inquiring reporter, he should at the same time call in the other reporters and give the facts to all.

In conferences with the city editor of each paper, the police chief should attempt to reach agreement regarding publicity of information in certain cases, including (1) the identities of juvenile offenders and victims in all incidents (except murder); (2) sex crimes in which the victim is of good repute and innocent of conduct that could have provoked the attack; (3) the exact addresses of witnesses in crime in which there is a danger of retaliation; (4) mention of an incriminating statement, admission, or confession (which may jeopardize a fair trial or an otherwise successful prosecution); and (5) cases in which public knowledge of the facts would interfere with the investigation or the apprehension of suspects. City editors almost invariably will agree to withhold the names of juveniles and of victims in sex crimes when they have a full account of the incident. This practice has become so general that the police no longer have the responsibility to censor or conceal such news items, and all information relating to the first two categories of cases should be released; in the absence of previous agreement, the press must decide on an ethical course in this regard.

Editors also usually agree in principle that the remaining three types of information should have no publicity, but they frequently argue that they, and not the police, must judge whether public knowledge of the facts would interfere with police operations. This attitude, of course, makes a satisfactory agreement impossible, and when the decision is to be made independently by each city editor on the basis of his own judgment, none will risk being scooped by a competitor, with the result that the item receives publicity unless the chief telephones each editor in an attempt to get unanimous agreement from all. Such a plan is plainly not feasible; when, in spite of unanimous agreement, one editor inadvertently or willfully publishes the story, the police chief is placed in an embarrassing position.

The daily police bulletin, teletype messages, and accident, case, miscellaneous-incident, and arrest reports in districts and headquarters should be open for inspection by representatives of the press or other news media when these items are not urgently needed for police purposes at the moment.

In larger cities, authorized news-media representatives should be issued press cards by the department. When the representatives are not readily recognized, they should be required to identify themselves. Issuance of the cards does not mean, however, that the holders are entitled to search files and indexes themselves. This practice should not be permitted in any department.

Procedures must be established to govern who will discuss specific

PUBLIC AND COMMUNITY RELATIONS

criminal cases with reporters. In departments which give patrol officers freedom to conduct investigations, the press should be able to talk to the investigating beat officer, the detective who conducts follow-up investigation, or the supervisors in the direct chain of command for either. Department regulation should prevent those outside the chain of command (with the exception of the public information officer) from making comments about the case. Detectives should be cautious about allowing their names to be quoted as a source of information when the actual work in the case has been conducted by someone else, possibly in the patrol division; it is easy for reporters to omit the name of the investigator and identify only the officer who has released the information.

News Relating to Police Administration Stories about administrative changes, internal controversies, disciplinary problems, and similar topics are usually of great interest to the news media. Whenever possible, such information should be released through the public information officer or the chief at a news conference or through news releases prepared by the information officer or personnel of the public information unit. As indicated previously, information of this kind should not be released selectively.

News releases should be carefully written in journalistic style, exactly as if they had been prepared by a trained newspaper reporter. This reduces the possibility of editorial misinterpretation during extensive rewriting.

Since the chief interest of police reporters is to obtain news, procedures should be established to facilitate their work and to ensure an ample supply of material for their use. The wise police chief will establish a policy authorizing division heads to release press items regarding the general or overall activities of their units, in contrast to items relating to specific cases which can be released by operating personnel as the incidents come to police attention. The chief will breathe life into the policy by urging his immediate subordinates to give careful attention to their press relations and to provide useful material, thus taking full advantage of press facilities in educating and informing the public and at the same time promoting a friendly and constructive relationship between the police and the press.

The records division should supply the public information officer and each division head with material so that they may always have copy for the reporters. One story each day is better than three stories every third day. News reporters are interested in the unusual; for them, any superlative makes a story, and they are always in search of some feature which will make that day unique.

Crime-Resistance and Safety Features The press can be a tremendous asset in the dissemination of crime-resistance and safety-education articles and features, regardless of the authorship. The public information unit should encourage reporters to write feature articles as well as shorter pieces in continued series on a regular basis. In large departments the crime-prevention bureau or division (see Chart 18) should contribute articles on crime resistance and safety education on a continuing basis. For example, columns or features have been run under such descriptive titles as "Traffic Tips" and "Safety Sayings."

Special Press Activities A cooperative press may assist the police in a number of special activities. Some newspapers publish, as a boxed feature, special items furnished by the police. One such series was called "Know Your Police Officer"; it featured, each day over a long period of time, a biographical sketch and picture of a different member of the department. The series received excellent public response and undoubtedly contributed much to good police public relations in that city.

Crime and accident facts may also be presented to include the number of personal-injury and fatal automobile accidents and the number and percentage of clearances by arrest of such crimes as robbery, burglary, and car theft, with figures for a comparable previous period included.

Public Reporting

An annual report, sometimes consolidated as a section in a municipal report, is intended to inform the community of police problems, accomplishments, and plans. Frequently these reports are limited to poorly prepared and incomplete textual material and accompanying statistical tabulations which are difficult to interpret. Such tabulations are appropriate in detailed operational planning and for submission to state and national clearinghouses of crime and accident statistics, but they do not present facts in a form suitable for public consumption.

Facts, whether in statistical or textual form, must be presented in an interesting manner that will enable the citizen to interpret them easily and to understand the message conveyed by them. Otherwise, the report fails in its purpose and represents a waste of time in preparation and of material in publication. A picture is worth a thousand words, and statistical facts can nearly always be charted in the form of line or bar graphs, thus enabling analysis at a glance, in contrast to the difficult task of comparing tabulated numbers. Photographs also present facts in an easily understood and interesting form.

The distribution of these formal reports frequently does not provide adequate or suitable coverage, particularly when the distribution has not been carefully planned to ensure that the reports are placed where they are most needed.

The formal periodic report just described does not discharge the police chief's responsibility of reporting to the citizens of the community; a number of other devices should be used to meet public reporting obligations more completely and also to inform the public about police problems and the regulations and practices designed to aid in their solution. Included among these are more informal and frequent police publications, police displays and demonstrations, and some special contacts with citizens aimed at providing an

PUBLIC AND COMMUNITY RELATIONS

opportunity for them to become better acquainted with their police department. Television and radio news services also assist importantly in public reporting.

Police Publications Department and police-association publications are a useful means of keeping the public and police personnel informed on police activities, but the department should be wary of depending upon commercial advertising to defray the cost of publication. It is possible through this means to publish quite a large magazine, but there is a definite danger that the practice will deteriorate into a "racket." It is better to have a smaller publication and meet the expense through budget appropriation.

Some departments publish a periodic citizens' newsletter or bulletin. Such a pamphlet is a convenient medium for the publication of police statistics in an easily understood, graphic form as well as of articles on traffic, juvenile activities, vice control, crime resistance, crime investigations, and department accomplishments, with credit being given to individual officers for work well done. It serves also as an organization publication, helpful in building esprit de corps and binding the members more firmly together as a group. News items regarding the private lives and department accomplishments of police personalities promote the house-organ value of the publication; when it is given public distribution, however, not over 5 percent of its space should be used for this purpose.

A special issue of the police publication may be mailed to a selected list of citizens who are active in civic affairs and to certain names taken each month at random from the telephone directory. Copies left in the reception rooms of every office in the main buildings of the community and in shops increase the effective circulation. Regardless of the method of distribution, a selected permanent mailing list should be maintained to ensure that copies go to city officials and community leaders. In large departments, a copy should be mailed to each officer's home to ensure distribution to all members and to reach their families.

Commercial Broadcasts Radio and television present further opportunities for public reporting. Five-minute dialogues broadcasted daily or a question-and-answer period on a specific subject will arouse the interest of many people who may otherwise be unaware of police activities. To facilitate such radio broadcasts, direct lines are sometimes installed between the radio studio and police headquarters. Participation on television panels that include news reporters or civic leaders also results in interested public response. Panel-discussion participation should usually be undertaken by superior officers who have the authority to answer direct questions that may be asked, should the panelists deviate from the announced topic.

Special Department Contacts with the Public

An excellent means for establishing an agreeable public relationship for a police department composed of wisely selected and well-trained personnel is to devise methods for enabling the public to become personally acquainted with police employees. Citizens are interested in the police department and welcome an opportunity to visit headquarters in order to see police demonstrations, to learn something about police procedures, and to participate vicariously in police operations. When police officers are of fine character and personality, providing the public with an opportunity to meet them and participate with them in an open-house situation serves to build a mutually friendly relationship on which respect and confidence are based.

Since the purpose of any special contact with the public is to make a favorable impression, qualified officers should be chosen for the occasion, and the police should appear at their best. They should prepare for the affair as for a general inspection, with headquarters tidy and clean, uniforms immaculate, and equipment in perfect order.

Inspection Tours   A tour of inspection of headquarters offers an excellent means for personal contact and provides an opportunity to show the public undesirable conditions which remain uncorrected because of lack of funds. Police departments are still frequently found housed in the basement of the city hall, and many municipal jails continue to be a disgrace. Such conditions often exist merely because citizens are unaware of them. A tour of inspection brings the unsatisfactory condition to light. Tours should be well planned, including publicity, scheduling, and the actual program to be offered to visitors.

Special Demonstrations   If a tour of inspection does not permit sufficient time for a demonstration, a special visit to police headquarters may be arranged for this purpose. Demonstrations may be given of police methods in handling prisoners, showing techniques for overpowering rough prisoners and for disarming criminals about to shoot, stab, or club an officer. Methods of searching prisoners may likewise be shown, thus illustrating the manner in which prisoners sometimes conceal weapons and tools useful in breaking jail. Target practice on the police range also provides an excellent demonstration, especially when the officers have been trained in trick shooting.

Police dispatching may be shown in detail, with maps arranged to indicate the beat covered by each car and the availability of the cars for service. An explanation should be made of the methods used in tactical dispatching.

The police laboratory offers much of interest to the public, especially if confiscated guns and other paraphernalia are on display. Laboratory equipment in operation invariably impresses the observer. A demonstration of fingerprinting may be planned to include the taking of prints, the development of latent prints on various materials, and an explanation of the classification and filing of fingerprints.

Displays and Exhibits   Displays and exhibits are effective means of informing and interesting the public. Their subject and nature and the location where they may be used advantageously are limited only by the ingenuity of the

PUBLIC AND COMMUNITY RELATIONS 235

officer in charge. For the interest of persons waiting in the police building as well as of officers, there should be space for charts relating to the current crime and accident situation. Retail stores will frequently donate a shop window for a police display because of the large number of people it attracts. Theaters are also usually willing to have displays for their lobbies. Openings and dedications of new civic buildings offer a perfect opportunity for displays and exhibits; since there will be at least one officer present at such an occasion, the public will have an opportunity to see an active demonstration of police service at the same time.

Filmstrips and motion pictures of many police operations may be used effectively in displays, with an officer in attendance to explain the scenes. Equipment displays also may be arranged in an impressive manner. While they would consist principally of photographs and diagrams, some actual equipment may also be used. For example, a large diagram may illustrate the police communications system and its operation, supplemented by photographs of switchboards, dispatcher's office and equipment, call boxes, and re-call lights; through telephone company cooperation, it is possible to place some actual equipment on display. Laboratory equipment may be shown by photograph and also by actual samples of polygraph records, moulage casts, and physical evidence from some disposed-of case. Contraband narcotics with samples and paraphernalia for ingesting them, confiscated weapons, and materials used in forgery and counterfeiting also make interesting display subjects.

Speakers' Bureaus and Crime-Prevention Education   An important part of a public information program is operationally oriented, such as talks by officers on burglary prevention and narcotics control. Additional information in this area will be found in Chapter 20.

COMMUNICATION OF PUBLIC NEEDS TO THE POLICE

One of the great benefits of a formal community relations effort is that the dialogue which results from police–citizen contact can be helpful in the general improvement of police services. Even the most casual community relations efforts—such as appearances before PTA groups and civic organizations—will often disclose ways in which police services can be improved. This kind of communication, obviously, should be encouraged rather than viewed as unwholesome meddling.

Police–Community Relations, Citizens' Organizations, and Citizen Crime Commissions

Citizens' organizations concerned with police generally fall into two categories. The first group consists of organizations which the police themselves sponsor and support. Most of them are general in nature and have titles such as "Police–Community Relations Council" or "Neighborhood Police–Citizen Task Force." The second broad category of organizations is the type which originates from citizen initiative, rather than the police. Organizations in the latter group typically include local crime commissions and safety councils and national organizations such as the National Council on Crime and Delinquency, the Chamber of Commerce of the United States, and the American Association of Retired Persons. Citizen-derived organizations in turn have several orientations—those which have multiple purposes (such as the National Council on Crime and Delinquency) and those which have a narrower, more specialized interest, such as groups which are concerned with juvenile-delinquency prevention, alcohol and drug abuse, and organized crime and those which are oriented toward education, employment, correctional rehabilitation, and other specialized expertise.

Regardless of whether the organization is derived from the police or from citizens, those which have a strong police orientation generally have the following objectives: (1) traffic control; (2) eradication of organized crime; (3) prevention of juvenile delinquency; (4) minimization of drug and alcohol abuse; (5) resistance to crime such as burglary, robbery, and theft; and (6) elimination of conditions leading to racial discrimination and its consequences.

Need for Coordination   Problems and their solutions in the areas mentioned above frequently involve programs that extend beyond the jurisdiction of the police; the coordinated activity of several agencies is then required. For example, the support of the prosecutor and courts is vital to the success of most police programs, especially in the fields of organized crime and traffic control, because these agencies are in a strategic position to nullify police efforts. A great number of social welfare organizations are concerned with crime prevention, and engineering and educational aspects of traffic control often require the combined efforts of engineers, planners, newspapers, and other agencies.

The coordination of public and semipublic agencies is difficult for the police alone to achieve because of the independent and unrelated character of nearly all the participating groups. The heads of these agencies, however, are usually amenable to the influence of community organizations. Conferences with agency representatives promote coordination by clarifying relationships.

Need for Public Support   The execution of plans in these four spheres of activity also requires the active support and participation of the public. The police, under a government for and by the people, are public servants appointed to protect life and property in a manner approved by the people. If the police are out of step with the people and attempt to impose on them unpopular programs of control, their efforts are doomed to failure, and the administrator who continues to go against the will of the majority in his efforts to regulate the conduct of people will usually be removed from office.

The solution of most police problems, which as a rule are complex and communitywide in scope, involves influencing mass attitudes which can be molded, directed, and controlled only by the power of public opinion. Without

PUBLIC AND COMMUNITY RELATIONS

the pressure of public support, successful enforcement of traffic, vice, and some other regulations is difficult, if not impossible. Efforts to induce compliance by force, without first favorably molding public opinion, consistently result in failure. It is in this function of creating a favorable public climate that the community organizations are so essential to the police.

Owing to limited budgets and personnel, the police, social workers, engineers, and other officials alone cannot successfully carry on programs as widespread and extensive as is necessary to solve many of the community problems in which the police have a primary responsibility. Public support, communitywide interest, and individual participation, therefore, must be enlisted. The latter is particularly important, since participation in the development and application of a community program promotes interest in its success. The greater the number who are interested and actively engaged in the study and solution of community problems, the more satisfactory will be the results. An organized, informed, and alert community will provide moral backing, financial support, and some special skills and will promote public understanding of police problems and of the actions proposed for their solution.

Objectives of Community Organizations   Community organizations, therefore, should be created to achieve the following objectives:

1   To coordinate participating public and semipublic agencies in programs that require the action of several such agencies

2   To protect the community, legislative bodies, courts, prosecutors, and police and other officials from the influence of groups with selfish interests that are contrary to the public interest

3   To influence officials to take action for the public good by supporting the adoption of desirable programs, regulations, and procedures and by opposing the adoption of undesirable ones

4   To obtain public support of programs designed in the public interest in order that essential facilities in the form of space, equipment, and personnel may be made available

5   To popularize these programs so that the people will favor their accomplishment and the enforcement of incidental regulations and to obtain cooperation in the form of compliance with regulations and an active intolerance of their violation

Several organizations offer excellent publications which provide guidelines for the organization and operation of citizens' organizations. Information can be obtained from the following publications or by writing to the addresses given below:

National Advisory Commission on Criminal Justice Standards and Goals, *A Call for Citizen Action: Crime Prevention and the Citizen*, U.S. Department of Justice, Washington, D.C., 1974.

Chamber of Commerce of the United States, *Marshaling Citizen Power against Crime*, 1615 H Street, N.W., Washington, D.C., 1970.

National Association of Citizens Crime Commissions, *How to Organize and Operate a Citizens Crime Commission,* Atlanta, Georgia, 1974.

Lay Character of Community Organizations   It is vital to the success of community organizations that they include both laymen and representatives of participating agencies. Parents, homeowners, business and professional people, and church leaders all have the welfare and character of the community as a major concern, and they bring to the solution of community problems a personal interest and enthusiasm.

Lay participation implies decentralization in the form of neighborhood safety councils and community councils for delinquency prevention, especially in cities that are no longer effective community units but are, instead, municipalities of neighborhoods or integral social communities, each distinct from the other. Racial, economic, occupational, religious, and social characteristics; topography; area; and population are all elements that influence the establishment of distinct neighborhoods. Cities of 250,000 population invariably are composed of separated neighborhood communities that deserve organization of neighborhood councils. The need is also frequently apparent in smaller cities. The need for decentralization does not exist so strongly for crime commissions, although their attention may be directed at neighborhood problems by the appointment of committees to work on specific conditions.

National or Local Character of Community Organizations   The community organization in each of the four fields under discussion may be of one of several types. It may be organized as a committee of a larger, already-existent parent organization, such as the chamber of commerce or some other communitywide organization, or it may be organized as a separate entity, completely dissociated from any other.

Certain advantages are immediately apparent when the new organization is created as a committee of a larger body, but there may also be disadvantages that should be recognized. In the first instance, promotion and support from the parent body can be relied upon, and the services of its clerical staff and of someone to serve as executive secretary are usually provided. Office space and other facilities are made available, budget allowance is usually provided, and moral support from the parent group may be expected. When the existent group is of high standing in the community and has gained the respect of the public at large, its assistance can be invaluable.

On the other hand, automatic identification with the parent group may prove to be a disadvantage when that organization has a poor reputation and encounters strong public opposition or when community support is divided by the existence of other groups antagonistic to it. There is also a danger of the influence of vested interests in a parent organization, which, if it results in restricted action, may prove disastrous. The committee of a large organization is not permitted to take action on controversial matters without the approval of the board of directors. Also, its efforts to raise money for its programs may interfere with the subscription activities of the main organization.

PUBLIC AND COMMUNITY RELATIONS

Leadership Strong leadership is required to organize a community for delinquency prevention and for the control of organized crime and traffic safety, as well as to deal with minority-group problems. The needed leadership is usually, but not invariably, found in the agencies whose primary purpose is related most directly to these activities.

Since many community agencies have at least an implied responsibility in delinquency prevention, any one of several may assume the leadership and provide the initiative, energy, and persistence to create and sustain a delinquency-prevention program. The pattern of the program is strongly influenced by which group is at the helm. In some communities the police furnish the leadership; in others, the probation officers or the schools provide it.

Expert advice will be needed in many phases of the organization and operation of the newly formed group to ensure its success. Promotion of community programs of this character requires technical ability. While the program, once under way, can and should be administered by local citizens, expert aid should not be scorned at the outset. Through it the community may profit from the experience of other cities. Both the Chamber of Commerce of the United States and the National Safety Council are prepared to assist communities in their plans and programs for organization. Similarly, the National Council on Crime and Delinquency makes available many publications in its field to assist communities in the development of delinquency-prevention programs. The Chicago Crime Commission and the National Association of Citizens Crime Commissions supply information regarding the formation of similar groups.

The community which avails itself of such experienced services gives its program further impetus at the start and avoids many commonly made mistakes.

Other Organizations

The interest and participation of the general public should be stimulated beyond the limits of the community organizations heretofore discussed. The active interest of other organizations should be aroused, directed, and maintained. Business and luncheon clubs, patriotic and fraternal organizations, women's clubs, parent-teacher associations, and church groups all have the community welfare at heart and need only to have specific tasks given to them and their work directed to engage actively in community programs. These groups have the power to influence public opinion and to develop a public attitude favorable to the solution of community problems. The stimulation of a directing hand is needed to bring these latent powers to life. The safety council, the crime commission, and the community council can promote their projects in this manner.

It is best to interest these associations in one phase of a community program rather than to place responsibility for the complete program on one group. One member should be selected to promote the activity by preparing a plan for presentation to the president and board of directors of the club. If the suggestion is looked upon with favor, a committee will be appointed to make plans for its accomplishment. A committee meeting should be called, the plan and ways and means of its execution discussed, and the matter of finance settled, and the task of winning the support and active participation of the entire club membership should be studied. In order to arouse and maintain interest, the committee should make frequent progress reports to the club as a whole.

Organization of the Community Relations Division

In larger departments, a formal community relations unit should be established. Placement of the unit and its related functions within the organizational structure is somewhat difficult because some public and community relations activities are clearly operational in nature—for example, when they deal with specific crime-prevention programs—and others are more administrative in character, such as information programs relating to the department's progress. In some major-city police departments, the community relations/crime-prevention/public information/safety-education grouping of activities has been given major bureau status. The Cincinnati Division of Police has a major entity intended to carry out this grouping of functions. The Chicago Police Department, following an IACP management study in 1970, has established a bureau of community services having equal organizational status with other major departmental bureaus, such as field operations and administrative services. The bureau of community services in turn has three major divisions—public and internal information, neighborhood relations, and preventive programs.

Community Relations Responsibility   A logical assignment of responsibilities for a community relations unit would include:

- Acting as liaison with formal community organizations, such as the police–citizen council or other neighborhood groups
- Establishing a working relationship with other community relations organizations in the region
- Participating in the development of community relations programs for the department as a whole
- Publicizing police objectives, problems, and successes
- Acting as the communications link for information transmitted from citizens' organizations to the police department
- Suggesting improvements in practices by police officers which have a bearing on police–community relations
- Identifying training needs through interviews with citizen representatives, consultation with the internal investigations unit, and conferences with supervisors

In medium-sized to large departments the public information function should be formalized by the creation of a public information officer or a unit within the community relations division. At times this function is found as an

PUBLIC AND COMMUNITY RELATIONS

adjunct to the chief's office or as a part of an administrative services bureau. What is more important than the placement of the office is the quality of the activity carried out by the unit.

Community Relations Programs   A great variety of community relations programs and projects are in use today. The police department in St. Louis, Missouri, for example, has compiled a list of 43 programs which have been developed, explored, or operated by the police at one time or another in that city in recent years.

Some of the noteworthy community relations efforts found in the United States are described in the following paragraphs. They deserve mention because they are either basic to any program or innovative and promising.

Training   Community relations training for police officers should be considered a basic, continuous program. The training should be comprehensive in scope and method and should stress the concepts mentioned earlier in this chapter. It should be a part of recruit and in-service training and should be not only presented as a specific course but also integrated into other subjects. Since community relations training has a more recent history than some of the traditional subjects in the police curricula and because the content is intended to influence general attitudes more than it is expected to supply specific procedural information, the course material should be developed with care. The attitude of instructors is also important, and they should be carefully selected. Some training programs have attempted to relegate all community relations training to outside guest speakers, such as representatives of minority-group organizations. While it may be wise to have a part of the content presented by outside instructors, it is important for most of the material to be offered by regular police instructors so that students will be convinced that the administration is as sincere about community relations as it is, for example, about the laws of arrest.

The police department in Covina, California, has experimented with *empathy training* of officers by sending them, disguised as skid-row derelicts, into cities where they could not be recognized. Their true identity was unknown to police personnel (except for a few high-ranking officers) in these cities. In addition to producing the intended empathy, the experiments also resulted in beneficial side effects, such as recommendations by some of the participants for changes in mechanics to increase the safety of officers during field interviews and arrests. The department has also sought to exchange personnel with other agencies in the criminal justice system for temporary periods.

Storefront Centers   A storefront center is a police–community relations field office, often located in a business district in a slum area. Since the innovation of storefront centers several years ago, their use has generated controversy. Advocates of the concept believe that such a center provides a heretofore-missing communications link between the police and the public, especially the residents of economically depressed neighborhoods, and that it allows the communication to take place in a nonthreatening atmosphere. Detractors are divided among (1) those who believe that the storefront reduces effective field strength or that the activity is essentially social work, which should be conducted by nonpolice personnel, and (2) those who believe that the storefronts are indeed "fronts"—that they represent nothing more than lip service to mollify those seeking change.

The storefront center can be an effective program if some essential conditions are observed:

- The centers should not attempt to duplicate the functions of the central communications division; in other words, they should not become precinct stations. (Requests for routine police service should be made by the citizen to the central communications room by telephone.)
- Twenty-four-hour operation is unnecessary. Hours from noon to about 8 P.M. are satisfactory.
- The storefronts should act as a general referral service for other governmental and community agencies. Personnel should explain police services and policies and should offer advice and counsel in police-related matters.
- Storefront locations should be selected with care and should not be restricted to minority neighborhoods. Furnishings should be comfortable and functional and certainly not so claptrap that they convey a sense of lack of financial support.
- Personnel selected to man the centers should be sympathetic to the objectives of the program and should have agreeable dispositions for interviewing and counseling work.
- Personnel should receive specialized training for their duties.
- The centers should be closely identified with the police department, and personnel should wear uniforms.
- If team policing exists, storefront or team offices should be operated by the team.

Preventive Services   Closely related to the philosophy of the storefront center is the concept of the preventive services program, in which the police view their role as activists in overcoming the causes of criminality. This philosophy has been evident in juvenile-delinquency-control work for many years, but only recently has the concept been extended to envision the police as champions of those who are unable to help themselves or who are victims of poverty, unemployment, discrimination, or injustice.

The Police–Community Relations Council   A basic community relations activity is the formal police–citizen organization which is created to improve understanding and communication of community problems and at the same time to afford police the opportunity to explain the department's problems, services, and objectives. Since a typical community organization is of the

PUBLIC AND COMMUNITY RELATIONS

grass-roots variety, it should have a broad membership from the community, with representation from various neighborhoods. The structure can provide subcouncils and committees for special purposes or interests in crime prevention, youth work, and so on.

Although the community relations unit should closely coordinate or supervise the police–citizen organization, the operating personnel of the department—such as patrol supervisors or commanders—should have an active role in the program.

Chapter 14

Personnel Management

The history of police reform in the United States has tended to parallel the history of reform of municipal government. Before the turn of the century, police forces in many larger cities were completely under the control of the political organization. Not only were police responsive to the needs of the local political figures, but in several larger cities they actually served as willing agents in the repression of opposing political parties. In order to be responsive to these political bodies, police officials were appointed and removed at the discretion of the political leadership. Often, large groups of employees came and left with them.

In reaction to the spoils system and direct political control, the reformers of the early twentieth century concentrated on providing a semimilitary atmosphere in police departments, increased tenure for police supervisors through civil service appointments, and began to insulate police leadership from the body politic.

The next phase of reform tended to originate from within the police service and was led by a generation of police administrators who were a product of their own departments or who established their own organizations. It built upon earlier civil service reform and stressed development of profes-

PERSONNEL MANAGEMENT

sionalism, disciplinary control, refinement in organizational structure, and high standards for selection and training. This last phase of police reform—in which we find ourselves today—has stressed improvement of the police institution itself and professionalism as the means for rendering better service to the public.

Thus the professional- or institutional-style police department tends to stress improvement of the indirect means for police effectiveness—such as the enhancement of superior personnel practices, improved supervision, better deployment of manpower, and organizational effectiveness—as opposed to improving actual operational efficiency and productivity. Nevertheless, it is not possible to discuss police improvement in a comprehensive way unless the *means* for improvement are stressed almost as much as the end product of improvement, i.e., operational effectiveness.

The reason that the progressive police department stresses improvement in personnel administration is not only to have better-selected and better-trained officers in themselves but, of course, also to achieve the results which more highly capable personnel can render in the field. As a consequence, if the gains which can be made from improvement of personnel are not actually translated into improvements in the field, the effort is wasted.

Police service is concerned primarily with human conduct and actions rather than physical objects, and because of this the success of the police department is much more dependent upon the qualities of its personnel than upon the suitability of its equipment. The two key characteristics of the good police department, in fact, are highly personal in nature—the integrity of the force and the willingness of its personnel to work hard. Stated another way, the police department is no better than the aggregate of its individual members. Incompetent, untrained, and undisciplined police officers invariably provide unsatisfactory service; they damage the reputation of their own department and promote unfavorable public opinion throughout the country. There is no place in a modern, progressive department for stupid, inept, uncouth, lazy, dishonest, or insolent officers, and their presence on a force is evidence of the failure of the police chief and the city administration to give priority to personnel-management responsibilities.

The police often deal with people under circumstances which result in emotional stress; contacts are made frequently with people who are in trouble as a result of their own delinquency or negligence or who are victims of the actions of others. Police officers may also contact persons of the lowest ethical and moral standards and thus may be exposed to temptation and degradation. In contrast with some of their clientele, police officers are expected to have a keen sense of justice and to possess a high level of honesty, energy, physical courage, emotional stability, wisdom, and self-reliance. Any one of these qualities may be necessary in other lines of work, but no other occupation requires either as many of these characteristics or their presence to such a uniformly high degree.

The cost of operating the police department is a major part of any municipal budget, and the greatest percentage of the police budget, in turn, is devoted to salaries. Police personnel cost is therefore the greatest single item of expense in most city budgets.

Obtaining the Best-qualified Personnel

Since so much depends on the quality of personnel and because of the high expense of staffing, it follows that the best-qualified personnel obtainable should be selected for the force. They should be adequately trained, properly compensated and advanced, and skillfully motivated to improve the quality of their work.

Role of the Chief The selection and management of personnel is the chief's most important administrative task. A high quality of service is dependent upon his unwavering insistence upon the application of two principles: (1) The best personnel must invariably be selected for appointment and promotion, and (2) doubt in reference to appointment, promotion, or separation from service must be resolved in favor of the department.

Final responsibility for the consequences of selection, appointment, and discipline should rest with the chief if he is to be held accountable for the management of the department. Subject to the direction of the administrative head of the city and the restrictions of the merit system or civil service, the chief should have the freedom to select personnel for appointment and promotion and to assign and remove police officers from service. This makes it essential for the police chief and the city administrative head to agree on basic policies relating to personnel management as well as other police activities. To this end the police chief should always have a clear understanding with his superior concerning (1) personnel matters that require preliminary consultation and approval before action is taken, (2) action which may be taken without prior clearance but on which a report is desired, and (3) other matters on which no report is desired. The extent to which the administrative head of the city participates in the management of the program will depend on his willingness and ability to delegate authority, the size of the community, and the confidence he has in his police chief.

In addition, in cities in which there is a central personnel agency for all municipal employees, the chief has the responsibility of developing a relationship which will result in the agency's willing assistance in the management of police personnel. Any other relationship is unsound, and the police chief, through the administrative head of the city, should insist on its correction. Should the central agency prevent the chief from exercising suitable control over police personnel, fail to provide qualified recruits, or insist that incompetent employees be appointed, the chief has no alternative but to test the candidates himself and to take steps necessary to avoid the appointment of those not qualified for police service. Similar action must be taken to avoid interference by the central agency in the assignment, promotion, and discipline of the members of the force.

Role of the Central Personnel Agency Most American cities have some form of central municipal personnel agency. Such an agency generally acts for all city employees, sets minimum requirements for different positions and standards for promotions, and provides job descriptions for applicants. In carrying out their function, central personnel agencies should follow the principle of superior public service; their purpose should be to improve the quality of municipal service by assisting the operating departments in the management of their personnel. A personnel agency with any other goal will only hinder the operating departments.

Central municipal personnel agencies may be roughly divided into two categories: (1) those which are under the direct control of the administrative head of the municipality and (2) those which are independent of the chief administrative officer, with authority to make important decisions in reference to appointments, promotions, and discipline, without regard to the administrative head of either the city or the operating department.

There are central personnel agencies in both categories that follow the principle of superior public service, and when so motivated, they render valuable assistance to operating departments. Failure to follow this principle, however, is found more frequently in agencies that are independent of the administrative head of the city. In either case, where failures occur, they can usually be traced to one or more of four causes: (1) technical incompetence in the application of sound personnel administrative procedures; (2) unwholesome outside influences; (3) lack of integrity, resulting in bribery and corruption of the staff; and (4) the desire of the personnel agency to remove the control of personnel from the operating departments.

Fortunately, bribery and corruption of the central personnel staff are extremely rare. Incompetence and outside influences are much more common, and where they exist, the tasks of the chief are greatly increased, for he must make every effort to secure sound personnel administration in his force despite the shortcomings of the central agency. The fourth fault of central personnel agencies—the desire to exercise management control instead of providing staff assistance to responsible department executives—is due to a fundamental misconception of the role of such an agency. The erroneous idea that the central personnel agency rather than the responsible department executive should make decisions concerning personnel matters is often held not only by the agency staff members but frequently also by the general public and even by public administrators. Unless the proper functions of the central agency are clearly understood by all concerned and unless sound relationships between it and the operating departments are secured, the administration of the department will be seriously impaired.

Some Perspective on Civil Service Reform The pioneering legislation in the civil service field in the United States was the Civil Service Reform Law of 1884. Contrary to public opinion, it was not the product of a true reform movement; rather, it was a measure favored largely by conservatives in

Congress who were against the concept of equal opportunities for minority groups. Further, it is often said that civil service commissions were established to lessen the evils of the political-spoils system. There is truth in this, of course, but there is also evidence that civil service commissions grew out of the reaction against the emergence of Negroes as threats to job seekers patronized by large-city political machines in the decades following the Civil War. According to many leading civil rights advocates of the decades of the 1890s through the 1910s (when Grover Cleveland and Woodrow Wilson were in power), civil service requirements were in some cases established to prevent minority applicants from taking public employment. Over the years, however, civil service has been linked to the need to eliminate the spoils system, and as a consequence many personnel-department administrators view their key role as a policing function rather than as a service function on behalf of operating departments.

One of the results of this attitude is that too much security is accorded to employees against separation from service or other disciplinary action, and police chiefs have found it difficult, if not impossible, to weed out incompetent and untrustworthy officers. Whenever the law grants to it, or the personnel agency itself assumes, an authority over the management of police personnel that results in interference with effective operation of the department, an improper relationship exists that should be corrected.

A central personnel agency is not responsible for the operation of a police department, and for it to have control of police personnel is a violation of the principle that authority should not be delegated without holding the person or agency to which it is delegated responsible for the use made of it.

When the chief is faced with problems brought about by a lack of cooperation from the central agency, the head executive of the city can solve them when the personnel agency is under his direct control, and when it is not, he may approve necessary legislative changes to give the chief the means needed to control his force through the administration of sound personnel policies. The education of the public regarding the role of civil service and the reassurance of the police-force members may be necessary.

Other Policy Considerations

Police chiefs should have personnel statistics to assist them in determining personnel policy. For example, statistical tables should show age, length of service, and level of education by rank. This information is useful in determining the nature of needed training and in developing such concepts as incentive pay. Information relating to employee turnover is useful in assessing such things as job satisfaction and retirement incentives. But the judgment of acceptability should not be made solely on the basis of the rate; the reasons for turnover must also be examined in detail. An annual turnover rate of 5 to 15 percent is generally within the acceptable range for fully developed organizations, with an ideal of 7 or 8 percent. Some authorities believe that a rate of less than 5 percent in a fully developed organization reflects stagnation, while a rate

PERSONNEL MANAGEMENT

in excess of 15 percent is disruptive and expensive. Even when the rate is acceptable, an analysis may reveal that personnel are leaving for the wrong reasons. Further, the state of the economy has a great deal to do with whether a particular turnover rate is acceptable. When jobs are hard to find, a turnover rate of 8 percent might very well be considered excessive.

Use of Civilian Employees The practice of assigning police officers to records tasks, clerical duties, reception desks, key-punch operations, and so on is unsound from the point of view of both economy and efficiency. Such positions can usually be filled by civilian employees at a much lower salary than would be paid to police officers. Also, civilians who perform these jobs are more likely to have had some experience or formal training in typing, records tasks, and office procedures. However, if the use of civilian employees is not accompanied by adequate selection and training, placing an incompetent and inexperienced civilian in a critical job, such as that of complaint operator in a communications section or that of police dispatcher, is false economy. Administrators are discovering that in order to secure the kind of personnel who will understand proper police procedures and stay on the job long enough to benefit from training, it is necessary to pay these employees an adequate wage which is almost comparable to the salary of the regular police officer. Attempting to recruit personnel who are willing to work for two-thirds of the pay of the regular officer, coupled with their inadequate training, is almost certain to result in high turnover and a continuous succession of untrained, incompetent employees.

At the higher levels of department management, specialists will be required to direct planning, finance, personnel, data processing, and public information. Similarly, for the greatest long-term economy and efficiency, the heads and employees of the crime laboratory and of the motor-, radio-, and building-maintenance divisions should be highly trained and experienced persons. The necessary skills for the accomplishment of these specialized tasks are not usually found in the ranks of the police force. When civilians are employed to fill these positions, they should keep their civilian status. It should be established as policy that a qualified police officer who wishes to be employed in such a specialized field should resign his or her police civil service status and enter civil service as a civilian.

In every department, however, there will be some officers who must be assigned to light-duty work. Their services may be used at desk jobs and clerical tasks, but for greatest economy their assignments should be based as far as possible on a study of their special talents and aptitudes.

ORGANIZATION AND RESPONSIBILITIES OF THE PERSONNEL STAFF

In medium-sized and small departments, personnel and training responsibilities can be assigned to a personnel officer, often as a part-time activity for a staff officer who may also be concerned with the planning and inspection functions. In larger agencies, personnel responsibilities may require the full time of a staff officer, and in still larger departments, a formal staff unit is necessary.

Role of the Police Personnel Officer Ideally, the department personnel officer should be a university graduate in public personnel administration, with training in psychology and in the techniques of psychological testing. When the appointment of a personnel officer so qualified is not feasible, the task should be given to an individual whose background comes closest to providing this necessary training and experience. In the absence of either of the above, a police officer, selected on the basis of interest, education, and intelligence, should be assigned with the understanding that he or she will study the techniques used in the personnel field. Colleges and universities offer courses in public personnel administration, and assistance in the form of literature, home-study courses, and training workshops is available from the Public Personnel Association, Chicago, Illinois, and the International City Management Association, Washington, D.C.

The Police Personnel Officer and the Central Agency The existence of a central agency does not diminish the need for a police personnel officer. This officer should serve as a liaison between the department and the central agency and should strive to establish suitable working relationships between the two. Conditions of service and police personnel requirements differ from those in other departments; a knowledge of the nature of police service is basic to a wise application in the department of the principles of personnel administration. The chief role of the police personnel officer, therefore, is to work with the central agency in developing techniques of personnel management that meet the unique needs of police service.

Department personnel officers should actively assist the central agency in the promotion of police recruitment, in the establishment of satisfactory eligibility standards for appointment, in the development and application of reliable testing procedures for selection and promotion, and in the suitable measures of accomplishment and service ratings. They should train and assist supervising officers in the evaluation of subordinates. They should assist in job-classification studies conducted by the central personnel agency. A major responsibility should be the direction of the departmental training program. Finally, personnel officers should be concerned with the welfare of employees and with employee benefits.

When police personnel officers are competent and well trained, and when they demonstrate a willingness and eagerness to perform the above duties to the fullest, they can usually gain the confidence of the central personnel agency. In most central personnel agencies, shortage of staff will usually result in the central agency's assigning many of its police personnel tasks to the department officer, but under the general direction of the central agency and subject to its approval.

PERSONNEL MANAGEMENT

Organization in the Large Department In many departments, all personnel functions, including training, are grouped in one division. In most cases, however, it makes better sense to maintain the training function as a separate organizational unit. Under this form of organization, all other personnel responsibilities are placed in the personnel division.

Generally, the organization of a large personnel division ought to follow functional lines. A great part of the responsibility of such a division is the recruitment and selection of personnel. Another major activity is concerned with examinations and promotions. A third grouping includes staff work relating to personnel benefits and liaison with employee organizations. A logical fourth grouping consists of administrative and personnel records functions, including position classification, calculation of turnover rates, and personnel statistics.

The organization of the personnel division of the Metropolitan Police Department, Washington, D.C., follows these general guidelines and is depicted in Chart 22.

RECRUITMENT

Although the terms "recruitment" and "selection" are sometimes used interchangeably, the two words have different meanings. Recruitment is the process of attracting candidates who have the minimum qualifications to be eligible for the selection procedure. Selection, on the other hand, is concerned with screening out undesirable candidates after they have applied and with appointing the best-qualified personnel.

Attracting Superior Candidates

Candidates with good qualifications are in wide demand; competition in the labor market makes it important to attract candidates with the desired qualities, preferably in greater numbers than are needed. Consequently, the pay, working conditions, and other benefits for officers and their families should compare favorably with those available in other occupations. Otherwise, excellent potential candidates, as well as officers already in the service, will seek more attractive employment in other fields.

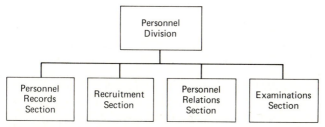

Chart 22 Organization of a personnel division.

The potential for advancement and the opportunity to enter at a higher level than the usual entrance position have become significant inducements, particularly to persons with college credits or degrees. Some departments now offer higher pay for educational attainment to new officers immediately upon their joining the force. The existence of this benefit should obviously be publicized.

More important than these material advantages in attracting and retaining qualified officers, however, is the intangible but nonetheless real spirit or atmosphere of the department which reflects the morale and true character of the force. A high esprit de corps is based on interest, enthusiasm, love of work, and the feelings of respect and confidence that all members of the force have regarding their superior officers. But most important of all in attracting competent officers is the opportunity to perform altruistically motivated public service. The above-average candidate knows this opportunity is greater in the department which has a good reputation.

Some employees in police service—as in any other calling—have a high degree of motivation which seems to be self-generated. A few such employees in any organization want to do an outstanding job regardless of pay, working conditions, quality of supervisors, and other outside influences. These employees seldom if ever complain, and they have a high degree of esprit de corps. One of the great challenges in personnel administration would seem to be identifying these individuals in advance and then encouraging their employment.

Advertising The opportunities for employment must be brought to the attention of those persons who possess the necessary qualifications in such an attractive way as to create a desire for appointment. This is done by advertising, the amount and character of which are influenced by the difficulties faced by the recruitment program. Departments with high prestige, adequate salaries, and favorable working conditions have little trouble recruiting qualified applicants.

The advertising campaign should be sufficiently intensive, selective, and effective to attract the desired number of candidates who possess suitable qualifications, and any of the commercial advertising procedures may be utilized when necessary. Notices and posters should be sent to colleges and universities, civic organizations, clubs, military separation centers, employment offices, and all other appropriate places likely to have contact with potential applicants. Newspaper advertising, while not as productive as some other methods, should always be used.

Field Recruiting Many departments send recruiting officers into the field to seek out applicants. These officers usually concentrate on visits to colleges having law-enforcement programs, areas where there are a high percentage of young men and women of recruiting age, and locations having a high percentage of minorities. This practice is recommended.

PERSONNEL MANAGEMENT   **253**

Recruiting vans have been utilized with success by many police departmentments (particularly in conjunction with walk-in examinations, described later in this chapter). During the period of popularity of James Bond movies, the Philadelphia Police Department was highly successful in taking advantage of the remarkable resemblance of one police officer (who was issued badge number 007, of course) to the star of the series. The officer was accompanied on his tours by attractive policewomen, considerable fanfare, and the actual gadget-loaded sports car used by James Bond in the pictures—loaned by the film studio as a public service.

Recruiting-Incentive Plans   A high percentage of new police officers are recruited through contacts with personnel already in the department. Some agencies have made use of this relationship and have offered various incentives for having suggested the names of applicants who are subsequently appointed to the force. Both cash bonuses and time off (such as five days of leave) have been given. The cash payment is more popular with officers and has the advantage of avoiding shortages of personnel—which the recruitment is aimed at overcoming in the first place. Officers should be supplied with recruiting packets containing brochures and applications, regardless of the existence of a recruiting-incentive plan.

The Recruiting Brochure   Materials used in recruiting should be attractive to the eye, colorful but dignified, and professional in appearance if not actually prepared by a professional advertising firm.

Recruiting materials should obviously mention the tangible benefits of police service, such as salary, benefits, and educational opportunities. What seems to be lacking in most recruiting materials today, however, is the mention of the opportunity to serve the public, to help people who cannot help themselves, to protect the vulnerable, to prevent crime, and to promote justice.

Eligibility Requirements

Part of the recruitment process involves setting eligibility requirements which applicants must satisfy before they are admitted to the selection procedure.

Residence Requirements   Preemployment residence in the community should not be required of candidates, for it reduces the number of qualified applicants from whom the most promising may be selected. Qualified young people who are residents of other cities or of small communities and rural areas often lack attractive opportunities in their local police service and are frequently interested in service in the department of a larger community.

A case can readily be made against limiting police appointments to candidates having preemployment residence in the community by comparing the records of service and the reputations of departments that follow this practice with those of departments that have not imposed such restrictions on their candidates. Departments with the greatest prestige and with long records of superior service recruit their police officers without limitation on residence, and increasing numbers of progressive departments are now adopting this policy.

Citizenship should be required of all candidates, and local residence after appointment is desirable except in communities where compliance with such a requirement would work an undue hardship on police employees because of limited suitable housing facilities.

Age   The tendency in personnel administration today is to liberalize age requirements. The direction of legislation and court decisions is toward job relatedness in every factor which can be used in selecting employees, including age, height, weight, and sex. For many years it has been fashionable to believe that police applicants who have not selected law enforcement as a career by the time they reach thirty years of age are perhaps motivated for reasons other than a deep interest in police work. However, an interest in law enforcement can develop at any age, and perhaps the only factor which would militate against hiring those between thirty and fifty years of age for general patrol service would be the ability of the city to absorb an older employee into the pension or retirement system. Although eyesight, hearing, and general health begin to deteriorate after adulthood is reached, allowances can be made for this sort of deterioration, and older employees can be brought into police service without jeopardizing the public good.

An age limit of twenty-one through thirty-five is recommended for inexperienced recruits, with extension of the upper limit for previous police service on a year-for-year basis. Court decisions in the future may prevent adherence to an age limit of this sort because of the need to demonstrate job-relatedness, but until that time comes, agencies would be advised to continue to try to recruit younger employees because of the difficulty encountered with the retirement system.

The advent of lateral entry and the development of certification and registry programs (discussed later in this chapter) may justify further extension of upper age limits on this same basis, provided candidates meet all other requirements.

At the other end of the age spectrum, considerable sentiment is developing for the recruitment of eighteen-year-olds into police service. For some time, persons of this age have been subject to military service and have had the right to vote in national elections. Many states give majority status to persons at eighteen years of age.

From the point of view of avoiding the loss of potential police candidates to police service, bringing recruits in at this age makes good sense. Otherwise, there is a possibility that between the time the potential candidates graduate from high school and reach twenty-one, they will develop an interest in some other occupation. There is also a belief that the younger candidates are, the less likely they are to be exposed to some of the corrupting influences that make many young persons ineligible for police service.

PERSONNEL MANAGEMENT

Educational Background   University or college training has become commonplace in American education, and degree courses in law enforcement, police science, and police administration are offered in hundreds of institutions across the country. Courses include all aspects of law enforcement, and may cover the related fields of criminology, criminalistics, corrections, traffic engineering, law, and the administration of criminal justice. Many of these schools offer graduate degrees; others restrict their courses to two-year or four-year programs. In addition to students who receive this specialized and relevant training, there are many other capable young people in colleges and universities who are potentially good candidates but who are not attracted to a service in which low educational requirements prevail. It seems reasonable to adopt, within the next few years, a minimum educational entrance requirement of two years of college. When it appears that four-year institutions can supply the number of graduates needed to introduce the two-level police-officer concept (described later in this chapter), the minimum educational requirement for agent and supervisory positions should be the baccalaureate degree. This position has been recently supported by the National Advisory Commission on Criminal Justice Standards and Goals. The Commission is clearly in favor of increasing educational requirements over the next few years and has stated unequivocally that all agencies should require a minimum of two years of college for entrance by 1978 and a four-year degree by 1984.

While university training will not make a competent person out of one who is intellectually inferior or otherwise deficient, when all other factors are equal, the university-trained candidates are better qualified for police service than those who have graduated only from high school. They have had broader experience with people and new situations, and their adaptability has been tested; they have also had the opportunity to meet students of many different nationalities, cultural backgrounds, and racial characteristics, and consequently they should have lost much of any previous bias or prejudice they may have held. Their studies will have given them a new perspective on the problems and aspirations common to all people, and they will have learned to some degree to withhold judgment and to restrain their actions and impulses in favor of calm consideration and analysis. College-educated persons who enter law enforcement are often idealistically motivated and appear to be able to resist corrupting influences. College-trained persons who have studied basic law enforcement subjects will, of course, be able to apply much of this knowledge immediately. Those who have studied police administration or other management-oriented subjects will already have begun to prepare for the future position of leadership which it is hoped they will strive to attain. Such officers will contribute a great deal to the true professionalization of police service.

Height and Weight   Even before the accelerated movement of women into police service in the past few years, there was a growing trend toward establishing less rigid height requirements and leaving the determination of the desirable height-weight relationship to the examining physician. Now that women are being accepted into police departments—and especially in view of the federal government's unwillingness to support law enforcement grant applications if a discriminatory height or weight requirement is in effect—many agencies are now stating simply that a height and weight standard of a particular level is "desirable" rather than required.

Visual Requirements   In recent years there has been a marked tendency to reduce visual requirements. Years ago, 20/20 visual acuity was required by many departments, but personnel officers and police administrators are recognizing that there is little practical difference between the effectiveness of an individual whose vision needs moderate correction and that of an officer who has 20/20 vision. In a recent study of the selection process in California, only 20 out of 411 cities required an uncorrected visual acuity of less than 20/40 for both eyes. Although most of these agencies required a correction of eyesight to 20/20, there has nevertheless been a definite shift toward more permissive visual requirements.[1] In Los Angeles, for example, uncorrected vision may be 20/67, with correction to 20/30.

Other Considerations

In the recruitment process, attention should also be given to the preliminary interview with the candidate, the application form, the closing date for filing applications, and the frequency of recruit examinations.

The Preliminary Interview   The practice of some departments of interviewing candidates when they file their applications serves no useful purpose; it only wastes time of the department and the candidates, unless the interviewer has the authority to eliminate those he feels are inadequate. However, rejection at this stage and by one officer is unwise. An effort should be made to obtain as many candidates as possible; the tests and examinations will determine unfitness for service, and this evaluation should not be undertaken by one individual.

Similarly, the practice of using the personal interview at the time of filing the application to inform the candidate verbally of the conditions of service is a waste of department time. The applicant should be given a booklet describing the service and should be instructed to read it at some point during the selection process. Just as an adverse description of the department is unwise, there is little justification for emphasizing benefits to the exclusion of an honest presentation of the disadvantages of entering police service. It is unfair to characterize law enforcement as a truly lucrative field or to appeal solely to the desire of a young person to join a semimilitary organization so that he or she can wear an attractive uniform.

---

[1]"Employment Opportunities in California Law Enforcement, 1975–1976," State of California Commission on Peace Officer Standards and Training, Sacramento, 1976.

PERSONNEL MANAGEMENT 257

Literature given to prospective applicants usually does not devote enough attention to the hazards and unpleasant aspects of police service. Although police administrators are obliged to make police work as reasonably safe as they can, law enforcement should not be oversold as a safe occupation without hazards. Police work is inherently more dangerous than many other professions, and police officers are subjected to unpleasant experiences and conditions from time to time. Literature provided to applicants should also give age, height, and educational requirements and should discuss the qualities desired in recruits. Most unqualified applicants, reading these requirements, will eliminate themselves.

At the other extreme, a few departments exaggerate the disadvantages of the service in the belief that when a pessimistic outlook is presented, the less-determined potential candidates will withdraw, and recruits will not feel that they have been inducted under false pretenses. An intelligent person will weigh the relative merits and demerits of employment in several fields, and if police service is unfairly presented in an unfavorable light, some intelligent potential candidates will decide against it. The aim in recruiting is to attract as large a group of qualified candidates as possible in order to have the best selection; consequently, the department should emphasize, within the limits of fairness, the advantages of the service.

The Application A great deal of personal-history data must be obtained from candidates before their appointment. These data facilitate the selection of candidates and, for those chosen, become an essential part of the personnel file. They are of value in understanding the officer during his or her development and training, and later they serve as a guide in selections for promotion and assignment. After candidates have successfully passed the entrance examinations, they should record these data on suitable forms to be used, as described later, as a part of the character investigation. The other tests may eliminate as many as 75 percent of the original candidates, and consequently the preparation of a long application is a waste of forms and of the time of unsuccessful candidates.

A convenient preliminary application form is printed on an 8- by 5-inch card with spaces for recording the name, address, and telephone number of the candidate; his or her age, height, weight, education, sex, marital status, date of birth, social security number, driver's license number, and the end results of the several tests. This form is a helpful tool in administering the entire selection process.

Closing Date for Filing Applications Since the objective is to obtain the maximum number of candidates, applications should be accepted up to the last possible date. In some instances, it may be feasible to accept applications at the time of the first series of tests. The advantage of so doing is to include among the candidates those most recently available and those attracted by the last-minute news stories about the examination.

Frequency of Examinations for Recruitment Recruitment examinations should be held at least once a year and more frequently when the need arises. A list of eligible recruits should not be kept on file for more than one year because each new year a number of young people reach the minimum age required for eligibility. Also, interest in appointment deteriorates after a candidate has been on an eligibility list for more than a few months, let alone a year.

THE SELECTION PROCESS

The selection of recruits is a grave responsibility and one that stands first in importance on the list of personnel administrative duties. The competence and integrity of recruits appointed to the force will determine the status of police leadership and the quality of police service for the ensuing 20 to 30 years. The chief or the personnel officer must apply, from the very beginning of the selection process, the two principles referred to earlier: Only the best must be considered for selection, and any doubts about a candidate's qualifications must be resolved in favor of the department.

Neither expense nor effort should be spared in selecting the best-qualified candidates for appointment. Training someone to be a competent police officer is expensive and time-consuming. It requires not just several months of intensive training but also several years of experience before the officer can be of real value to the department. The appointment of unqualified or poorly qualified persons is very expensive. One innocuous misfit who is unable to become a good police officer constitutes an economic loss that is usually many times the cost of the entire selection process for all the newly appointed recruits. The cost to the police department and to the community is substantially greater when the misfit is guilty of misconduct or of well-intentioned but ill-advised acts based on poor judgment; the prestige of the department is then damaged, and great harm may result from the actions.

Economy in police service is desirable, but failure to utilize the best techniques in the selection of candidates for appointment and promotion is penny-wise and pound-foolish. Superior procedures, administered by the best-qualified specialists and technicians, should be used without regard to cost if substantial police economies are to be effected.

The Positive Approach to Selection During the prosperous decades of the 1950s and 1960s, the labor market was competitive for the employer. The number of fully qualified candidates seldom exceeded the number of openings, and so selection based primarily upon negative standards was feasible; police administrators had a fair idea of the kind of candidate they did *not* want, but few expressed selection standards in positive terms. In recent years, however, there have been many more qualified candidates than openings, except in those few departments having a college-education requirement. This situation allows

PERSONNEL MANAGEMENT **259**

the department to focus on positive characteristics as well as negative ones.

A number of qualities are essential for the satisfactory performance of basic patrol tasks, in addition to the desirable characteristics mentioned earlier for police officers in general.

Patrol officers work with people. They must like people and be able to deal with them in a calm and dignified manner; they must be emotionally stable, courageous, firm, temperamentally equipped for police work, and free of bias or prejudice. They should have forceful personalities, and they should be poised and have well-developed powers of self-expression. The temptations that confront police officers and the critical attitude of the public make it essential that their character and reputation be beyond reproach. They must have a high order of intelligence, which ensures their ability to learn, to observe, to retain, to reason rapidly and accurately, and to adapt quickly and satisfactorily to new situations. Police officers must have a keen sense of loyalty to their fellow officers, the department, and the community. Finally, and of utmost importance, they should be willing to work hard.

In addition, recruits should have good health, strength, endurance, agility, and coordination to permit them to make arrests and participate in rescue operations which may be physically demanding.

The Berkeley Police Department has established a list of desirable personal qualities for patrol officers:

- Initiative
- The ability to carry a great deal of responsibility and to handle difficult emergency situations alone
- Social skills and the ability to communicate effectively with persons of various cultural, economic, and ethnic backgrounds
- The mental capacity to learn a wide variety of subjects quickly and correctly
- The desire and ability to adapt their thinking to technological and sociological changes
- An understanding of their fellow human beings and a desire to help in need
- The emotional maturity to remain calm and objective and to provide leadership in emotionally charged situations
- The physical strength and endurance to perform these exacting duties

In the next few decades, there may be periods when the labor market will become highly competitive for the prospective employee. If this happens, one could expect to find eligible lists with larger numbers of candidates who are well qualified by today's essentially negative standards—those within height, weight, and age requirements; those who are not below a certain level of intelligence; and those who do not have physical or medical problems, personality difficulties, or deficiencies in character. Assessment of positive

Examinations and Tests

It should be remembered that public employment is a privilege and not a right. It is reasonable, therefore, to reject any candidate who may have failed to meet the minimum qualifications for police service. Once standards have been set, a series of tests and examinations, designed to eliminate the unfit and to differentiate among the fit, should be administered by either the central municipal personnel office or by the police department itself.

The various tests and examinations require some of the skills of a physical education instructor, an investigator, a physician, a neurologist, an endocrinologist, a psychologist, and a psychiatrist. A competent medical examiner, when furnished with the results of clinical tests administered by a qualified psychologist and when fully conscious of the exacting needs of police service, may make the first physical examination and refer to specialists those who appear to need further examination.

The Impact of *Griggs v. Duke Power Co.* In 1968 several employees of the Duke Power Company in North Carolina were given an examination by their employer for a job requiring manual labor. The company administered a standardized aptitude test to fill the positions, and the employees, including Griggs, filed a suit to the effect that passing a pencil-and-paper test of this sort had little to do with ability to perform manual labor. The decision was eventually taken to the United States Supreme Court,[2] which held that if a test (1) is not job-related and (2) differentiates on the basis of race, sex, or religion, it is inherently discriminatory.

The impact of that decision on public employment has been great. Both entrance and promotional examinations must now have some relationship to success on the job or at least (in the case of entrance examinations) to success in performing in the police training academy. Further, a test which fails a higher percentage of minority applicants is also discriminatory.

Intelligence Many police tasks have complex ramifications involving socially significant problems that call for a relatively high level of intelligence for recognition, analysis, and solution. Intellectually inferior police officers cannot provide the kind and quality of service needed to deal with these situations. Crime prevention in its broadest sense demands the service of unusually competent police personnel, and progress in this direction will be somewhat in proportion to the intelligence that is brought to bear on these problems.

Several departments have demonstrated the feasibility of requiring a high level of intelligence, and the superior performance of the talented officers in these departments has proved the wisdom of this procedure. Promotions to

[2]*Griggs v. Duke Power Co.*, 915 Sup. Ct. 849 (1971).

PERSONNEL MANAGEMENT

supervisory and command positions must be denied to police officers of inferior intellect if impairment of service is to be avoided. When the intelligence of the entire body of the force is high, competent leadership within the department is more easily ensured, and the department can safely promote through the ranks to the very top positions.

Job relatedness is difficult to establish in a direct comparison of conventional IQ scores and police tasks. However, there is a significant degree of job relatedness in aptitude and achievement tests which have been developed specifically in the past few years to cope with the two requirements of (1) relationship to performance on the job and (2) absence of discrimination against minorities or women. Further, there is a measure of natural screening of the less intelligent in higher education; people with inferior intellect seldom have the inclination or the ability to graduate from college.

Written Examinations Most civil service systems and personnel agencies require some form of written testing for the purpose of ranking candidates in the selection process. Basing the ranking on an IQ or aptitude test is psychologically undesirable and is seldom done. Instead, most civil service systems require the use of a written examination which usually has a high concentration of "achievement" content—that is, content relating to achievement of educational skills and levels rather than to the potential or aptitude for learning.

In many tests, particularly in examinations which are constructed without extensive preparation and in which there is never any intent to achieve standardization, there is a considerable mixing of aptitude items with questions relating mainly to achievement.

There is now a desirable trend toward the use of standardized achievement tests as the written examination which is to be scored and weighted for selection purposes. These tests correlate highly with educational achievement, and the passing mark should generally coincide with the scores of high school graduates at the upper quartile. Naturally, when several years of college work are required for entrance into police work, scores on such tests should be adjusted upward.

Information on standardized achievement tests can be obtained from most secondary school systems or directly from publishers of these tests, such as Educational Testing Service in Princeton, New Jersey.

Specific-Information Tests The use of tests designed to measure job knowledge or specific information at the recruit level is unwise if there is no college-education requirement. Some of these tests contain meaningless questions relating to community characteristics, such as the geography of the area, or questions based on police rules and regulations, city ordinances, and other specific information which is usually committed to memory by cramming but may soon be forgotten after the examination. Specific-information tests are unfair to candidates who are not familiar with local conditions and to those without police experience.

In the past few decades, the most progressive departments discontinued the use of specific-information tests on the grounds that they limited the number of potential applicants. However, two factors mentioned above have come into play since then which argue for readoption of the specific job-related test. First, according to the *Griggs* decision and related court decisions, tests must be job-related. Second, the explosion in police and law enforcement education now makes it possible to establish college-education requirements as well as to administer written examinations on police subjects.

Since there is a high degree of correlation between success on any written test and intelligence, the development of a new specific-information test to measure comprehensive knowledge about police procedures seems to be an ideal way to carry out written examinations in those cities having college-education entrance requirements.

An Alternative to Written Tests   In the absence of a college-education requirement for entrance and in the event that aptitude testing is denied the department because of court decisions, the most logical approach for the agency is to adopt "open selection," or simply to admit candidates on a first-come, first-served basis to the police academy after initial screening and a brief background investigation.

A requisite for the "open selection" procedure, however, is the adoption of true job-related training standards which have been predetermined by measurement against those who have successfully carried out the job.

Following intensive instruction in police subjects, candidates are quickly given tests on actual job-related subjects. Those who cannot meet these standards are then eliminated along with those who are screened out during concurrent intensive background investigations. In this form of selection and testing, it must be made absolutely clear to candidates that the academy testing is an integral part of the selection procedure.

Psychological Evaluation   The evaluation of the personality of the candidate involves more than an appraisal of personal qualities by an oral board. As considered here, "personality" is regarded as a reflection of the total makeup of the individual and, more particularly, the impact of this reflection upon others. Any procedure designed to evaluate it should attempt to discover emotional instability or immaturity and any conflicts that would make it difficult for the officer to work successfully with others. As in the case of character, the personality of the applicant in these respects is usually either acceptable or unacceptable and not good or bad in degree; it is an intangible quality that is not subject to appraisal in terms of exact measurements.

Adaptability and some other factors that make up personality can be measured by means of psychological tests. A psychologist and a psychiatrist who are highly qualified may make an appraisal of personality through the use of psychological tests on both a group and an individual basis. Psychological tests of personality for use in competitive examinations, however, may be subject to error because candidates sometimes give the answer they believe will enhance their opportunity for employment instead of the one that would reveal their true attitude. Tests that permit choices on such a basis do not seem suitable for selection purposes, although they may have considerable value as clinical devices. To meet the demands of personnel selection, the test should require some competitive effort to avoid false answers. Further, the test should have been previously tried and found reliable. The department personnel officer has an obligation to keep informed about means of testing the emotional makeup of candidates and to promote studies relating to police aptitudes at the local university and college departments of psychology so that, in the future, even more valuable tests will be available for use in police recruitment programs.

The City of Pittsburgh achieved noteworthy success in the psychological screening of candidates by using independent consulting psychologists employed under contract with the civil service commission. Following the successful use of psychological testing, the police department underwent a reduction in force; as a result, for a period of several years, no new applicants were hired. However, hiring has resumed again, along with psychological testing. The basic test instrument is the Minnesota Multiphasic Personality Inventory, which is computer-scored to produce the 10 clinical scales and standard validity scales. The MMPI is supplemented by the Guilford-Zimmerman Temperament Survey. After completing the MMPI, candidates are subject to an in-depth character investigation, which is conducted by police investigators according to a format designed by one of the psychologists. The third phase of the process is a face-to-face interview with a psychologist who has access to the MMPI scores, background investigation, and intelligence-test scores. The psychologist is given wide latitude and may administer the Rorschach, Thematic Apperception, Bender-Gestalt, or similar tests; the psychologist may also request an interview by another psychologist before making the final decision.

The success of the program has been demonstrated by the relative absence of personnel problems among police officers selected after January 1966, when the procedure was adopted. As of 1971, not one officer had been the subject of trial-board action, and few new officers have required serious disciplinary measures since then.

Psychiatric Examinations Some departments use psychiatric examinations rather than psychological testing. The objective is much the same, except that the psychiatrist tends to focus more on mental health than on the general assessment of personality.

The high cost of the psychiatric examination has prevented many departments from employing it, but often this cost is far exceeded by the havoc wrought by one deranged or psychotic officer whose actions may bring death or sorrow to an individual and shame to the department. With careful screening and interpretation of tests, the number of potentially psychotic candidates can be substantially lowered, and it is essential that the department protect the public and safeguard its reputation by barring its doors to such risky candidates.

Psychiatric examinations should be a part of the medical examination so that rejections for psychiatric reasons may be classified as rejections for medical reasons. The emotional state that may disqualify a person for police service may not interfere with a career in some other field. The rejection should be made in such a manner as to be least damaging to the candidate.

The Physical and Medical Examination The rigors of police service make it important to eliminate physically unfit candidates. The physical and neurological condition of applicants should be ascertained by thorough and extensive examinations and laboratory tests.

Those who tend to be overweight should be eliminated, although this should be determined in each individual case in accordance with the height-weight relationship decided upon by the examining physician.

The practice of summarily rejecting a candidate because of flat feet should be reappraised. Studies indicate that congenital flat feet are foot *types* and are a normal characteristic. Unless the condition produces symptomatic problems such as foot or leg pains or rapid fatigue, it should not be considered the result of a defective foot. Congenital flat feet do not prevent active, heavy work and do not require medical attention. Acquired flat feet, on the other hand, may lead to chronic difficulties that impair the value of an officer's services.[3] A method of diagnosing this condition should become a standard part of the medical examination.

A relaxation of visual-acuity requirements seems justified, as indicated earlier. Former standards of 20/20 and of 20/30 vision correctable to 20/20 should be changed to permit a 20/40 vision with a 20/20 binocular correction.

There is frequently a temptation to overlook apparently minor physical defects in otherwise well-qualified candidates. This practice is to be condemned; the appointment of persons in doubtful health or of questionable organic or neurological soundness almost always proves to be a poor investment. Their physical condition frequently results in decreased energy and attention to duty that impair the quality of their service. It results in time lost as a result of illness and sometimes in early disability and retirement on pension benefits; such officers thus become a burden on the retirement system and an added operating expense since others must be selected and trained to replace them earlier than would otherwise have been necessary. Doubts relating to the physical qualifications of candidates should be resolved in favor of the service.

Strength and Agility Standards should be established to ensure the more-than-ordinary strength and agility that are sometimes required in police service; the staying power of the individual thus measured may reflect

---

[3]Henri L. DuVries, M.D., *Surgery of the Foot*, The C. V. Mosby Company, St. Louis, 1959.

PERSONNEL MANAGEMENT

desirable psychological qualities in addition to physical endurance. Since strength and agility are not the most important factors in the selection of police officers, however, it seems wise not to establish standards that will eliminate substantial numbers of candidates or to give undue weight to the test scores. The primary purpose of these tests is to reveal a lack of coordination, strength, and speed which would make the candidate unfit for service. Standards somewhat less than the average for university freshmen seem suitable.

Because of the need to accommodate women applicants, some modification of the traditional strength and agility tests seems desirable. Such tests should now be structured to permit a certain percentage of women applicants, as well as male applicants, to pass.

The inability of many women to pass strength and agility tests on equal terms with men is also partly cultural; women have traditionally remained aloof from vigorous work and sports competition, and this tends to give male applicants more strength and agility. With greater participation by women in activities heretofore reserved for men, this picture is changing. Nevertheless, for many generations to come it is likely that women will continue to be of slighter stature and to be less strong than most men, and for this reason if women enter police service in proportion to their percentage of the general population, the strength of the average police employee may diminish.

Character Investigation A thorough background investigation is one of the most important and expensive steps in the elimination process and should be restricted to those who have successfully passed the preceding tests. *Character* is one of the less objective factors, and it cannot be measured in percentage points; unless the candidate's character is suitable, he or she must be eliminated. The intangible nature of character makes it no less important; the expenditure of considerable effort is justified to ensure that the character of candidates makes them acceptable for police service.[4]

An essential tool in a proper character investigation is the use of a detailed personal-history statement, which calls for in-depth answers relating to arrest or criminal record, traffic violations, indebtedness, medical history, names of friends and relatives, previous residences, previous employment, organizational affiliations, interests and hobbies, and so on.

Fingerprints of the candidate must be cleared through the FBI and state bureaus, and a search must be made of police records locally and in other cities in which the candidate may have lived. A personal interview must be held with the candidate and also with his or her employers, teachers, associates, friends, relatives, and other persons who may have information bearing on character and reputation.

A most useful technique in conducting a character investigation is the interview of "developed references," persons whose names have been ob-

---

[4]For a detailed discussion of character-investigation procedures and other selection techniques, see Richard L. Holcomb, *Selection of Police Officers*, Bureau of Public Affairs, University of Iowa, Iowa City, 1946.

tained from references listed by the candidate. Investigators should ask each reference to supply the names of other friends of the candidate. Close attention should be paid to the findings revealed through interviews with developed references. The character and attitudes of the developed references are also valuable clues about the candidate if the association has been close. The interviewer should be alert during these discussions to any reference to erratic behavior, emotional instability, or other personality defect that, if verified, would make the candidate an undesirable recruit. In fairness to the candidate, such assertions should be checked carefully, but if they prove to be well founded, the decision must then be made in favor of the department.

The applicant's scholastic and work records should be studied, since they may provide indications of his stability and willingness to perform and can serve as a check on his written test scores. The members of the candidate's immediate family should be interviewed in their home; their reaction to police employment must be discussed, especially in the case of a spouse or a person to whom the candidate is engaged. Criminal behavior and mental illness on the part of relatives should be ascertained. As a part of the background investigation, many departments require the candidate to take a lie-detector test.

The background investigation should obviously pay attention to factors which would disqualify a candidate. However, there should be equal stress on characteristics which are positive in nature. A candidate may not have any of the bad characteristics which would result in disqualification, but, on the other hand, he or she may not have a surplus of positive traits such as loyalty, initiative, courage, and a sense of justice. These positive characteristics cannot be reliably determined by conventional written examinations or through the brief interviews in the oral-board phase of the examination process. It may be possible within the next few years to develop character "profiles" to differentiate between acceptable and superior qualities. The evaluator would, for example, rate each candidate on several scales such as honesty–integrity, social awareness–sense of justice, and altruism–sense of service. At present, however, if attention is to be given to the positive characteristics, the logical means is the coordinated character-investigation–psychological-evaluation process.

Investigations of Motivation and Interest Earlier in this chapter it was mentioned that a few individuals have a strong desire to succeed regardless of working conditions. These persons almost thrive on adversity and seem to want to do a good job in spite of poor working conditions, poor supervision, and other equally undesirable conditions. It is possible to establish whether a potential employee has this characteristic during the background investigation. Although the candidate's personal friends—and developed references obtained from these friends—provide extremely useful clues as to the candidate's character, contacts with teachers and with previous employers are very helpful in determining whether the applicant is highly motivated. At the same time, however, these same individuals may not know of certain flaws in the applicant's character.

PERSONNEL MANAGEMENT

If a previous employer describes the candidate as one who wants to succeed regardless of working conditions or outside inducements, then it is safe to conclude that with good working conditions in a police department, the individual will continue to exert the same level of effort.

Since lack of suitable character qualifications will eliminate the candidate from further consideration, important judgments must be made on the facts revealed by the investigation. This is not a difficult problem for central personnel agencies in recruiting for other branches of public service; convictions for felonies and offenses involving moral turpitude serve as a convenient and easily applied rejection indicator.

In police service, however, the character of the candidate is a matter of more serious concern. When decisions must be made to reject or approve persons who have given some evidence of unsuitable character by acts other than those involving felony or moral-turpitude convictions, sound judgment must be used to preserve the integrity of the police service and to deal fairly with the candidate. Examples of such acts are speeding to elude a police car resulting in the arrest of the candidate, shoplifting but with the complainant dropping the charge, or being named as correspondent in a divorce case. Such incidents may vary from area to area or from one recruit group to the next, but each must be studied carefully, and the behavior must be evaluated in terms of its impact on the future conduct of the candidate. Here again, the psychiatric examination can be of value, and the psychiatric report should play an important part in the consideration of the problem.

In the absence of a central personnel agency, responsibility for such judgments clearly rests with the police. Because of their training they will usually make wise decisions in these matters, especially when they resolve doubts in favor of the department. Central personnel agencies usually do not have a corps of qualified investigators to make suitable background investigations; consequently, they frequently rely on a perfunctory mail-order questionnaire that depends heavily on references supplied by the candidate. When the personnel agency is under the control of the chief administrative officer of the city, and especially when it is staffed with competent persons interested in the recruitment of the best-qualified candidates, the problem can nearly always be resolved if the police undertake a character investigation and reach decisions acceptable to the central personnel director. When this degree of cooperation is not found, the police chief is confronted with the important necessity of conducting the background investigation to his satisfaction and of refusing to appoint those whose character seems to him to be unsuited to police service, even though he may be subjected to strong pressure. The chief renders an important service to the community when he avoids the appointment of any but the most desirable persons.

Oral Interviews The intangible personal qualities of candidates should be appraised either by an oral board or by selected members of the department in longer and more leisurely personal interviews. One interview with all oral-board members is sufficient, thus giving this procedure the advantage of speed, which makes its use almost imperative when the number of candidates is great. The use of an oral board also gives the department an opportunity to invite commanding officers from nearby departments and citizens with special qualifications and prestige to participate in the selection of personnel. An examining board which includes some citizen members avoids the charge of favoritism, and a carefully selected board which includes outsiders as well as members of the department is likely to provide a more accurate appraisal than a board drawn entirely from the department.

The oral board should concentrate upon the appraisal of personal qualities that may be evaluated during a short interview. These include such qualities as appearance, voice, articulateness, poise, bearing, carriage, and alertness. The board should limit attempts to deal with factors that may be more accurately measured by other means. Included in the latter category are knowledge, education, intelligence, strength, and agility. Neither should the oral board place too much emphasis on judgment of character, loyalty, honesty, dependability, initiative, ability to get along with people, or other characteristics that require longer observation and more reliable information than are provided by a short interview. It should, however, undertake to appraise the attitude of the individual toward matters relevant to police service.

At the conclusion of each interview, after the candidate has left the room, each board member should record on a form provided by the department his or her appraisal of the personal qualities under consideration. Each board member should then estimate an overall percentage score for the candidate based on this appraisal. When the meeting is over, the personnel officer should average all the overall percentage scores for each candidate.

The group oral interview is now gaining acceptance with personnel administrators. In the group technique, candidates are given an opportunity to demonstrate leadership with their peers. The procedure also permits evaluation of verbal communications skills and the candidates' personalities.

A superior method of appraising personal qualities consists of a private and informal interview of each candidate conducted separately by several commanding officers who have demonstrated their ability to judge people. Any form of questioning that the examiner may consider worthwhile should be used in arriving at an opinion regarding the personal qualities of the candidate. Each examiner should submit a written report stating his or her conclusions and should include in it a definite recommendation either to reject or to appoint the candidate.

Appraisals made in this manner by commanding officers in whose judgment the chief has confidence are more thorough than oral-board evaluations, which are usually based on a 15- or 20-minute interview. They also carry more weight because the oral board may be open to the charge that it went through the routine motions without the concentrated attention that is ordinarily given by someone with a greater interest in, and responsibility for, the final result.

In Arlington, Virginia, the candidate appears before two separate boards. The first board is a panel made up of representatives from the central personnel

PERSONNEL MANAGEMENT

agency and the manager's staff. This board looks for positive traits, such as a sense of altruism, high motivation, and sensitivity to such issues as use of women in police work. The second board is a conventional police oral board which is made up of police supervisors. The police board tends to concentrate on the more negative aspects of selection, such as lack of involvement with crimes, traffic offenses, bad debts, immorality, and other poor conduct.

The Final Selection From the group of candidates who have successfully passed the battery of mental and physical tests and whose character investigation and oral-board appraisal indicate that they are suitable material, those best qualified for appointment must be selected. It is difficult to devise a formal procedure for evaluating intangible personal qualities, and because of this there is a tendency to overevaluate tangible, objective qualities, such as intelligence and strength. The test results are used as guides in the final selection, but the temptation to give undeserved weight to variations in objective qualities, merely because they are easily scored, must be resisted. When procedures are used that assign a weight to the score obtained in each test and the final selection is made on the basis of the total, the assumption is that the candidate who makes a perfect score is perfectly qualified. The fallacy in this assumption lies in the fact that, although a minimum standard of competence should be established, those who exceed the minimum qualification may not be more qualified proportionately for police service. Intelligence tests are probably not accurate to such a fine degree, and even if they were, the added increment of intelligence may not be so important in terms of good police service as consideration of others, adaptability, or some intangible quality of leadership. The same situation prevails in the case of tests of strength and agility. It is important that an officer be sufficiently strong and agile to apprehend fleeing culprits and to handle unruly prisoners or perform rescue feats, but it does not follow that the candidate who has broken Olympic decathlon records or who has excelled in other sports is that much better qualified as a police officer.

In many cases the appointment process may be controlled by civil service or merit-system rules, such as the common requirement to consider two more candidates than there are positions open. Smaller departments are more inclined to take advantage of this rule, which usually permits a final, brief interview conducted by the appointing authority. A single appointment can be of great significance in a small department, but in a larger agency the "rule of three" is of less value because the appointing authority does not have the time to conduct hiring interviews.

Probation Some police administrators fail to recognize probation as an important step in the selection process. Although it is true that testing procedures are highly effective in eliminating the incompetent or emotionally disturbed candidate, tests have not reached a stage of perfection that precludes the possibility of the appointment of undesirable individuals. The final test must be trial on the job. Full advantage should be taken of the opportunity afforded by the probationary period to eliminate those who demonstrate unfitness. There should be no hesitation in this regard once the supervising officers have studied the individual case and have reached a conclusion that the recruit is unsatisfactory, and there should be no appeal from this decision. Such elimination is especially important where testing procedures are poor, for it is difficult to remove unqualified officers after they pass the probationary period. Failure to remove incompetent and otherwise unsuited probationers is a mark of weak leadership; police chiefs who do not avail themselves of this opportunity to complete the selection process cannot complain that they are denied personnel control.

The probationary period should last one year. Some weaknesses and incompetence may not be discovered in a shorter time, particularly when recruit training may require six months or more. Special attention should be given to the supervision and rating of probationers. They should be observed closely during their training period and during class hours; notebooks, examinations, and classroom attitudes should be evaluated and carefully recorded. When they are sent into the field, they should spend time with several different supervisors, usually patrol officers with several years' service who have demonstrated their ability to direct and guide rookies and who have enthusiasm and unquestioned loyalty to their jobs. Records of accomplishments and service ratings should be made at least quarterly and preferably every month. High standards must be maintained, and doubtful cases should be resolved in favor of the department.

Without a doubt, probation is the first true job-related test in the selection procedure. It is probable that in the next few years probation will become more and more important in the movement toward job-related tests. The difficulty with reliance on probation is that it fails to take into account the human tendency of supervisors who have the power to pass or fail an employee to accept failure and weakness once a candidate has become personally known to them. Because of this, it becomes obvious that one of the great supervisory training needs in the police service is to convince first-line and middle-level supervisors that one of their major responsibilities is to separate borderline and unfit candidates who are able to get into the department despite the formal testing procedure and entrance requirements.

Walk-in Examinations   Many departments now conduct an accelerated recruitment and selection procedure known as the "walk-in" examination. Walk-in testing can be conducted in the field during recruiting trips outside the city or as a continuous testing program carried out by the central personnel agency or the police personnel unit. It is best suited for the "bear market" employment situation, when there are fewer qualified candidates than job openings. The procedure thus allows the recruiter to strike while the iron is hot; an interested candidate can be tested, interviewed, fingerprinted, and measured during the first visit and may even be given a provisional appointment while awaiting the outcome of the character investigation.

PERSONNEL MANAGEMENT   271

Sequence of Events in Group Testing   The cost of tests and examinations varies, some requiring more time or more expensive specialist or laboratory services than others. Since the number of candidates becomes smaller as the hurdles are cleared, the tests should be arranged in a sequence that will eliminate the unqualified at minimum expense and with the least loss of time. Legal restrictions or rules of the central personnel agency which require that candidates be permitted to complete the entire series of tests should be amended to avoid this wasteful procedure. Eligibility for taking the next test in the series should be predicated on the successful completion of the preceding one. The same holds true for the component parts of the physical examination, which should be given in such an order that the unfit candidates are eliminated before they are subjected to the more expensive medical, laboratory, neurological, and psychiatric studies. For example, eye examinations and physical measurements of height, weight, and chest expansion may be made during tests of strength and agility.

Written examinations, including achievement tests, should be given first because they eliminate a large percentage of the candidates and are less expensive to administer than the other tests. Tests of strength and agility require more time than the written tests since they are individually given and are consequently more costly. They should therefore be administered only to those who successfully pass the written examination. Medical, neurological, and psychiatric examinations must be individually made by highly skilled specialists and laboratory technicians. In consequence they are very expensive and should be given only to candidates who have successfully completed all the previous tests.

Summary of the Selection Process

The following sequence of events has proved to be effective:

1   Review of short-form application for age, height, and education or for evidence of disqualification.

2   Written examination (a job-related achievement test), weighted 60 percent.

3   Fingerprinting and initial name checks.

4   Physical measurement, preliminary visual testing, and agility testing.

5   Initiation of personal-history statement and medical questionnaire. (Note: For walk-in or field recruiting, the above events can be conducted on the same day.)

6   Oral interview, weighted 40 percent of the total score.

7   Completion of character investigation, based on information in personal-history statements and results of oral interview.

8   Medical, psychological, and psychiatric examinations.

9   Appointment interview (if appropriate).

10   Probationary period of one year.

PERFORMANCE EVALUATION

Performance evaluation is one of the most controversial issues in personnel management.

For many years authorities in the personnel field, in public as well as private management, have tried to devise foolproof systems for the evaluation of individual performance. For as long a period, the developers of these systems have sought multiple objectives. Personnel technicians have believed that the ideal form could satisfy many purposes, such as serving as a guide for salary increases, promotion, transfer, and disciplinary action; increasing productivity and efficiency; and stimulating supervision.

Achievement of these multiple objectives has simply not been possible, and in the last few years there has been a noticeable trend toward the simplification of these objectives. Using the performance rating to determine whether an employee should receive the next salary step is inadvisable and has been one of the reasons for the failure of multiple-objective systems. While most supervisors can be convinced that performance evaluation ought to be carried out to improve performance, few can divorce themselves from concern over the employee's family welfare when the question of a raise is at issue. If the system is used to determine raises, most supervisors will simply give an employee a fictitious rating so that a salary increase will not be withheld.

Some personnel authorities now believe that a performance-evaluation system should have one—and only one—objective: to inform employees of the quality of their work so that they may improve their performance. This has meant that the performance-rating system itself can be simplified somewhat. It has also meant that the use of the same form for evaluating job performance cannot be adjusted to achieve multiple objectives as diverse as stimulation of productivity and evaluation of promotional potential. Many modern systems have therefore evolved into two separate but compatible programs: (1) the performance evaluation, which is used only to notify employees of the quality of their work, and (2) the promotion-potential rating, which is used solely to facilitate the rating of candidates for promotion.

Other Trends in Performance Evaluation

Several other trends in performance evaluation can be identified. One is the shift away from rating such characteristics as "dependability" and "quality of work" and toward rating more easily recognized or observed characteristics. For example, managers and supervisors can often recognize failures in planning and scheduling or the existence of excessive grievances or low morale, but they have considerably more difficulty learning why such problems exist. Proponents of the trend toward objectivity therefore advocate performance evaluation based on an examination of symptoms rather than of underlying causes.

In opposition to this trend, there is a tendency for some personnel authorities to regard performance evaluations more subjectively, that is, to consider them opinions and attitudes rather than scientific measurements.

PERSONNEL MANAGEMENT

Some of the stress on trying to shroud opinions, or to systematize them, is being eliminated.

It does not make sense to give an employee a numerical rating during performance evaluation if the sole purpose is to improve the candidate's performance. Since the rating under this concept does not have any influence on promotion, future salary determination, transfer, or any other adjustment, an overall numerical score serves no purpose.

A performance-evaluation system advocated by IACP is shown in Appendix F. The system is a modification of a performance-evaluation procedure recommended by the Public Personnel Association.

Regardless of the system used for performance evaluation, the procedure should be carried out once every six months for employees in regular status and oftener for those in probationary positions, such as every two to three months during a probationary period of one year.

The Evaluation Interview   One of the benefits of a formal performance-evaluation system is that it can force supervisors to interview their subordinates. The very fact that an interview has taken place may have beneficial effects in improving performance. Even when a formal performance-evaluation system is not in use, an interview between the employee and supervisor can be carried out periodically, such as every six months.

Promotional-Potential Rating

At the time a candidate for promotion is going through the selection process, he or she should be given a rating to assess potential in the rank being sought. This is particularly true of the promotion from patrol officer to sergeant, when the nature of duties performed shifts abruptly from patrol tasks to supervisory responsibilities. It must be recognized that individuals who demonstrate superior ability in actual work tasks as patrol officers may not have the qualities required to be successful supervisors. The same concept also holds true for the promotion from any rank to a higher rank, but to a lesser degree. For example, the primary skills required by a lieutenant, i.e., leadership and ability in the direction of subordinate supervisors, will relate quite heavily to success as a captain if the officer has performed these tasks well as a lieutenant.

Identification of Promotional Potential   Among all the desirable characteristics of the good supervisor, the qualities of leadership rank first; these attributes ensure superior performance by patrol officers, and promotions should be given to those who excel in leadership. The qualifications of a good leader were discussed at length in Chapter 8. Attention here is directed primarily at an analysis of these qualifications for the purpose of establishing procedures helpful in their evaluation.

The following paragraphs discuss methods for obtaining information about officers and analyzing it to discover those who are most competent and to detect those who are deficient in leadership qualities and in performance.

Information Needed for Evaluation   Leadership in subordinates is best evaluated in terms of incidents, observed and recorded by their supervisors, that give evidence of the presence or absence of the desired qualities. Each leadership quality is composed of so many traits of such diverse nature as to make the evaluation and weighting of the component factors difficult. For example, the ability to get along with people is dependent on such characteristics as courtesy, tact, poise, voice, demeanor, facial expression, self-confidence, friendliness, helpfulness, consideration, unselfishness, integrity, and fairness, as well as a great many other factors which are not easily defined or recognized. To analyze and evaluate each of these component traits seems unnecessarily complicated and purposeless, since some important characteristics will be overlooked, false appraisals will be given to others, and inaccurate weights will be assigned to all.

The factors that result in sound judgment are so many and so varied as to make their isolation, definition, and evaluation difficult. The desired quality is most accurately detected and evaluated by evaluation of incidents that demonstrate soundness of judgment. These incidents should be noted by supervising officers at the time of their occurrence. When suitably recorded, they form the basis for a fair and reasonably accurate appraisal.

Promotional-Potential Rating Form   In contrast to the performance evaluation, the promotion-potential rating is intended to have a role in the scoring process and is therefore based on a numerical grade. The rating should not take place until the candidate passes the written examination.

A promotional-potential rating form recommended by IACP, shown in Appendix F, is based on a system used in the Berkeley Police Department. It provides for a rating-review board (composed of bureau or division heads) which has the task of equating and adjusting the averages for all bureaus, divisions, and sections in the department. As indicated in the next section, the promotional-potential rating should be given a weighting of 10 to 20 percent of the total score. Indoctrination of raters is essential to the success of any evaluation system, especially when the rating will have an administrative use such as in promotion. Explanation of the process to all personnel is also helpful in dispelling doubts and rumors.

PROMOTION

Promotion in police service ordinarily means advancement to a position of leadership. The officer's first promotion is normally to a supervisory position (from patrol officer to sergeant). In the original selection of a patrol officer (assuming the department adheres to the traditional rank structure and promotional pattern), qualities of leadership over and above those needed for the performance of the usual patrol tasks should be sought. When patrol officers are to be promoted to the rank of sergeant, it is essential to choose

PERSONNEL MANAGEMENT

those who possess the greatest potential qualities of leadership and not necessarily those who have displayed the greatest proficiency in their duties as patrol officers. From among the group of sergeants will subsequently be drawn those for advancement to higher responsibilities of command, unless lateral entry becomes a reality. It is extremely important for the department to have at each level in the chain of command an adequate number of officers who are well qualified for advancement to higher positions.

Selection for promotion presents greater difficulties than selection of recruits. It is also more important. In spite of the firsthand knowledge that supervisory and command officers may have of the characteristics of promotional candidates, the present methods for detecting and accurately measuring the necessary qualities of leadership are seriously inadequate. Promotions should invariably be given to the officers who are best equipped to perform the duties of the higher position and not to those whose restricted leadership potential makes it unlikely that they would ever be qualified for advancement beyond the position under consideration. Neither should promotions be given as a reward for faithful service or acts of heroism, except when the recipient is the best-qualified candidate.

Length of Service Length of service should not in itself be given numerical weight in the selection for promotion. However, this factor should not be overlooked in the promotional-potential or oral-board evaluations, since by its very nature it will have either increased or lowered leadership potential. In the first instance, a long period of service may have given the candidate better judgment, greater self-confidence and decisiveness, greater knowledge, and an improved ability to get along with people; in the second instance, it may have resulted in diminished energy, initiative, enthusiasm, interest in work, and willingness to accept responsibility. The factor of length of service, then, should be measured only in these terms.

Written Examinations As a general rule, police departments—especially the larger ones and those under the influence of central personnel agencies—rely too heavily on written tests of knowledge in selection for promotion. The popularity of the written test for this purpose arises from a sincere desire to select personnel on the basis of merit free of outside or departmental favoritism. The test is easily administered, it provides a numerical score, and it seems fair in that candidates can blame only themselves for unsatisfactory results. Suitable tools and procedures for evaluating other desirable qualifications have been slow to develop, and it is not surprising, in consequence, that the use of the written test is so widespread.

In the promotion to sergeant, supervisory content should be stressed in the written examination. A good balance of subject matter might provide 40 percent of material on supervision, 20 percent on principles of administration, 10 percent on departmental procedures, 10 percent on criminal law and procedure, and the balance on police investigations and procedures. Written examinations for higher supervisory positions should stress supervisory and administrative matters by devoting more than half the content to this subject. The central personnel agency should refer to training-course content, written directives, statutes, current professional literature, and textbooks for test material.

Oral Interviews   Some intangible characteristics cannot be measured by written examinations. In the absence of a well-developed promotion-rating system, the only logical way these qualities can be evaluated is through the oral interview. Many agencies use an oral board composed of senior supervisors (preferably two ranks higher than the candidates), and some departments use persons from other police agencies to avoid the charge of favoritism. The board may be assisted by a nonvoting member of the central personnel agency, who may act as moderator and coordinator. Only those candidates who pass the written test should be given the oral interview. The interview should be scored and weighted at 40 to 50 percent of the total, depending on whether a promotional-potential rating is used.

Evaluation of Personal Qualities by Other Means   The evaluation made by an oral board in the relatively short time at its disposal cannot be as accurate as a composite evaluation made by all the supervising officers who have observed the work of the candidate over a period of time. There is also the danger in oral-board review that favoritism or other factors of personal acquaintance may influence the rating of the candidate. In the case of promotions, a rating scale should be prepared by the candidate's supervisors. Here again, techniques of rating need continuous study; those such as the diagnostic forced choice should be given attention, and any refinements of them should be evaluated for possible use.[5]

Seniority Credit   Seniority preference or credit for length of service is used in a few departments in the promotional process. This procedure is unwise and should be discouraged. Seniority has no direct relationship to supervisory ability, and its only logical use in modern police administration appears to be as a means to decide between which of two or more officers should be given first choice in days off or vacation time. If it is restricted to this limited application, seniority is not harmful when used as a convenient means of making routine decisions.

Promotion of Superior Officers   As indicated at the beginning of this chapter, there are two broad approaches to upgrading police service: (1) the improvement of police effectiveness through indirect means such as improved

[5]See *Municipal Police Administration*, 7th ed., International City Management Association, Washington, D.C., 1971.

PERSONNEL MANAGEMENT

supervision and better organizational effectiveness and (2), more important, improvements in actual operational efficiency. The objective of the police, after all, is the protection of society from crime and other hazards and the rendering of police service. The true test of supervision, therefore, is whether personnel being supervised actually carry out the objectives for which the organization has been established. Superior officers should thus be selected primarily on the basis of their ability to achieve the operational objectives of the organization.

In the first promotional step, from patrol officer to sergeant, it is often not possible to judge the candidates on the basis of achievement of operational objectives. Although superior officers (those in middle-management positions, such as lieutenant and captain) may be selected partly on the basis of a written examination, personal qualities, service ratings, and the like, their performance should be rated primarily in terms of accomplishment of departmental goals. They may also be rated in terms of their judgment and control of subordinates, including (1) their ratings of their own subordinates, (2) their aggressiveness in taking and reporting needed corrective measures and of their willingness to criticize, and (3) their ability to communicate departmental policies and objectives to subordinates.

A critical analysis of all these factors—including the direct and indirect—will enable the rating officers to rank candidates in a relative order of merit and with a reasonable degree of accuracy.

Over the years, the United States Armed Forces have developed military fitness reports to a high degree. Although fitness reports tend to stress the indirect measures of performance, they also attempt to judge the candidates' accomplishment of organizational goals. The police service has been remiss in its failure to explore the benefits of military fitness reports.

Trial on the Job Trial on the job is closely related to probationary performance and is sometimes used by administrators in small departments to determine the best qualified of several candidates, each of whom is given an opportunity to act as supervisor for a temporary period. One difficulty with this procedure, however, is that acting supervisors face a real dilemma if there is a good possibility that they may be among the unsuccessful candidates. Acting supervisors often tend to be too sympathetic and considerate toward their peers when there is a good possibility that they will once again be equal in status with these peers. Acting supervisors should therefore be placed in this category only when the administrator is reasonably sure, on the basis of other criteria, that they will remain there.

Probationary service in higher ranks, because of the problem of what to do with the supervisor who fails the probationary period, has not been as successful as probation at the entrance level. Getting supervisors and administrators to embrace the concept of probation as part of the selection process is difficult enough, but it is easy when compared with getting them to accept the idea of meaningful probation at higher levels. Nevertheless, during the supervisor's probationary period, the administrator can use probationary status as leverage to encourage the new supervisor to carry out activities which might seem unpopular, particularly to the new first-line supervisor. Once the new supervisor begins to mature in the role and realizes that it is possible to make constructive but sometimes unpopular decisions without losing respect, attitudes that can persist for the rest of his or her career may be solidified in a healthy way.

Exempt-Rank Positions In large municipal and state police departments, a different method of selection should be used for the highest ranks in the structure. Deputy-chief positions and other high-ranking offices above the level of captain are sometimes filled through informal executive appointment rather than formal civil service procedure. High-ranking positions of this sort require an unusual degree of trust and confidence. It is therefore proper for the police administrator to make appointments of persons whom he feels will carry out his policies. When an exempt-rank system is used, personnel ordinarily retain their permanent civil service status in the lower rank. For example, if the rank of captain is the highest civil service rank which may be reached through competitive examination, persons who hold higher rank should serve in such capacity at the pleasure of the chief executive, but they should retain their permanent civil service rank if they are subsequently demoted.

SALARIES, BENEFITS, AND WORKING CONDITIONS

If qualified persons are to be recruited and retained, the conditions of police service must be as attractive as those of other public and private employment. Police salaries, length of workweek, annual and sick leaves, sick benefits, and pensions must compare favorably with those in all enterprises that compete with the police in recruitment.

Salaries

The level of salaries in private industry is ultimately determined by the wage-profit relationship. Businesses that pay a low, "uneconomic" wage may suffer from strikes, poor morale and production, and low sales. They may collapse or at least be forced to adjust. On the other hand, the business which pays extravagant salaries may fail to make a profit.

The wage-profit theory, of course, is not directly applicable to government salaries. Government service is also monopolistic; a police department does not have to vie with other agencies for profits. At the same time, however, the police must compete with the rest of government for the tax dollars which ultimately determine the level of public salaries.

There are three key factors which have a bearing on the salary level: (1) determination of the amount necessary to attract and retain competent employees, (2) determination of the amount necessary to provide a reasonable standard of living, and (3) determination of the amount which must be paid to reward greater responsibility or superior performance. (The third factor can be

PERSONNEL MANAGEMENT

Table 14–1   Desirable Salary Increments and Differentials (in percent)*

Rank	Step 1	Step 2	Step 3	Step 4
Police officer	Base	+ 5	+ 10	+ 15
Police officer (agent, senior, or master police officer)	+10	+15	+ 20	+ 25
Sergeant		+30	+ 35	+ 40
Lieutenant		+45	+ 50	+ 55
Captain		+60	+ 65	+ 70
Deputy chief		+75	+ 80	+ 85
Chief		+95	+100	+105

*This table is intended to apply specifically to medium-sized and large departments; a very large department would require additional ranks.

subdivided into several separate determinations: the amount necessary to pay all the employees of a department as a result of the superiority of that department, the amount necessary to reward superior performance of an individual, and the amount needed to compensate supervisors for increased responsibility.)

A superior pay plan should take all these considerations into account and should provide for some regular method for periodic adjustment or review of the plan so that the budgeting deliberations of the legislative body are not always disrupted each year by the agitation and uncertainty generated by less-systematic approaches.

Salary Increments and Longevity Pay   Provision should be made to increase salary by about 5 percent annually in recognition of the employee's increased skill and value to the department. However, a limit should be placed on the number of annual steps, which should not exceed four or five. Any salary plan adopted for police personnel, of course, must generally conform to the pay plan for the entire governmental-personnel system. However, Table 14–1 may be helpful in illustrating the proper relationships in the absence of an overall governmental pay plan or if the police pay plan is determined independently from the rest of the system.

Salary changes to keep pace with living costs should keep the top step for the advanced police-officer or police-agent position 10 percent higher than police-officer level. Note that there is a 15 percent differential between ranks (calculated at the top step) above the rank of sergeant up to the level of deputy chief. Because of the higher level of responsibility, the chief's position should be paid at least 20 percent higher than the next lowest rank.

Longevity pay should not be encouraged as a personnel benefit. At times, however, such pay must be considered in order to remain competitive with nearby police departments. Beyond a certain level, performance does not necessarily improve with age; the maximum improvement in any position generally takes place within the first few years, and after that, while improvement may be noticeable and steady, it seldom equals the increase in proficiency which occurs during the early years. It may also be unfair to pensioners to convert an excessive amount of salary to longevity pay, since the income of pensioners may often depend on current salary level exclusive of longevity pay.

Differential between Ranks   A pay difference must be provided between ranks to compensate supervisors for the additional responsibilities. The average differential between patrol officer and sergeant for cities in the United States with more than 300,000 population is about 15 percent, calculated at the top step for each rank. A differential of 15 percent between ranks, calculated on this basis, is equitable for pay between ranks.

Specialist Pay   In jurisdictions where salary scales are rigidly fixed according to rank, a salary commensurate with the responsibility and duties of the assignment in some instances may be paid only by classifying an individual in a rank which usually carries with it a power of command not exercised in that individual's particular position. For example, a specialist, such as a criminalist or a lie-detector operator, may be given a higher rank than a patrol officer to ensure suitable compensation, even though the specialist may have no subordinate personnel. This is an undesirable practice and results from an unwillingness to employ civilian specialists in these positions rather than sworn police officers. Job specifications should be drawn for these positions, and salaries should be provided to attract qualified persons to them. Officers equipped to fill these positions may resign from their police positions and be employed as specialists. The employment may be under civil service; civil service examinations should then be held to fill the positions.

It is equally undesirable to establish a large number of civil service positions with or without salary differentials to be filled on the basis of an examination by a small number of persons. Civil service categories should be kept broad rather than narrow. Patrol officers may serve as lockup keepers, desk officers, report-review officers, mail-car drivers, squadrol or prison-van drivers, and evidence technicians. A position classification for each of these should be avoided; the assignment should not alter the grade or rank.

In some departments, similar flexibility is provided by the assignment of patrol officers to detective service; in some instances, a pay differential is secured or an expense allowance is provided during the period of assignment. This arrangement enables the head of the department to transfer officers in and out of detective service as they demonstrate their ability. In other departments, all detectives have the rank and pay of sergeant and in most cases may be assigned to any sergeant position. This practice should not be encouraged; in general, persons with supervisory rank should carry out supervisory duties.

Grades of Rank   Each rank may be divided into two or more grades, frequently bearing pay differentials. The grade is usually determined by years of service (especially in the rank of patrol officer), although the distinction sometimes is one of assignment, as, for example, when the title of "captain" is

PERSONNEL MANAGEMENT

invariably given to the head of each functional division. The advantage of distinguishing by assignment is that all heads are then on an equal basis at staff conferences and in obtaining their share of personnel and matériel. The disadvantage is that many officers are receiving identical pay for a wide range of responsibilities. The numerical strength and duties of the divisions vary, and if the heads are to be paid in proportion to their responsibilities and the nature of their tasks, there must be a salary differential among them. To avoid salary differentials within a rank, different titles may be used for the heads of divisions to correspond to variations in their responsibilities and pay.

Overtime Compensation Although the police nominally work an eight-hour day, the nature of their duties often requires some overtime work. Overtime may be classified as (1) that resulting from the completion of tasks undertaken during, or growing out of, the normal tour of duty, such as report writing and investigations, initiated shortly before, and continuing beyond, the end of the tour of duty; (2) organized extraordinary police operations; and (3) court appearances.

Although a 1976 Supreme Court ruling removed public employees from coverage by the federal Fair Labor Standards Act, compensation for overtime is likely to be controlled in an increasing way by the federal government. Paid overtime is justified and desirable for such work. The categories above are a part of the total police job, and pay for them should be recognized as a normal part of the cost of operating the department.

When compensation for overtime is provided by means of extra days off duty (a situation which may be changing, if the current federal trend to compensate overtime by pay is continued), regulations should prevent excessive accumulations. For example, accumulated time due may be taken with the annual furlough, but not to exceed a total absence of one month, with the provision that any remaining time due would thereupon be automatically canceled. In order to avoid such cancellation, the officer is obliged to take his or her time off during the preceding 11 months. Suitable controls must also be established to ensure that officers are not credited with overtime that they have not fairly earned.

Other Benefits and Working Conditions

To remain competitive and to foster good morale, the well-rounded personnel program must provide other benefits in addition to salary. In a time of conservative fiscal policy, furthermore, many labor-union leaders believe that benefits should be increased at a higher rate than salaries on the grounds that management is willing to supply benefits other than salaries. The idea is that in better times the benefits which have been accrued will be retained, and at the same time they can then work toward a higher salary level once again.

Insurance Modern personnel practice requires payment for health insurance premiums. The pattern varies regionally and may range from partial payment of employees' premiums to total payment for employees and their families. Almost all large municipal departments and all state police and highway-patrol organizations in the United States offer health insurance. Many departments also offer life and accident insurance and usually pay the entire amount of the premiums.

Workweek For the past 20 years, the 5-day 40-hour workweek has been a national standard in police service, except for a few agencies scattered throughout the country. During the next few years, however, police agencies are likely to follow a rapidly developing national trend to a workweek consisting of 4 days at 10 hours a day and then most probably to 4-day, 36- or 32-hour weeks.

The 4-40 or "Ten Plan" Many police departments—ranging from Huntington Beach, California, to Arlington, Virginia—have already adopted 4-day workweeks, and they have reported that there are advantages in scheduling which are not available with conventional 8-hour shifts. The 10-hour shift permits overlap of manpower during the critical evening hours from 8 P.M. to 2 A.M. and has resulted in apparent reductions in response time and crime rate, as well as in an increase in arrests. Part of the change can be attributed to the simple adjustment of manpower to work load, but some of the progress is due to increased officer morale and motivation.

Sick and Annual Leave There are wide variations in sick-leave programs, with a common pattern of one-day accrual of sick leave per month.

Placing a maximum on the number of sick days which may be accrued may be unwise if employees view sick leave as a right rather than a privilege; when employees reach the maximum level, they may tend to call in sick even when they are not, rather than "lose" sick days. If there is a good medical program and sick-leave-control procedures are in effect, the best policy is unlimited sick leave, coupled with a medical-retirement program.

Annual-leave benefits have gradually increased in recent years, and many agencies now provide 15 to 20 working days of vacation per year, depending on length of service.

Police should also be paid for holidays, in terms of either time off for the actual holiday or overtime if it is necessary for them to work on the holiday. Holiday leave should be the same as that given to other employees in the city government. Holiday time generally ranges from 8 to 13 days per year, and any number in this range may be considered competitive.

Medical Programs The police department has a duty to maintain a sound and positive medical program similar to those found in industry. Such programs can be considered an economy in that they are conducive to the performance of better work, result in less lost time for minor or imaginary ailments, and produce a lower turnover rate. The basic requirements of a good medical program are (1) preemployment physical examinations; (2) sick-leave control; (3) treatment of injury on duty and adequate provision for first-aid training and

PERSONNEL MANAGEMENT

equipment; (4) periodic medical examinations; (5) medical research; (6) medical counseling, particularly for employees suffering from chronic illness and alcoholism; and (7) health education, including periodic x-rays and special immunization programs.

A sound system of preemployment medical examinations of candidates should be worked out with the central personnel agency to prevent duplication of examinations and conflict over standards, and the examination report should become the basis of a medical record to be maintained by the department personnel office. The first examination should be followed by periodic medical examinations on a voluntary basis. The cost of basic examinations and laboratory services, consultations, and diagnostic services should be paid for by the department. Medical care following diagnosis should be the responsibility of the individual officer (except in cases of service-connected injury), but sick leave with pay should be granted for remedial care.

Sick-leave abuse can best be controlled by supervisory officers, personnel-division counselors, or the internal investigations unit. The member on sick leave should be required to remain at home, when not hospitalized, and to telephone his or her office or division before leaving for medical treatment. The physician should be available to advise and counsel those officers who are frequently absent because of actual and serious illnesses.

Stress Units Several departments have organized specialized units to counsel officers experiencing stress resulting from the unusual demands of police work. In the Boston police department, the stress unit is staffed with experienced officers who have received special training in handling problems which affect police officers to a greater degree than some other occupations. The counselors offer advice and referral services for problems including role conflict, alcoholism, family crises, and emotional stress brought on by fear or frustration. Identities of officers and the nature of problems are kept confidential.

Safety Programs The personnel officer should develop programs of employee-safety education which should be aimed primarily at the promotion of safe driving practices and compliance with regulations designed to prevent personal injuries. Safety lectures and roll-call training material should be developed in order to ensure a continuing concern for, and awareness of, the department's responsibility and possible liability in cases of accident and injury.

Physical-Fitness Programs The federal government and the Armed Forces have recently stressed physical-fitness programs which are variations of the aerobics program developed by a clinic in Texas. At the heart of these programs is the strengthening of the cardiovascular system through jogging and exercise in order to minimize the effect of ordinary tension and sudden exertion. Police departments should provide similar programs and should offer time off (in limited amounts) to encourage participation in physical training.

The provision of gymnasium facilities in a police department is a definite job benefit.

Retirement An actuarially sound pension system should ensure the officer of security in old age and protect the officer's dependents in the event of his or her death or disability. A suitable pension system has the further advantage of removing from the force those who have outlived their usefulness. The age when usefulness is seriously impaired varies among individuals and also with the kind of work they perform. For example, patrol service requires greater physical fitness than a command post. Since removal of those whose usefulness is impaired by advancing years is an important purpose of the pension system, it should be administered wisely and courageously.

The pension provisions should be fair to the police by providing liberal protection against deprivation caused by death, disability, and old age, and at the same time they should not be unreasonable to the taxpayer. A system that enables police officers to retire in their prime and undertake the same employment in another jurisdiction while on pension is open to grave question, but policies in this regard must be determined by current practice. Police service must be kept as attractive as any other; hence if other services provide such liberal benefits, it may be necessary to include equal liberality in police pensions.

The pension benefits of a municipality should be under a state retirement system so that police officers may transfer from one service to another without losing their pension rights. Interstate compacts should also be arranged.

Police chiefs are now eligible for membership in the retirement system administered by the International City Management Association for the benefit of its members. The ICMA retirement system allows chiefs to move laterally from one department to another without the loss of benefits.

UNIONS, EMPLOYEE ASSOCIATIONS, AND GRIEVANCE PROCEDURES

The subject of employee relations is rapidly becoming a primary area of concern for police administrators. It may be argued with some justification that the concern has come too late. Poor management practices in the past, particularly in the area of personnel management, have no doubt contributed to the proliferation of unions and other collective-bargaining organizations and to the tactics which have been used by some of these groups—"blue flu," slowdowns, and other "job actions," as well as strikes.

Collective Bargaining

In the labor relations field a union is any organization or group chosen by employees to represent them in negotiations concerning salaries and working conditions. To many people the word "union" necessarily means affiliation with a traditional organized-labor group such as the AFL–CIO or the Interna-

PERSONNEL MANAGEMENT

285

tional Brotherhood of Teamsters, but in modern labor relations practice, any group—such as a police fraternal association which also is a recognized bargaining agent—is by definition a union. This broad definition will be used for the balance of this chapter.

Why Unions Form   It is often said that unions form because management has failed. This view, although simplistic and sometimes not true at all for some agencies, nevertheless contains great truth. Unions form primarily because employees believe that in no other way can they obtain improvements in salaries, benefits, working conditions, and management practice. Formation of a union may also take place because employees regard it as the fashionable thing to do or because union organizers have been exceptionally skilled in presenting their arguments.

What Unions Expect to Gain   Union objectives sometimes parallel those of management. An interesting exercise occasionally performed by labor relations specialists is to ask a mixed group of union and management employees to separate into two groups—union and management—and then to ask each group to identify its objectives. Surprisingly, some striking parallels emerge, with both groups claiming to want:

- Improved salaries
- Better working conditions
- Increased professionalization
- Increased productivity
- Higher morale

Another exercise used by labor relations specialists is to ask a group of employees to list a number of items which dissatisfy them. At a later point—after a sufficient period of time so that participants cannot directly recall the list of dissatisfiers—the group is asked to identify those things which would *satisfy* them. The two lists are usually quite different, with low salaries and benefits usually near the top among the dissatisfiers, but with recognition of good work high among the satisfiers. The lesson to be learned here is that paying attention only to the dissatisfiers does not assure the ultimate satisfaction of employees.

The Collective-Bargaining Process   Collective-bargaining agreements are now a fact of life in many agencies at every level of government. Agreements of this sort are common in those agencies which have permitted organized labor to become established and in departments which use an employee organization as a vehicle for collective bargaining. Some states also require the local government to recognize a union or other group chosen by employees to represent them in negotiations concerning salaries and working conditions.

Collective bargaining ordinarily results in the establishment of a contract which specifies the areas of agreement between employees and management. Most contracts relate to employee working conditions and benefits, although on occasion a contract will make stipulations about the general management of the department. One contract in a police department in New England, for example, provided for a management survey to be conducted by an outside consulting group. This provision of the contract was suggested by the employee organization and was agreed to by the police chief and the city administration.

A key word in the collective-bargaining process is "bargaining." Before any provision can be accepted in a contract, of course, there has to be an agreement between the parties involved. Too many police administrators or city officials complain about provisions in a contract which inhibit the right of management to make effective policy and decisions, but fail to realize that there is nothing which *requires* management to accept restrictive provisions of this sort. In one department studied by IACP, consultants asked why the union had the right to name the employees designated to perform special assignments outside regular working hours for pay, such as providing police protection at private affairs or serving on temporary security details. The response from the department administration was that the union "required" it. The answer to this, of course, is that administrators need not agree to every provision offered in a contract, and they should not agree to a provision if it is contrary to the best interests of the department and the community.

The actual collective-bargaining process usually begins with each party agreeing to a bargaining schedule (which often sets up beginning dates and the date upon which mediation or arbitration commences, if there is no agreement) and to the rules to be followed by both parties. Commonly found rules of this sort require each side to maintain confidentiality after initial proposals are presented to the other party. The rules may also specify the number of people who will be engaging in the bargaining sessions and their titles or positions.

The next usual step is for each side to formulate its initial proposals. In the case of the union, this often means a series of meetings with the membership so that the bargaining committee understands what the membership wants. In the case of management, the initial posture can be determined more easily, but the ease with which management's points are established is in no way related to their importance. The point is that management should not just simply react to the proposals of the union but instead should prepare a list of positive proposals which management believes should be agreed upon by the union.

Another consideration which should guide police administrators is the fact that a contract provision can be modified or eliminated in the next bargaining session. However, this process is obviously more difficult; once concessions are made, removing a benefit or favorable working condition is always hard. Bargaining should therefore never be carried out with the intention of giving in on an issue which is damaging to the department for the sake of temporary gain in some other area and with the hope that poor provisions can be eliminated easily the next time around.

Collective bargaining is a management skill which may have to be carried out by specialists in larger departments. Very often a member of the police legal staff or the city attorney's office may participate in bargaining sessions to provide overall assistance to the police personnel division or other members of the staff who participate in these sessions.

The Role of the Chief in Collective Bargaining Before collective bargaining became popular, many chiefs found satisfaction and pride in acting as the departmental spokesman in the quest for additional personnel benefits or an increase in salaries. The emergence of formal collective bargaining has made a difference in such situations because the bargaining usually takes place between the employee organization and the governmental administration—sometimes a city council or legislative committee directly. The chief then finds himself in a dilemma, and his morale and attitude can suffer. A procedure which works effectively and gives the chief a voice in representation as well as allowing him to fulfill his responsibility for proper administration of the department is to permit the chief to have a trusted associate act as his representative on the management bargaining team. The chief should not participate directly and personally in the bargaining sessions for several reasons. First, the level of rhetoric and emotion is often quite high (sometimes as a matter of role playing by both union and management, but occasionally with real emotion and hostility involved). This setting can be uncomfortable for the chief, who should not be in a position either to apologize for any of the participants or to discipline them. Second, the presence of the chief on the bargaining team does not allow management to have the opportunity to "catch its breath" by pausing long enough to find out what the chief's reaction might be. Finally, the chief is usually expected to be decisive, which is difficult to do if he has to state continually that a union position must be taken into advisement.

Prohibition of Strikes and Job Actions Police officers should be permitted to organize, but they should be prohibited from joining unions which recognize the strike or job action as a bargaining tool or which may prevent them from performing their duty. The oath taken by officers when they enter police service is their promise to serve the public unselfishly. Furthermore, once police officers join in a movement that recognizes or advocates the use of the strike or job action as a bargaining tool, the implication is that the lower echelons of the police department, through their union strength, could control department policy and direct its administration. Such a situation is inconceivable in the conduct of a public service agency.

President Franklin D. Roosevelt eloquently expressed concern about the activities of public employees in a communication to the National Federation of Federal Employees in 1937:

> Militant tactics have no place in the functions of any organization of government employees. Upon employees in the Federal service rests the obligation to serve the whole people, whose interests and welfare require orderliness and continuity in the conduct of government activities. This obligation is paramount. Since their own

services have to do with the functioning of the government, a strike of public employees manifests nothing less than an intent on their part to prevent or obstruct the operations of government until their demands are satisfied. Such action, looking toward the paralysis of government by those who have sworn to support it, is unthinkable and intolerable.

Police officers should be forbidden to join a union local or chapter which urges a strike or work slowdown as a means for achieving its demands. On the other hand, the fact that an organized labor union wins a recognition election in a police department does not automatically mean that the local will endorse the technique of striking. As long as the chapter or local agrees to remain free of strikes and job actions, police should be permitted to affiliate—if they wish—with organized labor.

Since police officers should be denied the right to strike, an alternative to the strike or slowdown seems desirable. Compulsory arbitration for resolving impasses between management and police unions is an acceptable solution.

The Contract   This document should be drafted carefully, and under ideal circumstances it is a composite of the views of both management and union. A common problem in contracts is the tendency to assume that the other party understands a generality or abstraction. The truth is that within a few days of the signing of a contract, the parties involved have begun to forget what was "understood" and commence the process of deciding what they *think* was meant. The rule in drafting contract language is to be specific instead of general and to be detailed rather than vague.

Contract language should be developed systematically. A good way to begin is to have the various demands made by the union typed onto loose-leaf paper, one to a page, so that the union language occupies about an inch or so of space at the top of the page. Next, a paragraph summarizing the position of the management bargaining team should be added—preferably in two versions. The initial portion should consist of the contract language which is ideal, and the second portion should specify the language for the "bottom line" position of management.

After the management bargaining team comments have been added to the pages, they should be reviewed by the chief of police, who should indicate whether there is agreement or disagreement and the reasons therefor.

The final step in preparing the contract "workbook" should consist of adding the opinions of the city manager or mayor to each page. At the conclusion of each negotiating session the workbook, as amended, can be used to draft the final language of the contract. Obviously, the actual content of the workbook should be kept confidential and should not be disclosed to the union or made public.

Model-contract language is available from several sources, including IACP, and should assist in the development of the contract workbook and the final contract itself.

PERSONNEL MANAGEMENT

289

Professional and Social Associations

The members of the force should be stimulated to join professional police organizations, such as the International Association of Chiefs of Police, the International Association for Identification, the American Academy for Professional Law Enforcement, the Associated Public-Safety Communications Officers, and similar state and regional organizations. They should also be urged to join police fraternities, such as Lambda Alpha Epsilon, and organizations of governmental officials of various kinds, especially associations of municipal employees, subject to the restrictions noted above.

The members of the force should be permitted to organize locally for social and other purposes, and facilities should be made available for their use and enjoyment.

Many employee associations exist primarily to influence the bargaining process or to induce changes in salary or working conditions. There are numerous other employee organizations, however, which attempt to carry out other objectives, such as philanthropic activities, juvenile-crime-prevention work, recreation, and legislative changes affecting police or public safety.

A recent development is the establishment of black police officers' associations, particularly in large urban departments. Some of these associations have been concerned about discrimination against black officers by whites. They have also assumed a protective attitude toward black citizens whom they feel have been subject to abuse by white police officers. Their concern about discrimination and abuse, though it has led to ill will in some departments, must be viewed as a positive and healthy force.

While it may be simplistic to state that increased communication between management and working levels and improvement of working conditions and officer conduct will eliminate the need for a multiplicity of associations, the solution to the problem should certainly include these goals.

Employee organizations should be discouraged from forming or continuing if they intend to engage in unprofessional activities and practices. For example, exerting pressure on merchants for various reasons and high-pressure solicitation for dances and benefits are undesirable practices. The police administrator can discourage improper activities by making clear and unmistakable declarations of policy, by publicizing the improper methods in the public media, and finally by taking disciplinary action.

Grievance Procedures

Grievance procedures should cover a wide range of circumstances, including the following groups of subjects:

1   Matters affecting personal status: performance evaluation, disciplinary action, the conduct of others, and personal disputes
2   Matters affecting the benefits and working conditions of groups of employees: salaries, overtime, working hours, retirement, and so on
3   Management, administrative, and supervisory methods and procedures

4 Matters relating to police operations: complaints about patrol methods, extent of service which should (or should not) be rendered, and so on

Most grievance procedures provide for some form of communication of complaints through regular command channels as a first step, with appeal to an alternative channel as a second step.

Grievance Committees   The grievance committee is a common element in many grievance procedures, but the structure and composition of such committees are by no means consistent. Most committees have rank-and-file representation, and the structure of the committee is often a part of a collective-bargaining agreement.

The committee may have several responsibilities, including listening to grievances, rejecting unfounded complaints, consolidating and coordinating grievances, and preparing recommendations which are transmitted to the administration.

If the first step in the grievance procedure consists of a communication through the chain of command to a certain level, it does not make sense to redirect committee reports to this same level. Grievance-committee recommendations should therefore be directed to the chief of police and, if not acted upon, to the highest level of government with the authority to remedy the grievance.

Grievance committees ought to be welcomed by the chief of police; the conditions arousing complaints should be investigated thoroughly and discussed by the chief and the committee, and insofar as possible, they should be corrected.

PROFESSIONALIZATION AND CAREER DEVELOPMENT

Progressive chiefs of police have been concerned about professionalization of police for many years, and in the past decade there has been increasing interest in professional career development through reorganization of the traditional police-position classifications and promotion structures; encouragement of education; adoption of minimum standards, certification, and lateral entry; and encouragement of phased, departmental career-development plans.

New Concepts in Position Classifications and Promotional Patterns

There is increasing realization of the need for sufficient prestige and recognition for officers in operational-level positions. For many years police departments have recruited new employees under the assumption that promotional positions will be filled by persons who joined the force at the entrance level. Departments have also assumed that some of the recruits thus hired will be capable of filling higher ranks, including administrative and management positions. In American police service there is a widespread feeling that

PERSONNEL MANAGEMENT

operational-level employees are entitled to the opportunity for promotional consideration for all ranks within a department. Moreover, the feeling is nearly as strong that *only* those employees who join the department at the entrance level are entitled to promotions to higher positions and thus lateral movement from one department to another is practically nonexistent except at the entrance level and occasionally at the chief's level.

Thoughtful administrators have always tended to rationalize the inability to bring in competent people at higher levels by asserting that if a recruit has all the essential characteristics and potential to be a chief of police, there will be no lack of personnel qualified for promotion from within for all higher positions in the department.

In recent years, however, it has been recognized that the qualities required in a patrol officer are not necessarily the characteristics needed by the successful administrator. Yet recruitment of patrol officers has tended to emphasize education more and more, and the level of education in a number of departments has risen to a point which would have been unthinkable 20 years ago. A recruit who thinks that a college degree is an automatic assurance of promotion through the ranks is in for a rude awakening in many of the departments in the country today. In these agencies there are simply not enough management positions for the number of college-educated officers entering the service.

Moreover, the drive to achieve supervisory status in a police department is not always commendable. Because of the traditional prestige that accrues to someone who holds a position with visible status, most new patrol officers immediately want to become something other than patrol officers right after they join a police department. They realize that there is prestige and satisfaction in becoming investigators, specialists (in such areas as communications, identification, traffic enforcement, or juvenile work), and supervisors. The desire for prestige and status often outstrips the desire and ability of officers actually to perform supervisory work per se. In most departments today, the problem is very real for many of those who hold the basic police position of patrol officer. Even if they are not personally frustrated, and instead take satisfaction in their status, many officers believe that people look down on their role.

Other professions are substantially free of the need to be promoted as a hallmark of success in the profession. For example, the *summum bonum* of medicine is the achievement of status as a physician, not as a supervisor of physicians. Similarly, most lawyers are content to be lawyers and feel no great urgency to be supervisors of lawyers.

It is interesting to note that some law enforcement agencies have avoided the status problem. The FBI has achieved remarkable progress in avoiding an improper emphasis on prestige through promotion. Even though the FBI is a semimilitary organization, with its rank structure as highly developed as that of any other law enforcement agency, there is much less tendency to regard promotion to a supervising agent's position as a status symbol.

The police service must emphasize the development of career positions at the operational level. As discussed earlier, one method of doing this is the adoption of educational-incentive pay plans, particularly systems which benefit those who are in operational positions but who are not supervisors. Promotion to a supervisory position is a reward in itself. Supervision should be made to appeal only to those with supervisory ability and desire.

The Police Agent   A key suggestion in the President's Commission report in 1967 was the creation of two new classifications in addition to the conventional police-officer position—the community-service officer and the police agent.

The community-service officer was intended to assume some of the noncriminal service work load now carried out by police. The work was to be oriented toward community service and was to serve the dual purpose of communications link and relief valve. The community-service-officer concept has met with little approval among police, partly because of the suggestion that the CSO should be unarmed and partly because of the belief that the report recommended acceptance of candidates with relaxed personal-conduct and arrest-record requirements. According to the author of the concept, the CSO should meet no less than the standards of conduct and character required for regular police-officer candidates.[6] It is unfortunate that so few agencies have given the total concept a fair trial.

The police-agent concept was given a better reception, but the response has been less than overwhelming. Only a handful of cities adopted the title and classification, and no major city has adopted the position along with the use of the community-service officer and regular police officer, as envisioned in the Commission report. This slowness can be attributed to the lack of sufficient numbers of college-educated officers, although this disadvantage is being rapidly overcome in many agencies.

A New Concept in Rank Structure and Career Development

The following paragraphs describe an integrated approach which deals with (1) the problem of conventional rank titles, (2) the need for a second-level "career" position, (3) the means for proper utilization of college-educated officers at the operational level, (4) the use of the squad concept and team policing, and (5) the problem of recruiting and selecting highly qualified personnel.

The Problem of Conventional Rank Titles   The usual designation of police ranks is not completely satisfactory for several reasons—first, because of the inevitable comparison with military-rank titles. The rank of sergeant in the military service is traditionally noncommissioned. In modern police service,

---

[6]Interview with Gene S. Meuhleisen, former Associate Director, The President's Commission on Law Enforcement and Administration of Justice; then Executive Officer, California Commission on Peace Officer Standards and Training, March 1971.

PERSONNEL MANAGEMENT

the commissioned versus noncommissioned concept does not exist. The entrance-level position in some departments is already equivalent in many respects to the first level of commissioned officer in the military service. The problem can be illustrated by a reference to the Berkeley Police Department, which requires college graduation for entrance and issues "commission numbers" to new officers. Berkeley sergeants are even more qualified, and of course they supervise the college-educated patrol officers. Yet they are identified with the image of the noncommissioned military rank.

The rank of patrolman has disadvantages when used in systems in which patrolmen are assigned to nonpatrol activities, and it is awkward for use by women officers. The term "patrol officer" is satisfactory for most purposes when discussing patrol-division positions, but it is inadequate to describe an officer who is assigned as an investigator in the detective division. The term "police officer" has fewer disadvantages, but it has the drawback that sergeants, lieutenants, and captains are also police officers when the term is used in its broader sense.

A solution to the terminology problem can be achieved by referring to personnel in all ranks as "officers" and by using grade numbers to identify rank for internal and administrative purposes. Conventional insignia, such as chevrons, bars, and gold leaves, should be eliminated. (Rank should be indicated by simple pins, with grade numbers depicted by arabic or roman numerals.)

Entrance at Grade 2 for Degree Holders The President's Commission report gives many excellent justifications for (and examples of) the use of police agents. In addition, one of the problems in recruiting and retaining college-trained officers is their reluctance to perform some of the necessary but dead-end police tasks over a long period. Also, recruiting problems have become more and more difficult for police in prosperous times, with highly qualified officers becoming increasingly harder to find during those periods. There is increasing doubt as to the logic of trying to recruit college-educated personnel at the basic level. However, if college-trained persons have an opportunity to enter at a higher level and if adoption of team- or squad-policing concepts can facilitate the use of large numbers of college-trained officers at the operational level, these problems may be solved. Under this concept, grade 2 officers would move directly to difficult patrol assignments, investigative duties, and other challenging activities after a brief familiarization period with some of the less-challenging assignments found in most cities.

Use of Personnel Grade 2 officers would be assigned to the criminal investigation division and other operational units in the department at the working-level investigator's position. Traffic-division assignments could be divided into routine enforcement activity (grade 1 officers) and accident investigation or follow-up work (grade 2s).

In smaller cities having no problem with officer boredom or stagnation, grade 2 officers could be assigned to beat-patrol duties, provided that the department operates under a "beat-officer responsibility system" which gives significant responsibility to patrol officers for the investigation of almost all classifications of incidents, including the follow-up investigation of most felonies. (Fewer grade 1 officers would be required under this variation.)

The adoption of squad or shift-based team policing would facilitate the use of grade 2 officers. Varying proportions of grade 1 and grade 2 officers should be assigned to each supervisory sector under a grade 3 officer (the first-line supervisor), depending on the shift or location. The patrol function in Arlington, Virginia, is organized in this way. Staffing the squad with four grade 1 and two grade 2 officers might be suitable, for example, in a busy downtown area in the evening. More grade 2 officers are required for daytime and early evening hours because of the greater requirement for investigative skills as opposed to preventive patrol, making on-view arrests of drunks, and so on. Grade 2 officers may have one or more patrol beats within their jurisdiction, or they may divide investigative responsibilities in some other manner.

The concept is also applicable to team policing based on coverage of one beat over a 24-hour period, such as the unit-beat-policing concept developed in England and the modifications adopted in Charlotte, North Carolina, and Los Angeles, California.

Organization of field operations under district team policing should contemplate the use of the supervisory sector as a base for team policing over a 24-hour period. It is envisioned that a grade 2 officer would act as a lead officer or as an assistant to the supervisor of each sector, in addition to having investigative responsibilities as a patrol officer.

An outline for a suggested personnel-classification plan based on this concept is shown below:

Grade 1 officer (base salary)	Basic patrol, traffic, and other fieldwork of a routine nature. Minimum amount of report writing. Written examination to consist of qualifying achievement tests. Approximately the same standards for education, experience, and conduct now required by most departments for recruits.
Grade 2 officer (20 percent increase over grade 1, calculated at the top step for each grade)	Advanced patrol work, investigative duties, and other responsibilities mentioned for the agent position in the *Task Force Report: The Police.* Assistants to grade 3 officers. Promotion to grade 2 from 1 upon achieving A.A.[7] (associate of arts) degree.

[7]This grade should require three years of college by 1978 and four years by 1982. These requirements coincide with recommendations of the National Advisory Commission on Criminal Justice Standards and Goals.

PERSONNEL MANAGEMENT

	Entrance level for A.A. and B.A. (bachelor of arts) degree holders who pass qualifying examinations. B.A. transfers from other departments at this level. No competitive examination for promotion to this rank.
Grade 3 officer (15 percent increase over grade 2)	Sector and squad supervisor. Two years of experience in grade 2 required. B.A. degree plus competitive examination.
Grade 4 officer (15 percent increase over grade 3)	Platoon, watch, section, or territorial supervisor. Two years in grade 3. B.A., plus competitive examination.
Grade 5 officer (15 percent increase over grade 4)	District or division commander. Two years in grade 4. B.A., plus competitive examination.
Grade 6 officer (15 percent increase over grade 5)	Bureau commander. Appointment by chief from grade 4 and grade 5 officers.
Grade 7 officer (15 percent increase over grade 6)	High-ranking officer in a large department.

The Effect of Specialist Pay   In addition to advanced pay status for patrol officers with higher education, prestige for the patrol-officer position can be increased tremendously by not rewarding specialist positions in the department with higher pay (unless the pay is based on agent or grade 2 status). Traffic officers, detectives, youth officers, dispatchers, identification officers, and other specialists should not receive higher pay than patrol officers. In fact, the well-rounded patrol officer who has had experience in several specialties ought to be rewarded for continuing as a patrol officer and generalist.

Certification and Lateral Entry

For years, students of police administration have discussed the possibility of lateral entry—that is, bringing a police officer or supervisor into the department from another agency at something other than the entrance level. Although lateral entry sometimes occurs in the lowest-quality police agencies by default (because of the lack of a merit system, through appointment by political pressure, or as a result of favoritism), there has been practically no use of the technique in agencies having civil service or higher standards. Few agencies operating under the merit principle or civil service will permit applicants from outside the system to participate in promotional examinations. The philosophy that promotion to higher rank is a privilege and reward for remaining in the service is one of the strongest traditions in police personnel management. There are exceptions, of course. The San Mateo County sheriff's department in

California—an agency with high standards for administration and personnel management—permits sheriff's officers from outside the department to participate in promotional examinations. In practice, however, there is actually very little lateral entry because (by law) preference is given to the local candidates.

One of the oldest laws permitting lateral entry has received little attention by police writers—perhaps because the law affects only Westchester County, New York, and because of the low number of transfers that have taken place over the years:

> *Transfers.* Transfers from one town police department to another town or village police department in the county may be made upon the mutual consent of the appointing officers of the departments affected. Any member of such police force who is or has been transferred shall receive credit with the town department to which he is transferred for time served on the police force or in the department of any village or town within the county, as though the full time had been served with the department to which he has been transferred, for purposes of seniority, promotion, pensions, and general administration.[8]

Other departments have adopted lateral entry for the correct reasons, but on a limited basis. The Savannah Police Department has hired police supervisors on the basis of education and experience outside the department, and the Baltimore Police Department has brought in civilian personnel (including persons with police experience in other agencies) to high-ranking positions as sworn officers with peace-officer status and all other advantages of rank except civil service tenure.

The movement toward lateral entry is encouraging. Its significant contributions to police management will be the capacity to transfer expertise from one agency to another and the standardization of those techniques which are most effective. Local and state governments should enter agreements to accept applications from the personnel of one another's agencies, provided that certain minimum standards are met and maintained for both transfer and promotion.

The adoption of police standards and training legislation is a certain step toward lateral entry. The California Commission on Peace Officer Standards and Training administers a certification program consisting of basic, intermediate, and advanced certificates. The intermediate certificate, for example, requires a minimum of 15 college credits, 300 hours of training, and 8 years of experience. (If an officer has a bachelor's degree, the experience requirement is reduced to two years, and the number of training hours to that required by the basic certificate.)

Management Certificates In addition to the three-level certification mentioned above, the Commission also issues management and executive certificates to qualified supervisors.

[8] *1936 Laws of New York, as Amended*, chap. 104.

The management certificate is available to middle managers of the rank of lieutenant and above who have a minimum of two years of experience and who have completed a 100-hour mandatory training course. The executive certificate is issued to department heads (police chiefs and sheriffs) who have a minimum of two years of experience and who have completed an optional executive development course of 80 hours or, in the absence of the optional 80-hour course, can demonstrate its equivalent in other training.

There will soon be no reason why an officer or supervisor with an intermediate or advanced certificate should be prevented from applying for a transfer or promotional examination to any other department in the state.

When individual states agree in the establishment of standards, it will soon be possible for supervisors to transfer from one state to another, such as from New Jersey to New York.

Registries One promising avenue for career development is the registry concept. The registry program, administered by the International Association of Chiefs of Police, is based on the voluntary registration of police officers, supervisors, and specialists with the association. If applicants pass qualifying examinations, the association will supply their names to potential employers.

Peace-Officer Standards and Training Commissions

Over the past few years, the movement toward state police-training commissions has generated interest in career-development programs as well as significant change and improvement in local police training. Most states—46, as of the publication date of this text—have adopted minimum standards for police training, and several states subsidize local training, provided that certain standards for eligibility and training are maintained. The California Commission on Peace Officer Standards and Training is administered as a part of the state Department of Justice. The commission sets standards for selection and training and then reimburses local agencies for part of the cost of training, provided these standards are met. (A substantial part of the cost is obtained from fines in criminal courts.) The commission approves the curricula of various police academies throughout the state. As indicated in the preceding paragraphs, it also has adopted a certification system based on education and experience. California, New York, and New Jersey also operate consulting services for local agencies at no cost. (In New Jersey, this service is carried out by the Police Administrative Services Bureau of the State of New Jersey Police Training Commission.) In California and New Jersey, these consulting services programs are administered through the police standard training organization.

ORGANIZATION AND ADMINISTRATION OF TRAINING

Police service, even of the simplest kind, is unlikely to be of a high quality unless police officers have special training. Patrol officers must recognize a criminal act and know the elements to be proved in each crime, the rules of arrest and evidence, and the principles of first aid. In addition, they must understand how and when to use their police weapons, they must be skilled in the art of self-defense, and they should know how to handle people. Responsibility for traffic, vice, and youth-crime control, as well as for preliminary investigations and searches for physical evidence, increases the variety of their duties and the number of procedures in which they must be trained.

Purpose of Training The purpose of training is to make sure that the officer performs all tasks with ease and in such a way as to ensure his safety and the safety and satisfaction of the public. This is accomplished by developing such skill and dexterity that each act is performed naturally and semiautomatically with a minimum of conscious physical or mental effort. The act is preceded by a decision; therefore, training must provide a background of knowledge acquired through either actual or simulated experiences to which current situations may be related for judgment.

Nearly all police tasks involve people, and the accomplishment of the police purpose necessitates a control of people that is best effected by winning their compliance with laws and ordinances. An important training objective is therefore an understanding of human drives, inhibitions, emotions, reactions, and attitudes and a knowlege of techniques that promote a desirable relationship between the police and the public. Training should also emphasize that the police must scrupulously avoid petty graft, corruption, brutality, and prejudice.

Preemployment Training Preemployment police training at the college level is desirable. As standards of education and recruitment are raised (and they are both constantly being raised), an increasing proportion of police recruits will have college training. Under these circumstances the subject matter of college courses becomes of interest to police administrators, who prefer candidates for recruitment whose preemployment training best prepares them for police service. College education in law enforcement is discussed in a later section in this chapter.

Municipal Responsibility for Training The municipality clearly has a responsibility to provide training for its police officers, not only for their own safety, but also to protect the city against suits for damages resulting from the actions of inadequately trained officers. The liability of the municipality has been established by several courts which have held that where death or injury resulted from the accidental discharge of a weapon or from its faulty handling by the officer, the ultimate responsibility lay in the failure to provide proper training. The implications of these decisions are very far-reaching.[9] The cost of training recruits and of continuing their training throughout their careers is far less than that which might be incurred by the city for damages, early retirement benefits, or widows' pensions.

[9]See a letter from Paul B. Weston, in *Police*, Charles C Thomas, Publisher, Springfield, Ill., 1961.

PERSONNEL MANAGEMENT

Chart 23 Organization of a training division in a large department.

Organizing and Staffing for Training

In small agencies, training is often combined with other personnel duties. In larger departments, it may be necessary to establish full-time training specialists in a separate division, supplemented, when necessary during actual training programs, by the addition of instructors from elsewhere in the department and from outside sources. In the largest departments having continuous training programs, almost all training is carried out by a full-time training staff.

In a large academy staff, division of duties can take two basic directions. The most common is division of teaching assignments by program—that is, a group of instructors assigned to teach recruit courses, another group assigned to in-service training, a third to management and supervisory training, and so on. A second method, which is more appropriate for larger agencies, divides the staff into functional specialties. In this arrangement, a group of instructors will present material in their specialty regardless of the clientele.

A good organizational structure for the training effort in a department of 1,500 officers is depicted in Chart 23. Here, the staff is divided into three groups—a basic-training section, an advanced-training section, and a specialized-programs section.

Selection of Staff Regardless of department size, selection of training personnel should be carried out with the utmost care. Training of officers can have a profound effect on the quality of police services, particularly in the indoctrination phase of recruit training. Unfortunately, the training-officer position is sometimes filled by an individual who is there only because of a circumstance over which he has no control, such as light-duty status resulting from an injury, or because he is not fit for critical command duties or cannot be trusted in the field. In one study made by IACP, consultants found that an officer had a history of assaults on citizens during arrests, with accompanying citizen complaints alleging brutality. As a result, he had been reassigned to the training division as a means of keeping him away from public contact. Ironically, the area of mechanics of arrest was among the topics assigned to him in the recruit program.

The head of the training function should have a strong voice in the selection of training officers. In small departments it may not be possible to set out inflexible requirements for the training staff, but in larger agencies some attempt should be made to establish minimum standards. Training officers should ideally be college graduates and should have practical experience within the department. They should have a proper philosophical attitude toward the department and toward law enforcement in general. It would also be desirable for instructors to have training in teaching methods, such as courses in education given at colleges or universities.

Not everyone who has a high interest in teaching has an equivalent level of ability. A trial session as an instructor is a good way to screen personnel interested in training assignments. The potential instructor can then be heard by supervisors in the training division, and the reaction of the class can also be considered.

Once a member of the department has been selected for the training staff, he or she should be given outside training at various schools and academies. Instructors should be offered every opportunity to participate in outstanding training programs, such as those provided by the FBI National Academy, the Northwestern University Traffic Institute, the Southern Police Institute, and the National Crime Prevention Institute.

Outside Lecturers   As stated earlier, a training staff should be supplemented from time to time by the use of lecturers from other divisions of the department and guest speakers from outside. It must be stressed, however, that the quality of instruction is generally best when permanent training-division instructors are used. Most educators feel that if there is a choice between a good teacher who has little familiarity with the subject matter and a poor teacher with good command of the subject matter, the good teacher should be used. Furthermore, some departments tend to use outside instructors for parts of the curriculum which may be controversial or, in some people's minds, unpleasant to present. For example, the use of a representative from a civil rights organization to teach the entire course in community relations might be a mistake. Students in this situation can easily feel that the material represents only the opinion of an outsider rather than the thinking of the department.

If qualified staff members are not available for full-time assignment to the training unit, the department should utilize all available resources in organizing its training program and in providing instructors. In some states, boards for vocational education help organize the program and also provide teacher training. The FBI, in its regional and local training programs, provides both organization of subject matter and instruction.

Persons are usually available in every community who, although they have not had actual police experience, are better equipped than the police to give instruction in subjects not exclusively of a police nature. The following are some of the subjects included in this category: legal medicine and toxicology; criminal psychiatry; the American Red Cross first-aid course; public speaking; report writing (journalism and English); typewriting; some phases of public relations; grammar; and most, if not all, phases of legal training.

The legal staff of the city and county are often available for legal training. Federal and state police agencies are able, and usually pleased, to provide

PERSONNEL MANAGEMENT

instructors in their specialties. Instruction in subjects of an exclusively police nature, especially those unique to municipal police service in which federal and state officers are inexperienced, presents a special problem. In small departments, the training officer must give such instruction or utilize the officers of the department as instructors, aiding them in organizing and presenting the material.

Minimum Standards and Training

Adoption of minimum-standards and training laws by states and the creation of standards and training commissions are among the more progressive developments in the field over the past few years.

Approximately 46 states have adopted minimum standards for selection or training of police officers, either through passing direct legislation or by offering incentives for local governments which select or train employees in accordance with the standards. Information on model legislation for minimum-standards programs and the creation of police-standards councils may be obtained from the International Association of Chiefs of Police.

Improvements resulting from the adoption of minimum standards are worthwhile in their own right, of course, even if lateral entry does not materialize immediately. State standards and training agencies have a wide range of responsibilities, including rendering consulting services in any area of police administration. The agencies also inspect local departments to ensure compliance with standards in such areas as selection of recruits, length and depth of training courses, and certification of individual officers.

Administration and Planning of Training

There are several useful devices for influencing the quality of training programs and for planning changes in training. First, the results of field inspections serve a useful purpose. Inspectors can often pinpoint the lack of training as a reason for a given deficiency. Second, training needs can be discussed in general departmental staff meetings from time to time. Third, training needs should be a significant part of the general departmental program effort, particularly when a significant change in policy or procedures is about to take place. Fourth, some departments have established training committees (consisting of representatives of various divisions, but always chaired by the head of the training function). The training committee can also be used to suggest training programs, including the outline of curricula.

Training Facilities A properly designed training facility can greatly increase the effectiveness of a police training program. There should be adequate space provided for both small discussion-group study and larger lecture classes. Classrooms should have adequate lighting, ventilation, and physical design so that audiovisual presentations can be most effective. Gymnasium and range facilities are also necessary in a well-rounded program. A gymnasium should have adequate space for conditioning games such as basketball and handball, as well as physical apparatus for body building. In locations where swimming and lifesaving skills are likely to be needed, a swimming pool is a definite asset in the training program. A police firearms range is often a part of a training-academy facility. Newly built outdoor ranges should permit firing of the FBI practical pistol course, and an attempt should be made to incorporate indoor range facilities in new buildings.

The training facility need not be located at the police headquarters. Training often requires field exercises, which are sometimes difficult to carry out in a downtown area, and the presence of recruits going to and from classes in an operating police facility is distracting.

Administrative Duties   The administrative and clerical duties in an intensive training program occupy considerable time: Decisions must be made regarding subject matter to be presented and the time to be devoted to each; outlines of subject matter and lesson plans must be prepared to ensure complete coverage and suitable coordination; schedules must be arranged that will fit into the work programs of the officers and the instructors; equipment and facilities for classrooms, the gymnasium, the target range, and demonstrations must be provided; records must be kept of attendance and examination scores; material must be prepared for classroom distribution; department and outside instructors must have assistance in preparing for their classes; interest and enthusiasm in the training program must be created and maintained; and orders to initiate the various phases of the program must be drafted.

The training program referred to here is limited to the somewhat formalized instruction having exact objectives, with definite planning and preparation for fulfilling that purpose. It does not include continuous training in the techniques, procedures, policies, and programs carried on by specialists, superior officers, and commanding officers. The training officer should facilitate instruction by supervisory officers at roll calls or periodic conferences; toward this end, the training officer should prepare useful material and aid in its presentation, serving as an assistant (not necessarily present) of the officer in charge of the conference or roll call.

Length of School Day   A determination of the number of hours to be devoted each day to classroom instruction under a full-time program requires careful study. The fatigue resulting from many hours of lectures, especially in the case of officers some years removed from schoolroom experience, diminishes the effectiveness of the instruction. Not more than seven hours of class should be provided each school day, and these should be relieved by an extended lunch period. Included in the seven hours are classes, such as gymnasium, range, and public speaking, which do not require the continued concentration of the usual lecture. These subjects should be timed to provide relief from fatigue and thus avoid diminished concentration, interest, and attention. For example, the lunch period may be followed by range practice or public speaking. The period devoted to gymnasium should come near the end

PERSONNEL MANAGEMENT

of the classroom day, since it is physically fatiguing and consequently induces drowsiness and since time is required to shower and dress. Limited range and gymnasium facilities sometimes make desirable the instruction of both subjects during the same hour, part of the class being instructed in one, and part in the other, during each half period. Extension of instruction in these subjects over a longer time may be desirable for other reasons.

If home study is required and the officers are examined on their homework, the number of hours of instruction should be reduced. In any event, officers should be supplied with printed and mimeographed material which they should be expected to study on their own time.

RECRUIT TRAINING

Technically speaking, recruit training can be considered to be in-service training—as opposed to preservice or outside training in an academy or college. In this text, however, recruit training will be distinguished from other in-service training activity because of its importance and length.

Recruit training is the foundation for good patrol service, for annual continuation training, and for special training. A minimum of three months of recruit training seems justified, and more time could be used to advantage. The length of recruit training in some of our larger and more progressive departments is increasing steadily. The Chicago Police Department recruit-training program is now nine months long.

There is a common tendency for those who plan training courses to think first in terms of a specified number of hours or weeks and then fill up the time with subject matter. For example, administrators will occasionally ask their training staffs to set up, say, a 12-week training course based on 40 hours of training in firearms, 32 in criminal law, and so on. Actually, the length of the course should ideally be based on the time required to achieve the teaching of objectives in a series of well-defined units of instruction.

Recruit Curriculum Prospective police officers should be exposed to a variety of training activities before they are expected to assume basic police responsibilities. A typical major-city recruit-training curriculum, as given by the Baltimore Police Department, is presented in the Appendix. The Baltimore program is intended to be conducted in several phases, with periods of field training between classroom sessions.

Multiple-Phase Training Some division of emphasis is necessary in recruit-training programs if the department uses a two-phase training schedule. Many administrators are finding there is an advantage in giving initial courses of training in some fundamental police subjects—such as law enforcement ethics, laws of arrest, first aid, use of firearms, and self-defense—and then exposing the recruits to field conditions for a brief period of time. Following the period of field training, recruits are brought back into the academy for the

304   ADMINISTRATION

continuation of the program. This approach has the great advantage of pointing out to the individual student the areas and job skills he or she will need to know after graduating from the academy.

Field Training A field-training program is an integral part of recruit training, and there should be a smooth transition from the theory of the academy to practical application on the street.

Some kind of field training for new officers should take place in any department. This can be carried out by assigning recruits to experienced officers with the proper attitude and by utilizing a field-training checklist. A good checklist itemizes some of the procedures and techniques for handling situations which are likely to be encountered during field training, and it always has provisions for listing the many topics which must be explained during the course of the program. A good checklist is shown in Appendix H.

In larger departments, the field-training officer program should be formalized. Experienced officers (selected from volunteers) should be brought into the academy for orientation and discussion of the methods to be used in the field-training officer program. In a two-phase training program, recruits should be assigned to field-training officers during the interim portion. When the interim field training is finished, the training officer should write a brief report on the need for emphasized training in certain areas. At the conclusion of academy training, the recruits should again be assigned to field-training officers during their first few weeks on the streets.

The effect of proper influence on a new police officer is very profound. Some administrators have become aware of the difficulty caused by exposing a new recruit to a disaffected or disinterested older employee, not to mention the influence of dishonest or brutal officers. They have therefore sought to assign new officers to senior officers with proper attitudes. The St. Louis Police Department has experimented with assigning only recruit officers to an entire police district, along with experienced police supervisors and field-training officers. The effect of this experiment was unexpectedly rewarding; although the administration believed there would be the usual high activity which results from the enthusiasm of recruit officers, they were unprepared for the sustained productiveness of the new officers for an indefinite period, as well as a rapid development of their proficiency in a short time. The Berkeley Police Department approaches the problem in a different way, by assigning all new officers to the same shift, with movement to the next shift on the basis of seniority. New officers are thus not exposed to officers who are significantly older or more experienced, and field training is carried out almost exclusively by sergeants.

IN-SERVICE TRAINING

In addition to recruit training, a continuation-training program should be provided. It should be redesigned annually to meet current needs arising from

PERSONNEL MANAGEMENT

changes in policies and procedures, the adoption of new techniques, and weaknesses detected in the recruit program.

The following is a list of suitable subjects for a typical 35- to 40-hour general in-service training course:

Subject	Hours
Combat shooting and police-range exercises	3
Criminal law and procedure	6
Ethics	1
Field reporting	3
First-aid review	2
Investigative procedures	4
Mechanics of arrest	3
Minorities and police	2
Operational policy review	1
Patrol procedures and tactics	5
Proper use of force	1
Public relations	1
Recognition and recovery of stolen autos	1
Riot control	2
Safety in pursuit driving	1
Testifying in court	1
Traffic law enforcement	1
Youthful offenders	1
Final examination	1

Besides the general in-service training courses, specialized programs are highly useful in developing operational skills. Similar courses should be developed for investigators, traffic-enforcement officers, technical service personnel, and supervisors. Week-long courses are also practical in large departments in such subjects as patrol methods and procedures, delinquency prevention and patrol, community relations, driver training, and civil-disturbance control.

Advanced in-service training of this sort should not be restricted to the specialists themselves, but should be offered as well to personnel on a preassignment basis.

Roll-Call Training Most large or progressive departments offer roll-call training to officers periodically during the week or (in a few cases) on a daily basis. Training usually consists of brief lectures, demonstrations, and discussion, carried out in sessions lasting about 15 minutes during the roll-call period. The time should be considered a part of the regular working day.

Training material should be based on bulletins prepared by the department or purchased from commercial sources. The training officer or training division should coordinate the roll-call instruction.

Middle-Management and Administrative Training Few departments today offer adequate in-service training for middle-management personnel. There are several outstanding academy-type training programs available to experienced supervisors, but these programs cannot possibly absorb all the lieutenants, captains, and other ranking officers who need administrative and management training.

Material for the course should be similar to the content of this text, except that it should be oriented to the middle-management level rather than the police administrator. The content should give heavy emphasis to the middle-management role in providing for effective first-line supervision.

Advanced management training should be based on whatever time is needed to achieve the instructional objectives set out for the course, but as a minimum, 70 to 80 classroom hours should be required for a general course. The subject matter can be presented over a period of several months to allow for study and library research between classroom sessions.

EDUCATION

The best hope for long-term improvement of police service lies in the development of superior personnel to carry out future planning and direction in this field. For the most part, the present national effort in the upgrading of the law enforcement system depends on the application of expertise which is currently available. This collection of expertise has been given some additional resources and direction and has been reorganized in a different way. Truly significant improvement, on the other hand, will result from the development of greater numbers of highly qualified personnel who will be engaged in future management and operations. In turn, the best way to achieve this objective is through college-level education.

As indicated earlier in this chapter, a minimum educational requirement of two years of college is now feasible—or soon will be—in many areas in the United States. A four-year degree in police administration or law enforcement should be listed as desirable in any promotional examination, and within a few years the baccalaureate degree should be required for entrance into police departments as well as for promotions.

College Programs

For students who intend to enter police service, many universities and colleges now offer specific degree courses or majors in the police field, such as in criminal justice, criminology, law enforcement, police science, police administration, and public administration. Courses in government, psychology, sociology, social welfare, statistics, English, public speaking, and military science and tactics also have value in providing a background of knowledge.

A university or college criminal justice or law enforcement program is also useful to students of public administration, social welfare, and journalism. The

PERSONNEL MANAGEMENT

availability of these courses to students not intending to enter police service helps in the general dissemination of information relating to crime and criminality. These citizens are thus equipped to deal more intelligently and effectively with problems relating to the administration of criminal justice.

Police administrators should promote police training programs in colleges and universities in their communities, and they should participate by making police facilities available for training purposes. A local department may thus serve as a laboratory for students enrolled in criminology courses, and arrangements can be made for part-time service with the department as an element in the training program for advanced students.

Recommended Curricula On behalf of the American Association of Community and Junior Colleges, James D. Stinchcomb, of Virginia Commonwealth University, has prepared a suggested curriculum for the associate degree in arts or general studies.

Courses offered in four-year institutions tend to differ much more, partly because of the nature of the academic department or school which offers the curriculum. For example, a law enforcement degree program organized as a division of a school of public administration might require several courses related to public administration, while a police program in a school of criminology may require several courses related to criminology.

Law Enforcement Curriculum Summary
(Associate Degree)

First year	Second year

General education courses:
  English/technical report
    writing
  Psychology
  Sociology/criminology
  Government
Technical, specialized courses:
  Introduction to law enforce-
    ment/criminal justice
  Police organization/administra-
    tion/operations/procedures
  Juvenile-delinquency preven-
    tion/procedures/control
  Criminal law
	General education courses:
	  Math
	  Humanities/social science
	Technical, specialized courses:
	  Police supervision
	  Criminal investigation
	  Law of evidence (procedure)
	  Police–community relations/
	    human relations
	  Introduction to criminalistics
	  Internship/practicum/field
	    methods/seminar

Most typical additional specialized courses include:

  Traffic administration/control/regulation
  Administration of justice (emphasis on courts and legal process)
  Narcotics/drug abuse/investigation
  Minority/race/ethnic relations

Source: James D. Stinchcomb, *Opportunities in Law Enforcement and Related Careers,* Vocational Guidance Manuals, Inc., Louisville, Ky., 1976, p. 84.

A recommended curriculum for a four-year degree program is shown below.

Law Enforcement Curriculum Summary
(Bachelor's Degree)

First year

English
General psychology
Introduction to law enforcement
Introduction to sociology
History (including American)
Foreign language
Public speaking

Second year

Criminology
Survey of the administration of justice
Social problems
Laboratory science
Government (national, state, and local)
Adolescent psychology

Third year

Society and the law
Psychology (abnormal and social)
Police management and administration
Government (public administration)
Delinquency and the youthful offender
Humanities
Math, logic, or philosophy

Fourth year

Criminal law (current decisions)
Advanced criminalistics
Government (constitutional law)
Business or public administration (personnel management)
Statistics (data processing)
Urban sociology
Dynamics of criminal and delinquent behavior
Prevention and treatment of crime

Examples of specialized law enforcement electives

Traffic administration and management
Public and private security (industrial and retail)
Computers, research, and technical services
Community relations
International aspects of crime control
Criminal justice planning
Contemporary critical issues in law enforcement (seminar)
Field training (internship)

Source: James D. Stinchcomb, *Opportunities in a Law Enforcement Career*, Universal Publishing and Distributing Corporation, New York, 1971, p. 72.

Educational-Incentive Plans

The rapid development of educational-incentive plans in the police service ought to raise some doubts about the wisdom of categorizing police and local government as conservative and slow to change in every area. With the possible exception of the adoption of the fingerprint system as a means of identification, no other innovation in policing has achieved such widespread popularity in so short a time.

PERSONNEL MANAGEMENT

There are several principal varieties of educational-incentive plans:

- Giving additional pay for college credits or degrees
- Paying tuition and other costs for education
- Allowing time off to go to class
- Requiring college education as a promotional prerequisite
- Establishing a prestigious or career position requiring college education

Each variation has advantages, and the methods are not exclusionary; any of these plans may be used by itself or together with one or more of the other ideas.

The Tulsa Police Department granted incentive pay to degree holders in 1962, and in 1965 IACP began to advocate educational-incentive pay in its management studies of police departments. The first such recommendation was made to the Metropolitan Police Department in Washington, D.C., in a survey which began in October 1965 and was completed in April 1966. (Prior to 1962 the Santa Ana Police Department initiated incentive pay based on achievement of training, experience, and education "points," but education was not specifically singled out.)

In the years since then, hundreds of agencies have adopted incentive plans. In conjunction with the ready availability of tuition money supplied by means of LEAA's Law Enforcement Education Program (LEEP), educational-incentive pay plans have resulted in some dramatic increases in educational level. In Arlington, Virginia, for example, only a few officers had graduated from college in 1964, when the program began in an experimental way. By 1968, the plan was in full operation, and by 1976 there were more than 140 officers with four years of college or more, including 29 with master's degrees, out of a total of 300 sworn personnel.

Most educational-incentive pay plans are intended to carry out essentially the same objectives: to attract candidates with superior education to police service, to take advantage of the benefit of that training, and to encourage officers who are already on the force to go to college.

The federal service now permits college graduates to be paid a higher entrance salary in certain categories if they have the requisite degrees. Paying a salary differential based on education has also been a long-standing practice in certain fields, such as teaching and librarianship. This has carried over into other fields, particularly engineering and computer sciences.

The wide variety of incentive plans now in existence gives some testimony to the newness of the idea. Some agencies now offer a specific amount of money per unit of credit completed, such as $1 per month for each semester credit. Others pay officers only if they are actually attending school, and they may or may not give permanent pay after the degree is acquired. Still others pay a fixed amount per month for completion of the degree. The most common system, however, is to pay police officers a percentage of base pay for completion of certain increments of college credits. The National Advisory Commission on Criminal Justice Standards and Goals recommends 2½ percent of base pay for each 30 units completed, up to the level of a bachelor's degree. This method is also recommended by the IACP staff.

Regardless of the method of payment, the departmental personnel and/or training unit should act as the coordinator for administration of the system and should supply a roster of eligible employees to the city payroll clerk. The training division should also check or verify each officer's claim for qualification.

Law Enforcement Education Program   Perhaps the most valuable contribution made by the Law Enforcement Assistance Administration has been the advent of the Law Enforcement Education Program. The LEEP program has sought to carry out two major objectives: (1) to provide educational incentive by making financial assistance available to individuals working in the criminal justice system and to pursue additional education at the college or university level and (2) to provide incentive for college students to enroll in programs related to law enforcement.[10] LEEP funds are available to assist individual students in the form of (1) tuition grants, (2) loans, or (3) internship assistance. The latest amendments to the Crime Control Act expanded tuition coverage originally authorized by the 1968 statute, and awards up to $250 per academic quarter or $400 per semester are made under this portion of the program. Tuition grant money is available only for tuition fees and books.

LEEP loans, which have been expanded as a result of later amendments to the original Crime Control Act, are now awarded in amounts of up to $2,200 per academic year.

Finally, those who have completed two years of higher education may be eligible for internship programs consisting of full-time service in law enforcement agencies for not less than eight weeks during summer vacations or for entire quarter or semester periods on leave from degree programs. Funds of up to $65 per week are designated for payment to student interns.

The overwhelming majority of law enforcement students who have attended college since 1968 have received financial assistance through LEEP funds. This money has been in the main responsible for the proliferation of undergraduate programs for law enforcement throughout the United States.

Outside Training

There are some excellent academy- or institute-type programs which are unique in several ways. First, most of them are given under the auspices of a university. Second, they are often distinct from regular university programs, in both scheduling and format. Third, they do not require satisfaction of usual

[10]Metropolitan Washington Council of Governments, 1975 Division of Law Enforcement Programs, Washington, D.C., p. A–2.

PERSONNEL MANAGEMENT

college-entrance requirements, so worthy candidates who may lack these formal requirements are eligible to attend. Examples of such schools are the Northwestern University Traffic Institute, the Southern Police Institute of the University of Louisville, and the Delinquency Control Institute of the University of Southern California. The FBI National Academy at Quantico, Virginia, offers excellent training of the institute type, and in recent years it has vastly increased the number of officers who are graduated each year. The academy also offers excellent short courses on various subjects.

The police administrator should encourage attendance in schools of this kind, as well as in the many shorter courses conducted by various federal, state, and local agencies. As indicated elsewhere in this chapter, however, the capacity of institutes is limited. The chief must therefore emphasize educational improvement through conventional college and university programs.

Self-education and Self-improvement

One of the great benefits of formal education at the college level is the stimulation of continuing self-education. Another is the broadened perspective which results from exposure to ideas and concepts outside the field. Unfortunately, many noncollege people tend to believe that these benefits may be achieved *only* through formal classroom training and the traditional lecture method. This is not true, of course, and it may therefore be helpful to establish a directed reading program and a library within the department to encourage informal education.

Part Three

Operations

Chapter 15

Team Policing

Earlier editions of this text have described police operations in terms of the traditional operational functions found in the typical department. Chapters on patrol, criminal investigations, traffic, youth, vice control, and special operations have been appropriate and convenient.

In team policing, however, many of these functions are carried out by the same individuals assigned to a team. Although there have been references to team policing in some of the chapters mentioned above as well as elsewhere in this book, it seems appropriate to deal with general team-policing concepts and techniques at this point.

Varieties of Team Policing

There are many versions of team policing in the United States and the United Kingdom. Some "teams" are simply groups of patrol officers who work together, with a common supervisor, in one larger beat or in a grouping of adjacent beats. These officers have responsibility for their territory for an eight-hour shift; then they turn over their responsibilities to another crew of officers on the oncoming shift. In this simplest version of team policing, the team members carry out the traditional patrol functions.

315

In a few of these applications, however, detectives or investigators are assigned to the teams. This is an important step toward full team policing because it marks the beginning of generalized team effort which crosses the traditional barriers between the preliminary investigation conducted by patrol officers and the follow-up investigations by the detective division.

The ultimate extension of team policing is to give a squad or team of officers the responsibility for providing almost all police services within a specified area on a 24-hour-a-day, seven-day-a-week basis. This concept is generally known as *district team* or *neighborhood team policing.*

District Team Policing

The origin of district team policing can be traced to the concept of "unit-beat policing," developed by the police in Great Britain. The first known application of unit-beat policing in a larger police department took place in Aberdeen, Scotland. The concept was later adopted and refined in the Lancastershire Constabulary in England. In Lancastershire, each team assigned to a beat consisted of a basic number of constables, plus detectives for follow-up investigations and a coordinating officer assisting the team at headquarters. In the British system, constables have been encouraged to reside on the beat as well. The concept has been intended to emphasize personal contact with residents. Hours of work and the nature of assignments have been flexible; for example, several constables may be assigned to handle an investigation during evening hours on one night and then be assigned to some other activity the next day.

Unit-beat policing in its original version has been described by some English chief administrators as an absolute failure. Reasons cited have included problems in communication from one beat to another, the difficulty in coordinating major incidents requiring the use of personnel from several beats, and the morale problem which stemmed from overzealous attempts to have constables live in the beats to which they are assigned.

Some of these difficulties have been overcome by modifications of the original idea. In the Lincolnshire Constabulary, for example, most patrol work is performed by constables assigned to conventional shifts. However, there are a number of senior patrol officers who are assigned to territories as an "overlay" to the conventional coverage. These senior officers work more or less independently, with flexible hours. They engage in follow-up investigations, problem solving, and contacts of a public relations type.

There have been several adaptations of the concept of district team or unit-beat policing in the United States. One of the well-known experimental applications is in Cincinnati, Ohio, where it is being used in one of several territorial subdivisions. This pilot project area is termed "Com-Sec," short for Community Sector Policing.

The Cincinnati experiment has been financed by the Police Foundation, with evaluation of the project by the Urban Institute of Washington, D.C.

A highly successful full-scale citywide version of district team policing has been adopted in Charlotte, North Carolina. In that city, most policing responsibilities are carried out by 10 teams of officers, each consisting of about 24 patrol officers and detectives, plus six sergeants. Each team is led by a lieutenant who is assisted in administrative duties, scheduling, and report-review work by one of the six sergeants.

In Charlotte, team members handle most follow-up investigations except for a few categories of serious cases—such as murder or kidnapping—which are reserved for the department's "major case squad." Even in cases which are technically to be assigned to the major case squad, team members frequently continue with complicated investigations as a result of their enthusiasm.

In January 1975 the Los Angeles Police Department adopted true district or 24-hour team policing on a citywide basis, following several years of successful experience with the Basic Car Plan and an equally successful pilot project for team policing in the Venice Division of Los Angeles. Under the older Basic Car Plan, patrol beats were assigned to teams of nine officers who provided 24-hour coverage within the beat. Supervision was provided by a lead officer and a senior lead officer (Policemen III and III + 1 classifications in the Los Angeles pay plan). In the Venice Division, each district commander was given one to three "basic cars," i.e., from 9 to 27 officers, who were assisted by detectives and other specialists. The entire district team was given responsibility for almost all police services within the district. Following the success of the experiment in the Venice Division, team policing was adopted citywide.

Both the original Basic Car Plan and the newer version derived from it have emphasized contact with the citizenry; each team must conduct a monthly meeting, with all residents in the beat invited to attend. The concept also takes advantage of what is perhaps a basic human tendency:

> There is a fundamental social premise involved here. I'll call it territorial imperative; most people are familiar with it. Like the beast, and in this case we are human beasts, we identify with a piece of geography and the people in that area. The beast will fight for that, till death if necessary. And he will keep hostile forces away from the territory. Assign nine men to an area; try to keep them there for a good period of time; tell them to care for and protect their territory, and they will begin to take on this attitude. Instill this same fervor in the minds of the residents in that area and you will promote . . . public approval of police action.[1]

The National Advisory Commission on Criminal Justice Standards and Goals, while stopping short of outright recommendation of team policing, states categorically that departments should develop plans for team operation.

Most advocates of successful district team-policing operations, such as those in Charlotte, Los Angeles, and Rochester, New York, mention the following advantages and benefits:

---

[1]From an address given by Chief Edward M. Davis, Los Angeles Police Department, before the 77th Annual Conference, International Association of Chiefs of Police, Atlantic City, N.J., October 1970.

- Improved efficiency in handling less serious but more frequently encountered crimes
- Improved relationships with the community
- Increased departmental morale because of reduced friction in the absence of former divisional rivalries
- Greater job satisfaction for patrol officers
- Much better fixing of responsibility

Not all team-policing experiments have been successful—partly because some of the inherent disadvantages of the system were allowed to get out of hand. Disadvantages are said to be as follows:

- In some cases, decreased effectiveness in major cases requiring the simultaneous participation of members from several teams
- Resistance to implementation, due to inadequate planning and training or as a result of changes in scheduling which are unfavorable to individual officers
- At certain times of day (such as early morning hours) a wasteful ratio of supervisors to patrol officers

Essentials of Neighborhood or District Team Policing In its excellent publication in the "Prescriptive Package" series entitled *Neighborhood Team Policing*,[2] the National Institute of Law Enforcement and Criminal Justice has established several elements which ought to be included in any program that is labeled "neighborhood team policing" or "district-team policing":

1 Planning of team operations by team members, with emphasis on communication within the team and on innovation to suit changing requirements
2 Territorial integrity of the team so that responsibility for almost all police operations is fixed and so that overlap of supervision is eliminated
3 Investigations—both initial and follow-up—to be conducted by team members insofar as possible, with detectives working side by side with patrol officers accountable to the same team commander
4 Twenty-four-hour responsibility for the team area or district
5 An active community relations program with emphasis on meetings and other contacts with citizens in the neighborhood, to ensure citizen participation in setting team objectives and as a means for educating and informing the public

[2]Peter B. Bloch and David Specht, *Neighborhood Team Policing,* National Institute of Law Enforcement and Criminal Justice, LEAA, U.S. Department of Justice, 1973.

Chapter 16

Patrol

Crime results from the coexistence of the desire to commit a criminal act and the belief that the opportunity to do so exists. When either factor is absent, criminal acts will not be committed. The presence of one factor alone, regardless of how strong it may be, will not result in crime. The elimination or reduction of these two factors, therefore, is a basic police duty. One task is to prevent or eradicate criminality in the individual; the other embraces all security measures designed to hamper or prevent criminal operations.

As long as people are human, they will have selfish desires which, when the opportunity is presented, will sometimes cause them to commit crimes, create disturbances, or violate regulations. The desire to misbehave may, to some extent, be prevented by the removal or suppression of unwholesome influences, but the police may not hope to eliminate it entirely. At the same time, they cannot develop sufficient strength or efficiency to eliminate all opportunity for misconduct. The actual or total elimination of opportunity, however, is not always necessary; elimination of the *belief* that the opportunity for successful misconduct exists may be sufficient.

Nature of Patrol   To the layman, the word "patrol" suggests little more

319

OPERATIONS

than perfunctory inspectional activity, whether carried out on foot or in a vehicle. In most agencies today, however, the patrol function embraces many other activities beyond the physical act of patrolling the street. Patrol work involves extensive crime-prevention contacts and duties, criminal investigation, traffic-law enforcement, and an element of every other line activity carried out by field personnel. (The inadequacy of the term "patrol," in fact, has led some authorities to use the term "uniformed division" or "operations division" in describing a patrol unit, in an attempt to emphasize the generalized nature of patrol work.) Thus, unless the word "patrol" is specifically identified as a physical activity, it will be used in its broader meaning in this text.

Purposes of Patrol The basic purpose of patrol is the elimination of the actual opportunity (or the belief that the opportunity exists) for successful misconduct. This function is sometimes referred to as *crime repression.* An offender's desire to steal is not diminished by the presence of a patrol officer, but the opportunity for successful theft is.

The apparent likelihood of arrest influences the degree to which the potential offender is convinced that the opportunity for successful misconduct is absent. Patrol provides this favorable influence more completely than any other branch of police service. An impression of omnipresence is created by frequent and conspicuous patrol at every hour and in all sections of the community. Furthermore, effective patrol, through the use of sufficient personnel at the right times and places, almost invariably results in immediate apprehensions, and since nothing succeeds like success, a reputation for quick and certain apprehension is spread by the press, radio, television, and word of mouth. The potential offender is thus persuaded—without the need for personal experience—that the patrol force is invulnerable.

A secondary purpose of patrol is to provide the resources for *crime-prevention* activities, such as the discovery of delinquency-producing conditions, the stimulation of higher ethical standards, and the elimination of unwholesome influences. Besides being the only form of police service that directly attempts to eliminate opportunity for misconduct, the patrol function also checks the development of desire for misconduct by actively creating wholesome influences and by favorably affecting individual and group attitudes through continual contacts and association with the public. Patrol officers should be practical social workers who reach out to help others and who encourage persons to come to them for assistance and advice when in trouble. Distress situations are frequently symptoms of deep-rooted social ills that, if not corrected, may result in criminal or other antisocial conduct and thus adversely affect the remainder of the life of the individual. By giving assistance, advice, and sympathy to those in distress, patrol officers can help prevent social deviance and criminality, and in the process they win friendship and cooperation for the department.

The third major purpose of patrol is most evident when patrol has failed to eliminate the desire to commit a criminal act and when there is the belief that the opportunity exists. Patrol is then immediately available for *investigation* of offenses, apprehension of offenders, and the recovery of stolen property.

Fourth, the complete citywide coverage provided by patrol on a 24-hour-a-day basis makes it available for *noncriminal services.* The patrol officer searches for and returns lost persons and property, informs and assists citizens, and performs a wide variety of noncriminal services ranging from traffic control to assisting in resolving family arguments.

Patrol officers are the ultimate in the decentralization of municipal service. They are roving city-hall information and complaint centers for the distressed citizen, who is disgruntled by the inconvenience of trips to city hall, unsatisfactory telephone calls, and sometimes apparent lack of attention to his complaints. The constant availability and mobility of the officer make his services useful to other city departments, and he improves both public and interdepartmental relationships by attending more immediately to citizen needs. The extent to which patrol officers will provide extra police services is determined by the chief executive of the city and his department heads.

Services which the police may perform for other departments include searching for and eliminating fire and health hazards, such as trash and garbage accumulations, weed-covered lots, and unhygienic conditions in restaurants; reporting housing-code and occupancy violations; discovering and reporting street lights not burning and broken water mains; checking on building permits and occupation licenses; reporting of building-code violations; and reporting safety hazards for which other departments have some responsibility, such as defective sidewalks and streets.

Most services for other departments are performed in the course of routine patrol, with the officer thus continuously available for emergencies. The demand for these services usually is not urgent, and the tasks may be performed at slack moments when the need for more important police service is not immediate. Their performance often aids in the accomplishment of the more primary police tasks by encouraging the officers to circulate more actively. However, when these services occupy a significant amount of patrol time, the point of specialization has been reached, and the tasks should be performed by the city department primarily responsible. Furthermore, whenever the patrol force is made responsible for a new duty or activity, one must ask the question: What other activity must we *stop* performing in order to accommodate the new task?

ORGANIZATION AND STAFFING OF THE PATROL FUNCTION

The patrol division is the largest police division and is responsible for the performance of all primary police tasks. It provides complete coverage of the city and command at headquarters at every hour of the day and night. The patrol division may take immediate action in the absence of members from a special division, and during certain hours the patrol command may provide administrative supervision over the records and jail staffs and the dispatchers,

322   OPERATIONS

regardless of the division to which they may be regularly assigned (see Chapter 8).

Policing itself should be considered basically a patrol service with specialized activities developed as aids. The patrol division is the nucleus of the department, about which the special services are grouped; it should not be subordinated to any other functional unit, such as a detective or traffic division. If the patrol division is a part of a field operations bureau, the patrol function should be given the benefit of the best command and supervisory talent in the department.

During the past few decades, police responsibilities have become increasingly numerous and complex. At the same time, police departments have tended to retain traditional methods for fulfilling these responsibilities, such as the use of routine preventive patrol by officers assigned to patrol-car duty or on foot beats. Routine preventive patrol has been a highly regarded mainstay of police operations for as long as police departments have been formally organized. In many agencies, fully half of the force is engaged in patrol activity, and of this activity, as much as 50 percent may be in the form of preventive patrol. Any large expenditure of this kind deserves to be scrutinized as to cost effectiveness.

The Kansas City Patrol Experiment Some basic questions about the effectiveness of preventive patrol, along with the trend toward specialization, are issues which deserve attention. Are the American police on the point of discontinuing preventive patrol? Has patrol outlived its usefulness? Certainly, many people now think so, especially after the publicity generated by the Kansas City, Missouri, patrol experiment. In a true application of social research in the law enforcement field, a study team sponsored jointly by the Kansas City Police Department, the Police Foundation (who funded the work), and the Urban Institute (who evaluated it) divided a district in Kansas City into a number of zones having different levels of patrol activity. In one series of zones, called *proactive*, more than the usual amount of preventive patrol was supplied. In another series of zones, called *reactive*, all routine preventive patrol was eliminated, and police were allowed to go into these zones only in response to calls for service or to cross the zone to get to some other location. The third series of zones was designated as control areas. The basic finding in the experiment was that the crime level was not reduced in the proactive areas except for the category of auto theft, and even then by only a small amount. In the reactive areas, furthermore, citizens were alleged even to be unaware that fewer police officers were on duty there.

A number of criticisms—some of them suggested by the study team itself—have arisen with regard to the study, including (1) the failure of the experimenters to tell the public that preventive patrol was no longer in effect (a reality which would most certainly have to be confronted if any city adopted this technique on a permanent basis throughout the jurisdiction); (2) the fact that specialized units such as detectives and tactical officers were allowed to come into the reactive areas anyway; (3) the fact that preventive patrol was not eliminated altogether because proactive and control officers regularly traversed the reactive zones; and (4) the fact that various zones were in some cases laid out so that a long, thin reactive zone would be located between proactive zones or control zones, with the result that residents within the reactive zones could actually see proactive- or control-zone vehicles in the distance. Nevertheless, the experimentation was a landmark in police research, and similar efforts under controlled conditions should be conducted elsewhere to test the hypothesis that preventive patrol by itself has limited value.

Despite the evidence from Kansas City, the fact remains that in the few situations in recent history in which police response was obviously not immediately available—such as in the Montreal police strike of October 1969 and the Chicago blizzard in 1967, which immobilized the patrol force—wholesale looting and lawlessness have been the result.

It is also highly important to make a distinction between preventive patrol activity which is aimless or misdirected and activity which is more tactical in its application or directed to specific hazards. There is no question that intensive patrol efforts by a group of officers, tactically deployed, are effective in reducing certain kinds of crimes, such as armed robbery of commercial establishments, purse snatchings, and muggings. Also, the police department in New Haven, Connecticut, is now exploring the possibility of "hazard-oriented patrol," which differs from aimless, random patrol in that officers deliberately seek out a series of high-hazard locations which are given patrol surveillance in random order. Patrol in less-hazardous locations is rendered only by means of the movement of patrol officers from one high-hazard location to another or by movement from one assignment to another. This technique is not new, of course, but it may mark the first time that experimentation and evaluation will have been carried out in a systematic manner.

Despite misgivings about the future of patrol service, it is apparent that the patrol force will continue to carry out the most important function within any police department.

The Relationship of Patrol to Specialized Units

As indicated in Chapter 14, there is a great need for emphasizing the position of the experienced, capable patrol officer as one of prestige and responsibility. Siphoning off competent patrol personnel by assigning them to better-paid specialized positions will defeat worthwhile attempts to increase the image of the patrol force.

Influences toward specialization, and the resultant dissipation of the patrol force, are found outside as well as within the department. Local safety councils and public safety committees of civic organizations interested in traffic control, reformers and church groups interested in the suppression of vice activities, and socially minded citizens interested in the welfare of youth actively crusade for special branches of the service.

Business people exert influences that affect the strength of the patrol force, not always by the actual withdrawal of manpower from patrol, but also by a demand for services, some of them quasi-police or nonpolice in character, that require so much patrol time as to diminish the total effectiveness of the patrol force. Parking regulations, usually adopted at the insistence of retail merchants, may withdraw manpower from patrol service out of proportion to actual need.

Relative Strength of the Patrol Force   Patrol is responsible for the accomplishment of the total police job, and in small departments having no specialization, it actually performs all police tasks. When a special division is created, it must be decided which tasks are to be taken from patrol and made the exclusive responsibility of the special unit, which tasks are to remain the exclusive responsibility of patrol, and which tasks are to be assigned as a joint responsibility.

As the tasks of special units are increased, additional personnel must be assigned for their performance, and the added personnel are almost invariably procured from the patrol force, thus depleting its strength. On the other hand, the more duties assigned the patrol division, the larger the patrol force, because there is then less need for personnel to man special units.

The flexibility of patrol permits the performance of many diverse tasks that are specialized in character. The importance of maintaining the strength of the patrol division makes it desirable to assign to it all tasks which may be performed substantially as well by patrol officers as by specialists and which do not interfere with regular patrol duties. The advantages of a strong patrol outweigh the disadvantages of slightly inferior performance; more patrol officers are then available for an emergency, and the more active and widespread the patrol, the more apparent is their presence, thus promoting the impression of omnipresence.

Determination of the optimum proportional patrol strength also involves discovering whether the special branches of service relieve patrol of an amount of work proportionate to the strength withdrawn from the patrol force. While some specialization is desirable, it should not go beyond the point of diminishing returns; a balance must be reached between the staffing of patrol and specialized units. There is no formula which may be used to determine exactly the optimum proportional strength of the patrol and special divisions. In making each decision, the benefits of specialization must be weighed against the disadvantages (see Chapter 7).

Dangers of Specialization at the Operational Level   The need for specialization in administrative tasks, such as planning and inspection, becomes evident in departments of relatively small size. It is met in the small department by the assignment of these tasks to a line officer in addition to his usual duties and in larger departments by the creation of a special unit for the purpose. Dangerous depletion of the patrol force does not often result from specialization for planning, inspection, and the like; such specialization is nearly always essential to ensure suitable attention to the accomplishment of each of the primary police tasks, and in most cases very little manpower is involved.

Most of the evils of specialization are found at the level of execution, i.e., the performance by specialists of tasks that should be handled by patrol officers in the course of their regular duty. For example, following the creation of a traffic division, primary responsibility for the enforcement of moving-traffic regulations should remain with the patrol division. Even though a youth division is created, each patrol officer should be charged with the identification or correction of conditions on his or her beat that induce delinquency. The creation of a vice division should not relieve patrol officers of responsibility for vice conditions on their beats; both the special unit and the patrol division should be responsible for the existence of any commercialized vice in the community. The patrol division and the special units of the force must act jointly if suitable integration of the most effective operation is to be realized. Routine patrol on a permanent basis by detectives is particularly wasteful of investigative manpower and should not be permitted.

Friction between Divisions Specialized divisions sometimes resist activities by the patrol division in their field of operation. Influenced by a desire to maintain complete and exclusive control over its operations, the special unit is prone to insist that the activities of the patrol division in its field interfere with plans and effective operation. This becomes apparent, for example, in the field of vice control when an arrest by a patrol officer seems to upset carefully laid plans to obtain evidence against higher-ups, on which the vice division may have been working for months. Detectives sometimes have similar complaints. While there are instances of serious interferences by poorly timed or ill-advised action on the part of patrol officers, dangers of this character are greatly overemphasized, as are the actual mistakes made by patrol officers. Specialized divisions, impressed with the desirability of "doing a task yourself if you want it done properly," are overcritical of the efforts of patrol officers; unusual incidents are sometimes exaggerated to cover their own shortcomings and failures. The specialized divisions are created to help the patrol officers do the total police job and to perform tasks which interfere with regular patrol duties or which may be performed substantially better by the specialist. To relieve patrol officers of their basic responsibilities would lessen their effectiveness. The aggregate good that comes from patrol participation in the fields of vice control and crime investigation greatly outweighs the evils that arise from infrequent interferences and mistakes.

Other Problems Related to Specialized Divisions In an organization that follows sound administrative practices, the relationships between the component units are clearly and precisely established by exact definitions of the duties of each. Regulations should establish, therefore, the types of cases to be reported directly to special units for purposes of immediate action and the responsibility of the patrol division in dealing with various types of incidents which are subsequently handled by special divisions. It is especially important to anticipate the human tendency to avoid responsibilities; regulations and supervision must ensure that suitable disposition is made of all incidents that come to the attention of the specialists and that other members of the department do not conclude that the creation of a special division relieves them of responsibility in the special field.

The police chief is concerned with the organization and staffing of each division. Decisions must be reached regarding the number of officers to be assigned to each, their ranks, the hours they are to work, and whether they should work singly or in pairs. Almost all operations of a specialized division require the planning and inspection of tasks performed by members both inside and outside the specialized division, as well as the direction of the specialists and their coordination with the other members of the department.

An executive, in establishing the relationships mentioned above, should not discount too heavily the competence of patrol officers and their ability to carry a heavy load. It is better to use officers up to the limit of their capacity than to relieve them of tasks which they are able to perform on the grounds that skills are required beyond their competence or that time is not available from their regular patrol duties.

One of the disadvantages in the use of specialists to perform tasks at the level of actual execution is the difficulty of providing at all hours the necessary supervision by officers to whom the specialists are responsible. For this reason, in some instances the service is better provided by specialization in the patrol division than by the special division itself. For example, when the amount of special work is sufficient, it is often desirable to assign one or more patrol officers to devote full time to its performance; if its performance would interfere with regular patrol duties, it becomes essential to do so.

Patrol by Specialized Units   The physical act of patrolling should, with few exceptions, be performed by the patrol division. Patrol by specialized divisions has limited value because officers so engaged are not alert to conditions demanding attention outside the field of their special interest. Even if they observe such conditions, they are prone to ignore them, and when citizens point them out anyway, the specialists frequently refer the citizens to another division. Problems in the direction and control of specialists engaged in patrol further limit its use. The dispatcher has greater difficulty in keeping track of specialists when they are in the field, and he cannot rely upon them in emergencies because they are not regularly available. The overlapping of regular patrol by special patrols results in less-intensive patrol because of the larger territory each officer must cover. An intensive general patrol in a small beat has advantages over a more specialized patrol in a larger area.

Staffing of Patrol

It is not possible, of course, to retain all competent patrol officers within the patrol division. Even though the administrator must make conscientious efforts

PATROL 327

to avoid draining the patrol force to supply manpower for specialized units, the fact remains that the patrol division must usually accommodate most of the new officers who join the department. The patrol division is also the largest division, and thus there are far more basic police-officer positions within the patrol force than in any other division. Since it is therefore inevitable that good patrol officers will gravitate away from patrol, even in the best of systems, the department should compensate for their loss by staffing middle-level and command-level positions in patrol with the very best talent available in the department.

For example, if the department has a total of 10 lieutenants, with 5 assigned to patrol, those 5 commanders should be among the most capable, dedicated, and active of the group. Similarly, if there are 40 sergeants, with 30 assigned to patrol, the 30 patrol sergeants should be above average in competence. Certainly, disaffected and incompetent supervisors are a disadvantage no matter where they may be found, but their assignment to the patrol function, where they are more likely to be exposed to newer officers and are responsible for the most basic of all police services, is far more damaging.

PATROL ADMINISTRATION, SCHEDULING, AND SUPERVISION

In progressive police departments, chief executives should be concerned with several aspects of patrol administration. First, they must be sure there is a general appreciation of management theory and principles by patrol supervisors such as lieutenants, captains, and others of higher rank. Second, they must be concerned with the application of these concepts and principles, making certain that there is actual adherence to proper span of control, use of the chain of command, proper etiquette of supervision, and adherence to other administrative and supervisory principles. Third, they must be acutely aware of the need for middle management both to transmit top-level policies through the hierarchy to the working level and, in turn, to report deficiencies and other communications upward through the chain of command. Fourth, there must be a concern for the scheduling and assigning of personnel so that employees are properly distributed to handle the work load. Fifth, chief executives must ensure that the management of the patrol effort is knowledgeable concerning actual patrol methods and techniques.

Scheduling

The police administrator and middle-management supervisors must make decisions about the assignment of shift hours, rotation of beat assignments, and rotation of shifts. Once the policy is established, there need not be further planning work except when changes in procedure are contemplated.

Frequent Change of Beats Undesirable The highest quality of patrol service results from the permanent assignment of an officer to a beat. Police hazards vary from place to place, and the resulting police duties consequently vary in nature from beat to beat. Advantages may be taken of differences in abilities and preferences of patrol officers by assigning them to beats having duties for which they are best suited. Frequent beat changes prevent an officer from becoming well acquainted with persons, hazards, and facilities on his beat; they also interfere with continuity of service because the investigation and disposition of cases sometimes extend over several days, and when a change is made, there is delay and sometimes neglect in disposing of these cases.

Finally, frequent changes of beat assignments make it difficult to place responsibility for unsatisfactory conditions. Procedures that interfere with the application of the important rule that officers should be held responsible for the performance of their duties must not be tolerated.

Rotation of Shifts Undesirable Rotation of shifts at some regular interval is common. Among cities of over 300,000 population, periodic rotation of shifts is the most frequently encountered method of assigning shift hours. Nevertheless, this method of assigning shifts is undesirable.

Most efficient patrol service is attained by the permanent assignment of a patrol officer to a platoon until such a time as the quality of his or her services and the need for them justify transfer to another platoon. Police hazards, facilities, persons abroad, and physical conditions vary according to the hour of the day or night; consequently, knowlege of conditions on one shift is not as useful to service on another shift. Police duties at night are quite different from police duties during the daytime, and the officer should not be rotated if the advantages of specialization are to be derived and if the officer's skill is to be developed in handling certain types of situations.

Usually, the first platoon (midnight to 8 A.M. shift) is considered the least desirable, and the second platoon (daylight shift) the most desirable. Recruits should be assigned for training and experience to the first platoon, where their less frequent contact with more critical citizens lessens the disadvantages of their inexperience. Also, if recruits are exposed only to qualified field-training officers or sergeants, they are likely to develop superior attitudes and work habits. Well-trained, experienced, very active officers are needed on the third platoon (evening shift); officers should be assigned to this shift as they become skilled by experience in police service and as they develop seniority. As they become older in years, more experienced, and less active physically, officers should be transferred finally to the day shift as a reward for long, efficient service; their knowledge of police service and acquaintance with the general public will prove most useful on this shift, and they will be subject to less physical strain.

Permanent shifts greatly facilitate having different numbers of officers on each shift, in proportion to work load. Rotation of shifts, on the other hand, may force a chief to adopt the same number of beats on each shift simply because of the scheduling difficulties.

PATROL   329

Finally, the physical and domestic welfare of officers requires that they work regular hours. For top physical and mental efficiency, eating and sleeping habits should follow a set pattern. Regularity of hours also contributes to good family relationships. A family schedule interrupted each month by a change in working hours of one of the spouses may lead to discord and dissatisfaction. Disagreeable as the graveyard shift may be, if a schedule is established that ensures adequate sleep and regular eating habits, officers may work these hours indefinitely without impairing their health.

Some departments which use fixed shifts operate on a forced seniority basis, but with the same effect as described above. New officers are assigned to the midnight to 8 A.M. shift on the basis of order of appointment, and they have no choice in subsequent movements to the evening shift or (eventually) to the day shift. In other systems, there is more freedom of choice; officers are allowed to pick shifts, but in the order of seniority.

If the administrator chooses a rotation system (despite the advice given above), officers should be assigned to a minimum of four weeks on any shift, with the time spent on other shifts in proportion to the manpower on each shift. In other words, if there are twice as many officers assigned to the afternoon shift as to the morning shift (an entirely realistic ratio), then personnel assigned to the afternoon shift should spend twice as long on that shift as those assigned to the morning shifts. For example, an officer would be assigned to four weeks on the midnight to 8 A.M. shift and eight weeks on the evening shift. This is the only way that shift rotation is practical if there is a different number of officers on each watch. To make this system work, shift changes should be carried out on a squad basis so that some movement will take place every few weeks.

An example of a shift schedule and sign-up sheet for a small department and a rotation pattern as described above are included in the Appendix.

Some Supervisory Considerations

There is often a question as to the desirable number of patrol officers or patrol units to be supervised by a sergeant. The actual number of officers to be supervised, of course, depends upon whether one-man or two-man cars are in use. For example, a sergeant may be able to exercise adequate supervision over six patrol cars with two officers each, but would experience much more difficulty in meeting his supervisory responsibilities if the 12 officers were each assigned to individual beats in their own cars.

More attention should be paid to the number of cars supervised than to the total number of officers. In most cases, sergeants should supervise no more than eight units if all units are individual assignments—that is, officers working by themselves in cars or on foot. If most of the units supervised have two officers ordinarily assigned, the total number of units supervised should not exceed six.

Permanency of Supervision   Advantages are gained by having a squad— including its supervisor—operate as a unit, all members having the same days off and the same vacation period and moving from watch to watch when rotation of shifts is practiced. The resulting close relationships develop esprit de corps, and the sergeant becomes better acquainted with the strengths and weaknesses of the officers. The sergeant is thus better able to evaluate the officers' performance and may more logically be held responsible for their work and behavior than when the composition of the squad varies frequently.

Duties of the Headquarters Patrol Staff   The primary duty of the headquarters patrol staff is the direction and supervision of patrol personnel engaged in field operations. In a department of a size that requires some specialization, the headquarters patrol staff exercises a staff supervision over specialists during the absence of their own supervising officers and a direct control over them in emergency situations. Difficult problems in the supervision of specialists usually are not found in small departments. The platoon lieutenant in larger departments is available to coordinate the efforts of all police personnel during emergencies.

An important routine duty of the lieutenant (or the supervisor who is acting as shift commander in a precinct) is to review the circumstances that justify the jailing of persons arrested by his officers and also by officers from the special divisions during the absence of their supervising officers.

The patrol captain and his lieutenants have responsible duties in planning and control, including assigning patrol officers to platoons and beats, developing tactical procedures, planning to meet unusual needs, and maintaining a careful check on operating procedures. The duties of the command group of the patrol division must be clearly established by department regulations if friction resulting from overlapping duties and neglect of other important tasks are to be avoided.

In departments in which the need for specialization is not sufficiently great to justify the creation of special-operations or tactical units, staff planning and inspection of special operations must be assigned to the several commanding officers of the patrol division. These officers will then perform, in addition to their regular patrol duties, the planning and inspection duties normally assigned to the head of a special unit such as a tactical force or plainclothes detail.

Duties of the Immediate Supervisor   The extent of supervision may not be the same for each officer because it will vary according to the conditions on each beat and, of course, the experience and attitude of the officer. Certain factors, therefore, must be given greater attention on some beats than on others. The sergeant should prepare a suitable supervisory program for each officer; this can consist of a page or two of notes outlining the desirable level of field contact, timetables for presentation of information on police problems on the beat, instructional checklists, and so on.

Supervising officers should follow up on the work being done by their subordinates. From the records or services division they should receive data on the productivity and performance of each of their officers. (They must, in turn,

PATROL

provide the records office with information that will assist in tabulating these performance summaries.) They must maintain a day-by-day follow-up over the officers' routine activities, not only to ascertain the suitability of enforcement, but also to ensure appropriate disposition of cases. In this connection, in all but the smaller departments, the sergeant should have the assistance of the report-review officer, who, for this work, provides staff supervision as a service for a number of sergeants.

In order to satisfy themselves that subordinates are following department procedures and are not slipping into lax operating methods, supervisors should check continuously on the subordinates' performance of routine duties. They may do this by observing the officers in action (by accompanying them on patrol, by arriving after they do at the scene of action in order to observe how they are handling the situation, and by observing them performing the routine tasks of patrol) and by checking on conditions on the officers' beats and on their success in discovering and correcting unsatisfactory conditions. Supervisors should not, without proper authority, deviate from the officially established techniques and procedures; rather, they should search for weaknesses in them and devise improvements to recommend for adoption.

PATROL METHODS AND CONCEPTS

This portion of the text discusses the choice of patrol method, the question of one-man versus two-man cars, random versus directed patrol, the conspicuous nature of patrol, and the effect of team policing on patrol.

Methods of Patrol

Responsibility for the performance of certain police tasks within an area is placed on an individual patrol officer, and the accomplishment of his or her duty requires moving from one point to another. A choice of patrol method must be made on the basis of the purpose of the patrol (to provide primarily called-for services, inspection, or routine preventive patrol) and the conditions under which it is to be accomplished.

Automobiles, motorcycles, scooters, and bicycles are most frequently used, and the choice must be based on an appraisal of the advantages and disadvantages of each in terms of the primary purpose of the patrol and the conditions and characteristics of the beat or area to be encountered.

The purpose of the patrol may be the accomplishment of a special task, such as the enforcement of parking regulations, the escorting of parades and funerals, the enforcement of moving-traffic regulations, the inspection of establishments suspected of vice operations, or the inspection of parks, bowling alleys, discotheques, and other places of recreation where minors may congregate. On the other hand, it may be a general patrol for the accomplishment of the total police purpose.

Factors that influence the choice of patrol method include the density, distribution, and character of police hazards and the frequency and nature of the action required of the patrol officer; the size of the beat; the volume of pedestrian and vehicular traffic and the adequacy of its regulation by signs, signals, and markings; light conditions that depend on the time of day and the adequacy of illumination provided by streetlights and lights maintained on private premises; the surface and condition of streets and sidewalks; the usual weather conditions during the various seasons; the racial characteristics and moral tone of the population; and the character of business establishments and residences.

Conditions that justify a certain method of patrol may vary with the presence of persons or things. Examples include intersections and crosswalks with heavy vehicular and pedestrian traffic and areas containing establishments in which a large number of incidents calling for police service may originate. The conditions also may vary between day and night. In a business district, for example, the need for trying store doors and windows at night disappears when the establishments reopen for business the following day.

The Automobile The automobile has advantages over all other methods of transportation for general patrol under ordinary conditions. Its speed permits overtaking a fleeing motorist and rapid response to called-for services. It also provides an element of surprise because it makes possible an irregular and not easily predicted patrol. Officers in cars are more efficient than those on foot because they are able to cover a larger area with less fatigue and to reach the scene of action more quickly and in better physical, mental, and emotional condition. An automobile can be operated under all weather and road conditions; it provides protection against inclement weather and thus lessens the time lost due to illness resulting from exposure. It permits carrying other officers, prisoners, extra clothing, a radio, a riot gun, a fire extinguisher, a first-aid kit, and other equipment that makes a mobile police station of the patrol car. The advantages of the automobile in the enforcement of moving-traffic regulations are so great as to justify its use for this purpose to the exclusion of the two-wheeled motorcycle in all but the most densely crowded urban traffic situations and in cases where traffic on freeways is continually congested, making the motorcycle the only kind of vehicle which is able to respond quickly.

Foot Patrol Foot patrol, however, has some advantages over all other methods. It provides the best opportunity for observation within range of the senses and for a close contact with people and things, enabling the patrol officer to be of maximum service as an information source and counselor to the public and as the eyes and ears of the police department. A foot-patrol officer loses no time in parking a vehicle, and the performance of police tasks is not hampered by responsibility for the vehicle while afoot.

Foot patrol, however, does not enjoy many of the advantages of a patrol car. Lack of mobility lessens the emergency value of foot-patrol officers and greatly reduces their ability to provide called-for services. Walking is the least

PATROL   333

efficient mode of transportation; the limited area that can be covered on foot makes this method of patrol costly.

Bicycle Patrol   Bicycles were used frequently for patrol before the advent of automobiles, and since the recent explosion in bicycling, their use has been rediscovered. Officers on bicycles are able to patrol a larger area than those on foot, and when dispatched to the scene, they are able to cover a greater distance in a shorter period of time with less fatigue. Bicycle-patrol officers have only slightly less opportunity for observation and contact with people than officers on foot, and the bicycle's silent operation makes it especially useful at night. When compared with an automobile, however, the disadvantages of a bicycle are readily apparent.

The Solo Motorcycle   There are serious disadvantages in the use of the two-wheeled motorcycle in police service because of the great hazard to the rider and the excessive cost to the city. The hazard of solo-motorcycle operation is sufficient to condemn its use, and fairness to the officer and his family forbids it. Its use not only endangers the life of the rider but sometimes permanently cripples him through accident or by injury to internal organs caused by the constant jar while riding.

The operating cost of the motorcycle exceeds that of the automobile. To its maintenance expense must be added the salary differential nearly always provided motorcycle riders and the expenses that might be incurred as a result of an accident—the cost of time lost owing to injuries and the cost of keeping a handicapped person on the payroll either at a relatively nonessential job or at a task that could be performed better by a suitably selected person. Further, motorcycle officers usually are not most productively employed during inclement weather, when they are unable to ride.

The automobile excels the two-wheeled motorcycle in almost all respects. Distinctive paint and markings make the automobile as conspicuous as the motorcycle. Driving an automobile requires less attention than riding a motorcycle, and consequently the officer is better able to observe. The automobile also has greater maneuverability at high speeds. The greater maneuverability of the solo motorcycle in congested traffic and its greater acceleration potential are its principal advantages over the automobile, but circumstances that require these qualities are so infrequent that its use is not justified except in situations involving extreme congestion (such as when accidents occur on an urban portion of an interstate highway during rush hour).

The Three-wheeled Motorcycle   The three-wheeled motorcycle has greater maneuverability in dense traffic than the automobile, and it may be operated almost as successfully as an automobile on all road conditions. Its operation is less hazardous and requires less skill and attention than the operation of a solo motorcycle, and it can carry more supplies and equipment. However, it is not so suitable as the automobile for regular patrol because it does not protect the rider from inclement weather, its operation is more fatiguing and attention-demanding, it lacks safe maneuverability at high speeds, and its top speed is otherwise limited.

The three-wheeled motorcycle is especially suited to checking time-limit and other parking regulations where tagging parked automobiles necessitates frequent dismounting. It may be parked without the operation of a stand, and it is not easily knocked over. An officer on a three-wheeler supplied with a chalk stick for marking tires is five to ten times more efficient in checking overtime parking than an officer on foot in either metered or unmetered zones.

Scooters and Lightweight Motorcycles Several large police departments, including those in Washington, D.C., Detroit, and New York City, have adopted motor scooters or lightweight motorcycles, either for use by officers assigned to beats normally handled by foot-patrol officers or as a means of placing officers in closer personal contact with the community. Although scooters are much more flexible and economical than solo motorcycles, they are just as dangerous (perhaps more so) if they are used at high speeds.

Special-Purpose Vehicles and ATVs Many departments in the northern United States and in Canada now use snowmobiles for patrol of rural areas during winter months—partly to control violations by snowmobile drivers and occasionally to render emergency service when storms prevent the use of automobiles. During other seasons, police are beginning to use "all-terrain vehicles" (ATVs) for the same purposes in rural areas.

There is need for a low-cost, low-upkeep, special-purpose patrol vehicle to be used by beat officers in urban areas in much the same way that scooters are now used. The ideal special-purpose patrol vehicle should be capable of silent operation and long use without refueling or recharging. It should have the ability to overtake a running person, to travel over curbs, and to remain stable in sharp turns. Construction should permit use in all weather conditions and yet allow the officer to get in and out quickly.

Some of the all-terrain vehicles now being manufactured for sporting and utility use have these desirable features. However, most also have drawbacks, such as excessive noise, limited operational time on batteries, and not enough speed. The next few years may decide whether some other form of lightweight power will be practical (such as fuel-cell generation of electricity) or a combination of power sources, such as external combustion combined with an electrical power source for periods when quiet operations are required.

Helicopters and VTOL Devices Many departments now use helicopters for routine patrol, operational support (such as surveillance and traffic control), and rescue. The Los Angeles County Sheriff's Department has pioneered the use of helicopter patrol and has achieved great success in reduction of certain classes of crimes in areas which are best suited for this kind of patrol.

Construction of new police facilities should incorporate helipads when-

PATROL   335

ever possible even though helicopters may not be adopted for several years thereafter.

Fixed-wing aircraft with short takeoff and landing (STOL) characteristics are more economical than helicopters, have far lower maintenance costs, and can do most of what helicopters can do in the way of slow-speed flight, surveillance, chase of suspect vehicles, and illumination of crime scenes. However, they are unable to land anywhere other than an airport or airstrip, and they cannot be used for airlifting victims in rescue situations.

The Law Enforcement Assistance Administration and IACP have encouraged development and demonstration of vertical takeoff and landing (VTOL) apparatus which can be described in no other way than as jet flying belts. In prototype demonstrations the devices have exhibited great mobility. They are capable of hovering in flight, and they have fuel capacity for about 30 minutes of operation. The jet flying belt has obvious police applications, including response to crimes in progress and other emergencies, hot pursuits over difficult terrain, and rescue or lifesaving work.

Other Specialized Patrol Methods A horse patrol was established in London before the organization of the London Metropolitan Police, and the use of horses has persisted to this day, although in general patrol in the United States, horses are no longer used in municipal departments. Some large urban departments use horses in traffic and crowd control because the elevated position of the rider provides maximum opportunity for observation and because the animal is unequaled in the control of a crowd. Crowd control is the main justification for the continuance of the use of horses. Some departments maintain a boat patrol, which also might not be justified for its preventive value were it not for the occasional emergency use of this equipment. Some departments that maintain a summertime boat patrol on rivers substitute a patrol on skates during the winter months. As indicated earlier, ATVs—or, in some remote locations, trail-type motorcycles—are effective during the spring, winter, and fall months, with snowmobiles substituted during the winter.

Automobile versus Foot Patrol Relative cost must be considered in choosing between foot and automobile patrol. The cost of operating an automobile-patrol unit is the salary of the patrol officer plus the cost of transportation. Transportation increases the cost of operating a patrol unit from 12 to 20 percent, the exact amount depending upon the salary rate and the degree of economy in automobile maintenance and operation. Automobile patrol effects a money saving, therefore, when it increases the effectiveness of a patrol unit by an amount greater than the proportional rise in the cost of its operation. Automobile patrol provides an increased efficiency considerably in excess of 100 percent, except when it is unsuited to the purpose of the patrol or to the peculiar conditions under which it must be provided.

Automobile patrol is the least expensive form of patrol for the reason that increased efficiency, coverage, and effectiveness permit a saving in manpower that compensates for the cost of operating the vehicle. Foot patrol, because of its limitations, is the most expensive. First choice, therefore, should be given to automobile patrol wherever it can be used profitably; some other method of transportation is justified by unusual conditions, such as water, ice, or the requirement of silence, or by the desire to have available, for emergency use, equipment with operators skilled by constant practice. The choice between foot and automobile patrol must be based on the relative advantages of each method weighed in the setting of its primary purpose and under the conditions that prevail during its operation. The advantages of mobility during emergencies make desirable the motorization of as many patrol officers as possible.

Inspections May Necessitate Foot Patrol   Foot patrol is preferred when inspectional duties in a small area occupy the entire time of the patrol officer. The small area makes motorized transportation from one duty to another unnecessary, and lack of time makes impossible any routine patrol. For example, the inspection of contiguous commercial establishments may be impeded rather than aided by a vehicle. When the number of establishments is large, there may be no time left for routine patrol, and if calls for service are infrequent, they may be assigned to motorized officers; the activity of a foot-patrol officer may then be restricted to such inspectional duties as trying store doors and windows.

Frequency of Incidents May Necessitate Foot Patrol   The full time of an officer may be required to prevent and dispose of incidents that call for police service when a large number of them occur in a relatively small area. Conditions that justify a foot patrol under such circumstances are found in areas containing numerous amusement resorts, where the concentration of people requires continuous police attention. The character of the people, the nature of the establishments, and the extent of use of intoxicants influence the frequency of calls for service. For example, areas containing cheap amusement resorts and other questionable establishments may be the scene of fights and disturbances that justify the continuous presence of an officer on foot.

Lack of Driving Ability May Necessitate Foot Patrol   One or more foot-patrol officers may be justified in some communities because of the presence of officers who are not willing to drive or who are not qualified to drive safely for one reason or another.

Patrol in Business Sections   The proportion of the force on foot patrol is influenced by the size of the business district requiring intensive inspectional services and its adaptability to division among motorized beats. A business section may sometimes be divided among several motorized beats that contain noncommercial areas, thus giving each motorized officer a portion of the congested area. This arrangement enables a more complete motorization of the patrol force and avoids subjecting a patrol officer to the hardships of continuous foot patrol. It also provides some variety to the tasks of patrol and relieves fatigue, since officers may alternate their time between foot patrol and automobile patrol in sections of their beats that do not require intensive inspectional services. In a large city, however, the wide expanse of area containing establishments that require inspectional duties may make this

PATROL 337

arrangement impractical, especially during the hours of greatest need for this service. A sound rule, however, is to avoid as far as possible the assignment of officers exclusively to foot patrol.

One-Man versus Two-Man Patrols   A few years ago, conscientious police administrators could make a sound case for near-universal adoption of one-man patrol-car operations. They still can, in many regions of the country and in most cities. There is, however, a need to consider the realities of life in depressed urban areas, the sharp increase in attacks on police officers, and the posture of extreme militants who have avowed to assassinate police. There are sections of many cities in the United States in which it would be foolhardy for a police administrator to deploy police officers in one-man cars or on foot by themselves. Moreover, when public sentiment shifts toward providing two-officer coverage regardless of expense to the taxpayers and when there is public clamor for more law enforcement spending in an effort to reduce street crime, police administrators place themselves in a vulnerable position if they continue to advocate one-man patrol operations in high-hazard areas.

As a condition to wider use of two-man cars, however, the police administrator should insist that the total number of police cars or beats, as determined by a systematic manpower study, not be reduced. Also, manpower should not be permanently shifted from other essential activity for the purpose of staffing two-man cars. The public should be made to understand, through widespread publicity, that doubling personnel strength in patrol vehicles requires a tremendous increase in manpower, as well as other supportive services in the department.

In areas where this crisis atmosphere does not prevail, the arguments for one-man patrol are still as valid as ever. Patrol officers have operated on foot in this country for many years, and except in isolated and exceptional cases, they have performed their services unaccompanied by a second officer. The advisability of this procedure is seldom questioned. Patrol officers who are able to perform their duties satisfactorily while alone on foot should not find it necessary to be accompanied by a fellow officer when they are equipped with the most modern means of transportation and communication. Actually they work more efficiently, effectively, and safely when alone.

Officers patrolling alone are more effective for the reason that they give their undivided attention to police duties. Two officers together spend part of their time making nonessential conversation, swapping stories, and neglecting their routine duties. Further, there is a greater temptation for them to be involved in small delinquencies and infractions of the rules because when one makes a suggestion that is slightly out of line, the other is inclined to fall into the spirit of the infraction so as to avoid being considered a spoilsport. The officer who made the suggestion may not have been completely serious at the time, but he is unable to back down gracefully when the other officer acquiesces.

An officer patrolling alone in a car is safer than when accompanied by a fellow officer because of similar factors. The presence of a second officer may cause each to fail to take suitable precautions in an emergency lest such action be interpreted as cowardice. Each also gives the other a sense of security out of proportion to the added protection provided by the second officer. An officer who is alone in a patrol car knows there is no one else to rely upon in the event of emergency and consequently is cautious about stepping into dangerous situations. One patrol officer in a radio-equipped car is safer than a lone foot-patrol officer inspecting alleys and back doors on his beat.

One-man patrol-car operation is also more efficient than two-man patrol because the number of patrol units is thus doubled and the city is divided into twice as many patrol areas as when officers ride in pairs. Consequently, the frequency of patrol is doubled, a police car gives twice the attention to a beat, and a police hazard is inspected with twice the frequency. Safety is further increased by the fact that since the number of available patrol units is doubled, there are twice as many vehicles to be dispatched as an aid to an officer. They may approach the scene from twice as many directions, and the average distance they must travel is diminished.

Wherever patrol cars are used, one-man cars should be instituted unless the conditions are such that it would be unwise for foot-patrol officers to operate singly. These areas may be identified by a high frequency of multiple arrests and of arrests of persons who resist or who carry weapons. When officers are placed alone in automobiles, the number of patrol cars should be increased in proportion, and the officers should be trained in the technique of stopping suspicious cars so as to lessen personal danger.

Technique for Stopping Suspicious Cars   When an officer stops a car for the purpose of questioning the occupants, regulations should require that he report the license number and location to the dispatcher. Also, regulations should forbid him to initiate this or any other action when he has any doubt as to his ability to deal successfully with the situation by himself. He should be required under these circumstances to request assistance by radio. Backup cars should be deployed in a manner designed to ensure a stop, a search of a building, or control of a disorderly group with minimum hazard to the officers assigned and maximum likelihood of the success of the mission.

Use of Foot Patrol by Officers Assigned to Cars   Automobile patrol has some disadvantages. While driving, patrol officers have less opportunity for observation and for contact with citizens than when on foot, and consequently they are less useful in furnishing information to citizens and in serving as the eyes and ears of the department.

These disadvantages, however, may be lessened by considering motorized-patrol officers to be foot-patrol officers also on a beat whose characteristics justify giving them an automobile to transport them from one task to another, to bring them to the scene with greater speed and less fatigue, and to assist them in the capture of fleeing suspects. This concept may be stimulated by the development of procedures requiring the motorized-patrol officers to carry out the tasks of foot-patrol officers and by thorough training in these

PATROL

procedures and adequate supervision of their performance. Foot patrol must be considered basic because some action by patrol officers with their feet on the ground is required in the performance of nearly all patrol tasks, and motorized-patrol officers should spend a large part of their time on foot. Seeking protection against weather and relief from fatigue by occasional periods spent driving from one location to another should be done with discretion.

Officers assigned to motorized patrol should be equipped with portable radios to permit them to remain in contact with headquarters when they are out of their vehicles. Relay devices are now available for installation in police cars, making it possible for a low-powered portable-radio signal to be boosted by the car radio. The same result can be achieved by installation of a series of satellite receivers placed strategically in several locations within the community.

The Conspicuous Patrol Car   For the same reasons that officers engaged in patrol are universally dressed in easily identifiable uniforms, automobiles used in patrol should be conspicuously designated as police vehicles by means of paint of distinctive color and design and by the use of reflective emblems and other inscriptions on the sides, front, and rear. The marking of the patrol car may be described as either distinctive or conspicuous. Distinctively marked automobiles are readily identifiable as police vehicles at close range—for instance, by the occupants of a car being stopped when the police automobile is beside it—but they are not easily distinguishable from other vehicles when seen from the front or rear or from a distance. Conspicuously marked patrol cars, on the other hand, are readily identified as police vehicles from every view and from a long distance, even at night. The police telephone number, in reflective lettering, should be conspicuously visible on the sides and rear of the car.

Patrol Apparently Intensified   Experience has demonstrated that conspicuously marked automobiles are better suited for patrol than unmarked cars. The merit of easily identifiable automobiles in traffic control is conceded by all qualified police traffic experts. Similar advantages in the control of potential offenders are claimed by most police administrators who have had experience with both types of patrol. The effectiveness of patrol in minimizing belief in the existence of opportunity for misconduct is in proportion to the apparent or observed frequency of patrol. When uniformed officers are unobserved in unmarked patrol cars, regardless of the actual frequency of their patrol, there is no apparent patrol and hence no feeling of the presence of the police. Consequently, the patrol has little deterrent or preventive value. On the other hand, patrol in conspicuous automobiles, being more readily observed, has a deterrent effect on potential offenders and on opportunists who violate regulations when they think the police are not around. Citizens are impressed with the extent and frequency of patrol which they observe, and they feel that the police are efficient and readily available in the event of need. The impression of police omnipresence created by conspicuous patrol thus satisfies the critical citizen, comforts the uneasy one, and deters the potential offender.

Police Car Identified   Unless police automobiles are conspicuously marked, citizens may on occasion mistake a police automobile for an offender's car and attempt to flee. The police may mistake a fleeing citizen for a felon and shoot at him; when finally stopped, such citizens, even though uninjured, consider themselves badly treated, especially when the police refuse to believe their story. The possible serious consequences of such incidents are practically eliminated by conspicuous markings. The markings also eliminate the argument used by some traffic violators that they were entrapped by being followed in a covert manner. The emergency character of the conspicuous car is also more easily recognized; the driver is thereby assisted in making urgent runs, and the accident hazard is diminished.

Offender Made More Submissive Offenders are impressed by the official authority represented by the conspicuously marked patrol car, as they are by the police uniform, and are placed at a psychological disadvantage which makes them less likely to resist. Police officers are something more than ordinary human beings because they have the moral backing and the complete resources of organized society to aid them in the execution of their duties. When criminals or minor offenders see a plainclothes police officer as an ordinary individual with no outward evidence of authority, they may be tempted to pit their wits and strength against the officer. The police uniform represents the majesty of the law and the authority of government. Clearly marked patrol cars impress with their evidence of authority, and they simplify the performance of many police tasks.

Supervision Simplified The conspicuous patrol car, like the police uniform, aids in regulating the conduct of the police officer who uses it. A uniform on an officer and distinctive markings on a car attract the attention of the public and make noticeable any neglect of duty or other violation of department rules. Patrol officers in conspicuously marked cars are less likely to shirk their duty by parking in secluded spots or by having friends ride with them; they are also less likely to drive carelessly or in a manner inconsiderate of the rights of pedestrians and other motorists. Patrol supervision, a difficult and important task under any circumstances, is also made easier by the use of easily distinguished patrol cars. For these reasons, patrol cars should be conspicuously marked.

The Take-Home Car Plan For many years, the Berkeley Police Department patrol system was based on the use of the personal vehicles of patrol officers. The officers used their own vehicles for patrol and were reimbursed for the cost of gasoline and depreciation. This system was the ultimate expression of inconspicuous patrol, since many makes and models were utilized. However, it suffered from some of the disadvantages of unmarked cars, including low visibility for traffic enforcement when a deterrent effect was desirable, difficulty in emergency situations, and some citizen resentment; most important, however, was the inability to assign unmarked cars to traffic enforcement because of a state law requiring conspicuous markings if traffic-enforcement duties occupied the largest part of an officer's time. The great advantage of the system was that Berkeley could mobilize as many cars as cities four or five times its size. The use of vehicles by off-duty officers added tremendously to the flow of information into the department, since officers were urged to keep their radios on while shopping or in off-duty pursuits in the evening, and, of course, they were expected to take appropriate action in situations requiring police presence. The Berkeley system was discontinued several years ago, although a few small departments still use the method in states where emergency operation of a vehicle is permitted under these conditions.

In 1970, the Indianapolis Police Department began experiments with the assignment of patrol vehicles to individual officers on a 24-hour basis. Some of the same advantages mentioned in connection with the Berkeley system are apparent in the Indianapolis plan. More cars are available during emergencies, and there are usually a number of off-duty police vehicles in the city, which greatly increases the potential for observation and prevention. Police officials in Indianapolis discovered (as they did in Berkeley) that many officers deliberately spent off-duty time on the street in their cars because they enjoyed it—perhaps because they could move around the city without operational pressures and could relax somewhat while performing patrol activity.

In some departments which have adopted the take-home car plan, administrators have found that maintenance costs are much lower than for traditional fleet cars. This is attributed (1) to the better care given to a vehicle when an officer has sole responsibility and concern for it and (2) to the simple fact that the vehicle receives only one-fifth to one-third the usual mileage and wear and tear, with more time available between tours of duty for servicing. The police department in Arlington, Virginia, recently found that the total cost for a take-home car fleet of 235 vehicles was the same as for a traditional fleet of 80 cars, when costs were distributed over the useful life-span of the vehicles.

The system used in Indianapolis differs very little from similar practices that have been carried out for many years by state police and highway-patrol agencies who assign vehicles to resident troopers in isolated regions where it is impractical to have district stations. While few supervisory or operational problems with this method have been experienced in state agencies, the difficulty of supervision increases significantly when the system is used in cities. Experimentation of this sort should be encouraged, but there must also be a realization that it requires proper supervisory control and publicity.

Patrol Coverage and Deployment

Regardless of the method of patrol (whether on foot or by automobile or some other method), patrol officers should emphasize (1) the random and unpredictable character of patrol, which makes it impossible for potential offenders to predict police activity or identify patterns of patrol; (2) omnipresence, or the cultivation of the feeling that the police are everywhere; and (3) inquisitiveness, leading potential violators to believe that any patrol officer is liable to notice or question the circumstances or actions of others near him. Although patrol should be random and omnipresent, it should be concentrated in high-hazard areas, and patrol officers should be available for response to calls for service or emergency situations.

Deployment of Patrol Officers on Calls Procedures should be developed by the command group and approved by the chief to guide dispatchers in sending officers on calls that will ensure (1) that a force will be sent which is adequate to meet the need and (2) that it will be deployed in such a manner as to increase the likelihood of apprehension and decrease the hazard to the officers. The nature of the call will establish the number of officers and the manner in which they should be deployed to accomplish their mission most effectively.

Overresponse One of the great wastes of police manpower is the tendency for police to overrespond to calls, with subsequent failure to go back into service promptly. Supervisors should prevent this from happening by a combination of training and on-scene direction.

Calls Not Requiring Pursuit Only the beat officer need be sent on calls in which immediate arrest or pursuit of an offender is not required, except (1) when a crime or accident scene should be searched for physical evidence, in which case an evidence technician should be dispatched; (2) when there may be an attendant need for guarding premises, controlling a crowd, or diverting traffic, as at the scene of an accident, in which event additional officers should be sent; (3) in cases involving disorderly, drunken, or deranged persons and family quarrels, when at least two officers should be dispatched, and a greater force when the reported conditions indicate the need; and (4) in cases where the principal objective is to save a life endangered by accident or some noncriminal act, when the force sent should be sufficient to accomplish its purpose.

Calls when Crimes Are in Progress Cases where criminals are in the act of committing a crime should be divided into two categories: (1) crimes anticipated by the preparation of a broadcast kept on file at the dispatcher's desk for immediate use in such an event and (2) crimes for which prepared broadcasts are not practical.

Prepared Broadcasts As a minimum, radio broadcasts should be prepared for premises that are connected to police headquarters directly or through some central point by a burglary or robbery alarm system. The broadcasts should be prepared after a careful study of the area, with consideration given to the most likely points and methods of attack, to locations providing cover and view to which officers should be assigned, to the directions from which certain officers should approach, to intersections that should be blockaded, to the manner in which entry should be effected by the officers, and to probable criminal escape routes under varying conditions.

The broadcast, based on a plan of action approved by the command group of the department, should be on an 8- by 5-inch card; the broadcast cards should be filed alphabetically according to the name of the establishment and stored in a box or drawer at the dispatcher's desk. (In automated systems, the plan can be recalled from storage by terminal entry.) The heading of each card should contain the name and address of the premises following the words "Robbery at ____," and there should be added, in parentheses, instructions to the dispatcher to repeat the name and location several times to lessen the possibility of misunderstanding. Blank spaces for the insertion of the radio

PATROL

numbers of officers dispatched to key intersections or to the scene should be filled in to enable the ready identification of an officer conveniently located for some specific reassignment. Detailed instructions should be included as to where each officer is to go and what he or she is to do, such as to cover a main, side, or alley entrance or to enter through a designated door when the building is surrounded. The direction from which certain officers should approach should also be indicated.

Quadrant Assignments In cases of crimes in progress in locations for which there are no prepared broadcasts, the area surrounding the point of attack may be divided by the nearest intersecting streets into quadrants designated as northwest, northeast, southeast, and southwest. (This is difficult to do in cities in which streets are laid out in a random way.) The dispatcher should send, as a minimum, the beat officer, the evidence technician, and four other officers, each assigned to the quadrant that lies closest to his or her beat; additional officers should be dispatched if the size of the premises or other conditions indicate a greater need. All officers should be informed of the nature of the call and instructed to go directly to the scene to surround the premises, four or more of them having their quadrants designated at that time so that they will know that they are to make a search of the designated area while proceeding in the general direction of the crime scene.

As soon as it has been determined that the suspects are no longer at the scene, the officers assigned to the quadrants should undertake a search of their respective areas, while the beat officer, in the course of his preliminary investigation, should relay to headquarters any additional descriptions or information. At the same time, the evidence technician should proceed with a search of the scene for physical evidence.

Use of Codes in Radio Broadcasts Codes should not be used in radio broadcasts to identify the nature of the case because they unnecessarily introduce an opportunity for error and sometimes delay police action while a check is made to learn the meaning of a code number. The need for secrecy in police radio transmission is overemphasized in the first place, and those who have an illegitimate interest in police broadcasts are able to learn the codes without the slightest difficulty anyway. The only reasonably secure method for transmission of confidential information in police service is through the use of communications scramblers or through digital (nonvoice) information communicated by terminals.

Conventional Team Policing Some cities, such as Syracuse, New York; Richmond, California; and Arlington, Virginia, have experimented with team and squad concepts. However, most of these conventional applications are not as innovative as the systems described in Chapter 15, such as the British unit-beat concept, the Cincinnati model, and the Charlotte and Los Angeles versions, and most team concepts are based on deployment of a group of officers who operate simultaneously under the supervision of a sergeant, rather than as a group deployed over a 24-hour period.

The conventional team approach may suffer from the disadvantage of the lack of clear-cut responsibility for a fixed area. Some behavioral scientists believe that human beings are essentially territorial and that recognition of this territorial perspective must be considered in almost every area of human activity. There is no question that encouraging a patrol officer to be responsible for a given area—his beat—is a successful means of administering police service. It is possible that the flexibility of assignment inherent in conventional team policing will outweigh the disadvantages of loss of identity and loss of feeling of responsibility when a number of officers share a sector or district with simultaneous jurisdiction by each one for the entire sector.

It is also possible that 24-hour unit-beat or district team policing is the proper approach and will be fully responsive to man's territorial proclivities, provided only one patrol unit has the responsibility for a beat or district in a given time period. As indicated in Chapter 14, a combination of the two concepts—operation of an entire supervisory sector on a 24-hour basis—may prove to be most effective. In any event, experimentation in both conventional and district team policing should proceed until some definite conclusions can be reached.

Neighborhood Control of Patrol Service

A popular concept among urban planners today is neighborhood or community control of police. The theory is that policing will be more responsive to social needs and that citizens will be less subject to impersonal treatment and bureaucratic indifference if neighborhoods or communities within larger governmental areas have some voice in the control over police in their area. This concept tends to run contrary to one of the greatest needs in our police system today—to eliminate the multiplicity of smaller agencies under the separate control of local governments.

Neighborhood control of police also ignores the increasing need to cope with the great mobility of the population and the need for regional and consolidated information systems. The neighborhood-control concept also fails to give due credit to the existence of the democratic process in any city or county government. Police are *already* under the control of elected city councils and boards of supervisors or, in the case of state agencies, of elected governors and legislatures. The amount of local control which exists is substantial, and perhaps the solution is to improve existing machinery rather than to depend on an appealing slogan or concept which may have many more disadvantages than advantages in the long run.

PATROL TECHNIQUES

The subject of patrol techniques and mechanics is somewhat remote from the immediate concern of the police administrator in most departments. Nevertheless, the administrator should be aware that improper action by officers in this

PATROL

area can be a serious threat to the rights of individuals and can damage the reputation of the department in the process.

Generally, the administrator should make certain that middle-management supervisors and operating personnel are aware of several principles which ought to guide patrol techniques and mechanics. Any operation should be subjected to the following questions: Is it safe? Legal? Humane? Economical? Will it act as a spark in the creation of more problems than it solves?

The Need for Proper Techniques in Arrest The process of arrest, including search, physical arrest, and subsequent prisoner handling and transportation, is obviously a critical area when dealing with potentially riotous situations. As an example, riots or disorders have started because of the delay in arrival of prisoner transportation following a simple arrest on the street. Out of concern for regulations, the officers may have allowed a routine situation to become dangerous because someone ignored the practical consideration of crowd reaction. In most situations involving simple arrests, such as an arrest of a drunk by patrol officers, it is sometimes more advisable to transport the prisoner a short distance away or out of the immediate view of spectators so that a crowd does not begin to gather. Although this may not seem to be the safest immediate step, it is safer than being the target of a crowd which is out of control.

The police administrator must also be certain that officers are well trained in patrol techniques and mechanics in the interest of their own safety as well as the safety of arrested subjects. Supervisors and patrol officers should also be completely familiar with the mechanics of searches of vehicles, persons, and buildings and with security procedures during the transportation of suspects.

Emergency Response Response to emergencies is always a problem for police management because of the danger to citizens, police officers, and victims if police action is improper or negligent. Emergency-response procedures should always receive careful attention in general orders or rules, and personnel should be briefed periodically on department policy and proper procedure. Common sense should dictate that emergency vehicles should not take unnecessary chances which (if something goes wrong) would outweigh the gravity or importance of the initial event or emergency. Risking serious injury or death in a situation which may not be of an emergency nature is foolhardy. This is especially true in response to requests for ambulance service. Some cities, in fact, have experimented with a "no siren" policy to cut down on extremely high accident rates involving emergency vehicles.

Deciding the proper policy for emergency response to a crime in progress requiring unobtrusive arrival by police is most difficult. Studies of response time have shown that the likelihood of arrest is far greater if a patrol officer arrives within three minutes of the time a serious crime takes place. Yet officers are often told officially that they must not exceed speed limits unless they are operating in an authorized manner with emergency light and siren. At the same time, they are expected to ignore official instructions by speeding—without light or siren—to the scene of a call which requires an unobtrusive approach.

Official written policy of the department should clearly describe those instances in which exceeding the speed limit will be permitted.

Prisoner Transportation The police executive should be aware that the handling and transportation of prisoners are potential points of prisoner abuse, both by incompetent or unethical police officers and by other prisoners. Mishandling of prisoners sometimes takes place at the hands of police who feel that punishment should be meted out in advance to prisoners or, on occasion, at the hands of trusties or other inmates who are left with vulnerable prisoners for too long a period. The "panic stop" technique for punishing hostile or aggressive prisoners while they are being transported has been used for many years and results in a prisoner's being thrown headlong into the front of a van, usually causing injury. Supervisors and staff inspectors should be alert to this kind of abuse. As a safeguard, all prisoners who are injured at the time of booking should be interviewed by supervisory personnel.

Tactical Training Patrol supervisors should be certain that officers under their direction receive adequate training in squad tactics, including deployment to various kinds of situations. An excellent device to achieve this is the "training run," which is a field exercise in deployment. A typical training run might consist of a response to a simulated prowler call, with one of the sergeants acting as the prowler. The training run permits experimentation with different techniques in responding to the scenes of incidents, such as quadrant or team plans for covering escape routes and apprehending suspects. Practice runs can also be used by a supervisor to interrupt a monotonous evening. Supervisors should be encouraged to plan various kinds of training runs in advance with the officers in their squads, prior to a tour of duty. Then, at selected intervals, the training runs can be initiated. Following the training run, at the end of a shift, the supervisor can achieve additional training value by critiquing the run and asking how it could have been improved. In addition to its great value as a training device, the technique strengthens morale.

On occasions, a department should actually operate for brief periods on a full emergency-mobilization basis, using the command structure and communications system which would be in actual use during an emergency. Experience has shown that the routine communications and command structure is not adequate for full mobilization and is among the chief reasons for misunderstanding and mistakes during disorders or disasters.

Surveillance A basic police technique is the use of surveillance, and the term is applied to the observation of the activities of a person or vehicle moving from place to place (most often by detectives), as well as surveillance at a fixed location. The latter, when coupled with a readiness to make an arrest, is often called a "stakeout." The technique is an excellent device for the control of street crime, such as armed robberies at certain kinds of retail stores, and in general should be used more often by major-city police departments on a mass basis—that is, with every potential hazard in a given category protected for several hours at the same time or with various combinations of hazards covered. For example, on a given night the patrol or field operations commander may set up stakeouts for several hours at all liquor stores, on another night stake out half the liquor stores and half the convenience stores, and so on. Stakeouts ordinarily should be conducted by officers in civilian attire, although some assignments might permit wearing uniforms if officers are concealed or in unmarked cars.

Field Interrogation and Interviewing   Another fundamental technique is the systematic use of field interrogation. Patrol officers should talk to as many people as possible during routine patrol activities, and in particular they should contact as many potential offenders as they can. In situations in which "stop and frisk" action would be permissible, officers should obtain information from persons which can be filed for future reference.

The experienced patrol officer can often deal with a citizen in such a way that the citizen—if he had no intention of misbehaving—may not even know that the officer's interest in him was initially generated by suspicion. On the other hand, a citizen who is a potential offender will usually recognize such a situation as inhibiting. Of course, this latter situation may also evolve from casual questioning into field interrogation, or even into arrest.

PATROL ACTIVITIES

The activities of the patrol officer may be divided into two broad categories: handling called-for services and engaging in preventive-patrol activity.

"Called-for services" is a term used by police to describe the activity generated by crime complaints and requests for service, as well as other police work which *cannot* be categorized as (1) preventive-patrol activity; (2) administrative activity, such as refueling the police vehicle; or (3) time out of service, such as for meals and coffee breaks. A called-for service usually results in report writing and ordinarily becomes part of the measurable work load of the patrol officer.

Called-for services relate to incidents reported by police officers as well as to complaints of crime and requests for service by citizens. They include the disposition of violations in every field of police control by warning, citation, or arrest; the investigation and disposition of miscellaneous complaints; the investigation of accidents; the preliminary investigation of crimes; the recovery of stolen property; the search for, and interviewing and investigation of, suspects and witnesses; and the conduct of follow-up investigations of crimes and incidents.

Preventive-patrol activity includes random patrol, as well as "hazard-oriented" patrol intended to curb specific crimes or to curtail criminal activity at specified locations. It also includes inspections directed at lessening the potency of identifiable hazards. These services include the routine examination of the doors and windows of business premises and of vacation homes likely to be burglarized and the inspection of public garages, where stolen automobiles may be stored or temporarily parked. In addition, preventive-patrol activity involves the inspection and supervision of places under license; of questionable establishments such as taverns, bars, massage parlors, and cocktail lounges; and of parks, bowling alleys, poolrooms, skating rinks, dance halls, and other recreational places.

Preventive patrol includes all patrol operations which are directed primarily at diminishing less-tangible hazards that are not readily isolated and identified. The officer lessens opportunity for misconduct by the observation and supervision of persons and things during his routine movement from one point to another on his beat, especially when he gives particular attention to specific locations which are vulnerable crime targets or to areas in which incidents calling for police service most frequently occur. Street interrogations of persons whose appearance and actions arouse the suspicion of alert patrol officers are important tasks in preventive patrol.

Investigations by the Patrol Force

As in the case of patrol methods and techniques, police administrators usually are not immediately concerned with actual operational activity carried out by the patrol force, but they certainly ought to be cognizant of some of the key principles relating to this topic.

Initial or Preliminary Investigations   Some tasks relating to the investigation of crimes that detectives are responsible for clearing by arrest may be performed to best advantage by patrol officers—either through direct action at the scene or in immediate investigation thereafter. The initial or preliminary investigation thus includes the care of injured persons, apprehension of the criminal at the scene or in flight, protection of the crime scene pending a search for physical evidence, and finally the recovery of stolen property. The preliminary investigation is that which may be conducted up to the point at which postponement of further investigation does not jeopardize its successful completion.

Both direct and investigative duties are summarized in a Chicago Police Department training bulletin as follows:

P	Proceed to the scene with safety and dispatch.
R	Render assistance to the injured.
E	Effect arrest of perpetrator.
L	Locate and identify witnesses.
I	Interview complainant and witnesses.
M	Maintain scene and protect evidence.
I	Interrogate suspects.
N	Note all conditions, events, and remarks.
A	Arrange for collection of evidence.
R	Report incident fully and accurately.
Y	Yield responsibility to detectives.

PATROL

There are many advantages, and no serious disadvantages, inherent in the use of patrol officers as preliminary investigators: (1) The patrol division should, if possible, make an arrest following the commission of a crime, and preliminary investigation conducted at once provides information useful to this end. (2) Promptness and speed are essential in crime investigation because the opportunity for apprehension decreases with the passage of time. The patrol division, because of its 24-hour service and complete coverage, is able to meet this need and also is available for the immediate continuation of the investigation in the event that important leads are revealed. (3) Except in large departments, the use of the patrol force makes 24-hour service by the criminal investigation division unnecessary. Departments with fewer than 200 members usually provide detective service on the daylight shift only and thus avoid the withdrawal of additional officers from patrol on other shifts. (4) Preliminary investigations by patrol officers relieve the detectives of many time-consuming tasks, permitting the application of their special skills to more important duties. (5) Patrol officers' sense of responsibility is heightened when they investigate a crime which they were charged with preventing. (6) Investigation by patrol officers provides them with opportunities to acquire investigative skills; it also enables executives to discover investigative talent.

Crimes which elicit no immediate protest from the victim and which are not reported to the police, if at all, until after some time has elapsed (such as frauds, bad-check cases, and vice activities) usually do not require immediate action and consequently do not ordinarily justify preliminary investigation by patrol officers.

Serious preliminary investigations are often conducted under the close supervision of the commanding officer of the platoon, the lieutenant, or the patrol sergeant. In many departments these supervisors have had detective experience and may be considered fully as well qualified as the detectives to investigate a crime. These supervisors should determine how far the investigation should go before referring the case to the detective division. The most effective service results when patrol officers carry the investigation as far as their competence permits and when they render such further service to the detective division as they are able.

After a crime has occurred, the presence of a number of officers at the crime scene is usually unnecessary and a waste of manpower. Patrol officers and supervisors alike have a responsibility to stay away from the scene once the determination is made that the suspect is not at the scene and that no further assistance at that location is required. In most cases, the scene of the incident is the one location where the suspect is *not* likely to be found.

When patrol platoons are properly coordinated, the preliminary investigation is a continuing process until completed; i.e., any part of it left incomplete by one shift will be continued by the next until all the obvious clues have been investigated. As a consequence, there will normally be no investigation left to be done by the officer on whose beat the crime was committed when he or she returns to duty 16 hours later. However, when additional information relating to a previously investigated case is received by the platoon on duty, any action within the limits of preliminary investigation and justified by the new information should be taken by the patrol division.

Follow-up Responsibility for Patrol Officers In most cities, follow-up investigation by patrol officers is impractical. Although patrol officers should be held accountable for all crimes committed on their beats and should take an active interest in the investigation of them, complete responsibility for the clearances of these crimes by arrest and for the recovery of stolen property should not ordinarily be placed on patrol officers for the following reasons: (1) Responsibility placed on one patrol officer may interfere with the continuity of the preliminary investigation, which will be discontinued at the end of the officer's tour of duty unless the various patrol shifts or platoons are exceptionally well coordinated. (2) If beat officers are to be held responsible, they must have commensurate authority and the necessary time and freedom of movement to conduct the investigation. This means that they must be privileged to leave their beats for protracted periods to conduct investigations across town, in offices and homes, and at headquarters; the investigation may require so much time that it interferes with regular patrol duties, and during most of this time the patrol officer will be unavailable for other calls. (3) Detectives are especially well qualified by reason of ability, training, experience, and sources of good information to complete the investigation, to clear the crime by arrest, and to recover stolen property.

In some smaller progressive departments, it may nevertheless be desirable to assign follow-up investigations to patrol officers who are supplemented by a much smaller force of investigators concerned primarily with following leads out of the city or at some distance from the patrol officer's beat. For years, the Berkeley Police Department has operated on the "beat-officer-responsibility" system in which patrol officers handle most follow-up investigations arising from incidents which occur on their beats. Surprisingly, most follow-up investigations carried out by patrol officers can be conducted on the same shift on which the crime was reported. Also, the investigation is generally centered in the same neighborhood. In the Berkeley system, officers handle felony investigations from beginning to end, including consultations with prosecuting attorneys and preparation of cases for court. Some cases are excluded, however. Patrol officers do not handle homicides beyond the preliminary stage, nor are they responsible for follow-up investigations of certain other crimes, such as bad-check, bunco, or vice cases requiring plainclothes investigators from the beginning.

In the Berkeley system, detectives serve more in the role of coordinators and advisors, although in a series of crimes which are apparently committed by a single offender operating on several beats or shifts, the detective division may carry out the investigation. The detective division also works on cases upon the special request of patrol officers or supervisors in the patrol division.

The Berkeley system is generally considered impractical in conventional departments of over 100 members. However, even though a department may not use patrol officers to conduct follow-up investigations to this extent, many departments are recognizing the need for patrol involvement in more than simple preliminary investigations. In the Chicago Police Department, for example, follow-up investigations for some lower-value thefts or burglaries are handled by patrol officers rather than by the criminal investigation division. In several departments which use team policing, detectives are encouraged to involve patrol officers within the team in all investigations requiring the efforts of someone besides the assigned investigator. Team policing also facilitates giving patrol officers responsibility for follow-up investigations of lesser crimes because the pursuit of investigative leads outside the team area is vastly improved when one member of a team is designated to do the work on behalf of another officer.

Impact of New Agent Positions on the Relationship between Preliminary and Follow-up Investigations Although the movement toward the police-agent concept has not yet gained full momentum, the next few years will see some shifts in traditional rank structure and a new definition of duties assigned to these various new positions. In the rank structure suggested in Chapter 14 as a possibility for departments of the future, grade 2 officers would be expected to carry responsibilities for follow-up investigations of all kinds, subject to the limitations of distance and shift hours which may be in conflict with the investigation. The use of the term "agent" in itself implies a greater involvement in investigative activity.

Handling of Noncriminal Incidents and Services A substantial part of the patrol officer's time is devoted to noncriminal incidents and services which are a regular part of the case load. Officers must handle incidents involving such things as traffic accidents, runaway or missing persons, family crises, lost property, lockouts, aid to persons who are handicapped or incapacitated by injury, and fire calls. The administrator should be on the alert for the tendency of officers to think of this activity as not being "real police work." There is little enough opportunity to engage in work in a nonpunitive setting, and the police should welcome a chance to perform it.

Identification of Hazards Any situation that may induce an incident calling for some police action is a police hazard. Police hazards may result in crimes, minor violations, traffic accidents and congestion, lost persons and property, and other incidents that require police attention. August Vollmer, who is often described as the father of modern law enforcement, categorized police hazards more than 40 years ago. His classifications[1] are remarkably current:

[1]The classifications were taken from his lecture notes at the University of California.

Persons

Criminals
Migrants
Sex deviates
Alcoholics
Addicts
Prostitutes
Gamblers
Pimps

Drug peddlers
Saloonkeepers
Pawnbrokers
Secondhand dealers
Feeble-minded
Insane
Agitators

Fanatics
Subversive agents
Juvenile delinquents
Problem children
Solicitors
Peddlers
Taxi dancers

Property

Unoccupied dwellings
Warehouses
Fraternity and sorority houses
Safes
Automobiles
Buildings under construction
Gas stations
Banks

Business places where insurance
companies
  1 Prohibit open stock risks
  2 Prohibit open stock risks without
alarm systems
  3 Require that open stock risks be
referred to the home office
  4 Have experienced consistent losses

Places

Main arteries:
  Railroad
  Automobile
  Pedestrian
Shipping docks
Ferry landings
Rendezvous or
  residence of
  individuals
  listed under
  Persons

Railroad stations
Cheap boarding- and
  lodginghouses
Radical headquarters
Saloons
Gambling places
Pool halls
Amusement parks

Pawnshops
Secondhand stores
Transitional areas
Foreign-born areas
Streets in vicinity of theaters
Houses of prostitution

Situational

Athletic events
Political meetings
Parades
Conventions

Radical meetings
Radical conflicts
Celebrations
Disasters

Hazards may vary according to the hour of the day, the day of the week, and the season. They may be of high or low frequency and of high or low value. Some create a desire, and others present an opportunity to misbehave. Some hazards are temporary, and some are permanent. Some may be corrected or minimized by physical changes, regulation, or public education, and some may be affected only by the actions of a police officer.

Knowledge of Beat Important in Patrol Prevention, in the broadest sense, is the process of eliminating hazards or diminishing their effect. A patrol officer's beat is composed of persons and things that may constitute hazards in some cases and, in others, may be facilities that aid in the disposition of the resultant incidents. Knowledge of hazards and facilities, therefore, is essential to the successful performance of patrol duty.

Patrol officers should have information sources that may be of help to them. Personal contacts with residents, business people, and proprietors or employees of businesses frequented by persons of questionable character are information sources that officers should develop. They should also know sources of readily obtainable emergency equipment, such as wreckers, diving equipment, armored cars, and boats.

Furnishing Assistance The lending of assistance to motorists with stalled cars by taking them to a telephone or to a point where service is available or by sending help is greatly appreciated by the distressed citizens and hence creates good will. Other services appreciated by the public include sweeping up glass and covering blood spots with sand at accident scenes and using flares at night and improvised signs during the day to warn motorists of icy or dangerous roadways.

Officers who call at the hospital to obtain additional information from the victims of accidents can build good will by their solicitous treatment of the victims and by their consideration in notifying relatives and friends, in finding lost property, and in attending to other details that arise when a person has been injured.

Officers should look and act as though it were a pleasure for them to be of service; then it will be.

Services to Merchants and Householders Police officers should establish speaking acquaintances with the business people and residents on their beats. This relationship creates information sources for the officer, facilitates desirable dissemination of police information to the public, enables citizens to become personally acquainted with members of the force, and builds good will. Police departments should establish security-inspection services designed to lessen crime hazards, and they should furnish information and suggestions intended to protect people and property from crime.

Warning Merchants of Criminal Operations Officers should give the merchants on their beats warnings concerning bad-check passers, shoplifters, "bank-examiner" frauds, and other criminal operations. Officers may learn of such operations either through their own assignments or through crime-analysis bulletins or other releases made by the department. Patrol officers should give merchants a description of a suspect and of his or her method of operation and request them to telephone headquarters if the suspect should appear. The personnel of retail establishments, by means of group lectures or individual discussion, may be informed regarding the common methods of shoplifting and fraud and the points to observe in fixing the identity of a suspect in mind to ensure future identification.

Inspection of Banks and Hazardous Business Places   Banks and other business houses having large sums of money and stock of small bulk and great value, such as jewelry or furs, present hazards that should be inspected by detectives assigned to robbery and burglary cases. The physical security of the premises and the operating procedures, from the time the first employee arrives in the morning until the last one leaves at night, should be gone over minutely to eliminate any insecurity or unwise practice that might offer an opportunity for robbery or theft. Apparent needs for alarm systems should be discussed with the proprietor.

Store Inspections   Patrol officers should similarly inspect the security of stores on their beats. By the use of a suitable printed form, the officer may check unsatisfactory conditions and list recommendations made to the merchant. This record enables a follow-up urging the proprietor to make the suggested improvements and, when filed according to location, readily supplies information regarding the names, addresses, and telephone numbers of the proprietor, his or her manager, and anyone else who should be notified in the event that an emergency arises when the shop is closed.

Assistance from Merchants   The officer should seek information and assistance in his police problems from business people on his beat. They are pleased when an officer comes to them for advice and counsel. If the officer wants the friendship and cooperation of a merchant, he can often win them by getting the merchant to do something for him. When the officer accepts the assistance and follows the advice, the merchant becomes identified with the project and feels that he has a vested interest in it, and he becomes interested in the officer as well. The officer should not seek advice when he knows that he probably will not follow it; failure to act on requested advice does not strengthen friendship.

Study of Traffic Hazards   The department should establish a rule that the merit of complaints and suggestions relating to traffic hazards is to be ascertained and that a report on the results of an investigation of a suggested regulation is to be made to the citizen who proposed it. When a suitable study has been made of the situation, it is as easy to prove to a reasonable person that the suggested regulation is not needed as it is to prove that it is, when the facts so indicate. This practice shows citizens that their suggestions are not ignored.

Inspection of Vacant Homes   Some departments, in order to minimize the burglary hazard, keep a special watch on homes made vacant by the temporary absence of the occupant. At the start, this service requires advertising so that people will notify the police of their anticipated absence. The beat officer then inspects the premises on each tour of duty and sees that the neighbors keep the front porch clear of the usual accumulation of newspapers, advertising circulars, and milk deliveries, which so frequently indicate to a house prowler that a home is vacant. The inspecting officer should leave a notice (making sure that it is hidden from the view of potential offenders) urging the occupant to call the department immediately upon returning.

Meeting Residents Foot-patrol officers in residential areas often have an opportunity to become acquainted with everyone on their beats. Motorized-patrol officers, however, are apt to be derelict in this respect. Several departments have therefore established procedures to ensure contact by the officer with residents on the beat. In one method, a list of new residents in the city furnished by the chamber of commerce or some similar source is checked against police records to ensure that none is wanted, and the name and address of the new resident and the name of the officer on the beat are typed on a specially prepared leaflet, the front cover of which contains a word of welcome to the newcomer in the name of the officer. The leaflet describes briefly the organization, operation, and policies of the department; gives a few suggestions on guarding homes and locking automobiles; and includes traffic hints and some safety pointers with special reference to schoolchildren. It contains specific instructions on action the householder should take in the event of suspicion of trouble: when and how to call the police, how to dial in the dark, how to identify personal property with the engraving of a social security number, and what to do in case of fire.

This leaflet, along with pamphlets relating to other city services, is presented to the new resident by the officer in the evening or on a weekend.

In another approach, the officer simply goes from door to door, distributes safety and security literature to each resident, and then offers to conduct a security survey of the premises. Both these approaches have achieved good results in crime prevention, and they have excellent public relations value.

Supplying Information Citizens invariably go to the police for information. Each member of the force should be prepared to supply it from his or her knowledge of street locations, bus routes and schedules, distances and preferred highways to nearby towns and more distant large cities, and the location of special points of interest, such as public and prominent office buildings, parks, schools, hotels, theaters, and the chamber of commerce. Each officer should carry a street guide and a directory to assist in providing information desired by the public.

When information is requested, the officer should ascertain exactly what is wanted so that time is not wasted and then should proceed to give the information deliberately, briefly, and concisely, in a clear tone of voice. When giving directions, the officer should be certain that the location is clearly fixed

356 OPERATIONS

in the mind of the citizen. If the route is complicated, the directions should be written on a sheet from the officer's notebook and given to the citizen.

Services Related to Delinquency Prevention A major part of preventive patrol should be directed toward the identification and referral of delinquency-causing situations and toward personal relationships and behavior as opposed to tangible hazards. Additional information on this subject will be presented in Chapter 20.

Chapter 17

Allocation and Distribution of Operational Manpower

One of the most challenging responsibilities of the police administrator is the allocation of personnel—the determination of the appropriate level of operational manpower to carry out police tasks. In the great majority of American cities, this determination is made by a subjective process which may range from (1) guesswork through (2) comparison of police strength with that in other cities to (3) a calculation based on the number of officers to be added to compensate for an increase in crime. Once this allocation process is carried out—regardless of the method used—the *distribution* of personnel can take place so that work load is properly apportioned on each shift and so that each beat on a given shift has an equal work load.

ALLOCATION OF PATROL MANPOWER

Until recent years there have been few attempts to justify the level of manpower by any means other than the methods described in the preceding paragraph. In 1962 the International Association of Chiefs of Police began to advocate the allocation of personnel on the basis of a work-load formula, and by 1964 it had refined the procedure and applied it to a number of agencies.

Several years before this, the St. Louis Police Department began to experiment with a queuing theory in relation to manpower allocation so that the administrator could be provided with answers to such questions as: What level of manpower would be required to establish the probability that less than X events will be waiting in queue?

The key step in the IACP process is to make an arbitrary determination of the desirable balance between time required to handle called-for services and all other time on duty—that is, the time left for preventive patrol, inspectional services, and "buffer time" to guard against the tendency for incidents to be queued or stacked up. This arbitrary ratio of called-for services to preventive patrol and buffer time is 1 to 2. Beat size is thus based on adjusting dimensions until a work load of one-third of the officer's time in called-for services is obtained. The one-third–two-thirds ratio is not and was never intended to be an ultimate or optimum figure, but rather a starting place with the hope that the effect of this amount of time can be studied over a long period and that subsequent refinements can be made.

DISTRIBUTION OF PATROL MANPOWER

Until recent years, the practice in organizing the work in almost all police departments has been to distribute the patrol force evenly among three 8-hour shifts and to assign the officers to beats of equal area. This method of distribution was evidence either of a lack of knowledge concerning the hourly and geographical fluctuations of the police load or of indifference to the possible increase in efficiency resulting from a distribution of the force on the basis of need throughout the day over the area to be served. When beats of equal area are established without regard for variations in need for police service, some will have a much greater work load than others.

With the advent of the police car for patrol service, the problem of distribution remained fundamentally unchanged, except that the patrol was expanded to cover the entire city. At first the city was divided into a number of districts of equal area. When the number of patrol cars was very limited, this procedure sometimes resulted in fairly equitable division, especially in smaller cities whose expansion had been relatively homogeneous. In such cities, the four districts formed by the intersecting of the main streets frequently were constituted patrol districts, and often such districts were similar in area and in police hazards.

But as the number of patrol cars increased, the inequality of the police load in districts of equal area became apparent to some police chiefs, and they attempted to equalize loads by varying the size of the districts. At first they relied entirely on their memory of the distribution of offenses and estimated the need for police service in the various sections of the community on the basis of their knowledge of conditions in those sections. When the unreliability of such distribution became apparent, a few developed pin maps to show the location

ALLOCATION AND DISTRIBUTION OF OPERATIONAL MANPOWER 359

of offenses; this step was the beginning of a statistical method for determining the needs for patrol distribution.

A statistical method of distributing the patrol force in proportion to need is based on some underlying principles relating to the measurement of the need for patrol service that should be understood. These are discussed in the following paragraphs.

Measurement of Hazards and Distribution in Proportion to Need

Patrol officers should be distributed in proportion to the need for police service. The essence of the distribution problem lies in measuring the proportionate need. At first thought it would seem that the need for patrol service should be measured in terms of the time patrol officers spend performing called-for services. Data for estimating the amount of time a patrol officer must spend investigating each type of offense, accident, or miscellaneous complaint and making an arrest should be readily available.

But not all a patrol officer's time is spent in this way. The time spent performing inspectional and routine patrol services must also be ascertained. Theoretically, it should be possible to isolate a hazard and measure it in terms of the time a patrol officer must spend counteracting it. The time required to provide any desired quality (in terms of frequency) of inspectional service may be determined, but an analysis of intangible hazards with which routine patrol is concerned reveals the difficulty of measuring the time necessary to neutralize them. Intangible hazards make difficult an objective or absolute measure of the need for patrol service.

An equitable distribution of the patrol force can be made, however, without an absolute measure of the need for patrol in terms of minutes of service. The time in minutes is required only to ascertain the manpower needed on each shift for inspectional services. The relative need for other services can be ascertained for each hour of the day and for each area in the community; the force can be distributed in proportion to the time and territorial distribution of this relative need, taking into consideration the man-hours needed on each shift for inspectional services.

A distribution of the patrol force based on an absolute measure of the need in terms of minutes of time necessary to perform a satisfactory quality of service seems impractical for the following reasons: (1) There has not yet been developed an absolute measure of the time needed for a satisfactory routine preventive patrol, and (with the exception of patrol officers whose duties are almost entirely inspectional) most of a patrol officer's time is spent in this type of patrol. (2) There likewise has not yet been established a standard of optimum patrol strength. (3) Even if the above two deficiencies were met, unless the patrol force were precisely of the optimum strength, it would be necessary to distribute it in proportion to need. (4) Whenever a proportional distribution is made, the proportional need is the same, whether expressed in terms of proportional number of incidents or proportional amount of time needed to deal with them. (5) An absolute measure of the required patrol time must be based on complete data. As will be shown later, time and location data are unknown in some cases; the proportion with missing data may be high.

Measuring the Relative Need   The need for patrol service derives from police hazards. The total hazard in a community resulting in need for police service is the sum of a multitude of varied and complex conditions and situations, many of them intangible and difficult to isolate for purposes of analysis and measurement. However, hazards result in crimes, offenses, accidents, complaints, and arrests whose frequency may be taken as a measure of the hazards. The measure is made not in terms of the hours and minutes spent handling cases or neutralizing or minimizing the hazards but in terms of the proportional distribution of the incidents that result from these hazards among the various patrol areas and during various time periods. If one area or shift has twice as many crimes, offenses, accidents, miscellaneous complaints, and arrests as another area or shift, it may be assumed that it has approximately twice the amount of hazards resulting in need for police service.

Called-for Services   For purposes of patrol distribution, the proportional distribution of crimes and offenses committed, accidents, miscellaneous complaints, and arrests serves as a reasonably accurate and satisfactory measure on which to base the proportional distribution of the need for called-for services.

General Patrol Services   Certain patrol services are performed for the purpose of preventing calls for services. Crimes, accidents, and other incidents resulting in calls for service may be avoided by trying store doors, by spending an hour at a dangerous intersection, or by inspecting poolrooms, taverns, dance halls, and other recreational centers and requiring compliance with regulations. The need for, and character of, these duties vary with the time of the day. Accident frequency follows closely the ebb and flow of traffic. Recreational centers require attention in the evenings especially, although some types may have heavy patronage in the afternoons and others during the late hours of the night. The peak hours at recreational centers will vary considerably with the day of the week. The danger of store burglaries is greater after closing hours, especially during the late hours of the night. The need for inspections varies widely over day and night hours. Time spent in general patrol is divided between inspections and preventive patrol.

Inspectional Services   Some of the more important patrol duties may be measured in terms of the number of minutes required for their performance. This is true of the inspection of tangible hazards which may be identified and which take a large part of the total patrol time. Included are store tries and the inspection of dance halls, poolrooms, taverns, bars, and other establishments. The number of man-hours required on each shift to perform any desired quality of inspectional service may therefore be readily ascertained. In planning the beat layout on any shift, however, it is unnecessary to measure the need for inspectional services in terms of absolute time; for all practical purposes it may

ALLOCATION AND DISTRIBUTION OF OPERATIONAL MANPOWER 361

be measured in terms of the proportional number of inspectional duties performed. For example, if one beat has twice as many stores requiring tries as another, then twice as many man-hours should be provided.

Routine Preventive Patrol There are other police hazards that are so intangible that their isolation and measurement are practically impossible. The time spent in routine patrol is devoted to these less tangible hazards. The proportion of total time devoted to intangible hazards will vary with the beat. The need for attention to these hazards is best measured in terms of the results of the hazards. When two beats have equal needs for the inspection of identifiable hazards (inspectional services), the intangible hazards on one beat will exceed those on the other somewhat in proportion to the extent to which the number of calls for service on the one exceeds that on the other.

Summary The relative need for the three types of patrol service may therefore be measured as follows: (1) called-for services in terms of the relative frequency of incidents that call for service, (2) inspectional service in terms of the relative number of places that require inspections that are comparable in time required, and (3) routine patrol in terms of the relative frequency of incidents that result from intangible hazards, which is, for all practical purposes, the same as item 1 above.

Detailed Allocation and Distribution Procedures A detailed manpower distribution procedure is presented in Appendix J. It provides a comprehensive method for the distribution of patrol manpower without regard to the size of the city.

A simpler version of this method has been adopted by IACP. It includes a basis for overall manpower allocation, as well as for distribution. The method is fully described in Appendix K. When properly applied, the latter system determines the total number of personnel to be allocated to the patrol function, the number to be assigned to each shift, optimum shift hours, the configuration of patrol beats, and recommended days off so that peak work load will be handled by an optimum number of patrol officers on duty.

ALLOCATION AND DISTRIBUTION OF MANPOWER IN EXTREMELY HAZARDOUS OR HIGH-CRIME REGIONS

The systems described here and in the Appendix may be inappropriate in several highly urbanized American cities which are experiencing troublesome crime conditions. In these areas, far more officers must be arbitrarily deployed into what amounts to a continuing field battle against street crime. Later, when an aggravated crime situation is controlled, conventional allocation and distribution methods can be employed.

The federal government applied this rationale to the manpower situation in the District of Columbia in the years following the publication of the report by the President's Commission on Crime in the District of Columbia and the rioting in the aftermath of the assassination of Dr. Martin Luther King, Jr.

The conventional approach to determination of manpower may not have been feasible; even with the massive addition of manpower in blocks of 1,000 officers, crime continued to escalate until the latter part of 1970 and early 1971, when a combination of the application of manpower, attacks on heroin use and distribution, court reform, improved street lighting, and other reforms began at last to cause a slowing of the rate of increase and, ultimately, an actual decrease in serious crimes.

ALLOCATION OF MANPOWER FOR OTHER DIVISIONS WITHIN THE DEPARTMENT

Determination of manpower requirements for the patrol function is obviously the key step in ascertaining the level of manpower for the entire department. The patrol division is typically the largest unit by far and represents most of the manpower in the agency. It also represents the most challenging part of manpower allocation because of the imponderables in deciding the optimum level of preventive patrol to be applied.

Deciding on the number of personnel required for investigative divisions is much simpler; manpower is added until sufficient personnel are available to cope with the work load, provided the divisions do not engage in preventive-patrol activity. Determining the size of traffic-enforcement and special-operations-division units is more difficult and is largely a matter of personal judgment by the administrator.

Chapter 18

Criminal Investigation

No area of law enforcement is in greater need of improvement than criminal investigation. The management of criminal investigation, moreover, is less effective on the whole than the management of other police activities.

Investigations of crimes and other serious incidents are a concern of most members of the department at the operational level, in the form either of preliminary activity or of continuing or follow-up investigations. Crimes occur at any time and in widely scattered locations, making it a practical necessity to have officers available around the clock to respond to situations in which crime has occurred for the purpose of rendering aid to victims, obtaining evidence, arresting offenders, and gathering basic essential information.

Some degree of specialization for carrying out continued or detailed investigation of criminal cases is desirable in moderate-sized agencies; in larger departments it is a necessity.

Investigation by the Criminal Investigation Division In most medium-sized and larger police departments in the United States, the investigation of crimes is a joint responsibility of the patrol division and the criminal investigation division. Officers assigned to the patrol force are generally given responsibility for preliminary investigation, with follow-up efforts carried out by detectives.

363

The basic purpose of the detective or criminal investigation function is to investigate certain serious crimes in order to arrest and convict the perpetrators and to recover stolen property. The arrest of offenders is stressed partly as a matter of justice, but certainly a more fundamental reason is their removal from society on the grounds that they may commit additional offenses unless they are isolated. Another motivation for emphasis on arrest is to convince potential offenders that arrest is possible, which has a substantial deterrent or preventive effect.

The success of investigations is enhanced by active patrol participation. Suitable coordination of the patrol and detective divisions results in increased efficiency of the investigative efforts of personnel assigned to both divisions.

As indicated in Chapter 16, the initial or preliminary investigation by patrol officers may often result in arrest at the scene or very soon after the crime was committed. When this happens, the detective's usual responsibilities are reduced to the recovery of stolen property, the preparation of the case for presentation in court, and the investigation of other crimes, either reported or unreported, which the offender may have committed.

In most cases, however, detectives begin work on a case by analyzing the information contained in the patrol officer's preliminary-investigation report; then they contact the victim and witnesses and pursue leads which may have been developed by others.

The greater skill and ability of investigators, their background of experience, and their possession of many facts from similar or related investigations qualify them to continue an investigation until the criminal has been apprehended or further effort seems futile. Investigators may utilize the facilities of the patrol division in routine additional searches for witnesses, physical evidence, and suspects and thus save their own time and energy for more difficult phases of the investigation. Detectives may reinterview a victim and principal witnesses in the hope that closer and more skillful questioning will uncover additional information or information acquired since the preliminary investigation. However, routine reinterviews which cover little more than the area of the preliminary investigation are decidedly undesirable.

Patrol Participation Should Be Stimulated The chances for success of investigators in clearing cases by arrest and in recovering stolen property are substantially increased by encouraging the participation of patrol manpower. Patrol officers are responsible for the prevention of crime on their beats, and while they should not be held responsible for the clearance of crimes, they should be urged by patrol supervisors and detectives to do everything in their power to arrest perpetrators and to recover stolen property. (In systems in which beat officers are responsible for the complete investigation of crimes, their roles are obviously different.)

Supervising officers should urge patrol officers to continue their efforts to apprehend criminals who have operated on their beats on the grounds that the effectiveness of patrol, on a beat as well as throughout the community, is

CRIMINAL INVESTIGATION

measured in part by the crime rate. The arrest of the criminally active will tend to reduce the crime rate, thus simplifying the patrol task of preventing crime. The detective assigned to a case should discuss it with the patrol officer on whose beat the crime occurred and encourage him to continue his efforts. Clearances and recoveries, which are a measure of detective accomplishment, increase when detectives have patrol officers working for them in this manner. The effectiveness of the department in the investigation of crimes is further increased by keeping the patrol force currently informed about the operation and whereabouts of criminals and wanted persons; about their associates, hangouts, descriptions, and methods of operation; and about the automobiles they use.

Patrol activity in the investigation of crimes is also stimulated by giving patrol officers credit for their accomplishments. Detectives and patrol supervisors should try to make sure that the chief recognizes praiseworthy accomplishments of individual officers by commendation in the department bulletin, where all members of the force may read that the efforts are appreciated. Also, patrol officers' service records should reflect arrests for serious offenses and the recovery of property. Finally, press representatives should be influenced to give due credit to the patrol force, using the names of patrol officers who make arrests when policy does not forbid this. The practice of some detectives of accepting without protest an implied credit in a newspaper item for an arrest made by a patrol officer damages the morale and lessens the interest of patrol personnel and destroys the close working relationship which should be nurtured between the two divisions so that crime may be most effectively cleared.

ORGANIZATION AND STAFFING OF THE CRIMINAL INVESTIGATION FUNCTION

Adherence to sound organizational principles is just as important in the proper structure of the investigative function as it is in any other area of the department. In fact, part of the reason for the relative ineffectiveness of investigative management is the tendency for investigative supervisors to deemphasize management principles, while stressing the importance of operational skills and experiences.

Organizational Considerations

In most departments the detective function is organized according to the kind of offenses to be investigated. In the past, the organization of a detective bureau in many departments was extremely detailed, with separate squads or details for each of the various crime categories and activities, such as homicide, burglary, robbery, bunco, and fugitive. In recent years, however, there has been a tendency toward grouping the functional specialists—partly on the grounds that criminals tend to be less specialized themselves. A substantial percentage of crime today is committed by narcotics addicts to sustain their

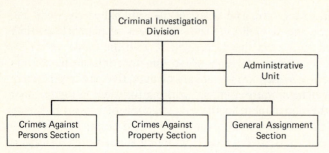

Chart 24 Organizational structure for a criminal investigation division.

habits or by youths. For both these groups, there is less tendency to follow an established pattern of criminal behavior. A high percentage of crime is also carried out by organized street gangs, who may intentionally vary their crime targets and methods considerably and who may shift from burglary of clothing stores to robbery of gas stations in the space of an evening.

Some functional specialization, of course, is still necessary; specialists ought to exercise their expertise during the course of interrogations of suspects, the review of cases to establish common characteristics and to ensure that all leads have been covered, and the presentation of the cases in the courts.

A suggested structure for a medium-sized to large department is shown in Chart 24.

Within the crimes-against-persons section, if further specialization is required, units should be established for homicide, assault and sex offenses, and robbery offenses.

In the crimes-against-property section, similar groupings should be established, if necessary, for burglary and theft and for auto-theft units. Pawnshop work should be carried out by personnel assigned to this section.

Activity of the general assignment section should include investigations of check cases, frauds, bomb and arson cases, and other nonindex felony crimes, including crime categories not mentioned for the other sections and fugitive or warrant-service assignments from outside the agency.

The division should ordinarily have an administrative unit, which should be responsible for review of all investigative reports to ensure compliance with Uniform Crime Report system requirements. The unit should also offer report-typing and stenographic help (for all reports in small divisions and in major cases in larger investigative divisions) and general administrative support for the division, such as arrangements for travel and other office duties.

The classes of crimes that are assigned to individual detectives (or to groups of detectives who make up a section of the division in a large department) are determined by the proportional incidence of the various crimes, by the seriousness of the offenses, by the average length of time required in their investigation, and by the ability of the investigator. The small number of crimes in some classes makes it necessary to assign more than one class to a detective. When this is the case, the classes of crimes assigned to one detective should be similar or related in some manner. For example, crimes

CRIMINAL INVESTIGATION

such as passing bad checks of all kinds, shoplifting, and short-changing are related because they are frequently committed against retail merchants. A detective assigned to these crimes enjoys some of the advantages of specialization because his field of attention in terms of area and prospective victim is narrowed. The merchants also become better acquainted with the investigator than they would if these three classes of crimes were divided among three detectives who, in addition, were given other assignments. Some classes of crimes may be grouped for assignment purposes because they are related in the sense that one may grow out of another. For example, robberies, aggravated assaults, rapes, and abortions sometimes result in homicide. Frauds, bad-check passing of all kinds, and counterfeiting are other examples of crimes that are similar in character.

In some cities the number of crimes in one class may be more than can be adequately investigated by one detective. Burglaries under these conditions may be advantageously divided into residence and nonresidence because burglars who attack dwellings usually do not attack stores, and vice versa. While individual house prowlers may direct their attention almost exclusively to apartment houses, one-story bungalows, or duplexes and individual store burglars may specialize in chain grocery stores, clothing stores, or warehouses, there is not a high-enough degree of persistency in such specialization to warrant further division by the police department. In a large city, however, an advantageous further division may be made by analyzing the patterns of burglars in directing their operations against one type of property. For example, the separation of hotel prowls from residence burglaries and of warehouse burglaries from other nonresidence burglaries may be desirable when the number in either category justifies the full time of one detective.

Staffing

The number of detectives or investigators actually assigned to the division is largely a matter of adjustment to work load. Some standards can be adopted, however, to facilitate this kind of decision. Many experienced detective supervisors believe that the number of new cases (if they are routine or average felony cases, such as burglary or armed robbery without complications such as the injury of a victim) should not exceed a given amount per day and that the number of active cases of this sort kept in pending status should be restricted. Finally, a specific period of time should be established as an automatic limitation on case load—beyond which permission should be required for continuing with the assignment. Each of these determinants should be established by the division commander. The number of detectives can be ascertained by the application of this kind of information.

Use of Female Detectives Selection of police officers should be carried out without regard to whether the candidate is male or female, and assignment to most positions in the criminal investigation division should also be done without consideration of sex. However, some police tasks are more easily carried out by female officers. Some investigations may be made more easily and more effectively by a woman than by a man. The practice of using female officers to interview women suspects and young children is frequently more productive and usually less objectionable to the interviewee. Female officers are essential in making some raids, in making arrests where the female criminal may seek refuge in a women's rest room, in searching and transporting female prisoners, and in interrogating young women and inexperienced older ones.

If a sworn female officer is not available, a female detective-division secretary, a woman records clerk, or a matron may fill this intermittent need. In larger departments, where the need is so frequent as to occupy a substantial part of the time of one female police officer, she should be transferred to the detective division and be given either investigative or clerical assignments to occupy her time during slack periods.

Selection of Investigators

Routine patrol service, with its manifold problems and opportunities for experience in preliminary investigations, provides invaluable training for future detectives. The qualities of a good detective are an abundance of physical and nervous energy; considerably more than average persistence; imagination and ingenuity, with the initiative and force to apply them; and a broad background of experience with special reference to information sources. Psychological and physical tests may one day be developed to measure these qualities, but at present the most satisfactory basis for selection appears to be that of observation of individual patrol officers for the purpose of discovering evidence of their investigative ability. A written examination intended to measure only information capacity is not the best method of selection.

The qualities needed in investigators are not exactly those needed in supervisory officers; some sergeants and lieutenants of superior ability would make mediocre detectives, and likewise some of the best investigators would not prove satisfactory as supervisory officers. For this reason it seems wise to select detectives from the patrol force but to refrain from giving them concurrently a rank of sergeant, which automatically places them in an important supervisory position, in the event they do not prove satisfactory as detectives.

Detectives should not be frozen into their positions by civil service. In no other branch may the accomplishments and abilities of individual officers be so accurately appraised as in the detective service, where percentage clearances by arrest and percentage and amount of property recoveries in one class of crime reflect rather closely the ability and effort of the investigating officers. The administrator should take advantage of this measure in the trial of patrol officers and in the transfer of those detectives who do not demonstrate the necessary skills.

Extra Pay or Rank for Investigators The police chief should avoid giving extra pay for the investigative function, and the basic job of detective should

CRIMINAL INVESTIGATION 369

not be carried out by an officer holding supervisory rank, such as a detective sergeant. As indicated in earlier parts of this text, there should be increasing stress on the need to enhance the position of patrol officer as the career job in the department. It is most difficult to do this if investigators or dispatchers or traffic officers receive more pay. Second, there should be complete freedom to transfer personnel from one division to another in the department, depending on the needs of the department and the individual abilities of the officers. The possibility of reduction in pay for a specialist is a serious practical handicap to the free transfer of personnel.

MANAGEMENT OF CASES AND SUPERVISION

Suitable control of detective operations is dependent on the maintenance of records by the division administrative unit, secretary, or clerk. The following are needed as a minimum: (1) Some form of daily attendance record showing hours worked for each detective. (2) An assignment sheet for each member on which are recorded each day all cases assigned to this individual as well as all cases that originated in previous months on which he or she recovered property or effected clearance by arrest during the current month, with columns for indicating identifying case data, the date reported, whether there was clearance by arrest, whether arrest was followed by prosecution, whether the case was unfounded, whether the perpetrator was adult or juvenile, and the amount of property recovered. (3) A prosecution ledger to ensure a monthly follow-up and a record of the disposition of cases tried in state and federal courts. Each case filed should be registered according to class of crime, listing the number, name of defendant, and date filed, with other columns for indicating the date disposed of, the court and docket number, whether the defendant pleaded guilty to the charge or to a lesser one, whether the defendant was tried, whether the defendant was found guilty or not guilty or whether there was no verdict, and whether the case was dismissed. (4) Monthly work summaries for each investigator, showing the number of days worked, number of cases assigned, and number cleared by arrest.

Working files for investigators are necessary if access to central records is not convenient. The working file for each case usually consists of copies of reports, original crime-scene notes, checklists, rough notes written by the investigator to himself, statements of suspects and witnesses, and supervisors' instructions. The file may be kept in the detective's immediate work area during active investigation. When the case becomes inactive, however, only the investigator's original field notes and the original copies of statements should be retained by the criminal investigation division because of the need to protect these documents for court purposes. The file in central records should have been receiving supplemental or follow-up reports all along, together with copies of statements, diagrams, photographs, case summaries, and other material. Extra copies of case reports, rough notes, checklists, scrap paper, and other redundant material should be discarded, providing that essential information has been incorporated into supplemental reports which have been sent to central records.

The criminal investigation division should not operate a separate case records and indexing system, nor should it administer the identification records function.

Planning Detective Operations Planning detective operations includes meeting relatively stable changes in crime frequency by permanent changes in assignments and meeting temporary fluctuations that result in unequal work loads by temporary changes in the regular assignments. The head of the division, who is responsible for such assignments, also participates in the development of procedures used by members of his division and by the patrol division in the preliminary investigation of crimes. Procedures that involve the patrol, records, and other divisions must, of course, be developed in cooperation with the commanding officers of the other units.

Plans of operation must also be developed by the detective captain to meet intermittent and unusual needs created by unusual criminal activity. In departments having a task force, the relationship of the detective division and the task force must be worked out by the detective captain and the patrol-division commander. Operational plans designed to uncover information concerning crimes or to effect the discovery and seizure of suspects, of persons wanted, of operating criminals, of automobiles used for criminal transportation, of tools used for criminal purposes, and of stolen property and evidence necessarily include tasks to be performed by the members of other divisions, principally the patrol division; consequently, these plans must be prepared in cooperation with other captains. Such plans will include special details in areas where criminals are operating, a canvass of areas or certain types of places or businesses, stakeouts, and surveillance.

The police administrator must be aware of some of the key concepts in operations conducted by the criminal investigation division. The chief should be able to answer the following questions: Under what circumstances should detectives be summoned to crime scenes to carry out immediate investigations? Should detectives work singly or in pairs? Should detectives engage in routine patrol? Should detectives be assigned to nighttime hours on an on-call basis? Should detectives handle crimes without regard to the probable age of the offender? How should detectives be selected? Should supervisors have extensive investigative experience? Should investigators be given additional pay or rank?

Immediate Investigation by Detectives All detectives who are likely to handle major crimes should, while on duty, be notified of reports of such serious crimes likely to be assigned to them; they may then participate in the investigation of a crime to the extent warranted by its seriousness and by their own availability. When the preliminary investigation is conducted by a patrol

CRIMINAL INVESTIGATION

officer, the detective's immediate attention is not usually necessary, but in any event there would be written guidelines for suggesting the level of seriousness which warrants active participation by a detective during the initial investigation. This guideline should be based on the fact that a detective's immediate attention is required only when his or her greater skills, knowledge, and freedom of movement are needed and when the investigation should be conducted without delay. Some but not all homicides deserve the prompt attention of detective investigators, but it is infrequently required for other classes of crimes. Such serious crimes as rape and aggravated assault may deserve immediate detective attention, especially if the victim may die. Robberies and burglaries resulting in a heavy property loss occasionally may justify similar prompt detective investigation.

Hours of Detective Duty The need for 24-hour detective service is found only in large cities (in excess of 500,000 population), although the need is influenced by the extent and quality of preliminary investigations by the patrol division. Detective-division quarters are usually open, and detectives regularly on duty, from 8 A.M. until 5 P.M. Most cases may ordinarily be investigated with least inconvenience to the victims, witnesses, and suspects during business office hours. Also, agencies and business houses whose records may contain information useful in crime investigations, as well as the courts and the prosecutor's office, are usually not open except during business hours.

The trend toward smaller families, together with increased employment of women, has resulted in an increase in the number of homes with no one present during daytime hours during the business week. This is a special problem for detectives in some suburban departments, who have the added disadvantage of both spouses' being in the central city during daytime hours. For these departments, some detective operations are best scheduled during hours such as 12 noon to 8 P.M. Detectives may occasionally find it necessary to work at other hours in the investigation of some cases, and each should be privileged to vary his or her hours of work to suit the immediate needs of the cases under investigation.

Detectives assigned to shifts after 5 P.M. usually cannot be given specialized assignments but must investigate all crimes committed during their tour of duty. Consequently, their investigation will consist of nothing more than a preliminary investigation for the detective who is regularly assigned to that class of crime on the day shift. Since every on-duty police officer should be supervised, the absence of detective supervising officers necessitates administrative supervision of detectives after 5 P.M. by the commanding officer of the patrol division, as previously described.

There is greater need for detectives on duty during the early evening hours than in the period after midnight or 1 A.M. However, the need for detectives on duty from 5 P.M. to 1 A.M. is not so great or so constant as the frequency of their assignment would seem to indicate. Cities of less than 150,000 population infrequently have crimes committed during these hours that require the immediate attention of a detective.

The head of the detective division and individual detectives in departments that do not provide detective service after 5 P.M. should confer with the patrol-division captain and his lieutenants regarding types of crimes that deserve immediate detective attention.

Case Screening A number of departments are now using formalized procedures for determining which cases handled by patrol officers at the preliminary level should be transmitted to detectives for follow-up investigation. The Rochester police department has organized the information on the basic crime report form so that the patrol officer answers thirteen questions relating to solvability factors—items which tend to be important in determining the probability of success. For example, if the officer marks an X (meaning "no") after a question which asks, "Can the subject vehicle be identified?" and at the conclusion of report-writing determines that there are ten other X's, the likelihood for success is not great. The case can then be placed in the status of "early suspension."

A great advantage of case screening is that investigative effort can then be spent on more productive cases. A second advantage is that patrol officers' investigations become more efficient.

One-Person Assignments Preferred Detectives should be assigned to work alone and not in pairs. All the reasons previously given for assigning one person instead of two in patrol-car operations apply with equal force to detective operations. Most investigations may be made more effectively by one investigator, and the economy of a one-person assignment is apparent. Department regulations, however, should require a detective engaged in a dangerous investigation or arrest to secure needed assistance from other detectives when available and otherwise from the patrol division.

The Assignment of Detectives As a general rule, all cases of the same class should be investigated by the detective specializing in that type. This does not mean, however, that there should be no deviation from the plan of assignment. Specialization of assignment fixes responsibility, simplifies training, permits a selection of personnel for assignment on a basis of special interest and ability, and provides a more accurate measure of the accomplishment of the individual detective. Frequent repetition of tasks increases skill and narrows the field of attention, thus permitting the detective to make contacts more effectively and to keep informed on a particular class of criminals and their operations. For example, detectives assigned to nonresidence burglaries are able to concentrate their attention on this class of crime and to learn about the type of persons who commit such burglaries, where they spend their time, and where they dispose of their stolen property.

CRIMINAL INVESTIGATION

Investigation of Juvenile Crimes   Detectives should usually investigate to the conclusion all crimes in the classes of offenses assigned to them, even though juveniles are involved in some individual cases as victims or offenders, for the following reasons: (1) The assignment of crimes for investigation on the basis of the offender's age is unsound because the age can rarely be established before arrest, but is usually determined by the investigation of the offense. (2) To assume the offender's age before his or her identity is known usually results in controversy and friction, and the detective may initiate the reclassification of an offense as juvenile in order to avoid work or the embarrassment of a low percentage of clearances. (3) Divided responsibility is undesirable. The assignment of all crimes of a class to one division for investigation and clearance is feasible and avoids the splitting of responsibility. (4) The detective division has as its primary purpose the investigation and clearance by arrest of the most serious crimes, and its members are usually best qualified by training and experience to investigate them. The youth division is not designed for this purpose. (5) The accomplishments of the detective division and of its individual members are measured in terms of the clearance by arrest of assigned classes of crimes, and consequently they should have authority to conduct the investigation to its conclusion. When responsibility for the investigation of a class of crime is divided between the detective and youth divisions, the clearance rate no longer reflects the effectiveness of one division or of one detective.

A distinction must be made, however, between the investigation of crimes committed by juveniles and the disposition of the individual juvenile offender. The latter should be the exclusive responsibility of the youth division. Also, since care must be observed not to subject juveniles to unwholesome influences and especially to contact with adult offenders, department regulations should require that the interrogation of juvenile suspects be conducted in the quarters of the youth division or in the presence of a member of its staff. The disposition of the juvenile offender by the youth division is discussed in Chapter 20.

Supervision

The nature of criminal investigation duties emphasizes the need for a close and continuous supervision of detectives, if satisfactory results are to be obtained. This is made possible by continuous review of the daily work of each investigator and appraisal of his or her accomplishments in terms of clearances, recoveries, arrests, and convictions. Supervision will usually be adequate when the supervisor knows from one hour to the next the whereabouts and activities of each subordinate.

The span of control of the head of the criminal investigation division is influenced by so many variable factors that it is impossible to establish categorically a maximum number of subordinates that he or a subordinate supervisor may satisfactorily supervise. While experienced and capable detectives require little advice in the investigation of their cases and refer only important matters to their commanding officers for decision or information, each detective should be able to confer with his or her immediate superior on important matters without unreasonable delay. Consequently, it seems desirable that the number of detectives reporting to a supervisor should not exceed 10. When two or more are assigned to the same class of crime investigation, there is some justification for designating one as the head to direct the investigations of all, thus creating a section within the division.

Qualifications of Supervisors   Most departments overstress the value of the seasoned investigator as a detective supervisor. Many administrators also believe that an effective supervisor in another division, such as traffic or patrol, would be completely unsuccessful in supervising investigators or detectives. While it may be that a first-line supervisor in a detective division must have a certain amount of appreciation for, and understanding of, investigative techniques, it should be emphasized that a supervisor in a detective or investigation division should be a good supervisor and handler of personnel first, and an investigator second.

INVESTIGATIVE METHODS AND TECHNIQUES

A general textbook on police administration such as this should not emphasize subject matter which is rightfully more properly handled in preservice or in-service training courses. Nor can material in this text impart the experience gained in years of actual investigations in the field. It is possible, however, to list some of the areas which should be of greatest concern to the administrator and of interest to the student of police administration.

Interviewing and Interrogation   The fundamental skill required of the detective—the *sine qua non* of the investigating officer—is the technique of interviewing and interrogation. Authorities generally make a distinction between the two, preferring to say that interviewing is the method used with victims and witnesses, while interrogation (implying the solicitation of information which is not voluntarily given under most circumstances) is reserved for suspects and prisoners.

The police executive must be certain that rights of citizens are not abridged and that criminal cases are not lost through improper police handling of persons who would otherwise be convicted. Improper handling related to interrogation generally occurs in the following areas, all of which are regulated by constitutional law and judicial interpretation:

- Coercion or involuntary nature of confessions or admissions
- Delay in arraignment
- Failure to inform defendants of their rights
- Deprivation of counsel

CRIMINAL INVESTIGATION 375

- Pretrial publicity tending to prejudice a fair trial

The chief must be certain that each of these areas is covered by written policy and procedure so there is no mistake in his intent to comply with constitutional requirements.

It is surprising, to say the least, that anyone with a small amount of common sense would confess under conditions prevalent in police practice today. At the stage when suspicion begins to focus upon him, a suspect must be informed of his right to remain silent, to have counsel, and to be informed that what he says thereafter may be used against him in court. Nevertheless, a great many persons *do* subsequently give admissions and confessions to police if proper methods are used.

A great percentage of criminal cases would not result in convictions today if defendants refused to give evidence against themselves through admissions or confessions. The fact that police have traditionally relied on confessions as a means for establishing a case has caused many observers in the police field to talk about alternative methods of proof, such as improved use of physical evidence. The fact remains, however, that physical evidence or testimony of witnesses simply is not available to the degree required for conviction in most cases.

The Polygraph   Some police departments have successfully employed the polygraph, or lie detector, as an investigative aid for over 40 years, and it is now in general use across the country. This instrument, by facilitating interrogation, speeds up investigation to such an extent that its use is an economic necessity. In addition to its use in the investigation of serious crimes, some departments profitably employ the lie detector in all routine investigations, thus conserving the time of investigating officers.

Best results are obtained when the lie detector is operated in a specially designed room with equipment suitable for this purpose (see Chapter 24). The operator of the polygraph should be highly trained in the techniques of this particular method of interrogation; the interpretation of physiological and emotional responses recorded on the machine in the course of an interview should not be left to an amateur. The polygraph operator should be attached to the police crime laboratory, where his services are uniformly available to all divisions of the department.

Crime-Scene Search   As indicated in the paragraphs above, not enough attention is devoted to obtaining proper physical evidence to supplement witness testimony, admissions, and confessions. The police executive should encourage additional emphasis on the gathering and use of physical evidence for the following reasons:

- Physical evidence is extremely reliable and will increase the likelihood of convictions if it is obtained.

- Examining crime scenes for physical evidence has a great preventive and deterrent value.
- Routine crime-scene search is an excellent training device and cultivates good investigative habits.

There is now a trend toward creation of evidence-technician positions in larger departments. The technician generally works in the operational division or bureau of the department but receives functional supervision from the crime laboratory. Evidence technicians should be given intensive training in the collection and preservation of evidence, but they should not be thought of as replacements for criminal investigators or detectives. In larger departments, the technician should be assigned around the clock, and a good means of doing this is to provide at least one evidence technician on each shift in each supervisory sector or district.

The technique of "cold searching" fingerprints (i.e., comparing latent prints found at crime scenes against the fingerprints in the general criminal fingerprint file) is both cost-effective and underutilized. According to a recent Rand Institute study on the management of criminal investigations, many of the traditional investigative techniques are not nearly as cost-effective as fingerprint comparisons.

***Modus Operandi* Searches**   A basic investigative technique is the search of files and records for evidence of similar patterns of criminal activity. In the police systems of the United Kingdom and the British Commonwealth countries, *modus operandi* search has a much greater significance and importance. The technique is of less utility in the United States because of the indiscriminate nature of street crimes, unpredictable youth-gang criminal patterns, and the prevalence of crime resulting from drug addiction.

Nevertheless, the administrator should make certain that the information system of the department has enough sophistication to permit the indexing of cases by the type of crime pattern or method of operation of the suspect.

Neighborhood Contacts   A basic tool in any investigative system is reliance on neighborhood contacts or canvass of neighbors, merchants, and others in the vicinity of a crime. It is estimated that the systematic use of neighborhood canvassing within a short time of the commission of a crime (such as the following morning) results in positive information of investigative value in 20 percent of cases. The neighborhood-contact procedure also has preventive value and leads to better contact between police and the community. The police administrator should require neighborhood contact or canvasses as a matter of routine and should demand specific explanation for the omission of a neighborhood contact.

Second Contact with Complainants   Another useful concept is the "second

CRIMINAL INVESTIGATION

contact" with complainants and victims. The police administrator should make certain that his investigators are recontacting the complainant or victim in any criminal case which does not result in arrest or a closed case. Before action on the case can be suspended, the investigator should be required to indicate that he contacted the complainant a second time a week or so after the initial call.

The second contact is valuable for supplying leads which are not available in any other way. Complainants and victims are usually very much interested in the circumstances of a crime or incident involving them; they may often learn additional details themselves because of this interest, or they may have information which is helpful to the solution to the case. Since complainants are sometimes reluctant to take the initiative by calling the department, the second contact is of vital importance, and a substantial percentage of cases can be closed through this technique. Furthermore, the concept has substantial public relations value.

Exploiting Available Sources of Information   The ability to use the appropriate source of information is one of the hallmarks of successful investigators. Sometimes investigators have no other information than part of a name or a fragment of some other identifying data, but through diligent search of various sources of information, they often develop this partial information into a complete case.

The police administrator should make sure that his investigators are supplied with listings of sources of information which are available in his area. The following public or governmental sources should be listed in written directives concerning criminal investigations:[1]

Departments of motor vehicles
City directories, particularly street-address directories (increasingly rare in recent years)
Probation and parole offices
Public welfare and social service agencies
Attorney general's office
Court records—criminal, juvenile, civil, and probate proceedings
County assessors' and recorders' offices
Boards of elections
Coroners' offices
Boards of education and schools
Bureaus of vital statistics
Licensing bureaus
United States Postal Service
United States Immigration and Naturalization Service
United States Coast Guard
United States Drug Enforcement Administration

---

[1]Charles G. Vanderbosch, *Criminal Investigation*, International Association of Chiefs of Police, Washington, D.C., 1968, pp. 13–16.

United States Internal Revenue Service and the Alcohol, Tobacco, and Firearms Division
Federal Bureau of Investigation
Social Security Administration

The number of private organizations and businesses capable of providing information are as numerous as the investigator will permit them to be. Almost any business transaction or credit investigation can become a valuable resource. The following sources have frequently been used by investigators:

Telephone directories. (Each vehicle in the department should carry a telephone book plus—if available—the telephone company's street-address directory.)
Telephone-company records and transactions.
Utility companies.
Bonding companies.
Commercial credit agencies.
Insurance companies.
National Auto Theft Bureau.
National Board of Fire Underwriters.
Churches and parish houses.
Banks and local companies.
Transportation agencies.
Laundry and dry-cleaning establishments.
Small business enterprises.
Union hiring halls.

Truant Contact   An investigative technique which has been proved to be particularly effective against juvenile offenders is a series of frequent contacts made by police with truants or, in the case of youths who are no longer in school, with those who are likely suspects for offenses frequently committed by youths, such as auto theft, theft of auto accessories, residence burglaries, and theft of citizens'-band radios.

In a very successful program adopted in Virginia Beach, Virginia, investigators receive daily listings of truants from school each morning, and during the course of their assignments they make the rounds of the homes and haunts of the truants with the express purpose of asking about their possible involvement in neighborhood offenses or their knowledge of responsibility on the part of others.

The truant-contact program in Virginia Beach, together with an emphasis on identification of youthful burglars, has resulted in a lower burglary incidence and a high clearance rate.

Establishing the Elements of the Crime   As simple as the idea may seem, many of the difficulties which arise in criminal investigation today are caused

CRIMINAL INVESTIGATION 379

by inattention to the elements of criminal offenses and the failure to realize that each of the elements must be established and proved before a conviction can take place. Part of the solution, of course, is in the proper training of investigators so that they are aware of the legal requirement for proof. This must be coupled with sufficient instruction in terms of operating procedure. The police executive should be certain that some of the existing aids in the establishment of proof are used, such as examination by the report-review officer, including a comparison of the report against a brief checklist which has been developed for a specific type of crime. Another excellent device is the use of the prosecution case summary, a form which requires the investigator to list briefly the elements of the offense and the evidence which is available to establish proof for each of these elements.

Use of Informants   The administrator must facilitate the use of informants by giving investigators sufficient funds to pay informers and by making it possible for them to preserve the confidential relationships which must exist between informers and investigators. A special investigation fund should be a part of any police budget in cities having a formalized investigative function. Use of such funds should be accepted as a normal operating practice, and with proper control the administrator may assure himself of reasonably secure operations. The system should require the investigator to complete a voucher for each payment, listing the date, amount, and code name or number of the informant. The voucher forms and cash should be kept in a locked safe, accessible only to an investigator or supervisor and the chief himself. To preserve the confidential nature of information provided by informants, each investigator should be required to keep the coding information in a separate location which is secure and accessible only to himself.

INVESTIGATIVE PROCEDURES

Giving specific advice for the investigation of various kinds of offenses is beyond the scope of this text. However, the administrator and student of police management should be aware of some of the proper concepts related to investigative procedures.

For convenience, investigative procedures described in this text are grouped into three general categories: *crimes against persons, crimes against property*, and *general assignment*. These categories are defined on the following pages.

The police executive must make certain that each of these areas gets sufficient attention in the in-service training program and that there is guidance in the form of standard operating procedures or instructional material covering these broad categories at least. Finally, the administrator should make sure that the formal inspection process, if it exists, covers these areas in the inspection of the investigative process.

Crimes against Persons Usually a crime against a person involves some form of communication or visual contact between the victim and the offender (a factor which is *not* generally present in crimes against property). For this reason, there should be careful interviewing of victims and witnesses in such crimes since it may be the only possible means for linking the offender to the crime. Instructions to investigators should emphasize the value of systematic and patient interviewing to elicit a proper description. Investigators should be supplied with extensive physical-description checklists and other aids, such as devices for constructing composite photos of suspects and the use of police artists.

A second key factor in the crime against a person is the use of photo files such as the "mug book" and identification photos filed by type of offender or crime classification. Investigators should be cautioned against some of the pitfalls in the use of photos, such as avoiding exposure of photographs to victims if there are suspects already in custody.

The lineup is an indispensable part of investigations of crimes against persons. When properly carried out, selection of a suspect from a lineup is often the key evidence in a successful prosecution. The administrator should be certain that the facilities for conducting lineups are adequate (for example, that there is no possibility of witness-suspect contact, that the light level at the scene of the crime can be approximated in the lineup, and that security for the identity of the witness is maintained).

In crimes against persons, such as robbery or indecent exposure, the use of the stakeout and fixed surveillance are essential techniques. At times police can lose sight of the economy involved in certain investigative procedures. For example, some departments have been known to spend countless hours in follow-up investigations in the pursuit of leads that may or may not be productive—such as in the investigation of a series of armed robberies of liquor stores—and yet not realize that the same level of manpower, if stationed inside these same stores, would absolutely prevent all such crimes during the course of the stakeout, with a very good likelihood of making arrests in the process. Somewhat related to this is the concept of saturation stakeouts for the purpose of arresting offenders engaged in a crime spree. For example, if there are repeated nighttime robberies of gas stations, such as five per night in a city with only 40 gas stations operating at night, it would be perfectly logical and justifiable to assign officers to the 40 gas stations with the probable assurance that arrests would be made in five cases. A series of arrests of this sort can have an astounding effect on the crime rate; as every experienced investigator knows, a "crime wave" can be carried out by just one or two offenders.

A significant aspect of crimes-against-persons investigations is that of alerting the public, particularly potential victims, when a crime pattern is known. To relate this to a specific situation, such as a series of gas-station holdups, patrol officers and investigators should visit service-station personnel to alert them as to descriptions of suspects and their vehicles and to give them instruction on safety precautions, the level of cash to be kept in registers, and

CRIMINAL INVESTIGATION

so on. At times (even though there is a risk of generating crime hysteria), it is a good idea to publicize a notorious crime pattern through the press or broadcast media. The method of handling information of this sort by police has a great deal to do with the amount of hysteria generated. If information is presented in a calm and reassuring manner, the public can accept alerts of this sort almost as if they were an everyday occurrence.

Crimes against Property In this category of offense, investigators should give careful attention to the identification of stolen property. The records system of the department (as well as regional and state identification systems) should make it possible to establish identification of stolen property and retrieve it if there is a serial or social security number, if the property is valuable, or if there are distinctive markings. The file search is therefore very productive, particularly if there is adequate description of the property.

Most solutions of crimes against property hinge on the ability to recognize physical evidence and on the adequate search of crime scenes. As indicated earlier, departmental procedures should require crime-scene searches in some formal way for most categories of offenses. For example, the dusting of recovered autos should be carried out routinely—partly because it often discloses valuable fingerprint evidence and partly because it has a deterrent value when persons in the neighborhood of the recovery see investigators or evidence technicians examining portions of the car for latent fingerprints.

The routine crime-scene search helps cultivate an appreciation for the value of physical evidence. Just the fact that such searches are carried out is sometimes a stimulus to greater learning by officers, evidence technicians, and investigators. If sufficient numbers of officers are trained as technicians, a sense of competition and discovery will also develop. Training is obviously important in this area. If common sense does not indicate to an investigator that the sheared ends of electrical wires, cut off in the theft of an electrical appliance, invariably have striation markings from the tool used to cut the wires, then training is needed and will serve the police purpose.

An essential part of crimes-against-property investigations is establishing rapport with potential outlets for stolen property, such as pawnshops, junkyards, secondhand stores, and antique shops. The administrator should make sure that the investigators spend sufficient time with the proprietors of these businesses, either in the control of uncooperative owners or employees through constant attention or through the cultivation of their cooperation if they are responsible citizens.

There is a growing recognition of the need to eliminate fencing of stolen property as a major step in crime reduction. Fences encourage crime, and in their absence the thief has no easy way to sell stolen property. Unfortunately, many otherwise law-abiding citizens patronize fences. For this reason, crime-reduction programs should stress the recognition of fencing and the undesirability of the practice.

To illustrate the willingness of the public to buy "hot" property, the police in Portland, Oregon, recently initiated a program to sell unidentified recovered property to citizens who were only too willing to believe the merchandise had been stolen. The resulting publicity had a definite positive influence on the attitude of the public.

In one of the most imaginative police undercover operations ever conducted, police and the FBI in Washington, D.C., recently established a large fencing operation in which the officers posed as organized-crime figures. Hundreds of suspects brought in stolen merchandise in great quantities, which the undercover operators purchased without question. Unknown to the offenders, concealed cameras recorded all transactions over a period of months, resulting in the positive identification of most of the suspects. To bring the operation to a close, the officers brashly invited all their criminal clientele to a party to express gratitude for the business. When the "guests" arrived, they were quietly arrested and transported away from the location by means of a hidden exit in the rear of the building.

Auto theft deserves special recognition as a crime against property because it is a crime which is committed so overwhelmingly by youthful offenders. The crime can generally be divided into two categories—theft for the purpose of stripping a vehicle for its engine or other valuable parts and theft for temporary joyriding or simple transportation. Regardless of the motive, auto theft accounts for a staggering loss to the economy. A demolished new automobile worth $5,000 is obviously a greater strain on the economy than a $20 no-account check or a $200 liquor-store robbery. In terms of life, accidents related to stolen-car joyrides take far more lives—not only of guilty drivers but also of innocent victims who may be in or outside the stolen vehicle—than murders committed during armed robberies.

Investigative procedures relating to auto theft should stress close scrutiny of possible suspects by the patrol force; public education to prevent people from leaving keys in a car, leaving cars unlocked, and so on; and constant surveillance of potential locations for stripping vehicles, such as garages of known offenders and remote or rural areas where stripping and dumping of cars are common.

Many other investigative procedures could be discussed in connection with crimes against property, but the administrator should be aware, at least, of the need for proper supervision and training in the areas which have been indicated.

The General-Assignment Grouping In larger departments there is a need to assign certain kinds of cases to investigators who may work on a variety of cases. Examples of offenses in this grouping are check cases, credit-card frauds, the acquisition of money or property by false pretenses, embezzlement, arson, and other cases not readily classifiable into the crimes-against-persons or crimes-against-property category.

Crimes involving abuse of credit cards are reaching epidemic proportions. This relatively new crime is made possible by the great expansion of credit-

CRIMINAL INVESTIGATION

card purchasing and the unsolicited mailing of hundreds of thousands of cards to potential customers, with the result that many of the cards are diverted to criminal use.

The credit-card crime is very often solved if the offender takes too many chances, such as using the card for the wrong kind of purchase (buying identifiable or traceable merchandise), or persists in a credit-card spree over a long period of time, thus allowing evidence to accumulate. Since the majority of firms in the credit-card business have a stake in the security of their operations, the police have been receiving help in the recovery of property by investigators who work directly for the major corporations. These companies are also willing to assist in the preparation of crime-prevention material and programs designed to curb credit-card theft and fraud.

Chapter 19

Organized-Crime and Vice Control

Violations of morals laws constitute a particularly difficult problem for the police. Vice offenses such as prostitution and gambling are characterized by the absence of direct harm to anyone except the willing participants, although in some cases the family and associates are indirectly injured. Many citizens and some public officials believe, therefore, that even though participants are weak individuals who cannot control their inclinations, they should be free to indulge in their vices in spite of injury to their health, the dissipation of their property, or the destruction of their own lives so that persons with stronger wills may continue to enjoy the freedom to participate in vice activities without apparent harm to themselves.

Modern society, however, has developed the philosophy that the strong must help the weak by protecting them from their own folly. This belief is deeply ingrained in our culture, and morals laws have been enacted to shield the weak from their own lack of good judgment. Vice, if not controlled, becomes a nuisance, and except in the case of gambling, the health of the participant is often jeopardized as well. The dissipation of money, the damage to physical and emotional health, the injury to the family, and other social evils that result from vice further justify morals legislation.

Successful enforcement of laws in the field of vice control is dependent on

384

public opinion. The public must be educated to the evils of vice and to the advantages of its control if regulation is to be successful. It is particularly important that citizens be made aware of the direct association of organized crime with the violations of morals laws and, through the exploitation of the attitudes of complacency or resistance on the part of the public toward vice enforcement, the loss of billions of dollars to the economy as well as injury to countless victims and participants.

THE IMPLICATIONS OF ORGANIZED CRIME AND VICE

Vice activities existing in a large city are often the result of—or under the control of—a group of individuals who operate as a syndicate. Profits from these activities are concentrated largely in gambling, the sale of narcotics, prostitution, illegal alcohol sale, and loan sharking.

Organized crime is the combination of two or more persons for the purpose of establishing, in a geographic area, a monopoly or virtual monopoly in a criminal activity of a type that provides a continuing financial profit, using gangster techniques and corruption to accomplish their aim. The simple two-party violation of morals laws is rare indeed. There is almost always in the background a third party, who shares in the profits but does not openly and actively participate in the operation. It is the third-party profit that makes vice so difficult to control; very often the profit is made in what appears to be a legitimate business transaction that provides immunity to prosecution by law enforcement officers. As a rule, the third-party profit goes into the coffers of organized criminals.

For organized crime to become entrenched in any community, two factors are necessary: (1) protection from police interference or police interference rendered innocuous by court dismissals and indifferent prosecutions and (2) monopolistic control of a criminal activity. The first of these conditions presupposes corruption of public officials, and the second requires the elimination of competition or intruders by killing or threats of violence. It is only because of the tremendous illegal profits that organized crime is possible; otherwise, public officials could not be easily corrupted, and the risk of killing and being killed would not be justified.

These huge and continuing criminal profits are found in gambling, prostitution, narcotics, the illegal sale of liquor, and loan sharking. Organized crime seldom concerns itself with other criminal activities, such as robbery, theft, and fraud, because the profits are neither large nor continuing and because monopolistic control cannot be established over criminal operations not conducted in an established location. Vice profits, when permitted in any community, are an open invitation to the gangster to organize the criminal activity in order to ensure continuing and still greater profits.

Organized crime becomes a significant problem in a community only through some form of corruption of public officials (or, at the very least, as a result of massive indifference on their part), and once entrenched, great efforts are required to remove it. Police attempts to eliminate organized vice operations meet strong resistance; in some communities the resistance is more than the police can overcome. In no community can the police satisfactorily control vice without strong public support. All citizens have the responsibility to see that their communities are free from commercialized vice because only then can they be certain that their government is free from corruption.

The crime commission and the intelligence unit of the police department can do much to help eradicate vice and loosen the hold of organized crime, but their work will be hampered unless it is understood by the public. It is necessary to bring to the realization of all citizens the true scope of the operations which are cheating the public of billions of dollars each year. The police department should release names, occupations, and relationships of known syndicate members and should enlist the help of the local press in exposing their activities. The police speakers' bureau can be supplied with information regarding actual amounts of money gained illegally and with the histories of known or convicted organized criminals. The public information division can supply civic associations, churches, and other groups with the titles of authenticated but popularized magazine accounts of organized crime. Many of these articles are reprinted and are available to the public at small cost. Any means of communicating the seriousness of this problem should be used, and new methods of bringing it before the public consciousness should be continually sought.

Ramifications of Organized Crime Organized crime does not stop with vice operations in such obvious locations as houses of prostitution, massage parlors, and gambling houses; it reaches out to embrace businesses, labor unions, food and produce markets, restaurant and hotel suppliers, many phases of the entertainment industry, and, in fact, any kind of endeavor in which profits are to be made. Organized criminals, however, are at least as sophisticated as the general public, and their techniques of operation have changed as the investigations of federal and local law enforcement agencies have revealed their depredations. Organized-crime operators have learned to avoid violent crimes and kidnappings because these arouse the public as well as the police. They and their families seek respectability and frequently establish their homes in fashionable suburban areas—a far cry from the old hotel hideout of gangster lore. Leaders in organized crime now buy controlling interests in legitimate businesses and use these enterprises as the coverup for their vice operations. They engage also in businesses or industries in which labor unions have been, or can be, corrupted.

It is no simple matter for the police to cope with the operations of criminal syndicates thus hidden behind a legitimate screen, but when it is remembered that the profits that make it possible to take control of such businesses come largely from vice operations, it seems obvious that one method of attack is to take the profits out of vice—in fact, this is the only method so far successful in eradicating organized crime.

ORGANIZED-CRIME AND VICE CONTROL

Vice and Criminal Activities Another primary police interest in vice control results from the close connection between vice and nonorganized criminal activities. Vice operations facilitate these activities and contribute to the development of criminality; they attract criminals whose emotional instability, lack of family ties, and weakness of character cause them to seek recreation and relief from reality in vice indulgences. Because criminals are important customers, vice operators frequently aid them through fencing stolen property, hiding them from the police, and planning their depredations. Criminals and vice operators feel a kindred relationship because of the illegality of their activities. Avenues of control which permit vice operations in violation of the law are useful to other criminals in thwarting the administration of justice.

Vice operations create other problems not directly associated with major criminal activity. Areas that contain vice establishments are difficult to police because of frequent fights and other disturbances of the peace; a person under the influence of liquor is less amenable to reason and frequently creates situations calling for police action. Narcotics addicts must resort to illegal sources of revenue to secure sufficient income to meet their needs. Gambling losses sometimes result in embezzlement, theft, and suicide. Loan sharking, with the typical "6 for 5" loan (i.e., $6 to be paid off for every $5 dollars loaned, per week) results in enormous profits at this extremely high 20 percent interest rate, compounded weekly. The loan-shark victim often may resort to other crime to pay off a loan, and, failing this, may be threatened, beaten, or murdered.

Social Problems of Vice Vice involves varied social problems having moral, health, economic, and criminal aspects. Their solution requires (1) education through the family, the school, the church, and the community; (2) health-control measures, which are the responsibility of the public health agencies; (3) economic assistance and welfare programs, a problem for social work agencies; and (4) law enforcement, a function of the police and the rest of the criminal justice system. Each of these elements has a part to play in combating the effects of vice, but not any one of them is created specifically for this purpose, and all have other interests that occupy their major attention.

POLICE CONTROL OF VICE

The police department is the only agency that has as one of its primary tasks the control of commercialized vice. Police control is intended to lessen or eliminate health, economic, and crime hazards, and as long as these hazards remain an integral part of vice, police participation in its regulation must continue.

The police should base their regulation of vice on law rather than on moral precepts. Otherwise, those persons with a contrary viewpoint will consider them reformers, and, in addition, the police may be prone to enter upon sporadic crusades rather than deal with the problem unemotionally and rationally.

Police control of vice is made difficult by the diversity of opinion among citizens about the nature and extent of regulation that should be applied.

Influences for Lax Control   Respectable business people may legitimately participate in vice profits by renting property and providing needed services; since the vice operator may be a valuable customer, business people are sometimes willing to use their influence to protect the vice operator's activities. Vice operators are willing to share their large profits to ensure a continuance of their income, and persons who exercise some influence over the police are sometimes willing to accept the windfall. Customer participants may also exert pressure so that their vices may be indulged. Some business groups, such as retail merchants, restaurant owners, and hotel proprietors, may consider laxity in vice control essential for prosperity and business development. Others who have no personal or monetary interest may oppose regulation on the grounds that it is an infringement of personal liberty contrary to the best interests of society. The restriction on personal freedom involved in vice control arouses the emotions of some people, just as any restriction on freedom of religion, politics, and speech does, and consequently a well-balanced view is seldom taken.

Persons who oppose strict enforcement of vice laws frequently make no determined effort to repeal existing laws but attempt to gain their objective by putting pressure on the police or on the local governing board to relax police control. For example, police participation in vice control may be lessened simply by reducing the size of the vice-control unit, by cutting off essential undercover funds, or by licensing apparently legal undertakings, such as coin-operated machines of a great variety, cardrooms, and massage parlors, any of which may be put to illegal use if police vigilance is lessened. A similar method is to strip the police of their control over the issuance and revocation of licenses to such places and activities and to vest this authority in officials who have no responsibility for the enforcement of vice and crime laws. Other influences that may be brought to bear on the police to effect a relaxation of their control include ridicule by the local press and suggestions and sometimes orders from the executive head of the city, individual members of the governing board, and influential citizens of the community.

The fact that there always has been vice and always will be as long as human beings are human is often used as an argument for nonenforcement or repeal of morals legislation. If this argument were valid, however, one would have to contend that laws which prohibit theft and murder should be repealed and that the police should make no effort to apprehend thieves and murderers because there always have been and always will be such criminals.

Influences for Strict Control   In opposition to these groups is the so-called reform element, which thinks that the police can and should completely

ORGANIZED-CRIME AND VICE CONTROL

eradicate all forms of vice, even though they cannot eliminate stealing, traffic violations, and other offenses. A public that takes crimes against persons and property in its stride should not be overcritical of morals offenses. Every community of any size has some burglars and thieves, and it is reasonable to believe that it will also have some gambling operators and prostitutes and many customers for both. The police cannot drive out every vice offender any more than they can drive out every thief. The elements that stand for rigid control, however, can be very powerful and frequently are very articulate in their protests against vice, and unless properly channeled, their efforts and energies may create a weapon against the whole administration of the police department.

Police Stand on Vice Control   The police are often caught between these two opposing groups and find themselves with the active support of only a small minority who are able to view the situation objectively and rationally. There is no simple rule to guide chiefs in formulating vice-control policy, and consequently a high order of administrative judgment is required. They should not join either of the two opposing elements because the interests of one are illegal and contrary to the public good and the goal of the other is impossible to attain. Police chiefs must map a course of action predicated on what resources are available to them, on what is legal, on what is best for the community, and on what the public desires.

A sound stand for the police is to treat vice offenses as they would any law violation and to do their best to eliminate them, just as they attempt to eliminate burglary, robbery, and speeding. As long as the police are charged with the enforcement of vice laws, they have no alternative but to impose such regulation or prohibition as may be required by law. Public attitude, however, influences in a subtle way the degree of enforcement. In some communities, for example, drunks may not be arrested at all or only if they are totally incapacitated, whereas in others, persons with the smell of liquor on their breath and showing only the slightest signs of inebriation are jailed. The proportion of police effort to be directed into the several fields of police control is a matter of administrative judgment, based in part on the interpretation of public opinion. If all police effort were devoted to vice control, there would still be some vice, just as there would be some accidents even though all police effort were devoted to traffic control. Since police manpower is limited, it should be directed into the several fields in proportion to need, which is influenced somewhat by the wishes of the community. A community that is extremely traffic-conscious justifies greater police attention to traffic control, and a community that is intolerant of commercialized vice justifies a greater proportion of police effort in that field.

However, there can be no compromise with vice any more than there can be compromise with other crime. Variations in enforcement pressure to meet variations in public opinion should be made by increasing or decreasing the time officers may devote to vice control, not by countenancing violations.

390   OPERATIONS

Officers assigned to the vice-control unit must make no concessions, and their best efforts must be directed toward carrying out the policy of strict enforcement, even though the number applying the enforcement may be varied.

Commercialized Vice First attention should be given to commercialized vice. The third-party profit magnifies its evils because it prompts operators to increase the volume of business through stimulating desire for more vice activity, thus multiplying the social problems related to it. The public will generally favor the prosecution of higher-level vice operators who exploit the weaknesses of other people. As their profits decrease because of continual police attack, these operators become less well entrenched in the community.

Some of the evil of overt vice activities stems from the creation of temptation for the susceptible. Police effort to suppress vice activities drives them under cover, where they are less obvious to those who favor rigid enforcement and less tempting to the weak. For these reasons, the police are well-advised to direct their attention to the most flagrant and evident violations.

The policy of giving first attention to commercialized vice recognizes the sanctity of the home and the private life of the citizen and the desirability of dealing with the most important things first. The police should direct their attention to the most serious offenses rather than dissipate their energy in ferreting out noncommercial violations, especially those which take place in private homes. The police cannot condone noncommercial vice, however; they have no alternative but to take appropriate action against flagrant violations.

The police are justified in grouping the enforcement of laws relating to narcotics, liquor, gambling, and prostitution because vice violations have the previously mentioned characteristics in common. These laws have a moral aspect and are frequently unpopular; often their violations are continuing offenses in both time and place; and large profits are provided to a third party, the gangster, who promotes official corruption and establishes a monopoly through terror. Techniques dissimilar to those used in crime investigations are needed in the investigation of vice activities. (An understanding of the four major vice operations is helpful in their control, and a description of each will be found later in this chapter.) Prostitution, Gambling, Narcotics, and Liquor Law Violations.

The Crime Commission

The police alone are powerless in many communities to resist the tremendous forces arrayed against them in the field of organized crime and vice. Only an aroused public can ensure the removal of these forces. In large cities it is imperative that the community be organized to assist its law enforcement officials. A crime commission or criminal justice commission can serve as a powerful ally to progressive police administrators.

Functions of the Crime Commission A high crime rate in any community may be evidence of a failure or deficiency in the policies or procedures used by the police, the courts, or the prosecutors, and these policies and procedures should be studied and made a matter of record. A low rate of clearance by

ORGANIZED-CRIME AND VICE CONTROL 391

arrest and recovery of stolen property, a small percentage of convictions, an unusual number of continuances of cases, abuse of bail privileges, unreasonable elapsed time in the disposition of criminal cases, unjustified reduction of charges, a disproportionate number of pleas of guilt to minor charges by persons originally held for more serious offenses (plea bargaining), perversion of probation, and misuse of licensing power by failure to deny licenses and to revoke them when appropriate—all these are matters of concern to the crime commission. They are indications of conditions which, though not perhaps immediately discernible, may be rooted in a widespread and serious corrupt alliance between public officials and the leaders of organized crime.

The crime commission should observe and work with the agencies concerned and attempt to overcome weaknesses in the administration of criminal justice. In cooperation with the interested agencies, it should also propose legislative changes that may be necessary to eliminate abuses that cannot otherwise be corrected.

The crime commission should conduct public hearings on various issues in the criminal justice field and should keep the public informed on its findings. Some commissions use citizen surveys and questionnaires to good advantage. But the major role of the commission is often the public disclosure of the true relationship between organized crime and vice and of the unlawful activities of persons attempting to establish monopolies in their various fields by corruption and terrorism.

Organization of the Crime Commission The advantages of community-wide interest in the crime commission should not be discounted, but there is a special situation in the membership policy of a crime commission that distinguishes this group from other community organizations. It is particularly important that no one who holds an elective or appointive political office related in any way to the administration of criminal justice be allowed to become a member, and, of course, all applicants for membership should be screened by the appointing body to rule out those who may have business associations with organized criminals.

Funding of the work of the commission is often done through appropriations made by the city council, but some commissions generate their own funds through public donations. If nongovernmental funding is permitted, no financial contribution should be accepted if there is any question of its having come from an individual or group which might wish to influence the commission or divert its attention from its principal objective. On the other hand, the crime commission's work requires considerable and continuous publicity; solicitation of numerous small contributions can assist in publicizing the work of the commission, but in general it must rely on a budget which is stable and large enough to permit the publication and free distribution of its findings.[1]

---

[1]Virgil W. Peterson, "How to Form a Citizens Crime Commission," reprinted from the *Journal of Criminal Law, Criminology, and Police Science*, vol. 46, no. 4, November–December 1955.

The composition of the crime commission itself may vary from place to place, but its officers and board of directors and its membership should be composed of people with extensive experience in civic affairs, social welfare, education, health, and business. In commissions with large memberships, an executive committee may be established to work closely with an executive or operating director. The latter must be so qualified that the executive committee may rely upon him to carry out the policies of the commission without recourse to emergency meetings. The executive or operating director should be alert, active, and personable, with a good educational background. While not essential, it is desirable that he be well known in the community and experienced in the activity of the organization.

Leadership in the creation and operation of crime commissions frequently comes from outside the official agencies that have important responsibilities in this field. Although they should not hold membership in crime commissions, police administrators should actively support the crime commission in their community.

ORGANIZATION AND ADMINISTRATION OF VICE-CONTROL AND INTELLIGENCE FUNCTIONS

Vice-control and intelligence units deal with operational information relating to organized crime, persons engaged in narcotics traffic, and other vice offenses and not with management information or matters relating to internal control. However, because of the close relationship to internal investigation and because of the covert nature of the work in many cases, vice control is sometimes placed within the structure of an inspectional services bureau. In some cases, if members of the department are involved in vice activity themselves, the close association between vice control and internal investigations is warranted. Finally, the vice and intelligence units can sometimes serve in a staff role in that they are able to review and analyze vice-control efforts by the patrol force. In effect, this gives them some of the responsibility of the inspectional services function.

The Vice-Control Function

In some agencies, there is a need to keep the vice-control function directly under the supervision of the chief of police. In other departments, there is ample justification for placing vice control within the inspectional services grouping.

Relationship of the Vice-Control Division to Other Units Beat officers should always be held accountable for suppression of commercialized vice in their areas, even though responsibility for vice enforcement may be shared with the central vice-control unit. In a department without district stations, a vice division will assist beat officers in the performance of this duty. In addition, the vice division will take aggressive action on its own against

ORGANIZED-CRIME AND VICE CONTROL

operations that are beyond the capacities of beat officers or are ignored by the patrol division. The vice-division commander will inform the chief when he discovers neglect by a beat officer or any evidence of collusion with vice operators. In departments with district stations or under district team policing, district commanders are responsible for the suppression of vice operations; they will have helping them their beat officers, supplemented by officers working in plain clothes as vice officers. The latter are comparable to the vice unit in the smaller department.

Heads of departments with district stations must have machinery to keep them informed of vice conditions on a citywide basis, just as chiefs of smaller departments do. A central vice unit reporting directly to the head of the large department, or to one of his deputies, will perform this service. In addition, it will assist district commanders at their request when they are confronted with a vice operation that is beyond their resources; it will also ferret out vice operations which are not yet discovered or which are ignored by the district command.

The relationship between the central vice unit and the district commanders should be made clear. The basic responsibility for eliminating vice operations lies with the district commanders and with the patrol officer on the beat. The central vice unit should have the following functions: (1) to provide staff supervision of the department's efforts toward the elimination of organized crime and vice by encouraging the interest and activity of district personnel, (2) to assist district commanders in the discharge of their responsibilities by providing them with advice and manpower or by assuming responsibility for dealing with a situation, (3) to discover and take suitable action against violations not detected by district commanders, and (4) to submit to the chief and to the intelligence unit information of interest to them.

Selection of Vice-Control Officers Most vice-control officers should be assigned on a permanent basis and not on a short-period plan of service if effective operation is the sole consideration. Occasionally, recruit officers are used in an undercover operation in the vice-control unit for brief periods, but in most of these situations, the new officers are returned to general duties after completion of their work in the vice unit. Continuity of service promotes increased efficiency because the officers become more skilled, develop more contacts, and have available the services of a larger number of undercover operators. However, it should be remembered that a certain amount of temptation is placed in the way of an officer on a vice assignment, and appointments on a permanent basis must be accompanied by some form of administrative check to ensure that an officer does not succumb to it.

Vice control is sometimes considered undesirable police work, and consideration should be given to the interest and desire of the officers. A permanently assigned officer who is interested in vice control is more likely to do a thorough job than one who is temporarily assigned or lacks interest in the work. Vice assignments frequently have promotional limitations because of the size of the division and the specialized nature of the job. If an officer with good promotional potential is assigned, the administrator should be alert for indications of "peaking out," frustration, and other signs that the nature of the work is affecting the incumbent.

Problems Confronting the Vice-Division Head A newly appointed and aggressive head of the vice division in a community where vice operations have not been effectively suppressed is confronted with a difficult situation. The previously described relationship between commercialized vice and organized crime places this individual in a vulnerable position; the reputation of the department and of the chief are also in jeopardy. Organized crime will usually have gained a foothold in such a community, and the vice head must then deal with highly motivated criminals, who are often supplied with large sums of money to fight all attempts by the police to restrict their lucrative, illicit enterprises. The vice-division head must realize that every effort may be made to discredit him in an attempt to effect his removal from his important post. He should evaluate these hazards and scrutinize procedures and activities that may offer vice operators an opportunity to embarrass him or his officers. The vice-division head and his subordinates are under greater pressure than other members of the force, and they must therefore be most circumspect in their behavior. They must avoid not only misconduct but even the appearance of misconduct; they must also avoid situations that may permit a frame-up by being constantly on the alert so as not to step inadvertently into a plot to incriminate them on false evidence. A system of disbursement and accounting for expenditures of undercover funds that will protect members of the vice division against charges of misuse of this money is essential. Many departments use a system of daily auditing of the undercover fund so that at the end of the time of duty the totals for all individual vouchers (each of which shows the date, the officer's name, the amount, and a coded name or number for the informant) are compared with previous balances and double-checked by a supervisor.

The dismissal of cases and the release of persons charged with vice violations should be avoided when possible or, when absolutely necessary, should be carried out with circumspection when the police purpose is best served by the dismissal of a relatively minor case in return for valuable evidence against more important vice operators. Otherwise, the dismissal may be used as the basis for discrediting the vice division on the grounds that the case was fixed. Any action that may result in the loss of a conviction in court, such as ill-advised statements made by officers either on or off the witness stand, must likewise be guarded against.

Greater-than-ordinary precautions should be taken in handling vice evidence because its loss usually results in the dismissal of a case, and the loss of the evidence by the police is usually interpreted by the public as proof of connivance between the police and the defendant. The seriousness of the consequences warrants a continuous review of the procedures for handling

ORGANIZED-CRIME AND VICE CONTROL

evidence. Vice evidence (except the most bulky sort, such as furniture, which is less likely to be lost) should be stored in a suitable vault under the exclusive control of the head of the vice division.

Raids rendered unsuccessful because of tip-offs are also frequently used to discredit the police, and vice operators will attempt to make it appear that the tip-off was received from the vice division.

Vice-division members must also guard against being forced into ill-advised action against minor, noncommercial violators that may arouse public indignation; raids on places of worship, homes, and privately occupied hotel rooms not used for commercial purposes are examples.

When in doubt about the wisdom of taking action or about the proper timing, the vice-division head should confer with the chief. He should not do so in reference to routine matters, however, because it is unnecessary to burden the chief with such matters until they have become faits accomplis. The wise chief will prefer not to have this information in advance, in order not to become involved in the event of a real or apparent tip-off.

Patrol Responsibility in Vice Control The evils of specialization and the dangers involved in granting exclusive management of vice control to a small unit should be considered in establishing relationships between the vice division and the other operating units of the department. Specialization is undesirable when flagrant vice operations are consequently ignored by other members of the department. Vice control, therefore, should not be the exclusive jurisdiction of the vice division but should be shared by the other divisions and especially by the patrol division.

Patrol participation in vice control reduces the number of officers needed in the vice-control unit, increases its efficiency, conserves the time and energy of its members, and enables it to focus attention on the more important violations, the higher-ups, and the well-organized violators whose roots are so deeply entrenched that their successful prosecution is impossible except after intensive investigation. The patrol officer may make a substantial contribution to vice enforcement in a number of ways: (1) by making frequent but irregular inspections of licensed establishments and other vice hazards; (2) by discovering and eliminating the more apparent vice violations, thus quickly correcting conditions distasteful to the public; (3) by investigating and disposing of the less serious vice complaints; and (4) by informing the vice-control unit of conditions that the officer cannot cope with alone and of the existence and location of important vice operators in the beat, furnishing facts that may be useful in further investigation or in planning a raid. Department regulations should require patrol officers to obtain the approval of their commanding officers before obtaining a search warrant or conducting a raid.

The vice and patrol divisions should have a joint responsibility for vice conditions, and both should be held accountable. This sharing of responsibility reduces the likelihood of graft because it is then impossible for one of the divisions to grant protection to vice operators, and the large number of officers involved diminishes the possibility of corruption. The existence of a vice-control division should not excuse the patrol division for failure to eradicate vice conditions; and, on the other hand, the vice division should not offer, in defense of its failure to eliminate vice activities, the fact that the responsibility belongs to the patrol division.

Utilizing Other Law Enforcement Facilities   Vice-control units should cultivate information sources and other resources of state and federal agencies, and they should also utilize all the resources of the local department. A close relationship with the members of the other divisions provides information sources and other assistance to the vice officers that multiply their effectiveness.

Inspectional Duties   The vice-control unit should investigate liquor- and entertainment-license applicants, approve license applications, and inspect liquor stores and other licensed places of business whose activity frequently creates vice hazards. The patrol division, when wisely utilized, should also carry out complete inspections of licensed establishments and in the process can provide the vice-control unit with information on questionable places. If patrol officers are to be held responsible for conditions on their beats, they must not be denied the privilege of inspecting any place in which they suspect the existence of vice. On the contrary, the frequent inspection of establishments whose business, by its nature, makes them suspect should be a part of patrol officers' regular duties.

The vice-control division commander should require regular and continuing inspection and analysis of police reports related to vice and organized crime. Such a report review assists in directing the efforts of the officers and may reveal districts or individual officers who so infrequently obtain convictions that questions of integrity may be involved. The division commander should keep the chief and the head of the intelligence unit informed of the activities of individuals in organized crime and vice and of deficiencies in the prosecution or adjudication of cases. The vice-division head should be aware of all proposed legislation which may be sponsored by organized-crime elements and should be prepared to work with the planning division in the development of counterproposals and of procedures that may strengthen the prosecution of cases, protect the validity of evidence, and promote the possibility of conviction.

Vice Records   The procedure for handling vice records differs somewhat from the system used for other police operations. Since the need for secrecy sometimes makes it inadvisable to have vice complaints and reports go through the usual records channels, other provisions must be made to ensure that they are accurately recorded and registered and properly followed through. The chief of police, by personal inspection, must make sure that this is being done. Weekly and monthly summaries should be provided so that the chief may be kept informed of vice-division accomplishments.

ORGANIZED-CRIME AND VICE CONTROL

The manner in which complaints and reports of violations are handled is an important factor in the relationship of the vice division and the patrol division. A patrol officer should deliver an investigation report to his commanding officer containing all information regarding vice violations observed by him or received from a citizen. A case is made (but not recorded on the daily bulletin, for reasons of secrecy), and duplicates of both the offense report and the investigation report are sent to the vice division. When a vice complaint has been thoroughly investigated by the patrol officer assigned to it, his commanding officer may permit the disposal of the case in one of three ways: (1) He may discontinue the investigation if the complaint proves unfounded, (2) he may authorize a raid or the arrest of the offender, or (3) he may request assistance from the vice-control unit, with one of the following reasons assigned: (*a*)The facts indicate the existence of a violation on which the patrol officers were unable to secure evidence; (*b*) the patrol officers were unable to ascertain definitely whether a violation exists, and assistance is needed; or (*c*) doubt exists about the advisability of taking action at the present time.

On receipt of a request for assistance, the vice division may (1) advise the patrol command to proceed with its own resources, (2) direct vice-division personnel to work under patrol-division command in order to dispose of the reported incident, or (3) direct vice-division personnel to take command of the operation.

Responsibility of the District Commander   In a city having decentralized operations, the district commander should be responsible for the suppression of vice in his area, and he should be required to eradicate undesirable conditions through the operation of the patrol force, a small number of whom should work in plain clothes as a vice squad. Conditions with which the district commander cannot cope should be reported to the central vice division for assistance or direct action; his only defense for vice operations in his district should be that the problem was beyond the limits of the district's facilities and had been reported to the vice division.

The Intelligence Function

The intelligence function is logically organized as a part of an inspectional services bureau or as a separate unit assigned to the chief of police.

The Intelligence Unit   In all but the small departments, the chief finds it difficult to keep informed about organized-crime conditions in the community except by using an intelligence unit working directly under him or an assistant chief. In the vast majority of medium-sized departments, one individual with adequate undercover funds can provide intelligence service. In large departments and in those in which long-standing unsatisfactory conditions must be dealt with, the unit must be larger. In some cases, on the other hand, the continuous operation of an intelligence unit is unnecessary; a periodic audit of conditions, requiring from one to six months and undertaken biannually or even less frequently, may suffice. In such situations, an out-of-town investigator may prove more useful than a local police officer. Some police chiefs borrow an officer from a department in a distant city for this purpose.

Although the fundamental purpose of intelligence is to keep the chief informed, it cannot be regarded as an isolated function. Like planning, it permeates the entire department, moving up and down and across. Intelligence is needed for the guidance of the chief, the chief's assistants, and the heads of the operating divisions. It must go to, and come from, such units as the vice division, the human relations unit, the labor relations unit, the task force, the planning unit, and the patrol and detective divisions.

The intelligence unit will be concerned primarily with persons engaged in organized crime. It is not the task of this unit to arrest persons guilty of participating in criminal activities, but rather to furnish the chief with the necessary facts so that he may require suitable action from the division which is responsible—unless there is evidence of collusion in that division. The chief should not reveal the source of his information when discussing the situation with the operating personnel. He should invariably demand an explanation for their failure to discover the conditions reported or to take remedial action.

The intelligence unit is concerned with the nature of the criminal organization rather than with its individual criminal acts, and it should establish the identity of all persons who are involved in any way in the ramifications of its operations. Important persons in the community who have excellent reputations for civic virtue may be involved in the net of organized crime, and the chief should know who they are and the nature of their relationships with those engaged in illegal activities. The chief should have similar information regarding those in the community who may be members of secret organizations that threaten the local or national security through subversive activity or espionage. The chief should also know what organizations are devoted to engendering racial hatreds and disturbances and what their programs and plans are. Organization charts and indexes showing connections between the individuals involved are useful guides in planning the work of the unit and in reporting facts to the chief.

Administration of the Intelligence Function   The intelligence unit should be headed by a supervisor in whom the chief has complete confidence. If for any reason it is impossible to assign such a person, it is better not to have the unit. The position should be established without regard to the civil service rank of the incumbent; in a larger department it should carry a suitable salary as an "exempt rank" and a provision permitting the chief to return the incumbent to his former rank if his usefulness becomes impaired. Although in the past it was frequently the practice not to include this unit on the department organization chart, experience has shown that the frank announcement of its existence can provide good public relations results and is a powerful bulwark against attempts at corruption of the police by organized-crime operators. It is not necessary, however, to reveal the names of any personnel except that of the head of a very large unit.

ORGANIZED-CRIME AND VICE CONTROL

It is even more important that the chief be kept informed of the activities of this unit than of the activities of the operating divisions of the department. The delicate nature of the investigations makes it imperative to use caution in reporting to the chief, who may prefer, pending the completion of an investigation, to receive information orally during informal conferences rather than in formal reports, the safeguarding of which would require unusual precautions.

The intelligence unit must of necessity operate secretly and in much the same manner as the central vice unit. They both should be furnished with the necessary number of carefully selected police officers as well as funds to permit the employment of qualified undercover investigators. Disbursement procedures should be established that will afford suitable safeguards both to the chief and to the members of the unit against charges of misuse of funds.

The intelligence unit must also maintain effective security for its files, including the names of informants. Ordinarily the names are coded and are identified in working documents by code name or number.

Assignments of cases should be made by the head of the unit, who should maintain a control device such as 3- by 5-inch tickler or suspense files.

The actual compilation of intelligence information can be improved by developing an extensive "classification and coding sheet," which lists in outline form a series of descriptive words and code numbers. Each separate paragraph of an intelligence report can then be assigned a code number when the report is analyzed. Some departments pursue this idea somewhat further by placing intelligence reports on separate 5- by 8-inch cards, with the code or classification number shown at the top. These cards can be indexed in several ways and filed by classification number in one file and by the names of organizations or of individual participants in a parallel file.

GAMBLING

The diversity of gambling laws in the various jurisdictions makes it difficult to formulate any universal enforcement guide. In one respect gambling may be considered the least serious of the vices. It does no harm to the health, and fewer social evils result from its practice because injury is usually restricted to the individual participant. The moral stigma attached to gambling is less severe than in other forms of vice, as evidenced by the frequency of church participation in lotteries and other games of chance to raise funds. Also, there is no serious economic problem involved as long as people can afford their losses; this, however, is seldom the case for any individual over a long period of time. On the other hand, gambling profits frequently exceed those in the other fields of vice, and consequently gambling offers a lucrative monopoly for organized-crime operators.

The police should give their first attention to the eradication of gambling that is organized and protected in this manner. To do so, they must take the profit out of commercialized gambling. For example, syndicated-crime interests are heavily committed to numbers gambling and sports betting as major sources of income, and without this income, syndicated-crime profits would decline abruptly.

The police chief must employ a high order of administrative judgment in reaching sound decisions in the enforcement of gambling laws. As a guide to enforcement, the seriousness of gambling violations should be judged by their extent, the amount of money involved, the open manner of the violations, and the number of participants.

Commercialized gambling carried on for a money profit per se, as in the case of the numbers racket, bookmaking, policy rackets, slot machines, and games of any sort conducted in gambling establishments, is the most serious and should be dealt with decisively. Gaming devices for trade stimulation, such as bank nights, and other forms of gambling by customers in pool and card games in which the house receives a sum of money for each game played but does not participate in the game itself present special problems to the police; if they are violations of gambling laws, the police cannot condone their operation.

Charity gambling, conducted by churches and by fraternal, social, and other organizations, is a form that proves especially annoying to the police. Various types of lotteries, pools, punchboards, and bingo are the most popular, and it is interesting and ironic to note that even where these games have been legalized, organized criminals frequently manage to gain control over their earnings, not only to the financial detriment of the groups which play but also to the detriment of their integrity. One such group testified before a committee investigating New York's experiment in legalized bingo that, before two years had elapsed following legalization, church and fraternal-society members were falsifying reports of their gains from this source in order to meet the demands of the organized criminals who had succeeded in taking over the operation of the games.[2]

The police chief in a city or state which does not permit legalized forms of gambling for charitable or nonprofit purposes must not condone the activity when it is a violation of the law. He has no authority to suspend a law, and when permission for such games is requested, he must state his policy clearly to avoid possible misunderstanding.

The police should not ordinarily dissipate their limited forces by ferreting out private gambling; action must be taken, however, when it is carried on flagrantly in public. Examples of private noncommercial gambling include bets of every variety between friends, pools made up among a group of friends on athletic and other events, and card games played within the home. Gambling in a private home for profit, however, should be impartially dealt with by the police.

Pinball and slot machines and devices purported to be games of skill or amusement of every variety present difficult enforcement problems. The

[2] "An Investigation of Bingo Operations in New York State," a report by the New York State Commission of Investigation, December 1961. See also "A Report on Chicago Crime for 1961," by Virgil W. Peterson, Operating Director, Chicago Crime Commission, Chicago, pp. 69–74.

ORGANIZED-CRIME AND VICE CONTROL

presence of an automatic payoff, however, is obvious and easy to prosecute in all jurisdictions; obtaining evidence of a payoff from the till is more difficult. Because of the relationship with gang-controlled activities, the possession of such devices has been made illegal in many states.

NARCOTICS AND DANGEROUS DRUGS

The last decade has seen an enormous increase in the use of narcotics and dangerous drugs, particularly among youth, military personnel, and inner-city dwellers. The sale and use of marijuana are endemic; although it may be of consolation to some persons to speculate that the use of marijuana does not lead necessarily to "hard" drugs and that its long-term effect on health may be no more injurious than that of tobacco or alcohol, the sad fact is that use of other, more dangerous drugs such as heroin, LSD, cocaine, amphetamines, and barbiturates has also escalated.

Control of narcotics and dangerous drugs has become a national issue, and without the influence of strong national sentiment by the populace for strict regulation and enforcement, the task of the criminal justice system over the next few decades does indeed seem formidable. This does not mean the police should give up the tremendous responsibility for continuous education and enforcement; on the contrary, it means the police should magnify their efforts. Where once police may have been content to allow a few officers to engage in quiet, undercover enforcement, the entire criminal justice apparatus—with police at the forefront—must concentrate on enforcement of laws regarding dangerous drugs. If the control of a truly perilous narcotic like heroin becomes diminished because of citizen reaction to overzealous police enforcement of laws against the less-dangerous marijuana, the police should not stand in the way of reduced penalties for the latter.

The Heroin Problem Heroin, or diacetylmorphine, is in a class by itself in terms of addictive power, involvement with organized crime and international criminal conspiracies, danger to health, difficulty in effecting a cure, and the tragic loss to society and the economy which is generated by the need for many of its victims to resort to street crime and other antisocial behavior.

John E. Ingersoll, former Director of the Bureau of Narcotics and Dangerous Drugs, has stated the problem very clearly:

> The end result is that the addict population is responsible for increasing numbers of crimes which directly or indirectly affect society at large.
>
> Since many addicts will resort to criminal acts to supply their habits, and considering that stolen merchandise must be fenced at a mere fraction of its actual value, the loss to the business community and private individuals is staggering. Consider also the millions of dollars being expended at the Federal, State and local level for enforcement of the drug statutes and for treatment and rehabilitation of the addicts—money which might otherwise be funneled into a score of badly needed programs, such as environmental pollution, education or urban renewal.

In addition to such economic factors, the social losses are inestimable. The addict is "tuning out" of the community at age when most people are making momentous decisions about jobs, marriage, and future relationships, and moving into the productive years of young adulthood.[3]

Methods of Use   Almost all heroin in the United States is consumed in the form of intravenous injection of diluted strengths of the drug in a water solution. Users may commence the habit through other means, however, such as by subcutaneous injections, by smoking concentrations of the drug mixed with tobacco, or by snuffing. The latter methods are in common use in Southeast Asia, where heroin is cheap, plentiful, and available in nearly pure form. Many United States servicemen in Vietnam became addicted initially through smoking a heroin-tobacco mixture, a method which would not be practical for addicts in the United States.

Heroin in its pure form is a crystalline powder and is reduced in potency, or "cut," many times to provide proper dose strength and to increase the value. Mistakes made when cutting the pure heroin, coupled with crude and dirty apparatus, account for the large number of deaths each year from overdosing and infection. The overdose death rate, in fact, is a reasonably accurate indicator of the number of addicts in an area.

The Means of Control

The relationship between the illegal sale of heroin and the cravings of addicts has produced a condition which calls for strict control by the police. It is the cost of the habit which leads addicts to give up their family responsibilities, their jobs, and even food in order to find more money to meet their needs. They seek to get the money in any way which will give them steady access to the drug, and almost inevitably they must turn to crime because a habit that costs from $50 to $100 a day cannot be supported by a person of average means. As the habit becomes more demanding, addicts will turn to burglary, robbery, petty thefts, prostitution, or any other source of money. They seldom go to the police or public health officials for help or treatment, and even when they do, there is no assurance that they will not soon return to their old ways of life after release.

Narcotics addicts may on occasion be essentially hostile and dangerous persons whose aggressions are set free by the use of drugs, and while under their influence, they may commit vicious assaults or murder. In most instances, however, the real damage to addicts comes from their dependence on the soothing effect they obtain from the use of opium-based narcotics; they withdraw into a stuporous or dreamlike state, become inactive, lose interest in their responsibilities, are unproductive of work, and, until the craving begins

[3]From a statement prepared by John E. Ingersoll in February 1971, based on material from a speech given previously.

ORGANIZED-CRIME AND VICE CONTROL

again, are physically unresponsive. They receive nothing for their pains except escape from reality, and this escape represents a waste in social terms and constitutes a real threat to society.

The primary criminal in these activities in the pusher, who first introduces the addict to the drug, and it is he and his source who should be the primary target of the police. His profit is enormous, and he knows that the addict must return to him or another pusher again and again. He will protect addicts from the police if necessary, in order not to lose them as customers, and he will guide them to criminal activities for the same reason. The pusher is a menace in other ways also, particularly because he will continually seek out new and younger customers or supply those who may voluntarily try drugs for the excitement of a new experience. The pusher is not moved by considerations of innocence or family tragedy—he is interested only in the continuing profit to be made from selling narcotics, and the police are justified in using every legal means to curtail his activities.

The police should assist in getting addicts into treatment and in helping them remain off the drug by eliminating any source of supply which can be identified. School areas, theaters, parks, and other places where adolescents congregate should be special points of observation by the police, in an effort to prevent the spread of narcotics sales.

Researchers in the narcotics-control field have developed reliable tests for the presence of heroin traces in the human system and have conducted experiments in the effectiveness of substitute drugs such as Methadone ®, which alleviates the craving for heroin by substituting an addictive but cheaper narcotic—which may also have less tendency to produce euphoria—in its place.

Biomedical research in the mechanism of physical dependency may be the most promising avenue for success in the long run. If the mechanism can be altered, for example, by some means which would repair and then "insulate" the sensitized tissue which now permits the phenomenon of physical dependence, the problem of addiction could be solved.

In the meantime, control should be concentrated on (1) elimination of the production of opium and its subsequent conversion to heroin, through diplomatic and other channels of influence in Turkey, France, Southeast Asia, Mexico, and other countries where opium is produced or processed; (2) enforcement against smuggling and distribution, particularly against syndicated-crime operations; (3) concerted and unified enforcement activity by the police and courts systems, with enforcement directed not only against higher-level distributors but also against street-level sellers; (4) a massive national educational program singling out heroin specifically as a target; and (5) encouragement of rehabilitative programs designed to keep individual addicts free of the problem.

Administration of Narcotics Units A guide for the staffing and organization of narcotics units, including recommended basic operational policies, is available from the International Association of Chiefs of Police.[4] The brochure was produced at the request of the U.S. Bureau of Narcotics and Dangerous Drugs, the predecessor of the Drug Enforcement Administration.

PROSTITUTION

The two principal factors to be considered by the police in the control of prostitution are crime and disease; a form and degree of control must be provided that will minimize these hazards. Public health officials no longer feel that the most important source of venereal disease (which has been on the increase despite the fact that effective medical control is easily available) lies in direct contacts with prostitutes. However, their case studies indicate that one contact between a prostitute and a youth can lead to the infection of 20 or more other adolescents and adults. The vast majority of these cases result from casual contacts between the adolescents, but the source may reside in the undetected infection of the prostitute. In addition to this danger, the control of commercialized prostitution by organized crime is a continuing problem for the police: criminals are hidden in houses of prostitution, the sale of narcotics is promoted both by and to prostitutes, blackmail and extortion are used against patrols, adolescent girls are seduced into this occupation, and offenses of a sexually pathological nature are encouraged.

The male homosexual prostitute creates another police and public health problem. He and his contacts are frequently the victims of extortion or violence, and active homosexuals who participate with a variety of associates tend to have a high rate of venereal disease. Control is more difficult than in the case of the female prostitute because the activities of the male prostitute are carried on with greater secrecy.

The welfare of female prostitutes should be included as an integral part of the control program because if these women are to be reeducated and rehabilitated, their health and economic welfare are of utmost importance. Many prostitutes are frequently ill-equipped to compete in the economic struggle for a conventional living. Reclamation includes training for useful employment and providing some means of livelihood and, in nearly all cases, the cure of venereal disease. These are social problems in which the police have an interest but not complete responsibility. The police should know the facilities available for the help of those who voluntarily seek it and the agencies specifically set up by the local government to deal with treatment and rehabilitation.

Methods of Prostitution The operation of commercialized prostitution assumes diverse forms in the United States. Some variety is found in every American city, and all are found in cities with a lax enforcement policy.

[4]*Standards for the Staffing and Organization of Municipal Narcotics and Dangerous Drug Enforcement Units*, International Association of Chiefs of Police, Field Operations Division, Washington, D.C., 1970.

ORGANIZED-CRIME AND VICE CONTROL

Common methods found today include streetwalking in its traditional form (actually walking or loitering on the street), soliciting in cocktail lounges and other places of entertainment, and using an automobile as a means to add respectability and mobility.

Houses of prostitution are encountered less commonly now than a few decades ago, but they still flourish in some regions near military installations or in vicinities where money is being spent freely on entertainment. "Massage parlors" are the latest national phenomenon related to prostitution. In almost all exotic-type massage parlors (i.e., those with masseuses scantily or seductively clad), masturbation is available to the client, along with a range of other similar services which escalate in variety and price. This kind of massage parlor is often the vehicle for actual prostitution, either on the premises or at another location. A new version of the exotic massage business, in fact, does away with the parlor altogether; the masseuse simply travels to the client's home or hotel room, and the activity is consummated on an "out-call" basis. The highest variation of prostitution on the social scale is the call-girl operation, which almost always involves the actions of a pimp or an associate. Call-girl operations are more difficult to investigate, since the solicitation takes place out of public view in one location, followed by the visit to the hotel room or other place of assignation. Other prostitutes, with taxicab drivers as pimps, accept customers in apartments which may be in respectable parts of the community. Women employed as trade stimulants—as B-girls, exotic dancers, or topless go-go girls—in retail-liquor establishments, dance halls, and other cheap recreation centers are frequently expected to obtain their principal remuneration by prostitution, their employment providing convenient access to clientele.

The transient prostitutes whose activities and place of business are scheduled and planned by others are another, dangerous addition to the list. They are difficult to identify or apprehend because they can be removed from any location easily and quickly, and they are a potential source of infectious disease because they generally do not stay in any locale long enough to receive medical examination or care. Their activities bring a substantial profit to the organized criminals who employ them, and at the same time they provide the syndicate with blackmail and bribery ammunition. These operations usually involve several states, and there are indications that the use of this method is on the increase.

Fornication and adultery privately and discreetly committed usually are considered offenses of less-immediate concern to the police. In some states, such as California, any form of sexual behavior between consenting adults is considered legal as long as the behavior is not commercialized. Noncommercial sexual behavior among adults has been thought to lack the socially evil consequences of prostitution, but in the changing cultural pattern of America, this kind of activity is being practiced by younger age groups, and it is among younger people that a new threat to our social and economic welfare has arisen. The rise in venereal disease during the past few years has been alarming; the widespread use of oral contraceptives has minimized the former dependency on mechanical methods of prophylaxis and contraception, and a casual attitude (relating perhaps to the efficacy of antibiotics) seems to prevail in lieu of the old fear of contagion.

Methods of Control Police control of prostitution ranges from practically no control to quite strict enforcement, depending upon the local law, the customs and traditions of the community, the attitude of the public, and the adoption of procedures best suited to the community.

In small communities particularly, there may be neither regulation nor control, a situation resulting from the view that since prostitution is illegal, it must not be condoned or recognized by regulation, but that since it cannot be eliminated, nothing should be done about it. Prostitutes are then left to their own devices, and brothels are allowed to operate, usually in less-desirable neighborhoods, where several may be found in close proximity to one another. Clients then know where to go, and the nuisance is restricted to a smaller area.

A second type of control recognizes prostitution by regulation and thus authorizes its operation. Regulation may be carried out by some or all of the following: (1) The operation may be restricted by the police (sometimes with and sometimes without instructions from, or the knowledge of, a higher authority) to a red-light district, which may be an area or a limited number of designated houses, prostitutes being prosecuted when they operate elsewhere. (2) Prostitutes may be registered, as a health measure to ensure regular examination or as a control device to restrict the admission of new prostitutes to the community and to provide the police with fingerprints and photographs of prostitutes as an aid in crime investigation. Each prostitute may be given a photograph identification card that is useful to officers charged with inspectional control of prostitution and to health authorities in their examinations. (3) Periodic medical examination of prostitutes, usually in the office of the health department or of a private physician, may be required in the erroneous belief that this will materially lessen the danger of infection. (4) Prostitutes may be regulated by prohibiting certain nuisances that attract public attention, such as window tapping; sitting in, or calling from, a window or doorway; soliciting or loitering on the streets or in recreational establishments; and being found in certain designated areas. Police action is directed toward the elimination of these undesirable activities rather than against the act of prostitution.

A third form of police control of prostitution is based on the view that, since it is illegal, it must not be condoned or officially recognized by any form of regulation and should be treated in the same manner as any other offense. The police attempt to eradicate prostitution as they attempt to prevent stealing, but with a frank recognition that, like stealing, it cannot be completely eliminated.

This control is marked by the following desirable objectives: (1) the elimination of areas where prostitutes may operate with impunity; (2) the elimination of outward signs of prostitution, such as window tapping, street-walking, sitting in a doorway or window, hustling, and the operations of pimps and call girls; (3) the prompt investigation of all complaints based on reports of

ORGANIZED-CRIME AND VICE CONTROL 407

infection or of nuisances created by the operation of prostitutes; (4) the investigation, with or without complaints, of persons suspected of being pimps, madams, or prostitutes and of establishments or locations where these persons are suspected of operating; and (5) the arrest of customers of prostitutes as often as the prostitutes themselves are arrested.

Justification for Strict Enforcement The existence of houses of prostitution is a sign of unhealthy government and of social conditions that are unwholesome for both youths and adults. In addition, prostitution in any form is a menace to the community health and potentially to the community economic welfare. The cost of treating victims of venereal disease is extremely high. The funds needed each year to search out victims and carry on research in treatment and prevention are a drain on governmental and private resources.

The following fallacious arguments are frequently advanced in favor of segregation of prostitutes to restricted areas: (1) *Prostitution is necessary to enable persons to satisfy their natural, biological sex impulses.* Actually, neither psychological nor medical evidence supports the contention. (2) *The elimination of houses of prostitution increases sex crimes.* Exactly the opposite has been shown to be true in numerous communities. Further, sex criminals usually do not seek out prostitutes. (3) *The elimination of houses of prostitution scatters prostitutes throughout the city.* This is not true under rigid enforcement, since closing the houses drives the least competent to other communities or into other means of livelihood because there is not sufficient street business for all prostitutes. (4) *Segregation makes it possible to eliminate unregulated prostitution.* There is no evidence to support this contention either in Europe or in this country. The existence of an authorized house of prostitution weakens the resistance of the community to this form of vice, and consequently there is greater likelihood that prostitutes will operate beyond the restricted area. In cities having segregated districts, the number of prostitutes found outside the restricted area is usually larger than the total number of prostitutes, on a per capita basis, in communities which do not have segregation. (5) *Medical inspection of prostitutes in segregated houses minimizes the danger of infection.* Medical inspection of a prostitute offers little assurance of immunity from infection among her customers; the prostitute may become infected on her first contact after a medical examination and infect every one of her clients before her next examination. Medical inspection of prostitutes in communities that require periodic examinations reveals that the incidence of infection is high; further, not all prostitutes voluntarily register, nor do they all report for examination.

Strict enforcement has many advantages: The evils of commercialization are eliminated; offensive appearances are avoided, and consequently potential customers are less tempted; and persons who are opposed to prostitution are protected against flagrant violations of the law.

The Legalization Question The argument for legalization of prostitution on a statewide basis is sometimes offered as a solution to the problem of prostitution. There is a certain case to be made for widespread legalization, on the grounds that casual prostitution would be minimized and that the high profits realized from illicit operations would disappear, along with the organized-crime apparatus which is inevitably linked with major commercialized prostitution. Further, many people correctly question our ability to legislate morality. But before legalization of prostitution could be given any chance of success from a police point of view, two requirements would have to be met: (1) elimination of the threat of venereal disease and (2) *national* adoption of legal prostitution, rather than on a state-by-state basis. Piecemeal adoption of such legislation would merely create police problems in the states having legalized prostitution because of the attraction of prostitutes and their associates to those states.

LIQUOR VIOLATIONS

There is a decided difference between the philosophy of narcotics enforcement and most liquor-violation enforcement. Narcotics enforcement stems basically from the desire to eliminate or minimize the injurious effect of narcotics, whereas liquor laws often have revenue control as the motivation; in some cases, the morality of drinking is the issue. Unfortunately, most liquor violations enforced by the typical police vice-control unit are only indirectly related to the serious problem of alcoholism and intoxication.

The diversity of liquor-control laws in the various jurisdictions makes impossible the formulation of universally acceptable enforcement policies. Prohibitory liquor laws which make the sale or possession of intoxicating liquors illegal present problems that are quite different from, and usually more serious than, those which arise when control is exercised through some form of license. These prohibitory laws usually require more enforcement effort, and the investigative procedures needed in their enforcement are similar to those used in the enforcement of narcotics laws. The police are sometimes tempted to be lax in the enforcement of such laws because the laws are often unpopular and lack the support of many prominent citizens. The police must avoid a compromise, however.

In jurisdictions where the sale of liquor is regulated by license, the police must be watchful for such violations as the sale of liquor to minors and the sale of liquor after hours, and they should undertake periodic inspections of licensed premises for the purpose of observing compliance. As a rule, the suspension or revocation of a license provides an effective control. Proprietors of retail-drink establishments are sometimes also in league with persons engaged in gambling, prostitution, and even more serious criminal activities.

In addition to making inspections to ensure compliance with regulations, the police must attempt to deal with the misuse of alcohol by individual drinkers. Contrary to popular belief, alcohol is not a stimulant but a depressant. Intoxication deadens the cortical layers of the brain, with a resultant loss of inhibitory powers. Persons under the influence of alcohol may,

ORGANIZED-CRIME AND VICE CONTROL

for this reason, give way to an impulse to fight, to disturb the peace, or to commit crimes or acts of immorality, and they become accident hazards as pedestrians and motorists because of impaired reflexes and coordination. Some persons, moreover, have a low threshold for drunkenness, and others become compulsive problem drinkers. The cost to society of alcohol abuse is estimated to be far in excess of the cost of drug abuse.

Police are confronted less with liquor-law violations than with the results of individual overindulgence. Although the emphasis on police disposal of the simple "drunk in public" case is declining each year, there is increasing awareness that the chronic drinking driver is responsible for an inordinate share of injury and fatal traffic accidents and that the chronic alcohol abuser is indeed a major police problem. Some of the efforts of vice-control personnel should therefore be devoted to acting as the departmental specialists in alcohol abuse. The control officers can act as coordinators for public education and rehabilitation programs related to alcoholism.

Chapter 20

Crime Prevention, Suppression, and Resistance

The terms "crime prevention," "crime suppression," and "crime resistance" are related, but there are distinct differences in meaning.

Crime prevention is one of the fundamental objectives of the police. Although almost any successful police activity involves crime prevention to some degree, the term as used here relates to long-range preventive activity such as the work carried out by youth or juvenile officers. Expressed another way, crime prevention is better stated as the prevention of criminality. *Crime suppression*, on the other hand, refers to tactical and short-range preventive efforts such as field interrogation, contact with truants, surveillance of potential offenders, and similar activities. Finally, *crime resistance* refers to security improvement, target hardening, and public education to prevent vulnerability to crime.

Some of the aspects of crime prevention which are related to public and community relations have been treated in Chapter 13, particularly the areas dealing with public information, press policy, administrative aspects of community relations, and citizen organizations. Crime suppression is an activity that is carried out primarily by patrol officers; it is treated in Chapter 16. This portion of the text will relate to prevention of criminality and to crime-resistance activities.

410

CRIME PREVENTION, SUPPRESSION, AND RESISTANCE 411

POLICE PARTICIPATION IN THE PREVENTION OF CRIMINALITY

The police have an obligation to become involved in a fuller measure of crime-prevention work than is provided in traditional patrol and criminal investigation activities. This broadened mission is the result of a combination of factors: (1) the presence of police capability to carry out such activities, which reflects a steady increase in police competence in preventive educational programs and in delinquency prevention, and (2) the impact of sweeping technical and social changes, which has forced this realization upon law enforcement agencies almost overnight.

Advocacy of social activism on the part of the police is being urged with greater frequency by authorities in the police and criminal justice fields. In other portions of this text there have been references to the need for police to become involved in the elimination of conditions that cause crime and criminality. Police should be concerned about crime-causing conditions resulting from poverty, discrimination, and injustice. If the police fail to take preventive action against these root causes of criminality or if they do not express an interest in these causes of crime, then we must view the police as having a neutral role in the entire crime-prevention field. It is in the best interest of our society to have police who are fundamentally concerned about basic social issues which contribute to criminality.

According to Patrick V. Murphy, former commissioner of the New York City police department, and now president of the Police Foundation, crime prevention is far superior to the best possible police reaction after a preventable crime has occurred, and yet the definition of the police job—and the rewards—still lean heavily in the direction of arrests and other enforcement activity.[1]

In most small agencies, much of the preventive-services activity will be carried out by personnel assigned to a youth or juvenile division. This kind of work relates to the identification of delinquency-producing conditions such as a poor home environment, bad parental relationships, and the presence of disabling mental illness. The general or widespread existence of these conditions can be made known to the community at large and to appropriate agencies so that enthusiasm for change will be generated.

Progressive police administrators recognize the need to assist in the prevention of crime by identifying and correcting conditions that induce criminality and by rehabilitating the delinquent. In no community can the police carry out this role alone or in isolation, and in determining the part they should play, the police should study the causes of delinquency and the means available for their elimination or correction. The police should inventory and evaluate the community social welfare resources that are directly or indirectly concerned with the prevention of criminality, and they should discover, by

[1]Patrick V. Murphy, "Police Accountability," in Joan L. Wolfle and John F. Heaphy (eds.), *Readings on Productivity in Policing*, Police Foundation, Washington, D.C., 1975, p. 39.

analysis, delinquency-prevention tasks that they themselves are best suited to perform.

Knowledge of the causes of criminality would facilitate its prevention, but there is no agreement among authorities in the field of criminal behavior about exact causes or their relative potency. There does appear to be agreement that there is no one cause in any case and that adjustment of an individual cannot be accurately predicted, although certain factors appear to occur in varying degrees in almost all cases of long-term delinquency patterns.

The uniform classification of crimes adopted by the International Association of Chiefs of Police and the Federal Bureau of Investigation includes the crimes of homicide, rape, robbery, aggravated assault, burglary, larceny, and automobile theft. So many index crimes are committed by youths under twenty-one years of age that if the police are to reduce the crime rate substantially, something must be done about young offenders before they reach high school age. Attitudes and behavior patterns developed at this critical time determine whether the youth will become a law-abiding citizen during the period of life when criminality is most apt to develop, i.e., during the late teenage or early adult years. The effectiveness of treatment is greater in the preteen or early teen period because the plastic young offender offers a greater promise of reformation in return for effort expended than the older youth or young adult. Over time, thoughts and emotions, choice of environment, and behavior become set, and if these can be made favorable at an early age, in terms of the total social good, no effort is too great. The police should see crime prevention both as an immediate necessity and as their ultimate responsibility; they must contend with the results of a poor delinquency-prevention program.

More important than the immediate reduction of the crime rate, however, is the future life of these youngsters. Nearly all confirmed adult criminals start their careers as juvenile offenders, and if society is to reduce its criminal population, young people must be prevented from becoming delinquent and developing into incorrigible adult offenders.

Police agencies should provide well-trained, alert, and sympathetic youth-division officers who can contribute to a reduction of delinquent behavior through prevention techniques and through coordinating the community efforts toward this goal. In many instances their efforts will be successful, and the child will be saved from the unwholesome experience of arrest and juvenile court; in cases where they fail, the child will be brought to juvenile court somewhat later, but probably no less redeemable than he was in the first instance.

Objections to police participation in the correction of the delinquent and predelinquent child usually result from a lack of understanding of police aims and programs. The police should break down barriers between themselves and other community agencies having related objectives by close coordination of plans and activities and detailed explanations of police policies and long-range goals. The press should also be given these explanations and kept currently informed of accomplishments. Frequent conferences with newspaper editors

CRIME PREVENTION, SUPPRESSION, AND RESISTANCE 413

are helpful in maintaining press interest in, and understanding of, present and future programs.

Administration and Organization of the Youth Division

All police departments should provide delinquency-prevention services, and most medium-sized and larger agencies will find it necessary to establish a separate youth division for this purpose. Certain characteristics of philosophy of service, attitudes of personnel, and relationships outside the department will distinguish this division from the others in the department.

The Title of the Delinquency-Prevention Division   Some departments avoid the disagreeable connotation of crime by calling their delinquency-prevention division a "juvenile division" or "youth division." This practice has some merit because children are not then reminded by the title on the door, and in police nomenclature, that their police experience borders on criminal conduct; parents are also more willing to seek police aid for their problem children when their doing so does not seem to imply that the children are delinquent or are being treated in order to prevent them from becoming so. The fact that the title "youth division" does not accurately describe delinquency- or crime-prevention activities does not seem to justify using another one that may interfere with the accomplishment of the division's purpose.

Specific Responsibilities of the Youth Division   The youth division has certain specific areas of responsibility in addition to the investigation of offenses. These include:

1   The suppression and prevention of delinquent and criminal behavior by youths. Various codes define juvenile delinquency in terms of acts committed by persons under a certain age limit, usually sixteen to eighteen, but the youth division will find that there is so much overlapping of ages among participants in delinquent acts, particularly in gang activities, car thefts, and burglaries, that they are justified in concerning themselves with persons of all ages up to twenty-one when those over the statutory juvenile age but under twenty-one are involved with younger offenders.

2   The processing of youth arrests. When juveniles, minors with juveniles, and minors engaged in gang activities are taken into custody by any unit of the department, the youth-division personnel should be available to assist in the specialized handling of these cases.

3   The preparation and presentation of court cases. Youth-division personnel should present in court only those cases which have been completely investigated, and each case must be as ready for presentation as it is possible to make it.

4   The diversion of offenders out of the criminal justice system and adjustment of cases. When the best interests of the community and the individual are served by adjusting cases without resorting to court action, youth-division personnel should accomplish this by turning the offender over to

his or her parents or other authorized adult and, where feasible, obtaining the assistance of appropriate community agencies.

5 The surveillance of amusement parks, recreation centers, schools, special events, and other places where youth problems are likely to develop. The youth division must maintain a liaison with the licensing section of the vice division in order that appropriate action may be taken against licensed establishments that contribute to juvenile delinquency.

6 The provision of intelligence relating to youthful offenders, with particular emphasis on gang membership and activities. The youth division should maintain a file on all known offenders and exchange information with the patrol and detective divisions and other crime-prevention agencies in the city as well as with the court.

7 The exercise of supervision over police efforts to deal with "status offenders"—youths who have not committed a crime per se but who are by statute given status as potential wards of the juvenile court. In this category are truants, runaways, children who are abandoned or abused by their parents, and so on.

Youth-Division Personnel The number of persons to be assigned to the youth division cannot be stated categorically because it is influenced by the size of the department, the degree of specialization that must be provided, the nature of the delinquency-prevention program, the services that must be provided by the police because they are not available through other community agencies, and the interest and abilities of personnel in the department— particularly in higher-ranking positions.

Delinquency-prevention services involve varied activities, and special abilities are required to perform some of the tasks. The division should contain the number of police officers necessary to provide supervision over recreational centers and other places that might otherwise exert unwholesome influences on youth. It should also contain a number of officers to investigate offenses by youth and to apprehend and prosecute persons offending against children. These officers should be trained and experienced police officers, and it is important also that they have a suitable concept of the social welfare character of police service and a genuine interest in delinquency-prevention work. Training in the social sciences and some background and experience in social work, especially in group work in the fields of recreation and character building, are desirable for youth-division personnel.

Finally, the youth division should contain qualified adjustment officers who are trained social workers skilled in the application of psychiatry and psychology in the diagnosis and treatment of maladjustment. If the adjustment section is to accomplish its purpose, it must be a child guidance clinic, although it will not be called by that name. The completeness of the clinical facilities will depend on the convenient availability and adequacy of such services in the community, although the youth-division staff should be qualified to diagnose and treat the less-serious cases of maladjustment without outside assistance.

Use of Female Police Officers in the Youth Division Until a few years ago,

CRIME PREVENTION, SUPPRESSION, AND RESISTANCE 415

most women officers served in youth divisions. In current practice, women officers are found everywhere in the department, which is a situation to be encouraged. Although some delinquency-prevention tasks are better performed by women prepared by training and experience for such work, some tasks are better performed by men, while others are handled equally well by a man or a woman.

In addition to careful selection of personnel to ensure adequate interest and native ability, attention must be given to training, not only for members of the youth division, but also for the entire department, if the program of preventing delinquency is to be successfully accomplished.

Youth-Division Records   Certain operating records must be maintained by the youth-division secretary in small departments and by a separate section in large agencies. Youth-division records must often be separated from adult records by law, and separate division files must be maintained for active and inactive diversion or status cases. An alphabetical index file should be kept for all juveniles contacted by the department. Copies of these index cards should be transmitted daily to the social service exchange, to the schools, and to the juvenile court or chief probation officer. The juvenile court, in turn, should send to the police the names of children otherwise brought to their attention, of those placed on probation or committed to institutions, and also of those paroled from institutions so that the youth division may have a complete record of the more serious problem children. (A recommended method for coordinating information to and from the principal agencies in the juvenile justice system will be discussed later in this chapter.) A file should also be maintained of all the social welfare agencies in the community, listing their services and cross-indexed for the convenience of the adjustment officer in search of some special service.

Spot maps showing the locations of juvenile offenses and the residences of the offenders (with the nature of the offense indicated by pins of different colors or shapes) are important diagnostic tools that should be maintained by the youth division. It should also propose forms to be used by the records division in preparing summaries of delinquency-prevention activities; other summaries relating to adjustment cases should be prepared by the division secretary in large departments.

Fingerprinting Juveniles   As a general rule, youthful offenders should not be fingerprinted by the police because the experience may have an unfortunate effect on the child and usually any advantage gained is not sufficiently great to justify this risk. If not forbidden by law, exceptions may be made in the case of persistent offenders or when the prints are desired for comparison with latents found at crime scenes. The policy for fingerprinting in these cases should be carefully and thoroughly set out by written directives, and in the absence of such controls, the approval of the chief or the head of the youth division should be obtained.

Notification of Parents   The police should recognize that parents have a natural interest in the welfare of their minor children and a legal responsibility for their care and conduct. The police should notify parents immediately of incidents involving their children, and they should work with them closely in disposing of the matter. When an officer has occasion to reprimand a child on his beat, he should call on the parents at once and report the matter. When a minor is apprehended, the first police act should be the notification of the parents. Police failure in this respect is reprehensible. Further, the misbehavior of the child may reflect some parental inadequacy that ought to be considered in dealing with the case, and the contact with the parent might quickly reveal the inadequacy. The delinquent child represents a problem of adjustment that of necessity involves the parents, and their cooperation is essential to the most successful treatment of the offender.

Cooperation with Other Divisions Essential   The youth and vice divisions should cooperate in the supervision of licensed places that are delinquency hazards and in all vice cases involving juveniles; such cases discovered by one division should be reported to the other. The youth and detective divisions should cooperate closely in all cases involving juveniles to which the detective division is assigned. Members of the criminal investigation and vice-control divisions should conduct their investigations of such cases with first thought to the welfare of the youth. Investigators should be encouraged to interview juveniles in youth-division quarters, although this requirement is not necessary if the atmosphere within the department generally is similar to that in the youth division and if privacy can be assured. Younger girls should not be questioned except in the presence of a policewoman or some other female member of the department. When requested to do so, female officers from other divisions should assist the detective division in all investigations involving women, and the detective division, on request, should assist the youth division in its investigations.

In addition to participating as actively in the prevention of delinquency as they do in traffic and vice control, beat-patrol officers can render an important service in the adjustment of individual delinquents by supervising and making friends with problem children on their beats. The youth division should keep patrol officers informed regarding the identity of problem children and the nature of their difficulties and should suggest procedures to follow in dealing with individual children. Patrol officers should establish friendly relationships with small children on their beats and promote in them a respect for law and a favorable attitude toward its enforcement. They should be alert for evidence of persons and places that influence children and youth undesirably, and they should be persistent in their efforts to eradicate these influences and to direct youthful activities into wholesome channels.

Organizational Structure   A youth division in a large department may be organized into several sections in order to perform its various functions. Chart

CRIME PREVENTION, SUPPRESSION, AND RESISTANCE

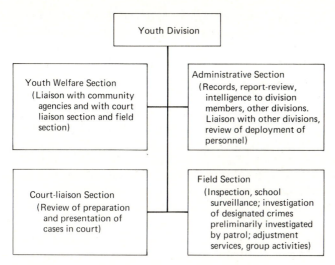

Chart 25 Organization of a large youth division.

25 illustrates such specialization within the division. In this plan, the administrative section concerns itself with records and report review, including records of missing persons. It keeps the commanding officer informed on all aspects of the division's operations. The section obtains, evaluates, and disseminates intelligence to its members and other divisions. In addition, it maintains liaison with other operating divisions and conducts a continuing review of the deployment of youth-division personnel. The youth welfare section maintains division relationships with community agencies (such as probation and social welfare departments and schools) concerned with providing services, recreation, treatment, and programs for delinquent and predelinquent children and youth as well as with the court liaison section and the field section. The court liaison section reviews the preparation and assists in the presentation of cases in court. The field section provides the following services: (1) inspection, (2) investigation of designated classes of crimes that have been preliminarily investigated by patrol officers, and (3) adjustment services, group activities, and some other services related to youth and the prevention of criminality. It also collects intelligence regarding delinquency problems in the schools and other specific areas. In the largest cities the field section may be decentralized for administrative and operational control. However, the personnel of these field-section units should not be rigidly tied to district limitations and should be transferred freely from one area to another as the need is indicated.

While the functions of inspection, investigation, adjustment or diversion, and group activities must be provided, it is not always necessary to create a separate unit for each. The need for separate sections is influenced by the size of the division and, in the case of surveillance and inspection, by the extent to which the patrol division performs these tasks. Further, there must not be too sharp a separation of functions among the members of the youth division; all of them, under some circumstances, should perform tasks outside their regular assignment. For example, those assigned to inspection must perform many investigative tasks, and those assigned to investigations may devote a part of their time to inspection duties, especially to meet irregular and infrequent needs. All members of the division, and of the police department as a whole, should participate in adjustment and group activities.

Specialization has certain advantages, but there are disadvantages as well. Each task should therefore be analyzed to determine whether it should be performed exclusively by the youth division or might be entrusted to other members of the force with equally effective and satisfactory results. Many duties may be performed by officers not assigned to the youth division, particularly if the department has adopted team policing. Participation by officers in other divisions has two important advantages: (1) The resulting conservation of the time and energy of youth-division personnel permits greater attention to tasks that require skill and experience beyond those possessed by other department members, and (2) the stimulated interest of officers thus indoctrinated in the philosophy of delinquency prevention promotes informal work in this field by police personnel engaged in other activities.

Delinquency-Prevention Activities

In order to carry out its specific responsibilities in the field of delinquency prevention, the youth division must engage in certain activities that will help to provide a well-rounded program. Some of these activities provide a greater return for effort expended than others, and some are more specifically police responsibilities than others. The police alone operate some, while others require the resources of one or more community agencies. The nature of the police delinquency-prevention program is determined by the field of activity given the greatest emphasis, and this is influenced by the needs of the community. A well-rounded program should include the following:

1 The eradication of elements that induce criminal tendencies and of conditions that promote criminal activities, especially among children.

2 The discovery of delinquents, near-delinquents, and those exposed to high-risk situations, as well as the treatment of the poorly adjusted. Some must be referred immediately to the juvenile court; the maladjustment of others may be corrected without such action by utilizing all community resources to this end.

3 The planning, promotion, and direction (to meet specific needs in crime prevention) of recreational, character-building, and other group activities that provide wholesome influences. Membership on community councils and on boards of directors of community agencies enables the police to win community cooperation and to exert an influence on long-range community planning in delinquency prevention.

CRIME PREVENTION, SUPPRESSION, AND RESISTANCE

Regardless of the size of the youth division, its primary tasks in carrying out this program may be divided into three categories: (1) inspection, (2) investigation and correction of the maladjusted individual, and (3) coordination and direction of community resources toward the removal of harmful influences and the provision of wholesome ones.

Inspection The purposes of delinquency-prevention inspection are (1) to eradicate unwholesome influences and to lessen the opportunity for misconduct by means of the presence of the police, the enforcement of regulations, and the apprehension of persons who may exert a harmful influence; (2) to discover persons in need of treatment for the correction of present or incipient maladjustments; (3) to assist in the supervision of problem children being dealt with by the division; and (4) to discover areas where group delinquency-prevention activities are needed.

Police inspection of establishments that have liquor licenses, discotheques, poolrooms, bowling alleys, swimming pools, skating rinks, and other commercially operated places of recreation is important to delinquency prevention. In addition, control must be maintained over parks, playgrounds, drive-in restaurants, vacant lots, public gatherings, and other places where youth may congregate. Such places may provide opportunities for misconduct or subject young people to unusual temptation or the unwholesome influence of sex deviates or other undesirable persons.

It should also be kept in mind that much delinquent behavior appears to be *learned* or to be committed in emulation of those acts which give status to the leader of a gang, for example. Some individuals will commit socially unacceptable acts in order to win recognition from those who do not esteem good conduct, even though the consequences are unpleasant. The police can disperse street-corner gangs and organized clubs which are known to be actively delinquent and destructive, and they can direct the attention of parents, schools, and agencies to the younger hangers-on who may be in the process of learning new and dangerous means of finding excitement and releasing their energies.

Investigations Youth-division members may conduct investigations for the purpose of collecting facts that are essential in the successful detection, diagnosis, and treatment of individuals. The youth division may also investigate some incidents, individuals, and conditions for purposes of delinquency prevention, just as the vice division will investigate vice violations and the detective division will investigate serious crimes. However, it is essential that the relationships between the youth, vice, and detective divisions regarding responsibilities for investigations be clearly and precisely defined by regulations. Failure to do so will result in neglect or friction. There will inevitably be some duplication of interest between two or more of these divisions, as when young people are involved in vice offenses or in crimes for which the detective division has the responsibility for clearance. The following factors should be borne in mind in establishing duties and assigning cases:

1 Undivided responsibility is desirable. It is advisable to hold one division responsible for the investigation and ultimate clearance of crimes in a designated class, regardless of the age of either the offender or the victim.

2 The age of the perpetrator of a crime cannot usually be established before his or her apprehension.

3 In some serious crimes a juvenile may be the victim or the offender.

4 The youth division is not designed to investigate the most serious crimes.

5 The primary purpose of the detective division is to investigate serious crimes and clear them by the arrest of the perpetrator.

6 A police task should be assigned to the unit that has similar or related duties.

Youth-Division Case Assignments   On the basis of these facts, the following cases would be assigned to the youth division, regardless of whether a juvenile is involved or not, leaving to the detective division the investigation of all other felonies, all cases believed to be felonies, and all cases of stolen property involving juveniles:

1 Offenses against the family, such as domestic relations cases, desertion, abandonment, nonsupport of a wife or child, and neglect or abuse of a child; encouragement of, or contribution to, the delinquency of minors; employment of children in injurious, immoral, or improper vocations or practices; and admission of minors to improper places.

2 Incest, statutory rape, and bigamy. Because of the seriousness of the offense, forcible rape should be assigned to the detective division regardless of the age of the victim or the offender.

3 Family-related abduction, not for extortion.

4 All other crimes, including gambling, in which juveniles are involved as victims but excepting those other crimes regularly assigned to the vice or detective division.

5 Missing persons.

6 Mental cases in which the police become involved in commitment or treatment.

7 Other cases in which persons need social welfare service and cases in which *designated* juveniles are suspected of any offense.

Diversion and Corrective Action   There is no rule that dictates the proportion of young offenders the police should treat themselves or by referral to another agency outside the criminal justice system, in contrast to the number they should send to juvenile court. A decision must be made in each case on the basis of the best interest of the child and society. The police are justified in attempting corrective action by themselves and with the aid of other agencies,

CRIME PREVENTION, SUPPRESSION, AND RESISTANCE

instead of referring the child to juvenile court, as long as they have a reasonable chance of success.

Preliminary Diagnosis   The police should make a preliminary diagnosis of each youthful offender coming to their attention in order to ascertain tentatively the most suitable treatment. Youthful offenders may be dealt with by the police in one of four ways: (1) outright release with no further action; (2) simple treatment by the police alone, consisting principally of supervision on a voluntary basis agreed to by the parents; (3) a relatively prolonged program of treatment, also on a voluntary basis, necessitating the services of a number of social agencies; or (4) referral to juvenile court.

Neighborhood Youth Councils   The youth council is an excellent device for identifying potential and actual problems among children and for coordinating investigative and corrective action by the various agencies concerned with predelinquent and delinquent children. In a small city, a typical council consists of representatives (usually one each) from the school, the juvenile probation agency, and the social welfare agency, plus the youth officer from the police department. In larger agencies the youth council is often organized on a neighborhood basis, with councils serving various locations in the city.

Regardless of the size of the city, the neighborhood youth council should operate primarily as a coordinating mechanism. In a typical council, the group meets informally, about once a month. Each representative mentions the names of problem children and potential delinquents and the nature of their problems, with particular emphasis on children who are not a serious problem for any one agency but who, in the aggregate, have enough difficulties to warrant referral to a corrective agency. Also, the discussions center on the need for procedural coordination.

In some smaller communities, the youth council serves as a review committee for the state criminal justice planning process. This responsibility is harmless if it does not preoccupy the group and prevent it from carrying out its primary role of identification of problem children and potential delinquents and coordination of corrective action.

Community Councils for Delinquency Prevention   These groups are generally larger and more formally organized than the neighborhood youth councils. Whereas the neighborhood youth council concentrates on the problems of individual children, the community council for delinquency prevention is concerned with the coordination of resources and the development of new or improved facilities. The first council for delinquency prevention was formed in 1919. No rigid pattern of organization has been followed since that time because organization is dependent upon the adequacy of social welfare agencies in terms of staff, facilities, and extent of activities; their relative interest and active, conscious participation in delinquency prevention; the pattern of civil organization; the degree of leadership provided by

422   OPERATIONS

social welfare and human-development centers at universities in the area; and
so on.

Volunteer Workers   Volunteer workers should be used in the police
delinquency-prevention program, especially in activities that would otherwise
be impossible because of the amount of time that must be devoted to direction
and supervision. Most volunteers will be lay persons having an interest in the
special activities but no training in social welfare, foster- or group-home care,
recreation, or other group work. Civic, fraternal, patriotic, and other community organizations should organize committees on delinquency prevention that
may accept some responsibility for providing volunteers for special occasions.

Volunteer workers having some special ability as a result of experience
and training may be drawn from fields of related activities; these would include
teachers, scout leaders, YMCA workers, playground directors, and social
workers. University students in the social sciences usually have an interest in
delinquency prevention and find participation in these activities a valuable and
highly desirable training experience.

There is controversy about the value of any volunteer work with individual
delinquents. It seems apparent that no harm will result from such efforts, and
there remains the possibility that some actual good will come from the
wholesome experiences thus provided the child. Further, such close participation provides citizens with a more complete understanding of police objectives
in the prevention of criminality. These activities may be justified without
regard to their actual value in the treatment of the individual child on the
grounds that citizen understanding is essential to the accomplishment of the
police delinquency-prevention program.

The police should assume a position of leadership in the organization and
(if necessary) in the operation of neighborhood youth councils, community
councils, volunteer efforts, and other group activities.

Police leadership does not mean, however, that the police officer should do
the work of a psychiatric social worker or a recreation leader. Such activity by
the police serves only as a stopgap measure for patching up the defects of a
faulty social welfare program or poor recreation department. More ultimate
good is accomplished when the police point out weaknesses in the community
services and promote action to remedy them. The police may properly perform
such duties during a limited period of organization, but after the activity is
developed, they should withdraw and leave its operation to some other agency.

These and other group activities are designed primarily to provide
wholesome interests that will make normal children better citizens. The
community has the responsibility for helping each child become a successful
adult with a well-developed sense of citizenship responsibility.

Police-sponsored Clubs   The total police energy available for the preven-

CRIME PREVENTION, SUPPRESSION, AND RESISTANCE 423

tion of delinquency is so limited that if it is expended on the entire juvenile population, the influence is spread so thin as to make it ineffective. Accordingly, it should be directed at individually selected children and segments of the population who are in the greatest need and live in areas where the existing resources are inadequate. Since police manpower is limited, the police must evaluate its expenditure in terms of ultimate good to be derived as compared with the returns from a similar expenditure in other delinquency-prevention activities.

Some police departments organize, uniform, and equip drill teams, bands, drum and bugle corps, and other activities for children. Unfortunately, participation is sometimes heavily dominated by the friends and relatives of police officers and of influential citizens in the community, to the exclusion of problem children. These organizations are a means of exerting wholesome influences on the delinquent and maladjusted child, and they should not be overlooked.

Youth-Resource Units   Although the concept of the police youth-resource officer is fairly new, it is gaining momentum. The youth-resource officer is typically assigned to a grade school or a junior high school and is given a wide variety of nonenforcement duties such as teaching short courses in ethics and citizenship, counseling students, taking groups to community affairs, and sponsoring safety shows. Some youth-resource-officer programs move from schools to playgrounds at the conclusion of the school year so that there is continuity of police contact with youth.

The youth-resource officer should avoid assuming the role of the school hallway monitor or disciplinary officer and should instead emphasize the counseling role. Although youth-resource officers should stress the positive and image-building aspects of their job, they should obviously take action on crimes committed in their presence.

In the field of recreation, the police may go beyond the conventional provision of playground space in sections of the community lacking adequate facilities. For example, some departments rope off street areas for playing ball, sledding, skating, and similar activities and provide street showers in the summer by means of attachments on selected fire hydrants. Some police departments provide buildings and supervisory staff for youth clubs and related activities. Many organize neighborhood baseball and basketball clubs and other athletic activities to meet the needs of problem children. Some organize athletic leagues that provide a variety of activities for youth. Provision of summer camps is a widespread police delinquency-prevention activity. Some camps are open to all children in the community, but the police may use the facilities for the children in greatest need. Sometimes special camps are provided as a reward for children who have worked in junior traffic patrols and similar activities.

CRIME-RESISTANCE AND SAFETY-EDUCATION SERVICES

In a large agency the administrator may want to emphasize the crime-resistance and safety-education function by giving it division status, as shown in Chart 18 (see Chapter 7).

Organization can be carried out by assigning part of the responsibilities to a crime-resistance section and part to a safety-education section.

Crime Resistance

The first general objective of a crime-resistance program is to increase public awareness of the conditions and circumstances which lead to vulnerability to crime. A secondary objective, but one which is by no means unimportant, is to build respect for the police so that police objectives receive public support. Crime-resistance activity should assume that the public has little knowledge of actual police operations or of crime-causing conditions. The work of a subdivision in this area should be directed toward assisting individual citizens, community groups such as service clubs, and school and church groups in crime-resistance programs designed to reduce vulnerability to crime. This section can also be responsible for the operations of police–citizen councils and can play a large role in the planning of crime-resistance programs.

Some departments issue to retail merchants a weekly bulletin warning them of the activity of fraudulent-check passers, confidence and shortchange operators, and shoplifters. These may be distributed by the store detail to large department stores, a sufficient number being furnished to ensure that there will be a copy for each store-security officer and department head. One or two copies should be mailed to each of the smaller retail merchants.

For distribution both at headquarters and by officers on the street, the department should have a supply of traffic leaflets containing brief statements of important safety rules, diagrams of correct and incorrect turning movements and hand signals, and other information useful to the motorist. Facts should be well arranged, easily readable, and stated concisely, without legal verbiage. Public utility companies sometimes cooperate by enclosing traffic leaflets and other police brochures with their monthly statements. Some departments send monthly traffic-safety bulletins or leaflets to members of the junior traffic patrols, sometimes also distributing them through the authorities to elementary school children. Such leaflets are a convenient means of instructing children in safe practices regarding crossing streets, riding bicycles and scooters, and playing in neighborhood lots.

A few departments have prepared brochures or packets for new residents coming into the community. The packet is delivered by a beat officer, who personally welcomes the new family.

Business-Crime Resistance In a large department, the prevention of business crimes is a logical division of the work of the crime-resistance section. A typical activity would be the development of the "counter-crime clinic," which involves bringing in a group of business people or merchants in a specific

CRIME PREVENTION, SUPPRESSION, AND RESISTANCE 425

trade or business and conducting an intensive clinic especially related to crime problems facing that business. For example, the crime problems of the vending-machine business are unique and are very different from those of clothing-store retailers. A major part of the work of the crime-resistance section should consist in recommending improved methods of store security, such as modern locking devices, silent alarm systems, and internal-theft-prevention techniques. Personnel of this unit can logically be assigned to make canvasses of neighborhood business establishments to suggest on-the-spot security improvements. During counter-crime clinic sessions, business people invited to headquarters or to district stations can be shown motion pictures or video-tape presentations and mock-ups of improved hardware, and they can be given literature as well as the usual presentations via the lecture method. An excellent method for bringing these programs directly to shopping areas is to use a large motor home or van equipped with slide or motion picture projectors, locks, exhibits, and so forth. The van should be equipped with as many seats as can be accommodated comfortably.

Security Surveys   A major activity of officers assigned to crime-resistance units is the security survey. A typical survey consists of an actual inspection of a business place or a residence by an officer who has had specialized training[2] in this technique. The officer is equipped with a checklist and literature on recommended hardware and security procedures. Merchants are often asked to update information on emergency-contact cards located at headquarters. The technique of engraving social security numbers on appliances is often combined with the security survey.

Advertisements   Slogans and posters are excellent devices for broadcasting ideas. Brief, catchy phrases and sentences that are meaningful and impressive often drive home a principle to the public consciousness. When the police department itself is unable to purchase posters, the local safety council or some other community organization should provide them for bulletin boards in schools, industrial plants, gasoline service stations, and large transportation terminals.

Police departments sometimes arrange with outdoor-advertising concerns for the use of spare billboards for traffic posters and slogans. Often merchants are willing to incorporate a traffic-safety slogan into their outdoor or newspaper advertising displays. Some companies require their stenographers to add a safety slogan as a postscript to each letter or to attach stickers bearing safety slogans to letterheads.

Personal Appearances

A speakers' bureau is needed to inform the public on the nature and purpose of police activities and otherwise to assist the chief in discharging his responsibility of reporting to the members of the department and to the citizens of the

---

[2] Available from the National Crime Prevention Institute, Louisville, Ky.

community. Although speeches are excellent means of communication, the effectiveness of a speech depends largely on the personality of the speaker.

Training in Public Speaking In establishing a speakers' bureau, it is important that the interest of officers be aroused and that arrangements be made for their instruction. An excellent training method is to require every member of a class, limited to 10 or 15 students to ensure participation by all, to give a five-minute talk on some police subject. The instruction should cover the organization of a speech and correct enunciation and breathing. The other officers and the instructor should constructively criticize each speech, and no officer should be encouraged to continue with the speakers' bureau if he or she demonstrates, after several classes, a lack of ability in public speaking. Garbled speech, unpleasant inflections, or evidence of self-conscious embarrassment may do more harm to public relations than the failure to provide a speaker for every occasion.

Direction and Supervision One officer should be assigned to direct and supervise departmental public-speaking activities. The supervisor should consider the personalities and abilities of officers available for engagements to ensure that the best ones are sent on the most important assignments, and the beginners on the less-important ones. The supervisor may inform the public of this service through newspaper notices, department publications, and a list of speakers and subjects mailed to churches, civic clubs, PTAs, and other community organizations.

Selection of Subject Matter Care should be exercised to select the subject that is most apt to interest the audience. Speeches on traffic furnish opportunities to inform the public about regulations and to train them in good driving practices. Church, reform, and some business groups are interested in speeches on gambling, narcotics, prostitution, and liquor-control problems. Business people are also interested in the operating methods of criminals who prey on retail merchants; speeches on burglaries, robberies, and car thefts also prove attractive. All these provide opportunities for the police to advise the citizen on how to cooperate in lessening the opportunity for crime.

Demonstrations and Displays Demonstrations and displays in the lobby or anteroom of the hall where the speech is to be given, before the meeting convenes and after adjournment, arouse interest and afford an opportunity to present additional information to the audience. Projection slides, filmstrips, motion pictures, and actual demonstrations of such simple techniques as developing latent fingerprints or testing for bloodstains assist the speaker in his or her presentation and focus attention on the subject at hand.

Safety Education

The safety-education program should encompass traffic safety as well as

CRIME PREVENTION, SUPPRESSION, AND RESISTANCE

general safety for all citizens. Members of the unit should participate in the development of text for releases and speeches and should make appearances before various organizations.

The logical assignment of responsibilities to this unit would include the coordination of school safety patrols (since a large part of this activity is related to safety education, rather than regulatory enforcement); the provision of instructors for driver-improvement classes, carried out by municipal traffic courts; the presentation of instruction in firearms safety as well as of safety talks to interested groups on the hazards of improper firearm use; and instruction in water safety before interested groups, including dissemination of releases to the public on this topic just before or during the summer season.

Although police routinely respond to accidents in the home, police themselves make little effort to prevent household accidents (nor does any other government agency). Until some other agency of government provides this service, the police have every justification for educating the public in such subjects as leaving poisons within access of children, mixing dangerous combinations of household substances, and leaving abandoned refrigerators without removing the doors.

The police often see hazardous situations in industry or business which can result in permanent injury or impaired health, such as cleaning windows without adequate safety-belt protection and handling noxious or harmful substances without taking the proper precautions. This is not to suggest that enforcement action should be taken to prevent circumstances of this sort, but to point out that the police have a potential role as safety educators of the public in the prevention of dangerous situations such as these.

Chapter 21

Special Operational Problems

Over the past 20 years there has been an increasing tendency to specialize some of the tactical operations in police service. Larger departments have developed special-operations divisions, task forces, or tactical units which are available for use in a variety of assignments and circumstances. In most cases these assignments have stressed the need for a mobile group of officers who can be assigned to situations requiring saturation preventive patrol, surveillances and stakeouts, extra traffic coverage at events such as football games and rallies, and concentrated preventive patrol in high-crime areas.

This movement toward specialized operational forces has received added impetus in the last few years from LEAA-sponsored crime-specific programs, which have tended to stress high-impact police efforts such as robbery or burglary task forces.

USES OF TACTICAL FORCES

A mobile tactical force is of value in those situations which call for saturation of an area either to prevent the outbreak of criminal activity or a civil disorder

SPECIAL OPERATIONAL PROBLEMS   429

or to provide the immediate assistance of additional personnel during an emergency of major proportions.

The essential characteristic of the task force is its flexibility. For this reason its members should not be assigned to routine duties that would limit their immediate availability. Task-force officers should be trained to work with the patrol, traffic, or detective division, openly and in strength, covertly and singly, or in teams in undercover operations.

In large cities, the constant demand for details for policing of special events may justify a detail section of the task force for this purpose. Some members assigned to this section may be used for the tactical purposes described above when they are not needed for their primary purpose.

Large task forces may have other units to provide some special services.

Decoy Unit   The concentration of mugging and jackrolling in some sections of large cities justifies the operation of one or more squads of six officers under a sergeant, all volunteers selected on the basis of their ability in self-defense. These officers should be subjected to continued training in judo and related defensive tactics. They should all be equipped with transistorized radio transmitters concealed on their persons. One should serve as a decoy while the others, serving as a backup, stand or walk nearby, ready to come to his assistance immediately should he be attacked.

Riot-Control Use   In the decade of the 1960s, the problem of riots and civil disorders brought about a great expansion in the size of police tactical units, which have been given the major responsibility for the first contact with a situation which is in immediate danger of becoming a riot and for control of small confrontations.

Canine Operations   The tactical force or special-operations division is sometimes given the responsibility for canine operations. The use of police dogs in high-crime areas for routine patrol and hazardous search situations is being accepted throughout the country. The dogs can accompany an officer into areas where cars cannot go, and because of their keen sensory perception, they can warn an officer of danger long before the human eye or ear is able to do so. Many police dogs are now trained for specialized tracking and scenting duties, such as bomb sniffing and narcotics detection. Trained dogs are valuable in the confrontations of street gangs and often will disperse a crowd without difficulty, when the presence of two or more officers would tend to inflame the group to violence. The use of dogs in riot control should be avoided, however. It has become an emotional issue which outweighs the utility of the dogs.

Both officers and dogs for a canine corps should be selected and trained with great care. In selecting the dogs, it is necessary to consider size, aptitude, courage, intelligence, and tractability. Screening of dogs for congenital hip problems is necessary as well as expensive, since the screening requires x-rays by a veterinarian. Once the dogs and their handlers have been selected, intensive training should proceed under the guidance of a professional obedience trainer or with an established canine-corps director from a department that has already had several years' experience with dogs in patrol. No aspect of the selection, training, health care, or use of the police dog may be haphazard. All procedures should be carefully worked out and followed faithfully, and refresher training should be standard if good results are desired.

Although police dogs attract a certain amount of publicity when they are used successfully in criminal work, they should not be used for public relations purposes on a regular basis. The element of hazard is always present, and one unfortunate incident involving an innocent citizen can destroy the entire program. Exhibitions by the dogs and their handlers should be given only under carefully controlled circumstances.

ORGANIZATION AND STAFFING OF SPECIAL-OPERATIONS OR TACTICAL UNITS

Many larger agencies have established a tactical force or special-operations division within the field operations structure of the department. The unit should be organizationally equal to other operating divisions, as indicated in Chart 17, in Chapter 7. Some local and state governments have unusual policing requirements, such as the need for harbor or marine patrol or for air rescue and surveillance. Some cities also operate an emergency rescue service which is assigned to the police department rather than private firms or another city department. The special-operations division is a convenient organizational grouping for all these unusual operational units.

A tactical unit serves a useful purpose in large cities because of the extreme mobility afforded by the assignment of a number of squads of officers to whatever tactical situation seems most important at the moment. Members of the tactical section should be recruited from personnel who have a vigorous and aggressive outlook, and discipline should be maintained at a high level— partly because of the sensitive situations which can develop as a result of the application of tactical manpower and partly because eager young officers, who are often assigned to such a unit, may be tempted to go beyond the bounds of common sense more often than older, less aggressive personnel.

The tactical force should be organized in military fashion, with each squad of officers supervised by a sergeant. The squads should be capable of independent activity because routine operational use often requires several smaller tactical units to be deployed simultaneously. However, the tactical force should have strong overall leadership because of the application to large-scale situations.

The special-operations division frequently has the responsibility for the assignment and training of police-reserve officers or the riot-squad detail, and it may also equip and train special-unit officers within the division (those assigned to a marine unit or permanent public-event unit, for example) so that they can be a part of the tactical force assigned during emergencies.

SPECIAL OPERATIONAL PROBLEMS

SWAT Units Many departments have adopted the concept of the special weapons and tactical unit, which is commonly referred to by the acronym SWAT. The Federal Bureau of Investigation has encouraged the formation of SWAT units as a means for dealing—in a responsible, controlled way—with barricaded persons, snipers, hostage situations, and similar problems in which there is a potential for the use of firearms or tear gas. The FBI has also provided free training of police SWAT teams at the FBI Academy in Quantico, Virginia.

Both the training and operational use of SWAT personnel should emphasize that the most successful SWAT operation is one which results in arrest of the barricaded person or sniper without injury to anyone. Team operation is fundamental to the concept, with squad-sized units under close direction in the field.

Directives regulating SWAT teams should specify the conditions under which a team should be called out and the mechanics to be followed in making the final decision to assault a position with the use of firepower.

Because of the tactical nature of SWAT units, they are obviously well placed in a special-operations division in a large department. In smaller agencies, however, SWAT teams must be a part-time responsibility for officers who have other assignments on a day-to-day basis.

Planning the Work of the Tactical Force

The administrator should establish policies relating to the selection of task assignments for the tactical section and provide guidelines for deciding who is to assign units of the force, during what hours, and at which locations.

Carrying out detailed planning work is logically a function of an operations analysis or administrative unit established at the field operations level; in smaller departments, the appropriate command officers plan the work of the tactical force. The decision as to whether the force should be deployed should generally be made by the common commander of the patrol division and the special-operations division. In medium-sized and large departments, this person is usually the head of the field operations bureau.

If the tactical force is not assigned to a specific problem or condition, it should generally be given tactical surveillance and high-intensity patrol assignments in high-crime areas during peak crime hours.

The tactical force can be effectively used to provide saturation coverage for traffic enforcement on holidays with notoriously heavy fatalities, such as Memorial Day, and can be used for traffic and crowd-control assignments for parades, baseball and football games, or any special event involving crowds.

PREVENTION AND CONTROL OF CIVIL DISORDERS

Since the Watts riot in California in August 1965 and the series of riots which followed the assassination of Dr. Martin Luther King, Jr., the police in the United States have become highly involved in the problem of riots and civil disorders. During the final years of the war in Vietnam, disorders erupted on college campuses almost as often as in inner-city slum areas, but the bulk of police concern has related to the prevention and control of riots in the inner-city or economically depressed areas rather than on the campuses.

Among a substantial part of the group of people who participate in riots, the police themselves are considered to be a prime cause. Because the police are selected from a cross-section of middle- and lower-income families, they are by no means immune from the prejudices and antagonisms which help foster a climate for civil disorder.

In its celebrated report on riots and violence, the National Advisory Commission on Civil Disorders indicated in its summary statement that racism is a substantial and profound cause of riots and disorders. When racism is manifested by police, of course, it may have a much more significant effect on those persons who suffer from it than the same degree of discrimination by a citizen who is not an official representative of government.

Police executives who have the proper attitudes should do everything in their power to carry out three objectives: (1) to make certain that no visible evidence of discrimination exists within the force, (2) to convince members of the department that discrimination is not an acceptable attitude and that it is inherently wrong, and (3) to encourage police officers themselves to take the lead in discouraging discrimination.

It is important for all public officials at all levels to say that they are against discrimination; however, an official will not be able to convince minority groups of his public posture for very long when he really does not believe his assertions himself. The police administrator who believes in discrimination should not expect community relations programs or other attempts to improve race relations to be successful.

Fair and impartial police actions probably have some effect on the prevention of riots per se; some riots have started because of improper police action, such as an aggressive or brutal arrest or too long a delay before taking a prisoner away from the scene. Shooting incidents often become the initiation point for riots or disorders, and this is one of the reasons why it makes sense to adopt the SWAT-unit concept. A shooting incident can create widespread and immediate hostility through dissemination of rumors, even though the information is erroneous; when the incident is marked by police overreaction and mistakes, the reaction can be immense.

There is a parallel between the prevention of crimes and the prevention of criminality, on the one hand, and the prevention of riots and the prevention of riot-causing conditions, on the other. In the prevention of crimes, most of the police effort should be focused on short-term action rather than on attacks on underlying social ills which contribute to criminality. Nevertheless, part of the police preventive effort should be focused on these social ills and underlying causes.

The same is true in the prevention of riots. The police must focus most of their attention on the immediate prevention and containment of riots, such as

SPECIAL OPERATIONAL PROBLEMS

by taking decisive action in potential riot situations and avoiding unnecessarily aggressive police action and other abrasive techniques mentioned above, but they must also focus to some extent on the conditions which tend to cause riots.

Control and Containment of Riots

Regardless of what prompts a riot or disorder, the police obviously bear a heavy responsibility for control of the situation and restoration of order.

Following the riots which occurred in the aftermath of the assassination of Dr. King, some intensive studies of riot-control procedures were carried out. IACP conducted a national series of seminars on this topic, partly to disseminate information on riot control and partly to develop a body of knowledge which could be used for prevention and control in the future. Some of the conclusions developed are as follows:

1 Policies regarding use of force, mechanics of arrest, and tactical handling of potentially dangerous crowds should be reviewed, developed, or modified.

2 The departments should develop plans for the control of riots and civil disorders. Coupled with the plan, department personnel should receive intensive training in riot prevention and control. Training of personnel assigned to the tactical force or to reserve riot squads should be especially intensive.

3 Policies, emergency plans, and training should all stress the operation of the department under emergency conditions. As noted elsewhere in this text, most agencies that had experienced riots came to the conclusion that the conventional organizational structure and chain of command were unsatisfactory during total mobilization.

4 Communications channels should be opened between minority-group leaders, militant groups, and others. Even though no effective agreement may be reached, the communications channel should be open so that it can be used during emergency situations.

Youth Radicalism

The police have become increasingly involved with problems stemming from campus unrest, disorders involving youth with unconventional living standards and habits, and radicals and militants who advocate the overthrow of established authority or the use of violence as the vehicle for change.

The kind of training and discipline required to cope with riots stimulated by discrimination or poverty has immediate applicability to the control of militancy and youth radicalism. In dealing with these groups, in fact, the police are generally faced with even more provocative situations which require the utmost in stamina, self-control, and discipline. The administrator must be certain that the training offered to personnel is designed to foster these important attributes and develop the perspective and judgment which are required under pressure.

A strong preventive device in the case of extreme militancy and radicalism is public education. Even though the news media usually give adequate coverage of events relating to militancy and radical disorder, the police should make certain that the true nature of the threat to the total welfare of the community is known by all responsible citizens.

SPECIAL-EVENTS CONTROL

In small agencies, coverage for crowd control, parades, and other assignments requiring unusual manpower is usually carried out by reassignment of regular uniformed personnel, by the use of overtime, or by the use of reserve officers. In medium-sized departments, the tactical section can often provide adequate control over events of this sort. In larger departments, some specialization of the tactical force may be necessary, as indicated in earlier pages.

When personnel are assigned to part-time special-events details, they can be given other meaningful work during the hours or days of the week when they have no crowd-control functions. Warrant service is an excellent assignment of this kind, since it can usually be scheduled conveniently and can be dropped almost instantly without loss of efficiency whenever officers are required for special details.

Chapter 22

Traffic

Although the increase in crime in recent years has diverted attention from some of the other police problems, traffic control continues to be a primary police responsibility. More people are injured or killed in automobile accidents than as the result of all other acts under police control combined. The economic loss from automobile accidents is greater than all other losses the police are charged with preventing. In every community this loss exceeds the total police budget. More people are disgruntled with traffic control than with police effort in any other field; traffic control causes the police more annoyance and subjects them to pressure from a greater number of sources than any other problem.

POLICE RESPONSIBILITY FOR TRAFFIC CONTROL

The police are challenged by the need to provide traffic control which is effective in accident reduction and congestion elimination and which is also publicly acceptable. Suitable traffic control requires an understanding of the purpose of the control, the factors involved, the processes to be used, and the relative worth of the several methods available.

Purpose of Police Traffic Control   Police control of highways, automobiles, and people is intended to facilitate the safe and rapid movement of automobiles and pedestrians. To this end the inconveniences, dangers, and economic losses that arise from the movement, congestion, delay, stopping, and parking of vehicles must be lessened. Accidents and congestion are evidences of failure to provide safe and rapid movement. First attention should be given to accident prevention because of the pain and sorrow incident to injuries and death; inconvenience and cost, however, force attention to congestion and parking problems also.

Steps in Police Traffic Control   Control of traffic is accomplished in three steps: (1) The causes of accidents and congestion must be discovered; facts are gathered and analyzed for this purpose. (2) These causes must be remedied; changes must be made in the physical conditions that create hazards, and legislation must be enacted to regulate drivers and pedestrians. (3) The public must be educated in the provisions of traffic laws, and motorists and pedestrians must be trained in satisfactory traffic-safety habits; compliance with regulations must be obtained by enforcement, if need be. The police should initiate action in these areas and coordinate the efforts of other agencies that are also concerned with these activities.

The police have three parallel tools to aid them in traffic control: engineering, education, and enforcement. It is the purpose of this chapter to discuss how these tools may be organized and used most effectively by the police.

The Traffic Division

Before a traffic division can be organized or staffed, policy must be established as to the role played by the patrol division in traffic enforcement. Most progressive administrators believe that patrol officers should play a large part in routine traffic enforcement and accident investigation. The International Association of Chiefs of Police regularly recommends the assignment of at least 50 percent of the traffic-citation work load to the patrol force. IACP also recommends giving uniformed patrol officers substantial responsibility for routine accident investigation.

In small and medium-sized departments, therefore, the personnel assigned to a formalized traffic unit should be specialists, rather than a large force of officers with primary responsibility for traffic enforcement and investigation.

In departments having only one patrol supervisor on duty per shift, the existence of a separate traffic division makes little sense. The traffic function should be assigned to the same supervisor to whom the shift supervisors report.

Traffic-Division Personnel   The traffic division may be limited in personnel to a headquarters staff, including officers in charge of a traffic-violator school and a program of public education and an analyst charged with staff-inspection duties. The only officers assigned to street duty may be the following: (1) the supervisor of the junior traffic patrol; (2) the traffic-engineering staff, which makes studies of high-accident locations, traffic flow and movement, and other factors; (3) full-time officers or civilians assigned to the enforcement of time-limit parking regulations and to crosswalk and intersection duties, although these officers may be assigned to the patrol division when necessary to ensure continuous supervision; (4) a small traffic squad which can be used for repetitive details, escorts, radar operation, and problems requiring intensive or complex coverage; and (5) one or more officers to serve as aides to the head of the division in checking on the performance of street officers having traffic assignments and on signs, signals, and markings in need of maintenance service. The traffic division, therefore, may be primarily a planning and inspectional agency rather than a field force.

Street Supervision of Traffic Officers The need for supervision requires that traffic officers, like others, be under the continuous and direct control of a sergeant. The number of officers on street duty who may be supervised adequately by one sergeant is influenced by variable factors. Most important of these are the nature and relative location of the duties of the officers. Motorized-patrol officers are more difficult to supervise when assigned to large beats. Officers assigned to the small beats used in the enforcement of parking regulations are relatively easy to supervise, and the supervision of officers on fixed posts involves no serious problem. If officers devote full time to downtown traffic duties (crosswalk, intersection, and parking), 4 to 12 police officers require the supervision of one sergeant, and 12 to 24 require two sergeants. When there are fewer than four officers, it is usually advisable to place them under the direct control of the patrol division for supervision by the patrol sergeant.

Staff Inspection by the Traffic Division Planning and staff inspection in the field of traffic control are the responsibility of the traffic division. Coordination of the traffic police and the regular patrol force in traffic control mandates staff inspection of the traffic accomplishments of the patrol division; the traffic administrative staff must see that traffic assignments for the patrol division are made and carried out. Special attention should be given to the following problems:

1 Maintaining an adequate enforcement index.
2 Exercising a proper degree of selectivity in enforcement.
3 Maintaining an up-to-date listing of traffic-control assignments for the benefit of patrol supervisors.
4 The continued use of techniques for good traffic enforcement and control. Evidence technicians and beat officers should be trained in accident-investigation procedures. Patrol officers should be instructed in techniques to be used in handling the traffic violator and providing intersection duty or manual point control. Officers who are not traffic specialists may sometimes drift into sloppy procedures, which must be discovered and corrected.

438 OPERATIONS

Traffic Records Traffic records enable the police to evaluate their accomplishments and to appraise the effectiveness of their traffic-control problem. They provide an administrative control over day-to-day operations by the assignment and report review of incidents that require police service. Data relating to accidents, enforcement, and engineering provide facts to replace guesswork and give the traffic administrator an assurance of certainty in understanding traffic problems, in wisely planning and directing their control, and in checking on the execution of his plans. The preparation of useful data requires (1) the gathering of facts relating to accidents, arrests, or engineering; (2) the derivation from these facts of statistical information in useful summary form; and (3) the intelligent analysis of this statistical information for planning purposes.

Indexes used as yardsticks should be based on the injury-accident rate. Since the goal is the reduction of accidents, any variation in this rate is an indication of the effectiveness of the program. The administrative head should receive periodic tabulations summarized in indexes that show the ratio between the number of citations (and the equivalent in notices of violation or warnings) for moving-traffic violations and the number of injury accidents, the percentage of citations and other prosecutions that result in convictions, the severity of the penalty assessed, the ratio between convictions for moving-traffic violations and injury accidents, and the percentage of drivers who observe traffic regulations. Summaries should also be provided containing information relating to engineering and educational work. Of special importance to the traffic engineer is a procedure that results in a notification to him from the records office of locations that have experienced an accident frequency in excess of a minimum number set by him.

The administrative staff should be able to detect hazards inherent in certain locations; to discover regulations unsuited to existing conditions; to learn where, when, and why accidents are occurring; to determine what kinds of arrests are being made and when and where they are taking place; to detect accident and violation repeaters; to ascertain the degree and quality of enforcement and to compare the present record with past records; and to determine the success or failure of prosecution. Analysis of traffic records enables the administrator to discover whether the program is reaching objectives or whether modifications are necessary. Traffic records call attention to changed conditions that require alteration in engineering or enforcement policy, and they also make apparent the efficiency or inefficiency of an individual officer and of a squad.

Maintenance It is not important that the police department have under its control the maintenance and installation of signs, signals, and markings, although the police traffic engineer should determine the types that should be installed, the location, and the need for repair, renovation, and so on. The construction and maintenance work may be done by a department of public works, although there is no particular disadvantage to having this work handled by the police.

TRAFFIC ENGINEERING

Engineering is one of the primary police traffic-control techniques. The purpose of traffic engineering is to design roadway facilities so as to lessen the frequency of accidents and the amount of congestion and thus facilitate safe, rapid movement.[1] A foolproof design of roadways that makes dangerous or improper driving difficult and congestion unlikely is the goal of the engineer.

City, county, and state engineering departments concerned with the design, construction, and illumination of streets, however, do not usually have a continuing responsibility for their safe and effective use or for traffic engineering per se. They may not ignore the needs of police traffic enforcement and engineering, but these functions are not their main purpose.

The police, on the other hand, have a responsibility for the continued safe and efficient use of roadways. Providing free and safe traffic movement is one of the major police duties. It is never fully accomplished because the movement of automobiles and people results in accidents and congestion. The police should be alert for evidences of accident and congestion hazards in their day-to-day operations; they should discover the causes and initiate their correction.

The ease with which the police can accomplish their traffic purpose depends greatly on the quality of traffic-engineering work in the community. Good engineering—as, for example, in the location and timing of traffic signals—simplifies traffic control and frees manpower for more important duties. On the other hand, poor engineering, as in the installation of many unnecessary stop signs, makes enforcement difficult, increases the accident rate, damages police prestige, and threatens satisfactory public relations.

Traffic-Engineering Activities It is important at this point to note the distinctions between general traffic engineering and police traffic engineering. The primary purpose of both is to effect the safe and easy movement of automobile and pedestrian traffic. Their goals, however, are accomplished by different methods; many of the techniques used in one are not used in the other.

General traffic engineering builds safety and facility into the highway system; it includes large-scale, long-range planning and construction of major improvements in the street and highway system. New streets, elevated highways, freeways, grade separations, and other elements of the road system that require much time, money, and effort for their planning, promotion, and accomplishment are examples. While traffic control is simplified by general traffic engineering, responsibility for the planning, promotion, and construction of large-scale roadway projects must rest on some agency more suitably designed for this purpose than the police.

Police traffic engineering, by contrast, is concerned primarily with the

---

[1] It is not the purpose of this book to explain police traffic-engineering techniques. Discussions of them may be found in the following: John E. Baerwald, ed., *Transportation and Traffic Engineering Handbook*, Institute of Traffic Engineers, Prentice-Hall, Inc., Englewood, N.J., 1976; and *Traffic Accident Investigator's Manual*, 4th ed., Northwestern University Traffic Institute, Evanston, Ill., 1963.

440   OPERATIONS

discovery and remedy of accident and congestion hazards. Surveys, studies, compliance checks, and the tabulation of accident and enforcement facts provide data relating to accidents, traffic flow and volume, and parking and driving practices. This information must be analyzed to reveal physical conditions that contribute to accidents and congestion. Unsatisfactory conditions may frequently be remedied by the use of signs, signals, markings, islands, median strips, intersection redesign, loading and parking facilities, and street illumination.

The Traffic Analyst (Police Traffic Engineer) Decisions relating to any of the actions listed above should be based on studies by a qualified traffic engineer. Solutions to traffic problems attempted without traffic-engineering skills are little more than guesses and often prove to be expensive experiments.

A traffic engineer is as essential in the continuing service of discovering and correcting hazards as he is in designing the road system to ensure maximum safety and facility in its use. Police traffic-engineering activities are an integral part of the traffic-control program; without them, the police cannot provide maximum safety in traffic movement with minimum inconvenience and delay. A police traffic engineer should be appointed to perform such essential tasks as the following:

1 Discovering the need for, proposing, and promoting traffic ordinances and the efficient use of signs, signals, and markings for the regulation of automobiles and pedestrians

2 Detecting dangerous intersections, streets, and districts and compiling and analyzing traffic facts relating to them in order to ascertain and eliminate the contributing factors

3 Establishing the need for improved street lighting, throughways, bypasses, and one-way and restricted streets, as well as median strips, safety islands, and other devices for channeling traffic flow

4 Evaluating parking needs, proposing suitable parking restrictions, and ascertaining safe speeds on curves, straight stretches of roads, and the approach to intersections

5 Organizing and directing traffic surveys and checking the observance of speed, sign, signal, turning, passing, and other regulations

6 Analyzing accident reports and enforcement data and ascertaining the speed of vehicles from skid marks leading to the point of collision

Police Review of Subdivision Design Plans Some cities allow the police department to review proposed street and grade layouts for new subdivisions or revamping of existing streets. The purpose of the review is to detect potentially dangerous conditions, such as long, straight, uninterrupted lengths of grade which encourage speeding. Police review can also result in changes which enhance patrol coverage in general, the blockade of an area with a lower number of officers, emergency-response routes, beat layout, and so on.

TRAFFIC 441

PUBLIC EDUCATION

Statistics indicate that the human factor—the willingness of drivers and pedestrians to take unwise risks, coupled with inattention as a result of emotional pressures—is a cause of a large number of automobile accidents. Defects in roadways and automobiles, physical defects of motorists and pedestrians, and lack of driver and pedestrian skill are contributory factors in some traffic accidents. The majority occur, however, when there is no defect in the driver, equipment, or roadway, and they involve the skilled rather than the unskilled driver. The contributing factor in these accidents is attitude, which also aggravates congestion problems.

Driver Attitude Attitude is the state of mind that influences conduct for good or bad. An improper attitude induces violations that represent bad driving manners; the guilty motorist is finally involved in an accident. An improper driving attitude causes over 80 percent of all accidents because it is an overlapping cause; the potency of each contributing factor is influenced by the attitude of the motorist and may be compensated for by a good attitude to the point where the factor becomes relatively insignificant. A driver with physical defects but with a proper attitude may drive a defective vehicle through hazardous locations in relative safety; he may be a more successful motorist than the person who has no physical defects and possesses a perfect vehicle but whose attitude results in bad driving practices.

Since the great majority of accidents are the direct result of a selfish attitude that causes the motorist to disregard the safety and convenience of others, the most productive direction for police effort is toward the correction of the unsatisfactory attitudes of drivers.

Correction of poor driving attitudes through education should be carried out by means of news releases, television and radio spot announcements, and lectures (in schools and before public audiences). Attitudinal problems, including the use of alcohol, should be clearly identified as accident causes, and the consequences of violations—in terms of both damage and injury as well as fine or imprisonment—should be identified with equal clarity.

Effectiveness of Education For each dollar expended, public education offers greater immediate results in preventing accidents than either engineering or enforcement. Important engineering changes to eliminate traffic problems require time-consuming and costly major construction projects. Even such relatively minor undertakings as signal installations and intersection redesign are quite expensive and frequently require considerable time to accomplish. The enforcement of traffic regulations by the presence of a police officer and by arrest and punishment of the offender is expensive in terms of salary and operating costs, and the police frequently pay a still higher price in terms of damage to public good will. Further, a decrease in the accident rate following rigid enforcement results from the publicity (i.e., the inadvertent "education" of the potential offender by the driver who has been arrested) as much as from the actual punishment of the offender. A well-rounded program of education reaches more people than an enforcement program because it affects every citizen in the community. The police have media at their disposal that may be used at little or no expense to win support by education; the subject matter is news, and other agencies, also interested in public safety and traffic control, are willing to help.

Public Education Objectives Public education in traffic safety should be directed at two objectives: (1) winning public understanding of police traffic problems and support of the programs, policies, and methods used in their solution, and (2) improving habits of safety among individual drivers, pedestrians, and schoolchildren. Educational programs, designed to accomplish these purposes, should be specific and forthright; little is accomplished by vague generalities.

The first objective is attained by explaining the department's purpose, the relationship between the accident rate and enforcement, the reason for selective enforcement, the need for engineering improvements, the results of engineering and enforcement failure, and the progress and effectiveness of the police traffic program. The public is thus convinced of the need for action. For example, public information on the accident results in inadequate street lighting will promote its improvement; a diminished accident rate due to improved street illumination at one location will promote similar improvement at other locations when the facts are made public.

The second objective, that of influencing motorists and pedestrians to move safely, is perhaps the primary purpose of public education in traffic safety. It is attained by improving the skill of motorists and pedestrians, increasing their knowledge of regulations and sound practices, and promoting their desire to move with consideration for the safety and convenience of others. This is accomplished by training in superior driving and walking practices, by disseminating information to ensure that the public understands traffic regulations and appreciates their purpose, and by stimulating an active public disapproval of noncompliance with safe practices. Of these, the most important is the development of attitudes that favor safe practices and condemn behavior that disregards the comfort, convenience, and safety of others. People's great desire for public approval and favorable recognition causes them to conform to public opinion.

This second objective of public education is also an objective of enforcement. Enforcement, however, is intended principally for the driver who demonstrates by willful and persistent violations a driving attitude not amenable to correction by the education process. There is not a sharp line of demarcation between education and enforcement; enforcement is a form of education for those who will learn in no other way. For the purpose of this discussion, however, educational processes directed against the individual violator are considered enforcement, in contrast to those educational activities which are directed at large numbers.

TRAFFIC

Education Must Precede Enforcement Enforcement not preceded and accompanied by a thorough education of the public regarding the regulation is almost invariably unsuccessful. Punishment for a violation that results from ignorance of the regulation usually creates an undesirable attitude and ill will toward the police. Inadvertent violations of this kind indicate a need for more adequate signs and markings and the dissemination of regulatory information. Disposition of these inadvertent violators should be directed primarily at their education.

Police Participation in Education Essential The police should participate in the coordination of the educational efforts of all interested community agencies. Public education is the most important activity of the local safety organization; public opinion is the device by which it attains its objectives. The police should participate actively in the organization of a local safety group and in its program of education; they discover needs and obtain facts which aid the local safety group in establishing an effective program. Organizing the community for traffic safety is discussed later in this chapter.

Police participation in all phases of public safety education has important values; in addition to stimulating safe practices, valuable contacts are made which elicit favorable public reactions, particularly in police relationships with juveniles.

A program of public education requires manpower and considerable effort. In small departments it may be carried on as a part-time activity by some designated member of the traffic division, for example, the traffic engineer, the chief accident investigator, or the traffic captain. In departments of more than 150 personnel, one officer should devote full time to these duties.

Public Relations Activities Some departments, recognizing that the public needs to be informed regarding the problems and activities of each operating unit, have an auxiliary unit engaged in coordinating and directing all police public information and education activities. Because of the importance of the traffic problem and the need for public support in its solution, the traffic division should take a more active part in this work than any other division if a specific unit for disseminating traffic-safety information has not been established.

Changes Brought About by New Highway Designs The advent of freeway travel brought with it some unusual problems. Some are related to the difficulty in moving from driving habits literally acquired in the horse-and-buggy age to those required on modern, high-speed freeways. An example is the emergence of the "accordion effect" as a recurring condition on highways. This phenomenon results in millions of hours lost to our economy and our leisure time, primarily because drivers do not understand what causes the condition and, as a result, do not alter their habits. Many of the delays on freeways which seemingly have no cause and many jams which are erroneously attributed to "rubbernecking" are in reality caused by this phenomenon.

The accordion effect arises when there is a momentary slowing of vehicles during high-speed, moderate- to high-volume traffic flow. Drivers then begin "closing up" space between vehicles—as they have done since the horse-and-buggy era—and soon the traffic comes to a halt, simply because modern vehicles can slow to a stop faster than they can accelerate. The solution to this aggravating problem requires educating drivers to maintain several car lengths between vehicles, even when they come to a complete stop. The space between vehicles then enables a column of cars to accelerate together, rather than one at a time.

Driver education can help in other situations; for example, drivers who are already on the freeway can be encouraged to move into traffic lanes which do not conflict with traffic coming in from access ramps. Another beneficial education program concentrates on training drivers to avoid blocking intersections.

Obviously, this sort of public education cannot be carried out in a vacuum. Unless educational campaigns of this type are given statewide or regional attention, a smaller city cannot hope to influence driving habits within its area if a large percentage of the motoring public is only passing through.

A police car with public-address equipment, used at signalized intersections with a large volume of pedestrian traffic, is an effective means of educating pedestrians. Drivers may also have their attention called to bad practices while the public-address car is in motion or while it is strategically parked.

Public-address equipment also has great crowd-control value. It is useful in directing and controlling mass pedestrian traffic at athletic events and other public gatherings, in clearing the route for parades, in moving onlookers back onto the sidewalk, and in controlling crowds of curiosity seekers at the scenes of explosions, fires, and other accidents. In tactics against mobs or potentially dangerous crowds, public-address equipment is useful in directing police action, in attracting and holding the attention of the crowd, and in cooling tempers with a rational presentation of facts.

Public-address equipment is profitably used in public education to present accident facts and other information. Children are particularly attracted to such presentations. A tape deck in the car permits the playing of safety messages and music through the loudspeaker system to children during school recess or in neighborhoods where children play in the street. Cautioning small children against running (as opposed to walking) across the street and other dangerous practices should be a regular service of this car while patrolling. This form of police attention has a desirable effect on relations not only with the children but also with their parents.

Junior Traffic Patrols Junior traffic patrols, through the supervision and direction of selected schoolchildren organized and trained for this purpose, provide safety for children crossing streets to and from school and develop a sense of civic responsibility in the children. The resultant relationship between the police and the children promotes friendship and respect for the police. Motorists, parents, and school authorities approve of the operation of the patrol because it diminishes the danger of injury to schoolchildren, makes them safety-conscious, and trains them in discipline.

The police department should promote the development of the junior traffic patrol and supervise its operation. The patrol should be organized into small squads of two to four children at intersections near schools. These squads, under the immediate direction of a student patrol leader, should be organized and trained by the police. One officer, with such aid as the size of the community warrants, should be placed in charge to oversee the operation of all junior traffic squads; this officer should coordinate with the school principal the selection of patrol members on the basis of scholarship and conduct, supervise the maintenance and distribution of equipment, and keep a membership roll.

Many cities enact ordinances forbidding motorists to drive through signs being displayed by the junior traffic patrol. The license numbers of automobiles in violation of this regulation are reported by the junior traffic patrol to the police, who call the violation to the attention of the offending motorist and explain the purpose and operation of the school patrol. Drivers are prosecuted for flagrant violations.

Traffic-Violator Schools   The school for the traffic violator is a heritage of the Depression of the 1930s, when the automobile continued to be a prime necessity for those on relief. Traffic courts could send indigent drivers to jail in lieu of a fine for minor infractions, but the trivial character of many violations made this procedure unwarranted because of its vicious influence on the attitude of the victim whose sagging morale needed bolstering. The other alternative, which made privileged motorists of the indigent, was to place the violator on probation or suspend the sentence, which was usually the equivalent of outright dismissal. The traffic-violator school proved to be a solution to this problem, and of course it served to inform and instruct drivers in traffic regulations and sound driving practices.

Court Cooperation Essential   A traffic-violator school cannot operate efficiently without court cooperation. The court must know that the school exists, why it exists, and the type of cases that should be referred to it for treatment. Special legislation is not needed for a traffic-violator school if enrollment is made a condition of probation. Failure to comply with the school program results in the return of the offender to court as a violator of the condition of his or her probation. Some police departments offer selected traffic violators, without the formality of a court appearance, a choice between attending the traffic-violator school and posting a bond.

Public School Assistance   The public school systems of some communities provide instructors for traffic-violator schools, and in others the instruction is carried out by the police department. Teaching experience is an asset, and a thorough knowledge of the traffic rules and regulations and the best driving practices is essential. If a police officer conducts the course, he or she should be in uniform so that contact with the students will clearly be one between the police and the motorist.

Multiple Sessions Some departments provide several sessions of the traffic school because of the advantages in teaching a class of fewer than 30 students. Usually some sessions are held at different hours of the day to accommodate persons whose work time may conflict with the regular school schedule. When several classes are provided, drivers should be assigned according to driving record, age, and experience. This is especially important in reference to age, and some departments reserve one class for juveniles. Special notices may be served on juvenile offenders to appear in traffic school with the consent of their parents and without the formality of a court appearance.

Drinking-Driver Schools A variation of traffic-violator school specifically oriented to drinking drivers is found in some locations, principally for social or occasional drinkers who are arrested. The Alcohol Safety Action Program (ASAP) in Arlington, Virginia, requires drivers to be screened as to alcohol usage, and those who are problem drinkers or alcoholics are provided with counseling therapy and other treatment. A substantial percentage, however, are deemed to be social drinkers and opt for the classroom instruction in lieu of trial, jail sentence, fine, or other penalty. The program is operated on a pretrial basis, and those who successfully complete the therapy or school are given a trial one year after arrest, at which time they may be found not guilty, or their sentence may be suspended.

Bicycle-Rider Schools Similar schools are conducted by some departments for children violators of bicycle-riding regulations. Some departments provide instruction in safe bicycle-riding practices to children at the schools or at police headquarters; some also promote bicycle-riding clubs organized for safety.

High School Safety Programs Most high schools now recognize their responsibility for providing driver training to their students; dual-control automobiles are used for practice after classroom instruction. In some communities the police participate in the promotion of this training as well as in the more general training in safety in the lower grades, frequently providing instructors for this purpose. Many high schools organize traffic-safety committees to promote desirable attitudes and safe driving and walking practices among the students.

TRAFFIC ENFORCEMENT

Public education will not win compliance from all motorists. Enforcement procedures must be used in dealing with nonconformists who persist in improper driving practices. Enforcement is not limited to punitive measures

TRAFFIC

based on arrest and prosecution but includes such nonpunitive procedures as active conspicuous patrol, warnings, and traffic-violator schools. These ensure a reasonable compliance with regulations and are usually more acceptable to motorists than fines and jail sentences.

Punishment, however, may not be eliminated as a traffic-enforcement device. Some persons are amenable only to punitive treatment, and punitive measures are also needed to restrict the driving of those who are incompetent because of physical or emotional defects or a lack of skill. License revocations and jail sentences for the more wantonly vicious drivers are essential for the protection of the general public. The threat of prosecution is an important control mechanism.

The effect on the attitude of motorists of methods used in the enforcement of traffic regulations must be considered because public support favorably influences driving habits. The customary police procedure, when a police officer has observed a violation of a criminal law or (to a lesser extent) a regulatory measure, is to arrest and prosecute the offender. This procedure, however, is not so effective against the traffic violator as it is against the criminal because many citizens are ambivalent about rigid traffic enforcement, although nearly all approve the vigorous enforcement of criminal laws. If unfairly applied, punishment may create or aggravate an improper driving attitude. Rigid punitive enforcement will fail unless it is based on a sound foundation of favorable public sentiment created by suitable public education. No permanent good may be expected from a control based on fear when the majority do not favor the regulation. Traffic laws, therefore, should be enforced with minimum punishment so that the unfavorable effect of punitive treatment on the attitude of the driver will not destroy the enforcement tolerance of the community.

Enforcement Tolerance The enforcement tolerance of a community is the amount or degree of enforcement that may be maintained indefinitely with public acceptance. It is determined by such factors as the general temperament of the community, its leaders, the press, and the reputation of the department. It is influenced, on the one hand, by the public good will and understanding attained by the police and, on the other hand, by the drain on this good will and understanding resulting from unpopular police activities. Public disapproval of traffic enforcement arises from a lack of understanding of its purpose and value or from a conviction that it is unnecessary, unsuited to its purpose, or directed against individuals without justification.

The police should carefully build and protect the reserve of tolerance so that public resentment will not at any time suddenly overwhelm it. Purposeless arrests should be avoided, and warnings and nonpunitive enforcement procedures should be substituted for citations when the driving history and circumstances warrant such action, especially in the case of inadvertent violations. The attitude, manner, and personality of the officer who takes the action also strongly influence the amount of resentment developed.

Consequences of Unwise Enforcement The primary purpose of police action against the traffic violator is to improve the violator's driving habits so that he or she will be less likely to become involved in an accident or to interfere with the smooth flow of traffic. When enforcement is applied indiscriminately to a substantial percentage of the motoring public, many drivers who do not merit such treatment are inconvenienced and punished. Citizen antagonism and resentment can then diminish the public cooperation which is so essential to the successful accomplishment of the total police job. Unselective and ill-advised enforcement results in the dissipation of police energy which should be reserved for persons who are amenable only to enforcement procedures.

Maximum Safety with Minimum Penalty Maximum safety with minimum public inconvenience, penalty, and resentment should be the police goal. Maximum safety is obtained by the use of the most effective control procedures directed at the group most likely to have accidents. The police should therefore classify drivers according to their accident expectancy and ascertain the relative effectiveness and public acceptance of the several methods of treatment, i.e., the warning, the citation or arrest, and the traffic-violator school. They should also tolerantly interpret and fairly apply regulations and direct their efforts against violations which cause accidents, taking into account the areas and the hours of greatest frequency.

Studies made in some jurisdictions indicate that it is possible to classify drivers according to their accident expectancy and thus provide a treatment for the violator or accident driver designed to meet his or her special need. Such a program, coupled with a substantial increase in public education activities, may result in a great reduction in the number of court convictions and a corresponding reduction in revenue to the jurisdiction. This fact alone stands as a bar to the institution of a program of maximum safety with minimum penalty in many revenue-conscious communities. The maintenance of a driver file in a large community presents clerical tasks of such proportions as to make its operation not feasible except with the use of costly electronic data processing. Some persons may argue that the use of a written warning or notice of violation described in the next section is a usurpation of the judicial function by the police; this conclusion does not seem sound as long as the police are to exercise any discretion in dealing with traffic violators, and it seems that discretion is essential.

Systems for Treating Violators

The police, in formulating their traffic-control policy, should weigh the relative cost of the treatment procedures to be used. The total cost includes not only the salaries and other expenses of administering the treatment but also the loss of public sympathy and support which may be incurred by unjustified or unreasonably severe punishment.

TRAFFIC

The Written Warning The warning notice results in less expenditure in both respects. An officer will serve a larger number of warnings than citations because the service of warnings involves less emotional strain and is more frequently used in borderline cases. The operating cost is consequently less, and in addition, resentment engendered by the warning is outweighed by the good will induced. Greater use should therefore be made of the warning notice on first violations and, in communities where an unusually large number of warnings are served, on second violations in a manner to be described later.

A written warning should always be used instead of a verbal warning because it exerts a more effective influence on the driver and aids in recording the incident for guidance in disposing of future violations.[2]

Traffic-Violator School Because of its great effectiveness, the traffic-violator-school treatment should be used in those cases where the warning has proved ineffective. The traffic-violator school creates some resentment because of the time required for attendance, but this is outweighed by good will created through close contact between a suitable police instructor and the student.

The Citation The cost of administering the citation procedure that results in a penalty is considerably greater than the cost of administering a warning. The citation followed by fine, jail, or license revocation is the form of treatment which is most commonly found in the United States. The citation or summons is the backbone of the police traffic-enforcement effort. However, it produces the most hostility because drivers often resent the penalty and lose confidence in the police department for penalizing them for an act which they almost invariably justify.

Notice of Violation A notice of violation specifying that a summons will follow if the driving history shows an unfavorable record of violations and accidents provides maximum opportunity to apply the most suitable enforcement procedure; it may be used as a warning except in cases where the driving history and the circumstances of the violation justify a more rigid treatment. It has the further advantage of removing this decision from the traffic officer, who, in addition to lacking the driving history of the offender, may be unduly influenced by the personality of the motorist and other extraneous factors.

This system works best if it is controlled at the state level. Many states now administer a "point" system, which operates on the same concept as the notice of violation described above. These systems often have license revocation as a powerful stimulus to compliance. Individual agencies supply conviction information into a state computer tied to driver's-license files and vehicle-

---

[2]When the form used is 5 by 3 inches, the original may be filed in the driver index, thus avoiding the need to prepare an index card. Statistical compilations are more readily made, however, when a punch card is used as the form. The duplicate copy should be given to the motorist.

registration records, and in some cases there may also be linkage to a centralized file containing notices of outstanding warrants. This prevents the issuance of license plates or tags and the renewal of driver's licenses to those with unpaid traffic warrants.

Nonresident Drivers   Policy should also be established concerning action to be taken against out-of-state motorists. To ignore their transgressions fosters dangerous driving practices, but to treat them as local drivers creates unfavorable relations with the offenders, their friends in the community, and others who may thus be influenced to avoid the community. A middle course that grants some tolerance to nonresidents, especially on local regulations, is wise. Violations of universally adopted regulations which menace public safety, however, justify no latitude beyond that granted local drivers.

The Drinking Driver   The police should emphasize policy and procedures for the enforcement of the law forbidding driving while under the influence of alcohol. Chemical tests of intoxication (using a breath analyzer or direct examination of blood alcohol) provide information on which a wise enforcement policy may be based. The current practice in many jurisdictions is to declare that a level of .10 to .15 milligrams of alcohol per cubic centimeter of blood is prima facie evidence of the influence of alcohol. Since severe intoxication is not necessary to make the drinking driver a hazard, the police should seek the cooperation of the courts in treating more severely other violations by drivers who have been drinking but who are not sufficiently under the influence to justify arrest on that charge, a fact readily brought to the attention of the court by indicating on the citation or notice of violation that the driver had been drinking or by placing the initials "HBD" on the margin of the form.

Enforcement Standards

The principal moving-traffic violations should be circumscribed with written standards or enforcement-policy statements to guide enforcement so that traffic efforts are uniform and fair. Without definite policies for enforcement, officers may vary widely in the degree of latitude they may allow before taking enforcement action. For example, deciding whether a driver has moved through a stop sign without stopping requires a judgment on the part of the officer, which must in turn be based on a standard he has in mind at the time he observes the violation.

To ensure uniformity of enforcement action, the administrator should be sure that written standards exist. In the case of the stop sign, such a standard might very well be to take enforcement action if the driver does not slow to walking speed. Requiring such standards is difficult and painstaking, but it is well worth the effort. If the standard cannot be reduced to writing, this may raise doubts about its propriety in the first place.

The policy for speeding violations should mention the minimum number of

TRAFFIC 451

miles over the speed limit which should warrant a warning, the speed which makes a summons or citation mandatory, and the tolerance which will be subtracted from the speed shown on the summons to allow for calibrations. The policy for violations at a stop signal should clearly spell out how far an automobile is allowed to go into the intersection before a citation should be issued. (In the case of the red-light violation, most traffic administrators permit a car to enter an intersection on a yellow light, but they instruct officers to write citations if the vehicle's front wheels cross the near curb line of the intersection after the yellow light changes to red.)

Enforcement-Policy Guides The following guidelines should be kept in mind when developing enforcement standards and policies:

1 Do not permit the public to know of latitudes permitted in the enforcement policy.

2 Do not allow a latitude beyond safe limits.

3 Avoid imposing inconvenience or penalty on motorists except when necessary to prevent actions that are likely to result in accidents or congestion.

4 Ensure that there is uniform application of enforcement policies by all members of the force.

5 Action should not be taken against a driver merely because there has been an accident. If the violation is one which a reasonable officer, had he observed it, would ordinarily have taken action against, the issuance of a citation after the accident would seem justifiable. However, it is not necessary to issue a citation just to determine who is at fault; that kind of determination can be made with a simple notation in the report as to the responsible party. It should also be kept in mind that testimony in accident cases in court can account for a great number of hours of lost time or overtime.

The Enforcement Program

Congestion Assignments The portion of the total traffic force to be assigned to intersection and street-crossing duty and to overtime-parking violations is influenced by many factors over which the police have no control. These include street characteristics, the suitability of regulatory devices, the volume of vehicular and pedestrian traffic, and the public demand for this regulation. Such assignments rob the force of officers who would otherwise be available for general law enforcement and accident-prevention duties, and hence mechanical devices should be used to minimize the need for officer control whenever possible.

The prevention of accidents is more important in most communities than the congestion problem, which involves public convenience rather than safety. The police, therefore, should use every form of ingenuity to shift their efforts from the problem of congestion to the problem of accident prevention in order to maintain a suitable balance between the less important and the more important. The congestion problem, of course, must be properly met, but the department that attaches undue importance to it will so dissipate its energy as to leave insufficient strength for a proper accident-prevention job. A safe rule to follow is to use no more officers on routine duties arising from congestion than are necessary to prevent too many accidents and to eliminate too frequent clogging of the easy flow of traffic.

Intersection and Crosswalk Duty   The extent to which the regular nontraffic patrol force is used in short-time, peak-congestion tasks influences the need for traffic officers for these assignments. When a traffic officer is not available for the performance of these duties, the usual part-time nature of crosswalk and intersection traffic duty makes desirable the assignment of the patrol officer on the beat up to the point where it requires so much of his time that it seriously interferes with his regular patrol duties. When the traffic-control effort requires almost the full time of an officer, this indicates the need for an added assignment to the unit in the department which handles intersection control.

Regulation of Moving Traffic   The primary responsibility for the enforcement of moving-traffic regulations should rest on the patrol division. The enforcement of these regulations does not require special skill and ability, and it is not dissimilar to other tasks performed by motorized-patrol officers. Since the necessity for this enforcement is not restricted in time or place, the complete coverage provided by the 24-hour, jurisdictionwide general patrol makes important the application of this force to the regulation of moving traffic. Because of the large number engaged in the task when the primary responsibility for enforcement of moving-traffic regulations is given to patrol, a high level of enforcement may be maintained without imposing an unreasonable burden on any one officer. Consequently, having a traffic squad devote its full and exclusive attention to the enforcement of moving-traffic regulations usually is not justified.

Selective Enforcement   To ensure maximum reduction of accidents, enforcement pressure should be applied, in proportion to need, to the locations and at the hours of greatest accident expectancy; it should be directed against the violations which cause the largest number of accidents and against the group of drivers who are responsible for the majority of the violations and who constitute the greatest hazard to the community. Failure to apply selective enforcement dissipates police effort and arouses public resentment.

Changes should be made in the enforcement program to meet changed conditions; an activity that is no longer of prime importance should not be continued. As soon as a hazardous condition has been remedied, the police should turn their attention to other problems.

The enforcement pressure should be uniformly kept at as high a level as is necessary to maintain a favorable accident rate. Spasmodic drives that result in large numbers of arrests preceded and followed by periods of enforcement inactivity are undesirable. They are unfair to the motoring public; the period of lax enforcement causes a misconception of the point of enforcement, and drives stimulate an overzealous police attention and unwarranted prosecutions of some violators. The inconsistency of spasmodic enforcement confuses the motorist, and prosecution for a previously ignored violation creates resentment.

Some of the violations which result in numerous accidents are traditionally not enforced with great regularity. The administrator should encourage officers to recognize the fundamental relationship between the kind of violation and the frequency of accidents in that category. A great many accidents, for example, are caused by following too closely. Except when it results in an accident, however, most officers neglect the following-too-closely violation in favor of arrests which are more easily judged, such as in stop-sign, traffic-signal, or prohibited-turn violations.

Some additional rules should be observed in setting enforcement policy. A cardinal rule is that an arrest or summons should have some bearing on actions that are likely to result in accidents or congestion. Although there is some enforcement effect to be gained in almost any legitimate arrest or citation, far greater benefit is achieved if the action taken is directed against a violation which is likely to result in an accident or against a violation at locations where accidents have been taking place.

Traffic Analysis An important part of the selective enforcement program is the analysis of accident reports to determine the most appropriate times and locations for enforcement. The traffic division should prepare memorandums and maps showing the location of "hot" streets and intersections. The memorandums should list the desired kind of enforcement action, as well as the locations and times of accidents. The material should be distributed to the patrol division as well as to traffic officers.

Extent of Enforcement The police should strive for a minimum accident goal by using nonpunitive procedures supplemented by enough wisely directed punitive enforcement to maintain a reasonably low accident rate. Warnings and visible patrol, coupled with intensive public education, should be used as far as possible, and punitive enforcement should be used only to the extent necessary. A suitable proportion is thus maintained between punitive and nonpunitive enforcement. As the accident rate is brought down, enforcement may be lessened; this result can be brought about automatically by maintaining a constant enforcement index.

Most police departments do not maintain a sufficient enforcement pressure to attain a favorable accident rate. Few police departments provide too much enforcement; when they do so, it is invariably too much punitive enforcement in proportion to nonpunitive enforcement.

Many police departments have demonstrated that rigid enforcement of traffic regulations, following a period of lax enforcement, lowers the accident rate. Communities having a high enforcement index generally have a low accident rate. Consequently, it might appear that all traffic accidents could be eliminated by completely enforcing driving laws. A point of diminishing returns, however, occurs; as the enforcement index is increased, the resulting reduction in accidents is not in proportion. It has been observed also that when a favorable accident rate has been established, it can be continued only by carrying out extensive educational and nonpunitive procedures or by continuing to increase the enforcement pressure.

Enforcement Index This index is the ratio of hazardous moving-traffic-violation convictions (with penalty) to injury accidents. It is useful in maintaining a suitable level of enforcement and in ensuring its uniform application where and when it is needed. Each citation should have an equivalent weight in warnings and notices of violations. Three warnings or notices of violation, for example, may be considered equal to one citation for the purpose of evaluating the enforcement pressure.

An enforcement index should be established to attain a desirably low accident rate. The selection of the index will be influenced in part by the enforcement tolerance of the community, although the hazard of a low tolerance may be met by increasing the proportion of nonpunitive enforcement without lessening the effective pressure. A low conviction index (percentage of those arrested who are convicted) requires a higher arrest rate if the enforcement index is to be maintained.

The enforcement index should not be less than 10 (i.e., 10 citations or 30 notices of violation for each injury accident), and traffic authorities have often mentioned an index of 20 as optimal.

Justification for the enforcement index rests on the inescapable fact that violations, and consequently accidents caused by them, are decreased by enforcement. The presence of accidents is evidence of a need for enforcement, and their frequency is a measure of the amount of enforcement needed.

Relationships with the Traffic Court

The traffic court bears a tremendous responsibility for the effectiveness of the police program. If a high percentage of violators receive warnings or suspended sentences from the court or if sentences imposed are unduly lenient, the enforcement program will suffer. The police should therefore make certain that proper relationships exist between the administration of the department and the court (including the agency which prosecutes traffic offenses).

A common situation which results in the waste of countless man-hours is the practice by some courts of insisting on mandatory appearance of the arresting officer for every arrest which requires the defendant's court appearance. Regardless of the nature of the arrest, whether on a traffic offense or for a criminal charge, the defendant should first make an appearance without the officer's being present to enter a plea of guilty or not guilty. If the plea is guilty, sentencing should be carried out without the presence of the officer. If the defendant pleads not guilty, the case should be scheduled for trial. This

TRAFFIC 455

two-stage system is far superior to the one of mandatory appearance of the officer, since it encourages more enforcement action by officers and wastes much less time of both police and court personnel.

For citations and summonses which do not require a mandatory court appearance, defendants should specify at the time of posting collateral whether they wish to have a court appearance. The appearance date can then be scheduled well in advance so that officers can be requested to appear on specific days and so that courtroom appearances can be grouped together.

Legislation

Since there can be no enforcement without law, the legislative process also merits attention. Legal regulation is needed to standardize driving and walking practices so that motorists and pedestrians may know what is expected of them and what to expect from other motorists and pedestrians. It also lessens hazards by forbidding dangerous practices.

The police are usually best qualified to discover and judge the need for a traffic regulation and the feasibility of its enforcement. They should initiate and assist in drafting needed legislation; they should also review critically all proposed traffic regulations in order to protest the unnecessary and the impractical. Public resentment against improper regulations, especially over-regulation, is usually directed against the police, regardless of who may have been responsible for their enactment.

A regulation may be so difficult to enforce as not to justify its enactment for several reasons: A high degree of compliance is essential if a regulation is to accomplish its purpose, and compliance failure is sometimes a greater hazard than no regulation. Enforcement may require an amount of police effort out of proportion to the value of the regulation. Also, disregard for one regulation breeds disrespect for all, and consequently one unenforced regulation increases the difficulty of enforcing the others. Finally, regulations that are difficult to enforce damage police morale, prestige, and public relations.

In order to ensure conformity with superior regulations, the police should promote the adoption of the provisions of the Uniform Vehicle Code, the Model Traffic Ordinance, and the Manual on Uniform Traffic Control Devices.[3]

ACCIDENT INVESTIGATION

Facts relating to automobile accidents are needed for four purposes: (1) to reveal hazards resulting from the unsuitability or inadequacy of the roadway, adjacent areas, signs, signals, markings, and regulations in order that they may be corrected or safeguarded by selective patrol and enforcement; (2) to discover the types of violations that are the most frequent contributing causes so that the enforcement program may be made more precisely selective; (3) to

---

[3]These model codes and the traffic ordinance have been revised and approved by the National Committee on Uniform Traffic Laws and Ordinances. Copies may be obtained from the committee, 1776 Massachusetts Ave., N.W., Washington, D.C. 20036.

ascertain classes of individuals (by age, occupation, or section of residence, for example) who are involved in accidents so that the educational and enforcement program may be more effectively directed; and (4) to obtain evidence of violations for the purpose of convicting the driver.

Serious Accidents The conviction of the driver is important in accidents involving the drinking driver and in those resulting in manslaughter and hit-and-run violations and, in some cases, personal injury. In other accidents, however, there seems to be no greater justification for convicting the accident driver than for convicting a driver who is guilty of the same violation but who did not have an accident as a result; the first accident driver is not so likely to have another accident as the repeat violator, and the cost of the accident stands as a heavy penalty to the motorist for his or her carelessness.

A complete investigation of accidents—including measurements and photographs of the roadway and adjacent areas, of skid marks, and of the exact place of impact, as well as detailed statements from the drivers and all witnesses—is a costly undertaking that is justified principally when it is necessary to obtain a conviction in injury accidents involving reckless driving or in manslaughter cases. Information essential to meet the first three purposes of accident investigation can be obtained in suitable detail and with satisfactory accuracy in less-serious accidents by less time-consuming methods. Detailed measurements of the roadway and significant parts of the adjacent area are made by the police traffic engineer in the preparation of a condition diagram of an accident-frequent location; properly prepared reports that do not contain exact measurements in less-serious accidents provide the information needed in the preparation of a collision diagram and in summarizing the types of contributing violations and the classes of accident drivers.

Less-serious Accidents An officer sent to the scene of a less-serious accident should assist in untangling traffic and should obtain the identification of the drivers and automobiles and essential information regarding the circumstances so that he can prepare an accident report; he should also instruct the drivers to fill out the required accident-report forms at headquarters. Less-serious accidents reported to police headquarters by the drivers some time after the occurrence do not justify on-the-scene investigation. The accident reports will fulfill the first three purposes of accident investigation; further action is not required unless it appears necessary to obtain a conviction.

The Accident Investigators Traffic-accident investigation is the application to the traffic field of the investigation methods and principles that have long been used in crime-detection work. Accident investigations should be made by beat officers and evidence technicians used in the investigation of crimes (see Chapter 24) because both kinds of investigations—accident and crime—involve the same problems and require the same techniques and equipment.

In the case of injury accidents, the beat officer should decide whether the

TRAFFIC   457

investigation requires the services of the evidence technician in order to
strengthen a case for prosecution. In noninjury accidents, only the beat officer
need be sent (with assistance, if needed, to direct traffic). If the beat officer
recognizes the need for prosecution in such an accident, he should request the
services of the evidence technician.

Follow-up Accident Investigation

Departments having more than 150 members require an accident investigator
on the day shift to follow up on accident investigations in the same manner that
a detective continues the preliminary investigation of crimes by patrol officers
and to ensure, by staff inspection, the adequacy of investigations by patrol
officers and the evidence technicians. In smaller departments, the evidence
technician on the day tour of duty may perform these tasks. The accident
investigator is responsible for the complete and suitable investigation of
accidents by the beat officers and evidence technicians, although he has no
direct control over them. He personally undertakes the continuance of the
investigation of hit-and-run cases and of serious accidents that result, or are
likely to result, in fatalities. In the accomplishment of these tasks, he utilizes
the services of the evidence technicians and patrol officers, as is done by
the detective division (see Chapters 16 and 18).

In departments where the full time of the accident investigator is not
required in following through on accident investigations or hit-and-run cases
and in making staff inspections of these activities, he may, as an aid to the
traffic commander, also inspect the condition of signs, signals, and markings
and the traffic performance of other members of the department, thus ensuring
continuous execution of, and adherence to, procedures. Some of the following
additional duties may be assigned to the accident investigator in small
departments when the limited traffic staff makes it necessary and time allows:
planning enforcement activities of the patrol division and of the special traffic
squad, analysis of accident records to determine educational and engineering
needs, analysis of enforcement records to determine the adequacy and
selectivity of enforcement pressure, the supervision of a junior traffic patrol,
instruction in a traffic-violator school, and the direction of public education.

PARKING CONTROL AND REGULATION

The enforcement of time-limit parking probably has less to do with the
essential police tasks of protection of lives and property than any other activity
now carried out by most police departments. In most cities, enforcement of
limited parking—through parking meters and time-zone parking—is primarily a
device for making certain that parking spaces undergo sufficient "turnover" for
the benefit of businesses in the community. Secondarily, enforcement of
limited parking is intended to supply revenue. In many cases, unfortunately,
the revenue-producing aspect becomes paramount, and the overall police
objectives can suffer because of zealous parking enforcement.

Double Parking The double-parking policy, however, has an influence on traffic flow. Stopping in a double line should be prevented when it interferes with traffic flow. Where "live" double parking does not interfere with moving traffic, it may be allowed for brief periods, but double-parked cars without drivers should not be permitted because they block cars parked at the adjacent curb and thus create public resentment. Double parking of trucks for loading and unloading purposes is a practical business necessity where adequate alley and loading-zone facilities are not available; the need for this practice should be eliminated, however, by the creation of suitable loading facilities.

Time-Zone and Meter Enforcement Policy in the enforcement of overtime-parking regulations should establish the permissible number of overtime minutes that may elapse before a ticket is to be written. Such latitude is justified because the violation does not jeopardize safety and because the resentment thus avoided more than offsets the evils of the overtime.

The original purpose of meter and time-zone enforcement—to produce turnover—is often thwarted, in any event, by allowing the feeding of meters. Since the only logical reason for limited parking in the first place is to produce turnover, feeding of meters should be prohibited. Tire marking, while somewhat more expensive than meter enforcement, should be employed as much as possible to prevent meter feeding.

Personnel to Enforce Parking Regulations The enforcement of time-limit and most other parking regulations requires the assignment of officers who devote most or all of their time to this duty. Some parking regulations may be enforced by officers assigned to intersection or crosswalk duty, and officers assigned to regulate parking should assist at intersections or other points where traffic congestion may require attention.

An officer charged with the enforcement of parking regulations should be furnished with a three-wheeled motorcycle and should also be assigned to a route that makes continuous movement possible without backtracking. In large congested areas that require the attention of several officers, greater police attention to streets having more difficult traffic problems and greater robbery hazards may be ensured by an arrangement of routes that enables a greater number of officers to travel along, and to cross, these thoroughfares more frequently. More complete coverage is thereby provided, and the availability of traffic control to citizens is increased; also, its presence is more apparent to criminals. This is especially desirable in cities where the daytime general patrol is completely motorized.

Revenues from Meter Fees and Fines Revenues from meter and parking fines should be used for improvement of off-street parking facilities. Revenue from meters and fines should not be placed in the city's general fund; when this is done, there is a temptation on the part of city officials to expect a certain level of revenue each year.

Part Four

Auxiliary and Technical Services

Chapter 23

Information Services and Control

The development of computers and the existence of random-access information storage and retrieval systems have created a revolution in police records and communications—a revolution of such dimensions that the word "records" itself seems inadequate to describe the diversified and powerful informational tools now available. Partly for this reason it is now common to refer to a centralized records and communications room as an "information center."

Advantages of the Good Information System

An efficient records and information system is an essential tool of police management and a vital aspect of police operations. Although the primary purpose of a police records system is to serve as the memory of the department, information furnished from records and communications activity is essential to the police administrator in planning and controlling the total activity of the agency.

A good information system serves the following purposes:

- It acts as a general communications device in an agency which operates around the clock, every day of the year.

461

- It serves as the processor and storage point for the basic police records system.
- It serves as the vehicle for the investigation of crimes.
- It permits the identification of individuals and the determination of their status.
- It facilitates the dispatching of police officers to crime scenes and locations of police activities.
- It supplies information for selective enforcement and preventive patrol.
- It supplies strategic information for deploying manpower and for making decisions on the level of services to be rendered.
- It serves as a supervisory device for determining the quality and quantity of work performed by officers.

Day-to-Day Operations A suitable records system contains information useful in the investigation of crimes, in the identification of persons and property, and in daily routine tasks. Reports of crimes and other matters of concern to the police, when classified, indexed, and filed, provide information needed by officers in the field. Records also make it possible to trace the history of possession of property in police custody and establish its final disposition, thus preventing its loss or unauthorized release and ensuring its return to its rightful owner.

Supervision Each police task must be made the responsibility of someone, and each officer must be given unavoidable obligations if administration is to be successful. Police records register these assignments so that supervisors may trace errors and detect oversights and neglect.

Suitable records give supervisory officers a basis for reviewing work and help in their day-to-day operations by revealing deficient or improper handling of cases; they show whether officers were correctly dispatched to the scene of criminal operations, and they disclose the progress of the investigation. Failures to follow up on investigations or otherwise correctly dispose of police business are revealed; such records prevent the individual police officer from conducting an investigation or discontinuing it in violation of departmental policy and sound police practice. The police position is strengthened when the department can disprove charges of improper police action by providing prompt and complete answers to specific allegations and to inquiries from the administrative head of the city, members of the governing board, or citizens.

Justification of Files Every record and file kept in the police department, however, should serve some useful purpose other than generation of statistics. One of the great wastes of police manpower is the development of a file or index containing information which is not used by detectives, police officers, supervisors, the chief, or anyone else in the department for a legitimate operational purpose. All files and records systems should therefore be scruti-

INFORMATION SERVICES AND CONTROL 463

nized with the point of view that a file or system is presumed to be useless, and therefore is to be discarded, unless proved otherwise. The test to be applied should be as follows: (1) Who uses the file? (2) How often is it used? (3) Of what benefit is the use? (4) Could some other source of information serve the same purpose? (5) Is a file with similar information being maintained elsewhere in the department? (6) Is compliance with departmental regulation (as opposed to state law) the only reason the file is maintained?

Development of Strategy Administrative decisions must be based on information gleaned from records and summary reports of present conditions and problems faced by the department, of the work of individual employees, and of activities requiring police attention; prompt analysis of records guides the police official in meeting these demands.

The first step in solving a problem is to diagnose it. For this purpose the police administrator wants facts concerning (1) the character of crimes and other incidents requiring police action and (2) the location, time, and circumstances of their occurrence. Records aid him in the determination of engineering, educational, and enforcement needs. With suitable information, he can identify police hazards, isolate the elements requiring attention, and direct police effort toward eliminating hazards or reducing their potency.

Success in preventing crime and accidents, in apprehending criminals, and in accomplishing the many other tasks of a modern police department depends upon the concentration of efforts when and where they are most needed. Records provide data to assist in the development of police strategy, and they make possible vigorous follow-through procedures.

Measurements of Accomplishment The success of a program launched to lower crime and accident rates may be ascertained by records analysis. Police administration is necessarily haphazard unless the accomplishments of the department and of its component units and individual members are computed and studied. Without these measurements, there is no way of knowing how effective policies and procedures are or of determining accurately the results of changes in methods of operation.

Public Reporting Keeping the public informed of police problems, policies, and procedures is also a vital administrative duty; the success of police programs is dependent on public support, which is more likely to be obtained when the purpose is understood. When the press is regularly supplied with accurate information, editorial-room crime waves are not so frequently manufactured, and a more complete public understanding of police programs is made possible. Information for public dissemination is made readily available to the chief or to the public information office through a suitable records system.

Fiscal Affairs Records supply information useful in preparing and justifying budget estimates. The police program must compete with the programs of other departments for public funds, and it is most likely to receive adequate support when the proposed expenditures are shown in terms of specific work programs designed to provide effective policing and protection from criminals. Records also assist in managing the department's fiscal affairs. Expenditures are thus kept within the limits of appropriations, and accurate payrolls are compiled.

Advantages of Centralization A well-administered central records system ensures this needed coordination and offers many other advantages. Records activities are then concentrated in the hands of a smaller number of individuals who can develop skill in performance. This concentration also permits greater specialization in work with consequent increase in efficiency. Training, supervision, control, and the placing of responsibility are simplified; inaccuracies resulting from lack of skill, deliberate efforts to distort, or an unconscious desire to make favorable returns are diminished. The various records that relate to a particular case, place, person, or problem are centralized in one place. Information obtained by one officer can become the common knowledge of all when records are suitably integrated. Success in dealing with the various phases of complicated criminal cases often depends upon the coordination of all records operations in a single records unit. Needless delay is avoided in searching for records, and a quicker response is possible to any call for information. Finally, a more consistently uniform classification of offenses and other data is ensured.

Assistance in Administrative Control A central records system supplies data essential for administrative control; it aids in the judicious distribution of manpower and police effort; it enables a more reliable evaluation of the efficiency and economy of operations; it makes readily available information for both short- and long-term planning; it provides a prudent control over the assets of the department; and it places responsibility for the effectiveness of records work in a single division head, and the chief then has but one person to contact for records information and reports. In addition, the records division assists in the control of the activities of individual officers and units through a system of record review that ensures that no incident or condition that has been called to the attention of the department is dropped until it has been properly concluded.

Decentralization of Records Detective, traffic, and other divisions frequently wish to maintain their own records, arguing that since they are the units that use the information, they must control its recording. There is no justification in this claim, and the urge, if unchecked, leads to complete decentralization. It may even result in a series of individual, uncoordinated records systems within a single operating division, as when auto-theft, homicide, and robbery sections in large departments establish and operate their own records systems. In recent years, the same tendency has been apparent in the establishment of separate records for the traffic and youth divisions. Such decentralization makes effective control and management of the department more difficult, and

INFORMATION SERVICES AND CONTROL

weaknesses of individuals and units not so easily detected. Also, the various activities of the department are not then so completely integrated into a well-rounded police program.

Perhaps the most serious result of the decentralization of records, however, is the lack of assurance that an honest accounting of police work is being made. When the patrol force keeps its own records, it may be tempted not to record some complaints because a low crime rate reflects to its credit. Detective divisions have falsely improved their standing by failing to keep records of offenses that are not likely to be solved. Such practices have been common in many police departments, and police administrators have been embarrassed when this laxity has been discovered. Integrity in the maintenance of the records system, combined with frank reporting to the public, has always proved to be the best policy in police administration.

Despite the evils of decentralization described above, there are several advantages of decentralization. First, decentralized files tend to be more practical and oriented to the user. Second, they are convenient—especially when there is considerable distance between the central records division and the working areas of detectives and police officers. Third, all investigators need to have a working file with them to facilitate their day-to-day work. Working files should be limited, however, to copies of reports covering *active* investigations, personal notes, witness statements, memos to the file, instructions to the investigator from the supervisor, and photos and diagrams. When the case becomes inactive, only the officer's personal notes and original statements should be kept under strict control at the operating-division level, for use later in court. All other materials should be discarded if appropriate copies are placed in central records files.

Records Work in Operating Divisions   In addition to working files, operating divisions have sometimes been forced to establish their own formal records because the department has failed to organize a single, coordinated system or to establish a competent records division. Also, some records officials have been guilty of forgetting that the sole function of the records division is to provide service to the rest of the department. Failures of certain departments in these respects do not constitute valid proof, however, of the undesirability of a central records system.

The compelling need for concentrating records responsibilities in a central records division does not mean, however, that it performs all the records work. The operating divisions must help to keep the system functioning smoothly, particularly by submitting supplemental reports on time and by supplying information to satisfy Uniform Crime Report requirements relating to crime classification and the descriptions of stolen and recovered property.

Organizing and Staffing the Records and Communications Functions

The organization of the records and communications function is related in large part to the size of the agency. In the very small department, the records and communications tasks are often carried out by a single individual, who answers the telephone, broadcasts calls, and types and files reports.

As a department increases in size, logical division of activity then requires full-time attention to be devoted to the records aspect, while the communications and dispatching activities are carried out by others. In the moderate-sized department, records activities are sometimes organized in a services (auxiliary services or support services) division, while communications functions are retained by the patrol or uniformed division. In still larger departments, retaining the communications function in the uniformed or patrol division is no longer desirable, and the activity is often transferred back to the services division.

The recommended form of organization for moderate-sized and large departments is the establishment of a consolidated information center which places records and communications personnel in close proximity. Although personnel may have separate lines of supervision, with individual records divisions or sections or individual communications divisions or sections, the two functions should be considered part of the department's information center.

An identification unit or bureau is often mistakenly considered to be better placed in a detective or investigation division than in the records division. This philosophy is especially prevalent in departments which place excessive value on the work of detectives, while downgrading the importance of patrol investigations. Identification records should be located physically in the same area as case records, although it may be necessary to have separate supervision of identification personnel.

A records and communications organization for a large police department is depicted in Chart 26.

Security requirements may cause some change in the physical layout of an information center. Most public buildings are vulnerable to attack by highly motivated or determined persons. In some cases, the information center of a police department may have vital communications equipment located near public passageways. Some recent building designs, even in very small departments, tend to separate the communications function from the records function because of fear of bombing or shooting incidents. The communications equipment is then placed in a less-vulnerable area, such as the basement of the building. In a small department, transferring the actual communications

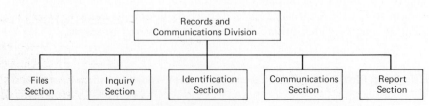

Chart 26 Records and communications division.

INFORMATION SERVICES AND CONTROL

operators to the basement area has serious drawbacks, since it prevents dispatchers from acting as file-search clerks during nighttime hours when records personnel may not be on duty. The solution for this problem is not to change the organizational structure to accommodate the security requirement but to establish the communications point in two places: (1) at a remote dispatching point located within the information center, close to the records, and (2) at the site of the actual communications equipment (plus backup microphones and telephone equipment), located in some protected area away from the information center.

COMPLAINT RECORDING AND PROCESSING

The basic police records and communications process involves:

1 Receipt, by police, of the report of an incident by a citizen requesting services
2 Recording the complaint and initiating the control process which later ensures a match-up of the officer's report with the complaint reported by the citizen
3 Dispatching the complaint to an officer in the field
4 Handling of the event by the officer and writing the officer's report
5 Processing the report, including matching with the complainant's initial information, indexing, and distribution
6 Use of information as appropriate
7 Storage of reports for subsequent later use

These items (except 3 and 4) are discussed in this section.

The Police Case What constitutes a police case is difficult to define. Generally speaking, a police case ought to be recorded as such if there has been a violation of law which is capable of being investigated or if a citizen requests police services which an officer is usually dispatched to provide.

Ordinarily, a call which is merely a request for information or the reporting of a traffic violation or traffic-enforcement action is not considered a police case. At times, the personnel of a department may include administrative calls appearing on a radio log as a part of the legitimate police work load. An entry in an annual report labeled "Police Calls" or "Radio Calls" should be viewed with suspicion unless what goes into the title is defined or clarified. Reporting the number of times an officer goes in or out of service or some other administrative matter as a part of police work load is a disservice to the taxpayer.

Complaint or Case Control

The initial information received from a citizen should be recorded on a form which is used primarily as a control and not as a source of information that is valuable for investigative purposes. Filling out the complaint or case sheet or card (also called a "face sheet," "face card," or "control card") is the first step in the development of a complete police-case report, and this form is usually the first document in a police investigation.

The complaint-control form should be brief and should contain essential information such as (1) the complainant's name, address, and telephone number; (2) the location of the incident; (3) the nature of the incident; (4) a complaint number; (5) space for a reporting area; (6) the provision for making disposition of the incident by the complaint officer or dispatcher; (7) the officer or unit assigned; and (8) space for recording various important times: the time the call was received, the time of dispatch, the time of arrival at the scene, and the time of return to service.

Computer-assisted Complaint Recording   At this point, in some systems in which computers are utilized, complaint-control-card information is keyed in to assist in dispatching. Several systems now in use are based on determination of previous activity at a given address, status of residents, and selection of the nearest available beat officer for assignment to the case.

In the police department in Virginia Beach, Virginia, the complaint operator keys in the information on the location and type of complaint directly onto a terminal, without the use of written notes or forms (see Figure 23–1). The operator then presses a "transmit" button, which places the information on line and onto the CRT screen of the police dispatcher, who sits at a desk across the room (Figure 23–2). In the meantime, the computer (Figure 23–3) has added the dispatch number of the nearest police car in service and another symbol which indicates the priority of the call. The output is then displayed on the CRT (Figure 23–4).

Field Reporting

Few people realize the extent to which police work is related to the use of language and verbal or written communication. Almost everything that a police officer does must be reduced to writing. What is written is often the determining factor in whether suspects are arrested in the first place and, if arrested, whether they are convicted and sentenced. The contents of written reports, in fact, often have great bearing in life-and-death situations. To say that officers need to be proficient in report writing is an understatement.

The ideal report-writing system would make it possible for patrol officers and investigators to produce reports rapidly and accurately, with review possible before the final form is placed into the records system. The report-writing system should minimize grammatical and typographical errors, but it should not require typing. The solution to the problem of finding the ideal system may not be found for many years. Until the ideal method appears, however, certain sound concepts may be applied. The basic report-writing systems now in use are categorized as follows:

INFORMATION SERVICES AND CONTROL   469

Figure 23-1 Complaint operator, computer-aided dispatch system, Virginia Beach, Virginia.

- Dictation by the patrol officer or investigator, by means of a stenographer, dictating machine, or handwritten notes, resulting in a typewritten report which can then be reproduced by various means
- Direct typing by the officer or investigator
- Handwritten report writing

In any of these systems, reports can be reproduced for distribution through the use of form sets with carbon copies or through multilith or electrostatic methods.

Each of these systems has its advantages and disadvantages. The disadvantage of the dictation system is that it introduces delay caused by the wait for typing, close attention to mechanics required by the dictator and the stenographer, and the absence of an immediate copy available for supervisory review.

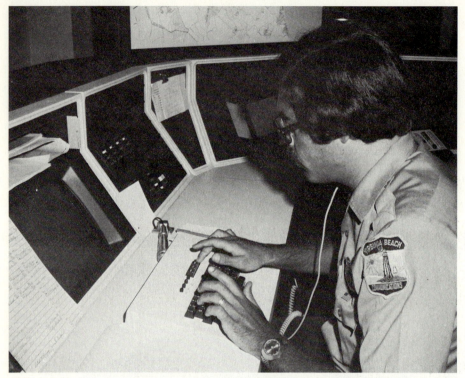

Figure 23–2 Police dispatcher, computer-aided dispatch system, Virginia Beach, Virginia.

Another disadvantage is the difficulty of conveying proper spelling and format for use in form reports. Advantages of the dictation system are greater legibility of reports and speed in terms of the officer's time, particularly with reports that are more than one page in length.

The disadvantage in having officers type their own reports is their lack of typing skill. The Berkeley Police Department used this method for many years, but few officers could ever achieve more than 30 words per minute in typing speed. Moreover, the burden of typing reports in extensive cases is considerable.

The advantage of the handwritten report-writing method is that it results in quick production of a report which can be reviewed immediately by a supervisor. The technique is slower on long reports and requires quality control in terms of legibility and neatness.

The number of report forms should be limited. If a different form is used for every conceivable kind of incident, the quality of report writing will suffer. Most large departments can do very well with four or five field-report forms, such as a miscellaneous-incident report, a crime-against-person report, a crime-against-property report, and a missing-person report.

INFORMATION SERVICES AND CONTROL   471

Figure 23-3 Computer, Virginia Beach Police Department communications system.

Several auxiliary report forms are generally found to be essential: a supplement-report form, which is also used as a continuation sheet for other reports; an arrest report, which should be used for all custody arrests and for some simple arrests as the only report submitted (such as on-view arrests for drunkenness, disorderly conduct, and similar offenses); a property report, which should be the formal means of reporting evidence or property taken into police custody; and a prosecution report, which is invaluable in summarizing the elements of a case which are required for successful prosecution.

Report Review by Sergeants The system based on typewritten or hand-

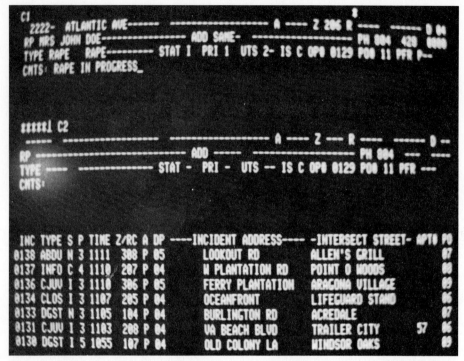

Figure 23-4 CRT display, computer-aided dispatch system, Virginia Beach, Virginia.

written reports by the beat officer or investigator permits immediate review by supervisors. The advantages of the review at this point are great, since it permits the supervisor to evaluate the work of subordinates—at least as it is recorded on paper—and permits correction of errors on the report.

OTHER RECORDS FUNCTIONS

In addition to police cases, the system should record incidents that call for police attention, arrests, the identification and control of persons and property, and activities related to the internal management of the department.

Summary of Incidents That Should Be Recorded If police records are to fulfill the purposes that have been described, all occurrences in the following categories must be recorded:

1 Violations of federal and state laws and city ordinances reported by citizens or other agencies or discovered by the police in any other way. Exceptions are made of city-ordinance violations which are observed by the police (not reported to them) and in which action consists only in a warning that is accepted without protest.

INFORMATION SERVICES AND CONTROL

2 Calls on which officers are usually dispatched, except those which (*a*) are merely requests for information and (*b*) result from traffic violations not endangering life or property.

3 Warrants and subpoenas and arrests not disposed of by citation.

4 Lost-and-found persons, animals, and property.

5 Reportable automobile accidents and reports of personal injuries, bodies found, suicide attempts, damage to public property, and mental cases.

6 Cases in which a police officer is involved in any way in the damage of public or private property or the injury of any person or animal.

7 Miscellaneous cases, general and special orders, violations of rules and regulations, and any other incident that a commanding officer desires to have recorded.

Uniform Crime Reporting   Since the early 1930s, American police departments have been submitting Uniform Crime Report information to the FBI. For an equally long time, the Uniform Crime Report system has categorized incidents into four classifications:

Part I offenses, which are the more serious or more reliably reported crimes as identified by the Uniform Crime Records Committee of the International Association of Chiefs of Police.[1] The crimes of murder and nonnegligent manslaughter, robbery, rape, aggravated assault, burglary, larceny over $50, and auto theft are included in the Part I category. For many years the FBI has also published a tabulation of crimes, most of them Part I offenses, described as *index crimes*. In the index-crime category several recent changes have been made to include larcenies under $50. FBI crime statistics for local agencies include most other categories of crimes with the exception of traffic citations.

Part II offenses, which include most other categories of crimes with the exception of traffic citations.

Part III offenses, which include all reports of lost-and-found persons, animals, and property.

Part IV incidents, which are casualties involving sick, injured, and dead persons and animals. This category includes all traffic accidents, suicides, bodies found, sick persons cared for, and mental cases.

Dissemination of Information and Chronological Records   Police officers, to work effectively, must be (1) notified of cases to which they are assigned and furnished with a brief résumé of essential facts; (2) informed of crimes, other incidents calling for police action, persons wanted and arrested, lost or stolen property, recovered property, administrative orders, and other information; and (3) provided with a chronological record of incidents calling for police

---

[1]Until 1931, IACP maintained the Uniform Crime Report system at IACP headquarters. In that year, the association succeeded in persuading the federal government to assume control over administration of the system. Determination of UCR classifications is still a function of the IACP committee.

action, which assists in ascertaining the case number when information is so meager as to make an index search impractical. The chronological record also establishes the identity and general character of any case that may have become lost or misfiled.

In departments of fewer than 200 officers, these three needs may be met by a typed bulletin, made out continuously as complaint sheets are prepared and in sufficient number so that one can be given to each division, the original being sent to the records office for permanent filing. A copy of the typed daily bulletin may be continuously furnished each division office by teletype. In larger departments a printed bulletin is necessary; detailed information must be limited to major cases, and information summarized for other cases.

Records Relating to Persons Arrested Police responsibility by no means ends with the arrest of the offender. Apprehension imposes additional duties, the performance of which is facilitated by records which relate specifically to the persons arrested. Records procedures aid in the control of the prisoner and his property and ensure a check on his identity and his appearance in court.

By registering information regarding the person arrested, the nature of the charge, and the circumstances of the arrest and release, arrest records answer such pertinent questions as: Who was apprehended? When, where, and why? By whom? How was the arrest made? Suitable arrest records provide for an entry on the daily bulletin so that all officers may know of the arrest; a notice to the court clerk regarding the charge and trial date; adequate lawful control over the privileges of bail and communication with outside persons, pending investigation; reinstatement of these privileges at the conclusion of the investigation or when the need for restrictions has ended; knowledge of, and information concerning, persons in jail; a search of police records before release in order to ascertain whether the prisoner is wanted; and release only by authorized persons.

In departments with district stations and in other large departments where prisoners might be booked at two or more locations, a central booking desk provides a control over detention practices; it has information about whether an individual is in custody, where he is located, and whether his civil rights have been violated by the police. A booking number is obtained by the booking officer from the central booking desk, which records on a log pertinent information relating to the arrestee.

Records relating to the arrested person also accomplish other purposes. The prosecutor is supplied with information useful to him; the time actually served by convicted prisoners is established; in the event of injury to a prisoner, information regarding the circumstances, extent, and treatment is recorded; in some instances, records serve to notify the health department of suspected venereal infection; the prisoner's property is recorded and a receipt is given to him; and control is exercised over cash fines and bail accepted by the police.

Before the prisoner is locked in jail or released on bond, information

INFORMATION SERVICES AND CONTROL

475

regarding the offender, the charge, and the circumstances of apprehension is recorded on an individual arrest card or slip. Each person arrested is assigned a number—the arrest or central booking number—for purposes of audit and control. On the first of each year, this number series may be started anew, preceded by the last two digits of the current year.

The individual arrest card or sheet has a number of advantages over an arrest book or blotter: (1) It may be typed and is therefore more legible. (2) Additional copies may be made to facilitate control and to provide information to the court clerk for the preparation of his docket and to the records office on the disposition of the case. (3) Maximum flexibility is obtained: The arrest report may be sent to the records office for a check to ascertain whether the subject is wanted; it may be kept in a jail file as long as the subject is in custody and thus serve as a jail register; and following the prisoner's release, the record of arrest may be placed in a pending file in the records office until the end of the month, when it may be used for tabulating information for the monthly report.

Privacy of Information and Public Right to Knowledge Recent federal legislation, which is serving as the vanguard for new state laws in many parts of the country, has specified that individuals have a right to privacy with respect to information recorded about them. In essence, the Privacy Act of 1974 allows agencies who are a part of the criminal justice system which is processing an individual to retain information on the involvement of the individual in a criminal or police incident to the extent that the criminal justice process is served and to the extent that there is a history of the incident in the agency's files. However, the nature of the information must be shielded from other parties, both private and public, who are not a part of the criminal justice system in which the crime or incident has placed the individual. For government agencies who need information about the backgrounds of individuals to solve crimes or as a part of character investigation, information in police files may be revealed, but only under certain conditions—that the date, time, and nature of the inquiry be recorded and, further, that disposition of what is done with the information be relayed back to the police department. This law promises to create a vast amount of additional records keeping for police departments.

Paralleling the Privacy Act, and in a sense counteracting it, is the Freedom of Information Act of 1967. The Freedom of Information Act is also a federal law which encourages states to adopt the same kind of legislation for nonfederal situations. Under the federal Freedom of Information Act, and in the several states which have adopted parallel legislation, newspapers, television and radio reporters, and citizens in general have a right to public records and information about crimes and criminals. This puts the act squarely in conflict with the Privacy Act, described earlier. There may be a lengthy period of adjustment before the conflicts are resolved.

Personal Identification Records Fingerprint records are the heart of the identification system. While the fingerprint card ensures positive identification, it should be supplemented by the following records: (1) description cards, (2) single fingerprint cards on selected prisoners, (3) photographs of some criminals, and (4) identification sheets.

Identification records also have their own number series; an identification number is assigned to each prisoner to indicate records relating to him. The same number should be used for each subject regardless of the number of times he may be arrested or fingerprinted. The identification number should appear on the fingerprint card, the identification sheet, the description card, and the photograph.

A policy regarding prisoners to be fingerprinted should be established by department regulation in order to avoid error through misunderstanding. The increasing recognition of the desirability of civilian fingerprinting and the extension of this practice have decreased opposition to fingerprinting prisoners, and in recent years there has been a tendency to increase the classes of offenders fingerprinted. Some departments fingerprint every person lodged in jail, although most of them exempt traffic offenders and the violators of less-important city ordinances. State laws sometimes specify which prisoners shall be fingerprinted. All prints permitted by law should be taken.

Procedures within the Records Division

Police records must be arranged, filed, and indexed if they are to be conveniently available for routine use and for the analysis and review so essential to the effective control of police operations. The tasks involved in processing records must be assigned to the various clerks so that each job will be done at the proper time and in the manner prescribed. For example, one clerk may classify, search, and file fingerprint cards, and another may index them. The disposition sheet may pass through the hands of a number of clerks, each of whom performs some small operation. Each case is inspected by the report-review officer, items are attached to it by the "hookup" clerk, another may index the names and the property stolen, and still another may file the case. In small departments one clerk may perform many different tasks, while in a large department a group of clerks may work at the same task.

Records Operations Records operations are complex and require painstaking effort. Newly obtained information must be added: Property may be recovered, or additional property may be reported stolen; additional information may necessitate changing the classification; and decisions must also be made and recorded in reference to clearance of cases by arrest. There is a danger that a clerk may fail in the performance of some detail which appears to be trivial and unimportant but which is really significant and that the failure will not be discovered until a summary is made at the end of the month. Routine safeguards and periodic checks are needed to prevent slipups from going unnoticed.

One of the simplest safeguards in the conduct of records work is to outline

INFORMATION SERVICES AND CONTROL

the tasks in detail on cards which may be arranged conveniently by identification numbers and letters in a records-operations file. Flowcharts which trace the course of the record from its origin to its final destination are also helpful both to records personnel and to officers in the field. These methods facilitate and ensure the accomplishment of all records operations. They simplify the assignment of various tasks and place responsibility for the performance of each; they ensure that each duty, regardless of its apparent insignificance, is assigned to someone; they permit each clerk to review his or her assignment and to refer to the outlined procedure in case of doubt; and they facilitate a regular and complete inspection of all operations by the division head.

Indexing and Processing

Report indexing is often a bottleneck in the records operation. It can seem like a nonessential function, and as a result, days, weeks, or even months of indexing can be backlogged. The report-writing system itself can be a valuable assist in the indexing process. There are several devices for building in "automatic" indexing, such as devising a 3- by 5-inch portion of the case report or arrest report to be reproduced independently as the index card. Another method (developed by the Novato Police Department in California) is based on the typing of index-card form sets during the preparation of the case-control envelope (the original complaint form completed by the complaint officer). In this manner, index cards are automatically produced for victims or complainants, as well as crime-classification cards. The only supplemental indexing required is carried out when there is an arrest or if the investigating officer believes that some other person, such as a witness or principal, should be indexed.

Index cards may be prepared from the incident or case report to which are attached all related records. Index cards must also be made of correspondence not relating to a case, such as teletype and radio messages from other agencies, and outside (nonlocal) fingerprint cards and circulars. The practice of searching for an index card filed on a previous case in order to add thereon information relating to a current case is an ill-advised, time-wasting procedure.

General Alphabetical Index A general index, with cards arranged in strictly alphabetical order, should be maintained for the purpose of ascertaining the case number, the fingerprint classification, or the previous records of any person who has been the subject of police inquiry or action. There has not been sufficient experience with phonetic filing of index cards in police service to demonstrate the superiority of this system. A single alphabetical index, rather than a separate one for each class of records (i.e., complaint, arrest, identification, and correspondence), has the following advantages: (1) Search is simplified, and errors in filing are lessened, since there is only one index, and (2) only one index card is required for each person in each case, since all pertinent information can be included on it, thus effecting a saving in manpower, supplies, and equipment.

Driver Index A driver index contains the names of persons who have been involved in automobile accidents or who have been arrested or served with citations, notices of violation, or written warnings. A driver index is justified when the volume of accident cases and traffic tickets makes burdensome the search of a large general index for the driving history of the offender. Also, it may be conveniently located at some point removed from the main records office for operation by a clerk who performs duties that require attendance but do not occupy his or her full time.

Other Indexes The following indexes should be considered to be the minimum requirement:

Accident-location index
Classification index
Description index for lost and stolen property ⎫ These indexes are also
Number index for lost and stolen property useful for making manual tabulations for UCR purposes.

Filing Index Cards and Other Records Great care is needed in filing index cards and other records, since misfiling makes them difficult to find. A misfiled card serves as a seed which grows as other items are inadvertently filed beside it. There is only one correct place to file each item; it belongs between two particular cards or records in the drawer, and when it is not between these two, it is misfiled.

Because of the importance of maintaining indexes in good order, department regulation should prohibit the removal of cards from the index and require the fixing of responsibility for filing by the designation of one clerk to file the cards in each index and the prohibition of anyone else doing so. A clerk should be assigned periodically to go through the index files, card by card, to discover and correct errors.

Color of Index Cards and Other Forms Index cards and other forms should be of white stock except when color accomplishes some specific purpose. Index cards of distinctive color on persons wanted and persons with licenses subject to revocation assist search and quick identification. When forms intended for a certain unit or office are of a distinctive color, segregation and routing are simplified, and the chance of error is diminished. Color may be used to indicate degree of urgency and also to assist in periodic purging of obsolete material from files.

The Formal Report-Review System

A formalized report-review system is a definite advantage in promoting operational efficiency. The placement of the review function varies in progres-

INFORMATION SERVICES AND CONTROL

sive police departments. In some agencies, report review is carried out by line sergeants who are provided facilities (working space and access to files) within the records unit. In other agencies, responsibility for report review is specifically assigned to the records function.

Regardless of its placement, the report-review process ought to achieve the following specific purposes:

• Ascertaining that investigators have made correct and complete investigations with particular attention to (1) the questioning of neighbors and the interviewing of witnesses; (2) the use in crime investigation of all facilities in the department and those available to it in the community, state, or nation; (3) the complete investigation of each investigative lead or clue; (4) the notification of other agencies when this procedure is advisable; (5) the sending, if necessary, of letters reporting parole violations and convictions which may result in the revocation of driver's or other licenses; and (6) the explanation to the complainant of the action taken by the department and the results.

• Ensuring that records-division operations are accomplished, with specific reference to (1) the correct hookup of items, (2) the accurate indexing of cases, (3) the prompt answering of correspondence attached to the case, (4) the receipt of answers to letters of inquiry, and (5) the disposition of property, being sure that all possible checks of stolen-property files against those of property reported found are made promptly and thoroughly.

• Ensuring that information on the report is accurate and consistent. For example, if a complainant's name is spelled two or more different ways, the conflict should be resolved, or the report should be sent back to the originator.

• Checking for adherence to proper format.

• Making certain that departmental policies and procedures are carried out.

• Reviewing the classification of the report for accuracy and making changes if necessary.

• Making certain that the report is submitted on time.

• Controlling the disposition of the report and approving the final status, such as suspended, closed, or cleared.

• Assigning new follow-up due dates.

The report-review process is a valuable adjunct to crime analysis. Supervisors or review officers can often link crimes or suspects because of the great number of cases they review.

The Report-Review Officer The reading and inspection of cases and reports is a tedious, time-consuming duty. If patrol sergeants personally reviewed all cases being investigated by their subordinates, a substantial part of their time would be devoted to this activity, and other important supervisory tasks would be neglected. Report review can be performed most economically and satisfactorily by one or more officers who devote full time to these tasks. The report-review officer serves as the central analyst of all reports submitted

AUXILIARY AND TECHNICAL SERVICES

by the force; he calls the attention of the appropriate supervising officers to errors, omissions, and needed actions; and he stands as a guardian over department policy and procedure.

On the shoulders of the report-review officer rests the responsibility for inspecting reports and scrutinizing recorded actions for the purpose of detecting failures and irregularities. He must understand in detail the interrelationships in the operations of all organization units and the relationship of police functions to those of other municipal, county, state, federal, and some nongovernmental agencies. He is the department diagnostician sitting with his fingers on the pulse of activity, anxiously watching to be certain that no beat is missed. He needs to know the details of the department's business: what should be done and what should not be done, how an investigation should be conducted and when it is completed, and what is expected from officers in all positions. Obviously, an ordinary clerk is not qualified to perform these tasks.

Relationship of Report-Review Officer to Others Report review involves the referral to higher authority of instances of improper disposition of cases and other irregularities. Such action frequently creates ill will because some superior officers resent having their judgment questioned and are offended when a matter is referred to someone over their heads.

A clear understanding by superior officers that report-review duties are of a secretarial and service nature and that the report-review officer is not attempting to dictate their policies or direct their officers will do much to eliminate ill will. It is not considered insubordination for a secretary to call the employer's attention to correspondence that must be answered, appointments that must be met, and conferences that must be attended, nor does this action carry with it a command. The report-review officer is in a comparable position. Although he may suggest the advisability of certain procedures by asking questions, the decision regarding what is to be done is left to the superior; the report-review officer has no direct authority over the members of the department. To give him such control would be a violation of the principle of unity of command.

Theoretically, when an officer fails to prepare a report on an investigation, his or her commanding officer should be notified, and the officer in turn should take the appropriate measures to secure the report. Practically, this line of command must be cut across in the case of such routine matters, or the commanding officers will be spending their time keeping the records system going when they should be devoting it to directing their subordinates in performing authentic police duties.

The commanding officers, obviously, want the records work done properly, since they themselves depend upon the reports and upon the many services of the records office for doing their own jobs well. When the records division suggests to a sergeant that he should have one of his officers submit a correct report, there is no conflict with the commanding officer. The latter has merely delegated authority to the records unit to initiate certain actions for him.

INFORMATION SERVICES AND CONTROL 481

However, if disagreement with the sergeant develops, if he is persistently negligent, or if a new policy or procedure is being initiated, the records unit must deal with the commanding officer or, in the case of disagreement, with the head of the department.

District-Station Records

District stations, with their consequent decentralization of operations, multiply the problems of administrative control and therefore strengthen the need for centralization of records. The fundamental elements of the records system continue to be complaint, arrest, and identification records. The need for a district number series may be eliminated by a requirement that a number from the central numbering series be obtained and used at the origin of each record. This is done by telephoning to the central complaint room for the assignment of a complaint number, to the central booking room for an arrest number, and to the identification office for an identification number. The central office should be supplied, in each case, with suitable facts regarding officer, district, offense, victim, and arrestee to enable identification of the record should an error be made in recording the number assigned. District property-control records should likewise be an integral part of the records system.

The essential records operations of the district stations are integrated into the central records system by transmitting to the central records office the original complaint sheet with the originals of related reports and records, the original arrest record, and the fingerprint record. No indexing of complaint, accident, or other case reports should be done at the district level.

Complaint Records   All telephoned complaints, with infrequent exception, are received and handled by the central complaint room or communication center in the manner described above. The district station also prepares a complaint sheet on each incident reported by citizens in person or by police officers, and essential information is telephoned to the central complaint room in order to have the central complaint number assigned to it as previously described. District stations should retain copies of the incident report and follow up on the final disposition of their cases. Investigation reports, like the incident reports, should be made in sufficient copies to furnish one for the district office and one for other interested divisions. District copies of reports should be kept only for a limited time.

Arrest and Identification Records   Arrest-record cards, with extra copies, are prepared on persons booked at district stations. When the prisoner is released, the arrest record, properly filled in, is forwarded to the central records office. When the prisoner is transferred to the central police jail, the arrest record accompanies him, and a copy is forwarded separately to the central records office for control purposes.

The fingerprint records of persons printed at district stations are likewise forwarded to the central identification office. The district station should not

AUXILIARY AND TECHNICAL SERVICES

retain arrest and fingerprint records after the subject is out of its control but should rely on the central records office for information it may need.

Administrative and Supervisory Considerations

Although the administration of records services entails a considerable amount of clerical work, the direction of the activities and the performance of many of the technical operations require a high level of competence. The head of the records division should be a good executive, capable of inspiring the staff with a philosophy of service and courtesy and able to maintain a friendly and cooperative spirit between this division and the members of the other branches of the service. The records-division head should be a top-ranking officer of the department who can deal with other commanding officers on an equal footing. The need of the head of the division to possess specialized skills decreases with the size of the organization. Most necessary is the ability to direct the tabulation of, and to interpret, statistical data; next is skill in identification procedures.

The records-division head must be able to assign records duties and to coordinate their performance so that all necessary tasks will be accomplished accurately, promptly, and smoothly. His administrative ability is demonstrated, in part, by his skill in assigning tasks so that each officer is fully occupied even though he is required to stay at a designated post to perform infrequent but important duties. For example, the duties of the complaint officer, the booking officer, and the telephone operator may be combined, in the small department. On the late shift the member handling these tasks may act as report-review officer as well. In departments where the load is not great, the dispatcher on one or more shifts may have time to sort, tabulate, and file traffic tickets or to index cases. Even though an officer performs several tasks, the advantages of specialization are not lost.

Perhaps the most difficult administrative problem of the records division is the maintenance of productive relationships with the other branches of the service. Unless these relationships are clearly understood, some records activities may result in friction.

The first step in avoiding conflict between the records and operating divisions is to develop definite policies and regulations governing the records system, the functions of the records unit, and the obligations and duties of other officers in relation to records. These regulations should be prepared jointly by the head of the records division and the heads of the operating divisions under the leadership of the chief. Once the records duties of the several divisions have been agreed upon, the task is to secure conformity.

Immediate Registration of the Incident Unless a procedure is established that will ensure the immediate recording and registration of each incident, some will not be recorded because they will be considered of insufficient importance to justify the paperwork involved; an incomplete account of police activities and a loss of administrative control over these incidents then result. A

INFORMATION SERVICES AND CONTROL

complaint-control form, registered by a serial number for control purposes, is needed from the inception of the complaint to ensure that all cases are correctly dealt with.

The preparation and numbering of the incident-report form accomplishes this purpose. A radio-assignment card may be used as an intermediate step, provided there is assurance that the proper incident report is prepared on each radio assignment. A radio-assignment card in the form of a punch card expedites the gathering of information for a daily summary of incidents and for analyzing elapsed time between assignment and reporting back on the air.

Provision may be made for receiving information from the complainant as soon as he calls, whether there be one or more dispatchers, by having a clerk engaged at other duties available to answer calls to which the dispatcher is unable to give immediate attention. The staff must be geared for peak work loads and adequate to handle any emergency that may reasonably be expected. During some hours dispatchers have spare time for records duties that they may accomplish without leaving their posts, but a records search proves difficult if the communications room is not located adjacent to the records office.

COMMUNICATIONS

The records and communications division should be responsible for the operation of the police telephone switchboard, call-box system, teletype, and radio. The control of communications by the records division instead of by an operating unit is essential to accurate crime accounting and is logical because communications is a service supplied to all the other divisions. Since the central complaint desk or office where the dispatchers are located should be an integral part of the records-division layout and since other communications personnel are usually stationed nearby, the supervision of these officers by the head of the records division is both natural and easy (see Chapter 7).

Desk Duties In small departments, complaint and communication tasks are assigned to desk officers, who have five primary desk duties: (1) operating the telephone switchboard, including the transfer of calls to other police offices and the receipt and recording of routine calls from officers on the street either through call boxes or through the regular telephone system; (2) receiving complaints by telephone or at the desk or counter and recording them on incident-report forms and a daily bulletin; (3) dispatching officers by radio or telephone, with attendant duties of maintaining a radio log or some other device for showing the availability of officers for radio service; (4) booking and searching prisoners and recording and storing their personal property; and (5) furnishing information to the public by telephone or at the desk or counter. Since the most important task is the handling of telephone calls and radio dispatching, the area is sometimes referred to as the communications desk.

Services provided at the complaint desk vary with the size of the department. In small ones it will be manned by the traditional desk sergeant, who is a combined switchboard operator–complaint clerk. The most desirable arrangement places the complaint desk contiguous to or in the records office and in a position accessible to the public so that the clerk may receive complaints as well as supply information to citizens who call in person.

The concentration of these tasks in the manner described has three important advantages: (1) Operations are kept moving at top speed by eliminating the lag that results when needs for police service are transferred by a switchboard operator to a complaint clerk who relays them orally, by written communication, or by signaling the dispatcher to monitor the conversation. (2) Maximum economy of manpower is possible when tasks are physically concentrated in a small area so that several or all may be combined and assigned to one person during periods of light load. Nearby records clerks may assist during unexpectedly heavy peaks, and the desk officers may likewise perform some records tasks during slack periods. (3) Personal contact with records clerks facilitates obtaining essential records information.

While a single telephone may be adequate in a very small department, in larger ones it is replaced by a switchboard, with an attendant increase in time spent transferring calls to other police offices. In larger departments other desk duties also increase in frequency to a degree that one officer cannot handle them. Assistance must then be provided in the form of part-time help from a records clerk, when the desk is contiguous to the records office. When the jail is conveniently near, an officer who serves primarily as an information clerk and clerical assistant to the desk officer may also perform jail duties, taking custody of prisoners brought to headquarters and searching them during the booking process.

Separation of Desk Duties As the volume of work increases in larger forces, a point is reached where prompt and effective service necessitates division of these several activities and assignment of some of them to officers in other parts of the building. In larger departments their concentration at one point, with the facilities and personnel needed, would require an inordinate amount of floor space. Considerations of security—particularly for communications and jail-entrance areas—also justify the separation of these activities. As a result, it is then no longer possible for the information desk, the records office, the jail entrance, and the communications facilities to be located together.

Consideration should be given to relationships between the several duties, when conditions require their separation, so that those least related may be assigned locations isolated from the others with minimum disadvantage. An effort should be made to keep together, for as long as possible, those duties most closely allied. For example, there is a close relationship between receiving complaints by telephone and dispatching by radio. These two tasks should be performed in the same location or in nearby locations in order to lessen the lag between the receipt of the call and the dispatch of officers.

INFORMATION SERVICES AND CONTROL   **485**

When furnishing information to the public is the primary task remaining at the desk, it is called the *information counter.* The information counter is a subdivision of the records division, and when it is physically a part of the records office, information may be more easily furnished by a records clerk. Although some complaints may be received here from citizens in person, they are merely forwarded to the complaint desk by allowing the citizens to use the information-counter phone to talk directly to a complaint operator. In some cases an officer may be asked to go to the information counter to take the report.

The Complaint Clerk and Dispatcher   The central point at which complaints are recorded is called the *complaint desk.* It may or may not be in a position accessible to the public. When the complaint and communications tasks are separated from the information desk and the booking counter, they may continue to be performed by the dispatcher, whose room is usually called the *dispatcher's office*, although it may also be called the *complaint room.* The work load, however, may necessitate further separation of these tasks. The manner of handling the several interrelated tasks that begin with a telephone call and end with the dispatch of officers to the scene of the complaint will influence the organization pattern as well as space and equipment requirements. Emphasis has been given to the close relationship of these tasks and the desirability of their integration into an operation that can be carried out at one point by one or two employees or at several separate but closely adjacent points when personnel crowding requires a compromise. In summary, these tasks may be listed as follows: (1) the receipt of all telephone (and call-box) calls and the transfer, to the complaint desk or dispatcher, of those which relate to incidents to be regarded as police cases; (2) the broadcast of the information and the interchange of radio communication with officers on the street; (3) the posting of changes in the availability of officers for assignment on a dispatcher's map, board, or CRT display; (4) and the entering of information on complaints onto complaint sheets and the daily bulletin.

In large departments the dispatcher must be relieved of some of these tasks in order that he may have adequate time for his primary duty of radio communication. The tasks of which he should be relieved include the following, listed in order of importance:

1   The first duty to be assigned to another person is the operation of the switchboard, in systems which have not been converted to Centrex. The dispatcher is thus relieved of incoming and outgoing telephone calls for headquarters offices and of calls for information and routine calls from officers on street duty. The dispatcher, however, would receive calls on incidents that require radio broadcasts to officers in the field.

The switchboard may be left in the presence of the dispatcher, or it may be moved to an adjacent office, although it would be less desirable to have it in some distant location. When the switchboard is suitably situated in reference to the dispatching equipment or when a radio microphone and controls are installed at the switchboard location, the dispatcher may operate both the radio equipment and the switchboard during hours of light load, such as on the graveyard shift. Except in departments where the load is too great, the switchboard operator may also handle call-box operations and perform suitable clerical tasks, especially during the night hours.

2   Complaint sheets and the bulletin may be prepared by a clerk on the basis of penciled memos containing information obtained directly from complainants by the dispatcher.

3   Telephoned complaints may be received by the complaint clerk (the complaint room, in a large department), who will transfer essential information to the dispatcher by means of a complaint-control card which travels along a conveyor belt, by transferring the call to the dispatcher, or (for crimes in progress) by signaling him to monitor the telephone conversation with the complainant. The complaint clerk will then prepare the case sheet and perform other clerical tasks related to it. A physical separation of these two officers is essential in large departments where several complaint clerks are needed to handle the work load. The nature of the tasks makes it desirable that they be separated by not more than a glass partition to exclude noise. The complaint room should then house the switchboard and any other telephone devices needed for expeditiously receiving and handling complaints, and teletype and computer terminals should be located in or adjacent to it.

4   The number of mobile radios may require the use of several channels, with separate dispatchers to handle communications for each channel.

District-Station Communications

Central control of police communications and complaint records is highly desirable. As previously explained, a central complaint room is essential to guarantee reliability of reporting, and this guarantee becomes more difficult to provide in departments having district stations. The necessity of utilizing members from adjoining districts in operations that lie near the district boundary and in other operations where manpower of the district must be supplemented makes a citywide communications control important. Since the principle of unity of command is violated when one district commander gives orders to the members of other districts, it is necessary that a higher coordinating power exercise command in these instances. The need for central control is further emphasized by the absence of a radio transmitter for each district.

District-Station Desk Operation   The central control described above must be provided in such a way that it will not rob the district command of its essential authority; otherwise, the district command cannot be held responsible for conditions and police operations in its district. Central headquarters should be the point for radio dispatching and for receiving complaints from officers on their accomplishments. However, information beyond the essential facts relating to the officers' actions should be reported to the district station, rather than headquarters.

INFORMATION SERVICES AND CONTROL

By maintaining a desk at the district station with suitable tie lines between it and the central complaint and communications room, it is possible to provide needed central control without unduly sacrificing the authority of the district command. The district desk officer must operate a small switchboard or call director on which should terminate, in addition to the tie lines to the central complaint room or to the department central telephone switchboard, lines to each of the offices in the district station and a suitable number of unlisted trunk lines.

The Call-Box System   When there is justification for district stations, the call-box system should be decentralized so that the call-box lines in each district will terminate in a switchboard at the district-station desk. This decentralized arrangement is sound for the reason that, since nearly all patrol officers are (or should be) radio-equipped, the call box is used principally for supervision, for routine messages to the street officers, and for the transmission of reports on their accomplishments by officers dispatched on calls, rather than for dispatching officers. The district command is responsible for the supervision of officers and for the control of police operations in the district, and consequently it is important that it exercise control over this principal reporting device.

Notifying the District on the Status of Complaints   Although all complaints should come to a central complaint room where action on them may be taken by the dispatcher who has citywide staff command, the central complaint room should transmit essential information to the dispatcher, assign a serial number to the complaint, and then teletype the information to the district station. The district desk officer, on receipt of these messages, should distribute them for the information of all members of the district force. The teletype messages serve the purpose of the previously mentioned district bulletin.

Coordination of the Need for Extra Assistance   Officers who are dispatched to the scene of action in an adjoining or nearby district and officers in hot pursuit should deliver any person they may arrest and report any other action they may take to the district station having jurisdiction over the incident. Reporting action taken is usually accomplished through department reporting procedures.

The central dispatcher performs for the district command a service that is nearly identical to that performed by the dispatcher for the platoon lieutenant in a department without district stations. The dispatcher should be required, on district command, to send additional officers of that district to the scene or to take any other specific action in reference to the deployment of the district officers. The district command should likewise have the right to request additional officers from adjoining districts to assist at the scene of an incident in his bailiwick, but he would not have the authority to order them in. The dispatching of officers from other districts is an action taken by the dispatcher

488   AUXILIARY AND TECHNICAL SERVICES

as aide to the head of the patrol division; it is for the purpose of supervising such dispatching that a representative of the patrol division head or higher authority should be on duty at all times, as previously explained.

Decentralization of Broadcasting

More than one radio transmitter is needed for dispatching when suitable coverage of the entire area cannot be provided by one station or when the traffic becomes so heavy that it cannot be suitably handled by one channel. When two or more transmitters on different frequencies are installed to serve designated areas, the operation is accelerated, and a heavier load can be handled.

When one or more transmitters on different frequencies are installed to serve designated areas in the jurisdiction of a large force, police vehicles should have receivers and transmitters equipped with switches that enable changing to a citywide frequency when ordered to do so; this ensures that all officers dispatched into the area of action will be under the radio control of the dispatcher of that area.

When more than one radio transmitter is used, the question arises concerning the advisability of decentralizing dispatching by duplicating the previously described complaint and dispatching setup in the areas served by each transmitter. The desirability of such decentralization is somewhat in proportion to the distances involved. For example, in the police force of a large state, the several transmitters scattered throughout the area should be operated independently of the central office. In most cities, however, the decision is limited by the location of telephone-company exchange boundaries. For example, a city having three telephone-company exchange boundaries of equal size cannot logically expect to establish two dispatching zones of equal size.

Telephone Communications

The public usually uses a telephone to obtain police assistance from either (1) someone in an office at headquarters, or at an outlying facility in large departments, or (2) an officer on street duty. In the first instance the calls are mainly administrative in character and must be transferred to the desired office by some switching arrangement. In the second, the calls are usually for immediate police service and must be transferred for dispatch by radio to officers on street duty. In a large department, a separate administrative switchboard lessens the burden on the radio-communications center, where calls for police service should terminate when a number specifically for that purpose is dialed. In departments that do not have such a number, calls for service are received at the main headquarters switchboard.

In a small department, both types of calls are received by the police officer who is also responsible for dispatching officers by radio. In departments of progressively greater size, the volume of telephone calls increases, and a proportionately greater number of personnel and trunk lines are needed. Trunk requirements will influence a change from an ordinary telephone instrument to

INFORMATION SERVICES AND CONTROL

a call director or to a switchboard and from a single-position to a multiple-position board. Studies made by the telephone company will reveal department telephone trunk needs.

The department's prestige suffers and its service is impaired when people attempting to telephone the police get busy signals. A sufficient number of trunks should be installed to enable the police to give immediate attention to each call, without using all trunks even at times of peak loads. A smaller number is inexcusable.

Administrative Switchboard The telephone company's survey may reveal that the department has reached the critical point in expanded telephone volume where more expensive equipment of increased capacity must be provided. This may necessitate the relocation of the switchboard and the assignment of additional staff to handle the enlarged facilities. Substantial and expensive remodeling may be required. When such extensive changes do not seem timely because of the economic or political situation, the pressing need may be somewhat diminished by the installation of direct-line unlisted telephones in offices in which a large volume of traffic originates. Automatic dialing equipment provides maximum relief to the operator, thus lessening the need for additional positions on the switchboard. Trunks restricted to outgoing and long-distance calls provide an economic advantage by relieving the load on more expensive ones.

In a small department, each police office should contain a telephone connected to a call-director-type telephone switchboard, answered by clerical personnel; if a call director is inadequate, a small switchboard may be used for the transfer of division calls to the desired office. This arrangement also somewhat simplifies the main switchboard operation.

When separated from the switchboard, communications personnel should be tied to it by two or three lines terminating in a call director that has lines going from it to the detective division, to the head of the patrol division, and to two or more positions in the dispatch room, one being to a supervisor or clerk to handle overflow calls.

Centrex System In large departments, the administrative switchboard may be eliminated by the installation of a Centrex system, which enables the citizen to dial direct to each police telephone instrument that was previously a station on the administrative switchboard. This arrangement enables each police telephone to be connected to any other station by direct dialing. Any tendency of complainants to seek assistance from police offices other than the complaint room in this system must be resisted.

When Centrex is used, the department should take advantage of its features by publishing most of the separate listings in the telephone book. Care should be taken to emphasize the principal number to be used for requesting emergency assistance and reporting crimes. The Centrex system permits transfer of calls, but the listing of the separate administrative numbers will

490 AUXILIARY AND TECHNICAL SERVICES

eventually encourage most users to dial the appropriate extension, rather than the main complaint number. This is particularly true when 911 is used as the main complaint number, since most people identify 911 with emergency situations.

Handling Calls from Citizens

For many persons, police contacts are restricted to occasions when they have a complaint to make or are suspected of an offense. In both instances the citizen is likely to be somewhat emotionally upset. For this reason it is important that the police give careful attention to the manner in which they deal with complainants and offenders if the best possible public relations are to prevail.

Telephone Relationships   In establishing telephone procedures, the administrator will profit by a study of the methods used by progressive business houses. They invariably give careful attention to the speaking voice of the telephone operator and to the procedure used in receiving calls. The police should also consider these two points, although the nature of their service requires the elimination of unnecessary formalities. The telephone operator is the citizen's first contact with the department, and this experience should be as pleasant and satisfactory as possible. Particular attention should be given to diction and grammar and to expressions of courtesy. Correct enunciation is important, and officers should be trained to speak with deliberate care and clearness.

Promptness of Reply Essential   Incoming calls at police headquarters are important and deserve prompt reply. A person's life may be at stake. Even in trivial matters, the subject of the complaint is the most urgent thing confronting the citizen at the moment. Frequently, with nerves on edge, callers are in such a mental state that little things annoy them. When kept waiting, they become disgruntled and sometimes justifiably so; when they receive a busy signal, they are angered and rightly so. Police calls should receive immediate response, even during peak hours; this necessitates an adequate number of trunk lines and trained operators. Provision should be made for calls to be transferred to records clerks when there is an extraordinary peak load that cannot be handled by the regular communications staff. However, the failure to reply promptly is sometimes caused not by too much business but by indifferent and poorly trained personnel. Commanding officers should make frequent checks by counting the number of rings before their telephone calls are answered, and they should take steps to curb lackadaisical tendencies when they appear.

The Telephone Greeting   The operator's manner of answering calls should indicate alertness and willingness to serve, and the greeting should be crisp and clear. The immediate "Police Department" is most satisfactory; it gives all the needed information, and when correctly enunciated, it convinces the citizen that the entire department is at his or her service. The practice of requiring complaint operators or dispatchers to give their names following this greeting is undesirable because the majority of people who telephone the police are not

INFORMATION SERVICES AND CONTROL

interested in this information and are only disconcerted by it. As a general rule, citizens under stress are impatient and want service with the least possible delay.

Calls for Immediate Police Service When a special telephone number is provided for the public to call the complaint room or the radio dispatcher without going through the administrative switchboard, the nature of the board on which the calls terminate will be influenced by the number of trunks needed to enable the police to give immediate attention to each call.

In the absence of a system which shows the numbers for all emergency trunk lines for all the complaint-operator positions, the trunks should be arranged so that a call will rotate through the several positions until it comes to a position free to receive it. This arrangement makes it unnecessary to staff each position except during peak periods.

Complaint operators who receive information by telephone should record essential information on a complaint-control card which is time-stamped and sent to the dispatchers on a moving belt or by some other means. In some systems, the complaint operator can determine the dispatcher to whom the card will be sent. In other systems, an officer at the receiving end decides, usually on the basis of the location of the incident but sometimes also on the basis of its nature, which dispatcher is to broadcast the message. This officer, in some departments, also designates the radio units to be dispatched.

Combined Complaint Operation and Dispatching The above-described procedure has a number of disadvantages that are not present in procedures used in smaller departments where the officer who receives the call from the citizen (whether through the main police switchboard or by means of a special number used by citizens to call for police service) also dispatches police cars to deal with the incident. For example, the dispatcher is restricted in his knowledge of the situation into which he is to send officers by the meager information recorded on the radio-assignment card by the switchboard operator. It is difficult for the operator to describe the sense of urgency apparent in the citizen's voice and the many details that are helpful in deciding how many radio units should be dispatched and how they are to be deployed. In contrast, when the dispatcher receives the complaint directly from the citizen, he may ask the citizen to hold the line while he dispatches cars; he may then obtain further information, such as descriptions of cars and suspects, direction of flight, or information relating to the location of criminals in crimes in progress, which he may dispatch to the cars en route to the scene and which he may use in directing the approach and deployment of the street officers. Delays and opportunities for mishandling are also inherent in the transfer of the radio-assignment cards by mechanical or manual means.

Even in the largest cities, it is possible to have the dispatcher in simultaneous communication with the citizen in need of police assistance and with officers on the street available to provide assistance. This may be accomplished by dividing the area of the city into a number of radio-communication zones, each containing a number of telephone-exchange areas. Calls to the telephone number used when immediate police service is desired may be made to terminate on three consoles manned by operator-dispatchers who serve the radio-communication zone in which the calls originate and who direct patrol cars and their supervisors assigned to that zone. Overflow calls (calls not answered in 10 seconds) may be taken at an auxiliary telephone and at some other consoles.

Radio communications between police officers, without any reference to the principal radio-communication system controlled from the communications center, have important advantages in such special police operations as both fixed and mobile surveillance, stakeouts or cover jobs, task-force operations in which either male or female officers are used as decoys while being covered by other officers in cars or on foot, and some other field operations. Portable hand-held transceivers and car-to-car transmissions on a private-line frequency are useful. The small, transistorized transmitter that may be carried in a shoulder or belt holster, handbag, or briefcase, with a microphone concealed in such a position as to permit the wearer to transmit by pressing a button carried in the hand or on the handle of the bag or briefcase, has great utility in some operations. Officers may, in some situations, wear hearing-aid-type earphones and thus receive instructions from other officers working with them.

Transistorized receivers, with or without hearing-aid-type earphones, are useful not only for foot-patrol officers but also for motorized-patrol officers when away from their cars. Portable radios have an obvious value in that they make it possible to recall an officer away from a minor assignment to a major crime in progress. Portables also allow immediate reporting of the status of cases being investigated.

Auditing the Complaint Reporting and Classification Process   As a part of the inspections process, there should be a periodic audit of the entire process of complaint recording, dispatching, preliminary investigation, and follow-up investigation to ensure accuracy of classification at each of these steps and proper recording and classifying of all incidents.

The proper procedure for this kind of audit is to monitor actual conversations between citizens and complaint operators and then review the information recorded at each subsequent step in the procedure, as listed above. Complaint-control cards resulting from the conversations between the control officer and the citizen should be examined to make sure that information recorded by the complaint operator is accurate and that it is repeated just as accurately to police officers in the field during the dispatching operation. Next, officers' initial classifications of the incidents should be compared with the information given to police by the citizen. A certain percentage of these calls should be rechecked by making contacts with citizens and witnesses in the field to make sure that the facts recorded by patrol officers are accurate.

A key step in the auditing process is to examine the facts as presented in reports to see whether proper UCR guidelines for each classification are being

INFORMATION SERVICES AND CONTROL 493

followed. The next important step in the auditing process is to review crime-clearance information to ensure compliance with UCR guidelines.

Street Telephone Communications   The use of public pay telephones is satisfactory, and the automatic return of the coin on calls to the police department is provided in many communities. However, telephone stations are not usually found in the outlying sections of the community. The use of telephones in commercial establishments during business hours is not desirable because of lack of secrecy and the inconvenience to the officer and the merchant. The police officer's use of commercial phones interferes with the business use of the instruments, especially for incoming messages; and if it is metered service, an unfair burden is placed on the merchant. The practice of an officer's carrying the key to a business house in order to have access to a telephone is to be condemned because of the temptation it offers, and because the officer is immediately suspected if any irregularity is discovered by the proprietor.

For the reasons cited, even with two-way radio there remains a sufficient need for telephone communication with headquarters to justify the cost of installation and maintenance of call boxes. The use of the call box establishes the location of the officer at the time, a feature lacking today in radio communications. In addition, it provides greater secrecy in communications. Further, a radio broadcast requires the initial attention of many patrol officers even though it is not directed to them, and, consequently, the somewhat diminished radio-traffic distraction obtained by the use of the call box for some police communications increases patrol efficiency.

Call boxes provide an important safety factor: The whereabouts of an officer who fails to call at an assigned hour, with a reasonable period of grace, may be investigated; a critically injured officer may thus be found and treatment given while there is still time to save his life. Call boxes also aid in the supervision of the street force; study of the location of boxes used by the officer sometimes reveals information relating to the manner in which he patrols his beat, a helpful factor to the patrol sergeant in detecting and correcting improper practices.

Call boxes installed and maintained by the telephone company as stations on the police telephone switchboard eliminate maintenance and operating problems for the police, and the rental is usually less than the initial and maintenance cost of a private wire system. The automatic recording on a tape of the time and location of origin of each call is not essential; these facts should be recorded by the telephone switchboard operator.

Visual and Audible Recalls   Visual and audible recall systems, essential to efficient operation before the adoption of police radio, continue to have some utility. Their use ensures a more constant attention to duty since the officer must usually be on the street to observe a signal and failure to respond is prima facie evidence of lack of attention. Their use for this supervisory purpose alone, however, is ill-advised, especially when failure to respond is followed by disciplinary action; such practice tends to diminish attention to conditions of more fundamental importance in the accomplishment of the police purpose.

A recall system decreases the need to use the radio for relatively unimportant messages in which speed is not essential, and when used in conjunction with radio broadcasts, it is useful in providing notice of the broadcast to the officer, which is important when an investigation or inspection has taken him beyond earshot of his car radio. Recalls continue to be indispensable in contacting and supervising foot-patrol officers not equipped with radio. The advantages of installing a new recall system or extending a present one must be judiciously weighed against the advantages of making an equal expenditure for other purposes. Extensive communication via portable radios diminishes the need for a recall system.

Communication within the Police Building Loudspeakers should be installed at strategic positions in the building; through them personnel may monitor radio broadcasts by operating a switch. The installation should be such that the dispatcher, by switch, may feed important broadcasts through the speakers without regard to the position of the switch at the speaker end. If desired, the speakers may, in addition, be connected to the intercom system to locate urgently needed personnel who are absent from their offices but may be in the building. If preferred, buzzers or flashing lights strategically located throughout the building may be used to summon personnel by means of code numbers.

Command and Control Systems

The earliest method for keeping track of the whereabouts of beat officers and deciding to whom cases should be assigned consisted simply of making notations on a log or slips of paper. The next refinement involved the use of a map, divided into patrol areas or beats, that was equipped with small lights indicating officers in and out of service or with magnets representing cars, which could be manually moved about the surface of the map.

The predominant form of dispatching control in use today is still the illuminated map, but the advent of computers has resulted in automated systems for giving dispatchers advice about the status of beat officers. Systems now used by several major-city police departments permit dispatchers to receive information on the nature of the location of an incident; for example, a system may inform the dispatcher that a police problem existed at an address in the past or that there are warrants outstanding or wanted persons living at the address. The system then selects the car number of the nearest beat officer in service.

Computer-Assisted Dispatching The advent of computers and video-display or cathode-ray-tube (CRT) terminals has made it possible to provide dispatchers with real-time information relating to wanted persons, stolen vehicles, arrest history, and so on.

INFORMATION SERVICES AND CONTROL

In a typical installation, the dispatcher or terminal operator first selects an inquiry format by his initial entry into the system. He then keys in required information, sometimes filling in "blanks" on the video screen. (See Figures 23-1 through 23-4, on pages 469 to 472.)

In the system used in the Dallas Police Department, the complaint operator who receives the call records some simple information, such as the location or street number, and a numerical signal indicating the classification of the offense. (This is the minimum amount of information required; the complaint operator can supply much more information of value to the dispatcher and beat officer.) When the complaint operator is satisfied that the information appearing on the video terminal is accurate, the information is entered into the computer. The computer adds the beat number, date, time, complaint number, and a series indicating available patrol cars in priority order. This information is automatically routed to the proper dispatching console (one for each of the radio zones, which are comparable to the district-station boundaries). At the dispatcher's console, information is displayed on the video terminal as well as imprinted on a continuous-fold perforated card terminal. As each message appears, it is torn off, and the card is inserted into microswitch status slots, resulting in a conventional mechanical-visual display on a dispatching map. Placement of the card in the microswitch also instructs the computer to relay information back to the complaint officer, assuring the latter that the call has been handled. A slave printer in the records area produces copies of the information for match-up purposes with officers' reports which are submitted later. Terminals in this system are also interfaced with the regional police-information system and with the National Crime Information Center (NCIC) in Washington, D.C. Results of inquiries are transmitted to the terminals in Dallas headquarters and, at the same time, on mobile teleprinters in patrol vehicles.

The Dallas system contemplates additional expansion in the following areas:

- Name and location indexing to replace manual indexing in the records room.
- Coding of crimes and other cases to permit retrieval of details on crimes, accidents, and other incidents.
- Automation of information on jail population and criminal charges pending.
- Input into the beat-analysis system to assist in realigning beats to coincide with changes in work load.
- Although an immediate application is not possible, the Dallas system envisions input of an officer's time into the various program-budget classifications. Work load assigned from headquarters as individual officer activity would be entered into the system. A useful by-product of this system would be an automated officers' daily report.

Computer-Assisted Transfer of Information from the Complaint Operator to the Dispatcher   The method used to record complaint information in the police department in Virginia Beach, Virginia, was discussed on page 468. In Virginia Beach; Charlotte, North Carolina; San Diego, California; and other locations having this system information being phoned in on a complaint by a citizen is keyed directly onto a terminal, and after it is correctly "captured" by the operator, a transmit button is pressed to convey it to the proper dispatcher. In the process, the computer identifies the nearest available car in service and establishes the priority of the call. A visual presentation of this information is then displayed on the terminal in front of the appropriate dispatcher, who, after making the radio broadcast, enters the number of the car handling the call if it is different from the one suggested by the computer and, eventually, the disposition of the case. The entire procedure is carried on without handwritten entries of any sort.

Conventional Status Boards

Boards listing personnel by name or room and located at points visible to division heads, their secretaries, and the dispatcher are helpful in showing the availability of personnel in departments having no more than 200 employees. Those available at headquarters may be indicated by a bank of lights on one side of the panel, and those available on the street, through radio, by a bank of lights on the other side. Multiple colors of lights also serve the same purpose. The lights should be operable from two positions; i.e., there should be a bank of switches in the dispatcher's office for all such signal lights throughout the building and smaller but similar banks of switches on the desks of the division secretaries for the division lights.

One method of informing the dispatcher concerning the availability of patrol officers for assignment is to place immediately in front of him a series of transparent city maps on each of which is outlined the patrol beats for one tour of duty. A small electric light under the map in each beat, operated by a three-position switch to burn brightly or dimly or not at all, indicates that the officer on that beat is available for call, has been sent on a call, or is off the air. A simple control arrangement consists in a bank of as many switches as there are beats on the largest shift and enough additional switches to control a border panel of lights for officers in radio-equipped cars not assigned to beats (the commanding officers, patrol sergeants, evidence technicians, traffic officers, and detectives). The number one switch will operate the light on the number one beat on each map, but by means of a simple switch arrangement, only the light of the map for the current shift will operate.

Another method, which permits the use of a larger map, consists in a rack arrangement with a backboard containing a light for each beat on each shift. When the map for the current shift is placed in position, the lights on the backboard shine through half-inch round holes in the board on which the map is mounted, the holes being in positions immediately opposite beat lights on the backboard.

An arrangement of slots for each beat and some other street assignments, with a microswitch to control availability-for-dispatch lights on a communication-zone beat map mounted on each of the previously described

INFORMATION SERVICES AND CONTROL

zone consoles, permits a light to be extinguished when a radio-assignment card is placed in the slot; this separates two metallic fingers, thus breaking the light circuit. As cars are dispatched or report off the air for a variety of reasons, cards placed in appropriate slots extinguish lights on the maps. When the cars report back, the cards are removed, and the corresponding lights are then automatically lit. Beats normally manned on the evening watch are shown on the map. On the first and second watches some officers are assigned to two beats. This is indicated by placing a card in the slot of one beat to extinguish its light; both beats are then shown to be covered by one patrol unit by outlining the enlarged beat on the glass map cover with a grease pencil or by drawing an arrow from the lighted beat number to the other.

The availability of officers may be inexpensively shown by small bar magnets when the beat maps are mounted on sheet metal. The magnet may be placed on its base when the officer is available, on its side when he is sent on a call, and on its end when he is off the air.

The magnet method permits manual placement of the magnets on the map in the same locations as the cars on the street—providing, of course, that the dispatcher is given the locations by the officers in the field. The method has great value during the dispatching of vehicles to cover crimes-in-progress calls and other situations which require tactical deployment. The dispatcher has a visual aid to assist him in getting the "feel" of the situation, and he is better able to make decisions to determine proper routes for officers to take while on the way to the scene, principal intersections which must be covered to prevent the escape of the offenders, and so on.

Car Locators

Although automated car locators have been under active development for some time, actual progress in practical application in the field has been slow—primarily because of the high cost of these systems.

The advantages of car location on a continuous basis are enormous. Supervisors will know where their officers are at all times; dispatchers will be able to ascertain the location of the nearest unit for response to an emergency call; officers in the field can be assured that their locations are constantly monitored, and hence they are less vulnerable to ambush or attack; areas which receive insufficient patrol coverage will be disclosed; and finally, as a tactical device, the system will provide the ability to know the locations of cars covering an arrest, responding to a crime in progress, or participating in a hot-pursuit situation.

There are several means for the automatic location of vehicles, and a few of the methods are startlingly different. One promising system involves the use of radar transmitters at various locations in the city, operating in conjunction with specialized transponders in police cars. (A transponder is an electronic device which automatically transmits an identifiable response when it receives a signal from the radar transmitter.) When a vehicle receives a pulse from a radar transmitter, a "clock" in the transponder is activated. At a predetermined point, the transponder sends back its own signal within one or two milliseconds. About 1,000 vehicles can be queried per second, which, of course, is more than adequate for any police system now in existence. A minimum of three transmitting stations are necessary in a system of this kind. About 35 transmitter sites would be necessary to cover a major metropolitan area such as New York City.

This system has more than satisfactory accuracy for car-location purposes and is capable of locating a vehicle within 100 feet of its actual position and occasionally within 10 feet even under the worst signal conditions, i.e., in the presence of skyscraper office buildings in a downtown metropolitan area.

A second method is based on an entirely different concept and consists of establishing a great number of high-frequency, low-energy, inexpensive "gates" in every block between intersections. The beam from the radio source would be constant and directional so that a passing police-car radio would be energized when it goes through the beam path. The signal from the car would in turn cause the interrogator to alter a low-grade transmitting signal to headquarters. Accuracy in this system would place a vehicle between specific intersections. The cost of transmission lines to headquarters would be minimal because of the low-grade signal required, and the interrogating gate could be built of low-cost components.

A third system depends upon the use of existing maritime navigational transmitters which produce signals for LORAN (standing for *long-range navigation*, a system used to determine the position of ships and airplanes). A variety of the LORAN system, LORAN C, is capable of miniaturization and can be placed in conventional police vehicles. Upon receipt of the signals from several widely spaced LORAN transmitters scattered throughout the United States, the equipment can produce a second signal, which is transmitted to a computer at police headquarters. The process can locate a vehicle within 50 feet of its true location at any place in the United States which receives LORAN.

A fourth method—and the only practical system in use today—is based on inertial navigation equipment located in each vehicle. The equipment transmits a radio signal conveying the coordinates of the vehicle. The disadvantage of this system is that periodic updatings or corrections of the vehicle's location are required to get the vehicle "back on track."

Boeing's FLAIR (standing for Fleet Location and Information Reporting) system, using inertial navigation equipment as above, has been used in a successful prototype installation in Wichita, Kansas, and is now fully operational in the police department in St. Louis, Missouri.

In the system installed in St. Louis, the FLAIR computer automatically inserts status indicator markings on the map on the CRT screen, showing the location and status of each vehicle as it moves around the city.

Figure 23-5 shows a photograph of the FLAIR CRT screen.

All the methods described above, as well as several other concepts for car location, have certain drawbacks including great expense. Car-location equipment required in the transponder system would cost about $1,000 for each vehicle, and the cost of transmitter sites for most departments would exceed

INFORMATION SERVICES AND CONTROL 499

Figure 23-5 CRT screen of the FLAIR automated car-location system in St. Louis, Missouri. *(Courtesy of the Boeing Company.)*

the total departmental budget for vehicles and equipment. Although the system based on a series of "gates" is less expensive, it is also less reliable unless every block face in the city can be covered, making this system as expensive as the transponder method. The problem with LORAN C systems is the sophisticated radio equipment required for transmission of a continuous coded signal from the vehicle to headquarters.

REAL-TIME INFORMATION SYSTEMS

In the decade between 1960 and 1970, the capability of the second-generation computer was realized. With its enormous capacity for speed, storage, and flexibility, the computer could be utilized in many police applications undreamed of a generation ago.

The Need for Computer-based Information Systems

Police organizations are beginning to see the great possibility of operational application of the computer, rather than its previous use in preparing administrative information such as uniform crime reports and police payrolls and in other routine or statistical tasks. The use of the computer in modern law enforcement is truly not justified unless officers in the field are thus assisted in their daily work.

The need for the computer-based information system is rooted in several factors:

- Increased mobility of the population in general and of those who commit crimes in particular
- Increased population and subsequent growth in files, making manual searches progressively more difficult
- Proliferation of local police agencies and records systems, making it more difficult to obtain operational information
- Recognition of the need for communication between elements of the criminal justice system: police, prosecutor, courts, and corrections

The mere existence of the technical capability and the possibility of interfacing police information with the rest of the governmental structure are powerful influences for the establishment of computer-based systems.

The Need for On-Line versus Off-Line Capability An on-line or "real-time" system means that changes in the status of an element on file are made individually and at the time the changes occur. For example, if a warrant is issued following the presentation of a complaint to the court, in a real-time system information relating to the subject is immediately placed into the system, indicating that the subject is wanted. On the other hand, if the system were based on the off-line or "batch" mode, the information would not be placed into the system until many warrants were to be processed at the same time.

City, Regional, State, and National Systems

At the present time there are a variety of systems in use. A few systems are based on city files only, and several other operating systems are regional in character. The clearest trend, however, is in the direction of the statewide information system which serves all agencies in that state and is interfaced with the National Crime Information Center (NCIC) operated by the FBI. The principal difficulty in the statewide system is that it tends to minimize the interface between police and the other functions of local government, such as the finance department and the public works department. The state system, however, offers the best possibility of exchange of information with the courts and correctional functions, since these activities are primarily state-oriented. A regional system, such as the Police Information Network (PIN) in the San Francisco Bay Region in California, serves an admirable purpose for certain kinds of information of great regional value, such as warrant services and wanted persons, but most regional systems seem to be stopgap efforts if the state later develops a comprehensive system encompassing all the activities of the regional network.

A Typical State System

In 1968 the Florida Department of Law Enforcement contracted with IACP for a design-concept study of a statewide information system, the Florida Crime

INFORMATION SERVICES AND CONTROL

Information Center (FCIC). Initial guidance for the design of the system was given by IACP to a subcontractor, Systems Science Corporation, which carried out a study of user requirements and then developed the details for the system. The FCIC consists of a network of communications channels, connected to computer-based information and files. Its capability is categorized into on-line and off-line groupings, as described in the following pages.

On-Line Information   A basic feature of this system is the interfacing with the NCIC in FBI headquarters in Washington, D.C., which provides local agencies with the information in NCIC files and allows the state system, FCIC, to act as the input to NCIC.

FCIC itself contains four major types of on-line information, all of it in greater detail than the NCIC format provides.

The system gives information on the following:

1   Wanted persons
   a Persons with warrants outstanding
   b Persons wanted for questioning
   c Missing persons
   d Persons under investigation or surveillance
   e Revoked and suspended driver's-license data
2   Persons: criminal-history information
   a Arrest data
   b Conviction data
   c Parole-probation data
   d Aliases—nicknames
   e Personal and physical characteristics
   f Method-of-operation patterns
   g Associates
3   Vehicles
   a Stolen vehicles
   b Stolen license plates or tags
   c Vehicles wanted in connection with crimes
   d Other vehicle status, such as repossessed, impounded, or abandoned
   e Vehicles under surveillance
4   Property
   a Stolen property
   b Lost property
   c Recovered property

The system provides for interfacing with other state files such as vehicle-registration data and driver's-license data in the files of the motor-vehicle department and the state highway patrol.

Another major interface is the connection between the FBI and the national Law Enforcement Teletype System (LETS) for communication of general police messages.

Off-Line Information FCIC makes use of several types of off-line data. Processing is handled in batches, and information is of lower priority or, because of time-consuming input, is better suited to batch processing. Input includes (1) uniform-crime-reporting information, processed on a monthly basis; (2) intelligence information, coming largely from input by state investigators themselves; (3) investigative case status and activity reports of state investigators; and (4) budgeting information and other information of administrative value, such as fleet operating costs, as a service for both local departments and the state.

The development of devices to make maximum use of computer-assisted information systems is proceeding at a brisk pace. Teleprinters can now reduce computer-processed messages to printed form in terminals located in police cars. Cars are also now equipped with terminal devices which make it possible to request information via computer directly without resorting to verbal transmission of the information by conventional radio.

Linking of State Information Systems with NCIC

There have been numerous efforts to link local systems with NCIC, generally through the exchange of information on wanted persons or stolen property. Other projects—the System for Electronic Analysis and Retrieval of Criminal Histories (SEARCH) and the FBI's Computerized Criminal History Program (CCH)—relate to the exchange of criminal-history data on a national basis. A criminal-history system such as CCH will provide much more information than the status data previously available in wanted-persons files.

Interfaces with the Criminal Justice System

An important consideration of any information system, whether on- or off-line, is coordination between police, courts, and the correctional subsystems. For example, the police ought to know the status of inmates when they are placed on parole, and the existence of parole or probation status ought to be indicated to any investigator who is conducting a name check on a subject. For sentencing purposes, the courts are entitled to know whether a subject has been rearrested or convicted on the same charge in the interval between arrest and sentencing. The corrections subsystem must know the conditions of sentencing and the details of past criminal activity before classification and rehabilitation can be carried out. There are many other examples of the need to exchange information on a systems basis, and this need is beginning to materialize now in several versions of OBTS (standing for *O*ffender *B*ased *T*racking *S*ystem). The local criminal justice system in Prince Georges County, Maryland, has a version of OBTS which can determine the status of individual offenders anywhere in the system. It is also capable of summarizing statistical information at various stages in the process.

Chapter 24

The Crime Laboratory

ORGANIZATION AND STAFFING OF THE POLICE LABORATORY

The value of a completely staffed and suitably equipped laboratory is now generally recognized by police officials, the public, and governing boards. The question is not whether the police should have a laboratory but, rather, how completely it should be staffed and equipped, where it should be fitted into the organization, and what its duties and relationships with the operating divisions should be.

Staffing and Equipment Requirements

Every department should have access to a full-service, wet chemistry laboratory with staff and equipment adequate to examine physical evidence brought to it by operating personnel. In departments having about 500 personnel or more, there is a compelling argument to organize the laboratory as a regular part of the department, rather than to depend on an outside agency. When no evidence is brought in for examination, there is manifestly no need for laboratory services. However, the volume of such evidence is influenced by the interest of the force in scientific procedures, which in turn is promoted by training and by operating procedures designed to facilitate the collection of evidence. The use of evidence technicians as described later will ensure the collection of physical evidence for laboratory examination. Responsibility for developing department facilities for the collection and examination of physical evidence and for promoting public and official acceptance of an enlarged scientific crime-detection program clearly rests on the chief.

Most police administrators are aware that a crime laboratory is usually underutilized. Part of the underutilization stems from a failure to staff the laboratory with the right kind of professional employees who can perform adequate services as well as promote professional laboratory activities, and another reason is the traditional distrust of police investigators concerning scientific methods. Most of the apathy, however, comes from a lack of understanding and training on the part of patrol officers and investigators as to the utility of evidence. A research institute which specializes in this field commented on the problem as follows:

> Some crime laboratories operating in a favorable environment of strong support by law enforcement agencies and ready acceptance of expert testimony by the judiciary have elevated their laboratories to a place of prominence and importance. . . . Others have changed little since their inception. . . . However, the involvement of the crime laboratory in the total body of crime has been so miniscule as to preclude a judgment as to the impact of criminalistics on the criminal justice system.[1]

Some Considerations in Establishing the Laboratory

The police laboratory performs a valuable service in crime investigation by assisting in the reconstruction of criminal action and in the identification of persons and things. When studied by a criminalist, physical things that were affected by the criminal act or were used in its perpetration often reveal facts useful in identifying the criminal and in ascertaining actions that occurred.

The nature of substances to be examined and the character of the examinations to be made vary so widely that the services of persons skilled in every science are needed in various crime investigations. Chemists, physicists, biologists, anthropologists, botanists, toxicologists, entomologists, metallurgists, and physicians are some of the specialists who may contribute. Psychiatrists, psychologists, questioned-document examiners, and firearms-identification, fingerprint, and interrogation experts are among others who may be called upon to assist. To employ such a complete staff and provide them with equipment and standards needed for all possible analyses and comparisons is

---

[1]Midwest Research Institute, *Systems Analysis of Criminalistics Operations*, Grant NI-044, Department of Justice, LEAA, Washington, D.C., June 1970, p. 7.

THE CRIME LABORATORY

beyond the means and the needs of any police organization. It is well, therefore, to consider the opposite extreme, i.e., the bare minimum laboratory.

The Rudimentary Police Laboratory   Every small force should have a rudimentary laboratory, even though it has limited equipment and is not staffed by a highly skilled criminalist. A police officer with simple equipment, an enthusiastic interest in scientific crime detection, and a knowledge of his own limitations can provide useful services in crime investigations. This person is usually the identification officer, and the nucleus of his laboratory is his darkroom. He is engaged in scientific crime detection when he searches for, develops, and photographs latent fingerprints; photographs the scenes of crimes and serious accidents; and makes casts of footprints and other impressions. He has probably canvassed the community, the immediate surrounding area, and the state and has inventoried the agencies with competent staff and suitable equipment to make needed examinations for him.

Without discounting the desirability of suitable laboratory equipment operated by a skilled staff, the advantages of the rudimentary crime laboratory, in departments that have no other, are worth mentioning. It develops a scientific attitude in the force by informing the members about the services that qualified examiners can provide and by training officers in collecting, marking, preserving, and handling evidence. More physical evidence is then made available for examination by competent experts, and some gross identifications and easily drawn conclusions that facilitate crime investigations are made without expert assistance. A public and official interest in scientific crime detection that facilitates obtaining more complete equipment and better-qualified staff is thus promoted.

Functions in the Larger Laboratory   In a large laboratory a certain division of effort is inevitable. The director of the laboratory should ordinarily be assisted by a small administrative unit, or possibly by one of the technicians working part time, for the purpose of logging evidence, routing evidence to the proper unit within the laboratory, maintaining a follow-up system, and carrying out other administrative-support activity. In an independent laboratory (that is, one which is not a part of another agency such as a county or state police organization) the administrative unit must usually embrace some of the other management functions such as responsibility for training, personnel management, inspections, and budgeting.

The work itself should be grouped according to the subject matter and method of analysis. In a complete full-service laboratory, six to eight separate divisions may be created to handle the following categories of work:

- Chemical analysis for evaluation of inorganic materials.
- Biological analysis for examination of physiological fluids and organic materials. (Some laboratories combine the two functions or divide the analytical grouping into "wet" and "dry" analysis.)

506 AUXILIARY AND TECHNICAL SERVICES

- Physical examinations.
- Work on firearms and analysis of tool marks and other impressions.
- Document examination for work on forgeries, ransom and blackmail notes, analysis of handwriting and typewriting, and so on.
- Photography (operation of highly specialized equipment, color processing, and so on).
- Latent-fingerprint identification for the development, photographing, lifting, and comparison of the latent fingerprint with suspect prints.
- Polygraph examination for interviewing suspects and, on occasion, witnesses and others, such as applicants for police positions concerning whom there is some doubt as to character.

Photographic Work All department photographic work conducted away from headquarters is the task of the evidence technicians, while all copying work and the photographing of evidence at headquarters should be done by the laboratory staff. The department needs only one darkroom, except in the rare situation where the volume and specialization of work and the space limitations of the darkroom justify a second one. The darkroom should be within and a part of the laboratory. Quantity production, specialization, maximum use of facilities, and suitable controls derived from such concentration of darkroom operations ensure maximum benefits.

The Polygraph Operator The progressive police administrator will also obtain a polygraph lie detector and the services of a competent operator to assist in the interrogation of suspects and other persons.[2] The operator should be attached to the laboratory staff. He performs a service for all operating divisions and ideally should not be connected to any one division in particular. He is engaged in scientific crime detection and utilizes a delicate, scientific laboratory instrument for his purpose; his activities will receive more sympathetic support from the head of the crime laboratory than from the head of an operating division. Should he not be attached to the laboratory, however, the next most desirable spot is the detective division, since this unit will need his services more than any other.

The Identification Officer and the Laboratory The identification officer should relinquish to this laboratory the darkroom, with the attendant task of developing photographs of criminals and fingerprints; the view camera, with the duty of photographing crime and accident scenes; the fingerprint kit and camera, with the responsibility of searching crime scenes for latent fingerprints and developing, photographing, and lifting them; and the casting material, with the task of searching for and making casts of impressions.

---

[2]Lie-detection procedures are discussed in detail by Fred E. Inbau and John E. Reid, *Lie Detection and Criminal Interrogation*, 3d ed., The Williams & Wilkins Company, Baltimore, 1953. See also Inbau and Reid, *Criminal Interrogation and Confessions*, The Williams & Wilkins Company, Baltimore, 1962.

THE CRIME LABORATORY

Not all the duties taken from the identification officer should be assumed by the laboratory staff. Tasks of searching crime and accident scenes for physical evidence should now be assigned to a sufficient number of motorized evidence technicians to ensure immediate 24-hour service throughout the area.

EVIDENCE COLLECTION AND CRIME-SCENE SEARCH

The search of crime scenes for physical evidence calls for the services of specialists supplied with essential equipment and assigned to each tour of duty so as to be available at any hour.

Laboratory usefulness is dependent on the receipt of physical evidence in an unchanged condition. Search must therefore be made before the crime scene is altered, and physical evidence must be recorded, preserved, and transported to the laboratory. Involved are the tasks of sketching and photographing crime scenes; searching for, developing, photographing, and lifting latent fingerprints; searching for articles or impressions left at the scene by the criminal; making casts of impressions of tires, tools, and feet and other body parts; and searching for and preserving lethal instruments, such as knives, bludgeons, firearms, bullets and cartridge cases, poisons, and suspected food, as well as other articles left at the scene by the criminal.

Evidence Technicians

The use of evidence technicians for this purpose makes possible the best investigation because (1) the investigation is undertaken immediately or with minimum delay; (2) qualified officers who have undergone intensive training are responsible for it; (3) more expensive, delicate, and complete equipment may be provided since those using it are specially trained; and (4) greater use is made of laboratory facilities since more physical evidence is brought in for examination. The evidence technician, because of his greater skill, saves time and ensures an increased proportion of crimes cleared by arrest.

Although the skills of the criminalist may ensure a more thorough performance of tasks at crime scenes, his use for this purpose is ill-advised. While the job requires special training, it does not ordinarily warrant using the services of a person with such extensive and costly training. Also, there would be some delay in getting the criminalist to the scene, especially during his off-duty hours, and 24-hour service is undesirable. Even though the laboratory is staffed with several criminalists, it is not usually practical to maintain a staff on duty at night. The inconvenience, delay, and imposition on the off-duty time of the criminalist result in this officer's services being used in only a portion of the total cases where physical evidence might be found. For these latter reasons the identification officer should not be used for this purpose.

Assigning the task of searching crime scenes to either the investigating detective or a patrol officer is also inadvisable. The task deserves specialization because of its importance, the special skills required, and its dissimilarity to other police tasks and because there is not sufficient work of this kind to keep each officer in practice. Supplying each officer with essential equipment would be unduly expensive, and its possession would prove inconvenient to the individual officer. Requiring the investigating officer to obtain necessary equipment at headquarters would be inconvenient and time-consuming and would delay the investigation; in addition, equipment used by all officers is subject to abuse because of lack of operating skill and because there is no clearly placed responsibility for its condition.

Accident Investigations   The separation of the search for physical evidence at crime scenes from that at accident scenes by assignment to different evidence technicians is inadvisable. Identical skills and the same equipment are needed, and both types of investigation require measurements, diagrams, photographs, and the search for, and preservation of, physical evidence. As a result of separation, the investigation of crimes is usually assigned to the detective division, and the investigation of accidents to the traffic division. Inadequate supervision of the evidence technicians in each of these divisions often results in less-satisfactory work. Furthermore, they are not readily available for assignment to other tasks between investigations, as is the case when the evidence technicians are members of the patrol force. The evidence technician from the detective or traffic division takes over exclusive investigation of incidents in his particular field, which is undesirable because the advantages of preliminary investigation by the patrol division are then lost and two officers are usually assigned to the work. Separation of tasks in this manner destroys the close integration of the several divisions that is so essential to effective operation.

Relation of the Beat Officer to the Evidence Technician   In the preliminary investigation, the beat officer is concerned primarily with people, whereas the evidence technician is concerned primarily with things. In the investigation of a crime or accident, they should work as a team, with the beat officer in charge of the investigation, the evidence technician furnishing him with all pertinent information discovered in the course of the search.

In the preliminary investigation of some crime and accident scenes, the beat officer will need no assistance; in others, however, owing to the need for extra investigators or for officers to assist in traffic or crowd control, assistance may be required. This should be provided by the officers dispatched to the scene, as described in the previous chapter, or by a call to headquarters for additional officers. The evidence technician, in most cases, will need no assistance except in making measurements and infrequently in performing other tasks. The beat officer can assist in these; conditions will seldom require the assignment of other officers or of a second evidence technician.

When two or more evidence technicians are assigned to the same tour of duty, the area of the city should be divided into sectors having approximately equal numbers of crimes and accidents. When the number of patrol sergeants is equal to the number of evidence technicians, one technician should be assigned

THE CRIME LABORATORY

to each; in this case, the patrol beats in the sector assigned to a sergeant should be the area covered by his evidence technician.

Supervision of Evidence Technicians   The need for continuous supervision of evidence technicians and the desirability of the close integration of their work with the preliminary investigations by the patrol officers make it most advantageous to assign these specialists to the patrol division. This plan makes their services during slack periods available for general patrol in areas needing special attention and for some special assignments. A laboratory technician should make a regular staff inspection of the accomplishments, procedures, and equipment of the evidence technicians, and the detective and traffic divisions should provide staff inspection of procedures and reports relating to crime and accident investigations.

Chapter 25

Other Auxiliary Services

Regardless of the size of a police department, some provision must be made for other auxiliary services, including the custody of prisoners, the service and maintenance of property and equipment, the requisition and purchase of essential supplies and apparatus, the custody of lost-and-found property, the handling of mail delivery, and the reproduction of documents and forms. In the smallest departments, some of these functions must necessarily be provided by outside agencies; in larger organizations, it is more economically sound to provide them from within.

JAIL ADMINISTRATION

The administrator should be aware of, and constantly on guard for, some of the hazards in the operation and administration of the police jail. In fact, in larger systems he can assume that problems exist. The mere absence of publicity about them should by no means lull the executive into thinking that adverse conditions do not exist.

The primary concern should be the security of the jail so that the escape risk is minimal and the possibility of riot or other disorder is reduced.

OTHER AUXILIARY SERVICES

Obviously, great attention must be focused on the design of the jail during the planning of a police building to prevent shortcomings of this sort. But most of the security problems in jails stem from personnel failure rather than defects in physical design. Personnel working in the jail function should receive thorough training and indoctrination in security principles. In the municipal jail, most incidents occur (1) during transfer of prisoners, (2) when prisoners are grouped together for exercise or for meals, and (3) when inmates are left unsupervised.

Second, there is a possibility of compromise of custodial officers unless they receive proper instruction and supervision. Custodial officers should be cautioned against excessive familiarity with inmates and should be warned not to accept gratuities or, in turn, not to do favors for inmates which might constitute an infringement of security or regulations.

Third, administrators should be constantly aware of the problem of sexual abuse of inmates. They should be certain that jail personnel and supervisors fully understand the hazards of placing a young, inexperienced inmate with an older, stronger prisoner of questionable character. The practice of putting two or three inmates in a cell is unwise, since the safety in numbers which might possibly exist in the dormitory situation is nonexistent if a small number of inmates are left together unsupervised.

Fourth, jail personnel should be constantly on the alert for passage of contraband and should automatically assume that attempts to pass illicit items will be made if sentences are beyond several days' duration.

Fifth, long periods of confinement in a city jail are undesirable, and sentences ideally should not exceed 72 hours. The administrator should seek to transfer prisoners being held for pretrial or post-trial detention for periods longer than 72 hours to some other facility, such as a county, regional, or state jail.

National standards for inmate welfare, care, and treatment should be strictly observed by every administrator to ensure efficient and humane operation of the jail. Recommendations by the American Correctional Association and the National Advisory Commission on Criminal Justice Standards and Goals[1] in the volume on corrections are particularly important.

Local jail administrators, particularly sheriffs who have the responsibility for county jails, should recognize that long-term incarceration of inmates in local jails is one of the key factors in establishing a pattern of criminality or perversion in what otherwise would be a salvageable human being. The police administrator therefore bears a tremendous responsibility in pointing out and preventing inhumane conditions which may result in the imprinting of these patterns upon inmates.

Jail Operational Policies

The most important duty relating to persons arrested is the review of their cases to establish justification for their detention and, in some cases, for other

[1]National Advisory Commission on Criminal Justice Standards and Goals, "Report on Corrections," U.S. Government Printing Office, Washington, D.C., 1973.

AUXILIARY AND TECHNICAL SERVICES

lawful restrictions on their liberties. This responsibility is usually not given to jail personnel.

Departmental regulations should prevent the improper detention of innocent persons and the imposition of unwarranted restrictions on the personal liberties of all prisoners. On the other hand, the unauthorized release, the failure to impose suitable lawful restrictions when required, and the escape of prisoners through police carelessness should be guarded against by equally stringent regulations. The protection of all prisoners from abuse, either by the police or by other prisoners, and the hospitalization of critically ill or injured prisoners must also be provided for by regulations. The head of the department must assure absolute compliance with these procedures through inspection.

Authority for Detention, Release, and Restrictions   The circumstances of the arrest must be reviewed to give assurance that they justify placing the person in jail and, in some instances, lawfully restricting his or her privileges of release on bail, of telephone communication, and of visits with persons who come to the jail for this purpose. This is a grave responsibility, and the chief must be certain that the authority to make such decisions is given to members possessing completely reliable judgment.

Restrictions on bail must be limited to that *reasonable* period of time the police have in which to take a prisoner before a proper judicial officer.

> It is ordinarily the duty of an officer after making an arrest, either with or without a warrant, to take the prisoner, within a reasonable time, before a justice of the peace, magistrate, or other proper judicial officer having jurisdiction, in order that he may be examined and held, or dealt with as the case requires. It is sometimes said that this must be done immediately, or forthwith, or without delay. These requirements are construed to mean no more than that this duty must be performed with all the dispatch and promptness possible under the circumstances. Accordingly, an officer may detain a person arrested in custody for a reasonable time until he can conveniently and safely take him before a magistrate, if the circumstances are such as to preclude an immediate examination, hearing, or trial, as when the arrest was made at night or on Sunday; when the court was not in session; where the prisoner himself occasions the delay, as where he is drunk; or where the arresting officer is unable to find a judicial officer. Similarly a person arrested may waive his right to be taken before a magistrate. An officer may not detain a person arrested in custody longer than is reasonably necessary under the circumstances, or arbitrarily refuse to place a formal charge against a prisoner, thus preventing him from obtaining bail; nor may an officer detain the person arrested for any purpose other than to take him before a magistrate, and, accordingly, it has been held that a peace officer may not keep a person arrested in his custody for an unreasonable length of time in order to procure evidence from him, or to obtain his confession.[2]

The high level of competence needed in making decisions regarding these and other important jail duties is the principal reason for their assignment to the

[2]*Corpus Juris Secondum* 618.

OTHER AUXILIARY SERVICES

patrol division. In departments where all other jail duties are assigned to the records division or to some other service unit, the review of cases of persons arrested should remain with the patrol commander. In any event it is important that one officer on each night shift be exclusively responsible for decisions to incarcerate a person or to impose restrictions on the liberties of prisoners. For example, lawful written orders for arrest, for holding a prisoner without bail for investigation or pending the health officer's examination for venereal disease, and for denying communication privileges to a prisoner should all be approved by a commanding officer before being issued, and the commanding officers should be held responsible for the action they take in such cases. During the day, the presence of division heads makes it possible for them to impose restrictions on persons arrested by their officers.

The commanding officer of the division responsible for jail duties should be required to check daily on prisoners whose privileges are thus restricted and report to the chief any case wherein it may appear that privileges are unlawfully restricted or that a prisoner is being unlawfully detained.

Commanding officers should be held responsible for the treatment received by prisoners; they should not permit unnecessary force or violent, profane, or obscene language to be used in the management of a prisoner, nor should they permit officers unnecessarily to humiliate or embarrass prisoners. Because of its effect on the attitude of the prisoners, police conduct at showup should be exemplary. The commanding officer should see that children are not incarcerated in any jail, holdover, or room in violation of the law or department regulations.

Commanding officers should see that prisoners are assisted in communicating with friends and relatives and in obtaining bond when lawful restrictions are not imposed on their privileges. They should also be authorized to release misdemeanor prisoners on their own recognizance or on a bond less than the amount ordinarily required.

Errors in judgment in reference to prisoners may result in three serious, immediate consequences: (1) Innocent persons may be jailed, and personal liberties may be denied others without justification; (2) overcautiousness may defeat the police purpose, as when guilty persons are not jailed because some real or fancied technical point is given undue weight under the circumstances or when a failure to impose justified and lawful restrictions checkmates the investigation by enabling friends or accomplices of the prisoner to destroy evidence or prepare alibis; and (3) interdivisional friction may result from injudicious decisions made against arresting officers of other divisions.

Arresting officers who feel that unwise decisions have been made against them, however, have recourse in immediate appeal to the head of their division. Regulations should grant to the commanding officer heading each operating division final authority in such matters without reference to the chief. This is justified because (1) the caution and judgment of division heads, ensured by their rank and long service, qualify them to judge the peculiar merits of each case in their jurisdiction and (2) some facts relating to the arrest may be revealed to the division head but concealed from all others.

514   AUXILIARY AND TECHNICAL SERVICES

It is not necessary for a commanding officer to review the circumstances of arrest at the time each person is booked. To do so would interfere with his other important duties and so restrict him to the booking counter that he would be nothing more than a glorified booking officer. Prescreening by the booking officer makes the presence of the commanding officer unnecessary. All persons arrested should be processed immediately, except when the booking officer doubts the justification for the arrest or the proposed restrictions; these he should hold in the booking room while he refers the case to the commanding officer for decision. The commanding officer, however, is responsible for all cases processed by the booking officer and should be required by regulation to review the circumstances surrounding the arrest of all persons jailed during his tour of duty as well as those jailed previously whose liberties were restricted during his shift. A review of the arrest record will suffice in some instances, while in others he may need to examine the reports of arresting officers. He should discuss questionable cases with the arresting officer before making a decision.

Injured Prisoners   The police frequently arrest persons who have been injured in fights or as the result of accidents or who may be suffering from some infirmity, prior injury, or disease. Occasionally the police use physical force to subdue a person in order to effect an arrest, and injuries sometimes result. Prisoners are sometimes injured in jail as a result of fights with other prisoners or falls due to intoxication, fainting, or epileptic attacks.

The public is inclined to look upon the injury and illness of prisoners with suspicion and to believe that these are evidence of police brutality. Because of this attitude, it is doubly important that the police give careful attention to injured or ill prisoners and detain in jail no person who is in a critical condition. Since the police are not competent to judge the extent of an injury or the seriousness of an illness, fairness to the prisoner demands that he or she be examined by a competent physician.

The commanding officer should be informed when injured and ill prisoners are brought to headquarters or when the fact is discovered in jail, and steps must be taken to safeguard the life and health of the prisoner in the interests of the department. Such prisoners should be sent immediately to a hospital or examined by a physician, and they should not be held in jail except on the written approval of the examining physician. A suitable injured-prisoner report protects the prisoner by giving greater assurance of examination by a physician, and it protects the police by recording the physician's approval of the prisoner's incarceration, showing that examination was made and that, where necessary, treatment was given.

Jail Duties

Since the primary purpose of the jail is to provide safe custody, all other jail duties must be performed in such a manner as to minimize opportunity for escape or injury to the prisoners.

OTHER AUXILIARY SERVICES   515

The specific duties that are customarily assigned to the jail personnel include the following:

1   The search and control of prisoners during the booking process
2   The booking of prisoners
3   Arranging for each prisoner to make a local telephone call to his or her attorney, a relative, or a friend at no cost to the prisoner and maintaining a log showing the date and time of the call
4   Fingerprinting and photographing of prisoners
5   The custody and return of prisoners' property
6   Arranging for authorized visitors to see prisoners and the supervision of such visits
7   Accounting for, inspecting, and supervising jail facilities and inmates to ensure security, good order, comfort, welfare, cleanliness, and suitable care of department property
8   Transfer of prisoners to court or to some other jail or institution
9   Operation of a patrol wagon and ambulance in the not-too-large department

Control during the Booking Process   Because of the danger to the officer charged with searching and booking prisoners, regulations should require that certain procedures be followed to the letter. Departmental procedures often specify the handcuffing of prisoners upon arrest for felonies or intoxication or upon an arrest characterized by fighting or physical violence. (If procedures fail to require such action, they should be modified accordingly.) Prisoners transported by a conventional police vehicle for these offenses should be handcuffed during the transport, and the failure of officers to handcuff should be brought to the attention of patrol supervisors by the person in charge of the booking process. It is unfair to booking officers to ask them to assist in handling an unruly prisoner who should have been brought in with handcuffs on in the first place. Furthermore, it is most important that the prisoner be searched by the arresting officer and by jail personnel in such a manner that the prisoner is unable to use any weapon or piece of clothing in an attack or an attempt to escape. A search should always be conducted in the presence of another officer, not only for reasons of personal safety, but also to protect against charges that property taken from the prisoner was appropriated by the searching officer. Each time the prisoner is transferred to the custody of someone else, he or she should be searched again. Regulations must provide for the handling of female arrestees, who may be subjected only to superficial search (of purses, coat pockets, packages, and so on) in the absence of a matron or policewoman.

Booking Prisoners   Since booking a prisoner is a clerical task, it is desirable that the arrangement of headquarters provide a booking counter adjacent to the records office so that a records clerk, designated as the booking officer, may prepare the record of arrest. When the booking counter is physically removed from the records-office layout and rearrangement is not feasible because of the location of the jail entrance, it must be decided whether records or jail personnel should be assigned to the post. Determining factors are (1) whether the volume of booking work leaves much free time for other duties, (2) whether the free time may be devoted with least inconvenience to jail duties or to records tasks, and (3) whether there are sufficient jail duties to occupy the full time of a booking officer when he is not engaged in booking prisoners.

Fingerprinting and Photographing Prisoners   The practice of bringing prisoners from the jail into the identification quarters for fingerprinting and photographing is unnecessary, unsound, and wasteful of the time of all officers involved. Such a transfer offers a chance for escape, especially if the distance is great or if it necessitates going from one building to another or through public corridors or several rooms. Prisoners should be fingerprinted and photographed by the jailer (neither process is difficult to learn) in the jail proper or in an adjoining room with only one door—the connecting door.

Prisoners should not be fingerprinted and photographed by an identification officer because this officer's time would be wasted in traveling from the records office to the jail, sometimes a considerable distance, and in waiting for admission when the jailer is occupied elsewhere. Moreover, prisoners arrested and released during hours when identification officers are not on duty would not be fingerprinted, unless 24-hour identification-officer service is required.

Control of Prisoners' Property   All property should be taken from prisoners at the time they are searched during the booking process. All jewelry, pencils, pens, tobacco, matches, pawnshop tickets, papers of any kind, keys, billfolds, and money should be removed. Some of these items could contain narcotics or be used as tools or weapons, and some of them may be items of evidence which should be maintained in good order. Also, storage of a prisoner's property obviates the chance that it may be stolen by other prisoners. Smoking equipment may be returned after the search.

Everything taken from a prisoner is still his or her property until shown to be otherwise, and the officer who makes the search and removes the property should itemize it completely, in the presence of another officer, and give the prisoner a receipt. The first officer must also see that the property is sealed in an envelope or otherwise deposited in a safe place when it is bulky.

After the issuance of a receipt, the booking officer is responsible for the custody of the prisoner's property until the time of release or transfer. The property should go with the prisoner if he or she is transferred to another jail. The department property clerk will not be concerned with the care of prisoners' property except when it is too bulky for storage in the prisoners'-property cabinet or safe.

OTHER AUXILIARY SERVICES

Visits with Prisoners Any visitors to the jail must be approved by the commanding officer. Visiting hours should be strictly observed in order to maintain efficient operation of the jail and to eliminate opportunities for the granting of special privileges to those prisoners who may offer to pay for them. Visiting should be supervised either by the personal presence of an officer or by means of closed-circuit television cameras, which can also be used to advantage in the control of entrance and exit surveillance in the jail area. All food and other material brought into the jail should be carefully examined before being given to the prisoner, even though the commanding officer may have given previous approval.

Jail Inspection and Prisoner Welfare Periodic jail inspections, coupled with the specific assignment to designated shifts of responsibility for cleaning the jail and performing other necessary duties, give the department head some assurance of the security of prisoners and of their comfort, health, and welfare. The jailer should be required to inspect the jail and prisoners approximately once each hour and to report any unusual or unsatisfactory condition. He should maintain order in the jail, locking unruly prisoners in individual cells. He should also prevent the operation of a kangaroo court or other forms of extortion or physical punishment.

Inmate Counts and Inspections An accounting of persons in jail should be made at each shift change by actual head count and roll call of names on the jail register. Personnel on the day shift should be responsible for scrubbing and general cleanliness, and the commanding officer of that tour should make a daily check of its accomplishment; a thorough daily inspection of the jail should be made for weapons, contraband, and other prohibited articles and for evidence of attempted escapes, as well as of the cleanliness of the jail quarters, bedding, and other facilities.

Trusties Convicted prisoners, in those jurisdictions where they remain in police custody, may be used to economic advantage as trusties to assist in maintenance and other headquarters tasks that require only simple skills and little supervision. They are especially useful in doing janitorial work, in servicing police vehicles, and in performing other unskilled tasks. Sometimes skilled artisans become regular police customers in consequence of their drinking habits, and their services may then be utilized in building and equipment repairs.

Responsibility for the custody of trusties should be imposed on the maintenance division or other police unit utilizing their services; jail personnel should not be required to guard them, except when a number of them may be engaged on a work project removed from police headquarters. As a general rule, the safekeeping of trusties is not difficult when they are wisely selected from the group least likely to attempt escape; these prisoners are usually identifiable by previous convictions for the same offense, long-time local

518 AUXILIARY AND TECHNICAL SERVICES

residence, relatively short sentence for a minor offense, or previous experience as a trusty.

The use of trusties should be carefully supervised, however, so that they are never placed in charge of other inmates or allowed undue influence in the management of the jail. Trusties should never be permitted to maintain control over vulnerable places such as the jail dispensary, where they can conceivably gain access to narcotics or salable items such as alcohol, tools, and syringes.

Work Release

One of the newer methods in the corrections field is work release. A version practiced in Arlington County, Virginia, affects prisoners serving sentences for misdemeanors and for misdemeanor-level convictions for nonviolent felonies. After appropriate screening, prisoners are allowed to have daytime jobs, but they must spend nights and weekends in jail. A portion of the facility is constructed with work release in mind; prisoners can come and go through special doors at specified times—after which the doors are locked by means of a master control switch.

MAINTENANCE SERVICES

Satisfactory maintenance and repair of property and equipment promote efficiency, good morale, and prestige of the service. In addition, considerable financial saving can be effected by proper use of maintenance materials and facilities to prevent deterioration. Manufacturers of furnishings, machinery, and floor coverings and of heating, air-conditioning, and other equipment are eager to provide instruction for the care of these items. The wise administrator will require the head of maintenance services to take advantage of this help and to see that subordinates are properly trained in their specific duties.

Personnel equipment must also be maintained in suitable condition. Frayed and patched clothing and soiled, sweaty, and wrinkled outfits damage morale and prestige as decisively as the need for a haircut, shave, manicure, or bath. Many clothing manufacturers provide specific instructions for care of the articles they make, and with the modern cleaning and laundry facilities available everywhere, there is no excuse for a slovenly appearance. Flashlights, firearms, handcuffs, leather equipment, and notebooks deserve the same care as any other item of personal property.

Building Maintenance Police headquarters are frequently located in old buildings, and departments with district stations will usually have several buildings that over the years have been allowed to deteriorate both externally and internally. If these facilities are salvageable at all through remodeling, they should be restored with the use of the best equipment and materials available, and a system of maintenance should be set up that will stave off a repetition of the wasteful attrition of previous years. Floors must be kept spotlessly clean; they must be swept daily, and those in public areas more frequently. Windows

OTHER AUXILIARY SERVICES

and walls must be washed periodically, and the walls repainted in a light color as needed. Roofs, floors, walls, windows, and lighting and plumbing fixtures will require occasional repair. Heating plants will need cleaning and renovation at regular intervals.

Some of the worst-looking departments are not necessarily dirty; in many departments, poor appearance stems mainly from the unprofessional and unbusinesslike clutter that seems to accumulate in the absence of strict supervision concerning (1) posting notices, cartoons, memos, etc., on file cabinets, walls, and desk tops; (2) piling old reports, phone books, lunch sacks, and the like on top of working surfaces; and (3) bringing in or retaining eclectic equipment and furnishings, such as an olive-drab Army surplus clothes locker next to a battle-scarred gray desk.

In departments with district stations, a centralized janitorial unit, equipped with a truck carrying power vacuum cleaners and other large cleaning machinery, can make a roving tour of the district installations and thereby eliminate the need for each district to purchase these items or to employ civilian cleaning firms. In areas where snow is a problem in parking-lot and street maintenance, the truck can be equipped with a snowplow, a further economy in time and money.

Similar arrangements can be made in regard to heating plants. Many old district stations in the past have relied on the services of the lockup keeper or other police personnel to maintain furnaces and to keep them fired. Such practices are unsound; greater long-term economy is realized by converting old-fashioned heating plants to automatic installations and by assigning a roving crew to maintain them.

Although the list of maintenance problems is endless, in essence the solution consists in taking a thoroughly businesslike approach to them. For this purpose a well-trained head of building maintenance should be engaged in large departments; in smaller ones, the solution may lie in contracting for these services with a reputable firm specializing in maintenance and cleaning. The only assistance that should be expected from patrol officers and other police personnel is that which comes from their normal careful use of facilities and furniture. This care will increase in proportion to the improvement of appearance and comfort which good maintenance practices will produce.

Automotive Maintenance Motor-vehicle equipment may be maintained by a central municipal repair shop or a police shop or by a private contract. The choice should be based on the quality, convenience, and cost of the service.

Theoretically, a central municipal repair shop is able to maintain police vehicles most economically. A police department is deeply concerned with prompt and efficient maintenance in order that cars may not be kept out of service an unreasonably long time. The number of department automobiles is usually geared to routine operations, with an adequate supply of spare vehicles for use during protracted repair periods; delays are costly because they restrict the most productive use of manpower. For patrol vehicles engaged in 24-hour

520   AUXILIARY AND TECHNICAL SERVICES

service, the number of maintenance spares on hand should be equal to 20 percent of the fleet. For detective cars and other vehicles which are not subjected to the same punishing wear as patrol cars, a figure of 10 percent is acceptable.

A shop under direct police control is more likely to adjust its operations toward a minimum tie-up of vehicles during hours of peak activity; its location in, or adjacent to, headquarters may provide a greater convenience than a central municipal shop. This is not invariably the case, however, and comparative studies should be made to determine which resource is the more desirable.

Motor equipment in a small department may be most satisfactorily serviced and repaired by a private garage, while in somewhat larger departments servicing may be done by the police department, and repairs by private contract. As the amount of work increases, the police department may undertake motor tune-ups and minor repairs.

Vehicles require service at the start of each tour of duty. Gasoline, oil, and water must be checked; the windshield and door glasses must be cleaned; the interior must be swept out; and the supply of tickets and other printed matter must be replenished. This service should be provided at headquarters in order to minimize time loss and to permit the use of trusty labor and more complete supervision of the officers and service crew. When suitable facilities are provided, 24-hour trusty service for battery and tire changes may also be available under the control of the headquarters staff.

The gasoline pump is the bottleneck in the service operation; in order to diminish delay, an adequate number should be installed, and cars on beats that require less patrol mileage may be serviced only once or twice each day. In larger departments it may be advisable to have officers report off duty on a staggered schedule in order to lessen the time needed for servicing and to avoid leaving the city uncovered at change of shift.

In large cities, tire-remount facilities at precinct gas stations are economical in that they allay a tendency of the driver to place a flat tire on the spare rack and then forget about it because of the need to drive a long distance to the central maintenance shop for a tire change. Also, a tire-repair truck may be used to advantage in large cities. This truck, equipped with racks, carries tires of all required sizes and other equipment needed for tire repair and changing. It can be radio-dispatched upon requests from officers in the field. Other economies may be effected by guarding against tire damage through improper inflation and by using a special pump to take water out of underground gasoline tanks. Water can be detected instantly by the use of litmus paste on the gasoline gauge-stick.

The care of the interior of cars and patrol wagons is important to maintenance and economy. In patrol wagons particularly it is necessary to guard against the storage of wet blankets and rusty tools. The use of proper lighting and mechanical ventilation and well-designed storage chests equipped with subfloors will prevent some deterioration.

A careful study of maintenance records to prevent time-consuming

OTHER AUXILIARY SERVICES 521

duplication should be the responsibility of the director of automotive maintenance. He should also conduct a continuing study of gasoline, mileage, and vendor and repair costs and comparative studies of several different types of automobiles to determine their relative economy. In addition, he should provide for regular inspections and audits to ascertain the quality of the repairs and the accuracy of the charges.

Radio Maintenance Communication facilities (radio, recall lights and audible signals, call boxes, and other equipment) also need maintenance and repair. Police radio maintenance may be by private contract in all but the largest departments; very large cities will require a separate unit working exclusively with radio and communications maintenance, and the city may operate its own radio-repair shop. Roving radio-maintenance trucks may prove economical in areas where the calls for service in the field are numerous.

Tailor Shop The amount of work in a large department may justify a tailor shop, even though the uniforms may be privately owned. This shop may be independently operated, the tailor being given headquarters space in return for special rates to the officers, or the tailor's salary and the cost of supplies may be paid by the department, and the services provided to the officers at cost. In medium-sized agencies, it is often more economical to keep a good supply of uniforms of various sizes in stock and then make arrangements for officers to visit a local tailor for alterations. In small departments, uniform clothing is often ordered on a one-officer-at-a-time basis from a regional supplier or by mail order.

Regardless of how the uniforms are stocked or supplied, it is often more economical to give officers a clothing allowance and then have them buy replacement items as needed.

Armorer The full-time services of a gunsmith are not justified except in very large departments which furnish sidearms or when the time spent reloading ammunition and servicing other police weapons is excessive. However, the weekly servicing and inspection of department-owned riot guns, rifles, and submachine guns is an important task requiring an established procedure to minimize the hazard of accidental discharge and to ensure the safe delivery of weapons from vehicles and gun cabinets and their return, loaded or unloaded, as prescribed by regulation. There should be frequent and thorough inspections to make sure that the weapons are properly serviced.

CENTRAL SERVICES

All departments will have certain custodial responsibilities for the storage of found and recovered property and evidence, the storage and inventory of department property, and the operation of auto pounds and animal shelters. They will also need to plan for mail delivery, for the requisition and purchase of

AUXILIARY AND TECHNICAL SERVICES

essential supplies, and for the security of equipment and other items in police care. In large departments these functions, together with graphic arts, may all be grouped together in one central services division.

Evidence and Recovered Property   The police department must retain in custody confiscated weapons, gambling equipment of all kinds, narcotics, and recovered and unclaimed items, such as bicycles, automobile parts, clothing, jewelry, and typewriters. Unclaimed and confiscated currency must also be kept in safe custody. Every item, regardless of its value, must be inventoried, protected, and accounted for. A major responsibility of the property-control section is to work out procedures that will ensure against removal, theft, or alteration of property. No access should be allowed to the property room except under the strictest rules of security. All officers or other persons wishing to enter should be required to identify themselves fully, if not known personally to the property-room staff, and their statements should be verified. Anyone requesting property for evidence should be required to sign for it, and his or her name should be placed on at least two receipts or forms as a cross-reference. Narcotics having high value, such as heroin, are special hazards, and equally special safeguards must be used, such as the requirement that samples be weighed before and after items are removed for court use.

When a storage room for evidence is available adjacent to the criminal court, it is desirable to have officers request necessary evidence on the day previous to the trial appearance. Evidence can be transported to this room by property-control personnel and made available upon call by the arresting officer.

Personnel in the evidence and recovered-property unit must trace ownership and arrange for the return of property which is not being retained as evidence. Unclaimed property must be disposed of after a period of time as prescribed by law. Narcotics, pornographic material of all kinds, and gambling equipment, such as cards, dice, and slot machines, should be disposed of by court orders. All such dispositions of material should be properly recorded and witnessed.

Department Property   Control of department property and supplies is dependent on an adequate inventory method. All requisitions, purchases, and deliveries must be recorded, and data relating to the date of acquisition, location, use, cost, description, destination, and so on must be readily available. In large departments this information, taken from the inventory ledger and from the items themselves, can be punched on cards for sorting at regular accounting periods or for providing any specific information desired.

Purchasing   Methods for the procurement of property and supplies must be established to ensure that commodities are of suitable quality and that they are purchased at the best prices. The ideal arrangement is for the police

OTHER AUXILIARY SERVICES

department to pool its purchase requirements with those of other departments and obtain the goods it needs through a central agency headed by a qualified purchasing agent using efficient methods.[3]

The Auto Pound Abandoned and stolen automobiles recovered by the police must be stored until their owners have an opportunity to reclaim them or until they are sold by the department. A concomitant duty is that of tracing ownership, checking the stolen-auto file, and obtaining information regarding title holders, lien holders, registrations, and license records. An inventory must be maintained, and adequate records of costs, disbursements, and receipts must be kept in order to provide for a monthly summary and report.

In large cities where storage space is at a premium, automobiles cannot be kept for long periods of time. It is important that their removal be expedited through the development of procedures that take into account all legal rights of the owners and at the same time permit a rapid turnover. Special forms and consolidations of reports to hasten searches and avoid duplication of written work should be devised, usually after conference with state automobile-registration officials.

Some police departments operate a towing service for the removal of abandoned or illegally parked automobiles and charge the owner a fee when the vehicle is reclaimed. Those which are not reclaimed are sold at auction, either by the police themselves or by contract with an auctioneer who charges a percentage of the sales receipts.

Animal Shelter While it is not desirable for the police to operate an animal shelter, in cities where this practice exists the unit should work in collaboration with other agencies concerned with animal welfare as well as with the public health department. Some police departments have the responsibility of issuing dog licenses and keeping the relevant records.

The local health department will be concerned about the presence of rabies in any animal which has bitten another animal or a human. The attacking animal must be impounded for examination by the health department. Local hospitals may request that some dogs or other animals be turned over to them for research purposes. The major responsibility of the animal-shelter personnel, however, will be to impound and care for stray dogs until their owners reclaim them and to dispose of those which remain unclaimed after a specific period of time.

Mail Delivery Large departments have a vast amount of printed, typed, or duplicated material that must be distributed throughout the department and an equally large amount of outside correspondence. A mail-delivery section is

---

[3] A detailed description of purchasing procedures may be found in *Management Policies in Local Government Finance*, International City Management Association, Washington, D.C., 1975.

essential to expedite the circulation of these communications and also to place responsibility for the performance of the numerous tasks involved. The mail section will receive some evidence and bail-bond moneys, and the security of these must be provided through the use of special forms and auditing controls. The section may be given the responsibility for counting and distributing daily bulletins, training guides, memorandums, and orders and for routing the incoming mail.

Chapter 26

Buildings and Equipment

Although most of the emphasis in police management is necessarily directed toward improvement of personal services, the performance of the varied duties included in a well-rounded police program is partly dependent on suitable buildings and equipment. Their adequacy and condition decisively influence the quality and efficiency of service as well as the morale of the force. Good police buildings and equipment create a favorable public impression, raise the prestige of the department, and aid substantially in creating satisfactory public relations. Maximum suitability to their purpose should invariably be the basis of design and selection; specifications should be determined by a study of the manner in which police buildings and equipment will be used.

The appearance of police headquarters or stations has an important influence on the attitudes of the public and the police; both react unfavorably to a foul-smelling, dark, poorly kept, and unclean police station. Police offices should have a businesslike appearance and create an impression of efficiency. A storage place should be provided for material and equipment, and these should be kept there when not in actual use; the tops of desks and filing cabinets and the floors in the corners of offices should be kept free of paper, boxes, and other material.

GENERAL CONSIDERATIONS IN BUILDING DESIGN

A police administrator who has the opportunity to design a new headquarters building to meet the needs of the force should give first consideration to providing maximum accessibility to the area being served. The building should be centrally located, with good access to principal thoroughfares intersecting the city. Adequate off-street parking should be provided for all police vehicles, with room for expansion to meet future needs. In many cases, however, the department inherits a building with no vacant space around it, and usually the structure was designed to meet police requirements of a bygone day. If the quarters are to be used effectively, the police administrator usually must rearrange the offices and facilities, with attendant remodeling, to enable the force to operate with maximum efficiency.

Whether the police chief is designing a new headquarters or remodeling his present one, he should consider the offices to be housed in it and its general design and construction. His studies must include space requirements, appearance, maintenance, light, ventilation, air conditioning and heating, electric ducts, and provision for the interoffice transfer of records. The building should be designed for the normal operation of the plant with a minimum headquarters staff, for its temporary operation with a staff reduced as the result of outside emergency assignments, and for the operation of communication and reporting facilities by a greatly enlarged staff to meet unusual needs. In order to expedite operations and make the most productive use of personnel, consideration must be given to the manner of handling inquiries, complaints, communications, records, prisoners, and property. Facilities should be arranged so that, in some operations, many tasks may be performed by one person in one location and, in other operations, interrelated tasks may be effectively performed by many persons in different locations. In the case of new buildings or a complete renovation of existing public structures, federal safety and health requirements must be met.

Thought must also be given to minimizing the possibility of escape of prisoners, to resisting outside attack, and to public convenience and the welfare of police personnel. Offices should be accessible to the public and to police officers in proportion to the use they make of them; the design should also enable the public to give information to the police without being overheard and, in some instances, without being observed.

The architect who designs the police building will usually not be familiar with the procedures of police administration and the facilities needed in police operations; hence the chief must describe the required features and the purposes they are to serve. While the factors discussed below refer to police headquarters, most of the points are also applicable to district stations.

The Police Architectural Specialist The unique architectural requirements for a police building are often beyond the competence and experience of local architects, most of whom have had little or no experience in the field. The

BUILDINGS AND EQUIPMENT 527

police administrator should therefore insist that a qualified police architect with a national reputation be the primary architect or an associate or consultant on the project. Besides having an appreciation for the proper relationships which should exist between offices and the layout of space within them, the qualified police architectural specialist has a great working knowledge of the many small details which must be planned and dealt with in the police building. The one-time police architect invariably makes many mistakes which the experienced person could have avoided.

Offices to Be Housed in Police Headquarters   Public convenience as well as efficiency in operation dictates that the headquarters building house all police offices and also the court, the prosecutor's office, and the traffic-violation bureau. Although officials occupying the latter offices are not under police control, their services are so closely related to police tasks that adjoining offices and intercommunication arrangements will greatly facilitate the operations of both. While the use of these intercommunicating facilities may justifiably be denied the public, the location of these offices adjacent to police headquarters is also a public convenience.

In addition to the usual police offices, provision should be made for adequate assembly spaces; for a gymnasium, pistol range, and crime laboratory; for the radio transmitter, if its location at police headquarters is not unsuited; for maintenance and service operations and the storage of supplies, parts, and property in police custody; and for a garage to provide off-street storage and service of police vehicles.

Design for Future Needs   A police building should be designed for future needs as well as for present ones. Providing for present needs is comparatively simple; foreseeing future needs presents a more difficult problem whose solution requires imagination. Police quarters built to accommodate the department for 25 years in the future are usually found to be too small within a relatively short time; sometimes the building is discovered to be inadequate on the first day of occupancy. The probable population growth and future developments in police practices should be anticipated, and the consequent growth in volume and variety of police operations and the needs during wartime and emergencies should be considered. Rearrangements of offices and other facilities should be planned to meet these future needs.

Generous assembly space and vast areas for property storage will provide some room for future expansion and emergency needs during catastrophes. Space should also be provided for the installation of additional cells in the jail.

General Type of Construction   Police headquarters should be pleasing in design and appearance and of an architectural type that will not date it. Normally it should conform to the architectural style of surrounding buildings, if they are of modern design and construction. It should be fire-, flood-, and earthquake-proof and constructed of material that will require minimum

528   AUXILIARY AND TECHNICAL SERVICES

maintenance and infrequent, or no, exterior renovation. To lessen the need for stairs and elevators, the number of floors should be held to minimum requirements. The jail, however, should be on an upper floor, with stairways and elevators exiting onto control points or work stations which are monitored 24 hours a day.

Floors and Walls Material to be used in the construction of floors and interior walls should be selected with a view to easy maintenance; it should be durable, easily cleaned, and preferably of a substance unlikely to require frequent repair or repainting. Cleanliness is important in all public buildings, and in none, not even excepting the hospital, should this virtue be given more assiduous attention in building design and maintenance than in police head-quarters.

The floor material is especially important in lobbies, corridors, and other public spaces and in areas where prisoners are temporarily held. Floor cleaning is a continuing process during the hours of public use, and suitable material will simplify the task and thus give further assurance of appropriate cleanliness. Terrazzo or poured epoxy floors are excellent for this purpose. Also suitable is any tile floor which may be waxed and brought to a high polish; which will not wear appreciably, chip, or crack; and which does not have in its design crevices where dirt may lodge. Jail floors should, of course, be of suitably pigmented, dustproof, reinforced concrete and should be kept waxed. The location of floor drains for waste cleaning water is an important item in jails; the slope of floors should allow water to flow toward drains in the central corridors, rather than into "plumbing chase" areas behind the cells. Vomitus and feces lodged among pipes and ductwork, in an area which cannot be readily swept or hosed out, is loathsome indeed.

Wainscoting to a height of 6 or 7 feet in public spaces and also in police offices should likewise be of a durable, easily cleaned material that may be readily washed, such as marble or tile. Otherwise, hand marks and marks left by heads and chairs leaning against the wall will present a dirty appearance and will necessitate frequent repainting. Except in the jail areas where they should be of concrete, partitions should be of a construction, such as hollow tile or metal, to facilitate future changes in office arrangement.

Windows Windows designed to permit easy washing from the inside promote periodic cleaning by the maintenance staff, perhaps with the use of trusties and without the need for special equipment. Some windows offer an escape opportunity to prisoners being interrogated or being taken from one point to another in the building. Such windows should have ornamental grillwork or be of a design that would impede quick flight. The appearance of bars should be avoided.

When designing window openings for the jail areas, especially those opening off the cellblocks, consideration should be given to security and the shielding of the public from disturbing sights and sounds of inmates. The

BUILDINGS AND EQUIPMENT

opportunities presented to look into jail windows from surrounding buildings must be avoided either by the location of windows, when possible, or by their design. Translucent glass does not entirely solve this problem because windows must be opened at times for ventilation and because it is sometimes possible for prisoners as well as outsiders to break a pane in order to provide a better view.

Security considerations rule that the jail should not be on the ground floor; when it is, particular attention must be given to safeguarding the windows from outside attack. Windows on upper floors are usually safe from such attack, but the opportunity remains for contraband material to be smuggled into the jail, even when the windows are separated from the cellblock by an inspection corridor. This hazard may be lessened by suitable outside screens over all jail windows, including those in the trusty quarters, which will make it impossible to pull even a note through on a string.

Utilities   Provision must be made for suitably placed ducts for electric wiring to meet present and future needs. Wires and cables are needed to operate a variety of devices: the radio; electric locks; signal lights to show the insecurity of doors and to designate assignment, location, and availability of personnel; bells and other sound devices to indicate that service is desired, that a certain officer is wanted, or that an emergency has arisen; loudspeakers at strategic locations in the building; closed-circuit television; and other interoffice communication.

A gasoline-driven generator to supply electric power in the event of failure of the regular source is essential to ensure continued police operations during such emergencies, and this installation may require circuits in addition to those ordinarily provided. It is essential that current, up to the limit of the generator capacity, be supplied for radio transmission and for illuminating offices where important police operations are conducted. In some quarters it may also be desirable to furnish emergency electric power for the elevator. Electric locks and interoffice communications essential to operations during an emergency must likewise be powered.

On the basis of the long-term plan for the rearrangement of offices and facilities to meet future needs, provision must be made for ducts in the floors to accommodate changed requirements that result from the relocation of partitions. Similar changing needs for water, heat, and gas should also be considered.

Light and Ventilation   Special attention must be given to illumination and ventilation. Dark corners and passageways invite uncleanliness and should be avoided; when unavoidable, they should be lightened by illumination and the use of light-colored construction material or paint. Suitability of illumination to the particular task in the records office and other locations where clerks use their eyes continuously on records is so important that a lighting engineer should be consulted. This service is usually provided at no cost by the local electric company.

530 AUXILIARY AND TECHNICAL SERVICES

The Need for Security The provision of security in jail quarters and in areas where prisoners are temporarily detained sometimes creates acute ventilation problems that can be solved only by forced draft. This applies also to rooms where the lack of a window is otherwise a virtue, such as interview rooms, storerooms, and vaults. Lavatories, shower rooms, locker rooms, darkrooms, and indoor firearms ranges, and some laboratory rooms likewise present unusual ventilation problems. The architect's attention should be directed to these problems, and an adequate supply of fresh air to all points in the building should also be ensured.

Air-conditioned facilities are necessary in most parts of the country to ensure comfortable conditions that promote maximum working efficiency. Air conditioning should also be provided in the jail areas in localities where high temperature and humidity make it desirable.

Locks Doors to police offices that provide 24-hour service do not need locks. There are some doors, however, which should be accessible to all members of the force but which should be closed to the public. These include doors to police lavatories, doors in public spaces leading to recreational and other police facilities, and sometimes doors leading to the space housing the courtroom and the traffic violators' bureau. These doors should be equipped with locks that can be operated by the call-box key that is in the possession of each officer.

Acoustics The acoustics of the police building influence the effectiveness of operations, and difficulties may be avoided by the use of acoustical material on the ceilings and on the walls above the wainscoting. Special problems that deserve the attention of an acoustical engineer are frequently found in the dispatcher's office, in the target range and adjoining area, in the courtroom and assembly rooms, and in the large, unpartitioned spaces.

Minimum Use of Partitions Unnecessary partitions should be avoided, and space separation should be effected by the use of counters. The spaces are thus left open to public view, an arrangement that encourages the presentation of a neat and businesslike appearance, with materials not in use stored out of sight.

The number of private offices and small rooms should be kept to the minimum required for effective operations. Specialization often creates an unwarranted demand for private offices, and they in turn promote a feeling of independence and unwillingness to perform tasks outside the specialty. Private offices make supervision more difficult; the occupants are tempted to turn their attention to outside matters and to engage in activities that are not strictly police business. This possibility is lessened when the partitions forming the offices are of glass; in many instances the partitions may be of less than ceiling height.

The need for privacy when interviewing some complainants and when

BUILDINGS AND EQUIPMENT

531

interrogating suspects is recognized and should be met by the provision of a suitable number of rooms to be used for these exclusive purposes. A commanding officer who spends much time interviewing complainants should, when the need is real, be provided with a private office. Glass partitions that permit an unobstructed view of the commanding officer's entire division are then desirable to facilitate supervising officers and seeing at a glance who is available.

Public View of Operations   Many police operations are of great interest to the public, and arrangements should be made for their observation without disturbing the officers engaged in carrying them out. The partitions of the communications room, the teletype room, the crime laboratory, the property-control room, the data-processing room, and the planning division may all be of glass to permit the clear viewing by the public of the operations therein. Large departments may install telephones with recorded tapes that will describe the procedures used and the purposes and aims of each operation. Such an arrangement helps to convince the public that the police department is their proper concern, and it sustains a continued interest in the department's improvement.

DESIGN FOR OPERATIONS

The importance of the design of a police building to suit its purpose cannot be overemphasized. Especially important are the location and arrangement of offices housing police records, the office of the dispatcher and of the commanding officer in immediate charge of police operations, the booking room, and the jail. Unsuitable arrangement and location of offices and other facilities impose restrictions on the organization of the force, on the economical assignment of office personnel and their effective operations, and on the use of superior procedures.

Design to Resist Attack and Protect from Sabotage   So that the building can be defended with minimum strength, it should be designed to reduce to a minimum the number of positions to be manned in case of attack by a lynching mob or other outside force. Certain positions in the building should also be designed to lessen the attack hazard by providing space in which the attendant may seek cover if attacked and by ensuring a view of the position by other personnel on duty at nearby positions not visible to the attacker.

The bombings of police facilities and attacks against officers inside them during the past few years have made planners and architects aware of the need to provide security for some of the vulnerable activities in the department, such as the communications room, computer area, and the arsenal. As indicated in Chapter 23, the records and communications activities ideally should be grouped into an information center, particularly in small and moderate-sized departments which may not have the personnel to man the records function 24

532   AUXILIARY AND TECHNICAL SERVICES

hours a day. Since the communications equipment itself is the most vulnerable, it should be placed in a secure location and protected by four-hour fireproof walls. Because of the cost of the computer and the contents of its storage files, the computer area should also have this degree of protection. Remote terminals should be connected from the communications equipment room to a point in the information center so that records and communications activities are physically close together. Emergency or backup microphones and telephones should be provided in the equipment room itself.

Much of the needed security can be acquired by simply screening vulnerable parts of the building and by using guard points or controlled-access doors which can be connected to an alarm system. The Detroit Police Department, for example, has a security plan which, if an alarm sounds in the jail, stops elevators automatically and sets in motion a doubling of protection at points of entry and other areas in the building.

The Desk-Officer Problem   Many departments still cling to the outdated notion that a police-station lobby area should be presided over by a desk sergeant, lieutenant, or captain, who serves as a combination dispatcher, turnkey, magistrate, and office supervisor. This concept is usually encountered in larger departments with district stations, particularly on the east coast of the United States. Very often, the desk officer sits on a raised platform within the station or in the public lobby area. The result of the concept is the misuse of space and loss of the supervisory potential of the desk officer. Design should eliminate the problem by removing supervisory activity to some other place in the building and by providing counter space for a clerk instead.

Design for Handling the Public   The police building should be identified by a distinctive illuminated sign. The front entrance should be brightly lit, and if steps lead to it, they should be broad and easy, with suitable handrails. The lobby should contain a conspicuously located, well-arranged, and easily understood building directory. Directional arrows on corridor walls should indicate the general location of rooms by numbers. Each door number and the title of the individual or unit housed in the room should be designated at vision height on the wall on the side from which the door opens, and each reception desk or counter should have on it the name of the police officer or clerk on duty at the time.

In order to attain its maximum usefulness, the information counter should be so placed in relation to the entrance door that it is the first thing that a citizen observes on entering. The certainty of the citizen's locating it without inquiry should be further ensured by a lighted sign.

Corridors should be ample to meet traffic needs without crowding. Offices most frequented by the public should be placed nearest the entrance insofar as this is possible. Reception rooms, with reception desks or counters, should be provided those organization units receiving large numbers of callers so that they will not need to stand in the corridors. Chairs should be provided for visitors in the reception rooms and also in corridors that are used as reception rooms.

BUILDINGS AND EQUIPMENT 533

Public lavatories separated from those used by the members of the department should be provided in the police building both for men and for women.

Design for Handling Records   A building for a small department should be designed to permit the concentration of the five principal desk duties (operating the switchboard, receiving complaints, dispatching officers, furnishing information, and booking prisoners) in a public location and as a part of, or adjacent to, the records office. The conditions necessitating a separation of these tasks were discussed in Chapter 23; the building must be designed accordingly. Complaint, arrest, and communication records must be filed in the records office, and the information clerk must rely on it in answering inquiries. The relative need of these tasks for juxtaposition to the records office must be appraised if wise decisions are to be made as to their location.

The information-supplying service has manifestly the least need for records-division services; the clerk can obtain necessary information by telephone. The booking process has the next least need; the relationship is limited to forwarding a copy of the arrest record (1) to the complaint clerk for registering, (2) to the records office for search to ascertain before the release of the prisoner whether he or she is wanted, and (3) to the records office for filing, following the release of the prisoner.

Devices for Transferring Records   When, in remodeling a building, the complaint room and the records office cannot be combined, they should be tied together by a pneumatic tube, dumbwaiter, or other device for the safe and speedy transfer of records between them. It is likewise important that a similar system be used to transfer records of arrest from the booking clerk to the complaint clerk for registration and to the records office (when it is separated from the complaint room) for search. While such a device is a convenient means of communication for an information desk separated from the records office and the complaint room, the actual need must be measured in terms of the number of complaints received at this point. The tie-in should be with the complaint room, which should serve as a diversion point for records received for some other location. This is especially necessary when all three locations (the complaint room, booking room, and information counter) are removed from the records office.

Mailboxes should be provided to facilitate the distribution among the operating divisions of duplicate case sheets, copies of the daily bulletin, follow-up indicators, and other police reports and records. Boxes for this purpose are best installed in a counter that has slots through which the records may be dropped and, on the lobby side, doors for easy access. The boxes should be in a location easily accessible to the commanding officers they are serving and at the same time conveniently near a records clerk, through whose hands the documents routinely pass, in order to ensure their prompt and accurate distribution. In smaller departments this will be the complaint clerk, and the boxes may be built into the complaint counter, except when it is in an inconveniently isolated position. When the information counter is readily accessible and is tied into the complaint room with a device for transferring

534 AUXILIARY AND TECHNICAL SERVICES

such records, the task may be assigned to the information clerk. In other departments, the records-office counter may be the logical location for the boxes.

The number of boxes required depends on the size of the department, the nature of its organization, and the office arrangement. At the minimum, however, one box should be furnished for each patrol-division platoon and one for each of the other divisions. At least one box should be available to officers for depositing traffic tickets.

Accessibility of Records The records office should have counters or windows readily accessible to police officers and to the public, but actual entry into the area should be made difficult for everyone, including police officers. No one but the records staff and the commanding officers should be permitted to enter. The entrance door should be located inconspicuously in order to lessen the number of demands for entrance which must be refused. The door should be kept locked, and keys should be furnished to the records-office staff. If the door is visible from the complaint desk or some constantly occupied post in the records office, it may be conveniently controlled by an electric lock.

Data-processing equipment should be located within or adjoining the records office so that duplicate records will be unnecessary for statistical use. When so located, statistical data may be obtained directly from the original reports.

Records-Office Space One hundred square feet of records-office floor space for each 15 police officers is a useful guide in computing space requirements for the convenient operation of the records staff. Storage space and the space used for communications tasks and the complaint desk are not included in this estimate. Factors that influence the amount of space reserved for records include the completeness of the records system, the spread of working hours of the records staff, the existence of pillars or other physical obstructions in the room, the number and location of doors and windows, and the total space of the headquarters building.

Design for Handling Prisoners The jail facilities include the booking room, court holdovers, and the showup room and passageways from the jail to these rooms; padded and other cells; facilities for drunks and for fingerprinting and photographing prisoners and for their medical examination and treatment; showers; visiting rooms; the kitchen; storerooms; and trusty quarters. Jail facilities should be arranged with a view to providing (1) minimum opportunity for escape, (2) operating convenience to ensure maximum efficiency and consequent minimum personnel requirements, and (3) protection of the public from raucous noises or obscene gestures by inmates. The facilities should also provide for the comfort and welfare of the prisoners.

Design for Handling Property Space should be arranged in the police building for a table, located in a position out of public view near the entrance

BUILDINGS AND EQUIPMENT

through which most property will be brought, where a supply of wrapping paper, string, and labels will be available for packaging and labeling property brought to headquarters. In large agencies, the property room is open 24 hours a day to receive property and evidence; in smaller agencies, the best solution is to provide airport-style luggage lockers. In this system, an officer puts the property in a locker and then keeps the key until a later transfer is made. This method helps preserve the chain of possession of evidence.

Provision can also be made for the 24-hour receipt of property by the records office through a desirably positioned booking or information clerk and for its safe storage until called for by the property clerk. Bulky articles of relatively small value, such as bicycles, cannot be readily handled by the records office in the manner described above. A room near the wrapping table and with a door that can be unlocked by a call-box key should be arranged for their temporary storage pending daily removal to other storerooms by the custodian. This room may also be used for the storage of such emergency operating equipment as lanterns, barricades, traffic signs on stanchions, and rope with supporting stanchions.

The size of storerooms for department supplies and equipment depends on the quantities to be kept on hand, and their locations should be convenient to the persons who use them or have custody of them. For example, office supplies should be kept in the records-office layout, and parts and supplies for the daily repair and maintenance of radios, vehicles, buildings, parking meters, and signs, signals, and markings should be kept in the spaces provided for maintenance.

Location of Police Offices

First consideration in the design of the police building should be given to the location of the records and communications facilities because they are the central nervous system of the department organization. After their location has been tentatively decided, an effort should be made to group the operating offices around them in a manner to provide maximum convenience. This will usually require some rearrangement of the tentative building plan; compromises must be made, but the principles that have been discussed should be adhered to as far as possible.

The patrol lieutenant or other officer commanding uniformed operations should have an office accessible to the public and at the same time adjacent to the dispatcher for ready consultation in questionable cases and for direction in emergencies. The location of the detective quarters should be influenced by the fact that detectives make most frequent use of records-office services. The patrol-division squad room should consider the availability of space for lining up patrol officers for inspection at roll call and for adjoining locker and report-writing rooms. The traffic-division location will show consideration of the fact that its varied activities require considerable floor space. The vice and youth divisions should be located so that persons may call at their offices with

Figure 26-1 Assembly Room, Chicago Area #1 Building.

BUILDINGS AND EQUIPMENT 537

minimum contact with the rest of the police organization. Lavatory facilities for male and female officers, a large mirror, and a locker for each member, with space for additions, should be provided somewhere in the building—preferably close to the roll-call room and the exit to the police parking lot.

From a functional viewpoint the location of the chief's quarters is not so important. It should have a reception room and be reasonably accessible to the public and convenient to the chief's staff. It should be large enough to seat all officers above the rank of sergeant; otherwise, a separate conference room should be provided.

Assembly Rooms Roll-call and assembly rooms should be well lighted, with ample space for training materials, projection equipment, blackboards, and so on. A good example of an assembly room is depicted in Figure 26-1.

Assembly rooms and classrooms should be on the less-desirable upper floors. Provision should be made for police training; for youth activities such as junior traffic patrols, junior safety councils, and bicycle-riding schools; for traffic-violator schools; and for public meetings.

Press Room An office, preferably out of public view but conveniently located in relation to the records office, should be provided for the use of press representatives. It should be furnished with typing tables, telephones, a loudspeaker for monitoring police radio broadcasts, and, in large departments, teletype receivers.

Police Laboratory The location of the laboratory in the police building is relatively unimportant, and some advantages are gained by having it in an out-of-the-way spot. Space requirements and utility connections are the principal considerations; space needs are strongly influenced by the size of the laboratory staff and the equipment used. The laboratory should be designed to meet future requirements, especially in departments that have not yet developed their potential laboratory needs through suitable operating procedures.

Separate rooms should be provided in the laboratory for (1) the darkroom, (2) copying and other laboratory photographic work, (3) chemical examinations, (4) the use of other laboratory instruments, (5) the storage of evidence, (6) a museum in which standards for comparison and evidence in cases that have been disposed of are stored, (7) an office for the director, and (8) a reception room.

Target Range The size and shape of an indoor firearms range are such that its installation in the police building may interfere with an otherwise desirable arrangement of the facilities. The need for convenient and efficient police operations manifestly comes ahead of the need for a target range located within the police building. An effort should be made to place the range within the headquarters building, however, because of the advantages derived from this convenient location. Suitable precautions must be taken, in the selection of its location and in its design, to minimize distraction from the noise and danger from wild shots. Suitable illumination should be provided, and the range should be equipped with retractable targets and a system of moving targets. Shooting booths should have bulletproof partitions, and boiler plate should be placed at points on the walls, floor, and ceiling where stray bullets might jeopardize life or property. Abundant forced-draft ventilation must be supplied to an indoor range to prevent the buildup of noxious gases containing lead residues. An out-of-doors range should also be provided, with capability for training officers in the FBI Practical Pistol Course (PPC).

Gun Cabinets   Cabinets for storing weapons, such as shotguns, rifles, and gas guns, as well as bulletproof shields, should be located at a point passed by police officers as they leave headquarters on receipt of a report of a bank robbery or other crime requiring such weapons. The cabinet doors should have electric locks operated from a post that has 24-hour service and a clear view of the cabinet.

Police Garage   The police garage should be in the rear portion of the headquarters building, in the basement, or adjacent to the building. It should be big enough to house all vehicles not in use, with additional space for the private cars of some of the commanding officers, for tires and spare parts, and for facilities used in preventive maintenance, mechanical and tire repairs, battery charging, and washing. Special attention should be given to the arrangement of service facilities to ensure minimum delay in this operation. Provision should be made, in large departments, for more than one line of vehicles to be serviced simultaneously. In departments that use trusties for service jobs, a room should be provided so that they may rest and be out of the way during slack periods at night when they are kept on call at the garage.

Other Maintenance   The need for servicing vehicle radios makes it desirable that the radio shop be located adjacent to or within the garage. The location of space for the storage of parts and supplies and for the maintenance of traffic devices (signs, signals, markings, and meters) is not important except for two points: (1) A convenient location in the police building ensures better supervision and a more ready use of trusty labor, and (2) a location near the garage and radio shop enables a more useful interchange of services.

Room must also be provided for the storage of supplies and equipment for building maintenance and service.

POLICE EQUIPMENT

The quality of police service and the success of many operations can be improved through the use of suitable equipment. Good equipment is also an economy, since it increases the effectiveness of police manpower.

Vehicles

The relative suitability of the automobile, the three-wheeled motorcycle, and the two-wheeled motorcycle for patrol and the advantages of the conspicuous-

BUILDINGS AND EQUIPMENT

ly marked patrol car were discussed in Chapter 16. What was said in reference to general patrol applies with equal force to traffic patrol. Two-wheeled motorcycles should have limited use. Instead, three-wheeled motorcycles should be employed to their full capacity for traffic control in congested areas, and they should be conspicuously marked.

The Police Automobile Protection from inclement weather and the greater safety in accidents provided by the steel top and pillars have made the four-door sedan the standard police vehicle for patrol service. The two-door sedan is usually less expensive than the four-door model and is suitable for detective operations and staff use. Cars in the intermediate size category and lower-priced lines are economical in terms of operation and maintenance and are well suited for police service. The advantages of such cars include better gas mileage; a shorter wheelbase, which permits greater maneuverability; light weight, which usually permits faster acceleration; and lower cost, which enables the operation of a larger number of vehicles for the same expenditure and also makes more frequent replacement possible.

The ideal patrol car has not yet been manufactured. Conventional sedans are made for other purposes and not for the combination of special conditions required in police service. The ideal vehicle must be designed to permit officers to cruise at low speed but to respond at high speed. They must be able to engage in pursuit driving using high-speed turns, to get in and out of the car easily to talk to people and inspect conditions, and to have space and room for equipment, for storage of supplies, and for conversations with citizens or suspects out of sight of the public. The ideal vehicle should also be easy to repair when its exterior receives minor damage.

Patrol-Car Accessories Automobiles used for general and traffic patrol should be conspicuously marked and should be furnished with accessories for providing driver convenience and comfort as well as for establishing their identity as emergency vehicles. All police vehicles should be designated by department number, which should be painted or applied near the gas-tank cap and under the hood to facilitate recording the service given to each car.

A police car in most jurisdictions must be equipped with a siren to qualify as an emergency vehicle. An assembly of red or blue rotating lights should be installed on a rooftop mounting bar or as a part of an integral unit containing lights, siren, and public-address speakers.

A small spotlight, with a flexible cord to be plugged into an outlet on the dash of the police car, is a useful hand light for illuminating alleyways, backyards, and other places requiring some attention but not justifying an actual shaking of the door at that time. This light, operated on the car battery, provides more powerful illumination and a longer range than a dry-cell flashlight. "Alley lights," mounted on the light bar to project a broad floodlight beam to the sides of the vehicle, are particularly valuable accessories.

Police automobiles should be equipped with identical ignition, door, trunk-compartment, and gun-rack locks. Each officer assigned a vehicle may

540 AUXILIARY AND TECHNICAL SERVICES

then be given one set of keys which will operate any lock on any police automobile. This arrangement eliminates the inconvenience of delivering keys to relieving officers and the annoyance which results when an officer inadvertently takes the keys when leaving headquarters.

Police cars should be equipped with efficient heaters and devices for defrosting windshields during the cold weather. Chains and snow tires must also be provided in some areas. In most places, cars should be air conditioned.

Each patrol car should be supplied with a small first-aid kit containing a resuscitator tube, tourniquets, and hemorrhage compresses—all of which may be applied while awaiting the arrival of an ambulance. The immediate ambulance service available in most communities usually makes unnecessary more intensive first aid by the officer. A fire extinguisher and road flares should also be part of the patrol-car equipment. The following items are frequently useful and can be placed in a dustproof wooden box in the trunk:

- Blankets
- Short broom and dustpan (for sweeping up at accidents)
- Yellow lumber-marking crayon
- Telephone directory
- Tape measure (100 feet long)
- Coil of rope

Police cars should be provided with facilities for making notes. For this purpose manufacturers provide "car desks" in which forms can be stored and which provide illumination, allowing the case to serve as a writing desk for the officer. A series of properly sized pouches, like pockets in an apron, made of synthetic leather and tacked to the inside of the driver's compartment just to the left and above the pedal, provide a convenient storage place for a supply of traffic tickets and other forms to be used when citing offenders, warning inadvertent violators, providing information to citizens, and otherwise meeting the needs of service. The attaché case has become an indispensable item for the modern police officer, permitting storage of forms, citation books, and a flashlight.

The Number of Police Automobiles   The number of automobiles necessary to meet the requirements of service will be determined by three factors: (1) the number required during the hours of maximum need for patrol, which occur in the late afternoon and evening; (2) flexibility of assignment, which will assist in meeting this need by the use, during the peak period, of vehicles assigned during other times to a different purpose; and (3) the requirement for spares, influenced by the promptness of repair and maintenance service.

It is felt by some that conspicuously marking police cars diminishes the flexibility of their assignment because a need exists for some vehicles that are not distinguishable from private automobiles, especially in vice investigations and in some detective and youth investigations. The advantages of greater flexibility in assignment justify a careful scrutiny of demands for cars that are

BUILDINGS AND EQUIPMENT

not conspicuously marked. An honest appraisal of the need will frequently reveal that it is not genuine, especially when the identity of the inconspicuously marked car is established by red light, siren, radio antenna, and license plates that reveal its public ownership. If such cars are to be used at all, they should not be identifiable by any of these signs.

Maximum flexibility of assignment is ensured when it has been demonstrated that conspicuously marking the cars does not interfere with most police service. Then automobiles used during the daytime by detectives and other members of the force may be impressed into patrol service to meet the maximum need during peak periods.

In the event that a heavy need for patrol cars arises one hour before the end of the day tour of duty for detectives, it may be met by reassigning some detectives' cars to the patrol division at that hour. The detectives who lose their vehicles before the end of their shift should schedule their work so that they may spend their hour without a car to greatest advantage at headquarters.

Police vehicles should be stored in the police garage at night to ensure against improper use and to protect the cars against the elements and vandals. Keeping inactive cars out of public view also helps to prevent the uninformed from commenting that officers are congregating or loitering at headquarters and prevents disclosure of the number of vehicles available for service.

Leasing Patrol cars may be rented from a dealer, an arrangement which has most of the advantages of department ownership. The factors to be considered in such an arrangement are (1) the rental cost as compared with depreciation, maintenance, and operating costs of department-owned equipment; (2) the quality of service; and (3) convenience in terms of constant availability of equipment and minimum delay in repairing and servicing as compared with that provided by a central municipal garage or a police repair shop. A rental plan has advantages for small departments lacking garage facilities. In larger cities, however, department ownership and service are usually more economical.

Replacement of Police Vehicles Factors to be considered in determining the frequency of replacement of police vehicles are efficient and satisfactory operation, appearance, and cost of operation. Dilapidated vehicles which look inadequate or which have a reputation for inefficiency arising from frequent breakdown and lack of success in pursuit destroy public confidence and damage police morale. Unsatisfactory operation and appearance cause the driver to treat the equipment with less consideration, thus aggravating its unsatisfactory condition. Increased operating cost at higher mileage has demonstrated the economic soundness of replacing police vehicles at or before 50,000 miles.

Interstation and Interoffice Communications Equipment

Teletype receivers and transmitters should be located in or adjacent to the communications center, with the sound of their operation acoustically deadened. Teletypewriters are invaluable in interstate, statewide, and district-station networks. District stations should not be operated without teletype connection with headquarters.

Teletype also has important uses in a large police building. A sender on an operational network supplies each district and unit office on the network with up-to-the-minute information on police activities. This sender is usually in a teletype room adjoining the radio dispatch room and is responsible for transmitting a brief of every incident on which officers are dispatched, with the records-division number and beat number of the officer responsible for reporting on it. This information facilitates follow-up on reports from assigned officers. When receivers on this network are installed in the press room, reporters are promptly alerted to incidents in which they have an interest.

Departments with district stations may need, in addition to the operational network, a separate administrative network for orders, descriptions of wanted persons, stolen property, and so on. One of the networks may be used for transmitting to a central booking desk information on persons arrested, thus effecting an important control over detention practices.

Closed-circuit television has application in police service to provide instruction at roll calls, personal messages from the chief to outlying facilities (which may be accomplished by loudspeakers over land lines in the absence of television), and surveillance of prisoners in custody and of selected locations in the community subject to frequent criminal attack. Television transmissions to outlying facilities should be by radio microwave.

Interoffice Communications Communications between offices at headquarters may be provided through stations off the main switchboard, through direct-line telephones, or through the type of desk transmitter that, when the user simply moves an office-selector switch and speaks into the instrument, automatically transmits the voice through a similar instrument on the selected desk. The use of stations off the main switchboard puts an added burden on the operator unless a direct inward-dial system is used; the use of the desk transmitter is independent and also has the advantage of speed. Interoffice communications needs should be appraised, and suitable equipment installed.

Additional description of the design, evaluation, and other aspects of police radio and telephone systems may be found in *Police Telecommunication Systems* (Government Printing Office, Washington, 1971).

Armament, Uniforms, and Personal Equipment

Armaments must be suitably selected and correctly used; on both these factors may rest the lives of police officers and sometimes of innocent citizens. The police administrator should give attention to protective devices as well as to offensive weapons in arming his force.

The Sidearm The sidearm should be carried on the right side (for right-handed officers) and sufficiently low to permit an easy draw. Cross-draw

BUILDINGS AND EQUIPMENT

543

holsters are not recommended; to draw a gun carried on the left side, the arm must cross the body in a position in which it may be seized or pinned to the officer's body. In holding an opponent at arm's length or in straight-arming him, the officer naturally stands sideways with his right arm free for an easy draw. A swivel holster with a snap fastener (to allow the holster to swivel when the officer is seated in a car, while permitting it to be snapped into place in rigid position while the officer is on foot) is excellent. The holster should also have a strap which snaps across the top, keeping the gun in place.

Lightweight synthetic leathers, Velcro-type fasteners, magnesium alloy handcuffs, and lightweight alloy revolver frames can reduce the weight of leather goods by a considerable amount. This weight reduction is very important in terms of officer fatigue.

Standard specifications should be established for the regulation sidearm, even though the weapons may be privately owned by the members of the department. The advantages of a regulation firearm are: (1) Standard specifications ensure weapons of suitable quality, caliber, and size. (2) Ammunition carried by each officer may be used in any gun, an important factor when the ammunition supply of one officer is exhausted under fire. (3) It is unnecessary for the department to stock more than one caliber of ammunition for sidearm service issue. (4) Greater accuracy is ensured when circumstances require one officer to fire the sidearm of another. (5) Fitting a holster to the sidearm is simplified, an important factor in maintaining uniformity of appearance.

Revolver versus Automatic　The sidearm carried by all police officers is the principal police weapon. The revolver is considered better suited to police service than the semiautomatic pistol because it will not jam. The sidearm is often not frequently and carefully cleaned, even in the best-disciplined police forces, and the grit which accumulates may jam an automatic weapon. Poorly disciplined forces sometimes carry ammunition which is defective because of age. To extract a defective cartridge in an automatic and to prepare the weapon for firing again may require some time, whereas a minimum of time is lost in the case of a revolver. The automatic pistol, however, has some advantages over the revolver. The cartridge clip has a greater capacity than the six shots in a revolver chamber; reloading by clip is faster than placing six cartridges, one at a time, into the chamber of a revolver; the construction of the automatic pistol makes it less bulky to carry; and it fits the hand more easily. Moreover, some semiautomatic pistols can be fired double-action (i.e., the hammer can be cocked by pulling the trigger), which is a decided safety advantage.

The weight and bulk of the sidearm are factors to be considered in establishing the barrel length, the construction and size of the frame, and the caliber. A gun with a short barrel is more easily drawn than a longer weapon; it is also less bulky and less easily wrested from the hand in a struggle. For all ordinary field operations the diminished accuracy resulting from an inch or two shorter barrel is inconsequential; the barrel should therefore be from 4 to 5 inches long.

The Caliber The shocking and penetrating powers of weapons are dependent on bullet weight and velocity, and these in turn are a product of cartridge-case size and the caliber. The penetrating power is of importance because sidearms are frequently used by police officers against criminals in automobiles. In the revolver, the .38 special is the ideal caliber for all-around police service. In the automatic, the 9 mm is usually considered superior to the .45 caliber because of its greater penetrating power and the fact that 9-mm pistols are frequently available as double-action guns. Few American police forces use a lighter caliber than the .38 special; in Middle Western states the .45 caliber is frequently the regulation sidearm, probably a carryover from frontier days, when the .45-caliber six-shooter was the favorite weapon because shocking power was then more important than penetration.

The .357 magnum handgun is an excellent police weapon under circumstances which demand long range and maximum penetrating power; consequently it is especially suited to rural patrol. However, such circumstances infrequently arise in cities, and the hazards created by the greater-than-necessary penetrating power and range and the disadvantages of weight, bulk, and cost make the magnum unsuited as a regulation sidearm for use in municipal departments.

Carrying the magnum loaded with regular cartridges and keeping magnum ammunition in a pouch for use under unusual conditions are unsatisfactory because of the time lost in changing the load. Loading the chamber with some magnum and some regulation ammunition is undesirable because, under fire, the officer is not likely to remember when the load changes from regulation to magnum, and the calculations are upset if the cylinder is inadvertently turned. Officers should always carry the same load. A diminished accuracy results when high-powered charges are used interchangeably with low-powered and regulation ammunition.

The High-powered Rifle The high-powered rifle is not a suitable weapon for general municipal patrol purposes because of its high penetrating power and long range and consequent danger from ricochet. The conditions of rural patrol, however, lessen the dangers to innocent persons, and the long range makes it an essential weapon. Circumstances arise in city police operations (see the discussion of SWAT on page 431) which make the high-powered rifle useful against barricaded persons, hostage holders, and snipers. Rifles should be a part of city police armaments, but they should be stored at headquarters rather than made a part of the standard patrol equipment. Selected officers on each platoon should be given intensive and continuous training in order to be specially qualified for accurate shooting with this weapon, and every officer should be given routine familiarization training with rifles, shotguns, and gas guns.

The Riot Gun The 12-gauge shotgun with an 18- to 20-inch barrel, sometimes called a *riot gun*, is the ideal auxiliary weapon for patrol. The pump gun is more reliable than the automatic because it is less likely to jam. The

BUILDINGS AND EQUIPMENT

545

barrel should not be merely sawed off; it should be of factory construction in order to ensure a satisfactory pattern.

The advantages of the riot gun over the submachine gun are: (1) Untrained officers are more accustomed to the shotgun and hence have greater skill in using it than in using the submachine gun. (2) Less training in the use of the shotgun is needed by most officers to make them good shots. (3) The shotgun pattern is usually better than one made by a machine-gun burst of an equal number of pellets. The recoil and climbing action of the machine gun interfere with its accuracy. (4) The spread of the shot makes the riot gun effective without accurate aim, an especially valuable feature in the dark. (5) The limited range of the shotgun makes its use on city streets less hazardous.

The riot gun should be carried in a rack in the driver's compartment of the patrol car and in a rainproof container with a hinged lid on motorcycles. The guns may be secured by an electric lock, with a hidden release button.

Riot guns should be loaded with cartridges that contain either 12 pellets of 0 buckshot or 9 pellets of 00 buckshot. Although plastic shell cases, polyethylene wadding, and modern crimping have all but eliminated the problem of swollen shells due to dampness, frequent inspection should be made of the ammunition, and at intervals all ammunition which has been carried should be taken out of service and used in trapshooting practice.

Gas Equipment   Gas guns and gas grenades are useful in dislodging barricaded criminals, but infrequency of need makes them unnecessary as a part of the standard equipment for each patrol officer. They should be available at headquarters, and in larger cities a locked case (with the key attached to the ignition key) containing a gas gun and an adequate supply of shells and grenades and two gas masks may be made a part of the equipment regularly carried in the automobiles of the patrol sergeants and evidence technicians. The gas shells should be of the long-range projectile type for operation against barricaded criminals. The short-range shells which discharge an instantaneous gas cloud are useful in stopping a small group of rioters, but they are of little value in dealing with criminals. Grenades thrown through windows, however, are effective.

Ordinary tear gas, or CN, is sometimes ineffective against anyone who is highly motivated. For this reason, police should also be equipped with CS gas, which is both safer and much more potent. However, CS gas is more difficult for police to cope with, during the aftermath. CN should therefore be used first, and as a second measure (or against the dangerous barricaded person) CS should be dispensed.

Nonlethal Weapons   There is now considerable research being carried out in the development of nonlethal weapons. Some are based on rapid propulsion of substances or projectiles which have stunning impact but which, when thrown back by ordinary human strength, are not dangerous. Other riot-control weaponry planning is in the direction of designing more sophisticated devices (such as tranquilizing substances), reviving water cannons, and spinning metal-fiber nets or "cocoons" that are harmless but inhibiting, as well as more exotic products.

An interesting new weapon, called a "Taser," has the appearance of a flashlight. It is used in much the same way, except that in lieu of a light beam, the gun ejects a small harpoonlike projectile up to a distance of about 25 feet. Wires trailing back to the device carry an intensive high voltage current which stuns a victim into paralysis, accompanied by extreme pain. Although this weapon is said to be harmless to healthy human beings, its potential criminal use should be obvious. Several crimes have already been committed with it, and the device should be controlled stringently by law.

The Yawara Stick The yawara stick is used for special purposes in a limited number of departments and as a substitute for the police club or baton in a few others. Its primary purpose is to control rather than to hurt or seriously injure. It has the following advantages over a club: (1) The primary purpose of the yawara stick is to increase, by leverage, the manual force applied by the officer on a recalcitrant person, whereas the purpose of the club is to strike or jab. The strength of the stroke or jab is influenced by the strength and emotional state of the officer and is frequently not in proportion to the resistance being experienced or likely to be experienced; the blow is sometimes not sufficiently vigorous, and the officer may then be bested; or it may be unreasonably severe, and the victim may then suffer serious injury. In contrast, the force applied manually should be, and nearly always is, in proportion to the resistance; the effect of the added force gained by the leverage of the yawara stick, therefore, is applied only in proportion to the resistance encountered. (2) The yawara stick can be carried at all times, inconspicuously and without inconvenience, on the person of the uniformed or plainclothes officer, and because of its size it is held inconspicuously in the hand and consequently does not impress the citizen as a threat of force, nor does it give an impression of brutality. (3) The club may be wrested from the hand of the police officer and used against him, a serious disadvantage in mob control, whereas such action is nearly impossible with a yawara stick. (4) The yawara stick may, when conditions require, be used to render a blow which, when knowingly applied, inflicts, with little danger of permanent injury, such severe pain as to make the subject nonresistant for some time. In contrast, blows by police clubs sometimes result in fractured skulls and other serious injuries.

Protective Devices and Armor Modern advances in armor have now made it practical to equip entire departments with helmets, shields, and protective vests. This equipment should be purchased in at least some quantity by all departments; in agencies which face ambush situations regularly, it should be purchased for each patrol unit. Lightweight nylon and kevlar body armor is flexible and relatively comfortable and can be worn regularly under the uniform or outer clothing. It can stop almost all handgun ammunition and should be standard issue in urban police departments.

BUILDINGS AND EQUIPMENT

The enforcement of department regulations requiring the use of the shield and vests in raids against armed criminals will discourage foolhardy officers who, in a spirit of bravado, spurn such equipment and consequently discourage its use by the more rational officers under circumstances which clearly warrant this precaution.

Bandit fire at motorized-patrol officers is not sufficiently frequent to justify armor plate or bulletproof windshields on patrol automobiles. Armored trucks, however, are useful in attacks on bandit hideouts. Such equipment enables the police to drive with safety within range of bandit guns in order to discharge gas into a building or to return gunfire from an advantageous position. Arrangements for the use of armored express trucks should be made with firms owning such equipment, and the names, addresses, and telephone numbers of the proprietors or drivers should be on file at headquarters.

The Police Uniform The uniform worn by patrol officers is an important item of equipment because it influences the prestige of the service and the morale of the department. The esprit of the organization is improved when the officers wear snappy, good-looking uniforms. On the other hand, it is difficult to build pride in an organization when patrol officers, because of ill-fitting, poorly adapted, inappropriate dress, give an air of slovenliness. The appearance of officers is reflected in this attitude, and when their uniforms lend an air of dignity and action, the officers automatically tend to develop these traits. The reaction of the public is just as great.

Police uniforms should be distinctive to avoid confusion with those of any other service and to ensure recognition by the stranger. Beset by the problem of blue-uniformed night watchmen, private detectives, prison guards, and others representing themselves as Chicago police officers and engaging in a variety of illegal activities such as extorting money from prostitutes, licensees, tavern owners, and gamblers, Chicago designed a distinctive uniform that could not be copied by any person without incurring easily enforced penalties. In four years only one person violated the law, and he was promptly convicted. The distinctive characteristic of the uniform consists of a checkerboard cap band—blue and white for all except exempt members, who wear a blue and gold cap band.

Traffic officers should wear the same uniform as the members of the patrol division. Uniforms should not be gaudy; the colors used should not be vivid or strongly contrasting.

The individual officer wearing the uniform constantly is concerned with its serviceability and comfort. Material of superior quality ensures longer wear and improves the appearance of the garment. Comfort and convenience demand that a uniform coat permit quick, easy movements, an advantage provided by the waist-length jacket. The modern nylon "car coat" with fur collar not only is warm and serviceable but can be bulletproof as well; the Law Enforcement Assistance Administration has recently funded experiments with kevlar linings in jackets, making them bulletproof.

In winter the uniform must be warm but not cumbersome. Winter overcoats should permit freedom of movement, and they should be designed so that the gun will be readily accessible.

In summer the uniform should be light and cool, and the coat may be dispensed with, provided the shirt is of military cut and of material that holds its press. In extremely warm climates, short sleeves and an open collar are desirable. This practice requires careful supervision to prevent police officers from reporting for duty in soiled and wrinkled shirts.

Hot, tight-fitting riding boots and puttees worn with breeches are uncomfortable but suitable for motorcycle service, especially during slushy winter weather, when regular trousers cannot be kept well pressed. For automobile patrol, however, trousers are preferred for year-round use, with galoshes for winter weather and knee boots for heavy storms.

Luminous garments, such as ponchos, gloves or mittens, and raincoats with luminous stripes cemented to the garment at locations most likely to reflect light, are important nighttime safety devices for officers on fixed traffic posts and for those engaged at the scene of street accidents. Such garments should be standard equipment for nighttime fixed-post officers, and ponchos or raincoats should be carried in patrol cars so that they may be quickly available after dark at the scene of street accidents.

White cotton gloves, with white leather gloves or mittens for cold weather, should be worn by officers assigned as a detail to public events.

Blazers Many departments are now equipping at least a portion of their "uniformed force" with blazer jackets in an attempt to add a businesslike, nonmilitary atmosphere to the police uniform and to increase the status of the police officer wearing it. Some of the departments using blazer jackets or civilian clothing for patrol officers have devised vests which are highly conspicuous and which can be slipped on and off easily. The vests have identifying emblems, names, or numbers and pockets for personal equipment.

Utility Clothing Easily laundered and distinctively marked smocks and coveralls should be supplied to personnel in staff services and in the crime laboratory who are engaged in tasks where other dress becomes quickly soiled. Such garments may be rented, in some communities, on a contract basis which includes laundry and repair.

Some departments also equip their patrol officers, investigators, and SWAT team members with jumpsuits for chores which are likely to tear or soil regular clothing. The jumpsuit is especially useful for those on the force who are attired in blazers.

Office Equipment and Special-Purpose Items

The selection of office furniture and equipment should be based on the appearance, durability, comfort, and suitability to purpose of the article. Chairs receive hard usage and should be selected with a view to years of service. Aluminum chairs have the advantage of durability and light weight; if the cost is prohibitive, steel ones may be chosen instead. Typing and desk chairs should

BUILDINGS AND EQUIPMENT **549**

be selected to ensure efficient posture. Squad-room tables should be of heavy plank construction, and the chairs should be made of steel.

Typewriters and duplicating equipment should be supplied to meet department needs. Metal filing cabinets and lockers of uniform make and type permit maximum flexibility in shifting pieces from one office to another, eliminate the problem of matching pieces of odd dimensions, and provide interchangeability of cabinet drawers.

Data-processing equipment should be obtained to ensure availability of suitable operational and statistical data in departments of more than 150 officers, though this equipment can be conveniently used in smaller departments also. Adding machines, calculators, and drafting equipment are also needed.

Laboratory Equipment The selection of laboratory equipment will be influenced by the volume of physical evidence brought to the laboratory, the nature of the examinations that must be made, the skill of the laboratory staff, and the cost. The department head should be advised by his laboratory staff, when they are qualified, in determining needs and in establishing priorities in equipment purchases. The laboratory should be well equipped to undertake the usual types of frequently made examinations, but the advisability of purchasing expensive equipment needed only once or twice a year should be examined critically.

The Evidence Technician's Equipment The car used by the evidence technician should contain all equipment needed in searching for, recording, collecting, preserving, and transporting physical evidence found at crime and accident scenes. The equipment should be placed in suitably designed cases to ensure protection, cleanliness, arrangement for accessibility, and ease in carrying. The cases should contain fingerprint, small frame (Instamatic or 35-mm), and view cameras with a tripod, flash units, flashbulbs, and film holders; long extension cords, flood bulbs, and reflectors; fingerprint powders, atomizers, brushes, lifting tape, and material and equipment for taking comparison prints; tools such as pliers, scissors, tweezers, files, screwdrivers, and chisels; magnifiers, tape measure, and scales or rulers; casting material, such as plaster of paris and moulage, with containers for mixing and heating; numbered markers, with devices for attaching to walls and other surfaces or to pegs to be pressed into the ground, used for identifying photographs and particular points in the scene; and gummed stickers, envelopes, vials, pillboxes, other containers, cellophane sheets, and envelopes, all of several sizes.

The evidence technician's car should also contain a broom, a rope, a bullet-resisting shield, gas supplies, and a gas mask. A small gasoline-driven, auxiliary electric-power plant to supply suitable illumination in the absence of electric power is also useful in one or two cars in each platoon.

Emergency Equipment The police and fire departments are both frequently called into service in emergencies, and the administrative head of the city should establish their respective responsibilities and relationships in order to avoid friction and to ensure attention to all tasks. The principle of unity of command makes it imperative that only one department be in charge of operations, the other providing such assistance as it is able. The assignment of these duties will determine the equipment the police must keep for such emergencies as drowning and asphyxiation and for the extrication of injured persons and the recovery of bodies from water, sewers, cave-ins, collapsed buildings, and transportation accidents.

There is no prescribed rule in making such assignments, but the general practice is to assign to the fire department duties that require a considerable period of time and heavy equipment such as boats, wrecking cars with winches, and other gear. This seems logical since such equipment in storage and in operation is more nearly comparable to fire than to police equipment.

Equipment used in police emergencies, however, should be maintained and operated by the police. Included are an emergency power supply to furnish electricity for operating the police radio during the failure of a commercial power line and an auxiliary radio transmitter to be used during the failure of the headquarters transmitter. A 10- or 15-kilowatt generator, driven by an automobile engine, will supply sufficient current to provide essential headquarters illumination in addition. Both the power supply and the auxiliary transmitter should be housed at a location removed from the police building so that in event of damage to headquarters by storm, accident, or design, police operations may continue under radio direction. There are advantages to mounting this equipment on a truck chassis or trailer so that it may be used in large-scale field operations when needed. The lighting facilities provided by floodlights and searchlights operated from the generator may be especially useful at night in conducting searches, attacks against barricaded criminals, investigations of important crime scenes, rescue work, and the search for bodies in water.

The recent increase in bombings has required the acquisition of bomb-disposal equipment. Larger police departments should purchase explosive-absorbent mats, mesh containers, and other special equipment for handling bombs, including a portable x-ray unit, cryogenic (freezing) equipment, and a disposal trailer consisting of an empty 55-gallon drum mounted in a bed of ordinary sand.

Every police department should have access to bomb-disposal technicians—either from within the agency or through arrangement with a larger department. Bomb squads in some areas are cooperative ventures in which each agency contributes to staffing and equipment. Training of police officers as bomb technicians is available from the United States Army at Redstone Arsenal in Alabama.

Part Five

Appendix

Appendix A

Outline of Items of Use in the Development of a Comprehensive Law Enforcement Plan*

The following recommendations have been developed by IACP as a brief outline of elements which might be useful in the establishment of a comprehensive law enforcement plan:

Section One — Police

I. Assessment of Problems and Resources.
   A. Study the nature of past crime and policing problems, and project future crime trends and service requirements.
   B. Assess the resources of the community and the police with respect to their capacity to improve the system.
   C. Study the attitudes of the community, to attempt to establish the desired relationship of cost vs. effectiveness, and to determine the kind of protection and service thought to be desirable by most members of the community.

II. Top-Level Organization and Control.
   A. Clearly establish the goals, objectives, and overall mission of the agency, including enforcement authority and jurisdiction. They should be founded in law.

*Developed by the International Association of Chiefs of Police, Inc., Gaithersburg, Md. Reprinted by permission of IACP, which reserves all rights for future publication or use.

B. Clearly define the means of control over the police agency. The head of the police agency should report to only one person in the government.

C. Delineate the functions, authority, and responsibility of the head of the police agency. Particular attention should be devoted to his authority to make appointments and administer the department's disciplinary system.

III. Organization.

A. Establish departmental organization along functional lines.

B. Structure the organization to permit the expansion or consolidation of activities and functions as the need arises.

C. Employ established principles in the development or modification of the organizational structure. [See Chapter 6.]

D. Designate the subdivisions of an organization—through all levels of responsibility—in a uniform manner.

E. Limit and control the creation of specialized units and/or functions unless a need inescapably exists for their establishment.

F. Develop clear and proper command relationships within the department's top-level command and within the department's structure in general.

G. Give top commanders direct access to the executive head of the police agency.

H. Establish a "quality control" program to assess department administration and operations. This is normally accomplished by the process of inspections by both line and staff personnel.

IV. Manpower Allocation and Deployment.

A. Conduct continuing analyses to determine if investigative, lower-level administrators and other nonuniformed personnel are being assigned on a basis of need.

B. Employ civilians in functions in the agency which do not require the background, skills, or attributes of police officers.

C. Develop patrol beats and deploy patrol personnel on the basis of an analysis of workload patterns, studies, and experience.

D. Assign tactical personnel based on studies of frequency, type, and location of known criminal activity.

E. Employ one-man patrol cars whenever and wherever possible.

F. Determine the need for special patrol requirements such as two-man patrol cars, foot patrol, "umbrella" elements, and transportation vans based upon scientific analysis of existing crime patterns.

G. Maintain accurate records of days off, vacations, holidays,

DEVELOPMENT OF A COMPREHENSIVE LAW ENFORCEMENT PLAN

sick and injury time, training time, and on-duty time spent in court. An accurate knowledge of such factors which detract from patrol activity will assist in accurately establishing a manpower availability factor in the determination of patrol needs.

    H.   Provide adequate numbers of field supervisors and command officers for patrol personnel.

V.   Management and Administration.

    A.   Establish a planning or research and development unit which assists the chief of police in conducting operational and administrative planning and research, and crime and traffic analysis activities.

    B.   Establish a system of written directives (general orders, special orders, memorandums, etc.) to delineate department policy and procedures.

    C.   Establish a program of staff meetings held regularly by the chief of police and his top-echelon commanders.

    D.   Establish a unit to inspect or evaluate department administration and operations, and to conduct internal investigations.

    E.   Establish vice control and intelligence gathering functions.

    F.   Assign the responsibility of fiscal management to one individual or unit, and consolidate fiscal and property management functions.

    G.   In larger departments, establish the position of legal advisor to provide consulting services to the chief of police and his upper-echelon commanders, assist the chief in policy-development for the department, and provide liaison with courts and prosecutors.

    H.   Establish a community relations unit to provide supervision of the department's community relations activities, to develop community relations policy for the chief of police, to identify specific external and internal community relations problems, and to conduct staff functions for the chief of police in fostering operational participation in community relations programs.

VI.   Personnel Administration.

    A.   Enact enabling legislation to provide legal foundation for a personnel administration program.

    B.   Establish a departmental unit or assign an individual the responsibility for the development of progressive personnel administration programs and policies relating to the attraction and selection of qualified recruits, maintenance of personnel records, maintenance of liaison with the appropriate civil service body, and the administration of personnel programs.

554 APPENDIX A

C. Establish field recruiting (if needed) and walk-in examination programs.

D. Create an attractive and informative recruiting brochure to attract qualified applicants.

E. Establish minimum standards designed to attract the best available candidates. Age and physical standards should be considered guidelines only and not as restrictions in the selection process. Residence requirements, if any, should be abolished and only applicants with high school diplomas should be considered. Written testing, oral interviews, agility performance, medical and psychological examinations, and a thorough background investigation should be part of the process. Authority for appointment should reside with the chief of police.

F. Promotional procedures should be clearly established, including policies relating to the employment of written and oral testing, time-in-grade requirements, and the absence of seniority credit. A promotional potential rating system should be included in the process.

G. Establish a personnel performance evaluation system to rate employees. Train all supervisory commanders in its purposes, objectives, and use.

H. Establish salary schedules high enough to insure that the police service is competitive with private industry, state and federal agencies, and other local agencies.

I. Establish adequate fringe benefits such as vacation and holiday leave, injury leave, overtime compensation, and uniform and clothing allowances.

J. Establish an adequate retirement system including provisions for service-connected permanent disability.

K. Establish clearly delineated disciplinary procedures.

L. Establish formalized procedures for the recording and investigation of complaints against police officers.

VII. Employee Development.

A. Assign the responsibility for the development and the initiation of recruit, in-service, executive development and specialized training programs to one unit or individual in the agency.

B. Provide adequate physical facilities, staff, and training aids to conduct such programs.

C. Adopt training standards and curricula recommended by IACP. Include a period of field training in the recruit program.

D. Establish minimum requirements to be employed in the selection of instructional staff.

E. Establish training programs for all supervisory and com-

DEVELOPMENT OF A COMPREHENSIVE LAW ENFORCEMENT PLAN

mand officers to include seminars on techniques of supervision, principles of management and organization, fiscal administration, personnel administration, and similar areas.

F. Assign selected supervisory and command officers to outside training programs and seminars such as the FBI National Academy, Northwestern University Traffic Institute, Southern Police Institute, and other programs offered at a variety of institutions of higher education throughout the country.

G. Establish college-level educational programs in police science and administration, in cooperation with local colleges.

H. Provide grants-in-aid assistance to officers electing to attend such colleges.

I. Establish an educational incentive salary differential which gives credit for certain levels of completion.

J. Establish a cadet program related to the college training program.

K. Establish a phased career development program for the rotation of personnel in various specialist and supervisory assignments.

VIII. Field Operations.

A. Patrol.

1. Deploy personnel on the basis of scientific workload studies.

2. Assign off days on the basis of low workload experience and prepare vacation schedules on the same basis.

3. Require alert and vigorous supervision of patrol activities.

4. Require supervisors to conduct regular inspections of uniforms and equipment.

5. Rotate supervisors and middle-echelon commanders with their command groups.

6. Closely evaluate operating procedures to determine the most efficient and economic patrol methods.

7. Thoroughly train patrol personnel in patrol procedures and tactics such as stopping cars, radio use, vehicle operation, occupant control, response procedures, arrest and search procedures, emergency operations, and the transportation and processing of prisoners.

8. Clearly delineate patrol officers' investigative responsibilities at scenes of incidents, including evidence collection and preservation and the extent of their investigative activities.

9. Establish a system for field interview of suspicious persons.
10. Require patrol personnel to participate vigorously in traffic enforcement efforts.
11. Adopt a program of intensive inquisitive patrol as the basic police technique in the department.

B. Criminal Investigation.
1. Place all specialized or follow-up investigative activities within one organizational entity (bureau, division, section—depending upon the size of the agency).
2. Organize investigative activity by specialized function—crimes against persons, crimes against property, and general assignments. (The extent of specialization will depend upon the size of the agency.)
3. Establish formal methods for the selection of investigators such as an evaluation of prior performance, education, and training, and through comprehensive written examinations.
4. Provide preassignment and continuous training for investigative personnel.
5. Require investigators to work singly and assign to work daytime hours unless a definite need exists which indicates other assignment needs.
6. Clearly delineate the distinction in investigative responsibilities between patrol and investigative personnel.
7. Assign preliminary investigations and the investigation of noncriminal incidents to the uniformed force.
8. Adopt the policies of "neighborhood checks" and "second contact with complainants."
9. Do not permit investigators to engage in routine patrol activities.
10. Require investigators to compile daily activity reports and the criminal investigation unit to compile administrative summaries.
11. Require investigative units to employ case clearance techniques and investigative status indicators in conformance with the Uniform Crime Reporting program.
12. Require investigative units to develop an administrative procedures manual.

C. Special Operational Problems.
1. Adopt a riot control and disaster plan, making certain that the plan provides for a distinct command structure to be utilized in emergencies.

DEVELOPMENT OF A COMPREHENSIVE LAW ENFORCEMENT PLAN

2. Provide intensive training in riot prevention techniques and riot containment and control, including mobilization under simulated riot conditions.
3. Establish a written policy for narcotics control and enforcement, following guidelines developed by IACP.
4. Adopt a written policy pertaining to race relations, containing a declaration of intention to provide equal and just treatment regardless of race or national origin, and including a prohibition against the use of racial slurs and use of so-called "trigger words" by personnel.
5. Establish a written policy on the use of firearms, and provide firearms training and other defensive techniques to minimize the danger of armed confrontations and ambush situations.
6. Adopt written policies and inspectional controls within the police agency to insure conformance with laws governing civil rights and criminal procedure, including arrest, search and seizure, interrogation, right to counsel, booking, release on bond, and so forth.
7. If indicated by the size of the department, the range, extent, and frequency of criminal activity, and the geographical and/or topographical features of the area develop a special operations unit to consist of a tactical patrol unit and/or special water and air patrol equipment (boats, helicopters, and vertical take-off and landing devices).

D. Traffic Enforcement Operations.

1. Depending on the size of the department and number, frequency and severity of accidents, create a traffic enforcement unit whose primary functions will be to investigate fatal and major injury accidents and perform selective enforcement activities.
2. Adopt the concept of selective enforcement, so that enforcement action is directed at the times, locations, and kinds of violations related to accidents.
3. Stress the role of patrol officers in traffic enforcement by requiring their participation in enforcement and general accident investigation.
4. Adopt classification, reporting, and disposition standards recommended by the National Safety Council and IACP.

IX. Technical Services.

A. Records Management.

1. Establish an information center for the central reposi-

558 APPENDIX A

tory of offense reports, correspondence, and identification and arrest records.

2. Staff the information center with civilians insofar as possible.

3. Establish a report-review function within the information center to insure complete, accurate, and timely reporting.

4. Establish strict numerical controls on all offense, identification, and arrest records, and require the completion of reports on all offenses and/or incidents brought to the attention of the police.

5. Prepare a field reporting guide, and issue a copy to operating personnel.

6. Require field supervisors to review all completed reports.

7. Employ mechanized reproduction techniques if available staff and funds permit.

8. Establish a records retention program in conformance with state statutes.

9. Maintain strict security over records.

10. Explore the employment of electronic data processing equipment and, if feasible, develop a computerized information system.

B. Crime Laboratory.

1. If the size of the department warrants, establish a crime laboratory staffed with professionally trained personnel capable of performing wet chemistry, tool mark, firearms, and bloodstain examinations, and document and handwriting analysis.

2. Smaller agencies should make extensive use of state and private laboratories as well as those established by larger municipalities.

C. Detention Facilities.

1. Whenever and wherever possible, employ the detention facilities of a county law enforcement agency or regional jail.

2. Establish appropriate standards for the selection and screening of jail personnel if the municipality has its own detention facility.

3. Train detention facility personnel in progressive jail administration policies, procedures, and operations.

4. Establish jail rules and regulations and revise and review periodically.

5. Inmates should be properly classified as to custodial risk, degree of sophistication as to behavior, and seriousness of offense.

DEVELOPMENT OF A COMPREHENSIVE LAW ENFORCEMENT PLAN

6. Conduct frequent formal and informal inspections of detention facilities, with emphasis on prevention of escapes and the sexual abuse of inmates.
7. Require all prisoners assigned to food handling to be examined by a physician prior to assignment and periodically thereafter.
8. Food should be simple but dietetically well-balanced. Prisoners assigned as food handlers should be inspected daily to assure that they are well-groomed, shaven, and have a clean white uniform and head-covering.
9. Do not book an unconscious person or one requiring medical treatment. Provide medical and dental services for all prisoners in custody of the jurisdiction.
10. Request fire department officials to conduct periodic, exacting fire prevention inspections.
11. Develop and publish a fire plan and conduct fire drills at least semiannually.
12. Require that prisoners take daily showers and shave frequently with razors provided by detention facility authorities.
13. Do not permit inmates to engage in guard (custodial) duty or other activities related to prisoner handling, supervision, or movement.

D. Property Management.
1. Establish a centralized property control program over department-owned property, including weapons and ammunition, lost and found property, and evidence.
2. Conduct annual inventories of department-owned property.
3. Conduct periodic inventories on all lost, found, and evidentiary property in the possession of the department.
4. Develop an adequate purging system for disposing of lost, found, and evidentiary property.
5. Develop and implement a centralized requisitioning procedure for all department purchases.

E. Communications.
1. Telephone - Teletype.
   a. Adopt message handling procedures to achieve:

   - Separation of emergency and nonemergency calls, with overload capability.
   - Expeditious handling of priority calls for police.

- Dependable interdepartmental and outside agency communication links.
- Rapid connection with LETS and NCIC facilities.

   b. Evaluate methods of gathering and disseminating operational data, in terms of the goal of integration of information flow, possibly on an areawide basis.

2. Radio.

   a. Establish tactical communications policies to assure:

- Timely dispatching of calls for police.
- Ability to handle peak message volume loads (channel allocations).
- Security of physical plant and of information broadcast.
- Flexibility in meeting special needs.
- System integration, including matching of information received by dispatchers with reports submitted by officers.
- Rapid response to field-originated requests for information.

   b. Investigate application of mobile teleprinter, car locators, personal radio capability, and other techniques locally.

   c. Provide radio communications links with neighboring or concurrent jurisdictions, to encourage rapid information exchange (both routinely and in event of major incidents).

3. Systems Planning.

Review the entire communications system, land line and radio, to assure compatibility with statewide communications systems as they are developed by:

- Continuing liaison with state counterparts.
- Development and extension of regional networks.
- Providing sufficient space to accommodate additional equipment.

X. Buildings and Equipment.

  A. Buildings.

    1. Inventory present space allocations in each departmentally-owned or used building.

DEVELOPMENT OF A COMPREHENSIVE LAW ENFORCEMENT PLAN

2. In the redesign of space or in the design of a new building, plan for:
   a. Adequacy for number of personnel assigned.
   b. Efficiency in work relationships with other organizational units.
   c. Effectiveness in assisting the public, if public access is provided.
   d. Effectiveness in affording prisoner security.
   e. Security from attack and sabotage.
3. Determine costs for operation and maintenance for each facility.
4. Plan for the efficient integration of:
   a. Expanded training activities.
   b. Augmented records and communications capability.
   c. Various vehicular equipment.
   d. Increases in total personnel strength.

B. Equipment.
   1. Motor Vehicles.
      a. Establish purchasing policies to assure that:

         - A low cost per mile is maintained.
         - Vehicles meet field needs.

      b. Investigate the application of scooters, special purpose patrol vehicles, airborne equipment, etc., to the police mission.
   2. Personal Equipment.
      a. Assure that standardized uniform equipment is on hand and properly maintained.
      b. Review departmental weaponry capability to assure:

         - Control.
         - Availability when needed.
         - Suitability for the job at hand.

      c. Adopt a formalized procedure for uniform clothing replacement.

Section Two—Courts

Material in this section, as well as the section relating to corrections, appears in check-list outline form only. Most of the items have been adapted from an outline which originally appeared in a book having

562   APPENDIX A

limited printing and distribution, entitled *Plan for Survey, The Administration of Criminal Justice in the United States*, American Bar Foundation, Chicago, 1955.

I. Prosecution and Defense.
   A. Prosecution.
      1. General considerations and basic policy questions.
      2. Organization and administration of prosecutors' offices, both at the Commonwealth and local level.
      3. The preservation of order and prevention of crime. (Relates to possible law enforcement activities which are not concerned with the detection of crime and the prosecution of offenders.)
      4. Investigation of crime, both concurrently with police agencies and independently of the police.
      5. Initiation of prosecutions.
      6. Termination of prosecutions.
      7. Selection of offenses to be charged.
      8. The accusatory pleading.
      9. Trial procedures and practice.
     10. Motions for new trial and arrest of judgment.
     11. Post conviction duties and practices of the prosecutor.
     12. Extraordinary writs.
   B. Public Defender.
      1. Principles guiding organization and administration.
      2. Investigation by public defenders.
      3. Access to the accused.
      4. Procedures involving waiver of the right to counsel.
      5. Preparation of cases.
      6. Trial practices.
      7. Disposition of cases without trial.
      8. Post conviction duties and functions of defense council.
      9. Procedures relating to appeal.
II. Courts.
   A. General Considerations and Basic Policy Questions.
   B. Lower courts.
      1. Organization and administration of the lower court system.
      2. Personnel, including selection and removal of court service personnel.
      3. Equipment.
      4. Functions of the court.

DEVELOPMENT OF A COMPREHENSIVE LAW ENFORCEMENT PLAN

5. Calendar.
6. Arraignment and pleas.
7. Pretrial motions.
8. Trials of lesser offenses.
9. Preliminary proceedings of felony charges.
10. Appeals.
11. Records and reports.
12. Public and press relations.

C. Felony courts—same as under (B) except that "functions" should consider the following:

    4. Functions of the court:

        a. Appellate functions.
        b. Investigation of crime.
        c. Crime prevention.
        d. Habeas corpus proceedings.
        e. Pretrial proceedings.
        f. Petty juries.
        g. Trials, including machinery and procedure for the conduct of trials and control of the courtroom.
        h. Appeals.
        i. Records and reports, including participation in a state criminal justice information system.
        j. Public and press relations.

D. Appellate Courts.

    1. Organization and administration of appellate courts.
    2. Selection of personnel.
    3. Functions of appellate courts.

        a. Extraordinary writs.
        b. Appeals.

E. The Grand Jury.

    1. Selection.
    2. Empaneling and organization.
    3. Challenges and motions.
    4. Term of service and sessions.
    5. Procedure.

F. Coroner or Medical Examiner System.

    1. Organization and administration.
    2. Selection of personnel.
    3. Facilities and equipment.
    4. Functions.

        a. Reports of death.
        b. Autopsies
        c. Inquests
        d. Field investigation by the coroner's office.

Section Three—Corrections

A. Local and county jails.
1. Organization and administration.
2. Selection and training of personnel.
3. Adequacy of buildings, facilities, and equipment.
4. Records and identification practice, including participation in statewide criminal justice information system.
5. Custodial practices.
6. Inmate discipline.
B. State Correctional Institutions—same as local and county, plus addition of the following:
1. Care and treatment, including pilot projects in rehabilitation research.
2. Classification.
3. Preparole planning and hearings.
C. Release Procedures (Probation, Sentence, and Parole).
1. General considerations and basic policy questions.
2. Probation agencies.
    a. Organization and administration.
    b. Selection and training of personnel.
    c. Equipment, offices, and clinical facilities.
    d. Records.
    e. Functions and procedures.
        1. Presentence investigation.
        2. Supervision and treatment.
        3. Relationships with other agencies.
    f. Public relations.
    g. Evaluation studies of effectiveness.
3. Sentence.
    a. Use of the indeterminate sentence.
    b. Studies relating to uniformity of sentence, improvement of prison discipline, rehabilitation, deterrence, and the effect of sentence on crime incidence.
4. Parole (Same as for probation agencies except for):
    e. Functions.
        1. Selection of prisoners for parole, including application procedure, timing, data on which hearing is based, hearing procedure, parole orders.
        2. Supervision and treatment of parolees, including case load considerations, legal restrictions and requirements, nature of rehabilitative efforts.
        3. Violation procedures.
        4. Relationships with other agencies.

Appendix B

Daily Activity Report
Program Budget Coding
Program Budget
Summary Sheets*

This appendix contains the basic forms required in a police program budgeting system.

A detailed daily activity report, similar to that shown on pages 566 and 567, is essential to the accurate measurement of the time required for the various activities of each police officer. The officer should make entries on the reverse side of the form (page 567) as he completes each assignment or activity. At the conclusion of the tour of duty, the officer should transfer the information to the front side, to facilitate processing later by a machine operator.

The use of the daily activity report will account for the largest part of the total budget, i.e., personal services. However, nonpersonal costs must also be related to each program. Every purchase or expense must be identified with a program code number, as depicted on page 568.

The forms shown on pages 569 and 570 are intended to be used for monthly as well as semiannual and annual reporting.

Material in Appendix B was developed by Robert H. Whitmer, now chief of police of Redding, California, while a member of the staff of the International Association of Chiefs of Police. The initiative for the development of the material was provided by Quinn Tamm, former executive director of IACP, who encouraged the dialogue between the staff, the U.S. Bureau of the Budget, George Washington University and other organizations interested in program budgeting in the police field.

*Developed by the International Association of Chiefs of Police, Inc., Gaithersburg, Md. Reprinted by permission of IACP, which reserves all rights for future publication or use.

565

DAILY ACTIVITY REPORT

NAME (Last)	First	Init.	SERIAL No.	ODOMETER READING FINISH
DATE	DAY	VEHICLE No.		START
SHIFT	BEAT	ASSIGNMENT		TOTAL MILES

(100) CRIME PREVENTION/SUPPRESSION

	INIT. INV.	SUPP. INV.	ASSIST.
(110) PREVENTIVE PATROL			
(120) SECURITY INSPECTIONS			
(130) VAC'TN HOUSE INSPECTIONS			
(140) FIELD CONTACTS			
(150) SECURITY ESCORTS			
(160) CRIME PREVENTION PROGRAMS (SECURITY ORIENTED)			
(170) CRIME PREVENTION PROGRAMS (TREATMENT ORIENTED)			
(180) ALARM PROGRAM			
SUBTOTAL			

(500) PUBLIC & EMERGENCY SERVICES

(510) EMERGENCY ASSIST & RESCUE			
(511) AMBULANCE SERVICE			
(520) ANIMAL CONTROL			
(530) MISSING PERSONS INVEST'NS			
(540) LOST & FOUND PROPERTY			
(541) ABANDONED AUTO CONTROL			
(550) PERMITS AND LICENSES			
(551) TAXI INSPECTION AND LICENSING			
(560) OTHER NON CRIMINAL INVEST'NS			
(570) OUTSIDE WARRANTS AND SUBPOENAS			
SUBTOTAL			

(400) MAINTENANCE OF PUBLIC ORDER

(410) PARADES			
(420) SPECIAL EVENT COVERAGE			
(430) CIVIL DISTURBANCES			
(440) POLICE RESERVE PROGRAM			
(450) CIVIL DEFENSE PROGRAM			
SUBTOTAL			

(200) INVESTIGATION/APPREHENSION

	INIT. INV.	SUPP. INV.	ASSIST.
(210) CRIMES AGAINST PERSONS			
(220) CRIMES AGAINST PROPERTY			
(230) VICE OFFENSES			
(240) TRAFFIC CRIME INVEST'NS			
(250) CRIMES AGAINST PUBLIC PEACE AND ORDER			
(251) DRUNKENNESS			
(252) DISORDERLY CONDUCT, DISTURBING THE PEACE			
(253) NUISANCE OFFENSES			
(260) MISC. HEALTH, WELFARE AND SAFETY OFFENSES			
SUBTOTAL			

SPECIAL PROGRAM ANALYSIS

(SHOW TIME EXPENDED IN THE FOLLOWING ACTIVITIES IN ADDITION TO THE TIME INCLUDED ELSEWHERE).

( ) JUVENILE INVESTIGATION			
( ) TRANSPORTATION AND BOOKING OF PRISONERS			
( ) WARRANT AND SUBPOENA SERVICE FOR LOCAL CASES			
( ) SPECIAL SERVICE CASES			

NOTE: DO NOT INCLUDE SUBTOTAL FOR THIS BLOCK ON REVERSE SIDE OF FORM.

(700) TECHNICAL SERVICES

(710) CENTRAL RECORDS ACTIVITIES			
(720) COMMUNICATIONS			
(730) PROPERTY CONTROL			
(740) CRIME LABORATORY SERVICES			
(741) PHOTO & I.D. SERVICES			
(750) CUSTODY OF PRISONERS			
SUBTOTAL			

(300) MOVEMENT/CONTROL OF TRAFFIC

	INIT. INV.	SUPP. INV.	ASSIST.
(310) TRAFFIC PATROL			
(320) ACCIDENT INVEST. FATAL & INJURY			
(321) ACCIDENT INVEST. MAJOR PROPERTY DAMAGE			
(322) ACCIDENT INVEST. MINOR PROPERTY DAMAGE			
(330) HAZARDOUS MOVING VIOLATIONS			
(331) NON HAZARDOUS VIOLATIONS			
(332) PARKING CONTROL & ENFORCEMENT			
(340) FIRES, FIRE ALARMS			
(350) ESCORTS			
(360) TRAFFIC REGULATION			
(361) TRAFFIC POINT CONTROL			
(362) TRAFFIC SIGNING & SIGNALING			
(363) TRAFFIC ENGINEERING AND FLOW			
(370) SCHOOL CROSSING PROGRAM			
(380) TRAFFIC SAFETY EDUCATION			
SUBTOTAL			

(600) ADMINISTRATIVE SERVICES

(610) DIRECTION AND SUPERVISION			
(620) PLANNING & DATA PROCESSING			
(630) INSPECTION			
(640) INTERNAL INVESTIGATION			
(650) COMMUNITY RELATIONS			
(660) PERSONNEL MANAGEMENT			
(670) TRAINING			
(680) FISCAL AFFAIRS			
SUBTOTAL			

TIME IS TO BE RECORDED IN HOURS TO THE NEAREST 5 MINUTES.

DAILY ACTIVITY REPORT (continued)

ACTIVITIES LOG: RECORD ALL ACTIVITIES WHICH ARE NOT ACTUAL PREVENTIVE PATROL AND OBSERVATION

TIME SPAN	CASE NO.	INIT. INV.	SUPP. INV.	ASSIST.	ACTIVITY AND LOCATION	TIME

VEHICLE AND EQUIPMENT INSPECTION

(208) GAS   (208) OIL

REMARKS ON CONDITION OF VEHICLE, CLEANLINESS, SAFETY, EQUIPMENT, NEED FOR

REPAIRS.

SUPERVISOR'S APPROVAL OF DAILY ACTIVITY REPORT   SERIAL NO.

COURT TIME

| ON DUTY | TIME |
| OFF DUTY | TIME |

CASE NUMBERS
AND CHARGE

CERTIFYING
OFFICER

TOTAL HOURS WORKED INCLUDING
OVERTIME – (EXCEPT COURT
TIME)

TOTAL ACTIVITY HOURS
INCLUDING OVERTIME
(EXCEPT COURT TIME)

TOTAL
PREVENTIVE PATROL
HOURS

PROGRAM BUDGET CODING
Key to Code Numbering

Department	Bureau and Division or Section	Object	Program
14 Public Safety - Police	10 Chief's Office	100 PERSONAL SERVICES	100 CRIME PREVENTION AND SUPPRESSION - General
15 Public Safety - Fire	11 Research and Development	101 Salaries - Permanent Employees	110 Preventive Patrol
16 Public Safety - Communications, etc.	20 Operations Office	102 Overtime	120 Security Inspections
	21 Patrol Division	103 Salaries - Temporary Employees	130 Vacation House Inspections
	22 Investigation Division	104 Salaries - Part-time	140 Field Contacts
	23 Traffic Division	105 Fees for Services	150 Security Escorts
	24 Special Operations Division	106 Reserved for future use	160 Crime Prevention Programs (Security Oriented)
	30 Administrative Services Office		170 Crime Prevention (Treatment Oriented)
	31 Community Relations Division	200 OPERATING EXPENSES	180 Alarm Program
	32 Personnel Division	201 Office Supplies and Forms	
	33 Training Division	202 Postage	200 INVESTIGATION AND APPREHENSION - General
	34 Systems and Procedures Division	203 Telephone and Teletype	210 Crimes Against Persons
	40 Technical Services Office	204 Membership Dues	220 Crimes Against Property
	41 Central Records Division	205 Travel and Subsistence	230 Vice Offenses
	42 Communications Division	206 Special Departmental Supplies and Equipment	240 Traffic Crime Investigations
	43 Data Processing Division	207 Vehicle Maintenance and Repair	250 Crimes Against Public Peace and Order
	44 Property Division	208 Gas, Oil and Lubricants	251 Drunkenness
	50 Inspectional Services Office	209 Equipment Maintenance and Repair	252 Disorderly Conduct, Disturbing the Peace
	51 Internal Investigation Division	210 Uniforms and Personal	253 Nuisance Offenses
	52 Inspections Division	211 Lighting, Heating, Cooling, Power	260 Miscellaneous Health, Welfare and Safety Offenses
	53 Intelligence Division	213 Rent	
	54 Vice Control Division	214 Building Maintenance	300 MOVEMENT AND CONTROL OF TRAFFIC - General
		215 Insurance	310 Traffic Patrol
			320 Accident Investigation - Fatal and Injury
		300 CAPITAL EXPENDITURES	321 Accident Investigation - Major Property Damage
		301 Furniture	322 Accident Investigation - Minor Property Damage
		302 Office Equipment or Machines	330 Hazardous Moving Violation Enforcement
		303 Special Departmental Equipment or Machines	331 Non-Hazardous Violation Enforcement
		304 Vehicles	332 Parking Control and Enforcement
		305 Building and Renovation	340 Fires, Fire Alarms
			350 Escorts
			360 Traffic Regulation
			361 Traffic Point Control
			362 Traffic Signing and Signaling
			363 Traffic Engineering and Flow
			370 School Crossing Program
			380 Traffic Safety Education

400 MAINTENANCE OF PUBLIC ORDER - General
410 Parades
420 Special Event Coverage
430 Civil Disturbances
440 Police Reserve Program
450 Civil Defense Program

OUTPUT: 1421 - 101 - 210 — Sample code obtained by processing an Officer's Daily Activity Report. Data bank entries will then show the code number, cost (computed from the hours worked on this activity multiplied by the officer's hourly rate) and date.

500 PUBLIC AND EMERGENCY SERVICES - General
510 Emergency Assistance and Rescue
511 Ambulance Service
520 Animal Control
530 Missing Persons Investigations
540 Lost and Found Property Control
541 Abandoned Auto Control
550 Permits and Licenses
551 Taxi Inspection and Licensing
560 Other Non-Criminal Investigations

INPUT: 1421 - 101 - 200 — Sample code applied to input—in this case a salary appropriation statement. Part of the salary appropriation should be allocated to various programs, using the best available estimates. In the first year of operation in a program budget, estimates of $\pm$ 10 percent will be entirely satisfactory.

(In general, the balance of the categories shown here are intended for non-assignable and non-operational activities.)

600 ADMINISTRATIVE SERVICES - General
610 Direction and Supervision
620 Planning and Data Processing
630 Inspection
640 Internal Investigation
650 Community Relations
660 Personnel Management
670 Training
680 Fiscal Affairs

Every transaction (both input and output) should carry appropriate coding by means of numbers showing both Object and Program designations whenever possible.

700 TECHNICAL SERVICES - General
710 Central Records Activities
720 Communications
730 Property Control
740 Crime Laboratory Services
741 Photo and I.D. Services
750 Custody of Prisoners

PROGRAM BUDGET SUMMARY

Prepared by:

Date prepared:

Approved by:

☐ Monthly Summary _____ 19 _____
  Month   Year

☐ Semi-Annual Summary From _____ To _____ 19 _____
  (Inclusive months)   Year

☐ Annual Summary for Fiscal Year Ending _____ 19 _____
  Month   Year

PROGRAM		COSTS BY PROGRAM																
	DETAIL	Crime Prevention/ Suppression Code #		Investigation/ Apprehension Code #		Traffic Movement/ Control Code #		Maintenance of Public Order Code #		Public and Emergency Services Code #		Administrative Services Code #		Technical Services Code #		TOTAL COST YEAR TO DATE	APPROPRIATIONS	UNENCUMBERED BALANCE	PROJECTIONS* COMING YEAR
OBJECT CODE #	OBJECT DESIGNATIONS	Report Period	Year To Date	Report Period	Year To Date	Report Period	Year To Date	Report Period	Year To Date	Report Period	Year To Date	Report Period	Year To Date	Report Period	Year To Date				
	Program Subtotal																	

*If desired, projections may be extended for several years.

PROGRAM BUDGET SUMMARY

Prepared by:

Date prepared:

Approved by:

☐ Monthly Summary _____ Month _____ 19___ Year

☐ Semi-Annual Summary   From _____ To _____ 19___
(Inclusive months) Year

☐ Annual Summary for Fiscal Year Ending _____ Month _____ 19___ Year

COSTS BY PROGRAM

SUMMARY	Crime Prevention/ Suppression Code #		Investigation/ Apprehension Code #		Traffic Movement/ Control Code #		Maintenance of Public Order Code #		Public and Emergency Services Code #		Administrative Services Code #		Technical Services Code #		TOTAL COST YEAR TO DATE	APPROPRIATIONS	UNENCUMBERED BALANCE	PROJECTIONS* COMING YEAR
OBJECT CODE #	Report Period	Year To Date	Report Period	Year To Date	Report Period	Year To Date	Report Period	Year To Date	Report Period	Year To Date	Report Period	Year To Date	Report Period	Year To Date				
Personal Services																		
Operating Expenses																		
Capital Expenditures																		
TOTAL BY PROGRAM																		

TIME DEVOTED BY PROGRAM (Recorded by 100ths of hours)

PERSONNEL TIME	Crime Prevention/ Suppression Code #		Investigation/ Apprehension Code #		Traffic Movement/ Control Code #		Maintenance of Public Order Code #		Public and Emergency Services Code #		Administrative Services Code #		Technical Services Code #		PROJECTIONS THIS COMING YEAR							
	Report Period	Year To Date	Report Period	Year To Date	Report Period	Year To Date	Report Period	Year To Date	Report Period	Year To Date	Report Period	Year To Date	Report Period	Year To Date	Code #	Code #	Code #	Code #	Code #	Code #	Code #	Code #
Regular Hours Worked																						
Paid Overtime																						
Compensatory Time (Non-Holiday)																						
Court Time on Duty																						
Court Time Off Duty																						
TOTAL																						

*If desired, projections may be extended for several years.

Appendix C

Consolidated Daily Report—Monthly General Activity Report*

The consolidated daily report illustrated on page 572 is based on classifications adopted by the Committee on Uniform Crime Records of the International Association of Chiefs of Police.

As a note of historical interest, the Uniform Crime Reports program was developed over the period of years from 1922 to 1930 by IACP. In 1930 (as a result of a request made by IACP in its annual conference in 1929) the program was transferred to the FBI.

The consolidated daily report is of value only in larger cities, which usually experience changes in each classification on a daily basis. Smaller agencies are better served by a monthly report, as depicted on pages 573-575.

The form shown on page 572 was designed by Donald D. Pomerleau, now commissioner of police of Baltimore, Maryland, while he was a member of the IACP staff.

*Developed by the International Association of Chiefs of Police, Inc., Gaithersburg, Md. Reprinted by permission of IACP, which reserves all rights for future publication or use.

APPENDIX C

CONSOLIDATED DAILY REPORT
(for use in a larger department)

For 24 hours ending _____ 19 ___

UNIFORM CLASSIFICATION OF OFFENSES	PERSONS ARRESTED				NUMBER OF INCIDENTS REPORTED			
PART I CLASSES	Past 24 Hours	This Month to Date	Last Month to Date	Same Month Last Year to Date	Past 24 Hours	This Month to Date	Last Month to Date	Same Month Last Year to Date
Murder & Nonnegligent Manslaughter								
Manslaughter by Negligence								
Forcible Rape								
Robbery								
Assault								
Burglary (B & E)								
Larceny – $50 & Over								
Larceny – under $50								
Auto Theft								
TOTAL PART I CLASSES								
Total Miscellaneous Non-Criminal Calls								
Total Part II Incidents								
Total Calls For Police Service								
TOTAL PART II CLASSES								

	Past 24 Hours	This Month to Date	Last Month to Date	Same Month Last Year to Date	PERSONS CHARGED	Past 24 Hours	This Month to Date	Last Month to Date	Same Month Last Year to Date
					TRAFFIC ANALYSIS				
Arson									
Forgery & Counterfeiting									
Fraud					Sign or Signal				
Embezzlement					Improper Turns				
Stolen Property					Careless Driving				
Vandalism					Speed				
Weapons-carrying & possessing					Failure to Yield				
Prostitution & Commercialized Vice					Pedestrian Violation				
Sex Offenses					Passing & Lane Usage				
Narcotic Drug Laws					DWI				
Gambling					Following Too Closely				
Offenses vs. Family & Children					Other HMV				
Liquor Laws					TOTAL				
Drunkenness					Traffic Accidents				
Disorderly Conduct									
Vagrancy					Injuries				
All Other Offenses									
GRAND TOTAL					Deaths				

MONTHLY GENERAL ACTIVITY REPORT

MONTHLY GENERAL ACTIVITY REPORT
(for use in a small or medium department)

Month _____ 19 ____

CRIMES

PART I OFFENSES (ACTUAL)	This Month	Same Month Last Year	This Year to Date	Last Year to Date
1. Criminal Homicide				
a. Murder and Nonneg. Mansl.				
b. Manslaughter by Neg.				
2. Forcible Rape Total				
a. Rape by Force				
b. Assault to Rape – Attempts				
3. Robbery Total				
a. Armed – Any Weapon				
b. Strong-arm – No Weapon				
4. Assault Total				
a. Gun				
b. Knife or Cutting Inst.				
c. Other Dangerous Weapon				
d. Hands, Fists, Feet, etc. -Aggr.				
e. Other Assaults – Not Aggr.				
5. Burglary Total				
a. Forcible Entry				
b. Unlawful Entry – No Force				
c. Attempted Forcible Entry				
6. Larceny-Theft (Except Auto Theft)				
a. $50 and over in value				
b. Under $50 in value				
7. Auto Theft				
TOTAL PART I				

MONTHLY GENERAL ACTIVITY REPORT
(continued)

	This Month	Same Month Last Year	This Year to Date	Last Year to Date
PART II OFFENSES TOTAL				
Checks				
a. NSF, Account Closed				
b. No Account, Forgery				
Vandalism				
All Other Part II				
TOTAL PART I AND II				
NON-CRIMINAL CASES TOTAL				
Accidents -- Total				
Personal Injury				
Fatal				
Property Damage				
Casualties (Non-vehicle)				
Emerg. Amb. & Aid				
Suicide Cases				
Unattended Death				
Routine Amb. Trans.				
Amb. P.U. (Outside)				
Missing Adults				
Missing Runaway Juveniles				
All Other Numbered Cases				
TOTAL CASES				

MONTHLY GENERAL ACTIVITY REPORT

MONTHLY GENERAL ACTIVITY REPORT
(continued)

	This Month	Same Month Last Year	This Year to Date	Last Year to Date
ARRESTS (Except Summonses)				
Part I				
Part II Total				
DWI				
Other Drunks				
All Other Part II				
TOTAL ARRESTS				
SUMMONSES – Total				
Hazardous Moving Viols.				
Non-Hazardous Mov. or Equip.				
Parking				
Warrants Served				
Warrants on Hand				
Miscel Police Services TOTAL				
Field Interrogation Cards				
Safe, Night Lights Out				
Doors, Windows, Open				
Street Lights Out				
Fire Calls				
False Burglar Alarms				
Other Non-criminal Hazards				
Incoming Phone Calls				
Traffic Enforcement Index				
Forcible Entry Burglary Rate per 1,000 population	(Averages to Date)			

Appendix D

Statement of Departmental Goals, Arlington County Police Department, Arlington, Virginia

August 28, 1975

SUBJECT: Departmental Goals

TO: Police Department Command Staff

FROM: Chief Roy C. McLaren

This statement of departmental goals has been prepared as a guideline for command officers and supervisors so that they can better communicate to all personnel what I believe to be the department's basic objectives.

MISSION

As Arlington County employees, our mission is to protect and serve the public through police action. In carrying out this mission, we should cooperate as a team to make certain that the citizens of Arlington are afforded the best protection and service we can give them and to establish the Arlington County Police Department as the finest in the United States.

GOALS

Statements of goals prepared for the guidance of employees should be consistent with goals and programs outlined in the police-department budget. The basic programs in the departmental budget are as follows:

1 Crime prevention and suppression
2 Crime reduction, investigation of crimes, and apprehension of offenders
3 Movement and control of traffic
4 Maintenance of public order
5 Public and emergency services

The goals of the department are:

1 *Crime Prevention and Suppression.* This area consists of long- and short-range crime-prevention efforts. It covers the work of personnel in school youth-resources activities. It includes the efforts of beat officers when they recognize a predelinquent situation and then refer it to the appropriate social service agency. It covers preventive-patrol activities which cannot be related to the prevention of any specific kind of crime.

Emphasis should be placed upon short-range crime-prevention methods such as hazard-oriented routine preventive patrol and field interrogation designed to discourage potential offenders. The police have a responsibility to take positive action, either indirectly by making referrals or directly, to help prevent crime-causing family relationships and unlawful racial discrimination in housing and employment.

Emphasis should be placed upon short-range crime-prevention methods such as hazard-oriented routine preventive patrol and field interrogation designed to discourage potential offenders. The police have a responsibility to take positive action, either indirectly by making referrals or directly, to help prevent crime-causing family relationships and unlawful racial discrimination in housing and employment.

Crime-prevention efforts should include the following:

a Each district team should organize a neighborhood youth council consisting of a representative from schools, a youth-resource officer, a beat officer, a representative from social services, and a representative from juvenile probation. By means of these councils, delinquent youth should be identified, and delinquency-causing conditions corrected.

b Field interrogation reports should be used regularly by patrol officers, traffic officers, agents, and supervisors in checking out suspicious subjects, both on foot and in vehicles.

2 *Crime Reduction, Investigation of Crimes, and Apprehension of Offenders.* A major goal of the department is of course related to the reduction of specific kinds of crime through public education and preventive efforts in the field, investigation of a case once a crime has been committed, and the apprehension of offenders and their subsequent trial, conviction, incarceration, and rehabilitation.

The objectives of the crime-reduction program should be stated in quantitative terms. The degree of crime reduction possible in a given community is dependent on several factors. The first is the amount of money which the governing body is willing to spend to support police activity. The second major factor is the extent to which the population within the community and the surrounding region is prone to commit crimes. A third major factor is the degree of competence of the personnel in the police department. Fourth, the morale of the officers in the police department and the willingness of police employees to work hard are considerable factors in police productivity. Fifth, the agencies in the rest of the criminal justice system must act responsibly in dealing with those offenders who are placed into the system.

If other factors remain reasonably consistent and if the department has a level of manpower which is close to the average, it is probable that the difference between the efficiency of a well-trained, highly motivated police department and an ill-trained, poorly motivated group is plus or minus 10 percent, or a range of 20 percent. Police objectives in reducing crime should probably therefore not realistically go beyond a 20 percent maximum.

Sub-programs or activities should be identified within the area of crime reduction, investigation of crime, and apprehension of offenders. The following objectives should be established for these subprograms or activities:

a To record 100 percent of all index crimes reported to the police department

b To carry out field investigations in 100 percent of cases for the categories of murder, rape, robbery, aggravated assault, burglary, and auto theft and at least 85 percent of the cases in the category of larceny and theft

c To reduce crime in all index categories to the rate per thousand which is the average for our population group, according to Uniform Crime Reports

d The crime-clearance objectives for the various categories of crime should be as follows:

Murder	90 percent
Rape	66 percent
Robbery	38 percent
Aggravated assault	76 percent
Burglary	28 percent
Larceny and theft	28 percent
Automobile theft	24 percent

e Follow-up investigations should be conducted by investigators in the centralized detective or investigations division for all murders of a stranger-to-stranger type and all murders which are unsolved. Patrol officers or combinations of patrol officers, police agents, or investigators should handle all cases of rape, including both initial report and subsequent follow-up reports.

In the case of robbery, patrol officers should handle initial investigations of robbery reports, with patrol officers, agents, or team investigators, either as individuals or in combination, handling follow-up investigations for purse-snatching robberies and strong-arm robberies as well as most armed robberies. The central headquarters investigators should be given the responsibility for

STATEMENT OF GOALS, ARLINGTON COUNTY POLICE DEPARTMENT 579

bank robberies and major robberies in which there has been severe personal injury or major financial loss exceeding $2,500.

The preliminary investigation of aggravated assaults should be handled by patrol officers, with follow-up investigations by combinations of patrol officers, agents, and team investigators except for serious stranger-to-stranger aggravated assaults in which there is likely to be permanent injury or if the injury is such that the victim might die. In that case, the follow-up investigation should be handled by the central investigative unit.

Patrol officers should handle preliminary investigations of burglaries with follow-up investigation by a combination of patrol officers, agents, and team investigators with the exception that burglaries involving property loss of more than $2,500 should be followed up by centralized investigators.

Patrol officers should handle preliminary investigations of larceny and theft with follow-up investigation by a combination of patrol officers, agents, and team investigators with the exception that larceny and theft involving property loss of more than $2,500 should be followed up by centralized investigators.

In case of auto theft, patrol officers should handle preliminary investigations in all cases with follow-up investigations by combinations of patrol officers, agents, and investigators.

Vice offenses should be the responsibility of each district team except that central vice investigators may concurrently investigate major vice conspiracies involving organized-crime elements or those involving wholesaling of narcotics, prostitution conspiracies, or gambling conspiracies. The central vice unit may also ask district officers to participate in or refrain from participation in, as the case may be, a vice investigation.

f Supervisors should foster independence, self-reliance, and initiative on the part of patrol officers, agents, and investigators. The emphasis in their supervision of patrol officers, agents, and investigators should be on the quality and quantity of work, rather than primarily upon military "spit and polish" regulations. Supervisors should also place emphasis on the review of reports for content and accuracy and upon requiring officers to account for the status of cases which remain unsolved.

g Investigators should have their positions because of their ability to carry out a higher level of investigative responsibilities. They are expected to work productively for their entire workday. Investigators' monthly work summaries should be employed, and those investigators in district teams who have consistently low productivity and clearances should be placed in patrol assignments.

h Supervisors should make certain that investigators properly use informants and investigative resources. All investigations for index crimes should involve a second contact with victims for the purpose of ascertaining whether the victim has learned of additional leads or evidence and for the purpose of communicating the status of the case to the victim.

i Each district team should engage in specific crime-prevention programs which include house-to-house crime prevention and security counseling and programs

580 APPENDIX D

involving the community group or association in the neighborhood. We should encourage participation of the news media in these efforts.

j Investigators or agents should not work in pairs and should not engage in preventive-patrol activity or in taking initial complaints in criminal cases. Supervisors should require all team officers to complete daily-activity reports. Supervisors of investigators, both in district teams and in the centralized investigative unit, should compile summaries of the progress of investigations and investigative status and should forward these reports to the division commanders.

k Each patrol officer should be given responsibility for certain follow-up activity in a smaller area within each district.

(1) Simple index-crime investigations (i.e., those not involving any other district or any other jurisdiction) should be assigned to beat officers for the following kinds of calls:

- Purse-snatching and strong-arm robberies
- Burglaries with less than $500 property loss
- Larceny and theft with less than $500 property loss
- Aggravated assaults where the victim is not permanently injured or in danger of dying
- Felony hit-and-run cases where the victim is not permanently injured or in danger of dying

(2) Most misdemeanors and noncriminal incidents requiring follow-up investigations should be assigned to patrol officers.

3 *Movement and Control of Traffic.* The department traffic-enforcement index (the number of hazardous moving-traffic violations convictions with penalty, divided by the number of injury accidents) should be 20. Division and district commanders should therefore encourage officers to engage in added enforcement action if the index in their respective division or district is below this level.

The drinking driver is a major factor in fatal, serious-injury, and property-damage accidents. Officers should be encouraged to engage in DWI enforcement.

Officers should concentrate enforcement efforts in traffic on those violations which are most often causing accidents and at the locations and times where accidents are most prevalent.

Beat officers should be responsible for surveys of the condition of traffic signs and markings and for discovering and reporting hazards to motorists, such as shrubbery obscuring visibility at intersections, potholes, and trees growing in front of stop signs.

4 *Maintenance of Public Order.* The department has a responsibility to be prepared to handle civil disorders, man-made or natural disasters, and special events such as parades and celebrations. Each division and district commander, in turn, has a responsibility to keep personnel trained and ready to cope with these problems and to maintain order. With respect to civil disorders, division and district team

STATEMENT OF GOALS, ARLINGTON COUNTY POLICE DEPARTMENT

commanders should be familiar with the community elements likely to cause disorder, and they should establish communications channels in advance or at the earliest possible time, should a disorder begin to materialize.

Contingency plans should take into account the fact that ordinary regular team operations and organizational structures are ineffective when large numbers of officers are mobilized. Plans should therefore be based on organizational relationships likely to be in effect during the disorder or disaster.

5   *Public and Emergency Services.* A great percentage of police workload is noncriminal and falls into the category of emergency service, miscellaneous service relating to lost persons or property, frightened persons, citizens locked out of their homes, and so on. It is the policy of the department to render such services to the full extent of the availability of manpower.

Obviously, if available police are out of service on more important calls, a request for nonemergency, noncriminal service should be given a lower priority. However, if personnel are available, the police should respond to each request and should render the service in a cooperative way. The good will and community support generated is enormous, and as long as the time spent in rendering noncriminal, nonemergency service does not cut into the time required for crime-reduction work or the investigation of cases, the practice should be encouraged.

Appendix E

Purpose and Nature of Inspection

PURPOSE AND NATURE OF INSPECTION

I **Purpose** To promote effectiveness and economy by the inspection of:

- Persons
- Things
- Procedures
- Results

In order to reveal

- Conditions
- Situations
- Actions

That adversely influence the success of police operations because of weaknesses and failures in

- Personnel
- Matériel
- Procedures

Which indicate a need for modified or additional

- Organization
- Regulation
- Procedure
- Equipment
- Headquarters facilities
- Manpower

582

PURPOSE AND NATURE OF INSPECTION

- Training
- Direction
- Leadership

II **Nature** Inspection is accomplished by interviews with

- Members of the force
- Persons involved in police incidents
- The general public

And analysis of

- Inspection reports
- Police records
- Police statistics
- Police procedures

And observation of condition of

- Police quarters
- Jail
- Public places
- Equipment
- Personnel

In order to ascertain whether

- Department morale is satisfactory
- Morale-destroying influences are at work
- The attitudes, actions, reactions, and accomplishments of members of the force are satisfactory.
- Training, direction, and supervision are satisfactory
- Rules governing the care of the person are complied with
- The integrity of all members is above reproach
- The moral standards of the members are satisfactory
- Regulations concerning the maintenance and use of equipment and property are complied with
- Equipment and property require repair or replacement
- Impaired condition of equipment and property has resulted from improper use or inadequate maintenance
- Equipment and space are adequate
- Department procedures are suitable
- Department procedures are being followed
- Operations are carried out as planned
- Department resources are used to best advantage
- Department organization units are operating satisfactorily
- Any part of the police job is being neglected

584 APPENDIX E

- Community conditions affecting operations against crime and vice are satisfactory
- Public reaction to department policies, methods, and officials is satisfactory
- Persons and incidents are satisfactorily dealt with

III **Duties of the Police Inspector**   As an agent of the chief of police, the police inspector should

- Conduct open inspection of personnel, matériel, procedures, and results of police operations
- Inform the chief on

  Action taken by the inspector
  Action desired of the chief

- Promote and stimulate supervision on the part of operating personnel by

  Devising well-conceived inspection reports for their use that will require a positive statement that a condition is satisfactory or unsatisfactory

  Instructing supervisory personnel in

  The use of inspection reports
  The nature of authoritative and staff inspections

  Spot-checking inspection reports

- Inspect and effect correction of conditions reported unsatisfactory
- Maintain satisfactory relationship with subordinate and commanding officers
- Focus his attention on task of appraising such intangibles as public relations, conditions in the community affecting police operations, and the morale of the men

Appendix F

Guide to Performance Evaluation*

PART 1 PERFORMANCE EVALUATION

The service rating has been a hotly debated topic in personnel administration. Employees generally dislike being rated, many times justifiably, because of the methods used. Conversely, supervisors often resent the hard work and unpopularity which can accrue to them as a result. There are almost as many rating systems as there are agencies to use them. Professional personnel officers disagree on methods and objectives, to add to the confusion.

Authorities have often listed numerous objectives which are seldom achieved. Some personnel officers claim that ratings are intended to:

- Keep employees informed of what is expected of them and how well they are performing.
- Recognize and reward good work.
- Help supervisors recognize weaknesses and give them the opportunity to remedy deficiencies.
- Identify employees who should be given specific types of training and identify general training needs.
- Provide a continuing record of an employee's performance history.
- Guide decisions to be made in matters of promotions, transfers, layoffs, and other personnel transactions.

*The Performance Evaluation Report form and part of the descriptive material —596-603—accompanying it is an IACP modification of a system published by Public Personnel Association, and in turn was taken from a procedure adopted by the school system in San Diego, California. The Promotional Potential Rating form is an IACP modification of a method used by the Berkeley Police Department, Berkeley, California.

585

586 APPENDIX F

- Help determine if an employee will be given an in-grade pay increase.
- Verify performance standards.
- Check accuracy of job descriptions and classifications.
- Verify the accuracy and effectiveness of recruitment and examination procedures.

All of these are worthwhile administrative objectives and it might be thought that ratings of employees would be welcomed by everyone concerned. However, personal and emotional considerations have significantly reduced the value of such systems. Furthermore, a perfect rating system has not yet been devised.

The importance attached to a good personnel evaluation system can be brought out by quoting one personnel director in a large municipal agency who states flatly:

> The development of an adequate employee evaluation plan is the primary task of modern personnel administration. While this may be overstated, there is no question but that employee performance rating is one of the areas of greatest challenge to the personnel administrator. His job is not made any easier by the many differences of opinion, within the personnel field itself, as to objectives and methodology. In fact, according to some authorities, there has been an increase in the number of 'appraisal plan debunkers' who, discouraged by the complexities involved, have recommended that all employee rating devices be scrapped as obsolete.

Over the past five years there have been some definite trends in the field of performance evaluation. The first is that there has been more thoughtful consideration of the philosophy, purposes, and principles of performance ratings. For example, one writer points out that the interview between the employee and the supervisor is more important to the procedure than any other aspect, and further, that it calls for sincerity more than technique.

The second trend is to avoid the use of the performance rating system for a multiplicity of purposes (such as those listed on the previous page.) The system based on multiple objectives will likely fail. As indicated previously, in the past it has been fashionable to enumerate many possible objectives of employee evaluation—to facilitate merit increases, promotion, transfer, demotion, discharge, rehire, references, motivation, employee training, supervisory training, personnel research, talent hunts, and many others. But there is increasing recognition that an evaluation method can be developed as an administrative tool, or as a supervisory tool, but it is unlikely that it can function to its optimum in both capacities. Clifford E. Jurgensen states that the use of a particular evaluation method as a supervisory tool requires an ability to evaluate accurately; and that its use as an ad-

GUIDE TO PERFORMANCE EVALUATION

ministrative tool also requires *willingness* to evaluate accurately. The second of these, he states, is too often assumed or overlooked and as an example he refers to the frequent complaint that appraisals show little differentiation between employees in the face of positive knowledge that the supervisors are fully capable of such differentiation.[1]

A third trend is the shift away from rating subjective or personal traits, and toward rating objective and more easily observed characteristics. One writer, for example, stated that while managers were effective in recognizing failures in planning and scheduling, or the existence of excessive grievances or low morale, or that operating costs were too high, they had considerably more difficulty diagnosing the underlying causes of performance failures, and that their diagnoses were, at best, near guesses and assumptions which could not be translated easily into effective counseling.

Fourth, there is now a tendency to regard performance evaluations for what they are, as opinions and attitudes rather than as physical science measurements. Some of the former stress on trying to shroud opinion, or to systematize it, is being eliminated. George N. Beck of the Los Angeles Police Department writes, "Rather than . . . to compensate for the subjective nature of ratings, observers in the field have begun to recognize that the main justification for ratings resides in this quality that does not lend itself to testing."[2]

The IACP System

The performance evaluation system recommended by IACP provides for the rating of both sworn personnel and civilians, including supervisors with the rank of captain or below, semi-annually. The system is an adaptation of a procedure published by the Public Personnel Association in 1965. It takes into account the most recent trends in the field of employee evaluation:

- The system avoids the confusion caused by multiplicity of purposes. It has only one definite objective in mind—to inform the employee of his standing, with intent to improve his performance or to sustain performance which is already superior.
- Summary or numerical ratings have been eliminated. It will not be possible with the use of this form to categorize an employee as "Excellent," "Above Average," "Average," and so forth. The system should not be used for any administrative action except that it should substantiate and certainly not contradict decisions made to discipline or terminate an employee because of poor performance.

[1] Clifford E. Jurgensen, Part I, "Employee Performance Appraisal Re-examined," *Public Personnel Association Report No. 613*, 1963, p. 4.

[2] George N. Beck, "Municipal Police Performance Rating," *Journal of Criminal Law, Criminology and Police Science*, Vol. 51, Jan.-Feb. 1961, p. 567.

588 APPENDIX F

- Factors are designed to help form opinions about performance, rather than intangible qualities.
- Ample provision is made for explanatory comments.
- An employee interview is a major feature.
- Explanatory material is a part of the package to be given to raters at the beginning of each rating period.

Training in performance evaluation is logically a part of in-service supervisory training. Also, some of the techniques used in performance evaluations, particularly in employee interviewing, are applicable to general supervision. The subject matter can be covered in about five classroom hours:

History of performance evaluation and discussion of various systems	1 hour
Philosophy and objectives of the recommended system	1 hour
Procedure, including explanation of evaluation factors, employee interviews, and completion of the form	2 hours
Promotional potential ratings	1 hour

Control over supervisors' evaluations and comments should be a primary responsibility of line commanders rather than the personnel officer within the police department, since limited administrative use of the system is recommended. A copy of the rating form should be retained at the division level until the subsequent rating period, and then discarded. A copy of the form should be routed through channels to the personnel office as a staff control. Evaluation reports should be placed in employee personnel files for a maximum of two years. Reports more than two years old should be discarded to avoid clogging the files.

The Purpose of Performance Evaluation

Basically, the purpose of performance evaluation is to improve employee performance. In addition, most supervisors realize that one of the major sources of job satisfaction for an employee is for him to know the work he does is considered worthwhile and essential—to know his efforts to do the job are appreciated and accepted as an important part of the progress of the department's work objectives; and above all to know whether or not he is performing his job correctly.

Job Performance Standards

Few police departments have developed job performance standards in written form. However, most supervisors have a great many unwritten standards in mind, often without knowing it. If you did not

GUIDE TO PERFORMANCE EVALUATION

have such standards you would have no basis for drawing the conclusion that an officer's work was well done, or that it was not properly done.

Although there is often a surprising amount of agreement among supervisors as to what constitutes "good" performance, standards are not mutually understood by supervisors and employees in many cases.

In police work the establishment of written standards for all conceivable tasks is not warranted because of the complex nature and wide variety of tasks performed. However, supervisors' concepts of standard performance for many factors will tend to become uniform and adequate with greater experience in rating their subordinates and close review by their common reviewing superiors.

Listed below are three definitions of job performance standards. Although the wording of each definition is different, the ideas are the same. A joint reading of all these definitions may provide a better picture of job performance standards.

1. A description of how well an employee must do the duties of his position in order to do them in a fully satisfactory manner.
2. A description of the performance expected by management in a particular job.
3. A statement of what an employee in a specific job, under existing working conditions, must do in order for management to be satisfied with his performance.

If we incorporate all these ideas into one definition, it might read as follows:

Job performance standards are descriptions of how well an employee must do the specific tasks of his position under existing working conditions, if he is to do his job in a manner satisfactory to management.

The establishment of job performance standards is a means of letting the employee know just what constitutes satisfactory or "standard" performance of the tasks in his specific job. The foundation on which performance standards are based is that each employee is entitled to know, and must know if he is expected to do his best work, what he is expected to do and what constitutes a job well done. Job performance standards are simply statements of these points. They are yardsticks for measuring performance. The "factor definitions" furnished later in this guide are intended to assist raters in establishing uniform job performance standards.

Supervision, Training, and Performance Evaluation

Too often a service rating or report of performance is thought of as a chore, and usually an unpleasant one. It might help to think of the service rating, or performance report, as an aid to good supervision and training.

Look briefly at your job as a supervisor and see where a more positive use of the performance report can make your work easier. A supervisor is of greatest value in the work of developing his own staff and not in doing the work of his unit. A supervisor usually is not paid the additional salary for doing the job himself. Your greatest value lies in developing your own people to do the job. The major responsibility of a supervisor is to improve the performance of subordinates, both individually and collectively.

It has been said that from 60 to 90 percent of a supervisor's work effort is spent in training or instructing his staff. Training is done in many ways, but the basic principles of teaching are the same. Although supervisors may not have been formally trained as teachers, they are expected to directly apply the principles of teaching.

These simple principles of teaching or training include the following:

1. Explaining
2. Demonstrating
3. Observing performance
4. Evaluating

Examine these four points briefly. You as a supervisor must *tell* both the new employee and the old employee under your supervision how to do the job. You must then *show* him exactly how the job is to be done. A supervisor who is a good trainer then has the employee *show by doing* that he understands what he is to do. Then you as a supervisor *examine* the results of his effort to determine whether he has learned the lesson. These supervisory principles are applicable to both office and field work.

After you have (1) told an employee how to do the job, (2) shown him the duties, and (3) observed his performance, comes the all important job of (4) reviewing the employee's work and making an evaluation in an objective manner.

Evaluation of the job being done by the employee is one of the most important aspects of your job as a supervisor. It is the means of letting the employee know where he stands. It is the opportunity for you to sit down with the employee and discuss his job performance with him. The interview period for review of your evaluation and analysis furnishes an opportunity for further training of the employee.

Often a supervisor's work can be made easier if he can demonstrate to the employee that his work is being considered fairly and objectively.

GUIDE TO PERFORMANCE EVALUATION

591

To achieve this goal is one of the essentials of good supervision. The objective analysis of the work done by the employee increases his own satisfaction of the work done as well as creating respect in his mind for the supervisor who treats him fairly and impartially. Planned, careful use of performance evaluation can help you to achieve this.

Before You Begin the Evaluation (Do the following each time a rating is to be made.)

1. *Familiarize yourself with the contents of the evaluation form.* Analyze its general scope as well as the detailed instructions.

2. *Understand thoroughly the duties and requirements of the particular position* held by the employee to be rated—it will be helpful to review the Job Class Description on file in division offices. Additional copies are available in the Personnel Division.

3. *Use a process of objective reasoning*, eliminating personal prejudice, bias, or favoritism. For example, don't allow your own personal likes or dislikes of certain mannerisms or aspects of personal appearance to blind you to the more important measures of competency or effectiveness.

4. *Don't assume that excellence in one factor implies excellence in all factors.* Observe and analyze the employee's performance objectively in terms of *each* factor listed on the rating form.

5. *Base your judgment on demonstrated performance*—not on anticipated performance. The evaluation is to be based on what *has* happened, not what *might* develop.

6. *Evaluate on the experience of the entire rating period*—it is better not to consider only single accomplishments or failures, or the most recent performance. Neither should important single instances of faulty or brilliant performance be ignored. They should be considered in context with the total performance for the period.

7. *Consider seniority apart from performance*—an employee with a short service record may not necessarily be less effective than one with a longer term of employment. Seniority does not guarantee superiority.

8. *Consider the requirements in terms of the level of the position*—a beginning clerk may very well be meeting the requirements of her position more effectively than her immediate supervisor does in his position in a higher classification.

9. Spaces have been provided on the performance evaluation report forms for additional factors you consider important enough to be included in the overall appraisal of the employee.

Examples of such additional factors are given in paragraphs 24 and 34 in the section of definitions.

Evaluating the Probationary Employee

For probationary employees, the rater must, on the final probationary evaluation, check and sign the statement on the form as follows:

I do (I do not) recommend this employee be granted permanent status.

The probationary, or *working test period,* is the final and most important stage in the *selection process* of quality employees. By the end of the probationary period, supervisors should have complete confidence that the probationary employee being evaluated *fully* meets or exceeds performance standards in every important factor if he is to be recommended for permanent status.

It should be noted that probationary employees may be released or demoted *at any time without appeal,* if, in the judgment of the department head, their dismissal or demotion is in the best interests of the department. Should the supervisor have a question in his mind as to the general fitness of the probationary employee for the position, he should seriously consider the consequences of burdening the department with an employee who may be a net liability rather than a net asset. He should also consider the possibility that it would be a disservice to the employee to retain him in a position for which he is poorly suited or altogether unsuited, thus directing him away from seeking a more productive and rewarding type of employment.

In deciding whether a probationary employee should be dismissed or granted permanent status, the supervisor might well consider that the average permanent employee remaining thirty years in departmental service will be paid more than $150,000 during that time. The supervisor should ask himself if this employee represents a sound, long-term investment of such magnitude.

Evaluating the Supervisor

There are various levels and types of supervisory activity within the organization. It is important, when rating a particular supervisor, to understand how and to what degree each of the factors applies to him.

Who Is to Be Rated as a Supervisor?

For evaluation purposes, a supervisor is one to whom the responsibility has been delegated to evaluate other employees. This definition

GUIDE TO PERFORMANCE EVALUATION

will necessarily eliminate a number of persons who, while they may direct some activities or provide a degree of technical supervision over other employees, have little or no authority to exercise control over other employees or direct responsibility for the results of their work. For the purposes of this report, an employee who is not delegated the responsibility to complete and sign evaluation reports on other classified employees should not be evaluated as a "supervisor."

How to Proceed

- *Choose a quiet place* where you can work without interruption for a period of time, and where unauthorized persons will not see the forms.
- *Mark lightly in pencil* each factor in Section A. You may later agree to changes after conferring with the reviewer. However, the report should be typed or written in ink before the employee interview, and any changes, corrections, or deletions on the report must be initialed by the employee.
- *Be generous* in rating the best of the employee's qualities, but *be severe* in rating weaknesses. Don't create over-confidence in an employee when improvements are really needed. Trying to *avoid* an unpleasant situation or risk of losing the employee's friendship by over-rating him is unfair, both to him and to the department.
- *Use the spaces for comments*—thoughtful comments give the most complete picture of the employee's performance. Note that check marks in columns 1 and 2 *require* specific written explanations in Section E for each factor thus checked. Use attachments if you find there is insufficient space for your comments.
- *Consider unusual circumstances* such as employees you have observed for short periods, employees who have done poorly as a result of temporary ill-health or other unavoidable conditions. In all unusual circumstances, evaluate the actual work *performance,* but comment fully to indicate reasons.
- It should be borne in mind that before probationary or permanent employees can be properly released for reasons of unsatisfactory performance, there must be documented evidence of a specific nature. Performance Evaluation Reports are intended to provide a written record of specific deficiencies during and/ or at the close of the rating period in which the deficiencies were observed. *Employee deficiencies affecting job performance which are not recorded on the Performance Evaluation Report cannot properly be used as a basis for dismissal.*
- *Special, unscheduled reports*—in some cases, and particularly

The Evaluation Interview

- Review your initial evaluation of the employee's performance, and consider why you evaluated his work as you did.
- Determine what you want to accomplish in the interview and plan your discussion accordingly. You should have as your main objectives *an improvement in the employee's performance and will to work.* If these are already superior, the objective shifts to one of commendation and maintenance of excellence.
- Plan to meet in private. If this is the employee's first evaluation interview, anticipate curiosity, tension, or anxiety, and be prepared to minimize them.
- Create the impression that *you* have time for the interview and that you consider it highly important.
- Make the employee feel that the interview is a constructive, cooperative one, by placing primary interest upon his development and growth. Tell the employee that the main purposes of the report are to inform him of your opinions of his performance, to improve his performance when possible and to sustain superior performance.
- Be open minded to the opinions and facts presented by the employee. Be willing to learn about him. Don't dominate or cross-examine. Avoid argument. Remember that the employee must do most of the talking at some points of the interview:
  a. In bringing his opinions and feelings to the surface and to your attention.
  b. In gaining a better understanding of himself.
  c. In identifying his own areas of needed or potential improvement and in making plans for their accomplishment.
- Pick the right day, time, and place. Don't conduct the interview too soon after a disciplinary action or reprimand. Pick a time when you are in a good mood and when you have reason to believe the employee feels likewise.
- Talk about the employee's strengths first, covering each point in some detail. This helps start the interview off on the right foot. Remember that the aim is to encourage or sustain high quality performance, not to reprimand the employee.
- While building upon the employee's strengths, *do not fail* to discuss his weaknesses or failures and *how he can prevent or curtail them in the future.* Here introduce your suggestions for

GUIDE TO PERFORMANCE EVALUATION

a specific improvement program. *Remember,* if you don't show the employee how he can improve his work performance then you are not doing your full job as a supervisor.

- You should close when you have made clear whatever points you intended to cover; when the employee has had a chance to review his problems and release any emotional tensions that may exist; when plans of action have been cooperatively developed; and when you and the employee are at a natural stopping point. Always reassure the employee of your interest in his progress, and indicate willingness to take up the discussion again at any time.

Duties of the Reviewing Officer

No doubt there will be an occasion when the employee will not agree with all or a part of the evaluation made by the supervisor. The employee may request that he be allowed to discuss his report with the reviewing officer.

In the same space provided for the employee's signature on the form, there is a statement which reads, "I understand my signature does not necessarily indicate agreement." If the employee wishes, he may check the box found in this same space alongside a statement which reads, "I wish to discuss this report with the reviewer."

After such request has been indicated by the employee, the reviewing supervisor will make arrangements for this meeting as soon as possible (within 15 calendar days).

The responsibilities of the reviewing officer include:

1. Thorough efforts to obtain uniformity in the application of standards by the supervisors under his direction.
2. Securing corrective action when bias or a misinterpretation of standards is evident.
3. Making sure reports are completely, promptly, and thoroughly prepared.
4. Discussing the report with the rater, and with the employee when requested, or when otherwise appropriate.
5. Striving to make the rated employee understand and recognize the validity of the rater's markings.
6. Checking the statements made in the comments section to see that the reasons are specific, substantial, and accurate.

FACTOR DEFINITIONS AND GUIDES FOR USE

Performance factors listed in Section A are defined below and guideline questions for each factor provided. Each factor should be checked in relation to the individual employee's duties and amount of responsibility. Raters should not assume that all of the factors are of equal importance. The degree of importance in each factor will vary according to the requirements of each employee's job. For example, "Effectiveness Under Stress" or "Suspect Contacts" may be of crucial importance in one position and relatively insignificant in another. Raters will find, however, that the first four factors listed do have the same degree of importance in any position, and employees should be evaluated accordingly.

NOTE: On the first five factors in Section A, Column 4 (Exceeds Standards) has been blocked out. These factors are considered absolutes—an employee either meets required standards or he does not. Column 5 (Does Not Apply) has been blocked out on the first four factors. All four factors apply to *all* employees, and therefore no option is provided.

1. **Observance of Work Hours:** Refers to punctuality in reporting to or leaving a duty station in accordance with the prescribed schedule of working hours, breaks, or leaves of absence. Can the employee be relied upon to be working when and where he is supposed to be?

2. **Attendance:** Reflects absences from duty for any reason. This factor introduces the opportunity for necessary or desirable counseling of an employee regarding his improper or excessive use of leave privileges, especially if his attendance has become unreliable. If sick leave use has been greater than the norm, should the employee seek medical care? Is there a Friday-Monday or holiday pattern of sick leave use? Have continued absences been costly to the department or harmful to the morale of co-workers who may have been required to carry extra loads?

3. **Grooming and Dress:** An appropriate type of dress and standard of good grooming is required in every position. Does the employee meet the standards of dress commensurate with the degree of public or employee contacts he makes? Is his uniform consistently clean, neat, and in good repair?

4. **Compliance with Rules:** Members of the department are subject to rules and regulations. Failure to observe reasonable directions and regulations is listed as a reason for disciplinary action. Does the employee *consistently* comply with rules and regulations applicable to him and his job?

5. **Safety Practices:** Nearly all employees, even those who do not work under physically hazardous circumstances, must comply with reasonable safety practices, particularly in sit-

GUIDE TO PERFORMANCE EVALUATION

uations involving the public. These practices may reflect specific supervisory directives, or simply forethought for potentially dangerous conditions and the use of good common sense. Does the employee endanger his own safety or the safety of others by his actions? Does he help to prevent accidents by practicing good safety procedures?

6. **Public Contacts:** Refers to all public contact made through personal or telephone conversation, correspondence, and day-to-day appearances before the public. Does the employee's exposure to the public eye and ear reflect credit on the department and promote a good public image? Is the employee courteous and discreet in his public contacts and behavior? Is he aware of the necessity to present a consistently good appearance to the public?

7. **Suspect Contacts:** As with public contacts, this factor may not apply to some employees and yet may be extremely significant in the cases of other employees. Is the employee too harsh or too timid with suspects or prisoners? Is his attitude or behavior toward suspects or prisoners detrimental to security, a good image, or investigative efficiency?

8. **Employee Contacts:** Reflects only those contacts which either improve or reduce the *effectiveness* of the employees involved. It does not apply to an employee's personal popularity or lack of it. Does he mind his own business, but at the same time have a proper concern for the problems of other employees whose jobs touch his? Is he a disruptive influence? Does he bother or embarrass others with his personal problems? Is he a positive influence on the morale of others?

9. **Knowledge of Work:** This factor should not be confused with, or restricted to, the technical knowledge an employee is required to bring to a specialized job class. (See Job Skill Level, factor 12). It is much broader and includes particularly the range of pertinent policies, regulations, and procedures relating to his assignment. Has the probationary employee acquired an acceptable working level of job knowledge?

10. **Work Judgments:** Every employee makes decisions depending upon the degree of responsibility assigned in his position. Does the employee make a minimum of poor judgments in the course of his work? Is he consistent and reliable in his judgments? What effect do his judgments have on the quantity and quality of work produced by himself and by others?

598   APPENDIX F

11. **Planning and Organizing:** Measure the manner and method in which an employee approaches his assigned duties, and how successful his planning and organizing is in achieving desired results. Does the employee take time to plan the sequence of steps required in carrying out his tasks? Or does he attack the job thoughtlessly or with such blind enthusiasm that waste and mistakes result or work deadlines are missed? Does he make allowances in organizing the job so that all foreseeable circumstances are properly taken into account? Does lack of planning or poor organizing indicate reasons for low production or poor quality of work?

12. **Job Skill Level:** (Mainly for civilian or technical assignments.) This factor relates particularly to the mental and/or manual skills required in a given position. A craftsman's basic skills are readily identified, while many police assignments include job skills which are relatively obscure. Does the employee consistently demonstrate at a proper level the skills prerequisite to entry in the job class? Has he made any effort to improve his basic skill levels? Does he have potential for acquiring or developing his job skills to higher levels of proficiency? Should he undertake a brush-up or back-to-school program? Has he taken advantage of related in-service training opportunities? Does he read technical publications related to his work?

13. **Quality of Work:** The degree of excellence of the work performed over the entire rating period is measured here. In rating this factor, attention should be paid to the consequences of poor quality work. Is the employee's work effective, accurate, thorough, and acceptable? Must the work be redone, thus reducing the potential volume of acceptable work which could have been produced? Do errors in the employee's work affect the efforts of others? Does poor work too often reflect adversely upon the department? Are reports clear, concise, and accurate?

14. **Volume of Acceptable Work:** Refers to the amount of work required to meet job standards. Does the employee consistently accomplish a day's work for a day's pay? Does he produce enough work so that he is clearly a net asset to the department? Supervisors should not make undue allowances for such reasons as the employee's poor health, home problems, age, or length of service. While short-term exceptions to the volume standard can sometimes be made, care should be exercised to see that proper warnings are issued when indicated.

GUIDE TO PERFORMANCE EVALUATION 599

15. **Meeting Deadlines:** If work schedules are important enough to set reasonable deadlines, were these deadlines met? If the employee could not meet deadlines, did he give advance notice? Did he show an honest attempt to meet deadlines?

16. **Accepts Responsibility:** Refers to the degree of willingness an employee exhibits when given responsibility and the manner in which the responsibility is carried out. Does the employee readily accept responsibility or does he avoid it? Does he deny his responsibility when things go wrong? Or is he quick to own up to his failures? Does he consistently act in a responsible manner?

17. **Accepts Direction:** The word "direction" as used here is synonymous with such words as "supervision," "training," and "instruction." Does the employee demonstrate that he has accepted the direction by carrying out the direction to the best of his ability? Does he chronically challenge supervision, instruction, or orders? Does he meekly or passively accept directions he thinks may be faulty? Does he blindly or maliciously carry out such directions? Is he resentful of direction or supervision? Does he accept direction, but complain about it to fellow employees?

18. **Accepts Change:** Use this factor to evaluate the traits of adaptability and flexibility. Does the employee accept change willingly? Does he slow down progress or cause inefficiencies by resistance to change? Does he adapt satisfactorily to new work surroundings, new equipment, new procedures, new supervisors?

19. **Effectiveness under Stress:** There are some positions where pace, pressure, and tempo are consistently demanding. Is the employee capable of meeting the demand? Can he produce an acceptable volume and quality of work in an emergency? Is his work generally organized well enough to meet unforeseen contingencies? Before marking this factor, consider whether stress is inherent in the position or results from the employee's failure to properly plan and organize his work.

20. **Appearance of Work Station:** Refers to the neatness and efficient arrangement of work areas. Does the appearance of the work station contribute to a desirable work atmosphere or a proper public image?

21. **Operation and Care of Equipment:** Reflects the employee's concern for safe, responsible, and reasonable operation or use of equipment. Is the employee concerned with conservation

600 APPENDIX F

of equipment? Does he request appropriate maintenance and repair of equipment when necessary?

22. **Work Coordination:** Measures specifically the necessary coordination of work which directly or indirectly involves other employees, sections, divisions or departments. Characteristics of this factor include preplanning, timing, and a consistent excellence of work judgments. In situations where work coordination is applicable, does the employee consistently maintain a smooth flow of work materials? Has the production process been slowed because of obstructions caused by the employee?

23. **Initiative:** Refers to initiation of action by the employee. While initiative shows up in the form of suggestions and constructive criticism, it is most obvious when the employee originates investigations or acts to produce more efficient, productive or economical methods and procedures. Does he take opportunities to exercise initiative or must he be prodded into action? Is he alert to operating efficiency and cost-cutting? Is he inventive? Does he offer practical constructive criticism?

24. Spaces 24-29 have been left blank for additional factors the rater may consider necessary in achieving a view of the employee's total job effectiveness.

> Factors such as oral or written expression, thoroughness, or accuracy may figure significantly in fulfilling the requirements of a particular position. *Intangible qualities, such as integrity, patience, and courage, usually refer to character or personality traits, not to an employee's performance, and should be avoided* as evaluation factors unless a direct relationship can be demonstrated.
>
> If the employee does not qualify to be evaluated as a supervisor (see "Evaluating the Supervisor") but does give work direction, field supervision, or is responsible for performing tasks which of necessity include some of the supervisory factors, the blank spaces provided for additional factors might be utilized to evaluate the employee to this end.

SUPERVISORY FACTORS: (In addition to factors 1 through 29, the following should be completed for those who supervise and evaluate the work of others.)

30. **Planning and Organizing:** Knowledge, talent, and mental

GUIDE TO PERFORMANCE EVALUATION   **601**

effort are required in planning and organizing the work of subordinates. How well does he analyze and then put into effect improved and more efficient work processes? Does he plan improvements or changes and effect them in a logical and systematic manner?

31. **Scheduling and Coordinating:**   This is the next logical step and is a critical phase of the supervisor's function. Does the supervisor effect the necessary scheduling or rescheduling of work? Does he provide the necessary personal coordination of the work, not only among his subordinates, but, more importantly, between other sections and divisions? Does he anticipate schedule problems, or is he surprised and "caught short" when these occur? Does he keep *his* supervisor informed of problems and delays, or does he wait until these may be discovered, or until it is too late for planning adjustments?

32. **Training and Instructing:**   Refers generally to orientation of new employees or to the demonstration and exploration of technical methods, procedures, and rules in which the new employee cannot be expected to be competent. It also refers to introducing permanent employees to changing methods, procedures, and techniques, as well as improving basic qualifying skills to their highest potential level. Refers also to instructions given in day-to-day or periodic observation and supervision of employee performance. It may be an occasional word or it may be a planned periodic meeting of a small group of employees in which effective methods, techniques, and standard procedures are explained, demonstrated, and reviewed. Does the supervisor plan and carry out a program of orientation and training for new employees? Does he provide for the correction of any technical skill deficiencies in new employees? Does he provide training for permanent employees in new methods and procedures? Does he assist employees in self-development programs?

33. **Effectiveness:**   This factor is designed to measure the results achieved by the supervisor and his subordinates. Do his subordinates prevent crime, apprehend violators, or provide services to the desired degree? Are assigned functions accomplished? Completely? On time? Is the quality of work produced by the supervisor and his staff up to standard?

34. **Evaluating Subordinates:**   Measures the accuracy and manner in which the supervisor approaches and completes the formal evaluation of his subordinates. Does the supervisor exhibit a good balance of constructive criticism and praise in evalu-

602 APPENDIX F

ating employees? Does he indicate how an employee's work may be improved, when improvement is needed? Are his evaluations positive contributions to employee development? Are his evaluations consistently objective, fair, and accurate?

35. **Judgments and Decisions:** Refers to the practical exercise of authority and responsibility by the supervisor. Does the supervisor exhibit firmness and fairness in judgments affecting employees? Is he accurate in making judgments affecting functional goals? Does he cause resentment or other adverse reactions to his decisions because of poor timing or the *manner* in which he states them? Are his judgments always in accord with the best interests of the department? Does he balance employee and department interests when these are not fully compatible?

36. **Leadership:** Does the supervisor spur subordinates to their best efforts through example rather than by relying on the authority of his position? Does he mold them into a group or team whose cooperative endeavors surpass their individual performances collectively? Does his intelligent exercise of leadership create an atmosphere in which employee attitudes are optimistic and positive?

37. **Operational Economy:** Refers to the conservation of time and material. Is the supervisor truly budget conscious? Does he live within his budgets? Does he make careful and accurate budget estimates? Does he know, or periodically calculate, operational costs for units or phases of his operational responsibilities? Is he able to identify uneconomical procedures, methods, tools, or equipment? Does he recommend changed policies or procedures which might effect dollar economies?

38. **Supervisory Control:** Refers to the maintenance of order in all areas of supervisory jurisdiction. Do the supervisor's employees perform their duties and functions in an orderly and disciplined manner which promotes work objectives? Do the employees have a clear understanding of behavior and performance standards which are expected? Does the supervisor enforce these standards consistently? Is the supervisor "accepted" by his subordinates and in full control at all times? Is the discipline and control too oppressive?

39. Spaces 39–41 have been left blank for any additional supervisory factors the rater feels should be included as determinants of supervisory effectiveness necessary to the position of the employee being evaluated. These may come under the heading

GUIDE TO PERFORMANCE EVALUATION

of particular qualities or skills, without which effective supervision cannot be achieved. Intangible qualities and references to character or personality traits should, however, be avoided.

PERFORMANCE EVALUATION REPORT

USE INK OR TYPEWRITER FOR FINAL MARKINGS

EMPLOYEE NAME (Last) (First) (Init.)	EMPLOYEE NO	DIVISION		DISTRICT OR SECTION
CLASS TITLE	EMPLOYEE STATUS	ASSIGNMENT	DUE DATE:	

SECTION A — FACTOR CHECK LIST

Columns: 1 Not Satisfactory / 2 Some Improvement Needed / 3 Meets Standards / 4 Exceeds Standards / 5 Does Not Apply

Immediate Supervisor Must Check Each Factor in the Appropriate Column

1. Observance of Work Hours
2. Attendance
3. Grooming & Dress
4. Compliance with Rules
5. Safety Practices
6. Public Contacts
7. Suspect Contacts
8. Employee Contacts
9. Knowledge of Work
10. Work Judgments
11. Planning and Organizing
12. Job Skill Level
13. Quality of Work
14. Volume of Acceptable Work
15. Meeting Deadlines
16. Accepts Responsibility
17. Accepts Direction
18. Accepts Change
19. Effectiveness Under Stress
20. Appearance of Work Station
21. Operation & Care of Equip.
22. Work Coordination
23. Initiative
24. (ADDITIONAL FACTORS)
25.
26.
27.
28.
29.

FOR EMPLOYEES who SUPERVISE OTHERS

30. Planning & Organizing
31. Scheduling & Coordinating
32. Training & Instructing
33. Effectiveness
34. Evaluating Subordinates
35. Judgments & Decisions
36. Leadership
37. Operational Economy
38. Supervisory Control
39. (ADDITIONAL FACTORS)
40.
41.

CHECKS IN COLS. 1 AND 2 MUST BE EXPLAINED IN SECTION E

SECTION B — Record job STRENGTHS, superior performance incidents, progress achieved, or checks in Col. 4.

SECTION C — Record specific GOALS or IMPROVEMENT PROGRAMS to be undertaken during next evaluation period

SECTION D — Describe STANDARD performance. (Optional for most factors checked in Col. 3, MANDATORY for some factors – see instructions.)

SECTION E — Record specific work performance DEFICIENCIES or job behavior requiring improvement or correction. (Explain checks in Col. 1 and 2.)

RATER: I certify this report represents my best judgment. ☐ I DO ☐ I DO NOT recommend this employee be granted permanent status. (For final probationary reports only).

(RATER'S SIGNATURE) (TITLE) (DATE)

REVIEWER: (IF NONE, SO INDICATE)

(REVIEWER'S SIGNATURE) (TITLE) (DATE)

EMPLOYEE: I certify that this report has been discussed with me. I understand my signature does not necessarily indicate agreement. ☐ I wish to discuss this report with the reviewer.

Comment:

(EMPLOYEE'S SIGNATURE) (DATE)

– SEE INSTRUCTIONS ON REVERSE SIDE –

604   APPENDIX F

INSTRUCTIONS

FOR USE OF THE PERFORMANCE EVALUATION REPORT FORM

GENERAL: 1. Using a preliminary draft sheet and pencil, complete Section A first, then other appropriate sections. The rater should review the draft report with his own supervisor. Markings and comments should then be typed or inked in on the final form. Either the rater or reviewer (or both) should then review the rating with the employee in a private interview. All signatures shall be in ink. Changes and corrections shall be initialed by the employee.

2. If space for comments is inadequate, dated and signed attachments may be made (either typewritten or in ink).

3. Due dates shall be observed, and are particularly important for final probationary reports. Filing dates for these are flexible, and both the first and the final reports may be filed at any time between the receipt and the printed due date.

4. All probationers (either entrance level or promotional) shall be evaluated not later than the end of the first three months of probationary service, and every three months thereafter for the first year. Probationers may be separated (or demoted, if permanent in a lesser class) at any time such action is deemed necessary by the department head, through use of either a scheduled or an unscheduled performance evaluation report.

5. All permanent employees and entrance level probationers in their second year shall be evaluated semi-annually as of the printed due date.

6. Unscheduled reports may be filed at any time for either permanent or probationary employees.

7. The "Guide to Performance Evaluation" should be consulted for s u g g e s t i o n s, definitions, interpretations, and further instructions.

8. The main purposes of this form are to inform the employee of his performance, to improve performance when possible, and to sustain superior performance.

SECTION A: Check one column for each factor. Column (5) may be checked when a factor is not considered applicable to a particular job. Additional spaces have been provided to write in any additional factors. Each check mark in Columns 1 and 2 requires specific explanation in Section E. In the absence of specific standards for a factor, use your own opinion as to what constitutes standard performance. Standard does not mean average; in fact standard performance can often be higher than average performance.

Exceeds Standards: Total performance is well above standards for the position. This evaluation should be reflected by marks for critical factors in Section A, and superior or excellent performance should be noted in Section B. Only a few employees would normally qualify for this rating.

Effective — Meets Standards: Consistently competent performance meeting or exceeding standards in all critical factors for the position. If margin is narrow and standards barely met, explain in Section E. Most employees would be rated in this category.

Some Improvement Needed: Total performance occasionally or periodically falls short of normal standards. Specific deficiencies should be noted in Section E. This evaluation indicates the supervisor's belief that the employee can and will make the necessary improvements.

Not Satisfactory: Performance clearly inadequate in one or more critical factors as explained or documented in Section E. Employee has demonstrated inability or unwillingness to improve or to meet standards. Performance not acceptable for position held.

SECTION B: Must be used to describe outstanding qualities or performances, when check marks are placed in Column 4. Use this section to record other progress or improvements in performance resulting from employee's efforts to reach previously set goals.

SECTION C: Record agreed-upon or prescribed performance goals for the next evaluation period.

SECTION D: Use for describing standard performance. This section must be completed for certain factors, depending on assignment:

Patrolman		Civilian Employees	
Patrol Division	9, 13, 14, 23	Clerks	6, 12, 13, 14
Traffic Division	6, 9, 13, 14	Technical, trades	12, 13, 14
Crim. Invest. Div.	9, 10, 13, 23		
Youth Drv.	9, 10, 13, 23	Supervisors	
Adm. Services Bureau	8, 11, 13, 15	Sergeants	32, 33, 34, 38
Tech. Services Bureau	6, 12, 13, 19	Lts. and above	30, 31, 33, 34
		Civilians	30, 31, 32, 33, 34

SECTION E: Give specific reasons for check marks in Columns 1 and 2. Record here any other specific reasons why the employee should not be recommended for permanent status, or — if the employee is already permanent — any specific reasons for required improvement.

SIGNATURES: Both the rater and the employee shall sign the report. The employee's signature indicates that the conference has been held and that he has had an opportunity to read the report. If he refuses to sign for any reason, explain that his signature does not necessarily imply or indicate agreement with the report, and that space is provided for him to state any disagreement. Further refusal to sign shall be recorded on the report, after which it shall be forwarded.

ROUTING: Keep the preliminary draft at the division level until the next rating period and then discard. Route the permanent copy through channels to the Personnel Division.

GUIDE TO PERFORMANCE EVALUATION

PART 2 PROMOTIONAL POTENTIAL RATING

The promotional potential rating should not be confused with regular performance evaluations or service ratings. The former is intended to be graded and weighted, whereas the recommended performance evaluation system is deliberately designed to avoid a numerical grade. Service ratings should not be used in the promotional process except to add background material for the oral board members. On the other hand, the promotional potential rating form should only be used as a part of the promotional process.

The promotional potential rating form is not intended to be completed unless and until candidates pass the written examination.

The recommended procedure requires the rating of the potential candidate by at least two raters who have been in close supervisory contact with the candidate. This will allow for some adjustment of tendencies to overrate or underrate.

The system provides for the establishment of a rating review board, consisting of the heads of the major divisions in the department. The purpose of the board is to equate differences in the average rating used in all bureaus, divisions, and sections of the department. This smoothing is done "across the board" for everyone in the specific unit.

The promotional potential rating system will improve as it is put into operation, and after the raters are given instructions and training. Nevertheless, we recommend that it be administered on a trial basis— that is, without having the results count—the first time it is used. After that, give the promotional potential rating an appropriate weighting. Generally we recommend a weighting of 50 percent for the written examination, 40 percent for the oral interview, and 10 percent for the promotional potential rating.

Guide to Promotional Potential Rating

1. A promotional potential rating shall be prepared for each candidate who has successfully passed the written test.
2. The promotional potential rating shall be prepared by the immediate supervisors of each candidate. All candidates will be rated by at least two and not more than three raters who have supervised the candidate during the past year. When a candidate has only one direct supervisor, other supervisory or commanding officers who have provided indirect supervision will be assigned as raters.
3. Use the year immediately preceding the rating as the foundation for ratings whenever possible. Follow instructions on the form and rate each factor for all candidates.

4. Supervisors shall rate each candidate independently. The raters for each candidate shall, after they have prepared their independent ratings, prepare one composite rating on which they agree. After signing the composite rating form, they will submit it and their independent ratings up the line of command in the district or division in which the candidate has worked for the longest period of time during the past year.

5. Each district commander or division director will have the responsibility for reviewing all ratings referred in the line of command to him, for the purpose of adjusting any inequities. When it is obvious that significant differences exist in the application of rating standards among the various sections or units under his command, he will have the authority to adjust ratings upward or downward for any section or unit. When the district or division commander or director is satisfied that the promotional potential rating is fair and proper, he shall sign it and forward it to the departmental personnal office.

6. The Personnel Division shall prepare a list of candidates and their numerical ratings, grouped by district or division, and showing the average (mean) for each. These lists shall then be forwarded to the Rating Review Board.

7. The Rating Review Board will have the responsibility to review summaries of ratings for the purpose of adjusting any inequities based upon any obvious differences in standards between the various districts and divisions in the department. The board will have the authority to adjust scores upward or downward. When the board is satisfied that the ratings are fair and proper, a representative of the board will sign them.

8. The objective of the reviews is to insure that similar standards for rating are used in all bureaus, divisions, and sections of the department. In general, reviewers should not permit more than a five-point spread in the mean ratings between the highest and lowest divisions. Ratings for all district personnel should be adjusted to the same average.

9. The Rating Review Board shall consist of the heads of the major bureaus in the department (or their representatives if above the rank of captain).

10. After the district or divisional rating has been determined, a candidate will be permitted to review his promotional potential rating during a time specified by the commanding officer. A candidate for sergeant or lieutenant who wishes to appeal his rating may do so by submitting a request through channels to the district commander or division director. In

GUIDE TO PERFORMANCE EVALUATION

examinations for captain, a candidate may appeal by directing his request for review through channels to the division chief or division director who reviewed his initial rating. The decision of the commanders, directors, and chiefs in these cases will be final. No appeal will be allowed for adjustments made during the equating of ratings between divisions, sections, or units.

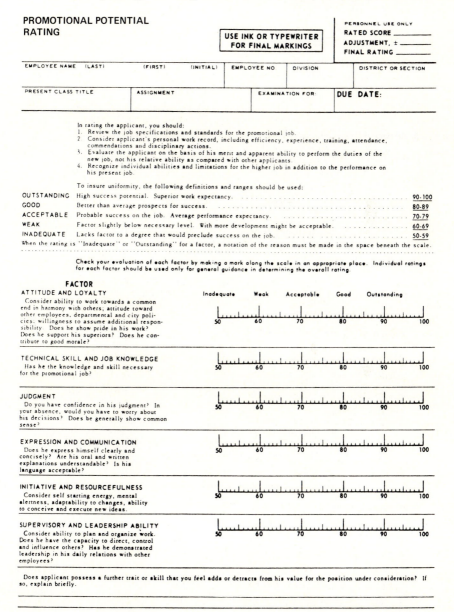

(OVER)

608 APPENDIX F

On the basis of the information on the reverse side, we believe the applicant should receive an overall rating

of [   ] (Based on a scale of 0-100, with 70 a minimum passing point.)

(RATERS' SIGNATURES)   (EMPLOYEE NO.)   (DATE)

_____   _____   _____

_____   _____   _____

_____   _____   _____

District or divisional rating, as equated by the district commander or division director, was determined by

adding / subtracting _____ points to / from all rating scores within the employee's division, section or unit:

[   ]

(SIGNATURE)   (TITLE)   (DATE)

_____   _____   _____

Final departmental rating, as equated by the Rating Review Board, was determined by adding / subtracting _____

points to / from all rating scores within the employee's division, section or unit:

[   ]

For the Rating Review Board:

(SIGNATURE)   (TITLE)   (DATE)

_____   _____   _____

Appendix G

Baltimore Police Department, 755-Hour Program, Police Recruit Training Curriculum Outline

The following curriculum is divided into eight major units of instruction compatible with the organizational structure of the Education and Training Division. The 18 weeks of training are designed to equip the probationary police officer with the necessary skills and academic knowledge to function with an optimum degree of proficiency while continuing to develop his or her career.

In addition to the basic academic and skill training necessary for procedural functioning, the trainee will receive 20 semester hours of college credit as follows:

Community College of Baltimore	Credit
Psychology 201 (applied psychology)	3
Sociology of Law Enforcement 204 (social problems)	3
Criminal Law 202 (procedural)	3
Criminal Law 203 (substantive)	3
Introduction to the criminal justice system	4
Maryland Traffic Code	2
Physical education	2
Total	20

610 APPENDIX G

INTRODUCTION TO THE CRIMINAL JUSTICE SYSTEM

This unit is designed to meet the basic requirements for academic credits and, at the same time, to introduce the police trainee to the various components of the criminal justice system. This course of instruction covers the following areas:

	Hours
Police ethics	1
History and philosophy of law enforcement	10
History and philosophy of corrections	10
Field trips to criminal justice facilities	15
Police headquarters	
City morgue	
Criminal court	
Pretrial release program	1
Scientific crime detection	3
Jurisdiction of federal agencies	3
Alcoholism and police operations	3
Total hours	46

ADMINISTRATION OF JUSTICE

This unit provides the trainee with a working knowledge of criminal law including the body of crimes in the State of Maryland, laws of arrest, laws of search and seizure, court organization, and criminal procedure.

	Hours
Criminal Law 202 (procedural)	42
Criminal Law 203 (substantive)	32
Total hours	74

POLICE OPERATIONS

This unit covers the functional aspects of "on-the-street" law enforcement. This course of instruction prepares the trainee to deal with the practical application of the line function and to acquaint him or her with the support functions designed to sustain the field operations.

	Hours
Patrol operations and criminal investigation	64
Traffic and Maryland Traffic Code	41
Report writing	39
Staff services	12
Total hours	156

HUMAN AWARENESS AND VALUES

The manner and method of police contact with the community are receiving greater emphasis in contemporary society. This unit of instruction is designed to equip the

BALTIMORE POLICE RECRUIT TRAINING CURRICULUM OUTLINE

trainee with a basic understanding of human behavior from both individual and group aspects. Abnormal behavior and emotional stress are dealt with from the standpoint of police responsibility.

	Hours
Sociology 202	32
Psychology 201	36
Community relations seminar	8
Sheppard Pratt Hospital seminar	7
Total hours	83

FIELD TRAINING (120 Hours)

This unit of instruction is conducted under the supervision of a field-training officer and a patrol-division supervisor. The trainee is exposed to field situations during three 1-week periods. Field training is conducted during the eleventh, fourteenth, and sixteenth weeks of the program. The first field-training assignment is designed to present a general orientation of the police function. The trainee is introduced to the patrol function, accident investigation techniques, and jail procedures. The fourteenth- and sixteenth-week assignments provide the new officer the opportunity to observe, evaluate, and participate by applying law enforcement techniques learned during the period of formal instructions at the Education and Training Center.

Field Assignment (64 Hours)

Following completion of the eleventh week of field training, the trainee is assigned to a weekend field assignment. On these occasions, the new officer works under the direct supervision of the patrol division in assignments such as specialized patrol, preventive patrol, and crowd or traffic control.

POLICE SKILLS AND PHYSICAL EDUCATION

This unit deals with the utilization of departmental equipment designed for the practical application of various operational techniques. Trainees are instructed in the use of firearms, departmental vehicles, handcuffs, and tear gas and are trained in various other physical skills connected with the performance of duty. A portion of this unit also deals with the methods of developing physical stamina through a personalized physical training program and participation in a water safety program. Two semester hours are earned upon the successful completion of the physical training and defensive tactics portion of this program.

	Hours
Skills and physical development	
Introduction	5
Indoor range	8
Outdoor range	40
Night firing	8
Physical training	33
Defense tactics	21
First aid	24
Driver education	24

612 APPENDIX G

Drill and departmental courtesy instruction	6
Drill—crowd control	8
Total hours	177

PROGRAM ORIENTATION

This portion of the Entrance-Level Training Program is conducted during the first two days of the program. The class advisor, training staff personnel, and guest lecturers employ this phase of the program to introduce the new officers to the Baltimore Police Department and inform them of the department's expectations of its personnel. The trainees are also briefed on the Training Center's rules and code of conduct.

	Hours
Introduction to the training program	3
Personnel affairs	1
Departmental organization	3
College-program orientation	1
Study habits and note taking	1
Departmental rules and regulations	2
Total hours	11

MANAGEMENT AND ADMINISTRATION

This portion of the Entrance-Level Training Program involves activities designed to evaluate trainee progress, course critiques, and the graduation ceremonies.

	Hours
Examinations	8
Class advisor counseling and test critiques	8
Director's hour	1
Graduation rehearsal	3
Graduation ceremonies	4
Total hours	24

TOTAL ENTRANCE-LEVEL TRAINING AND PROGRAM ADMINISTRATION

	Hours
Introduction to the criminal justice system	46
Administration of justice	74
Police operations and staff services	156
Human awareness and values	83
Field training and assignments	184
Police skills and physical education	177
Program orientation	11
Program management	24
Total hours	755

Appendix H

Field Training Guide*

The field training guide presented here is intended to serve as a practical checklist during the field training and orientation of recruit officers.

The guide was developed by Kai R. Martensen. Some of the material was adapted from similar checklists used by the Berkeley Police Department, Dallas Police Department, and the Pennsylvania State Police.

*Developed by the International Association of Chiefs of Police, Inc., Gaithersburg, Md. Reprinted by permission of IACP, which reserves all rights for future publication or use.

APPENDIX H

FIELD TRAINING GUIDE

NAME OF RECRUIT			CLASS NUMBER	DATE OF CLASS
NAME OF FIELD TRAINING OFFICER	FIELD ASSIGNMENT	FIELD TRAINING DATES (inclusive)		
1.		from		to
2.				
3.				
4.				

This training guide is a listing of basic police responsibilities, tasks and procedures. The Field Training Officer (FTO) should use this guide during the field training of a recruit. The FTO should explain each item, and whenever practical, demonstrate the task or procedure to the recruit. When the FTO believes that the recruit is capable of handling a specific task, he should require the recruit to perform the task while he observes. The FTO should pace himself to insure that sufficient time is allotted for explaining and/or performing each and every task. When an item has been satisfactorily completed, the FTO should enter the date of completion in the proper column. This is not an exhaustive list, and when unlisted situations arise, the FTO should demonstrate the proper procedure for handling the situation and record such action at the end of the guide.

Responsibilities

1.   The Training Division will enter the recruit's name, class number, and date of class on the top line of this form.

2.   The FTO should enter his name on the next line, and indicate his general field assignment and the training dates. If another FTO is used, he should enter his name on line 2 with the inclusive dates.

3.   Upon completion of the 4-week field training period, this guide should be returned to the Training Division.

4.   The Training Division will forward this guide to the recruit's first unit of assignment after completion of academy training. The unit commander should assign another FTO who will insure that the recruit receives the remainder of his field training. Upon completion, the recruit should sign this form in the space provided below, and this guide will be returned to the Training Division.

5.   Training Division personnel will review the completed guide. If all items have been completed satisfactorily, this guide will be filed in the officer's personnel folder.

I HAVE BEEN INSTRUCTED IN ALL ITEMS LISTED IN THE FIELD TRAINING GUIDE	
SIGNATURE OF RECRUIT	DATE
REVIEWED BY:	
(Signature of Training Division Reviewer)	DATE

IACP Form

FIELD TRAINING OFFICER INSTRUCTION GUIDE

	Initials of Field Training Officer and Dates	
	Explained and/or Demonstrated	Performed

I. PERSONAL ITEMS
1. Police and the public
   a. Congregation or loitering at crime scenes, coffee shops, stores, etc.
   b. Contacts with women
   c. Driving habits
   d. Wearing of the uniform
2. Command presence and courtesy
3. Precaution; preparation for anything
4. Personal conduct
   a. Smoking in public
   b. Offensive mannerisms, expressions, and gestures
   c. Voice and word usage
   d. Racial slurs and trigger words
5. Non-acceptance of gratuities and rewards
6. Rapport with fellow officers and supervisors

II. PREPARATION FOR PATROL
1. Personal appearance and hygiene
2. Uniform and equipment check
3. Locker use and arrangement
4. Information necessary for patrol
5. Roll-call procedures
6. Vehicle and equipment inspection
7. Vehicle servicing

III. ARREST PROCEDURES
1. Making an arrest
   a. Proper time
   b. Search incident to arrest
   c. With or without a warrant
   d. Felony and misdemeanor
   e. Force
   f. Club and handcuffs
   g. Handgun

APPENDIX H

	Initials of Field Training Officer and Dates	
	Explained and/or Demonstrated	Performed

    h. Legal and moral aspects of shooting

2. Searching a person—(males and females)
   a. Field
   b. Jail
3. Resisting arrest
4. Interfering with arrest
5. Removing occupants from vehicles
6. Information gathered at time of arrest
7. Transporting prisoners
   a. Use of auto; alone, with another officer
   b. Patrol wagon; when to use
   c. Care and watchfulness, prevention of prisoner from getting behind officer
   d. Extra precautions for selected prisoners
   e. Recording mileage (radio) when bringing in females
8. Restrictions on recommending attorneys, bail bondsmen
9. Booking and searching operations at station
10. Prisoners' property control procedures
11. Handling prisoners in detention facility
12. Proper clearances and release procedures

IV. USE OF POLICE RADIO
1. Use of car radio
   a. Position to hold microphone
   b. Normal voice
   c. Phonetic alphabet
   d. When out of car
   e. Status of other cars. (If another officer has something important happening do not use radio except in emergencies.)

FIELD TRAINING GUIDE

617

	Initials of Field Training Officer and Dates	
	Explained and/or Demonstrated	Performed

    f. Your status
        (1) Officer's Daily Activity Report
        (2) Radio dispatcher
2. Radio code, phonetic alphabet and unit identification
3. Orientation for dispatching operations
    a. Preparation of complaint dispatch cards
    b. Multiple responsibilities of the communication section

- Telephones
- Police radio
- Point-to-point radio
- Teletype operations and procedures
- Alarm set-up
- "Hot Car" file
- Emergency business data file
- Wanted persons file
- Teletype file
- Stolen property file
- "Status Board" and how it assists dispatchers in controlling police mobile units
- Computer-assisted dispatching and file searches

V. GENERAL OPERATING PROCEDURES
    1. Officer's notebook
    2. Field interrogation
    3. Questioning witnesses
    4. Statement-taking
    5. Descriptions of property
    6. Descriptions of persons
    7. Report-writing
    8. Protecting a crime scene
    9. Handling evidence
    10. Taking a dying declaration

618   APPENDIX H

| | Initials of Field Training Officer and Dates | |
	Explained and/or Demonstrated	Performed

     11. Obtaining ambulance, tow trucks, fire apparatus
     12. First aid
     13. Inspection of premises (permits, licenses, buildings, liquor establishments, etc.)

VI. OFFICER'S RESPONSIBILITIES
     1. Patrol purposes and responsibilities and general policies
         a. Crime
         b. Traffic
         c. Miscellaneous services
         d. Vice
     2. Rules affecting officer
     3. Types of patrol
     4. One-man patrol operations
     5. Patrol methods and techniques (day, evening and night shifts)
     6. Knowledge of beat; geography, persons, property, places and situations
     7. Observations and perception on patrol
     8. Developing contacts
     9. Officer's position in civil matters
     10. Relations with the public; prejudices, attitudes, etc.
     11. Relations with immediate supervisor
     12. Relations with command personnel
     13. Relations with investigative personnel
     14. Relations with other governmental agencies
     15. Conduct and behavior (on and off duty)
     16. Pitfalls to be avoided
     17. Requests for assistance
     18. Duties in emergency situations

VII. DRIVING TECHNIQUES
     1. Proper driving habits
         a. Public opinion regarding officers disobeying traffic laws

FIELD TRAINING GUIDE

619

	Initials of Field Training Officer and Dates	
	Explained and/or Demonstrated	Performed

    b. Defensive driving
    c. Driving in inclement weather
    d. Proper parking

2. Downtown and residential driving techniques
3. Answering routine calls
4. Identification and apprehension of traffic violators
   a. Stopping violators so not to impede other traffic
   b. Use of red light, siren and spotlight
      (1) Daylight
      (2) Darkness
   c. Positioning patrol car in relation to violator
5. Stopping wanted or stolen vehicles
   a. When assistance is necessary
   b. Selecting suitable location
   c. Parking police car in relation to suspect car
6. Pursuit driving
7. Tailing suspects
8. Driving and parking in emergencies
   a. What constitutes an emergency
   b. Use of red light and siren
9. Burglary-in-progress or prowler type call
   a. Approach
   b. Procedures for suspect at scene or running away
   c. Arrival at assigned position

       ■ Need for lights out
       ■ Eliminate noise
       ■ Direct or indirect approach to scene

10. Robbery-in-progress calls
    a. Approach
    b. Secondary assignment

APPENDIX H

	Initials of Field Training Officer and Dates	
	Explained and/or Demonstrated	Performed

11. Fire calls
    a. Approach hazards
    b. Assisting fire trucks through dangerous intersections
    c. Parking in position for traffic control

VIII. PATROL TACTICS
1. Inspectional procedures and techniques
    a. Shopping centers
    b. Vacation home checks
2. Open doors and windows
3. Finding a burglary, search of premises
4. Burglary in progress
5. Robbery in progress
6. Bank alarm
7. Suspicious character and prowler calls
8. Searching yards and alleys
9. Blockades
10. Searching quadrant
11. Stakeouts
12. Man with a gun calls
13. Conducting a raid
14. Crowds, mobs and riots
15. Demonstrations
16. Strike Duty
17. General duty alert
18. Bomb threats
19. Guarding prisoner

IX. GENERAL INVESTIGATIONS
1. Elements of crimes
2. Investigation of a felony
3. Modus operandi
4. Investigation of murder, rape and assault
5. Investigation of robbery
6. Investigation of residential and commercial burglaries
7. Investigation of safe burglary
8. Investigation of car theft
9. Investigation of suspicious cars
    a. Occupied
    b. Unoccupied

FIELD TRAINING GUIDE

	Initials of Field Training Officer and Dates	
	Explained and/or Demonstrated	Performed

10. Investigation of stolen property
11. Investigation of larcenies, shoplifting
12. Investigation of purse-snatching and pickpocket
13. Investigation of stolen auto accessories and theft from auto
14. Investigation of stolen bikes
15. Investigation of miscellaneous theft
16. Investigation of bad checks
17. Investigation of frauds
18. Investigation of embezzlements
19. Investigation of extortion
20. Investigation of counterfeiting
21. Investigation of suicides and unexplained deaths
22. Crime scene measurements and sketching

X. TRAFFIC PROCEDURES
1. Police officer's responsibility for traffic enforcement and control
2. Traffic laws and ordinances
3. Enforcement index
4. Selective enforcement (time, place, violation)
5. Recognizing traffic violation
   a. Evidence for conviction
   b. Moving violation
   c. Equipment violation
   d. Other violation
6. Approaching and handling traffic violator
7. Enforcement
   a. Use of warning
      (1) Verbal
      (2) Written
   b. Use of citation
   c. Arrests
      (1) Optional situation
      (2) Mandatory
      (3) With warrant

622 APPENDIX H

	Initials of Field Training Officer and Dates	
	Explained and/or Demonstrated	Performed

8. Parking violation enforcement
    a. Meter
    b. Time zone
    c. Prohibited areas
9. Accident investigation
    a. Handling injuries
        (1) First aid
        (2) Summoning aid
    b. Handling scene
        (1) Safeguards
        (2) Traffic routing
    c. Locating drivers and witnesses
    d. Interviewing drivers and witnesses
    e. Photographing, measuring and sketching traffic accidents
    f. Determining responsibility
    g. Issuing citations
    h. Reports
10. Driving while intoxicated cases
    a. Observations
    b. Sobriety report
    c. Chemical test
    d. Enforcement action
        (1) Custody
        (2) Non-custody (hospitalization)
11. Hit-run accident investigation
    a. Injury—non-injury
    b. Evidence at scene
    c. Locating and interviewing witnesses
    d. Following trail of evidence to responsible party
    e. Alerting other police units to suspect vehicle
12. Pedestrian violations
13. Radar in traffic enforcement
14. Vehicle identification; registration, license number and vehicle identification number

FIELD TRAINING GUIDE

	Initials of Field Training Officer and Dates	
	Explained and/or Demonstrated	Performed

15. Driver identification; operator license
16. Traffic direction and control
    a. General rules of traffic control
    b. Standing where clearly visible
    c. At a street corner with and without signals
    d. At an accident scene
    e. Proper use of flares
17. Police emergency escorts

XI. VICE CONTROL
1. Prostitution cases
2. Gambling cases
3. Liquor law violations
4. Narcotic peddlers and addicts
    a. Opiates
    b. Marijuana
    c. Dangerous drugs
5. Relationship to organized crime

XII. JUVENILE PROCEDURES
1. Juvenile involvement in crime
2. Gaining respect of juveniles
3. Interviewing female juveniles
    a. In presence of another officer
    b. In presence of matron or parent
    c. In presence of school official
4. Using neighborhood juveniles as sources of information
5. Juvenile officers
    a. Duties
    b. Assistance rendered
6. Selected cases
    a. Malicious mischief and BB guns
    b. Runaways and truancy
    c. Juvenile liquor law violations
    d. Glue sniffing
    e. Child neglect cases
    f. Battered and abused child cases

624   APPENDIX H

Initials of Field Training
Officer and Dates

Explained and/or Demonstrated	Performed

7. Juvenile gangs
8. Relationship with other agencies involved with juveniles: (schools; recreation; welfare; probation, etc.)
9. Transporting juveniles
   a. To station
   b. To detention
   c. Notification of parents or probation officer
   d. Reports and forms used
10. Disposition of juvenile cases
11. Juvenile traffic offender
12. Missing and found children

XIII. HANDLING PEOPLE
1. Emphasizing the specific techniques and skills necessary in dealing with the following:
   a. Wanted persons
   b. Missing persons
   c. Mental cases
   d. Transients
   e. Vagrants
   f. Beggars
   g. Peddlers
   h. Street corner orators
   i. Sex perverts
   j. Drunken persons

XIV. DISTURBANCE OF THE PEACE PROCEDURES
1. Neighborhood disputes
2. Family quarrels, domestic situations
3. Preserving the peace
4. Simple assault
5. Nuisances
6. Vehicular disturbance
7. Loud noise, party, etc., complaints
8. Street meetings, demonstrations
9. Trespassing

XV. PROPERTY CONTROL
1. Lost property

FIELD TRAINING GUIDE

	Initials of Field Training Officer and Dates	
	Explained and/or Demonstrated	Performed

    2. Found property
    3. Safekeeping property
       a. Prisoner
       b. Deceased person
       c. Property turned in
    4. Contraband
    5. Releasing property
    6. Destroying property

XVI. LEGAL PROCESSES
    1. Obtaining complaints
    2. Obtaining and executing search warrants
    3. Obtaining and executing arrest warrants
    4. Extradition procedures
    5. Serving subpoenas and summonses
    6. Mental commitment process
    7. Rules of evidence and exceptions
    8. Case preparation for court prosecution
    9. Courtroom testimony and demeanor

XVII. HAZARDS
    1. Detecting and reporting hazards
    2. Fire hazards
    3. Crime hazards
    4. Traffic hazards
    5. Insecure premises
    6. Defective conditions in public property; street, sidewalk, etc.
    7. Attractive nuisances
    8. Live wires
    9. Light outages

XVIII. ANIMAL COMPLAINTS
    1. Found animals
    2. Wounded or injured animals
    3. Dead animals
    4. Shooting animals
    5. Animal bite cases
    6. Rabid animals
    7. Animal nuisances
    8. Cruelty to animals

626   APPENDIX H

| | Initials of Field Training Officer and Dates | |
	Explained and/or Demonstrated	Performed
XIX. CITIZENS' REQUESTS		
1. Requests for assistance		
a. Medical aid		
b. Invalid		
c. Other		
2. Landlord-tenant disputes		
3. Mechanic and baggage liens		
4. Failure-to-pay cases		
a. Taxi		
b. Bus		
c. Restaurant		
5. Citizen arrests		
6. Information and direction		
XX. INFORMATION		
1. General sources of information available		
2. Obtaining record, warrant and vehicle checks		
3. Conducting record searches		
a. Alpha files (master index)		
b. Case (report) files		
c. Criminal history files		
d. Known offender and nickname files		
e. Mug shot files		
f. Warrant files		
g. Accident files		
h. Other files		
4. Information and assistance available from other official agencies		
a. Local		
b. County agencies		
c. State agencies		
d. Federal agencies		
5. Sources of information on beat		
6. Press relations		
7. Use of police and public library		
XXI. MISCELLANEOUS RESPONSIBILITIES		
1. Handling public gatherings and parades		
2. Discovery of fire, duties at fire		
3. Abatement of attractive nuisances		

FIELD TRAINING GUIDE

	Initials of Field Training Officer and Dates	
	Explained and/or Demonstrated	Performed

4. Enforcement of parking violations
   a. Driveways
   b. Private property
5. Enforcing health and welfare ordinances, i.e., bonfire; dumping garbage
6. Taxi ordinance
7. Notifications, death messages
8. Parks, waterways, game law violations
9. Permits and licenses

XXII. ORGANIZATIONAL PROCEDURES
1. Checking on and off duty
2. Days off
3. Overtime
4. Leaves of absence
   a. Vacation
   b. Military
   c. Sick
   d. Injury
   e. Death in family
5. Equipment and uniform regulations
   a. Issue
   b. Use
   c. Loss and replacement
6. Care of police vehicles
   a. Assignment
   b. Accident
   c. Damage
   d. Maintenance
   e. Reports
7. Discharge of firearms
   a. Accidental
   b. Duty
8. Investigation of complaints against personnel
   a. Procedures
   b. Reports
9. Disciplinary procedures

628 APPENDIX H

<table>
<tr><td colspan="2" align="center">Initials of Field Training
Officer and Dates</td></tr>
<tr><td align="center">Explained and/or
Demonstrated</td><td align="center">Performed</td></tr>
</table>

10. Mail
    a. Incoming
    b. Distribution
    c. Outgoing
11. Transfers
12. Performance evaluation
13. Outside employment regulation
14. Change of address and phone number
15. Changes in personal or family status
    a. Marriage, divorce
    b. Dependents
16. Contagious disease contact
17. Court appearance
    a. Subpoena
    b. Civil cases

XXIII. USE AND/OR PREPARATION OF THE FOLLOWING FORMS
1. Field offense reports
2. Vehicle accident report
3. Arrest report
4. Traffic citation or summons
5. Non-traffic citations and summonses, i.e., juvenile, misdemeanor, etc.
6. Daily bulletin
7. MO bulletin; crime and traffic analyses bulletins
8. Stolen vehicle list
9. Activity report
10. Sick and injury reports
11. Equipment and uniform damage claim
12. Manuals, report-writing; G.O.; rules and regulations, training; SOP's, etc.
13. Business cards
14. Statistical reports—daily, weekly, monthly
15. Organization phone directory
16. Field contact form

FIELD TRAINING GUIDE

	Initials of Field Training Officer and Dates	
	Explained and/or Demonstrated	Performed
17. Field sobriety form		
18. Hospital reports		
19. City vehicle accident report		
XXIV. UNLISTED ITEMS (To be entered by FTO)		
1.		
2.		
3.		
4.		
5.		
6.		
7.		
8.		
9.		
10.		
11.		

Appendix I

Shift Rotation Schedule and Sign-Up Sheet*

This appendix illustrates the recommended method for scheduling personnel in a small department, and a system for rotation of officers from shift to shift in a large department if permanent shift assignments are not desired.

The memo depicted on page 632 is intended to serve a dual purpose. First, it is a sign-up sheet which can be reviewed by each officer, in the order of seniority. Second, the completed sign-up sheet can be posted as the work schedule.

The shift rotation schedule shown on page 631 was developed as a means for overcoming the problem of having an equal number of patrol officers on each shift. The rotation schedule depicted here provides for the assignment of personnel in proportion to workload. The schedule was designed by Roger W. Reinke, formerly of the IACP staff.

*Developed by the International Association of Chiefs of Police, Inc., Gaithersburg, Md. Reprinted by permission of IACP, which reserves all rights for future publication or use.

630

Suggested shift rotation schedule — medium-size department
(based on nine squads)

Squad no. 1

	Jan. 1-14	Jan. 15-28	Jan. 29-Feb. 11	Feb. 12-25	Feb. 26-Mar. 11	Mar. 12-25	Mar. 26-Apr. 8	Apr. 9-22	Apr. 23-May 6	May 7-20	May 21-Jun. 3	Jun. 4-17	Jun. 18-Jul. 1	Jul. 2-15	Jul. 16-29	Jul. 30-Aug. 12	Aug. 13-26	Aug. 27-Sep. 9	Sep. 10-23	Sep. 24-Oct. 7	
Shift A	1	1	8	8	7	7	5	5	3	3	2	2	9	9	6	6	4	4	1	1	etc.
	3	2	2	9	9	6	6	4	4	1	1	8	8	7	7	5	5	3	3	2	
Shift B	4	4	1	1	1	9	9	6	5	5	5	1	1	1	8	7	7	7	4	4	etc.
	5	3	3	2	2	7	7	6	6	6	3	3	2	2	2	8	6	6	6	3	
	6	5	4	3	8	8	8	9	7	4	4	4	3	8	9	9	9	5	5	5	
Shift C	8	8	5	5	5	1	1	1	1	7	7	7	7	4	1	1	1	1	7	7	etc.
	2	6	6	6	6	5	2	2	2	2	6	6	6	6	4	2	2	2	2	6	
	7	7	7	7	3	3	3	3	9	9	9	9	4	3	3	3	3	9	9	9	
	9	9	9	4	4	4	4	8	8	8	8	5	5	5	5	4	8	8	8	8	

|<------------------ 18 weeks ------------------>|

When the full schedule is effected each squad spends four weeks on Shift A, six weeks on Shift B, and eight weeks on Shift C in each 18 week period.

632   APPENDIX I

Sign-up Sheet and Shift Schedule—Small Department

ADMINISTRATIVE MEMO # _____   Date:

TO: All Members   Files: PERS 2-2-1
FROM: Chief of Police
SUBJ: Sign-up sheet for schedule to be effective 12:01 am, _____

1st Platoon	Sun.	Mon.	Tues.	Wed.	Thurs.	Fri.	Sat.
Sgt. _____	12-8	0	0	12-8	12-8	12-8	12-8
Off. _____	12-8	12-8	12-8	0	0	12-8	12-8
Disp. _____	12-8	0	12-8	12-8	12-8	12-8	12-8
2nd Platoon							
Chief	0	8-4	8-4	8-4	8-4	8-4	0
Off. _____	8-4	8-4	8-4	8-4	0	0	8-4
Off. _____	8-4	8-4	8-4	8-4	0	0	8-4
Disp. _____	8-4	8-4	0	8-4	8-4	8-4	8-4
3rd Platoon							
Sgt. _____	0	0	4-12	4-12	4-12	4-12	4-12
Off. _____	7-3	7-3	7-3	0	0	7-3	7-3
Off. _____	4-12	0	0	7-3	7-3	4-12	4-12
Disp. _____	4-12	4-12	4-12	0	4-12	4-12	4-12
Relief							
Off. _____	0	12-8	8-4	4-12	4-12*	4-12*	0
Off. _____	4-12	4-12	0	0	8-4	8-4	4-12

                                          _____
                                          Chief of Police

* flexible

Appendix J

Excerpts from Distribution of Police Patrol Force*

The Distribution Procedure

The manner in which hazards and incidents are used to guide the distribution of the motorized patrol forces will be explained, using data derived from a study in a midwestern city as an illustration. Before proceeding, however, it is necessary to decide whether the need for called-for services and routine patrol is to be based on the hour of occurrence of the various types of incidents or the hour at which they were reported to the police. In the illustrative city, the total number of police incidents in each classification, and the number and percentage of each in which the location and time of occurrence were clearly established, were as follows:

TABLE 1.   Identification of Location and Hour of Occurrence According to Type of Incident

Type of incident	Total number of incidents	Incidents in which location and hour of occurrence were established	
		Number	Per cent
Part I crimes	2,184	679	31
Part II offenses	5,873	2,063	35
Miscellaneous reports	3,332	2,715	81
Accidents	2,707	2,203	81
Arrests	3,949	3,538	90

*Appendix written by O. W. Wilson. Public Administration Service has granted permission to reproduce this material taken from *Distribution of Police Patrol Force,* Publication 74, Public Administration Service, Chicago, Ill., 1941. This material describes a *method* of determining patrol distribution which is basically sound without regard to the size of the city. Variations of the method have been attempted but none has been devised that uses the refinements of the method here described. Police administrators should encourage research into new approaches to this problem.

In making a distribution, the adequacy of the sample in terms of the total number of incidents must be considered. In the chronological distribution the number of cases of each of the types of called-for service in which the hour of occurrence was definitely established was considered as adequate sample. In the geographical distribution these cases were considered adequate in all classifications except Part I crimes, which were considered on the basis of the time reported.[1]

Since Part I crimes are more serious than the other police incidents and since there are fewer of them, special care must be taken to ensure that the Part I sample is adequate. It seemed advisable to use the time of occurrence of these crimes in making the chronological distribution, because the distribution of these crimes based on time reported does not correspond to the distribution of these incidents based on the hour of occurrence, and there is greater need for service at the time of occurrence (routine patrol directed at intangible hazards) than at the time of reporting (called-for services). A smaller sample also suffices because the incidents are being distributed over fewer units: 7 shift periods as compared to 35 beats. In the geographical distribution the time of reporting of Part I crimes was used in determining the need for called-for service and routine preventive patrol; each crime spots a hazard geographically, and the larger number indicates more accurately the dangerous areas. The hazard may fluctuate in degree according to the hour of the day, but it is better to err on the side of recognizing a hazardous area which may be relatively free of danger during a particular tour of duty than to ignore it completely. Furthermore, at the time a Part I crime is reported to the police, there is a need for service (called-for services devoted to investigation) quite distinct in the matter of time from the routine patrol and inspectional services intended to prevent the occurrence.

Steps to Be Taken in Patrol Distribution *Step 1.* Ascertain the number of men to be used in the motorized patrol by subtracting from those available the number needed for (1) foot patrol, point duty, or other assignments that would make them unavailable for motorized patrol, and (2) annual, weekly, and sick relief. In this city, 47 men were used in patrol in addition to those for relief.

Step 2. Record on a map divided into small districts the area and inspectional services for each district. A large-scale map of the city should be divided into approximately 150 small districts for each 100,000 population.[2] The area[3] of each district should be computed, per-

---

[1] The time of occurrence was used in the case of Part II crimes because the sample was adequate (2,063 incidents compared with 679 Part I crimes). Since the time of occurrence is the same as the time reported in most Part II offenses, the geographical distribution will be practically the same, regardless of which time is used.

[2] These small districts should not be of equal area but should contain approximately equal numbers of incidents that are evidence of the need for police service.

EXCERPTS FROM DISTRIBUTION OF POLICE PATROL FORCE

haps by the city engineer's office, and the number of store doors to be tried and other establishments to be inspected in each district should be counted. The results should be recorded on the map. Several maps should be prepared, one for each shift, to show the proportion (in percentage of the total for each shift) of incidents, inspectional duties, and area in each small district. These will be used in establishing beat boundaries (step 12).

Step 3. Prepare incident cards, showing on each the district number, hour reported, and hour of occurrence. A card is prepared on each Part I crime, Part II offense, accident, miscellaneous report, and booked arrest in a recent 12-month period,[4] showing the hour reported. hour of occurrence, and the district number in which it occurred. When these incidents are currently recorded on punch cards, it is only necessary to add the district number. When punch cards are not used, 5- by 3-inch index cards of a different color for each type of incident may be prepared with no information recorded except the case number, district number, hour of occurrence, and hour reported.

Step 4. Tabulate the incidents to show the proportion during each hour of the day. The incidents in the 12-month period should be tabulated, as in Table 2, to show the number and percentage of each type that occurred during each hour of the day. (This is shown graphically in Chart A.)

The district or time of occurrence of some incidents will not be known. The tabulation cannot include those in which the time of occurrence is not known, but it may include those in which the district is not known, providing the incident occurred within the city limits.

While the hour of occurrence of many incidents, especially Part I crimes, will not be known, the sample thus provided is adequate to show the proportional hourly distribution of incidents. The hourly distribution of the need for called-for services and routine patrol is considered to be in proportion to that of these incidents. The chronological distribution of the force is based on this tabulation, plus the number of man-hours required for inspectional services on each shift as computed in step 8.

Since the factors to be considered are so numerous, the procedure for working out the distribution is simplified if those factors which deter-

---

A map on which incidents are spotted serves as a guide in establishing these basic districts; since the small districts are intended to contain only approximately equal needs for police service, it is necessary to spot incidents for only a month or two, and it is unnecessary to distinguish their class. However, the small districts should not be traversed by streets that may be used as beat boundaries.

[3] Street mileage could be used instead of area, if desired.

[4] A 12-month period gives consideration to seasonal variations.

TABLE 2. Number, Percentage, and Average Percentage of Police Incidents for Which Hour of Occurrence Was Established, by Type of Incident and Hour and Period of Day, and Number and Percentage of Part I Crimes According to Time Reported, by Hour and Period of Day

Period	Time reported Part I crimes		Time of occurrence											
			Part I crimes		Part II offenses		Miscellaneous reports		Accidents		Arrests		Per cent	
	No.	%	No.	%	No.	%	No.	%	No.	%	No.	%	Total	Average
7 A.M.– 8 A.M.	132	6.2	10	1.5	44	2.1	76	2.8	108	4.9	69	1.9	13.2	2.6
8 A.M.– 9 A.M.	153	7.2	18	2.7	53	2.6	69	2.5	111	5.0	71	2.0	14.8	3.0
9 A.M.–10 A.M.	126	5.9	24	3.5	49	2.4	104	3.8	103	4.7	56	1.6	16.0	3.2
10 A.M.–11 A.M.	115	5.4	26	3.8	65	3.2	122	4.5	110	5.0	102	2.9	19.4	3.9
11 A.M.–12 M.	111	5.2	24	3.5	57	2.8	111	4.1	107	4.9	73	2.1	17.4	3.5
12 M. – 1 P.M.	94	4.4	26	3.8	43	2.1	79	2.9	124	5.6	81	2.3	16.7	3.3
1 P.M. – 2 P.M.	119	5.6	35	5.2	44	2.1	94	3.4	103	4.7	93	2.6	18.0	3.6
2 P.M. – 3 P.M.	115	5.4	22	3.2	38	1.8	62	2.3	86	3.9	97	2.7	13.9	2.8
3 P.M. – 4 P.M.	142	6.7	64	9.4	125	6.1	175	6.5	133	6.0	208	5.9	33.9	6.8
4 P.M. – 5 P.M.	164	7.7	45	6.6	127	6.2	152	5.6	164	7.5	218	6.2	32.1	6.4
5 P.M. – 6 P.M.	113	5.3	33	4.9	123	6.0	116	4.3	201	9.1	217	6.2	30.5	6.1
6 P.M. – 7 P.M.	81	3.8	21	3.1	129	6.2	117	4.3	156	7.1	207	5.9	26.6	5.3
7 P.M. – 8 P.M.	88	4.1	50	7.4	120	5.8	148	5.5	161	7.3	233	6.6	32.6	6.5
8 P.M. – 9 P.M.	105	4.9	79	11.6	153	7.4	168	6.2	100	4.5	249	7.0	36.7	7.4
9 P.M. –10 P.M.	109	5.1	60	8.8	137	6.6	144	5.3	95	4.3	253	7.1	32.1	6.4
10 P.M. –11 P.M.	96	4.5	28	4.1	124	6.0	126	4.7	63	2.9	186	5.2	22.9	4.6
11 P.M. –12 P.M.	100	4.7	38	5.6	178	8.6	207	7.6	96	4.3	243	6.9	33.0	6.6
12 P.M. – 1 A.M.	51	2.4	22	3.2	124	6.0	180	6.6	74	3.4	209	5.9	25.1	5.0
1 A.M.– 2 A.M.	22	1.1	9	1.5	122	5.9	134	4.9	26	1.2	156	4.4	17.9	3.6
2 A.M.– 3 A.M.	13	0.6	11	1.6	70	3.4	109	4.0	16	0.7	155	4.4	14.1	2.8
3 A.M.– 4 A.M.	11	0.5	6	0.9	59	2.9	107	4.0	19	0.8	142	4.0	12.6	2.5
4 A.M.– 5 A.M.	17	0.8	13	1.9	37	1.8	52	1.9	11	0.5	89	2.5	8.6	1.7
5 A.M.– 6 A.M.	11	0.5	5	0.7	21	1.0	35	1.3	10	0.5	57	1.6	5.1	1.0
6 A.M.– 7 A.M.	43	2.0	10	1.5	21	1.0	28	1.0	26	1.2	74	2.1	6.8	1.4
Total	2,131		679		2,063		2,715		2,203		3,538			
7 A.M.– 3 P.M.	965	45.3	185	27.2	393	19.1	717	26.3	852	38.7	642	18.1	129.4	25.9
3 P.M. – 5 P.M.	306	14.4	109	16.0	252	12.3	327	12.1	297	13.5	426	12.1	66.0	13.2
5 P.M. – 9 P.M.	387	18.1	183	27.0	525	25.4	549	20.3	618	28.0	906	25.7	126.4	25.3
9 P.M. – 1 A.M.	356	16.7	148	21.7	563	27.2	657	24.2	328	14.9	891	25.1	113.1	22.6
1 A.M.– 7 A.M.	117	5.5	54	8.1	330	16.0	465	17.1	108	4.9	673	19.0	65.1	13.0
Total	2,131	100.0	679	100.0	2,063	100.0	2,715	100.0	2,203	100.0	3,538	100.0	500.0	100.0
Actual number	2,184		2,184		5,873		3,332		2,707		3,949			

mine the relative need for called-for services and routine patrol are consolidated into a single factor, or index. The proportionate hourly need for police service to deal with each type of called-for service factor is expressed as a percentage of the total. For example, 44 of the 2,063 Part II offenses were committed in the hour between 7:00 and 8:00 A.M. (see Table 2). Therefore, 2.1 per cent of the need for service resulting from

EXCERPTS FROM DISTRIBUTION OF POLICE PATROL FORCE

these offenses occurred during this hour. The proportionate hourly need for police service arising from each of the other factors is similarly com-

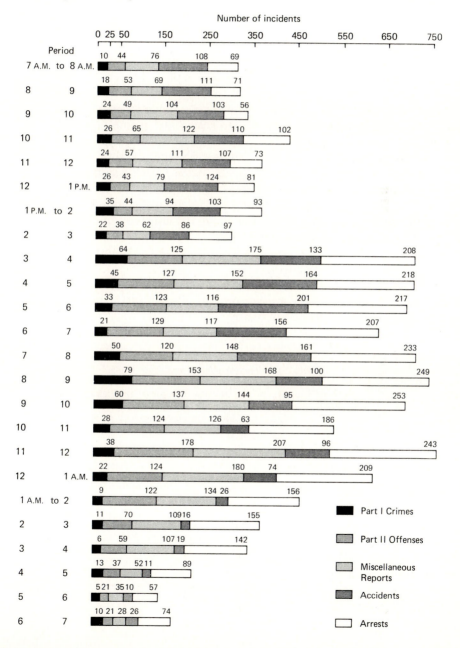

CHART A Number of police incidents for which hour of occurrence was established, by hour of day.

puted. The proportionate hourly need for called-for services and routine patrol is then considered to be the arithmetical average of these percentages for each hour. This index is recorded in the extreme right column of Table 2. Charts A and B also illustrate the time distribution.[5]

Several considerations enter into the analysis of the data. Normally, the tabulation would seem to indicate a slump in need for police activity just before the end of a tour of duty. This seeming slump is likely, however, to reflect a decrease in police activity at this time rather than an actual decrease in the need for police service. The decrease in police activity is brought about by (1) a tendency on the part of the dispatcher to assign cases or complaints received during the last hour of his shift to the detail of officers about to go on duty; (2) a tendency on the part of the individual patrolman not to initiate action just before going off duty that might interfere with his reporting at headquarters promptly at the end of his tour of duty; and (3) fatigue at the end of a tour of duty which probably results in a diminution of activity. Traffic accidents, as well as other incidents calling for police service, seem to slump just before 3:00 and 11:00 P.M., and this slump may also be accounted for to some extent by the reasons enumerated above. In interpreting the tabulations, the slumps in the last hour before the end of a tour of duty should be smoothed out by applying to them some of the peak built up in the hour immediately following.

It is interesting that a slump also occurs during the dinner hour. There is a tendency toward a decrease, or a leveling off of the increase, in all phases of police activity between 5:00 and 7:00 P.M., although automobile accidents show a marked increase during the before-dinner

[5]The method described herein for deriving an index of the need for called-for services and preventive patrol has the effect of giving a weight to each factor in inverse proportion to the number of incidents in each. This method may be simplified by assigning arbitrary weights to the several categories of incidents, on the basis of sound judgment, and by correcting for deficiencies in the time-of-occurrence data by dividing the number of incidents in each category in which the hour of occurrence is known by the percentage of incidents in that category in which the hour of occurrence is known.

A weight of one should be assigned to all incidents in each of the categories of arrests, accidents, and miscellaneous reports, since it is assumed that they are of approximately equal importance and that approximately equal time is required to deal with them. A weight of two should be assigned to Part II ofenses, and a weight of four to Part I crimes. In applying the weights, Part I crimes should be multiplied by four and Part II incidents by two, since it is assumed that they are, respectively, four and two times more serious than incidents in the other three categories and that a similar increase in time is required to deal with them.

The corrected and weighted number of incidents in each type may then be added, and the proportion of the total on each shift to the total for the 24 hours of the day may then be computed. This percentage should then be used to apportion the man-hours to be devoted to called-for services and preventive patrol among the shifts. If the administrator or the planner is not convinced of the validity of the above assumptions, he may make his own and assign weights accordingly.

EXCERPTS FROM DISTRIBUTION OF POLICE PATROL FORCE

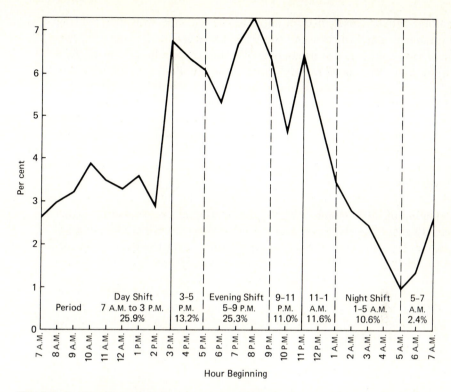

CHART B Percentage distribution of need for police service to handle police incidents for which hour of occurrence was established, by hour of day.

rush hour. Chart A indicates the rapid decline in police activity after midnight, with the low ebb reached between 5:00 and 6:00 A.M.

Table 2 shows proportional hourly distribution of 679 Part I crimes in which the time of occurrence was established. There were 1,505 additional cases in which the time of occurrence was not established. It was assumed that the nearly one-third of the Part I cases in which the time of occurrence was known was a fair sample for purposes of chronological distribution. Two peaks are apparent, one in the midafternoon and the other between 8:00 and 9:00 P.M. Part I crimes also reach a low point between 5:00 and 6:00 A.M. While the number of Part I crimes committed from midnight to early morning is considerably smaller than during any other period of the day, these crimes are usually of a more serious character.

Step 5. Determine the number and the reporting hours of the shifts. The number of shifts to be used in supplying police service and the time at which each shift will report for duty should be ascertained by analysis of the hourly distribution of incidents (as tabulated in Table 2) and some other factors. Four points should be considered: (1) Each patrolman must be assigned for eight hours of continuous duty; (2) the assignment of patrol beats and duties is facilitated, the beat organization task is simplified, the number of different dispatchers' beat maps is lessened, and the task of remembering beat boundaries by dispatchers, patrolmen, and other members of the force is made less difficult when the number of shifts is kept as small as possible for effective service; (3) the shifts should provide maximum manpower at the time of greatest need for service; and (4) the hourly need on each shift should not deviate greatly from the average need. The last point is considered in the following paragraphs which explain a procedure for selecting the most desirable hours for shift changes.

Selection of Shift Hours The hourly distribution of need for police service (Table 2) is an important factor in determining the most desirable hours for shift changes. Column 1, Table 3 lists the average hourly load for each of the three shifts in four different arrangements (shifts

TABLE 3. Average Hourly Load, Total Deviation from the Average Proportional Distribution of the Load, and Corrected Total Deviation, during Various Periods of the Day

Period	(1) Average hourly load	(2) Total deviation from average	(3) Proportional distribution of load	(4) Corrected total deviation
7 A.M.- 3 P.M.	3.2	2.7	25.9	0.70
3 P.M. - 11 P.M.	6.2	5.1	49.5	2.52
11 P.M. - 7 A.M.	3.1	12.0	24.6	2.95
Total			100.0	6.17
8 A.M.- 4 P.M.	3.8	6.5	30.1	1.96
4 P.M. -12 P.M.	6.2	4.9	49.3	2.42
12 P.M. - 8 A.M.	2.6	7.4	20.6	1.52
Total			100.0	5.90
9 A.M.- 5 P.M.	4.2	9.7	33.5	3.25
5 P.M. - 1 A.M.	6.0	6.1	47.9	2.92
1 A.M.- 9 A.M.	2.3	5.8	18.6	1.08
Total			100.0	7.25
6 A.M.- 2 P.M.	3.1	4.3	24.5	1.05
2 P.M. -10 P.M.	6.0	7.5	47.7	3.58
10 P.M. - 6 A.M	3.5	11.8	27.8	3.28
Total			100.0	7.91

EXCERPTS FROM DISTRIBUTION OF POLICE PATROL FORCE

ending at different hours). Since the force is distributed among the three shifts in proportion to the average hourly need[6] for police service on each, during hours of greater-than-average need the force is less adequate, and during hours of less-than-average need it is not used to capacity. Since both situations are undesirable, the sum for the three shifts of the total deviations from the average hourly load on each shift may be used inversely as a measure of the relative suitability of shift arrangements.[7] These sums are shown in column 2, Table 3, for the four shift arrangements. However, the proportional distribution of incidents that call for police service among the shifts should be applied to the total deviations for each shift in order to arrive at a deviation that takes into account the number of men working on each shift. (The manpower is distributed (1) in proportion to the incidents which call for police service, column 3, Table 3, and (2) in proportion to the need for inspectional services.) This computation (column 2 multiplied by column 3) is necessary because if one shift has twice the manpower of another on the basis of these incidents, an equal deviation results in twice the amount of this manpower not used to its potential or with a load beyond its capacity. The corrected total deviations (shown in column 4) provide a more accurate determination of the most desirable hours for changes of shifts and clearly indicate that shifts should end at 12:00 P.M., 8:00 A.M., and 4:00 P.M.

Overlapping Shifts This shift arrangement was discarded, however, because of an apparent need for overlapping shifts. For example, police court, held at 5:15 P.M., drew officers from the street to testify (and one to serve as bailiff), and more inspectional services were required after store-closing hours; thus there was need for more police activity after 5:00 P.M. than from 3:00 to 5:00 P.M. Similarly, the 11:00 P.M. to 7:00 A.M. shift experienced greater activity in the early hours of the shift than in the later hours. Further, some patrolmen who reported for duty at 3:00 P.M. were assigned to unproductive foot patrol and to unnecessary street-crossing duty until a number of automobiles used by the detective division became available at 5:00 P.M. For the above reasons it was decided to use an overlapping shift to report for duty at 5:00 P.M.

The need for increased attention to commercial establishments at night was also a factor in the determination of the shifts. This need was met by a squad of four foot patrolmen devoting their time exclusively to checking store doors in the central business district from

---

[6]The average hourly load for a shift is the average of the indexes (the percentage figures listed in the last column of Table 2) for the hours of the shift.

[7]The sum (without regard to plus or minus signs) of the differences (deviations) between the load for each hour (last column, Table 2) and the average hourly load (column 1, Table 3) is the total deviation for the shift.

9:00 P.M. to 5:00 A.M. The hours selected were believed to be those during which their services would be most effective.

Since the hours of the two overlapping shifts were selected for the reasons given above, there remained the determination of the most suitable hours for the basic shifts. Since the foot patrolmen who worked from 9:00 P.M. to 5:00 A.M. devoted all their time to inspectional services, there was no necessity to consider deviations of hourly needs from the average need for police service as reflected in the proportional distribution of incidents so far as they were concerned. Choices of hours for reporting for duty, therefore, were restricted to the day and evening shifts (currently reporting at 7:00 A.M. and 3:00 P.M.). The choices considered were 6:00, 7:00, 8:00, and 9:00 A.M. and corresponding hours for reporting in the afternoon. The results are tabulated in Table 4 and show clearly that the most desirable hours are 7:00 A.M.

TABLE 4. Average Hourly Load, Total Deviation from the Average Proportional Distribution of the Load, and Corrected Total Deviation, during Various Periods of the Day

Period	(1) Average hourly load	(2) Total deviation from average	(3) Proportional distribution of load	(4) Corrected total deviation
6 A.M.- 2 P.M.	3.1	4.3	24.5	1.05
2 P.M. - 5 P.M.	5.3	5.1	16.0	0.82
5 P.M. - 1 A.M.	6.0	6.1	47.9	2.92
1 A.M.- 6 A.M.	2.3	3.9	11.6	0.45
Total			100.0	5.24
7 A.M.- 3 P.M.	3.2	2.7	25.9	0.70
3 P.M. - 5 P.M.	6.6	0.4	13.2	0.05
5 P.M. - 1 A.M.	6.0	6.1	47.9	2.92
1 A.M.- 7 A.M.	2.2	4.8	13.0	0.62
Total			100.0	4.29
8 A.M.- 4 P.M.	3.8	6.5	30.1	1.96
4 P.M. - 5 P.M.	6.4	0.0	6.4	0.00
5 P.M. - 1 A.M.	6.0	6.1	47.9	2.92
1 A.M.- 8 A.M.	2.2	5.2	15.6	0.81
Total			100.0	5.69
9 A.M.- 5 P.M.	4.2	9.7	33.5	3.25
5 P.M. - 1 A.M.	6.0	6.1	47.9	2.92
1 A.M.- 9 A.M.	2.3	5.8	18.6	1.08
Total			100.0	7.25

EXCERPTS FROM DISTRIBUTION OF POLICE PATROL FORCE

and 3:00 P.M. The reporting time decided upon for the five shifts was, therefore, 7:00 A.M., 3:00 P.M., 5:00 P.M., 9:00 P.M., and 11:00 P.M. Each shift was assigned to duty for eight consecutive hours.

Step 6. Compute the percentage of total incidents (using the index developed in step 4 and recorded in the last column, Table 2) on each segment of day created by shift changes by adding the index for the hours of each period. In the example, the distribution, as shown in Chart B, was as follows:

Period	Per cent of incidents
7 A.M.– 3 P.M.	25.9
3 P.M. – 5 P.M.	13.2
5 P.M. – 9 P.M.	25.3
9 P.M. – 1 A.M.	22.6
1 A.M.– 5 A.M.	10.6
5 A.M.– 7 A.M.	2.4
Total	100.0

Step 7. Ascertain the man-hours to be devoted to called-for services and routine patrol on each period created by shift changes. The proportionate distribution of the police incidents developed in step 6 is used as a measure of the relative need for police services devoted to handling these incidents and to routine patrol (not including inspectional services). There is no absolute standard for measuring the man-hours needed to perform these two services, but after some study it was decided to take the number of man-hours available for each 1 per cent of incidents on the 7:00 A.M. to 3:00 P.M. shift as a standard unit of measurement. The third factor, need for inspectional service, is at a minimum during these hours, and it may be assumed that all police service on this shift is devoted to the first two factors. If the man-hours provided on this shift are meeting the need for these two services fairly satisfactorily, then the allocation of man-hours to these services on other shifts on the basis of relative need should also result in satisfactory service.

Eight men were assigned to the 7:00 A.M. to 3:00 P.M. shift, or a total of 64 man-hours of service. Four of these hours were consumed by relief, leaving 60 man-hours available for the performance of the 25.9 per cent of called-for and routine patrol services, or 2.3 man-hours for each 1 percent. In order to determine the number of man-hours needed to provide an equal quality of service on any shift, the per cent of police incidents (the sum of the hourly index) was multiplied by 2.3. The result of this computation was as follows:

Period	Percentage of incidents	Man-hours required
7 A.M.– 3 P.M.	25.9	60.0
3 P.M. – 5 P.M.	13.2	30.4
5 P.M. – 9 P.M.	25.3	58.2
9 P.M. – 1 A.M.	22.6	52.0
1 A.M.– 5 A.M.	10.6	24.4
5 A.M.– 7 A.M.	2.4	5.5
Total	100.0	230.5

Step 8. Compute the man-hours needed for inspectional services for each period created by shift changes. The total man-hours available for this service should be ascertained first. In the example, when 230.5 man-hours for called-for services and routine patrol, 6 for court appearances, and 23.5 for daily relief are subtracted from the 376 man-hours of work provided by 47 men, there remain 116 man-hours for inspections.

There were approximately 3,000 store doors that required inspection. A study of actual store tries indicated that, on the average, approximately 30 seconds were necessary for each try. Travel time between doors was considered routine patrol and was not included in the computation. One inspection of each, therefore, would require approximately 25 man-hours. It was estimated that 80 per cent of the stores closed before 9:00 P.M., and it was decided that they should be tried once before that hour. Approximately 20 man-hours were, therefore, needed for this purpose. It was decided that the 3,000 doors should be tried twice between 9:00 P.M. and 1:00 A.M., and that those stores presenting the greatest crime hazard (estimated at 60 per cent of the total) should be checked twice during the period 1:00 to 5:00 A.M. and once between 5:00 and 7:00 A.M. The need for the inspection of rooming houses, taverns, dance halls, and other recreational establishments presenting crime hazards was greatest in the period from 9:00 P.M. to 1:00 A.M., and 6 man-hours were allotted for these inspections. The man-hours needed for inspectional duties during the several periods were, therefore, estimated as follows.

Period	Man-hours
7 A.M.–3 P.M.	40
3 P.M. –5 P.M.	0
5 P.M.–9 P.M. (80% of 3,000 × 30 seconds)	20
9 P.M.–1 A.M. (2 × 3,000 × 30 + 6 hours*)	56
1 A.M.–5 A.M. (2 × 60% of 3,000 × 30 seconds)	30
5 A.M.–7 A.M. (1 × 60% of 3,000 × 30 seconds)	15
Total	121

* Six hours for other-than-store inspections.

EXCERPTS FROM DISTRIBUTION OF POLICE PATROL FORCE

645

The estimated total was considered close enough to the 116 man-hours available.

Step 9. Compute the man-hours needed on each shift for called-for services and routine patrol (step 7) and for court and inspectional services (step 8). In the example cited, the following is the computation:

Period	Man-hours required for		Total man-hours
	Inspections and court	Called-for services and routine patrol	
7 A.M.–3 P.M.	0	60.0	60.0
3 P.M.–5 P.M.	0	30.4	30.4
5 P.M.–9 P.M.	26*	58.2	84.2
9 P.M.–1 A.M.	56	52.0	108.0
1 A.M.–5 A.M.	30	24.4	54.4
5 A.M.–7 A.M.	15	5.5	20.5
Total	127.0	230.5	357.5

* Six hours in court.

Step 10. State the apportionment among the periods, in terms of men rather than man-hours, providing for continuous eight-hour service and relief. It is obvious that in determining the number of men to be assigned, it will be impossible to attain an exact apportionment of man-hours because each patrolman must serve a continuous eight-hour period.

The approximate number of men required for each period of the day may be ascertained by dividing the total number of man-hours needed by the number of hours in that period. To this number must be added sufficient manpower to provide daily relief. In the example cited, the period 7:00 A.M. to 3:00 P.M. calls for 60.0 man-hours; since there are 8 hours in this period, 8 men are required to furnish 60 man-hours of duty and 4 man-hours for relief. The period 3:00 to 5:00 P.M. needs no relief; 15 men are needed to provide 30.4 man-hours of work. By the same process it was determined that the period 5:00 to 9:00 P.M. required 24 men, 12 man-hours then being available for relief. The 9:00 P.M. to 1:00 A.M. period requires no daily relief, and therefore 27 men are needed to provide 108.0 man-hours of work. Likewise, 15 men are needed from 1:00 to 5:00 A.M. to provide 54.4 man-hours of work and 7.5 man-hours for relief. Ten men are needed from 5:00 to 7:00 A.M., a period not requiring daily relief.

The chronological distribution of men needed in each period to meet all patrol, court, inspection, and relief needs, expressed also in man-hours of service (relief time was subtracted) and compared with the man-hours of need as computed in step 9, was as follows:

Period	Man-hours of service needed	Man-hours for relief	Total man-hours needed	Men needed	Man-hours that would be provided
7 A.M.–3 P.M.	60.0	4	64	8	64
3 P.M.–5 P.M.	30.4	0	30.4	15	30
5 P.M.–9 P.M.	84.2	12	96.2	24	96
9 P.M.–1 A.M.	108.0	0	108	27	108
1 A.M.–5 A.M.	54.4	7.5	61.9	15	60
5 A.M.–7 A.M.	20.5	0	20.5	10	20

Step 11. Assign men to each shift in a manner to ensure a minimum deviation from the man-hour requirements. Men must be assigned to each shift in such numbers as to most nearly provide the manpower needs tabulated above and at the same time permit each officer to work an unbroken eight-hour tour of duty. In the example, no problem is encountered on the day shift because it is unbroken; eight men should therefore report for duty at 7:00 A.M. Since four foot patrolmen are to work from 9:00 P.M. to 5:00 A.M., the motorized manpower needs during this period are reduced by 4, thus necessitating 23 men from 9:00 P.M. to 1:00 A.M. and 11 men from 1:00 to 5:00 A.M. The problem then resolves itself into providing motorized manpower during the night shifts in a manner that will enable each officer to work an unbroken shift and at the same time deviate as little as possible from the indicated manpower needs.

Several different plans of distribution of the 47 men were considered before a final selection was made. The two seemingly most logical plans are given as an illustration of the procedure. The number of men reporting for each shift in these two plans is indicated below.

Hour of reporting	Number of men	
	Plan *A*	Plan *B*
7 A.M.	8	8
3 P.M.	14	13
5 P.M.	9	11
9 P.M.	4	4
11 P.M.	12	11

The following tabulation compares the deviation of each of the two plans from the man-hour requirements tabulated in step 9:

EXCERPTS FROM DISTRIBUTION OF POLICE PATROL FORCE

Period	Men provided		Man-hours provided		Man-hours needed	Man-hour deviation from need	
	Plan A	Plan B	Plan A	Plan B	(Step 9)	Plan A	Plan B
7 A.M.–3 P.M.	8	8	60	60	60.0	0.0	0.0
3 P.M.–5 P.M.	14	13	28	26	30.4	2.4	4.4
5 P.M.–9 P.M.	32	24	80.5	84	84.2	3.7	0.2
9 P.M.–1 A.M.	26*	27*	104	108	108.0	4.0	0.0
1 A.M.–5 A.M.	16	15	56	52.5	54.4	1.6	1.9
5 A.M.–7 A.M.	12	11	24	22	20.5	3.5	1.5
Total deviation						15.2	8.0

* These are average figures; two less report on duty than report off duty at 11 P.M.

Since the distribution according to plan B resulted in less deviation from the need than other plans, it was adopted. The distribution is shown graphically in Chart C.

The various types of activity requiring police attention during different periods of the day indicated the assignment of two patrolmen as evidence technicians during the hours from 7:00 A.M. to 11:00 P.M. Only 12.6 per cent of Part I crimes (Table 2) were reported between 11:00 P.M. and 7:00 A.M. (and only 5.5 per cent between 1:00 and 7:00

CHART C Distribution of manpower and man-hours of police service, by period and type of service.

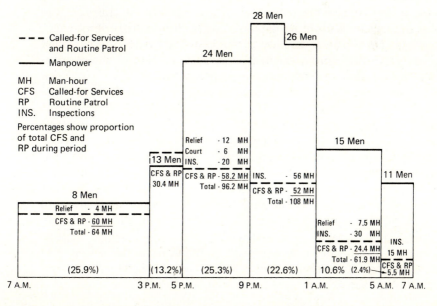

A.M.), so one evidence technician was considered sufficient for this shift, and he was assigned to a beat in addition. It was also decided that at least one patrol sergeant should be on duty at all times, and two sergeants seemed to be needed for the shift from 5:00 P.M. to 1:00 A.M.

The distribution of manpower according to number, rank, and reporting hour was therefore as follows:

Hour of reporting	Sergeants	Evidence technicians	Patrolmen	Total
7 A.M.	1	2	5	8
3 P.M.	1	2	10	13
5 P.M.	1	0	10	11
9 P.M.	0	0	4 (foot)	4
11 P.M.	1	1	9	11
Total				47

Step 12. Divide the city into a number of motorized beats for each period of the day, containing approximately equal needs for police service, to correspond to the number of men made available for assignment by the chronological distribution, as indicated in the tabulation immediately above.

There are more calls for service and greater need of routine police activities in some sections of a city than in others. In certain sections crime and accident rates are high, and many arrests are made. In some sections more stores require attention, more recreational centers need inspection and regulation, and there is greater flow of traffic. More routine time must be spent on patrol in these sections than in others.

To apportion the force equally throughout the area to be patrolled will not distribute manpower effectively. Each section of the community should be ensured police service in proportion to its needs. Such distribution provides an indisputable answer to pressure groups, political or otherwise, who may wish to concentrate a disproportionate amount of patrol service in a particular section of the city. Reasons of economy and efficiency also dictate the distribution of the force in proportion to need. Furthermore, proper geographical distribution should be made in fairness to the public and to the individual police officers. If one beat has twice the need for police service that another has, the officer assigned to the first beat has twice as much work to do as the officer assigned to the second. Such inequalities result in variations in the quality of police service and in a damaged morale. They tend to make a drone of one policeman and to arouse a feeling of futility and resentment in another who is faced with much heavier burdens.

EXCERPTS FROM DISTRIBUTION OF POLICE PATROL FORCE

THE BEAT LAYOUT

The principal purpose of the patrol and the conditions under which it is performed influence the shape of the beat. Patrol duties may be so clustered along a roadway as to justify a route consisting of a length of street instead of an area for patrol. A beat in the form of a route simplifies assignment for the enforcement of moving-traffic regulations and for checking overtime and other illegal parking practices because it restricts officers to the streets on which their duties are located. The main-street pattern of some cities makes foot beats in the form of a route desirable.

A patrol route simplifies the problem of supervision and permits the patrolman a view of his entire beat at any point, although these are advantages to the criminal as well. A route can be patrolled in only one of two directions and consequently provides less opportunity for surprising a criminal in operation than an area which permits the patrolman to follow diverse routes. For this reason, police beats should cover an area instead of a route, except when some advantages are derived by assigning men to a route.

A square beat permits a maximum quadrilateral area with a minimum distance between any two possible points within it. It is impossible to have all beats in the forms of squares, however, because hazards requiring police service are not uniformly spread over the area of a city; and streams, railroads, and highways that sometimes form desirable beat boundaries are not arranged in square patterns. Also, it is sometimes desirable to include uniform demographic and business characteristics within the same beat, although this uniformity may be sacrificed in order to divide a congested business area among several motor beats. The beat pattern, therefore, must of necessity be irregular and should be influenced most strongly by the desirability of establishing beats with equal needs for police service.

The chronological distribution in this instance provided five shifts of men, with one or more sergeants and one or more evidence technicians assigned to each shift. With the exception of one evidence technician who reported at 11:00 P.M., the sergeants and evidence technicians were not assigned to motorized beats. The four patrolmen who reported at 9:00 P.M. were assigned to foot-patrol beats. The number of men available for assignment to motorized-patrol beats by periods, therefore, was as follows:

Period	Number of men
7 A.M.–3 P.M.	5
3 P.M.–5 P.M.	10
5 P.M.–1 A.M.	20
1 A.M.–7 A.M.	10

The problem was to divide the city into 5, 10, 20, and 10 beats for the respective periods, of a size that would provide approximately an equal amount of police activity for each man and allow a relatively equal amount of police service for each of the beats.

The geographical distribution was based on (1) the need for called-for services and routine preventive patrol, as measured by Part I crimes, Part II offenses, miscellaneous complaints, accidents, and booked arrests; (2) the need for inspectional services as measured by the number of store doors to be tried and the number of taverns, bars, dance halls, rooming houses, and other places presenting easily identifiable police hazards; and (3) area.

The application of these factors in determining the size of each patrol district was a trial-and-error process. The small districts into which the city was arbitrarily divided (step 2) were combined experimentally until an approximately equal total proportional amount of the factors listed fell into each patrol area or beat. Four considerations, however, somewhat limit the determination of the area to be included in each beat: (1) Natural boundaries, such as rivers and main thoroughfares, should be used whenever possible. (2) The social character of the beat should be as uniform as possible. (3) In some cases men working through two periods (such as before and after 5:00 P.M.) will necessarily be assigned to a smaller and then a larger area, or vice versa, in which cases the smaller area should be entirely contained in the larger area if possible. (4) It may be impossible in some cases to set up areas with an equal number of each of the factors; in these cases a deficiency of a certain number of occurrences of one of the factors cannot be made up by using an excess of an equal number of occurrences of another of the factors. Each of these points is discussed below in relation to the manner in which it affected the geographical distribution.

Procedure　The procedure followed in making the distribution may be briefly described. The cards (step 3) were sorted according to hour of occurrence (hour reported in the case of Part I crimes) into the four periods into which the day had been divided to take care of changes in the number of beats or districts:

> 7:00 A.M. to 3:00 P.M.
> 3:00 P.M. to 5:00 P.M.
> 5:00 P.M. to 1:00 A.M.
> 1:00 A.M. to 7:00 A.M.

A tabulation was then made of the total number of Part I crimes, Part II offenses, miscellaneous reports, accidents, and arrests for each of the periods in each of the small districts. The number of store

EXCERPTS FROM DISTRIBUTION OF POLICE PATROL FORCE

doors and the number of establishments needing other inspectional services were likewise tabulated for each of these districts.

The next step was to combine the small districts to form the desired number of beats. The operation is facilitated by the use of a map for each shift or time period, of such scale as to permit recording on each small district the sum of the proportions (weighted in a manner to be described) of each class of incidents, of inspectional services, and of area, and the sum of these weighted proportions. The sum for each district is an index of the need for police service in that district during that period of time. In combining districts into beats, the sum of the indexes of the component districts is the relative proportion of need for police service on each beat for that time period.

For the period 7:00 A.M. to 3:00 P.M. the small districts were combined experimentally until an average of about 20 per cent of each factor was placed in each of five beats. The same procedure of combining small districts experimentally was followed in dividing the city into 10 beats for the 3:00 to 5:00 P.M. period, into 20 beats for the 5:00 P.M. to 1:00 A.M. period, and again into 10 beats for the 1:00 to 7:00 A.M. period. An effort was made to use important thoroughfares as district boundaries so that these streets might be patrolled by officers in adjoining beats and thus receive adequate protection. So far as possible, the beats were designed to contain like racial, economic, business, industrial, residential, and other social characteristics, as well as uniform features, in order to secure some of the advantages of specialization in patrol.

Changes in Beats during Shifts In cases where the number of beats changed during the hours of any one shift, the best arrangement for an officer who worked through the two periods would provide that the large area for which he was responsible in the one period would contain the smaller area for which he was responsible in the other. For instance, officers going on duty at 3:00 P.M. would patrol a large area until 5:00 P.M., at which time the addition of a squad of 10 men would result in the division of the 10 large districts into 20 smaller ones for the period from 5:00 P.M. to 1:00 A.M. It was desired to have the beat boundaries so arranged that an officer patrolling a large area before 5:00 P.M. would have contained within that area all of the smaller area to be patrolled by him after 5:00 P.M. Again, it was desirable that each of the 20 beats patrolled from 5:00 P.M. to 1:00 A.M. should be contained as nearly as possible within one of the 10 beats patrolled in the period from 1:00 to 7:00 A.M. This arrangement is desirable for several reasons. The officer is responsible for the smaller area during his entire tour of duty, and maximum stability is provided by eliminating the shifting of patrol officers and thus permitting them to become better acquainted with their areas. The arrangement also simplifies the assignment of cases; the maximum number of complaints can be given to an officer who will continue working in a particular area for a complete tour of duty.

Administrative Problems   From an operating point of view there are disadvantages in having the day broken up into a large number of periods, each with a different geographical distribution. In the first place, a separate dispatcher's map must be maintained for each period; if these maps are good they are expensive, and additional ones, plus the control switches, take up valuable space. In the second place, dispatchers find each distribution an added burden. More beat boundaries must be carried in mind; the assignment of cases to men who will be working part of their tour in a large area and the remainder in a smaller one makes rather difficult the task of determining whether a case falling within the larger area, but outside the smaller one, should be assigned to the officer now patrolling that larger area or to the officer about to report for duty; and the operation of the beat-map light switches becomes more complicated and time-consuming.

For these reasons, in establishing the 10 beats for the period from 3:00 to 5:00 P.M., it was desirable whenever possible to use the same beats as were used from 1:00 to 7:00 A.M. By making a few readjustments in the distribution, it was found that the 10 beats used during the 1:00 to 7:00 A.M. period provided a satisfactory beat arrangement for the period from 3:00 to 5:00 P.M. The proportional load distribution remained nearly constant for both periods. The needs of the longer period should be given priority in readjustments, however, because 66 man-hours of service are provided from 1:00 to 7:00 A.M. and only 26 man-hours from 3:00 to 5:00 P.M.

Weighting the Factors   In the combination of the small districts into the required number of beats, it was sometimes not possible to establish areas that contained an equal, or nearly equal, amount of each of the factors being used. Because some of the factors required more of a patrolman's time than did others, it was not possible, in every case, to substitute an excess of one factor for a deficiency of an equal number of another factor. For example, if in a period two areas experienced an equal number of Part II offenses, of accidents, and of arrests, but the first area had 20 more Part I crimes in a year than the second but 20 fewer miscellaneous reports, it probably would not have been fair to assume that the two areas had an equal need for patrol service.

In determining the beat boundaries for the periods from 5:00 P.M. to 7:00 A.M., the store factor should be given more weight than the other factors. During the daylight hours the store factor is considered equal to each of the other factors, but after 5:00 P.M., and particularly

EXCERPTS FROM DISTRIBUTION OF POLICE PATROL FORCE

after 9:00 P.M., a much greater percentage of time is required to be devoted to stores.

During the chronological distribution it was determined that in the period from 5:00 P.M. to 1:00 A.M., 76 man-hours were required for inspectional service (see step 8). The foot patrol, which was not considered in the determination of motorized beats, carried 16.0 man-hours of this load (four men for four hours), which left 60 man-hours of inspectional services to be performed by the motorized patrol. It was determined that 110.2 man-hours were required for called-for and routine patrol services during the same period.

If during the periods 7:00 A.M. to 3:00 P.M. and 3:00 to 5:00 P.M. the factor of stores[8] was considered equal to each of the other factors (Part I crimes, Part II offenses, miscellaneous reports, accidents, and arrests) in making the geographical distribution, then all these other factors combined could be considered as having a ratio of 5 to 1 to the store factor. In the period from 5:00 P.M. to 1:00 A.M. however, all these other factors required 110.2 man-hours of service as compared to 60 man-hours for stores. Therefore, the ratio of all these other factors to the store factor was 1.8 to 1; in other words, after 5:00 P.M. stores became approximately three times as important (5 divided by 1.8) as they were from 7:00 A.M. to 5:00 P.M.

The weight of the store factor for the period 1:00 to 7:00 A.M. was determined by the same procedure. Fourteen of the 45 man-hours devoted to inspectional services were provided by foot patrolmen (four men for four hours less two hours for relief). Consequently the ratio of the other factors to the store factor was as 29.9 man-hours to 31 man-hours, or 0.96 to 1. Therefore, during this period, the store factor was slightly more than five times as important (5 divided by 0.96) as it was from 7:00 A.M. to 3:00 P.M. Actually, the store factor was given a weight of 6 in order to simplify the computations and because it was felt that a weight of 6 was more nearly accurate.

With the store factor unweighted, each of the eight factors used in the geographical distribution (area, Part I crimes, Part II offenses, miscellaneous reports, accidents, arrests, stores, and miscellaneous inspections) had a value of one-eighth. Weighting the store factor by 6 in the period from 1:00 to 7:00 A.M. and eliminating the factor of miscellaneous inspections would have resulted in giving each of the other factors a value of one-twelfth. With this arrangement the factor of area would have had a value only two-thirds as great as it had during the period from 7:00 A.M. to 5:00 P.M., when each of the eight factors was given equal weight. The area factor, however, should be kept nearly

---

[8]In the geographical distribution, stores are considered a factor during the hours when they are not subject to regular inspection because they constitute an unusual hazard at all times. The number of store doors is a satisfactory measure.

TABLE 5. Number, Percentage, and Average Percentage of Factors of Need for Police Service in the Period 5:00 P.M. to 1:00 A.M., Distributed by Beats

Beat No.	Area Sq. miles	Area %	Part I crimes* No.	Part I crimes* %	Part II offenses† No.	Part II offenses† %	Miscellaneous reports† No.	Miscellaneous reports† %	Accidents† No.	Accidents† %	Arrests† No.	Arrests† %	Stores‡ No.	Stores‡ %	Miscellaneous inspections No.	Miscellaneous inspections %	Average per cent
1	0.54	2.7	27	3.6	59	5.4	61	5.1	52	5.5	89	5.0	117	11.3	10	1.8	4.1
2	0.92	4.6	45	6.1	49	4.5	43	3.6	46	4.9	33	1.8	195	18.9	43	7.6	5.2
3	2.62	13.2	30	4.0	64	5.9	72	6.0	59	6.2	73	4.1	95	9.2	21	3.7	5.3
4	0.03	0.2	64	8.6	26	2.4	63	5.2	47	5.0	96	5.4	248	24.1	44	7.8	5.9
5	0.04	0.2	46	6.2	26	2.4	48	4.0	38	4.0	111	6.1	277	26.9	50	8.8	5.9
6	0.06	0.3	21	2.8	25	2.3	22	1.8	43	4.5	101	5.6	205	19.9	45	8.0	4.5
7	1.69	8.5	39	5.3	71	6.5	60	5.0	49	5.2	78	4.3	115	11.1	23	4.1	5.0
8	0.48	2.5	27	3.6	83	7.6	90	7.5	68	7.2	83	4.6	160	15.6	23	4.1	5.2
9	1.69	8.5	36	4.8	47	4.3	75	6.2	53	5.6	125	7.0	164	15.9	33	5.8	5.8
10	0.66	3.4	33	4.4	63	5.8	49	4.1	58	6.1	103	5.7	96	9.3	24	4.2	4.3
11	2.74	13.8	18	2.4	77	7.1	58	4.8	29	3.1	90	5.0	91	8.8	13	2.3	4.7
12	0.21	1.0	40	5.4	80	7.4	60	5.0	81	8.6	107	6.0	123	11.9	24	4.2	4.9
13	1.12	5.7	42	5.7	70	6.5	79	6.5	46	4.9	109	6.1	128	12.4	21	3.7	5.1
14	3.10	15.7	29	3.9	61	5.6	103	8.5	41	4.3	45	2.5	74	7.2	5	0.9	4.9
15	1.34	6.8	39	5.2	60	5.5	75	6.2	69	6.2	35	1.9	203	19.7	19	3.4	5.5
16	0.12	0.6	31	4.2	28	2.6	45	3.7	31	3.3	113	6.3	222	21.5	57	10.1	5.2
17	0.04	0.2	63	8.5	33	3.0	46	3.8	29	3.1	122	6.8	180	17.4	40	7.1	5.0
18	0.04	0.2	45	6.1	22	2.0	38	3.1	28	2.9	116	6.5	129	12.6	34	6.0	3.9
19	1.76	8.9	31	4.1	74	6.8	73	6.1	40	4.2	83	4.6	115	11.1	9	1.6	4.8
20	0.60	3.0	37	5.0	70	6.4	46	3.8	49	5.2	85	4.7	157	15.2	27	4.8	4.8
Total	19.8	100.0	743	100.0	1,088	100.0	1,206	100.0	946	100.0	1,797	100.0	3,094	300.0	565	100.0	100.0

* Based on hour reported. †Based on hour of occurrence. ‡Stores given a weight of 3.

EXCERPTS FROM DISTRIBUTION OF POLICE PATROL FORCE

constant in value, and its weight, therefore, needed to be multiplied by 1.5. In order to simplify computations, area was given a weight of 3, stores a weight of 12, and each of the other five factors used in the 1:00 to 7:00 A.M. distribution a weight of 2.

The distribution of the various factors calling for police service among the beats on one shift is shown in Table 5.

Appendix K

Allocation and Distribution of Police Patrol Manpower*

Introduction

Proper allocation of resources is one of the most critical problems facing law enforcement today. The allocation question is critical for three very basic reasons—first, because of considerations of efficiency and economy. Although law enforcement and the administration of justice is a governmental service without profit, we are still responsive to competition from profit making organizations. The salary portion of the police budget is by far the greatest expense in a typical departmental budget, and since the police department is usually the largest of city departments, police salaries represent the greatest single block of expense to our taxpayers.

I noted this morning that Dr. Blumstein referred to the cost of just one two-man car, around the clock, as $100,000 a year.

Second, the allocation problem has a fundamental relationship to crime repression, preventive patrol, and investigative efficiency. Proper allocation can be the difference between a high crime rate and a lower one, and can significantly affect clearance and closure efforts. Dr. Blumstein also mentioned this in his talk when he spoke of the relationship of response time to arrest rate.

Third, proper allocation and distribution of resources is an important factor in police morale, which in turn affects productivity.

*Originally given as a speech by Roy C. McLaren before the First National Symposium for Law Enforcement Science and Technology, IIT Research Institute, Chicago, March, 1967; published in the symposium proceedings, entitled *Law Enforcement Science and Technology*, Thompson Book Company, Washington, D.C., 1968, p. 599. Reprinted by permission of the publisher.

656

ALLOCATION AND DISTRIBUTION OF POLICE PATROL MANPOWER

I would like to pause here for a minute and define the two terms I have just used—allocation and distribution.

First of all, the term *allocation* is used by the IACP staff to mean the determination of the overall manpower for the department and for each division within the department.

On the other hand, the term *distribution,* as used by the IACP staff, means the assignment of a given number of personnel according to area workload, time or function—and in general our discussion will refer more to distribution of patrol resources rather than the more easily defined needs of investigative or traffic functions.

Distribution

It becomes rather obvious that one of these two activities—distribution—is much more easily accomplished than the other. It is a fairly easy matter to distribute available manpower according to workload, providing sufficient factual information is available. For example, if an operations commander is given a group of one hundred patrol officers, and he knows the measurable workload is divided by shifts into groups of 22, 33, and 44 per cent of the total, he must assign approximately 22, 33 and 44 per cent of his beat officer strength to these same shifts if he wants to keep the workload about equally divided.

Similarly, reasonably accurate methods have been developed—including one used routinely by the IACP Field Operations Division staff—to distribute the work into motorized patrol beats of equal workload. Some sophisticated work in distribution of available resources has been carried out in the past by many agencies, institutions and individuals. One significant contribution was by August Vollmer and the Berkeley Police Department in the early 1930s. Even in those days, Berkeley tested and adjusted its patrol beat structures by calculating the number of felonies, arrests, investigations, accidents, and so on in each beat, and conducted studies of the time required to conduct general investigations by patrolmen, those involving detective investigations, and arrests.

O. W. Wilson has developed and refined the distribution technique, and has applied it to numerous cities. It is difficult to understand how any reasonable person can read the chapter on distribution of the patrol force in the latest edition of Police Administration and not put it into effect. Other noteworthy efforts in distribution have been made by Frank Walton of the Los Angeles Police Department, who used the term "selective distribution," the Oakland Police Department, my associate R. Dean Smith, Director of Research and Development for IACP, and others interested in the distribution problem.

These approaches have dealt with the measurement of workload by time of day, day of week, by shift, by month, and by census tracts and other small areas. Different classes of events have been timed and weighted, and differences in time have been discovered according to the time of day or according to shift. Construction of patrol beats and precinct boundaries has been based on logical measurements, with appropriate factors considered such as event weightings, area, response time, presence of hazards, and so on. Computers have aided the "selective distribution" process, and in recent years the application of cybernetics to deployment, as summarized by Robert Gaunt of the Los Angeles Police Department, has received widespread attention by progressive agencies.

One would think that these fine efforts would by now have resulted in good deployment practices everywhere. However, before I run the risk of minimizing the distribution problem, let me say that inadequate distribution of resources is a great problem in itself—one that affects a great many departments—perhaps a substantial majority of them. Certainly, many of the departments observed or surveyed by the Field Operations Division have suffered from inadequate distribution of manpower resources. It is very common to find that a department has simply distributed manpower equally among the shifts—in some cases only for one reason even when they know better—it is easier to rotate shifts that way.

This practice is widespread even though most departments can demonstrate a level of activity on swing shift which is roughly twice as high as the midnight-to-8 A.M. shift. Distribution according to workload by day of week is similarly ignored, either because of the lack of adequate measurement or simply to equalize the number of nights off for each day in the week—even though the called-for-services workload is typically twice as high on Friday and Saturday evenings as it is for comparable periods on Tuesday and Wednesday. Patrol beat boundaries are often determined by seat-of-the-pants estimates, or by arbitrarily dividing a city map into a number of beats of approximately equal area. In this sort of situation, officers run themselves ragged on some beats on some shifts, while others are bored with idleness.

Waste of manpower because of inadequate functional distribution is also highly apparent in many departments today. Some have excessive numbers of men assigned to foot patrol, traffic corner duty, station duties, and so on, while there are insufficient men assigned to motorized patrol and general investigative duties.

Allocation

Though there is obviously still an enormous amount of good work yet to be done in distribution, the problem of allocation of manpower is much more complex and difficult. The heart of the problem is this: What is the optimum number of officers to be employed for a specific city? We can easily measure called-for-services workload, but the most imponderable part of the problem is that we don't know the precise effect of preventive patrol upon street crime rates. We are unable to state with certainty that a beat officer is most efficient when he spends 20, 30, 40, 50 or whatever percentage of his time on preventive patrol as compared to handling called-for-services. Perhaps we will never arrive at a eutectic formula, and our approach should continue to be one of narrowing the area of decision, through adequate information, so that sound administrative judgments can be made.

The literature contains few references on the question of optimum preventive patrol time as a basis for determining the overall allocation of patrol manpower, and is practically devoid of suggestions for approaching this problem. Another weakness in our knowledge is that we lack really solid time studies of various kinds of cases at the patrol division level, and have to depend on time studies made in a few selected departments. We then hope that the times are realistic in terms of the methods we are proposing for the city in question.

We need trial and error research, or to put it more acceptably, experimentation and analysis. For example, the division of patrol work into investigation and preventive patrol mentioned by Chief Rogers. We need to supply the administrator or policy maker with more "points of diminishing returns," for various aspects of the allocation problem. For example—and again let me refer to Dr. Blumstein's talk this morning—the study of response time in Los Angeles showed a 60 per cent probability of arrest if response time to crime calls was within one minute. But the probability of arrest was considerably less when response time was at a much higher level of 15 minutes. Suppose the probability dropped slightly to 55 per cent after 3 minutes? This still is a high figure, and the response time is practical.

We need to know a great many other things which affect the allocation of manpower, but there have been some inroads. Explorations in the use of mathematical concepts in allocation have been conducted by several authorities, including Robert Shumate and Richard Crowther of Systems Science Corporation, and members of the science task force of the President's Commission. Such work has involved application of mathematical queuing and probability theories to the allocation problem. Their work has dealt with questions such as "What is the probability of having one or more events already waiting in queue?" Or, "What is the probability of encountering a delay of X minutes?" Or, "What is the probability of one event occurring in the next minute?"

The IACP Allocation and Distribution Method

The Field Operations Division of IACP has developed a method for the allocation and distribution of patrol manpower which has been applied to numerous cities surveyed by IACP since 1959. Parts of the method (those dealing with assignment/availability factors and the overall allocation of manpower) were introduced in 1964.

The following example of the method is an excerpt from a recent IACP management survey. All of the numerical facts are accurate, although the description of the city has been modified to prevent identification:

Allocation and Distribution of Patrol Manpower

This is a seaport city of 150,000 inhabitants. It is one of America's most colorful tourist cities, and is the urban center for a metropolitan area of some 350,000 population. The city contains lower, middle-and upper-income neighborhoods. The lower income areas include some blighted spots which are equal to any in the country in requiring active police patrol. Because of the prosperous industry located in and near the city, the department has been fortunate in having an adequate tax base to support its budget.

Although the department has more than enough administrative talent and technical capacity to carry out an adequate manpower distribution study, the present distribution of patrol manpower by shift, and by beat within each shift, leaves much to be desired.

Present deployment The patrol force is organized into three watches operating with conventional shift hours, and an overlapping shift (the former tactical force) covering portions of both night watches.

Present staffing is shown below:

> Watch 1—12 P.M. to 8 A.M.   12 Auto Patrol Beats
>> 2 Lieutenants
>> 4 Sergeants
>> 33 Patrolmen
>
> Watch 2—8 A.M. to 4 P.M.   8 Beats
>> 1 Captain (division commander)
>> 1 Lieutenant
>> 3 Sergeants
>> 26 Patrolmen
>
> Watch 3—4 P.M. to 12 M.   12 Beats
>> 2 Lieutenants
>> 5 Sergeants
>> 32 Patrolmen
>
> 7 P.M. to 3 A.M. Shift   (Overlapping Beats)
>> 1 Sergeant
>> 12 Patrolmen

Note that the number of beats on the day watch is smaller than on the two night shifts, and that the number of patrolmen on Watch 1 exceeds even the number of patrolmen on the evening shift. Both of

ALLOCATION AND DISTRIBUTION OF POLICE PATROL MANPOWER

these circumstances are contrary to typical distributions, and this is substantiated by the department's own tabulations. Each month the statistical unit prepares a tabulation of arrests, unnumbered incidents, offenses, and accidents for each of the beats. From the police beat report for the same period, it was determined that the 33 patrolmen on Watch 1 accounted for 22 per cent of the workload, while the 32 men on swing shift accounted for 47 per cent. For all three shifts, the percentages of manpower and workload were as follows:

	Patrolmen assigned	Per cent patrolmen	Per cent workload
Watch 1	33	36	22
Watch 2	26	29	31
Watch 3	32	35	47
	91	100	100

The percentages of 22, 31 and 47 are consistent with similar figures from other departments, but it is obvious that officers assigned to Watch 3 are carrying more than their share. This simple table does not take traffic manpower into account or the contribution of assistance from the 7 P.M.–3 A.M. shift, but it does point out the general discrepancy.

Inequities in beat workload are extreme. Workload figures obtained in the IACP distribution study, covering the previous year, were applied to the existing beat structure. On Watch 1 beats 227, 237 and 230 each averaged 7 per cent. Beats 222 and 220 had 17 and 24 per cent, respectively, of the shift workload. In the patrol beat report for December 1964, beat 430 had a workload of 124 incidents, while during the same period beat 427 had 425 incidents.

Allocation of manpower In the opinion of the Field Operations Division, patrol workload is most effectively distributed when it is measured in terms of the following classes of events:

Part I Crimes
Part I Arrests
All Other Offenses
All Other Arrests
Traffic Accidents
Miscellaneous Services

Extensive time studies conducted in several municipal police agencies have established standard time requirements for completely processing each class of events listed above by the patrol officers assigned. Applying such time requirement standards to these events yields the basic man-hour requirements for handling all events at the preliminary level.

APPENDIX K

The workload-manpower distribution study conducted by IACP was based on an examination of 17,587 complaints and incidents handled by the department in the previous year—an accurate and statistically "correct" 20 per cent sample of the year's total workload. Under supervision of the IACP staff, a detail of officers located each incident geographically by placing it into one of the existing small "reporting areas" (quarter-sections) into which the city is divided. (In other departments the staff has divided the city into discrete reporting areas in sufficient quantity so that there will be about two reporting areas for each 1,000 population. These reporting areas are designed to facilitate consolidating them into patrol beats, and thus the reporting area boundaries should follow natural boundaries, arterial streets, railroad tracks, freeway routes, and so on. In a busy downtown neighborhood, however, a reporting area typically consists of four to nine city blocks.) Next, each incident was then identified as belonging to one of the following:

Type of incident	Relative weighting
Part I Crimes	4
Criminal Homicide	
Forcible Rape	
Robbery	
Aggravated Assault	
Burglary	
Auto Theft	
All Other Offenses	3
Arrests for Part I Crimes	2
Arrests for All Other Offenses	2
Arrests for Drunkenness	1
Arrests for Disorderly Conduct	2
Arrests for Vagrancy	2
All Other Arrests (including those for outside departments)	2
Traffic Accidents	2
Miscellaneous Police Services	1

This weighting is partly based on the time required to handle these various incidents, and partly on the seriousness of the event. The time and day of week occurrence (or reporting) was then determined. All of this information was entered on data processing cards—one for each incident. Data on the 17,587 cards were analyzed by computer, which was programmed to show (1) the number of incidents (multiplied by the relative weighting factors) in each reporting area by shift; (2) workload by day of week; (3) totals by time of day in hours; and (4) "within shift" variations in workload.

ALLOCATION AND DISTRIBUTION OF POLICE PATROL MANPOWER

Shift hours. The latter procedure (item 4, above) determines the optimum arrangement of working hours by shift. The least internal variation of workload occurred when shift hours commencing at 1 A.M., 9 A.M., and 5 P.M. were contemplated. These working hours are thus considered most efficient insofar as they minimize the difference in workload between hourly peaks and lulls in activity. The existing scheduling of shifts commencing at 4 P.M., 12 midnight, and 8 A.M. was the third most efficient arrangement of hours out of a total of eight possible combinations, but the difference in variation was not great between the first three positions so the advantage to be gained by changing shift times was therefore considered to be negligible.

Man-year productivity. For the purpose of this report it is assumed that each officer in the department is capable of an amount of work equal to all other officers. A basic "man-year" in a police department is made up of 365 eight-hour tours of duty. It was then determined that there were 182 patrolmen employed for the previous full year in the department being studied. Nine others worked for fractions of a year, with the final equivalent amounting to 185.4. Multiplying this figure times 365 days a year equals 67,671 potential man-days available. From this we subtracted the number of days lost in order to derive the actual man-days available:

Total potential man-days available		67,671
Less: Days off	19,281 (185.4 × 104)	
Annual leave	2,589 (actual)	
Sick leave	1,134 (actual)	
Injury leave	378	
Holidays	2,224 (185.4 × 12)	
Classroom Training	282 (actual)	
Miscellaneous loss	74 (actual)	67,671
	25,962	−25,962
Actual man-days available		41,709

The ratio of 41,709 to 67,671 is the same as 1 to 1.62. For every man who is actually available for duty, 1.62 officers must be assigned. The ratio of 1.62 to 1 is designated the *assignment/availability* factor.

To determine the number of men needed to do *no more* than handle the offenses and incidents reported to or investigated by the department, the average available time for one man is divided into the time required for investigation of the cases. The problem is not quite this simple, of course, because no allowance is thereby made for repressive patrol time, nor for time to travel from the scene of one incident to the scene of the next. Police incidents obviously do not occur on a regular, predictable basis and therefore a certain amount of "stacking" or buffer time is necessary. *Previous experience has shown that about*

664   APPENDIX K

one-third of an officer's time on shift should be allocated to protect against the tendency for cases to occur in groups rather than to be spaced equitably throughout the tour of duty. An additional one-third of an officer's time should be available for repressive patrol activity, and the remaining one-third should be available to handle called-for-services.

Calculating the Required Number of Beats. Previous studies have shown that the average time required to investigate a case at the preliminary level by members of a patrol division, and using techniques to be recommended is 45 minutes. (If the department had conducted time studies of patrol investigations, we would have used the times thus obtained. But they had not conducted such studies over a long period of time, which meant we had to apply our standard time factor.) After application of this factor and making allowances for buffer time and repressive patrol time, the number of beats can be determined.

Two factors have to be taken into consideration during the calculation of the number of beats. The first was the exceptional difference between the workload on weekends (Saturday and Sunday on Watch 1, and Friday and Saturday on Watch 3) for the two night shifts. On Watch 1, the weighted workload on Sunday morning (Saturday night) is two times greater than the workload for the average of the other mid-week nights. The workload for Saturday morning is nearly as great. While the differences on Watch 3 are not so pronounced, the workload on Saturday night is 51 per cent higher than on Monday, and 35 per cent higher than on Tuesday. To prevent a serious overloading of beat officers on weekends, it is recommended that two beat configurations be used on each of the night shifts. The problem is minimal on the day watch, with the workload on all days of the week fairly consistent.

The second factor to be considered is the tremendously concentrated workload in Happyland. (Editorial note: This is a seriously blighted skid-row area of about six city blocks which has been given a colorful name by the local citizenry. We will identify it as "Happyland.") If this workload were included in the totals for each shift, the distribution for the remainder of the beats would be skewed significantly. Distributions on all watches were therefore based on the citywide totals minus Happyland. A further consideration is that the Happyland beat on each shift is so small, because of the heavy workload, that the irreducible minimum area has been reached. Any additional coverage would have to be provided by overlapping cars and foot patrol beats. Finally, the Happyland area is scheduled for razing due to the construction of a freeway interchange.

Other Patrol Manpower Requirements. A two-man car generally operates in the Happyland area on all shifts, and on occasions when

ALLOCATION AND DISTRIBUTION OF POLICE PATROL MANPOWER

extra men are available, other beats are doubled up. Because of the heavy load in the area, the proposed beat distributions will require a two-man car in this area on the two night shifts. Two wagon drivers will be required on all three shifts for citywide coverage. Foot patrol will require two men on Watch 1, two on Watch 2, and three on Watch 3. Watch 1 will require one evidence technician, with two on the other shifts.

Watch 1–12 P.M. to 8 A.M.

A. Weekend (Saturday and Sunday) Beat Distribution

Number of incidents sampled (adjusted to the Saturday and Sunday rate and subtracting the westside zones 2755.1 and 2755.2) — 4,080

Converted to 100 percent — 20,400 incidents per year

Multiplied by .75 hours (45 minutes) — 15,300 hours per year in called-for-services

Multiplied by 3 (to add buffer factor and time for routine patrol) — 45,900 total hours

Divided by the number of hours necessary to man one patrol beat on one shift for one year $(8 \times 365$ or $2920) = 15.7$ (or, raised to the next whole number) — 16 beats

Additional beat including zones 2755.1 and 2755.2 (Happyland) — 1 beat

17 total beats

B. Midweek Beat Distribution

Number of incidents sampled (adjusted to the mid-week rate and subtracting the westside zones 2755.1 and 2755.2) — 2,350

Converted to 100 percent — 11,750 incidents per year

Multiplied by .75 hours (45 minutes) — 8,812 hours per year in called-for-services

Multiplied by 3 (to add buffer factor and time for routine patrol) — 26,436 total hours

Divided by the number of hours necessary to man one patrol beat on one shift for one year $(8 \times 365$ or $2920) = 9$ — 9 beats

Additional beat including zones 2755.1 and 2755.2 (Happyland) — 1 beat

10 total beats

Watch 2–8 A.M. to 4 P.M.

(Same number of beats for all days of the week)

Number of incidents sampled (subtracting the westside zones 2755.1 and 2755.2) — 4,269

APPENDIX K

Converted to 100 percent	21,345 incidents per year
Multiplied by .75 hours (45 minutes)	16,008 hours per year in called-for-services
Multiplied by 3 (to add buffer factor and time for routine patrol)	48,024 total hours
Divided by the number of hours necessary to man one patrol beat on one shift for one year (8×365 or 2920) = 16.4 (or, adjusted to the nearest whole number)	16 beats
Additional beat including zones 2755.1 and 2755.2	<u>1 beat</u>
	17 total beats

Watch 3-4 P.M. to 12 M.

A. Weekend (Friday and Saturday) Beat Distribution

Number of incidents samples (adjusted to the Friday and Saturday rate and subtracting zones 2755.1 and 2755.2)	6,086
Converted to 100 percent	30,430 incidents per year
Multiplied by .75 hours (45 minutes)	22,825 hours per year in called-for-services
Multiplied by 3 (to add buffer factor and time for routine patrol)	68,475 total hours
Divided by the number of hours necessary to man one patrol beat on one shift for one year (8×365 or 2920) = 23.4	23 beats
Additional beat including zones 2755.1 and 2755.2	<u>1 beat</u>
	24 total beats

B. Midweek Distribution

Number of incidents sampled (adjusted to the midweek rate and subtracting the westside zones 2755.1 and 2755.2)	4,021
Converted to 100 percent	20,105 incidents per year
Multiplied by .75 hours (45 minutes)	15,078 hours per year in called-for-services
Multiplied by 3 (to add buffer factor and time for routine patrol)	45,234 total hours
Divided by the number of hours necessary to man one patrol beat on one shift for one year (8×365 or 2920) = 15.4 (or adjusted to the next whole number)	16 beats
Additional beat including zones 2755.1 and 2755.2	<u>1 beat</u>
	17 total beats

ALLOCATION AND DISTRIBUTION OF POLICE PATROL MANPOWER

Supervisory strength has been provided so that there are approximately six patrolmen for each sergeant. Although the assignment/availability factor for sergeants is slightly higher (1.64 to 1 compared to 1.62 to 1 for patrolmen. The difference is insignificant; the ratios between patrolmen and sergeants assigned and patrolmen and sergeants available will practically be the same.) The number of beat officers per sergeant will vary from three to five, depending on the size of the supervisory sector and upon how many support patrolmen (wagon drivers and evidence technicians) and foot patrolmen are assigned.

Once the number of beats, two-man cars, foot patrolmen and support patrolmen have been determined, it is possible to ascertain with accuracy the number of men who should be assigned to patrol sections of the division. Such assignment should insure the availability of sufficient manpower after attrition due to days off, sick leave, and other manpower drains.

Watch 1

11 beat officers, one-man cars (16 beat officers $\times \frac{2}{7} = 4.5$ men, plus 9
   beat officers $\times \frac{5}{7} = 6.4$ men; 4.5 plus 6.4 = 10.9 men)
    2 beat officers, two-man car
    2 foot patrol beat officers
    1 evidence technician
    <u>2 wagon drivers</u>
  18 patrolmen to be available

Multiplied by 1.62 (the assignment/availability factor), the 18 men which must be available will require an assignment of 29 men plus 5 sergeants.

Watch 2

    17 Beat officers, one-man cars
    2 foot patrol beat officers
    2 evidence technicians
    <u>2 wagon drivers</u>
   23 patrolmen to be available

Multiplied by 1.62, the 23 men which must be available will require an assignment of 36 men plus 6 sergeants.

Watch 3

18 beat officers, one-man cars (23 beat officers $\times \frac{2}{7} = 7$ men, plus 15
   beat officers $\times \frac{5}{7}$ men = 11 men)
    2 beat officers, two-man cars
    3 foot patrol beat officers
    2 evidence technicians
    <u>2 wagon drivers</u>
  27 patrolmen to be available

668   APPENDIX K

Multiplied by 1.62, the 27 men which must be available will require an assignment of 44 patrolmen plus 7 sergeants

Recommendations

1. Retain the present shift hours of 12 M.–8 A.M.; 8 A.M.–4 P.M.; and 4 P.M.–12 M.

2. Adopt the following number of patrol beats on each watch:

   Watch 1: 10 beats for Monday through Friday and 17 beats for Saturday and Sunday

   Watch 2: 17 beats

   Watch 3: 17 beats for Sunday through Thursday and 24 beats for Friday and Saturday

3. Allocate 109 patrolmen, 18 sergeants and 3 lieutenants to patrol sections as indicated:

	Patrolmen	Sgts.	Lts.
Watch 1			
Assigned	29(27%)	5	1
Available	18	—	—
Watch 2			
Assigned	36(33%)	6	1
Available	23	—	—
Watch 3			
Assigned	44(40%)	7	1
Available	27	—	—

Configuration of beats   Next the weighted workload total for each shift was divided by the number of beats to obtain the average workload, which would in turn determine the size of beats. The small reporting zones were combined into a larger area, or beat, by adding reporting zone totals until the proper size was reached. Adjustments for peculiarities of terrain, accessibility, unusually high or low incident rates, and the character of neighborhoods were made. Large beats in the outlying residential areas were given a somewhat smaller workload to account for the greater area to be patrolled and the increased travel time between extreme parts of the beat. Travel time from one extreme to the other is limited to a maximum of three minutes under emergency conditions. Areas with a high incident rate, on the other hand, were combined into beats with a somewhat larger than average workload due to the reduced size. The beats in the Happyland area have a much heavier workload, but will be patrolled by two-man cars and foot beat officers.

Recommended beat configurations will be indicated below. It should be noted that the weekend beat distribution for Watch 1, the day shift distribution, and the mid-week distribution for Watch 3 all contain 17

ALLOCATION AND DISTRIBUTION OF POLICE PATROL MANPOWER

beats. The workload varies in location from shift to shift, of course, but is close enough to permit the use of the same configuration for all 17 beat distributions, and will be less confusing.

Recommendation

Adopt the following beat structure and supervisory assignments indicated below.

Watch 1

A. Ten Beat Distribution

Beat number	Per cent of weighted workload	Boundaries, notes
(Supervisory Sector 1-5)		
1-51	8.04	(specific description of streets making up beat boundaries)
1-52	8.03	
1-53	7.82	
1-54	8.35	
(Supervisory Sector 1-6)		
1-61	8.16	
1-62	9.05	
1-63	8.35	
Foot Beat	—	
Wagon	—	
Evidence Technician	—	
(Supervisory Sector 1-7)		
1-71	8.53	
1-72	8.13	
1-73	25.57	Happyland
Foot Beat	—	
Wagon	—	

B. Seventeen Beat Distribution
(Same as distribution for Watch 2 except for evidence technicians, foot beats.)

Watch 2

A. Seventeen Beat Distribution

(Supervisory Sector 2-1)	
2-11	6.41
2-12	6.41
2-13	6.57
2-14	6.55
2-15	6.08

670 APPENDIX K

(Supervisory Sector 2-2)

2-21	5.64
2-22	6.26
2-23	6.30
2-24	6.24

(Supervisory Sector 2-3)

2-31	6.85
2-32	6.25
2-33	5.88
2-34	6.21
2-35	6.28
Evidence Technician	—
Foot Beat	—
Wagon	—

(Supervisory Sector 2-4)

2-41	5.83
2-42	15.27
2-43	6.24
Evidence Technician	—
Foot Beat	—
Wagon	—

Watch 3

A. Twenty-four Beat Distribution (weekends)

(Supervisory Sector 3-1)

3-11	3.21
3-12	3.32
3-13	3.37
3-14	3.91
3-15	3.56

(Supervisory Sector 3-2)

3-21	3.39
3-22	3.24
3-23	3.24
3-24	1.81
3-25	3.59

(Supervisory Sector 3-3)

3-31	3.36
3-32	3.51
3-33	3.09
3-34	3.40

(Supervisory Sector 3-4)

3-41	3.75
3-42	3.66
3-43	5.65
3-44	3.20

ALLOCATION AND DISTRIBUTION OF POLICE PATROL MANPOWER

Beat number	Per cent of weighted workload	Boundaries, notes
Foot Beat	—	(specific description of
Evidence Technician	—	streets making up beat
Wagon	—	boundaries)
(Supervisory Sector 3-5)		
3-51	3.17	
3-52	3.02	
3-53	3.29	
3-54	21.33	
3-55	3.59	
3-56	3.29	
Wagon	—	
Foot Beats (2)	—	

B. Seventeen Beat Distribution (Midweek — Same as Watch 2 except for foot beats).

Bibliography

Altshuler, Alan A., *Community Control: The Black Demand for Participation in Large American Cities*, Pegasus Publications, New York, 1970.

American Bar Association Project on Standards for Criminal Justice, *Standards Relating to the Urban Police Function*, June 1974.

Anderson, Deborah, and Peter B. Bloch, "Policewomen on Patrol—Final Report," Police Foundation, Washington, D.C., 1974.

"Automatic Vehicle Monitoring Systems Study—Executive Summary," Jet Propulsion Laboratory, California Institute of Technology, Pasadena, Calif., June 30, 1976.

Baerwald, John E., ed., *Transportation and Traffic Engineering Handbook* Institute of Traffic Engineers, Prentice-Hall, Inc., Englewood Cliffs, N.J., 1976.

Bass, Bernard M., and Samuel D. Deep, eds., *Current Perspectives for Managing Organizations*, Prentice-Hall, Inc., Englewood Cliffs, N.J., 1970.

Bergsman, Ilene, "Police Unions," *Management Information Service Report*, International City Management Association, Washington, D.C., March 1976.

Blalock, Joyce, and Martha Handman, "How to Implement Criminal Justice Standards through Police/Bar Cooperation," American Bar Association, 1976.

Bloch, Peter B., and James Bell, "Managing Investigations: The Rochester System," The Urban Institute and the Police Foundation, Washington, D.C., 1976.

Bloch, Peter B., and David Specht, *Neighborhood Team Policing*, National Institute of Law Enforcement and Criminal Justice, Law Enforcement Assistance Administration, U.S. Department of Justice, 1973.

Bloch, Peter B., and David Specht, "Prescriptive Package–Neighborhood Team Policing," National Institute of Law Enforcement and Criminal Justice, Law Enforcement Assistance Administration, U.S. Department of Justice, December 1973.

Bloch, Peter B., and Cyrus Ulberg, "Auditing Clearance Rates," The Urban Institute and the Police Foundation, Washington, D.C., December 1974.

Bloch, Peter B., and Donald R. Weidman, "Prescriptive Package—Managing Criminal Investigations," National Institute of Law Enforcement and Criminal Justice, Law Enforcement Assistance Administration, U.S. Department of Justice, 1975.

Bloch, Peter B., and Thomas W. White, "Police Officer Height and Selected Aspects of Performance," Police Foundation and International Association of Chiefs of Police in cooperation with The Urban Institute, October 1975.

Bopp, William J., *Police Personnel Administration*, Holbrook Press, Inc., Boston, 1974.

Bopp, William J., *Police Administration*: *Selected Readings*, Holbrook Press, Inc., Boston, 1975.

Bristow, Allen P., and E. Caroline Gabard, *Decision Making in Police Administration*, Charles C. Thomas, Publisher, Springfield, Ill., 1961.

Chaiken, Jan M., "The Criminal Investigation Process—Volume II: Survey of Municipal and County Police Departments," The Rand Corporation, Santa Monica, Calif., 1975.

Chamber of Commerce of the United States, *Modernizing Criminal Justice through Citizen Power*, distributed and reprinted by American Bar Association, undated.

Chapman, Samuel G., and George D. Eastman, *Short of Merger*, D. C. Heath and Company, Lexington, Mass., 1976.

Clark, Ramsey, *Crime in America*, Simon And Schuster, New York, 1970.

Clift, Raymond E., *A Guide to Modern Police Thinking*, 2d ed., W. H. Anderson Co., Cincinnati, Ohio, 1965.

Coffey, Alan E., E. Eldefonso, and W. Hartinger, *Human Relations: Law Enforcement in a Changing Community*, 2d ed., Prentice-Hall, Inc., Englewood Cliffs, N.J., 1974.

Compendium of Model Correctional Legislation and Standards," 2d ed., U.S. Department of Justice, Law Enforcement Assistance Administration, U.S. Department of Justice, 1975.

"Congress Votes 753 Million for LEAA in Fiscal Year 1977. Funding is $45 Million over Administration Request," *Criminal Justice Newsletter*, Vol. 7, No. 14, July 5, 1976.

"Connecticut Patrol Strategy Reduces Selected Crimes," *Target*, March 1976.

Connelly, J. Campbell, *A Manager's Guide to Speaking and Listening*, American Management Association, Inc., New York, 1967.

BIBLIOGRAPHY

Dale, Ernest, *Management: Theory and Practice*, McGraw-Hill Book Company, New York, 1965.

David, Edward M., "Team Policing," *The Police Yearbook*, International Association of Chiefs of Police, 1975.

Deutsch, Karl W., *The Nerves of Government: Models of Political Communication and Control*, paperback ed., The Free Press (Macmillan), New York, 1966.

Diversion of Youth from the Juvenile Justice System, Law Enforcement Assistance Administration and the Office of Juvenile Justice and Delinquency Prevention, U.S. Department of Justice, April 1976.

DuVries, Henri L., M.D., *Surgery of the Foot*, The C. V. Mosby Company, St. Louis, 1959.

Eisenberg, Terry, et al., "Collaboration between Law Enforcement Executives and Social Scientists—Principles Which Govern Effective Collaboration," National Conference of Christians and Jews, Inc., San Jose, Calif., 1975.

Eliot, Warner A., et al., "National Evaluation Program Phase I Report—Early-Warning Robbery Reduction Projects: An Assessment of Performance," National Institute of Law Enforcement and Criminal Justice, Law Enforcement Assistance Administration, U.S. Department of Justice, 1976.

Farmer, David J., "Fact versus Fact: A Selective View of Police Research in the United States," *The Police Quarterly* (England), April 1976.

Farmer, David J., "Police Research Program of the National Institute of Law Enforcement and Criminal Justice," *The Police Chief*, March 1975.

Ferguson, John H., and Dean E. McHenry, *The American System of Government*, McGraw-Hill Book Company, New York, 1971.

Ferguson, Robert W., *Drug Abuse Control*, Holbrook Press, Inc., Boston, 1975.

First Interim Report—Commission on the Review of the National Policy Toward Gambling, Washington, D.C., 1975.

The FLAIR System (Fleet Location And Information Reporting), The Boeing Co., Wichita Div., August 1975.

Folley, Vern L., *American Law Enforcement*, Holbrook Press, Inc., Boston, 1973.

Fourth Annual Report—The National Commission on Productivity and Work Equality, Washington, D.C., 1975.

"Full-Service Neighborhood Team Policing: Planning for Implementation," Public Safety Research Institute, Inc., St. Petersburg, Florida, for National Institute of Law Enforcement and Criminal Justice, Law Enforcement Assistance Administration, U.S. Department of Justice, 1975.

Garmire, Bernard L., ed., *Municipal Police Administration*, 8th ed., International City Management Association, Washington, D.C., 1977.

Goldstein, Herman, "Police Corruption—A Perspective on Its Nature and Control," Police Foundation, Washington, D.C., 1975.

Gourley, G. Douglas, and Allen P. Bristow, *Patrol Administration*, 2d ed., Charles C Thomas, Publisher, Springfield, Ill., 1974.

Granof, Michael H., and Dale A. Kinzel, "Zero-Based Budgeting: Modest

Proposal for Reform," *The Federal Accountant*, Vol. 23, No. 4, December 1974.

Greenberg, Bernard, et al., "Felony Investigation Decision Model—An Analysis of Investigative Elements of Information," Stanford Research Institute, Menlo Park, Calif., 1975.

Greenwood, Peter W., and Joan Petersilia, "The Criminal Investigation Process—Volume I: Summary and Policy Implications," The Rand Corporation, Santa Monica, Calif., 1975.

Greenwood, Peter W., et al., "The Criminal Investigation Process—Volume III: Observations and Analysis," The Rand Corporation, Santa Monica, Calif., 1975.

Guidelines for the Establishment of a State Law Enforcement Planning Agency for the Commonwealth of Massachusetts, Part I, International Association of Chiefs of Police, Washington, D.C., 1968.

Gulick, Luther, *Papers on the Science of Administration*, Institute of Public Administration, New York, 1937.

Hansen, David A., and Thomas R. Culley, *The Police Training Officer*, Charles C Thomas, Publisher, Springfield, Ill., 1973.

Hansen, G. R., and W. G. Leflang, "Application of Automatic Vehicle Location in Law Enforcement—An Introductory Planning Guide," Jet Propulsion Laboratory, California Institute of Technology, for National Criminal Justice Information and Statistics Service, Law Enforcement Assistance Administration, U.S. Department of Justice, Jan. 15, 1976.

Holcomb, Richard L., *Selection of Police Officers*, Bureau of Public Affairs, University of Iowa, Iowa City, 1946.

Hoover, Larry T., *Police Educational Characteristics and Curricula*, National Institute of Law Enforcement and Criminal Justice, Law Enforcement Assistance Administration, U.S. Department of Justice, Washington, D.C., July 1975.

Horton, Raymond D., "Productivity and Productivity Bargaining in Government: A Critical Analysis," Public Administration Review No. 4, July–August 1976.

The IACP-UCR Audit/Evaluation Manual, Technical Research Services Division, International Association of Chiefs of Police, Gaithersburg, Md., 1976.

Iannone, N. F., *Supervision of Police Personnel*, 2d ed., Prentice-Hall, Inc., Englewood Cliffs, N.J., 1975.

International Association of Chiefs of Police, *Equipment Technology Center* (monograph), IACP, Gaithersburg, Md., 1976.

International Association of Chiefs of Police, "The Police Chief Executive Report," Law Enforcement Assistance Administration, U.S. Department of Justice, Washington, D.C., 1976.

International Association of Chiefs of Police, *The Police Yearbook 1974*, IACP, Gaithersburg, Md., 1974.

International Association of Chiefs of Police, *The Police Yearbook 1975*, IACP, Gaithersburg, Md., 1975.

BIBLIOGRAPHY

International Association of Chiefs of Police, *The Police Yearbook 1976*, IACP, Gaithersburg, Md., 1976.

International City Management Association, "Public Safety Departments: Combining the Police and Fire Functions," *Management Information Service Report*, Washington, D.C., July 1976.

Interoffice memo dated Jan. 30, 1975 by Richard N. Harris, Chairman of the National Conference of State Criminal Justice Planning Administrators,

"An Investigation of Bingo Operations in New York State," a report by the New York State Commission of Investigation, December 1961.

Kelling, George L., et al., "The Kansas City Preventive Patrol Experiment— A Summary Report," Police Foundation, Washington, D.C., October 1974.

Kelly, Michael J., *Police Chief Selection—A Handbook for Local Government*, Police Foundation and International City Management Association, Washington, D.C., December 1975.

Kenney, John P., "Team Policing Organization: A Theoretical Model," *Police*, August 1972.

Kooken, Don L., *Ethics in Police Service*, Charles C Thomas, Publisher, Springfield, Ill., 1957.

Koontz, Harold, and Cyril O'Donnell, *Management: A Systems and Contingency Analysis of Managerial Functions*, 6th ed., McGraw-Hill Book Company, New York, 1976.

Koverman, Robert B., "Team Policing: An Alternative to Traditional Law Enforcement Techniques," *Journal of Police Science and Administration*, 1974.

Lamb, William F., "Police Communications: A Pragmatic Concept," *Law & Order*, February 1976, p. 42.

"LAPD Returning to Old Ways—Almost," *Law Enforcement Journal*, April 1975.

"LEAA Withdraws 'Dedicated Computer' Requirement for Criminal History Data Banks," *Criminal Justice Newsletter*, National Council on Crime and Delinquency, Vol. 6, No. 22, November 1975.

Lee, W. L. M., *History of the English Police*, Methuen & Co., Ltd., London, 1901.

Likert, Rensis, *The Human Organization*, McGraw-Hill Book Company, New York, 1967.

Lynch, Ronald G., *The Police Manager*, Holbrook Press, Inc., Boston, 1975.

Mark, Sir Robert, "Cornerstones of Excellence," monograph of a speech at the Executive Forum on Upgrading the Police, The Police Foundation, Washington, D.C., Apr. 13, 1976.

Martin, Edgar E., et al., "Neighborhood Team Policing Proposal," Multnomah County Department of Public Safety, Portland, Oreg., 1975.

Maslow, A. H., *Eupsychian Management*, Richard D. Irwin, Inc., Homewood, Ill., 1965.

Maslow, A. H., *Motivation and Personality*, Harper & Row, New York, 1954.

Maslow, A. H., *The Farther Reaches of Human Nature*, The Viking Press, Inc., New York, 1971.

Maslow, A. H., *Religions, Values, and Peak-Experiences*, The Viking Press, New York, 1970.

McGregor, Douglas, *The Human Side of Enterprise*, McGraw-Hill Book Company, New York, 1960, p. 33.

Merewitz, Leonard, and Stephen H. Sosnick, *The Budget's New Clothes—A Critique of Planning—Programming—Budgeting and Benefit–Cost Analysis*, Markham Publishing Company, Chicago, 1971.

Metropolitan Washington Council of Governments, *1975 Division of Law Enforcement Programs*, Washington, D.C.

Midwest Research Institute, *Systems Analysis of Criminalistics Operations*, Grant NI-044, Department of Justice, Law Enforcement Assistance Administration, Washington, D.C., June 1970.

Mintz, Allen, and Georgette Bennett Sandler, "Instituting a Full-Service Orientation to Policing," *The Police Chief*, May 1974.

Morgan, Clifford T., and Richard A. King, *Introduction to Psychology*, McGraw-Hill Book Company, New York, 1950.

Murphy, Patrick V., "A Decade of Urban Police Problems," a speech delivered at the Sixteenth Annual Wherrett Lecture on Local Government, Institute for Urban Policy and Administration, University of Pittsburgh, 1974.

National Advisory Commission on Criminal Justice Standards and Goals, "A Call for Citizen Action: Crime Prevention and the Citizen," U.S. Government Printing Office, Washington, D.C., 1974.

National Advisory Commission on Criminal Justice Standards and Goals, "Report on Police," U.S. Government Printing Office, Washington, D.C., 1973.

The National Association of Citizens Crime Commissions, "How to Organize and Operate a Citizens Crime Commission," Atlanta, Ga., 1974.

National Institute of Law Enforcement and Criminal Justice, *A Compendium of Selected Criminal Justice Projects*, U.S. Department of Justice, Washington, D.C., June 1975.

National Institute of Law Enforcement and Criminal Justice, *Innovation in Law Enforcement*, Law Enforcement Assistance Administration, U.S. Department of Justice, Washington, D.C., June 1973.

National Institute of Law Enforcement and Criminal Justice, "Program Plan, Fiscal Year 1976," Law Enforcement Assistance Administration, U.S. Department of Justice, Washington, D.C., 1975.

Oberlander, Leonard, ed., "Quantitative Tools for Criminal Justice Planning," Law Enforcement Assistance Administration, U.S. Department of Justice, Washington, D.C., 1975.

"Opportunities for Improving Productivity in Police Services," National Commission on Productivity, Washington, D.C., 1973.

Ostrom, Elinor, and Dennis C. Smith, "On the Fate of 'Lilliputs' in Metropolitan Policing," *Public Administration Review*, No. 2, March–April 1976, p. 192.

Pate, Tony, et al., "Kansas City Peer Review Panel: An Evaluation Report," Midwest Research Institute and Police Foundation, 1976.

Pate, Tony, et al., "Three Approaches to Criminal Apprehension in Kansas City: An Evaluation Report," Midwest Research Institute and Police Foundation, 1976.

Peterson, Virgil W., "A Report on Chicago Crime for 1961," Chicago Crime Commission, 1962.

Peterson, Virgil W., "How to Form a Citizens Crime Commission," reprinted from the *Journal of Criminal Law, Criminology, and Police Science*, Vol. 46, No. 4, November–December 1955.

Reith, Charles, *A Short History of the British Police*, Oxford University Press, New York, 1948.

Roethlisberger, Fritz J., "The Human Equation in Employee Productivity," speech before the Personnel Group of the National Retail Dry Goods Association, 1950, as published in H. Koontz and C. O'Donnell, *Management: A Book of Readings*, McGraw-Hill Book Company, New York, 1964.

Rules and Regulations for the Department of Police, Cairo Ill. (undated).

"San Diego Field Interrogation—Final Report," John E. Boydstun (System Development Corporation), Police Foundation, Washington, D.C., 1975.

Savage, Edward H., *Boston Watch & Police*, J. E. Farwell and Company, Boston, 1865.

Schwartz, Alfred I., and Sumner N. Clarren, "Evaluation of Cincinnati's Community Sector Team Policing Program—A Progress Report: The First Six Months, Summary of Major Findings," The Urban Institute, Washington, D.C., 1974.

Sherman, Lawrence W., et al., "Team Policing—Seven Case Studies," Police Foundation, Washington, D.C., August 1973.

Skogan, Wesley G., "Efficiency and Effectiveness in Big-City Police Departments," *Public Administration Review*, No. 3, May–June 1976, p. 278.

Sohn, R. L., et al., "Multi-Community Command and Control Systems in Law Enforcement," Jet Propulsion Laboratory, California Institute of Technology, Pasadena, California, for National Criminal Justice Information and Statistics Service, Law Enforcement Assistance Administration, U.S. Department of Justice, 1976.

Stahl, O. Glenn, and Richard A. Staufenberger, eds., "Police Personnel Administration," Police Foundation, December 1974.

Standards for the Staffing and Organization of Municipal Narcotics and Dangerous Drug Enforcement Units, International Association of Chiefs of Police, Field Operations Division, Washington, D.C., 1970.

Stinchcomb, James D., *Opportunities in a Law Enforcement Career*, Universal Publishing and Distributing Corporation, New York, 1971.

Stinchcomb, James D., *Opportunities in Law Enforcement and Related Careers*, Vocational Guidance Materials, Louisville, Ky., 1976.

A Survey of the Police Department, Baltimore, Maryland, International Association of Chiefs of Police, Washington, D.C., December 1965.

A Survey of the Police Department, Chicago, Illinois, International Association of Chiefs of Police, Washington, D.C., June 1970.

A Survey of the Police Department, Dallas, Texas, International Association of Chiefs of Police, Washington, D.C., September 1967.

Tanzler, Hans, et al., "Crime—Have We Lost Control? A Reassessment," *Nation's Cities,* December 1975.

"Teams Work Better than Traditional Ways," *Law Enforcement Journal,* April 1975.

U.S. Advisory Commission on Intergovernmental Relations, *Safe Streets Reconsidered: The Block Grant Experience,* 1968–1975, U.S. Government Printing Office, Washington, D.C., 1976.

Weston, Paul B., *Police Organization and Management,* Goodyear Publishing Co., Pacific Palisades, Calif., 1976.

Weston, Paul B., *The Police Traffic Control Function,* 2d ed., Charles C Thomas, Publisher, Springfield, Ill., 1968.

Weston, Paul B., and Kenneth M. Wells, *Criminal Justice: Introduction and Guidelines,* Goodyear Publishing Co., Pacific Palisades, Calif., 1976.

"What You Need to Know about Labor Relations: Guidelines for Elected and Appointed Officials," Labor-Management Relations Service, 1974.

Whisenand, Paul M., *Police Supervision, Theory and Practice,* 2d ed., Prentice-Hall, Inc., Englewood Cliffs, N.J., 1976.

Wilson, James Q., *Thinking about Crime,* Basic Books, Inc., New York, 1975.

Wolfle, Joan L., and John F. Heaphy, eds., "Readings on Productivity in Policing," Police Foundation, Washington, D.C., 1975.

Zinberg, Norman E., M.D., "High States—A Beginning Study," The Drug Abuse Council, Inc., Washington, D.C., 1974.

Index

Index

Index

Abandoned automobiles, 523
Aberdeen, Scotland, Police Department, 316
Abstract research, 178
Accessories for police automobiles, 539
Accident rate, 438
Accidents:
  investigation of, 455–457
  investigators of, 456
"Accordion effect" in traffic, 443
Account numbering in budgeting, 190, 568
Accountability of command, 201
Accounting procedures, 193
Achievement tests, 261
Acting chief, 135
Acting supervisors, 277
Activity report:
  daily, 565, 571
  monthly, 573
Adjustment of cases, 413
Administration:
  definition of, 60
  principles of organizational concepts in, 73–86
Administration of Justice, Survey of the, 13

Administrative filing, 194
Administrative function, organization of, 98–101
Administrative principles, 73–86
Administrative records, 194
Administrative reporting, 195
Administrative services bureau, organization of, 112
Administrative supervision, 131, 134
Administrative units, separate, 98
Advancement (*see* Promotion)
Advantages of specialization, 93
Advertisements:
  in recruitment, 252
  (*See also* Public education)
Advisory Commission on Intergovernmental Relations, 45
Affirmative action (*see* Minority recruiting)
AFSCME (AFL–CIO), 284
Age, as eligibility requirement, 254
Agent, police, 292, 351
Agility testing, 264
Aide to chief, 98
Air conditioning, 540

INDEX

Alarm systems, 342
Alcohol Safety Action Program (ASAP), 446
Alcoholic beverage control, 408
Alexandria, Virginia, police department, 55
Allocation of manpower, 357–362, 658
  definition of, 357
  in hazardous or high-crime regions, 361
  methods used for, 633–671
  as planning task, 169
Alphabetical index for records, 477
American Academy for Professional Law
    Enforcement, 289
American Association of Community and Junior
    Colleges, 307
American Association of Retired Persons, 236
American Bar Association, 12
American Bar Foundation, 13, 562
American Correctional Association, 511
Ammunition, 544
  reloading of, 521
Analysis:
  crime analysis, 175
  operations analysis, 164
  organizational, 86
  in planning, 164
  strategic, 176
  tactical, 176
  in traffic, 440
Animal shelter, 103, 523
Annual leave, 282
Annual report, 196
Appeal from disciplinary action of chief, 216
Appearance of officers, 203
Application of organizational principles, 86–97
Applications for police service, 257
  closing date for filing, 257
Applied research, 178
Appointment in personnel selection, 269
Appraisal of intangibles:
  in character investigation, 267
  by inspector, 208
  in personal qualities, by oral board, 268
Aptitude tests, 261
Architecture, police, 526
Area, definition of, 72
Arlington, Virginia, police department, 268, 282,
    309, 341, 343, 576
Armaments, 542–547
Armor, 546
Armorer, 521
Aronson, J. Richard, 188*n*.
Arrest:
  as factor in patrol distribution, 359
  index of, in traffic, 454

Arrest:
  records of, 474–476, 481
  techniques in, 345
Assaults on police (*see* Attacks on police)
Assembly rooms, 537
Assessment centers, 297
Assignment/availability factor, 663
Assignments:
  to beats, 327
  detective, 372
  to shifts, 328
Assistance to citizens, by beat officer, 321
Assistant chief of police:
  as acting chief of police, 135
  coordination by, at night, 130
  disadvantage of a single assistant, 91
Associated Public-Safety Communication's
    Officers, 289
Associations, employee, 289
Attacks on police, 9, 337
  protection against, 466, 531
Attitude:
  of driver, 441
  friendly, development of, 119, 224
  of police and public, 223
Audible recalls, 493
Authoritative (or line) and staff inspections, 203
Authority:
  delegation of, 83, 201, 205
  for detention, release, and restriction of
    prisoners, 512
  exercise of, 79, 128
  organization by level of, 76
  by regulation, 80
  of unit heads, 83
Automatic pistol, 543
Automatic vehicle locators, 497–499
Automobile patrol, 332, 335
  versus foot patrol, 335
Automobile pound, 103
Automobiles, police, 539
  leasing of, 541
  maintenance of, 519
  number of, 540
  ownership of, 343, 541
  replacement of, 541
Auxiliary functions, definition of, 61
Auxiliary services, 61, 101, 459–550

Background investigation in selection, 265
Baerwald, John, 439*n*.
Bail, restrictions on, 512

INDEX

685

Baltimore, Maryland, police department, 155*n.*, 164, 296, 303, 609
Basic car plan, 317
Basic research, 178
Batch processing, definition of, 500
Baton, police, 546
Beat:
  definition of, 72
  frequent change of, 327
  knowledge of, 353
  layout of, 649, 662
Beat-officer responsibility system, 350
Beck, George N., 587*n.*
Behavioral aspects of management, 66, 149–156
Behavioral research, 179
Bender-Gestalt test, 263
Benefits, personnel, 281–284
Berkeley, California, Police Department, 259, 274, 293, 304, 340, 350, 470, 585*n.*, 613, 657
Bicycle control, 446
Bicycle patrol, 333
Biomedical solutions to crime, 180
Black police officers associations, 289
Blazers, 548
Bloch, Peter B., 318*n.*
"Blue flu," 284
Board, oral, 267
Boeing Company, 498
Bombings, as threat to police buildings, 531
Bombs, disposal of, 550
Booking of prisoners, 515
  headquarters facility for, 534
Boston Police Department, 92, 283
Bribery of police (*see* Corruption)
Bristow, Allen P., 153*n.*
British police:
  consolidation of, 53
  modus operandi searches by, 376
  principles of, 37
  service given by, 219
  unit-beat policing by, 294, 316
Broadcasting, decentralized, 488
Brutality, allegations of, 514, 146
Budget, 182–193
  conventional, 187
  departmental-type, 185
  functional, 187
  justification of, 188
  line-item, 185
  object, 185
  performance, 186
  planning of, 169

Budget:
  program, 186, 546–570
    (*See also* Program budgeting)
  zero-base, 187, 191
Budget office, need for, 99
Buildings, 525–538
  design of, 526–538
  maintenance of, 518
  security of, 466, 530, 531
    (*See also* Headquarters arrangement)
Bulletin:
  daily, 474
  prepared by clerk, 483
Bureau, definition of, 71
Bureau of the Budget, U.S., 565
Business-crime prevention, 424

Caliber of sidearm, 544
California Commission on Peace Officer Standards and Training, 256*n.*, 292*n.*, 296, 297
Call-box system, 487, 493
Called-for services:
  definition of, 347
  as measure of patrol need, 360, 633
Canine corps, 429
Car locators, 497–499
Career development, 290–297
Case, police, definition of, 467
Case files, 465
Case screening, 372
CCH (Computerized Criminal History Program), 502
Central personnel agency, 247
Central services division:
  functions of, 521
  need for, 103
Centralization of records, 464
Centrex system, 489
Certification, 295
Chain of command, 79, 124
Chamber of Commerce, U.S., 236, 239
Changes:
  in organizational structure, 86
  in police methods, 10
Character investigation, 265–267
Charlotte, North Carolina, Police Department, 132, 294, 317, 343, 496
Charts:
  of accomplishment, 197
  organizational (*see* Organizational structure)
Checklist for comprehensive law enforcement planning, 571

686   INDEX

Chicago Police Department, 165, 176, 240, 303, 351, 547
Chief of police:
  approval of plans by, 160
  authority vested in, 21
  inspection by, 204
  as leader in community, 30
  relationship of, to mayor or manager, 18
  responsibility of, for personnel management, 246
  role of, in collective bargaining, 287
Children and police (*see* Delinquency prevention)
Cincinnati, Ohio, Police Department, 240, 316, 343
Citation, traffic, 449
Citizen complaints (*see* Complaints)
Citizen organizations, 235
City councils, relationship of, with chief of police, 19
City manager, relationship of, with chief of police, 19, 32
Civic associations, 34
Civil disorders:
  containment and control, 431–434
  equipment used in, 545
  prevention of, 431–433
  radicalism by youth in, 433
  tactical force, use in, 429
Civil Disorders, National Advisory Commission on, 12, 432
Civil rights in investigations, 375
Civil service commissions, 248
Civil service reform, 247
Civilian employees, 249
  definition of, 73
  supervision of, 145
  use of, to relieve officers, 249
Civilian review boards, 212
Clark, Ramsey, 5*n.*
Classification of incidents, 473
Closing date in personnel recruitment, 257
Clubs, police-sponsored, 422
Code of ethics, 8
Code numbering in budgeting, 190, 568
Codes in radio broadcasts, 343
Collective bargaining, 284
College programs in law enforcement education, 306–308
  (*See also* Education)
Command, 124–135
  accountability of, 201
  chain of, 79, 124
  definition of, 124

Command:
  departmentwide, 129
  direction by, 124
  of district station, 132
  of division, 130
  during full mobilization, 130
  line, definition of, 128
  outside pyramid of authority, 79, 135
  rule of, 83
  staff, definition of, 128
  unity of, 80
Command and control systems in dispatching, 179, 494–495
Command post:
  department, 129
  in emergency, 173
Command presence, 118
Commanding officer, definition of, 73
Commendation by chief, 122
Commercialized vice, 390
Commission(s):
  California Commission on Peace Officer Standards and Training, 256*n.*, 292*n.*
  crime, 390
  National Advisory Commission on Civil Disorders, 12
  National Commission on the Causes and Prevention of Violence, 12
  peace-officer standards and training commissions, 297
  police, 22
  President's Commission on Crime in the District of Columbia, 361
  President's Commission on Law Enforcement and Administration of Justice, 12, 292
  Wickersham Commission, 13
Commission form of government, 22
Commissioner of police, 23
Communication of public needs to the police, 235
Communications:
  dispatching in, 483, 485, 491, 494
  district station, 486
  duties of communications personnel, 483–486
  informal, 156
  interoffice communications, 484
  in personal relations, 153
  security of premises in, 466, 531
Communications division:
  need for, 101, 465
  organization of, 479
Communications equipment, 488, 541
Communications scramblers, 343
Community control, 27, 344

INDEX   687

Community councils for delinquency prevention, 421
Community leadership, 30–38
Community organizations, 235–239
Community relations, 221–243, 425
  division for: organization of, 240
    responsibilities of, 240
Community service officer, 292
Compensatory time, 281
Complaint clerk, 485
Complaint-control form, 467
Complaint desk, definition of, 483
Complaint recording and processing, 467–472
Complaints:
  of crimes, 467, 492
    control of, 467
    receipt of, in district station, 481
    telephoned, 486
  against department, 222
  against officers, 212
    investigation of, 215
    registration of, 214
Completed staff work in planning, 160
Comprehensive law enforcement planning, 40, 50, 170
  checklist for, 551
Computer-assisted dispatching, 180, 468, 494
Computer-based information systems, 499–502
Computer files, 501
Computer technology in planning, 168
Computerized Criminal History Program (CCH), 502
Conferences, 122
  between chief of police and grievance committees, 290
  and inspector, 207
  and press, 228
  staff, 141–143
Confidence:
  in chief of police, promotion of, 120
  expressed toward subordinates, 123
Congestion assignments in traffic, 451
Connelly, J. Campbell, 155n.
Consolidated daily report, 195, 571
Consolidation of services, 51
Conspicuous patrol car, 339
Consulting as a method for planning, 171
Contingency plans, 173
Contract negotiation in collective bargaining, 288
Contract services, 55
Control:
  channels of, 124
  definition of, 201
  deviation from lines of, 85

Control:
  of dispatching, 486
  through inspection, 201–211
  through internal investigation, 211–220
  points of, in inspection, 209
  rule of, 201
  span of, 81
Coordination:
  of decentralized divisions, 132
  with district station, 132
  of functional units, 127
  of geographical patrol units, 125
  by operating personnel, 131
  of platoons, 125
  with team policing, 128
Corruption, 14, 247, 385
  of police, 218–220
    factors relating to, 212
    investigation of, 213
    by organized crime, 385
    prevention of, 219–220
Cost of treatment of traffic violators, 448
Cost effectiveness in budgeting, 189
Counter-crime clinic, 424
County police organizational structure, 115
Courts:
  attempts to discipline police by, 10
  police relationships with, 57, 445, 454
Covina, California, Police Department, 241
Credit-card crimes, 383
Crime:
  etiology of, 5
  organized, 384–386
  white-collar, 5
Crime analysis, 175
Crime commission, 390–392
Crime Control Act (see Omnibus Crime Control and Safe Streets Act)
Crime hazards, 351
Crime investigation, 363–383
Crime laboratory, 503–509
Crime prevention, 4, 410, 424
Crime prevention bureau, organization of, 105–106
Crime problem, 4
Crime resistance, 424
  definition of, 410
  news coverage relating to, 231
Crime-scene search, 375, 507
Crime suppression, 410
Crimes:
  in business, 5
  against persons, 380
  in progress, 342
  against property, 381

688 INDEX

Criminal identification, 474, 475, 516
Criminal investigation division, 363–383
   organization of, 365–369
   (*See also* Detective division; Investigation)
Criminal justice:
   planning agencies, 41
      organization of, 45
      regional planning by, 50
   planning guidelines, 40, 551
Criminal justice coordinating council, 58
Criminal Justice Standards and Goals, National
   Advisory Commission on, 12
Criminal justice system, 11, 15
   information systems within, 499–502
   local plan for, 58
Criminalist, 507
Criminality:
   cause and prevention of, 4–6, 411
   etiology of, 5
   genetic factors in, 5
Crosswalk duty, 451
Curriculum:
   called-for services, 347
   in law enforcement education, 307–308
   for training, 303, 609
Custody of prisoners, 510–518

Daily activity report, 189, 566–567
Daily bulletin, 474, 483
Daily report, 195, 573–575
Dallas Police Department, 132, 141*n.*, 495, 613
Dangerous drugs, 401–404
Data processing division, 102, 167
Data processing function in planning, 167, 168
Davis, Edward M., 12, 142*n.*, 317*n.*
Decentralization:
   of command, 132
   of police, in team policing, 132, 316
   of radio broadcasting, 488
   of records, 464
Decision making, human factors in, 152
Decision package in budgeting, 191
Decoy unit, 429
Delegation of authority, 83, 198, 201
   by department regulations, 80
Delinquency Control Institute, 311
Delinquency prevention:
   community councils for, 421
   community organization for, 235
   by neighborhood youth councils, 421, 577
   by patrol officers, 356, 577
   by youth division, 413–423
Democracy in leadership, 123, 151–152

Demonstrations:
   control of, 431–434
   special police, as public relations activity, 234
Departmental goals and objectives, 576
Deployment of patrol, 341
Desk duties in communications, 483
Desk officer, problem of, 532
Detective division:
   need for, 106
   organization and staffing of, 365–369
   (*See also* Criminal investigation division;
      Investigation)
Detective operations:
   assignment of, 372
   hours of duty, 371
   planning of, 370
   selection, rank, and pay, 368
   supervision of, 373
   use of women in, 367
   (*See also* Investigation)
Detention, authority for, 512
Detroit Police Department, 52, 334, 532
Deutsch, Karl W., 227*n.*
Diagnosis of predisposition toward crime or
   violence, 180
Digital terminals (*see* Terminals)
Direction, 117–148
   by command, 124
   coordination in, 12
   definition of, 61
   verbal direction, 141–143
   written direction, 136–141
Directive system, 136–143
   verbal direction, 141
   written directives, 136
Disability, 284
Discharge (*see* Separation from police service)
Disciplinary action, 145, 215–218
   documentation of, 148
   forms of, 146
Discipline:
   definition of, 145
   responsibility of supervisor in, 146
Discrimination:
   ethnic, 9
   racial, 6, 14, 180, 248, 289, 411, 432
Dispatcher, 483, 485, 491, 494
   and complaint clerk, 483, 491
   in district station, 486
   maps for, 485, 496
   physical location of, 466, 531
Displays, police, 234, 426
Dissemination of information among police,
   473

INDEX

Distribution of patrol force, 357–361, 633–671
  definition of, 357
  methods used for, 359–362, 633–671
  as planning task, 169
District, definition of, 72
District of Columbia Police Department, 208, 213, 251, 309, 334, 382
District commander:
  as coordinator of specialist's work, 130
  responsibility of, in vice control, 397
District station:
  communications systems for, 486
  need for, 107
  records in, 481
District station command, 130
District station desk, 486
District team policing, 316
  (*See also* Team policing)
Diversion, 413, 420
Division:
  definition of, 71
  (*See also specific divisions*)
Dogs, police, 429
Double parking, 458
Drinking drivers, 450
  schools for, 446
Driver attitude, 441
Driver education, 448
Driver index, 478
Drucker, Peter, 66
Drug abuse (*see* Narcotics and dangerous drugs)
Drug Enforcement Administration, 89
  (*See also* Narcotics and dangerous drugs)
Duties:
  administrative, 52–53
  similar or related, 74
  staff, 61
Duty manual, 138
DuVries, Henri L., 264*n*.

Education, 306–311
  as entrance requirement, 255
  public (*see* Public education)
Educational incentive plans, 308
Educational Testing Service, 261
Efficiency, test of, 160
Electric power supply at headquarters, 550
Elements of criminal offenses, 378
Eligibility standards for recruitment, 253–258
Emergency equipment, 539, 550
Emergency plans, 173
Emergency response, 345
Empathy training, 241

Employee associations, 284
Enforcement in traffic, 446–455
Enforcement index, 454
Enforcement policy in traffic, guides for, 451
Enforcement tolerance, 447
Engineering, traffic, 439
Environmental influences in criminality, 6
Equipment:
  armament, 542–546
  for communications, 541
  for disposal of explosives, 550
  for emergency use, 549
  for the laboratory, 549
  office, 548
  personal, 542
  protective, 546–547
  uniforms, 547–548
  for vehicles, 539
Esprit de corps, 93, 123, 252
Ethics, police code of, 8
Etiology of crime, 5
Evaluation:
  of personnel, 272–274, 585–605
  of police practices, 160, 202
Evidence:
  collection and preservation of, 507–509
  custody of, 522
  and recovered property section, 103, 522
Evidence technicians, 376, 507–509
  in accident investigation, 456, 508
  equipment for, 535, 549
  relation of, to beat officer, 508
  supervision of, 509
Examinations in selection process (*see* Selection)
Executive aide, 98
Exempt ranks, 278
Exhibits, police, 234
Experimental research, 177
Explosives and explosive devices, disposal of, 550

Facilities, police (*see* Buildings)
Fair Labor Standards Act, 281
Fairfax County, Virginia, Police Department, 55
Fayol, Henri, 63
Federal Bureau of Investigation, 52, 291, 300, 302, 412, 431, 473, 501, 571
  National Academy of, 300, 311
Federal law enforcement planning, 39
Fencing of stolen property, 381
Field inspection (*see* Inspection)
Field interrogation and interviewing, 347

690 INDEX

Field operations analysis, 175
Field operations bureau, organization of, 104, 112
Field recruiting, 252
Field reporting, 468
Field training, 304
Field training guide, 304, 613–629
Files, 462
  (See also specific entries)
Filing:
  of administrative records, 194
  of index cards, 477
Finance office, need for, 99
Financial statements, 194
Fingerprint records, 475
Fingerprinting:
  automated search in, 180
  in district stations, 481
  of juveniles, 415
  policy for, 475–476
  of prisoners, 476
Firearms, 542–544
  range, 537
Fiscal management through records, 463
  (See also Budget)
Fiscal plans, 169
Fiscal statements, 194
Fixed shifts, 328
Fleet Location and Information Reporting
  (FLAIR), 498
Fleet maintenance, 519
Flexibility:
  in assignment to key positions, 89
  in leadership, 24, 150
  in organizational structure, 89
Florida Crime Information Center, 500–501
Follow-up investigations:
  by investigators, 363, 371
  by patrol officers, 294, 350–351
  by traffic accident investigators, 457
Foot patrol, 332, 335
Formal directive system, 136
Forms for incident reports, 469–470
Forms control in planning, 164
Four-day workweek, 282
Freedom of Information Act, 475
Freeways, problems of, in traffic control, 443
Frequency shift keying, 180
Function(s):
  definition of administrative and line, 60
  organization by, 75
Functional supervision, 205
Functional units:
  coordination of, 127
  definition of, 71

Gabard, E. Caroline, 153n.
Gambling, 399–401
Garage, police, 538
Gas equipment, 545
General duty manual, 139
General orders, definition of, 139
General patrol service (see Patrol)
Genetic factors in criminality, 5
Geographical organization of police force, 75
George Washington University, 565
Goal-setting, 35, 576
Goals:
  definition of, 137
  of law enforcement, 13
Goldstein, Herman, 219n.
Grades of rank, 280
Graft by police (see Corruption, of police)
Grievance procedures, 289
Griggs v. Duke Power Co., 260
Group attitudes as a factor in management, 151
Grouping of similar tasks, 74
Guides, guidelines (see specific entries)
Guilford-Zimmerman Temperament Survey, 263
Gulick, Luther, 60, 199n.
Guns:
  cabinets for, 538
  gas, 545
  (See also Weapons, police)

Harbor patrol, 430
Hawthorne experiments, 152
Hazard factors, 352
Hazard-oriented patrol, 323, 347
Hazards:
  in allocation and distribution of manpower, 359
  inspection of, 359
  police, definition of, 351
  traffic, study of, 354
Headquarters arrangement:
  for handling and booking of prisoners, 515, 534
  for public convenience, 532, 535
  for records, 533
Health insurance, 281
Heaphy, John F., 411n.
Height requirements, 255
Helicopters, 334
Helmets, riot, 546
Heroin, 7, 401
Hierarchy:
  channels of communication within, 79
  of command, 79, 124
  of needs, 66
  of rank, 70

INDEX

691

High-risk situations:
for police officers, 337, 342
for youth, 418
Highway patrol organizations, structure of, 116
Hit-and-run accidents, 457
Holcomb, Richard L., 265*n.*
Holidays, compensation for, 282
Horse patrol, 335
Hostage situations, 431
Hours of duty:
for detectives, 371
for vice-division members, 106
(*See also* Shift hours, selection of)
Householders, services to, 353
Hoy, Vernon, 12
Human relations in management, 149
Huntington Beach, California, Police
Department, 282

IACP (*see* International Association of Chiefs of Police)
Identification officer and the laboratory, 506
Identification records, 475
in district stations, 481
Illumination in police building, 529
Importance of job as influence on specialization, 95
Imprinting of personality characteristics, 5, 180
Inbau, Fred E., 506*n.*
Incentive pay for education, 308–310
Incentive plans for recruitment, 253
Incident-report forms, 469–470
Incidents:
classification of, 473
immediate registration of, 482
to be recorded, 472
Index of enforcement in traffic, 454
Index crimes, 473
Indexing of records, 477
Indianapolis Police Department, 341
Informal leader, 156
Informants, 379
Information:
dissemination of, among police, 473
privacy of, 475
supplying of, 355
Information counter, location of, 532
Information division, need for, 102
Information system:
in management, 182–197
in records, 461
Information tests, 261

Informing the public, 224–235
Ingersoll, John E., 401
Injured prisoners, 514
Injury on duty, 282
Injustice, as contributing factor in delinquency, 242, 411
Inmates (*see* Prisoners)
In-service training, 304–306
Inspection, 201–211
authoritative, 203
checklist for, 582
control by, 201
of hazards, 354
in allocation and distribution of manpower, 360
as a patrol activity, 347
of jail, 517
line inspection, 203–204
need for, 202
procedures, 211
purpose and nature of, 202, 582
scope of, 202
staff inspection, 203, 205
by staff unit, 206
standards, 211
of stores, 354
as tool of planning, 202
of vacant homes, 354
by vice division, 396
by youth division, 419
Inspection reports, review of line reports by staff.
officers, 209
Inspectional services, 198–220
definition of, 199
organization of, 103–104, 199
Inspections unit, 199
need for, 104
Inspector, staff: duties of, 206, 584
relationship of, with personnel, 206
Institutional-style department, 245
Instructional material, as part of directive system, 140
Insurance, 281
Integration of telephone system with radio, 491
Intelligence function:
administration of, 398
relation to other inspectional services, 392
Intelligence unit, 397
Interference in departmental matters by councilmen, 24
Internal investigation, 211–218
disciplinary action, 215
need for, 211
organization of, 212
process of, 213

INDEX

International Association of Chiefs of Police (IACP), 8, 13, 16, 60, 138, 141*n.*, 165, 167*n.*, 176, 190, 240, 274, 289, 297, 301, 309, 310, 335, 357, 361, 377*n.*, 404, 412, 433, 436, 473, 551, 565, 571, 585, 630, 657
International Association for Identification, 289
International Brotherhood of Teamsters, 285
International City Management Association, 16, 188*n.*, 250, 276, 284, 523*n.*
Interpersonal aspects of management, 149–156
Interrogation:
  field, by patrol officers, 347
  by investigators, 374
Interrogation room, 531
Intersection duty, 451
Interviewing:
  field, by patrol officers, 347
  by investigators, 374
Investigation:
  of accidents, 455–457
  case-screening in, 371
  of character, 265–267
  of crimes, 363–383
  by detectives: follow-up, 350, 364
    immediate, 370
    of youth-committed crimes, 419
  facilitated by records, 462
  follow-up, by patrol officers, 350
  initial, 348
  internal, 211–215
  methods of, 374
  preliminary, 348–350
  procedures for, 379–383
  responsibility of patrol officers for, 348–351
  by youth division, 419
Investigation function, organization and staffing, 365–369
  (*See also* Detective division)
Invoices, 193
Issues, avoidance and meeting of, 25

Jail:
  administration of, 510–518
  inspection of, 517
  operational policies for, 511
Jail division, separate, need for, 102
Jail duties, 515–518
"Job actions," 284
Job-relatedness, 260
Johnson, Lyndon B., 12
Judicial function, relationships of police to, 57
Junior traffic patrols, 444
Justice, system of, 11

Jurgensen, Clifford E., 587*n.*
Juvenile delinquency (*see* Delinquency prevention)
Juvenile division (*see* Youth division)

Kansas City Patrol Experiment, 322
Kansas City Police Department, 322
Keys:
  automobile, 540
  police building, 530
King, Martin Luther, Jr., 361, 431
Kooken, Don L., 9*n.*
Kuntz, H., 63*n.*

Labor relations, 284–290
Laboratory, police, 503–509
  equipment in, 503
  location of, 537
  need for, 102
Lambda Alpha Epsilon, 289
Lancastershire constabulary, 316
Lateral entry into police service, 284, 295
Law Enforcement Assistance Administration (LEAA), 12, 44, 178, 180, 335
Law Enforcement Education Program, 309
Law enforcement planning, 41
  checklist for, 551
  (*See also* Criminal justice, planning agencies; Criminal justice, planning guidelines)
Law Enforcement Teletype System (LETS), 501
LEAA (*see* Law Enforcement Assistance Administration)
Leader, confidence in, and loyalty to, 120
Leadership:
  attributes of, 120
  in community, 30–38
  in community organization, 239
  definition of, 61, 118
  democracy in, 123
  outside department, 30–38
  within department, 117–120
  flexibility in, 26, 150
Leading versus commanding, 118
Leasing of police vehicles, 541
Leave (*see* Annual leave; Sick leave)
Lee, W. L. M., 92*n.*
Legal advisor, 58
  need for, 100
Legislation:
  leadership role of chief in, 32
  in traffic, 455
Length of service, as factor in promotions, 275

INDEX 693

LETS (Law Enforcement Teletype System), 501
Level of authority, organization by, 76
Lie detector (*see* Polygraph)
Light in police building, 529
Lights, recall, 493
Lincolnshire constabulary, 316
Line command, definition of, 128
Line functions, definition of, 60
Line inspection, 203
Line-item budgeting, 185
Line officers, inspections by, 204
Lines of authority, 79
Lines of control, 124
  deviation from, 85
Lineups, 380
Liquor control, 408
Loan sharking, 387
Locks in police building, 530
Longevity pay, 279
LORAN (long-range navigation), 498
Los Angeles County Sheriff's Department, 46, 334
Los Angeles Police Department, 12, 212, 294, 317, 343
Loud speakers (*see* Public-address equipment)
Loyalty:
  to employees, 121, 123
  promotion of, 120

McGregor, Douglas, 65
McLaren, Roy C., 576, 656*n.*
Magnum calibers in firearms, 544
Mail delivery, 103, 523
Mailboxes in police building, 533
Maintenance:
  of automobiles, 519
  of buildings, 518
  of radios, 521
  of traffic-control devices, 438, 538
Maintenance division, need for, 103
Management:
  by objectives, 64, 65
  of investigations, 369
  theory of, 63
Management behavior, 66
Management certificates, 296
Management consulting as a method for planning, 171
Management-information systems, 182–197
Management plans, 168
Manpower, allocation and distribution of, 359–362, 633–671
Manuals, 138

Maps:
  dispatching, 496
  spot, 164, 197
Marine unit, 430
Marked cards, 339
Martensen, Kai R., 613
Maslow, Abraham, 65
Massage parlors, 405
Mayor, relationship of, to chief of police, 19, 32
Measures of accomplishment, 197, 463
Medical program for police welfare, 282
Medical standards for selection, 264
Memoranda, as a part of directive system, 140
Merchants, services to, 353
Methadone, 403
Metropolitan Police Department, Washington, D.C., 208, 213, 251, 309, 334, 382
Meuhleisen, Gene S., 292*n.*
Midwest Research Institute, 504
Minimum standards and training, 297
Minnesota Multiphasic Personality Inventory, 263
Minority recruiting, 54
Mission, as statement of broad goals, 576
Mobile teleprinters, 180
Mobilization, command during, 130, 346
Model organizational structures, 109–115
Model police ordinance, 17
Modus operandi searches:
  in crime investigation, 376
  in relation to crime analysis, 175
Monthly report, 196, 573
Moral laws, 385
Morale, 123, 143, 145, 151, 202, 252
Motivation:
  determination of, in selection, 266
  theory of, 66–68
Motor-vehicle maintenance, 519
Motorcycles, 333, 335
Moving traffic, regulation of, 452
Moving violations, 454
Murphy, Patrick V., 219, 411

Name index for records, 477
Narcotics and dangerous drugs, 7, 401–404
National Academy of the FBI, 300, 311
National Advisory Commission on Civil Disorders, 12, 432
National Advisory Commission on Criminal Justice Standards and Goals, 12, 237, 255, 294, 310, 317, 511
National Association of Citizens Crime Commissions, 238

694 INDEX

National Commission on the Causes and Prevention of Violence, 12
National Commission on Productivity, 12
National Conference of State Criminal Justice Planning Administrators, 41
National Council on Crime and Delinquency, 236, 239
National Crime Information Center, 495, 500
National Crime Prevention Institute, 300
National Institute of Law Enforcement and Criminal Justice, 180, 318
National League of Cities, 16
National Safety Council, 239
NCIC (see National Crime Information Center)
Negative reinforcement, 67
Neighborhood control:
of police, 27, 344
as a tool in crime investigation, 376
Neighborhood team policing, 316
(See also Team policing)
Neighborhood youth councils, 421, 577
New Haven Police Department, 323
New Jersey Police Administrative Services Bureau, 297
New Jersey Police Training Commission, 297
News release procedures, 231
Newspaper assistance in public information, 226
New York City Police Department, 334, 411
Noncriminal incidents and services, 8, 321, 351
Nonlethal weaponry, 180, 546
Northwestern University Traffic Institute, 300, 311
Notice of violation, 449
Notification of parents, 416
Novato, California, Police Department, 477

Oakland, California, Police Department, 657
Object budgeting, 185
Objectives of department, 576
O'Donnell, C., 63n.
Odor-sensing devices, 180
Off-duty use of police vehicles, 340
Offender-based transaction system (OBTS), 502
Off-line information, definition of, 500
Office equipment, 549
Office of Law Enforcement Assistance, 12
Officer, individual, in public relations, 223
Officers, police, definition of, 73
Offices, police location of, 535
Onnibus Crime Control and Safe Streets Act, 12, 40

One man versus two men in patrol car, 337
On-line information, definition of, 500
Open selection, 262
Operational functions:
definition of, 60
organization of, 104–109
Operational plans, 171
Operations, 313–458
definition of, 60
Operations analysis function in planning, 165, 175
Operations research function, 166
Oral interviews, 267, 276
Order of rank, 135
Orders, special and general, definition of, 139
Organization, 69–115
of administrative functions, 98–101, 112
for command, 79–85
of community, 235–243
for control, 201
of crime prevention bureau, 116
of criminal justice planning agency, 45
by function, 71, 75
of inspectional services, 103, 104, 199
by level of authority, 76
of operational functions, 104–109
for personnel management, 249
for planning, 162–168
principles of, 73, 86
for research and development, 162–167
of state law enforcement planning agency, 45
table of, 170
of technical services bureau, 101–103
terminology in, 70
by territory, 71, 76
by time, 72, 75
at top level, 98
Organizational principles, 73–86
Organizational structure:
analysis of existing structure, 86
bases for, 73
recommended structures, 97–116
variations in, 89
Organizations, police, 289
Organized activities for youth, 422
Organized crime:
and corruption of police, 214
definition of, 385
and prostitution, 408
ramifications of, 384–386
Organized labor unions, 284
Overlapping shifts, 282, 641
Overresponse, 342

INDEX

Overtime compensation, 281
Overtime parking, 458
Ownership of police automobiles, 340, 541

Parents, notification of, 416
Parking meters, 458
Parking regulations, enforcement of, 457–458
Parole status in OBTS, 502
Participatory management, 151
Partitions in police building, 530
Patrol, 319–356
  activities, 347, 356
  administration of, 327
  allocation of, 357–362, 633–671
  analysis in, 175
  automobile in, 332
  as backbone of police service, 322, 323
  by bicycle, 333
  in business section, 336
  concepts in, 331–344
  deployment, 341
  distribution of, 357–362, 633–671
  on foot, 332
  hazard-oriented, 323, 347
  by helicopter, 334
  by horse, 335
  investigations in, 348–351
  methods of, 331–344
  by motorcycle, 333
  nature of, 319
  by one-man cars, 337
  organization for, 105, 321–327
  preventive, 322, 347
  purposes of, 320
  relative strength of, 324
  routine preventive, 322, 347
  scheduling of, 327, 663, 664
  by scooters, 334
  versus special division, performance by, 323
  by special purpose vehicles, 334
  specialized, 335
    by specialized units, 326
  staffing for, 321–327
  supervision of, 329
  techniques in, 344–347
  by two-man cars, 337
  by unmarked cars, 339
  and vice control, 395
Patrol activities, 347–356
Patrol car:
  accessories for, 539
  conspicuous, 339

Patrol division:
  organization of, 105, 110, 321–327
  proportional strength, 324
  relationship of, to other divisions, 323
  responsibilities of: in delinquency prevention,
    416, 577
    in investigation, 364
    in traffic control, 452
    in vice control, 395
Patrol methods, 331–344
Patrol officers:
  deployment of, on calls, 342
  follow-up investigations by, 294
  number needed, 357–362, 633–671
  preliminary investigation by, 348
Patrol operations analyzed, 347
Patrol participation:
  extent of, 320
  in investigation, 294, 350, 364
  in traffic, 452
  in vice control, 395
Patrol services for other departments, 321
Patrol staff, headquarters, duties of, 330
Patrol techniques, 344–347
Pay (*see* Incentive pay for education; Salaries,
  police)
Pay telephones, 493
Peace-officer standards and training
  commissions, 297
  (*See also* California Commission on Peace
    Officer Standards and Training)
Peel, Sir Robert, 92
Pennsylvania State Police, 613
Performance budgeting (*see* Program budgeting)
Performance evaluation, 272, 585
Personal communications, 153
Personal equipment, 542
Personal-history statement, 265
Personal qualities, 258–259
  evaluation of, in selection, 265–269
  (*See also* Performance evaluation;
    Promotional potential rating)
Personal use of patrol cars, 340
Personality imprinting, 5, 180
Personnel administration (*see* Personnel
  management)
Personnel division:
  organization of, 249
  separate, need for, 98
  staff responsibilities of, 249
Personnel management, 244–311
Personnel orders, definition of, 140
Personnel plans, 169

INDEX

Perversion, sexual, among inmates, 511
Peterson, Virgil W., 391*n.*, 400*n.*
Philadelphia Police Department, 253
Philosophy of police service, 7
Photographing of prisoners, policy for, 516
Photography:
  by evidence technician, 507, 549
  by identification officer, 506
  by laboratory staff, 506
Physical evidence, search for, 375, 507
Physical examinations in selection, 264
Physical fitness, 283
PIN (Police Information Network), 500
Pittsburgh, Pennsylvania, use of psychological
    screening in, 263
Planning, 157–176
  completed staff work in, 160
  data processing in, 165, 167
  of detective operations, 370
  federal law enforcement planning, 41
  operations research in, 166
  philosophy of, 160
  records in, 463
  regional law enforcement planning, 50
  responsibility of chief in, 161
  state law enforcement planning, 41
  steps in, 162
  for training, 170, 301
  written directives in, 164
Planning unit:
  need for, 100, 157
  organization of, 162
  procedures within, 161
  qualifications of members, 163
  (*See also* Research, and development
      division)
Plans:
  allocation of manpower, 169
  approval of, by chief of police, 160
  budget, 169
  community relations, 170
  comprehensive law enforcement and criminal
      justice, 170
  through consultation, 171
  contingency, 173
  detective operations, 370
  field operations analysis, 175
  general emergency, 173
  management, 168
  operational, 171
  personnel, 169
  routine operations, 171, 174
  specific emergency, 173
  staffing, 170

Plans:
  for standard operating procedures, 175
  strategic, 176
  tactical, 173, 176, 431
  traffic, 438
  training, 170
  for unusual needs, 172
Platoons:
  coordination of, 125
  definition of, 72
Police:
  corruption of, 218
  philosophy of service, 7, 37
  and politics, 23–29
  present-day problems of, 9
  professionalization of, 9, 290–297
  purpose of, 7
  responsibilities and relationships of, 1–58
  role of, 6–11
Police Administrative Services Bureau of the
    State of New Jersey, 297
Police agent, 292, 351
Police case, definition of, 467
Police chief (*see* Chief of police)
Police commission, 22
Police-community relations (*see* Community
    relations)
Police-community relations councils, 34, 242
Police Foundation, 14, 219, 316, 322
Police functions, 7
Police Information Network (PIN), 500
Police laboratory, 503–509, 537
Police legal advisor, need for, 100
Police methods, changes in, 10
Police objectives, 7
Police officer, title of, 293
Police ordinances, 16–18
Police organizations, 289
Police programs, 30–35
Police publications, 233
Police reform, 244
Police responsibilities and relationships, 1–58
Police services:
  miscellaneous, 321, 351
  noncriminal, 8, 321
Police titles and rank, 70, 292
Policewomen:
  in detective service, 367
  discrimination against females in police
      service, 260, 261, 265
  in juvenile division, 414
Policy:
  definition of, 137
  development of, as a part of direction, 138

INDEX

Policy:
formulation of, 84, 183
implementation of, 124
Politics and police, 23–29
Polygraph:
in crime investigation, 375
operator of, 506
in personnel selection, 266
Pomerleau, Donald D., 571
Portable radios, 339, 492
Portland, Oregon, Police Department, 382
Position classification, new concepts in, 290–295
Positive reinforcement, 68
Post, definition of, 71
Poverty as influence in criminality, 6, 14, 180, 242, 411
Power of the press, 27
Power structure, 26
Practical Pistol Course (PPC), 538
Precinct (*see* District)
Preemployment training, 298
Preliminary interview in recruitment, 256
Preliminary investigation:
by detectives, 370
by patrol officers, 348–350
Prescriptive package publications, 180
President's Commission on Crime in the District of Columbia, 361
President's Commission on Law Enforcement and Administration of Justice, 12, 53*n.*, 292
Press:
activities of, 229–232
conferences with, 228
policy toward, 27, 229
Press room, 537
Prevention of criminality, 5–6, 242, 356, 411
police participation in, 356, 411
Preventive patrol, 322, 347, 361
Preventive services, 242
Principles of organization, 73–86
application of, 86–97
Prisoners:
authority for detention, release, and restrictions of, 512
booking of, 515
headquarters arrangement for, 534
control of, during booking, 515
custody of, 510
fingerprinting and photographing, 516
injured, 514
property of, 516
transfer of, abuses during, 346
visits with, 517

Prisoners:
welfare of, 517
work release, 518
Privacy Act, 475
Probationary appointment:
as step in selection, 269, 592
for superior officers, 277
Probationer status in OBTS, 502
Problems of police, 9, 14
Procedural manuals, development of, 138
Procedures, as part of directive system, 138
Productivity, 663
National Commission on, 12
Professional associations, 289
Professional-style department, 245
Professionalization of police, 290–297
Program budgeting:
account numbering in, 568
daily activity report in, 566
definition of, 186
installation of, 188
program coding in, 568
Programs, promotion of, 30–35
Promotion, 274–278
oral interviews in, 276
of police programs, 30–35
seniority in, 276
of superior officers, 276
written examinations in, 275
Promotional potential rating, 274, 605
Property:
control of, 522
handling of, design for, 535
of prisoners, control of, 516
recovered, 522
Property crimes, 381
Prosecutor, relationship of, to police, 56
Prostitution, 404–408
Protective devices and armor, 546
Psychiatric examinations, 263
Psychological evaluation, 262
Public:
in delinquency prevention, 235, 421
handling of, design for, 532
in relation to police, 221–243
Public-address equipment, 444
Public Administration Service, 171, 633*n.*
Public and community relations, 221–243, 425
(*See also* community relations)
Public education:
in crime resistance, 424
against organized-crime, 385
in traffic control, 441
for understanding of police purpose, 223–225

698 INDEX

Public-information officer, duties of, 225
Public-information unit, need for, 99, 225
Public Personnel Association, 250, 273, 585*n.*
Public relations policies, 221
Public reporting, 232, 463
Public-safety director, 22
Public speaking, 425
Public support of police program, need for, 222
Publications, police, 233
Purchasing, 191, 522
Pyramid of authority, command outside of, 79, 135

Quadrant assignments in patrol deployment, 343
Qualifications for leadership, 120
Qualities, desirable, for police service, 258–260
Quality of personnel, 245, 246, 251, 291
Quartermaster function, 521

Racial discrimination (*see* Discrimination, racial)
Radio:
  code usage on, 343
  maintenance of, 521
  in public relations work, 233
  transistorized, 339, 492
  transmitting systems, 488
  (*See also* Communications)
Rand Institute, 181, 376
Rank:
  consideration of, during organization, 91
  grades of, 280
  order of, 135
  terminology describing, 70
Rank structure, new concepts in, 292–295
Ranking officer, definition of, 73
Ratings:
  promotional potential, 274, 605–608
  service, 585–605
Real-time information systems, 499
Recalls, visual and audible, 493
Recording of police incidents, 467, 472
Records:
  of accomplishment, 463
  administrative, 194
  arrest, 474–476, 481
  centralization of, 464
  detective, 369
  district station, 481
  filing of, 462

Records:
  handling of, design for, 533
  need for, 461
  traffic, 438
  vice division, 396
  youth division, 415
Records and communications division, 465–467
  (*See also* Communications division; Records division)
Records division:
  administration of, 465–467
  need for, 101
  organization of, 101, 466
  procedures in, 465–472
Records work in operating divisions, 465
Recruit training, 303, 609
Recruitment, 251–258
  advertising in, 252
  application forms in, 257
  definition of, 251
  eligibility requirements in, 253
  in field, 252
  incentive plans in, 253
  minority, 54, 252
  (*See also* Selection)
Red light and siren policy, 345
Redding, California, 565
Regional information systems, 500
Regional law enforcement planning, 41
Regionalization of services, 51
Registries, 297
  (*See also* Lateral entry into police service)
Reid, John E., 506*n.*
Reinke, Roger W., 630
Reith, Charles, 38*n.*, 224*n.*
Release of prisoners, authority for, 512
Reorganization, 86
Report-review by field supervisors, 471
Report-review officer, 479
Report-writing systems, 469
Reporters, police, 226–230
Reporting of administrative information, 195
Reporting accomplishments to public, 197, 232, 463
Reports:
  annual, 197
  daily, 196, 571
  inspection, 209
  by intelligence unit, 399
  monthly, 196, 573
  statistical, 196
Reproduction and graphic arts, 103
Requisitions, purchasing, 191

INDEX 699

Research, 157, 176–181
  behavioral, 180
  biomedical, 180
  categories of, 178–179
  and development division, 112, 162–167
    (*See also* Planning)
  directions for technological research, 180
  in patrol distribution, 659
Residence requirements for police service, 253
Response to emergency calls, 345
Retirement from police service, 284
Review of reports (*see under* Report review)
Revolver versus automatic pistol, 543
Richmond, California, Police Department, 343
Rifle, 544
Rights of citizens in investigations, 375
Riot control (*see* Civil disorders)
Riot gun, 544
Rochester Police Department, 317
Roethlisberger, Fritz J., 151
Role of police, 6
Roll-call training, 305
Roosevelt, Franklin D., 287
Rorschach test, 263
Rotation of shifts, 630
  undesirability of, 328
Route, definition of, 72
Routine preventive patrol, 322, 347, 361
Rule:
  of command, 83
  of control, 201
  as a part of written directive system, 138
Rumors, 155

Sabotage of police building, 531
Safe Streets Act (*see* Omnibus Crime Control
    and Safe Streets Act)
Safety-education services, 424, 427
Safety programs for police welfare, 283
St. Louis, Missouri, Police Department, 241,
    304, 358, 498
Salaries, police, 278–281
San Diego Police Department, 496
San Mateo County, California, Sheriff's
    Department, 295
Santa Ana, California, Police Department, 309
Savage, Edward H., 92*n*.
Savannah, Georgia, Police Department, 296
Schedule, shift, 327, 630
School-child patrols (junior traffic patrols), 444
Schwartz, Eli, 188*n*.
Scientific crime detection (*see* Crime laboratory)

Scooters, 334
Scramblers in radio communications, 343
Screening of cases, 372
SEARCH (System for Electronic Analysis and
    Retrieval of Criminal Histories), 502
Search for physical evidence, 375
"Second contact" as a tool in crime
    investigation, 376
Section, definition of, 71
Sector, definition of, 72
Security:
  of jail, 512, 529–530
  in police building, 466, 531
  of records, 466
Security surveys, 355, 425
Selection, 258–271
  definition of, 251
  examinations in, 260–271
  positive approach to, 258, 266
  for promotion, 274–278
  sequence of events in, 271
  tests for, 260–271
Selective enforcement in traffic, 452
Self-actualization, 66
Self-management, theory of, 65
Seniority, 276
Separation from police service, 145, 148, 216–
    218, 284
Sequence of events in selection process, 271
Sergeant, as key to discipline, 146
Service, police: conditions of, 278
  length of, in promotions, 275
Service-connected injury, 282
Service ratings, 272–273, 585–603
  (*See also* Promotional potential rating)
Service units, need for, 101
Services:
  administrative (*see* Administrative services)
  auxiliary, definition of, 60
  called-for, 360, 633
  definition of, 347
  inspection, by patrol, 347
  inspectional (*see* Inspectional services)
  to merchants and householders, 353
  for other city departments, 321
  sharing of, 54
  technical (*see* Technical services)
Services division, 101, 110
Sexual abuse of inmates, 511
Sharing of services, 54
Sheriff's offices, organization of, 116
Shift, definition of, 72
Shift hours, selection of, 630–632, 639–640, 663

700 INDEX

Shift rotation schedule, 328, 630
Shifts:
  fixed, 328
  overlapping, 282, 641
  rotation of, 328, 630
Shocking power of sidearm, 544
Shot gun, as police weapon, 544
Sick leave:
  control of, 282–283
  as personnel benefit, 282
Sidearm, police, 542–544
Sign-up sheet for shift selection, 632
Sirens, use in emergencies, 345
Smith, R. Dean, 657
Social activism, 8, 242, 411
Social science research, 180
Sources of information in crime investigation, 377
Southern Police Institute, 300, 311
Span of control, 81–83, 91
Speakers' bureau, 235, 425
Specht, David, 318n.
Special events control, 434
Special operations division:
  need for, 107
  organization of, 430
  role in riot containment and control, 433
  tactical forces in, 428
Special orders, definition of, 139
Special-purpose patrol vehicles (ATV units), 334
Special-service units, need for, 101–103
Special weapons and tactical units (SWAT), 431
Specialist pay, 280, 295
Specialization:
  advantages of, 93
  based on need, 77
  determining factors in, 94
  development of, 92
  disadvantages of, 94, 324
  influence on patrol, 323–326
  in small departments, 93
  in youth division, 418
Specific information tests, 261
Spoils system, 244
Spot maps, 164, 197, 415
Squad policing, 293, 315
  (*See also* Team policing)
Squad room, 537
Staff command, definition of, 128
Staff conferences, 141
  vertical, 142
Staff duties, definition of, 60

Staff inspection, 205
  functional supervision as part of, 205
  versus line inspection, 203
  by traffic division, 437
Staff work, completed, 160
Staffing plans, 170
Stakeouts, 346, 380
Standard operating procedures:
  as an element of directive system, 138
  as planning task, 175
Standards:
  for enforcement in traffic, 450
  in inspection, 211
  intelligence, 260
  medical, 264
  for recruitment, 251–258
  for selection, 258–281
  training, minimum in, 301
State highway patrols, organization of, 116
State information systems, 500
State law enforcement planning, 39, 41
State police, organization of, 116
State services for local agencies, 55
Station (*see* District station)
Status boards in dispatching, 496
Status offenders, 414
Stinchcomb, James D., 307
Stolen-car and persons-wanted files, 501
Storage of property, 522
Store inspections, 354
Store security, 424, 426
Storefront centers, 241
Strategic analysis, 176
Strategy development, use of records in, 463
Strength, tests of, 264
Stress units in personnel counseling, 283
Strikes, police, 287
Submachine gun, 545
Subordinates, attitude toward, 123
Summaries:
  daily, 195, 572
  monthly, 573–575
Summary punishment, 217
Superior officer:
  definition of, 73
  promotion of, 274–278
Supervision, 143–148
  administrative, 131, 134
  of civilian employees, 145
  of detectives, 373
  of evidence technicians, 509
  facilitated by records, 462
  of patrol, 327–331
  relationship to discipline, 145

INDEX 701

Supervision:
  by report-review, 478
  role of sergeant in, 144, 146
  of traffic officers, 437
Support services (*see* Technical services)
Surveillance, 346
Surveys:
  police management, 171
  security, 355
Suspension, 148, 217
Switchboard operation, 485, 489
Sworn officers, definition of, 73
Syndicated crime, 384
  (*See also* Organized crime)
Syracuse Police Department, 343
System for Electronic Analysis and Retrieval of
    Criminal Histories (SEARCH), 502
Systems and procedures section in planning, 164

Table of organization, 170
Tactical analysis, 176
Tactical forces, 107, 428
  (*See also* Special operations division)
Tactical plans, 173
Tactical training, 346
Tailor shop, 521
Take-home car plan, 340
Tamm, Quinn, 565
Target range, 537
"Taser," 546
Task force (*see* Special operations division)
Task Force Report: The Police, 53, 294
Tasks, grouping of similar or related, 74–77
Taylor, Frederick, 63
Team policing, 294, 315–318
  conventional, 343
  coordination, 128
  district command in, 132
  staff conferences in, 141
  terminology in, 72
Teamsters, International Brotherhood of, 285
Tear gas, 545
Technical services, 459–550
  organization of, 101–103, 111
Technician (*see* Evidence technician)
Technological research, 180
Telephone communication, 488–494
  equipment for, 488
  interoffice, 541
  on street, 493
Telephone dictation of reports, 469
Telephone relationships, 490

Telephone system integrated with dispatching,
    485, 491
Teleprinters, 180
Teletype, use of, in communications system,
    483, 541
Television:
  as means for public contact, 233
  for training and intercom use, 542
Terminals, 180
Terminology:
  administrative, 60
  organizational, 70
Territorial organization of police force, 75
Territorial tendency in human behavior, 150,
    317, 344
Territorial units, defined, 71
Tests:
  of information, 261
  of intelligence, 260
  psychiatric, 263
  psychological, 262
  for selection, 260–271
  sequence of, 271
  of strength and agility, 265
  (*See also* Selection)
Thematic apperception test, 263
Theory X, 64
Theory Y, 64
Time, organization by, 75
Time division of tasks of command, 129, 130
Time units, defined, 72
Timeliness of inspection, 208
Titles:
  disadvantages of conventional rank titles,
    292
  of organizational units, 71
  of ranks, 70
  of territorial units, 71
Top-level control, 16
Tours of inspection for public, 234
Towing service operated by police, 523
Trace-odor-sensing devices, 180
Traffic administration, 435–458
Traffic control, 435
  public education in, 441
Traffic court, 454
Traffic division, 436–438
  need for, 105
Traffic enforcement, 446–455
  citations and summonses in, 449
  selective, 452
  standards for, 450
  use of warnings in, 449
Traffic engineering, 439

702 INDEX

Traffic hazards, study of, 354
Traffic records, 438
Traffic-violator schools, 445
Training:
  administrative, 306
  facilities for, 301
  field training, 304, 613–629
  in-service, 304–306
  middle-management, 306
  minimum standards for, 301
  municipal responsibility for, 298
  organization for, 297–303
  planning for, 170, 301
  preemployment, 298
  purpose of, 298
  recruit, 303, 609
  roll-call, 305
  staffing of, 299
  subject matter in, 305, 609
  tactical, 346
"Training runs," 346
Transistorized radios, 339, 492
Transmitters, radio, 488
  auxiliary, 550
Transportation of prisoners, 346
Truant contact, 378
Trusties, 517
Tulsa Police Department, 309
Turnover rate, 248
Two-man patrol cars, 337

Undercover funds, 399
Understanding between police and public, 222–224
Uniform, police, 547–548
Uniform Crime Reports, 366, 473, 571
Uniformed division, 110
  (*See also* Patrol division)
Unions, labor, 284–288
Unit, definition of, 71
Unit-beat policing, 294, 316
United States Conference of Mayors, 16
Unity of command, 80
University of California, 351*n.*
University of Louisville, 311
University of Southern California, 311
University training (*see* Education)
Unmarked cars, 339
Urban Institute, 316, 322
Urban Police Function, 12
Utilities in police building, 529

Vacant homes, inspection of, 354
Vacations, 282
Vanderbosch, Charles G., 377*n.*
Variations in organization structure, 89
Vehicles, police, 538–541
  choice of, for patrol, 539
  maintenance and service of, 519
Venereal disease and prostitution, 404, 407, 408
Ventilation in police building, 529
Vertical staff meetings, 142
Vertical take-off and landing apparatus, 334
Vests, protective, 546
Vice, 384–409
  commercialized, 390
  and organized crime, 385
  patrol responsibility in, 395, 397
  police attitude toward, 387–389
  relation to intelligence and inspectional
    services, 392
  social problems of, 387
Vice control division:
  investigations by, 392
  need for, 106
  problems of, 394
  selection of officers for, 393
Vice records, 396
Vice unit, central, 392
Video-tape files, 180
Violation, traffic, notice of, 449
Virginia Beach, Virginia Police Department, 378,
    468, 496
Virginia Commonwealth University, 307
Visual recalls, 493
Visual requirements in selection, 256, 264
Voice scramblers in radio communications, 343
Vollmer, August, 351, 657
Volunteer workers in delinquency prevention, 422

Wagons, patrol, 346, 520
Walk-in examinations, 270
Walls in police building, 528
Walton, Frank, 657
Wanted-persons files, 501
Warnings, traffic, 449
Warrant service, 434
Washington, D.C., Police Department, 208, 213,
    251, 309, 334, 382
Watch, definition of, 72
Wayne County Sheriff's Department, 52
Weapons:
  nonlethal, 180
  police, 542–546

INDEX

Weight-height ratio in recruitment, 256
Welfare program, police, 281
Westchester County, New York, lateral entry in, 296
Weston, Paul B., 298
White-collar crime, 5
Whitmer, Robert H., 565
Wichita Police Department, 498
Wickersham Commission, 13
Wilson, O. W., ix–xii, 633n., 657
Windows in police building, 528
Wolfle, Joan L., 411n.
Women:
  avoidance of discrimination against, 260, 261, 265
  as detectives, 367
  strength and agility testing of, 265
  as youth-division officers, 414
Work load:
  in manpower distribution, 358, 633, 657
  noncriminal, 8
  police case, as part of, 467
Work release, 518
Working conditions, 281–284
Working files, 369, 465
Workweek, 282

Written directives, 136–141
Written examinations, 261, 275

Yawara stick, 546
Youth councils, 421
Youth crime, 411–423
  (*See also* Delinquency prevention)
Youth division:
  case assignments in, 420
  delinquency-prevention activities by, 413, 418–423
  investigation by, 419
  need for, 107
  organization of, 416
  personnel, 414
  records, 415
  specialization within, 417
    disadvantages of, 418
  specific responsibilities of, 413
Youth radicalism, 433
Youth resource units, 423

Zero-base budgeting, 187, 191